The Challenge of Politics

Sixth Edition

The Challenge of Politics
An Introduction to Political Science
Sixth Edition

Douglas W. Simon
Drew University

Joseph Romance
University of South Florida

Neal Riemer
Drew University

FOR INFORMATION:

CQ Press

An Imprint of SAGE Publications, Inc.

2455 Teller Road

Thousand Oaks, California 91320

E-mail: order@sagepub.com

SAGE Publications Ltd.

1 Oliver's Yard

55 City Road

London EC1Y 1SP

United Kingdom

SAGE Publications India Pvt. Ltd.

B 1/I 1 Mohan Cooperative Industrial Area

Mathura Road, New Delhi 110 044

India

SAGE Publications Asia-Pacific Pte. Ltd.

18 Cross Street #10-10/11/12

China Square Central

Singapore 048423

Acquisitions Editor: Scott Greenan

Editorial Assistants: Lauren Younker

Production Editor: Jyothi Sriram

Copy Editor: Laurie Pitman

Typesetter: C&M Digitals (P) Ltd.

Proofreader: Jeff Bryant

Indexer: Terri Morrissey

Cover Designer: Candice Harman

Marketing Manager: Erica DeLuca

Printed in the United States of America

ISBN: 9781544305967

Library of Congress Cataloging-in-Publication Data

Names: Simon, Douglas W., author. | Romance, Joseph, 1966- author. | Riemer, Neal, 1922–2001, author.

Title: The challenge of politics : an introduction to political science / Douglas W. Simon, Drew University, USA, Joseph Romance, Fort Hays State University, Kansas, Neal Riemer, Drew University, USA.

Description: Sixth Edition. | Washington, D.C. : CQ Press, A DIVISION OF SAGE, [2019] | Previous edition: 2015. | Includes bibliographical references and index.

Identifiers: LCCN 2018026597 | ISBN 9781544305967 (Paperback : alk. paper)

Subjects: LCSH: Political science.

Classification: LCC JA66 .R498 2019 | DDC 320—dc23 LC record available at https://lccn.loc.gov/2018026597

This book is printed on acid-free paper.

19 20 21 22 23 10 9 8 7 6 5 4 3 2 1

BRIEF CONTENTS

DETAILED CONTENTS

LIST OF TABLES, FIGURES, BOXES, AND MAPS

FIGURES

TABLES

BOXES

MAPS

Douglas W. Simon is emeritus professor of political science at Drew University, where he specialized in international affairs, U.S. foreign policy, international organization, and national security. After receiving a BA from Willamette University, he served as an officer in U.S. air force intelligence, including a tour in Vietnam. Following his military service, he earned a PhD at the University of Oregon. After arriving at Drew University, he directed the university's Semester on the United Nations for fifteen years, served as convener of Drew's Masters in International Affairs Program, and later was department chair. In addition to *The Challenge of Politics*, he is co-author of *New Thinking and Developments in International Politics: Opportunities and Dangers* and has contributed to such publications as the *Harvard Journal of World Affairs*, *East Asian Survey*, *Comparative Political Studies*, *International Studies Notes*, *Teaching Political Science*, and *Society*.

Joseph Romance has taught for over twenty-three years at such institutions as Rutgers University, Drew University, and Fort Hay State University. He received a BA from the College of William and Mary and a PhD from Rutgers University. He is co-author, with Theodore Lowi, of *A Republic of Parties: Debating the Two Party System*; co-author of and contributor to *Democracy and Excellence: Conflict or Concord?*; and co-editor of *Democracy's Literature*. His articles and reviews have appeared in a number of journals, including *American Review of Politics*, *The Responsive Community*, and *Perspectives on Political Science*. He has also contributed pieces to a number of edited volumes, including *Progressive Politics in the Global Age*, *Friends and Citizens*, and *American Political Parties Under Pressure*. He currently is working on a book about progressive reforms and American political parties.

Neal Riemer was the Andrew V. Stout Professor of Political Philosophy at Drew University. After receiving a PhD from Harvard University, he taught at the Pennsylvania State University; the University of Wisconsin-Milwaukee; University of Innsbruck, Austria; and Drew University. His books include *Problems of American Government* (editor); *World Affairs: Problems and Prospects* (co-author); *The Revival of Democratic Theory; The Democratic Experiment; The Future of the Democratic Revolution: Toward a More Prophetic Politics; New Thinking and Developments in International Politics: Opportunities and Dangers* (editor/co-author); *Karl Marx and Prophetic Politics; James Madison: Creating the American Constitution; Creative Breakthroughs in Politics; Let Justice Roll: Prophetic Challenges in Religion, Politics, and Society* (editor/co-author); and *Protection Against Genocide: Mission Impossible* (editor).

PREFACE

In this sixth edition of *The Challenge of Politics*, we again advance a vision of political science that is sweeping in scope and integrative in nature. We believe that politics should be concerned with the creation of a humane, civilized society. For that reason, students of politics must not only work diligently to determine empirically what is and why, they must also make judgments as to which political systems and processes are most efficient and most humane.

We do not believe in a sharp distinction between classical and empirical theory in the pursuit of these goals. Instead, we strongly affirm students' need to appreciate the wisdom of classical theory as they address timeless questions: What is the good life? What is freedom? What is justice? When should citizens disobey their government? How do we balance individual rights and the broader interests of society? Throughout the text, we constantly return to these and other fundamental questions.

We also welcome contemporary methods of investigating politics. For example, the ability to analyze data about what citizens and political actors think and do brings new dimension and depth to our understanding of what the good life is. Put simply, classical theory and the scientific method are never at war in this text. Knowing Plato's conception of the ideal just state, for example, illuminates the kinds of political choices we make today as we think about war, economic efficiency and fairness, and the dangers of global pollution.

Further evidence of our desire to offer an integrative concept of political science is our belief that the four traditional fields of the discipline—political theory, American government, comparative politics, and international relations—can, and should, inform each other. When political science is taught in a compartmentalized fashion, as it frequently is, students may have difficulty seeing how the discipline's subfields interact as a whole. For example, controversies in American political parties can seem completely unrelated to the balance of power in international relations. Yet, knowing about American domestic politics and how it might affect the country's leaders is vital for understanding how the world's nations interact. Because we want students to see the whole of the political world, we focus on what constitutes a just and well-governed society. Students are motivated to see linkages between how governments work, how states interact, and how the great theorists of politics have shaped and influenced political actors.

This text puts forth the idea that all politics is about certain fundamental concepts. What are the political values that encourage a good political life? Can we develop a science of politics to help us understand the empirical realities of politics? Can we bring a high level of political prudence and wisdom to bear on public issues? Can we creatively address the future of politics? These are the concerns that form the bridges between the subfields of the discipline in *The Challenge of Politics*.

As we lead students to explore these questions, we remind them that politics is emphatically about choice and thinking about the possible. We give them the ability to make informed judgments about some of the most compelling public policy issues of our time: poverty, war and peace, human rights, and environmental degradation. In this way, we invite students to think about the future. How might a more just and civilized society come about? Can students of politics use their knowledge, reason, and innovation to develop creative breakthroughs in the way we govern ourselves as human beings?

ORGANIZATION

The Challenge of Politics is divided into four parts linked together by several common themes: political values, the science of politics, political wisdom, and the future of politics and political science.

Part I, Rules of the Game, introduces students to the field of political science by focusing on the kinds of choices political actors make. We use this approach because the element of choice is at the heart of politics and because we believe it is the most exciting way to engage students at the beginning. What is more compelling than to discover how renowned political figures as well as common people wrestled with profound political dilemmas, the resolutions of which determined how people would ultimately be governed, or whether people lived or died? The chapters in Part I also examine the tasks of political science and ask the critical question, how scientific can political science be? In Chapter 1, we have added an extensive discussion of the concepts of "positive" and "negative" freedom, and in Chapter 3, we present an extended analysis of rational choice theory and game theory, including a discussion of the Prisoner's Dilemma. Chapter 4 explores the physical, social, and cultural environments in which politics takes place, highlighting the crucial fact that politics never occurs in a vacuum. In this chapter, we have provided a much greater discussion of the cyber revolution and its impact on politics, including Russian interference in the 2016 presidential election. Part II, Political Philosophy and Ideology, explores the world of political philosophy and ideology. We give considerable attention to classical theory and the manner in which it illuminates our fundamental understanding of politics and the search for justice. In addition, we examine a number of modern ideologies, including liberal democracy, communism, and democratic socialism. Perhaps the biggest addition to this entire section is to be found in Chapter 5 where we include an entirely new section on the eighteenth century feminist political philosopher, Mary Wollstonecraft. In Chapter 8, we provide a discussion of how the election of Donald Trump to the American presidency seemed to reaffirm the notion that the American electorate was becoming increasingly divided on a variety of issues. Part III, American, Comparative, and World Politics, examines political values and the problems that arise because of the gap between professed values and the actual behavior of political actors. This section is also concerned with the institutional context in which politics occurs. Throughout the three chapters in this section is the idea that tough political choices are shaped not merely by ideas but by the characteristics of the institutions of governance. How adequate and effective are these institutions of governance in seeking a just and humane society? Do they contribute to the political health of communities or to a more peaceful world? These are central questions that the student of politics must address. We assist this study by exploring the domestic political systems of a variety of countries, including discussions of their constitutions, voters, interest groups, political parties, media, legislatures, executives, bureaucracies, and courts. In Chapter 11, we move to the world of international politics and explore the effectiveness of institutions like the United Nations and the European Union. Part IV, Political Judgment and Public Policy, invites students to apply the tools of the discipline to four critical public policy areas: war and peace, human rights, economic welfare, and the environment. We present a variety of approaches for dealing with these concerns. Some thought is devoted to considering which approaches offer the best opportunity for solving the most intractable policy problems. The chapters on public policy encourage students to articulate their own ethical values; to present and assess significant empirical findings relevant to the problems; and to balance ethical, empirical, and prudential concerns to reach sensible political judgments on important current problems. These chapters invite students to develop their own creative breakthroughs to solve these problems. In addition, Part IV is specifically designed to give instructors flexibility in the way they use the book. Each of the four policy chapters stands on its own; instructors can choose to have students read all four chapters or to assign chapters individually.

PEDAGOGY

We designed *The Challenge of Politics* to engage students' interest. Throughout this sixth edition, students will find updated tables and graphs containing up-to-the-minute data, as well as conceptual figures and maps that enhance the text. A wide array of photographs with substantive captions are incorporated throughout the text. In addition to traditional news and scenic photographs, we took considerable care to find photographs and portraits of important political theorists and personalities. For many students, Plato, Machiavelli, Madison, Mill, Thoreau, and Marx are abstractions, merely names on a page. By presenting these images, we hope that these figures will come alive.

Another feature of the book is the presentation of Chapter Learning Objectives as well as Key Questions at the beginning of most chapters with an icon in the margins highlighting their importance. These questions are intended to get students thinking about some of the critical issues raised in each part of the book. Other features include end-of-chapter Suggested Readings—a mixture of contemporary and classical works—and a list of key terms. These terms, highlighted throughout the text, are defined in an extensive glossary at the end of the book.

In addition to these text features, the sixth edition of *The Challenge of Politics* is accompanied by an updated website (edge.sagepub.com/simon6e) composed of several elements: learning objectives, flashcards to assist students in mastering key terms in the discipline, an interactive quiz section with multiple-choice and true-false questions, and Internet links appropriate to each chapter. Instructor resources, which can be downloaded (register at edge.sagepub.com/simon6e/instructor-resources), include a test bank with multiple-choice, short-answer, and essay questions, available with ExamView test generation software, and PowerPoint lecture slides to better assist professors in course planning.

Our hope is that after reading *The Challenge of Politics* students will have gained a greater understanding and appreciation of the political world, and perhaps even be inspired to become themselves active participants on the political stage.

INTRODUCTION

In *The Challenge of Politics*, we seek to introduce you to the intriguing discipline of political science. We strongly believe that our unique and comprehensive approach can best equip you, the student of political science, to stay abreast of the ever-changing, challenging world of politics, a world now in the early years of the twenty-first century. This is a world in which the paramount issues of peace/war, human rights/tyranny, prosperity/poverty, and ecological balance/malaise continue to dominate the political agenda.

In the few years since the last edition of this book, major changes and challenges have demanded the attention of students of political science. Through the years 2015 and 2017, the United States continued to pull itself out of the crushing recession of 2008, and by the end of 2017, the Dow Jones Industrial Average had quadrupled from its low point in the crisis. Unemployment, which had soared into the double figures, by 2018 had fallen below levels before the crash occurred. In 2016, the United States experienced an extraordinary presidential election when Republican New York real estate magnate and controversial reality television star, Donald Trump, defeated Democrat Hillary Clinton, former U.S. Senator and Secretary of State. It was an election that also saw Russia marshaling its cyber capability to interfere with the election process in a variety of ways. During the first year of the Trump administration, the American Congress continued to experience a degree of dysfunction with both political parties experiencing internal conflict as well as conflict with each other. The Arab Spring that had generated cautious hope in 2011 and 2012 continued to fade as countries either plunged into chaos or experienced a reassertion of authoritarian rule. Only Tunisia seemed bound for some meaningful democratic reform. Terrorism continued to plague the international system, particularly in Europe and the United States despite the military defeat of the Islamic State (ISIS) in Iraq and Syria. While terrorist groups like Boko Haram and Al-Shabaab continued their reign of terror from West to East Africa, the most alarming development was the increase in "rogue" terrorist attacks perpetrated by individuals with no formal or close ties to large organized groups. Tensions increased in the Baltic states as both NATO and Russian military forces deployed on either side of the Russian border. North Korean leader Kim Jong-un relentlessly pursued its nuclear weapons program despite the world's condemnation. Under President Donald Trump, America's commitment to confronting global warming was dramatically reversed when in 2017 the United States pulled out of the Paris Agreement on Climate Change. These and other changes and challenges require us to ponder some major issues: the nature of leadership in the United States as well as in other parts of the world, the persistence of war as part of the human condition, and the difficulties in establishing peace. In addition, we note large pockets of poverty persist in several regions. Human rights are still violated with impunity in far too many countries, and ecological balance remains a critical problem for our "spaceship earth."

As we seek to keep abreast of these developments, we need to keep our eyes focused on four key questions. These questions highlight the analytical framework

KEY QUESTIONS

1. Can we as citizens and students articulate and defend a view of the good political life and its guiding political values?

2. Can we develop a science of politics to help us understand significant political phenomena—the empirical realities of politics?

3. Can we bring a high level of political prudence or wisdom to bear on judgments about politics and public issues?

4. Can citizens and students creatively address the future of politics?

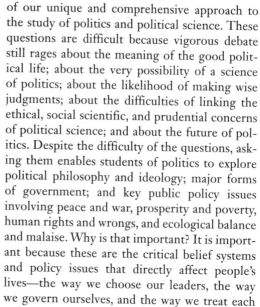

of our unique and comprehensive approach to the study of politics and political science. These questions are difficult because vigorous debate still rages about the meaning of the good political life; about the very possibility of a science of politics; about the likelihood of making wise judgments; about the difficulties of linking the ethical, social scientific, and prudential concerns of political science; and about the future of politics. Despite the difficulty of the questions, asking them enables students of politics to explore political philosophy and ideology; major forms of government; and key public policy issues involving peace and war, prosperity and poverty, human rights and wrongs, and ecological balance and malaise. Why is that important? It is important because these are the critical belief systems and policy issues that directly affect people's lives—the way we choose our leaders, the way we govern ourselves, and the way we treat each other as human beings inside and outside our country. We welcome the challenges of exploring these systems and issues and hope that our approach will contribute to enlightened dialogue and creative debate.

POLITICAL VALUES

Addressing the first question of our framework, that of political values, we reaffirm our normative preference for politics as a civilizing enterprise, one that enables people in the political community to live better, to grow robustly in mind and spirit, and to find creative fulfillment. This normative preference has guided our choice of topics in this book. The theme of politics as a civilizing enterprise has also provided a standard for exploring the meaning of political health, a metaphor for the political community that is able to secure peace, protect human rights, enhance economic prosperity, and advance ecological balance—and thus facilitate creative individual realization within the framework of the common good.

To hold this perspective, however, does not mean ignoring the ugly fact that politics often is not a civilizing enterprise, that politics is sometimes a dirty and unpleasant business. Truth, honor, and decency are sometimes casualties in the world of politics. Appreciating the realities of politics clearly requires a keen understanding of war as well as peace, tyranny as well as freedom, injustice as well as justice, poverty as well as prosperity, ecological malaise as well as ecological well-being. Put simply, it remains important to see—and to seek to achieve—politics at its best, as well as to recognize how it can degenerate and function at its worst.

A SCIENCE OF POLITICS

The science of politics compels us to determine, as accurately and truthfully as possible, the objective reality of what goes on in the political arena. Students of politics are faced with the task of accurately assessing and understanding past, present, and emerging political realities. Understanding changing realms of domestic and international politics is an important, and often neglected, task.

Keeping abreast of the changing and challenging nature of politics is clearly an imperative of a realistic political science. However, change is not always unique or singular. Political science recognizes the enduring realities of the struggle for power. Current developments and contemporary changes are always best understood in the light of those enduring ethical, empirical, and prudential realities. It is also most important to appreciate that changes may pose dangers to be avoided as well as opportunities to be seized. Changes may, unpredictably, usher in the "best of times" or the "worst of times."

Strikingly, the changes and challenges outlined in this book all relate to the political values of peace, freedom, economic well-being, and ecological balance, and thus offer a way to link events across eras and regions, from the domestic realm to the international realm.

POLITICAL WISDOM

Political actors, as they seek to advance their values in the light of the realities of politics, will need to exercise wise political judgment as they respond to the striking changes that have taken place in recent years. The challenge of politics calls upon students and citizens to make wise decisions based on a combination of factors: thorough knowledge, deep understanding, rational thought, and a sense of compassion. Wisdom must be brought to bear in responding to the different character of the rivalries between the world's major powers since the end of the Cold War; to the ongoing problems of liberal democracies; to the continuing plight of many developing countries; and to a host of other challenging political, economic, religious, scientific, and environmental developments.

THE FUTURE OF POLITICS AND POLITICAL SCIENCE

Attention to the preceding features of *The Challenge of Politics*—political values, the science of politics, and political wisdom—helps one attend to the future. Here we have in mind not only the immediate future but the long-range future as well. In the prophetic tradition, we must carefully scrutinize the future as well as the past and the present. Political scientists need to project forward, to scenarios both positive and negative, in order to critically assess what lies ahead in politics. Here students of political science are challenged to explore the future imaginatively. Consequently, we encourage you to use the analytical framework of the text to (1) probe the future of political values more clearly, fully, and critically; (2) seek to grasp the emerging realities of politics more incisively, keenly, and astutely; and (3) weigh the costs and benefits of alternative judgments, policies, and actions more prudently, humanely, and practically in order to reach wise decisions.

In seeking to advance the critical exploration of the book's cardinal questions, we will explore in each part a key organizing question. In Part I, Rules of the Game, which serves as our introduction to the field and study of political science, we ask this question: How can we best understand politics and political science? To stimulate interest about the nature and challenge of politics, in Chapters 1 and 2 we use some dramatic "political games" to underscore crucial choices. Thus, in Chapter 1, we employ five cases drawn from history, literature, and political philosophy to focus on the players, stakes, rules, strategies, and tactics in the "game" of politics. In Chapter 2, we employ five memorable cases to emphasize the central role of choice in politics. Then, after using these cases and choices to highlight goals, realities, and judgments in politics, we move on in Chapter 3 to outline the major tasks, fields, and controversies of political science in a more systematic way. Finally, in Chapter 4, we emphasize how the larger physical, social, and cultural environment affects the discipline and its tasks.

Our guiding question in Part II, Political Philosophy and Ideology, is this: How do political philosophy and ideology illuminate our understanding of politics? In Chapter 5, we discuss the contributions of the great political philosophers, and in Chapters 6 and 7, we examine such political ideologies as liberal democracy, communism, and democratic socialism.

In Part III, American, Comparative, and World Politics, we consider this question: How far have we come in developing a fruitful science of politics? In Chapter 8, we begin by considering some of the key dilemmas in the areas of political form, culture, and values. In Chapters 9 through 11, we focus on such significant empirical problems as the gap between the actual and professed values of political actors. We also explore which political patterns are successful in furthering cooperation, advancing accommodation, and handling conflicts in national and international politics.

In Part IV, Political Judgment and Public Policy, we focus on this question: How can we sharpen our prudent judgment on key issues of public policy? In order to probe this question, we explore in Chapters 12 through 15 a number of policy issues of global concern, such as the achievement of a peaceful world order, greater protection for human rights, economic well-being, and a sane ecological balance. The public policy chapters seek to encourage you to articulate your own ethical values; to present and assess significant empirical findings relevant to the problems at hand; and, finally, to balance ethical, empirical, and prudential concerns in reaching sensible political judgments on important, albeit controversial, problems of the day, the decade, and the future.

In the Conclusion, we ask this: How will we, in the twenty-first century, carry on the work of politics as a civilizing enterprise? We set forth some scenarios about the future of politics—scenarios involving the character of the political world in a new century. This final chapter recognizes that you who read this book will be engaged in the politics of the twenty-first century. You will have to be prepared to take charge and to respond intelligently, effectively, and humanely to the political issues of this new century.

RULES OF THE GAME

The chapters in Part I seek to introduce you to politics and the discipline of political science and to provide you with a framework for a more complete exploration of the nature of politics and political science. They are designed to help you understand the political scientist's tasks, fields of study, and key controversies. You are invited to think critically about politics, especially about the extent to which politics function as a civilizing activity. Are the tasks we discuss the tasks that political scientists ought to be performing? Do the traditional fields of study do justice to the discipline? The central question that each of these introductory chapters addresses is this: How can we best understand politics and political science?

Chapters 1 and 2 begin by presenting some "games" that politicians play and by emphasizing the importance of choice. These games and choices highlight differing views of the good political life, of political realities, and of wise judgment. The metaphor of a game calls attention to these crucial features of politics: players, stakes, rules, and behavioral strategy and tactics. Four dramatic models illustrate the way power—a cardinal factor in politics—is used. These sample games are designed to help you think critically about ends and means in politics. These chapters also highlight the struggle for power in politics—that is, in the words of Harold Lasswell in his 1935 classic book of the same title—who gets what, when, how, and why. Our presentation builds on your commonsense understanding of power as strength and influence and on your appreciation of the military, political, economic, and ideological aspects of power.

Politics involves grappling with tough problems in an often difficult world. By focusing on four momentous choices in politics, Chapter 2 again underscores the relationship among values, behavior, and judgment. These choices highlight the creative challenge involved in reaching wise decisions. Thoughtful investigation of these choices should stimulate you to probe political philosophy and ethics, comparative and world politics, and public policy in the succeeding parts of this book. Chapters 1 and 2 are designed to engage your interest and to prepare you for a somewhat more systematic presentation of our approach to political science and its main concern: politics.

Chapter 3 defines political science and outlines the conceptual framework for the entire book. Political scientists, we emphasize, explore the good political life, a science of politics, and wise judgment on public policy. Although these interests are evident in the traditional fields of political science, political scientists still argue about which of these concerns should be most prominent and about fitting them into a unified discipline.

Our exposition of the nature of political science assumes some familiarity with our suggested framework. Indeed, you could not have lived seventeen to twenty-one years or more without arriving at some views about the good political life; acquiring some understanding of political realities; and making some judgments about political actors, institutions, and policies. Chapter 3 builds on this awareness.

Chapter 4, the final chapter in Part I, explores how the larger physical, social, and cultural environment influences political values, behavior, and judgment. To understand problems in politics, people need to be aware, for example, of the geographic world they live in, the biological creatures they are, and the social communities they have built. The work of political scientists is thus informed by a variety of scholars, among them historians, economists, geographers, sociologists, anthropologists, psychologists, and physicists. Thus, Chapter 4 seeks to make students of political science cognizant of the interdisciplinary setting of politics.

Republican Donald Trump and Democrat
Hillary Clinton during the presidential debates
of 2016.

REUTERS/Pool New

1

GAMES POLITICIANS PLAY

At its best, politics can be a civilizing activity. It can preserve the peace, protect human rights, advance economic well-being, and encourage excellence in the arts and sciences. At its worst, however, politics—particularly for those on the losing side of the struggle for power—makes for war, tyranny, economic ruin, and barbarism. Even in democratic and constitutional countries, politics at its worst involves falsehood, deception, and meanness. In this chapter, we explore politics at its best and at its worst by examining some classic models in history, literature, and political philosophy. These examples suggest certain patterns that we call "political games."

THE GAME OF POLITICS

Politics is a process, within or among political communities, whereby (1) public values are articulated, debated, and prescribed; (2) diverse political actors (individuals, interest groups, local or regional governments, and nations) cooperate and struggle for power to satisfy their vital needs, protect their fundamental interests, and advance their perceived desires; and (3) policy judgments are made and implemented. Although subject to certain constraints imposed by the larger environment, political actors are still remarkably free to shape their own destinies—for good or ill. They have a creative ability to respond to political problems in diverse ways. The political games we will analyze illustrate a variety of such responses. Your critical appraisal of these games should advance three of this book's central purposes:

1. To deepen your critical appreciation of the good political life

Chapter Objectives

After studying this chapter, you will be able to do the following:

1. Describe ways in which the study of politics involves both moral judgment about goals and a scientific understanding of the way politics works.

2. Define the key concept of power.

3. Evaluate the efficacy of the main ideas of the destruction, accommodation, and conversion continuum.

4. Discuss the political game of wipeout.

5. Explain the political game of lion and fox.

6. Describe the political game of civil disobedience.

5

2. To enhance your scientific understanding of politics

3. To develop your capacity for wise political judgment

We chose the games that follow because they illustrate a wide range of political activity—physical annihilation, the struggle for power, and nonviolent civil disobedience. These patterns illustrate various forms of **power**: military power, political cunning, and the appeal to conscience. Although we do not include a specific game to illustrate the wheeling and dealing of such constitutional games as "bargaining"—commonly referred to as the politics of accommodation—this pattern is treated frequently throughout the book.

Elements of the Game

In this introductory chapter, our guiding question is this: How can the metaphor of a game serve our understanding of politics? The political games that we present are dramatic and educational. As drama, they may entertain. As education, they may enhance critical intelligence and shape political character and wise judgment. But can such a serious business as politics be called a game? We certainly do not mean to imply a frivolous pastime. We do, however, mean to suggest that all politics as contests have certain basic elements commonly found in other kinds of games. A game includes **players**—contestants who win or lose, who compete or cooperate in pursuit of certain goals, who exercise power or will, who enjoy or suffer. The **stakes** in the game are the goals that can be gained in victory or lost in defeat. The **rules** are the agreed-on procedures that must be followed if the game is to retain its identity; they regulate the conduct of the game. Finally, games entail **strategies and tactics**—plans of action, schemes of attack or defense, and judgments that bring about victory or defeat.

Thus, one way to look at politics is to see it as a game-like struggle to fulfill certain purposes; to gain, keep, and use power; and to formulate public policy. By viewing politics in this way, we can better explore its key patterns, particularly with the help of the following questions:

Unfortunately, the games politicians play are more complicated than football or chess. Unlike the contestants in such games, politicians involved in a given battle may not follow the same rules or even any discernible set of directions. They may even change the rules midgame and new players frequently enter the game at unpredictable times. If all the players do not follow the same rules, the players who have to respond to their opponents are at a serious disadvantage. This creates the kind of confusion and alarm that we call the Alice-in-Wonderland effect. When Alice plays croquet in Wonderland, she is not accustomed to using hedgehogs for croquet balls, flamingos for mallets, and soldiers for arches. Nor is she accustomed to a system in which the accused is first beheaded and then tried!

To compound the confusion created when there is no agreement on rules, politicians frequently shift from one game to another without warning. Consequently, a participant may not be aware of the decisive game—and its rules—until the contest is over. Politicians may also attempt to play several games simultaneously.

The Destruction-Accommodation-Conversion Continuum

Can we devise a scheme to help us understand the variety of political games? Several classifications are possible. Figure 1.1 offers a scheme in which the games are seen as ranging across a destruction-accommodation-conversion continuum. At one end of the continuum are games aimed at complete **destruction** of the opposing player. These games are marked by deadly conflict and war. Violence, including **terrorism** and torture, is prominent, and political, economic, psychological, and military instruments of force are used to exercise power.

Joseph Stalin's destruction of those he perceived as enemies within the Soviet Union is one infamous example of a game of destruction. Stalin came to power in the Soviet Union shortly after V. I. Lenin's death in 1924 and ruled with dictatorial power until his own death in 1953. Through his actions and policies, Stalin executed high-ranking political and military leaders and millions of other people suspected of disloyalty. Many people were killed outright; others died of starvation (most famously in a state induced

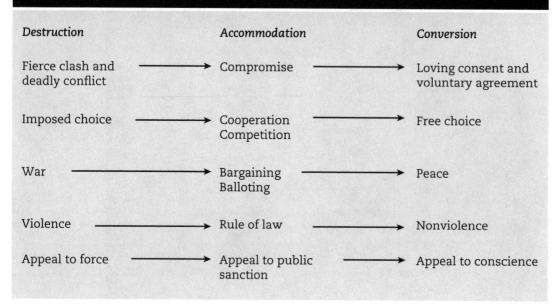

Figure 1.1 The Destruction-Accommodation-Conversion Continuum

Destruction	Accommodation	Conversion
Fierce clash and deadly conflict ⟶	Compromise ⟶	Loving consent and voluntary agreement
Imposed choice ⟶	Cooperation Competition ⟶	Free choice
War ⟶	Bargaining Balloting ⟶	Peace
Violence ⟶	Rule of law ⟶	Nonviolence
Appeal to force ⟶	Appeal to public sanction ⟶	Appeal to conscience

Source: Compiled by authors.

famine in the Ukraine during the mid-1930s); and still others died in prison camps, what the Russian novelist Aleksandr Solzhenitsyn called the Gulag Archipelago, a chain of prison labor camps spread across the Soviet Union.[1] No one was allowed to stand in the way of his quest for absolute power.

Adolf Hitler also illustrates a twentieth-century pattern of destruction. He, too, killed high-ranking party members who had helped him come to power. He, too, destroyed all effective political opposition to his rule. His barbaric campaign of destruction led to murderous onslaughts against Germany's neighbors, to slave labor for millions forced to work for the Nazi war machine, to concentration camps and death for millions of Germans and other Europeans, and to the Holocaust (the systematic killing of 6 million Jews).

More recent examples of the destruction game can be found all around the world: in the genocidal slaughter in Cambodia (Kampuchea) in Southeast Asia in the 1970s; in the Rwanda genocide of the mid-1990s as well as the **ethnic cleansing** in Bosnia and Herzegovina during the same decade; in the massacres occurring in the Darfur region of Sudan in Africa in the 2000s; in the terrorism visited on New York City and Washington, D.C., with the total destruction of the World Trade Center towers and partial destruction of the Pentagon in 2001; in the savage repression by the Syrian government against its own people in 2011 and 2012; and in the brutal rule of Kim Jong-un in North Korea. Such destruction was a dreadful twentieth-century reality of politics at its worst, and now, it seems, it is a reality of the twenty-first century as well. Will this type of destruction continue in this century?

In the middle of the continuum are games of **accommodation**, marked by cooperation, bargaining, and balloting. This pattern of politics is characterized by free elections, a two-party or multiparty system, public debate, and constitutional action according to the rule of law. Games of accommodation predominate in liberal democracies and in democratic socialist regimes. However, variations on these games also occur in authoritarian regimes.

At the other end of the continuum are games characterized by the peaceful **conversion** of the opponent. This pattern of politics stresses voluntary agreement and emphasizes free choice. In this pattern, even a majority decision may be ignored if the majority deviates from the claims of conscience. Love, conscience, and reason are the instruments employed in games of conversion. If games of destruction rely on arbitrary dictatorial edicts and games of accommodation rely on constitutional majority rule, then games of conversion look to unanimous agreement. Players of the game of conversion—for example, religious groups such as the Society of Friends (Quakers)—may seek to exercise influence (a version of power), but such influence is based, they argue, on truth and love rather than on majority rule or physical force.

Thus, the use of power to get political actors to do what they would not normally do ranges from overwhelming violence at the extreme pole of destruction to overwhelming charismatic, or spiritual, power—the free appeal, by word and deed, to the mind and heart—at the other pole of conversion. Political games, then, may involve fierce clashes and deadly conflicts, mild competition and pacific accommodation, or loving consent and freely given obedience.

Along the continuum, power may be used in many ways other than for destruction or conversion. Power may be used to balance, to seduce, or to support. For example, political actors may use the carrot or the stick to exercise influence: They may promise and deliver a host of benefits (money, goods and services, position, prestige) or they may threaten and retaliate with sanctions (the loss of benefits).

Political behavior is thus often a mixture of bullets and ballots, of arbitrary might and the rule of law, of bullying and encouraging. The character of the game depends significantly on the sanity of the players, the vital interests at stake, the status of rules and law, and judgments about wise policy and strategy.

Now, we will turn to some dramatic games drawn from history, literature, and political theory. These examples illustrate the way the game of politics is played in all its variety.

WIPEOUT: THE POLITICS OF DESTRUCTION

Superficially, **wipeout** is a simple game. One player, insisting on total domination, encounters resistance and employs brute physical force to destroy an opponent. Wipeout exemplifies the ultimate use of force in the struggle for power. Of course, complications can occur because of the different ways in which power is used, the maneuvers that precede total destruction, or the strange "logic" of a "reason of state" that "justifies" exterminating the opponent. The following classic model of wipeout will help explain some possible complications.

Athens and Melos

In his *History of the Peloponnesian War*, the Greek historian Thucydides presents the game with brilliant clarity.[2] The game unfolds at Melos, a Greek island caught in the midst of the savage war between two much more powerful and mortal political enemies: Athens and Sparta. Because the Melians will "not submit to the Athenians like the other islanders," they are forced into a confrontation. In the great struggle between Athens and Sparta for the mastery of greater Greece, the Melians at first remain neutral. But when the Athenians plunder Melian territory, the Melians assume "an attitude of open hostility." This leads to the brutal confrontation between the Athenians and the Melians (see Map 1.1).

Initially, the Athenians seek to negotiate the capitulation of Melos without all-out war. They have overwhelming military power and want to press their advantage. Their message is loud and clear: Surrender or be wiped out! They attempt to win the Melians over by appealing to their self-interest. The safety and security—indeed, the very preservation—of Melos requires that the Melians submit to Athens. The Melians must accept the harsh realities of power politics. The Athenians candidly declare, "You know as well as we do that right, as the world goes, is only in question between equals in power. . . . The strong do what they can and the weak suffer what they must." Do not, they urge the Melians, rely on appeals to **justice**, the gods, or the Spartans. Such appeals will not be answered.

At a serious disadvantage in the contest, the Melians try desperately to shift the game's emphasis from power to justice. They plead for the "privilege of being allowed in danger to invoke what is fair and right." They appeal to the gods. They remind Athens of the power of Sparta. They warn Athens of potential dangers. They cling to the idea of heroic resistance: "To submit is to give ourselves over to despair, while action still preserves for us a hope that we may stand erect. . . . We will not in a moment deprive of freedom a city that has been inhabited these 700 years . . . and so we will try to save ourselves. Meanwhile we invite you to allow us to be friends to you and foes to neither party."

The Athenians reject the idea of a neutral Melos and reemphasize their earlier arguments. The neutrality of Melos would adversely affect Athenian power, and appeals to justice, the gods, and the Spartans will not be answered because gods and men respect power. "Of the gods we believe, and of men we know, that by a necessary law of their nature they rule wherever they can." The Spartans will aid the Melians only when Spartan self-interest is engaged and Spartan power can be mustered without grave risk. Unfortunately for Melos, Sparta's vital interests are not at stake, and its power is not great enough to warrant a challenge to Athens at Melos. So, the Athenians plead with the Melians: Do not be blind. Be prudent. Save yourselves. Do not be led by fear of disgrace into hopeless disaster. Do not hesitate to protect your country and its prosperity. Choose security, not war and ruin.

So, the game is played. The Athenians seek domination without war but reserve the power to destroy their opponent. The Melians insist on freedom and independence even at the risk of war, and they hope for the best. Thus, the debate over power and justice, over "reason of state," and over enlightened self-interest comes to an end. The war of words, which so candidly reveals the strategy and tactics of the players, ceases. Physical hostilities commence. The Athenians lay siege to the isle of Melos. Pushed beyond endurance, the Melians finally surrender. Thucydides writes that the Athenians "put to death all the

Map 1.1   Ancient Greece

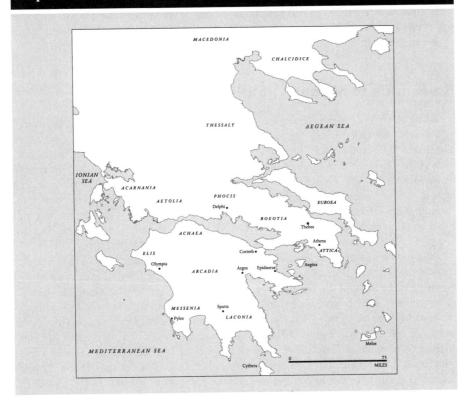

Source: CQ Press.

grown men whom they took, and sold the children for slaves, and subsequently sent out five hundred colonists and inhabited the place themselves."

This sketch identifies the players, stakes, rules, and strategy of the game of wipeout. The opponents played for varied stakes. Athens sought to dominate Melos. For Melos, there were three possible outcomes: (1) life and freedom, at best; (2) submission and domination if Melos agreed to accept Athens's terms; or (3) war, destruction, slavery, and death, at worst.

In examining this game, we discover that there were no agreed-on rules to protect the Melians. They sought in vain to persuade the Athenians to honor a code of justice and to respect the rules of neutrality. The Melians also failed to convince the Athenians to observe the rule that warns of the penalties for aggression. Such penalties may have to be paid when the aggressor's action engenders countervailing power or when the aggressor loses power.

The Athenians urged the Melians to accept the game of mastery. They urged the Melians to consider the penalties for failing to play the Athenian game: war, destruction, and death. They urged recognition of the rule that "justice" is the interest of the stronger party. Superior power, not abstract justice or sentimental goodwill, is what counts in politics. Athenian strategy was thus guided by Athens's need to protect its vital interests with superior strength. Such strength could normally convince an opponent, who sees self-preservation as the most vital interest, to back down. Melian strategy included an appeal to the gods, to justice, to the Spartans, and to Athenian self-interest.

Relevance to Modern Politics

The pattern of purpose, power, and policy revealed by this game can be illustrated in a host of actions throughout history. We have already highlighted the destructive patterns of Stalin and Hitler. To their actions, we can add thousands of other "wipeouts," such as the conquests of native North and South Americans by Spaniards, Portuguese, Anglo-Americans, and French. Communist regimes in North Korea, China, and Cuba have also wiped out their political opponents, sometimes through murder, sometimes through imprisonment or exile. Fascist dictators such as Benito Mussolini in Italy and Francisco Franco in Spain did likewise. In recent history, we had the brutality of Saddam Hussein in Iraq, Bashar al-Assad in Syria, and Km Jong-un in North Korea.

Genocide and ethnic cleansing are other forms of wipeout. Genocide is the systematic mass destruction of a national, ethnic, racial, or religious group, and ethnic cleansing is the forceful displacement of a group from a given territory based on its religion, ethnicity, race, or nationality and may involve mass murder as well. In Cambodia (Kampuchea), from 1975 to 1978, the Khmer Rouge, led by Pol Pot, compiled one of the worst records of human rights violations in history as a result of a thorough and brutal attempt to restructure Cambodian society. More than 1 million people, out of a total population of approximately 7 million, were killed or died under the Khmer Rouge's genocidal regime.[3] To this horror, we can add the genocide in Rwanda in 1994, in which members of the Hutu tribe killed nearly 1 million of their fellow Rwandans who were members of the Tutsi tribe. Ethnic cleansing in Bosnia and Serbia, also in the mid-1990s, and in the Darfur region of Sudan in the first decade of this century illustrate a contemporary pattern of wipeout.

Terrorism is another pattern of political wipeout. Defining the term is a very difficult and controversial task. How we define *terrorism* and count terrorist actions will significantly affect how we approach the problem. Nonetheless, there is at least some agreement that terrorism is the use of violence against innocent civilians in order to achieve a political goal. But two issues make it difficult to get beyond this simple definition. The first issue is motive. We can update the old adage and say, "One man's terrorist is another man's freedom fighter." One view holds that terrorism is nothing more than a vicious criminal act and there is no excuse for the killing of innocent people. Others take the stand that terrorism can, at least to some degree, be a legitimate instrument to counter powerful government repression and other unjust policies. Some view terrorism as an act of liberation. The other controversy has to do with identifying the terrorists. Some people believe that the definition of terrorism should include acts of terror perpetrated by governments, not merely nongovernmental groups. With an understanding that these issues are not fully resolved, terrorism will be defined as the use of violence by nongovernmental groups against innocent civilians for the purpose of achieving political goals.

While in recent years much of our attention has been riveted on the September 11, 2001, attacks on the World Trade Center in New York City and the Pentagon in Washington, D.C., terrorism can be traced back 2,000 years to groups like the Sicari and the Zealots, Jewish groups that fought against the first-century Roman occupation of the Middle East. Another early religious terrorist group, the Assassins, operating in the eleventh century, originated in the Ismaili sect of Shia Islam. The Balkans, Russia, and Ireland were fertile grounds for terrorist organizations during the latter part of the nineteenth century. The United States was not immune from terrorism during this period, as evidenced by the violent activities of the Ku Klux Klan to fight Reconstruction after the Civil War. In the post–World War II period, terrorist methods were used by some, but not all, decolonization movements in Africa, the Middle East, and Asia.[4]

The modern era of international terrorism emerged primarily out of Europe and the Middle East, with a variety of groups crossing national borders to carry out high-profile terrorist acts in order to maximize visibility for their cause. During the latter part of the 1960s and through the 1970s, groups such as the Palestine Liberation Organization, the Italian Red Brigades, and the West German Red Army Faction carried out a large number of spectacular terrorist acts that involved airline skyjacking and kidnapping of high-profile hostages. Probably the most famous terrorist act prior to September 11 was the attack at the 1972 Olympic Games in Germany when the Palestinian group Black September seized and murdered eleven Israeli athletes.

Despite the recent attention given to terrorism, the frequency of such incidents fluctuates over time. For instance, international terrorism reached near epidemic levels in the middle 1980s only to fall in the early to middle 1990s. One of the challenges for the student of politics is interpreting statistics and trends in order to form a clear understanding of what is actually happening in the world. For example, in 2006 the U.S. State Department broadened its definition of terrorist acts; this caused a dramatic increase in the number of terrorist incidents that the State Department reported. Although this does not necessarily mean terrorism is any more or less of a problem, this data can affect how policymakers and citizens perceive the issue. Nonetheless, no matter how we define the dangers of terrorism, the events of September 11 clearly demonstrate that a few incidents can kill thousands. And some analysts worry that the sophistication of such attacks has grown in recent years, as demonstrated by the meticulously coordinated attacks in Bali, Indonesia, and Moscow, Russia, in 2002; Madrid, Spain, and Beslan, North Ossetia, Russia, in 2004; London, England, in 2005; Mumbai, India, in 2008; Peshawar, Pakistan, in 2014; and Paris, France, and in the Sinai Desert, Egypt, in 2015. At the same time, less technologically advanced methods of terrorism can harm fewer people while still fostering a climate of fear that severely weakens the health and stability of any society. We see this in the rogue terrorist attacks in recent years carried out by individuals often radicalized via the Internet and possessing no affiliation to established terrorist groups.

To understand such political games is not to approve of them, any more than a doctor approves of disease. But in politics, as in medicine, diagnosis must precede prognosis. Only with a fuller, more critical understanding of purpose, power, and policy can we begin to explore what leads some political actors to engage in wipeout. We can then ask a crucial ethical question: What power should be exercised to protect

KEY QUESTIONS

1. In order to guarantee a necessary military victory, is it ever justified to intentionally kill large numbers of civilians?

2. Is the assassination of the head of another country justified if that leader's behavior is perceived as a threat to national security?

3. Is the use of torture justified if national security is threatened?

a state's vital interests or a ruler's ideological commitments or positions? We can also ask an important empirical question: Is superior power (understood here as physical force) what counts in politics? And we can ask a troubling, prudential question: Is it ever wise to sacrifice freedom to ensure self-preservation?

The relevance of these matters to modern politics is suggested by the Key Questions on this page, which illustrate the problematic character of politics. These questions suggest the difficulties inherent in the struggle for power. Next, we will examine another political game to illustrate the complexity of that struggle.

LION AND FOX: THE POLITICS OF THE NATION-STATE

We find the title of our second game in the work of Niccolò Machiavelli, a controversial student of Renaissance Italy.[5] The key players are the rulers of states. At stake are each state's vital interests: its unity, independence, freedom, security, power, and prosperity. The key rules in this game require leaders to behave realistically, to protect their community's vital interests, and to use both force and craft. Violation of the rules will incur severe penalties.

Machiavelli: The End Justifies the Means

If princes, or rulers, are to win amid the struggles for power that surround them, they must be adept at the "beastly" game of realistic politics. They cannot survive and prosper if they know or play only the higher human game of morality and law. They must know the game of **lion and fox**, played primarily with force and craft and, if necessary, unscrupulously. As Machiavelli puts it, "A prince being thus obliged to know well how to act as a beast must imitate the fox and the lion, for the lion cannot protect himself from traps, and the fox cannot defend himself from wolves. One must therefore be a fox to recognize traps, and a lion to frighten wolves."

Machiavelli holds that a prince is justified in playing the game of lion and fox because "in the actions of men, and especially of princes . . . the end justifies the means." "For," he writes, "where the very safety of the country depends upon the resolution to be taken, no considerations of justice or injustice, humanity or cruelty, nor of glory or of shame, should be allowed to prevail. But putting all other considerations aside, the only question should be, What course will save the life and liberty of the country?" When the occasion demands it, force and craft must be used boldly and shrewdly. On such occasions "good faith" and "integrity" can be sacrificed. The prince (as a lion or a fox) has only "to be a great feigner and dissembler." Machiavelli continues, "Thus it is well to seem merciful, faithful, humane, sincere, religious, and also to be so; but you must have the mind so disposed that when it is needful to be otherwise you may be able to change to the opposite qualities." Hence, "in order to maintain the state," a prince may be obliged "to act against faith, against charity, against humanity, and against religion."

Machiavelli outlines the general strategy of lion and fox with great candor. The prince must act "to secure himself against enemies, to gain friends, to conquer by force or fraud, to make himself beloved and feared by the people, [and] followed and reverenced by . . . [his] soldiers." With a keen regard for circumstances, he must act with Renaissance *virtù*—that is, to act with resolve and energy and achieve great things. Appreciative of dangers, the prince must be prepared to "destroy those who can injure him." With an eye to power, he must "maintain the friendship of kings and princes in such a way that they are glad to benefit him and fear to injure him." Recognizing the importance of the citizenry, the prince will win and keep widespread popular support and rely on a loyal citizen army. Above all, he will use muscle power and brainpower, severity and kindness, with discrimination and a shrewd regard for his ends and his power.

Machiavelli does not exclude the rule of law or the influence of traditional Christian morality. But he does assert that, in playing the game of lion and fox in a political world, the prince who confuses what ought to be with what is will surely lose. "For how we live is so far removed from how we ought to live, that he who abandons what is done for what ought to be done, will rather learn to bring about his own ruin than his preservation."

The foregoing strategy is prominent in *The Prince*, which Machiavelli wrote as a textbook for statesmen who would establish a state in a world beset by corruption, quarrelsome groups, foreign interference, and external aggression. But even in *The Discourses*, his book on the internal and external affairs of Rome, Machiavelli insists that those who would rule a republic on the basis of good laws must also be concerned with good arms. Moreover, even in a republic, a high commitment to popular virtue, a balance of social classes, the constitutional competition of parties, and the sound exercise of public opinion must not make the republican ruler forget the beastly game of lion and fox.

Physical power, particularly military strength, is crucial in nation-state politics and must be used, when necessary, effectively. For Machiavelli, military power means a citizen army. Good soldiers are the "sinews of war." The prince must be skilled in the organization, discipline, and conduct of war. He must use power to eliminate actual enemies and to paralyze potential enemies. The prince must be wary of helping others to become powerful. He must avoid making common cause with someone more powerful than himself. He should always use shrewd judgment in exercising power—guarding against false hope, overexpansion, the "insolence of victory," empty threats, and "insulting words."

The prince must be a "ferocious lion" and an "astute fox." He must shrewdly consider the uses of power and the uses of love, fear, hate, cruelty, and magnanimity. Thus, to build a strong internal base for his power, a prudent prince should seek to maintain

Machiavelli is known as both a political thinker and practicing politician. In this painting Machiavelli is shown seated near Cesare Borgia—a true prince who was willing to use both force, like the lion, and cunning, like the fox, to achieve his goals. Machiavelli's most famous book, *The Prince*, highlighted the abilities of men like Borgia to do whatever is necessary to achieve and maintain power. Painting by Faraffini, circa 1898.

popular favor, satisfy popular needs, and reward merit and achievement. The prince must artfully seek "to be feared and loved." But since "it is difficult for the two to go together," if he has to choose, he will act on the assumption that "it is much safer to be feared than loved." Moreover, the "prince should make himself feared in such a way that if he does not gain love, he . . . avoids hatred." To this end, a prince should abstain "from interfering with the property of his citizens and subjects or with their women." If he has to take a life, let the reason be clear and the justification convincing.

If possible, villainy and hatred should be avoided, but sometimes circumstances require cruelty. Then, Machiavelli suggests, "The conqueror must arrange to commit all his cruelties at once, so as not to have to recur to them every day, and so as to be able, by not making fresh changes, to reassure people and win them over by benefitting them." Here Machiavelli makes his famous—or infamous—distinction between "well-committed" and "ill-committed" cruelties: "Well committed may be called those (if it be permissible to use the word well of evil) which are perpetuated for the need of securing one's self, and which afterwards are not persisted in, but are exchanged for measures as useful to the subjects as possible. Cruelties ill committed are those which, although at first few, increase rather than diminish with time." And, of course, the prince should let others handle his cruelties and unpopular duties while he bestows "favors." Appearances matter in Machiavelli's account of politics.

Relevance to Modern Politics

Lion and fox is a difficult and dangerous game that is probably played more frequently throughout the world than most rulers (of liberal democracies as well as authoritarian regimes) are willing to admit. The high goals of classical political philosophy and modern constitutional morality are abandoned in this game. Machiavelli is willing to accept less than the best political life because justice is not possible for earthly political actors. In the battle between actual power and traditional morality, morality loses.

This game is notorious because of the candor with which Machiavelli laid bare its rules and its strategy. This notoriety should not obscure either the strengths or the weaknesses of the game. Machiavelli sought to achieve unity for Italy in the face of widespread popular corruption, dreadful internal divisions, and despised foreign domination. He held that the philosophy and tactics he advocated would achieve victory. He hoped, of course, that the outcome of the game would be a virtuous republic in which a divisive church, quarreling nobles, numerous principalities, and interfering foreign powers would not prevent the people from enjoying unity, liberty, prosperity, and strength.

But is it possible to find a great man—a Machiavellian prince—able to do the job? The problem haunted Machiavelli in Renaissance Italy:

> And as the reformation of the political condition of a state presupposes a good man, whilst the making of himself prince of a republic by violence naturally presupposes a bad one, it will consequently be exceedingly rare that a good man should be found willing to employ wicked means to become prince, even though his final object be good; or that a bad man, after having become prince, should be willing to labor for good ends, and that it should enter his mind to use for good purposes that authority which he has acquired by evil means.

The problem still haunts us today as we reflect on the careers of Napoleon, Otto von Bismarck, Stalin, Hitler, and hundreds of other national leaders, oppressive tyrants, and false messiahs.

It is a tribute to Machiavelli's genius that he understood so well what rulers of modern nation-states think they must do. They must protect the state's vital interests. They must be devoted, pragmatically, to success. They must maintain a love affair with power, particularly military power. They must not confuse what ought to be with what is. They must be prepared to operate as both lions and foxes.

Sometimes we may think that lion and fox describes only authoritarian rulers or such forceful and astute leaders as Bismarck, the "Iron Chancellor" of nineteenth-century Germany, whose use of military might and diplomatic cunning played a dominant role in unifying his country. Yet rulers of constitutional democracies also play lion and fox in both domestic and foreign affairs. For example, following the 2001 attack on the World Trade Center and the Pentagon, the George W. Bush administration may have pushed the legal envelope in extending the power to wiretap American citizens in order to gain better intelligence on potential acts of terrorism.

AP Photo/Bob Daugherty, File

Although the game of the lion and the fox has many champions, it is a dangerous game to play. President Richard M. Nixon was forced from office in 1974 after the Watergate scandal tainted his administration and his part in the cover-up was discovered.

The game is also evident in U.S. domestic politics. For example, dirty tricks in political campaigns illustrate "foxy" politics in operation. The Watergate scandal is the best known because it reached into the office of the U.S. presidency itself. Watergate is the name given to a series of scandals in President Richard M. Nixon's administration. First, there was an attempted burglary of the Democratic Party's national headquarters at the Watergate office complex in Washington, D.C., in June 1972. Two employees of President Nixon's reelection committee were involved, and Nixon's former attorney general was accused of approving the break-in. Then, the president's top advisers, and allegedly Nixon himself, attempted to cover up the bungled burglary. A number of officials were convicted for their roles in the affair. On August 9, 1974, Richard Nixon resigned his presidency under threat of impeachment.

Leaders in other administrations have also been seen in a Machiavellian light. For example, James MacGregor Burns titled his sympathetic study of Franklin D. Roosevelt, *Roosevelt: The Lion and the Fox.* Thus, many students of politics recognize that widely admired leaders with noble ends might very well be characterized as playing the game of the lion and the fox.

Students of political science must ask critical questions about this game. See the Key Questions on the next page.

We now turn to a quite distinctive political game more concerned with peace and the appeal to conscience to achieve its ends.

KEY QUESTIONS

1. Should we accept the doctrine that the end justifies the means—no matter what the end or the means?

2. How realistic is Machiavelli's "realism"?

3. Do Machiavellian realists miss important aspects of power because of their narrow understanding of power?

4. Do such realists fail to see that short-range success does not necessarily secure long-range vital interests?

CIVIL DISOBEDIENCE: THE POLITICS OF MORALITY

The game of **civil disobedience**, which was dramatized by the Greek tragedian Sophocles in *Antigone*, is well known to the modern world. Henry David Thoreau explored the game in a perceptive essay in the nineteenth century. Mohandas Gandhi made it popular in India—and the world—in the twentieth century. Norwegians and Danes used it tellingly against the Nazis in World War II. And Martin Luther King Jr. revealed its capabilities in the United States during his tragically brief but influential life. We have subtitled this game "the politics of morality" because the appeal to conscience, and thus to a higher law, is its central characteristic. In our examination, we will use Thoreau's brilliant essay "On Civil Disobedience" as our model.[6]

Thoreau: "On Civil Disobedience"

Who are the players in Thoreau's game? His answer resounds across the years. On one side are people of conscience—people of superior morality and integrity, who are human beings first and subjects second. On the other side are those who lack moral vision or courage—governments, majorities, people blind to the higher law or lacking the courage of their convictions. Specifically for Thoreau, on one side are those who oppose slavery and war; on the other side are the federal and state governments and the spineless multitudes that follow them.

What are the stakes? Nothing less than the abolition of outrageous moral evil and the return to the commandments of the higher law. In Thoreau's case, the evils are slavery and war, and the commandments are freedom and peace. Thoreau insists, "This people must cease to hold slaves" and cease to "make war on Mexico, though it cost them their existence as a people."

The following rules apply to the people of conscience who play this game. First, the game must be peaceful. To employ violence is to break a cardinal rule. Second, the act of disobedience must be selectively aimed at an outrageous moral evil. The protest must not be an indiscriminate one against all authority. Third, those disobedient must be public, not secretive, in their actions. Fourth, the participants must be prepared to pay the price of their disobedience. Thus, Thoreau peacefully went to jail rather than pay taxes to a government that supported slavery and fought the Mexican War. These rules hold only for those who engage in civil disobedience, not for their opponents.

What strategies and tactics guide the players? The disobedient must convert the ruling establishment by dramatizing the evil against which they protest. To do this, they must mobilize the sleeping conscience of the political community and destroy support for a government that sanctions immoral acts. This they can do by (1) effectively rallying their own forces, (2) making moral partisans of the neutral and the indifferent, and (3) converting or weakening the position of the immoral ruling elite.

According to advocates of civil disobedience, this general strategy can be implemented when people of conscience cease to obey an unjust government. They do so by peacefully withdrawing their support "both in person and in property." They break the law rather than serve as agents of injustice. Some may, as in Thoreau's case, refuse to pay taxes and be put in jail. Here their purpose is to clog the courts and the jails. Consciences throughout the land will be aroused at the sight of just men and women in jail. A chain reaction will set in as conscientious citizens refuse allegiance to, and conscientious officers resign from, the unjust government. Such action will provide the friction essential for stopping the machinery of government. The ruling elite will be divided and thus weakened. When confronted with the possibility of keeping all just people in jail or of giving up war and slavery, the state will abandon its immoral acts. Blood need not be spilled. If it is, however, it will be spilled by a state that has superior physical strength but not superior moral strength. Thus, moral strength will prevail. Civil disobedience is therefore not only desirable but also feasible.

Practitioners of civil disobedience are moral crusaders. To rally his own forces, Thoreau declares the following:

Library of Congress

This 1856 photograph is one of the few of Henry David Thoreau. Thoreau, the author of a famous essay on civil disobedience, was a vigorous defender of the moral responsibility of individuals to challenge unjust laws. He had a tremendous influence on such later political actors as Mohandas Gandhi and Martin Luther King Jr.

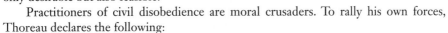

> I know this well, that if one thousand, if one hundred, if ten men who I could name—if ten honest men only—ay, if one HONEST man, in this state of Massachusetts, ceasing to hold slaves, were actually to withdraw from this co-partnership, and be locked up in the county jail . . . it would be the abolition of slavery in America.

To rouse—indeed, to radicalize—the indifferent, Thoreau writes:

> When a sixth of the population of a nation which has undertaken to be a refuge for liberty are slaves, and a whole country is unjustly overrun and conquered by a foreign army, and subjected to military law, I think that it is not too soon for honest men to rebel and revolutionize.

To induce neutral observers to join the cause of the righteous, Thoreau emphasizes several crucial arguments. Moral men and women cannot "recognize that political organization" as their government, "which is the slaves' government also." They appreciate that under "a government which imprisons any unjustly, the true place for a just man is also a prison." To undercut the legitimacy of the immoral government and to convert and weaken the ruling elite, Thoreau appeals to a higher law: "They only can force me who obey a higher law than I."

Thoreau is aware that his opponents will argue that he rejects democratic and constitutional politics. He knows that they will contend that civil disobedience illustrates a dogmatic, self-righteous position. He anticipates the criticism that civil disobedience is hostile to the normal give-and-take of democracy and constitutional compromise. Thoreau's critics will argue that he refuses to recognize that just and brave people may not agree about all moral issues in politics and that civil disobedience is incompatible with democratic accommodation and makes for anarchy.

Thoreau is ready to repel this counterattack. He insists that it is important to distinguish between minor and major matters in politics. Matters that present no serious moral problem can be handled by majority rule. However, fundamental matters, such as slavery, cannot be left to the ethical competence of majorities. He is not seeking to destroy all aspects of government. As a good citizen, he is quite prepared to pay his highway tax and to educate his fellow citizens. He is aware of the virtues of obedience to the law, of majority rule, of constitutional debate and decision. But a higher law may have to take precedence over civil law. A constitution that recognizes slavery and refuses even to receive petitions protesting slavery does not deserve respect. Thoreau does not "wish to quarrel" or "set myself up as better than my neighbors," and he seeks to obey the laws of the land. He concedes that "from a lower point of view, the Constitution, with all its faults, is very good; the laws and the courts are very respectable; even this State and this American government are, in many respects, very admirable, and rare things, to be thankful for." But from the vantage point of a higher law of justice, the Constitution fails.

So Thoreau elaborates the strategy and tactics of civil disobedience. The boldness, as well as the difficulty, of the game is underscored by his basic assumptions: the superior power of conscience in politics, agreement on what is righteous, and the establishment's ultimate benevolence. He assumes there will be no reactionary backlash and that disobedience will not be brutally repressed.

KEY QUESTIONS

1. Should people rely mainly on civil disobedience to combat what they believe to be outrageous moral evils?

2. What makes a moral evil outrageous?

3. In the real world of politics, characterized by a struggle for power, is the risk of civil disobedience worth taking?

Relevance to Modern Politics

As we noted in discussing the game of lion and fox, Machiavelli challenged most of these assumptions. They are also impugned by the Athenians at Melos in the game of wipeout. Yet despite the objections of many people to Thoreau's assumptions, Martin Luther King Jr. used civil disobedience successfully in the civil rights movement of the 1960s. When employed according to Thoreau's rules, civil disobedience proved an effective weapon for advancing the rights of African Americans. Moreover, an accumulating literature highlights the success of civil disobedience against a wide variety of authoritarian regimes. Indeed, as we will see more fully in Chapter 13, some scholars maintain that the only sane road to peace and human rights in the nuclear age is through nonviolent civilian defense.

Civil disobedience has also been employed in another highly controversial issue in American society—the morality, lawfulness, and wisdom of abortion. Antiabortion advocates have, for example, used civil disobedience in their protests against abortion clinics. This issue pits pro-choice advocates against pro-life advocates. The debate involves judgments on a number of troublesome moral and legal questions: whether a fetus is a person and therefore entitled to moral rights and legal protection; how much control a woman has over her own body; how to balance the competing needs of fetus, mother, and other parties; when a fetus is viable; and what to do about life-threatening pregnancies or those caused by rape or incest.

See the Key Questions that must be asked in evaluating civil disobedience.

CONCLUSION

The games presented in this chapter are educational models. As such, they may help us to understand (1) the character of the major players in politics, (2) the stakes involved in key political games, (3) the rules of politics, and (4) influential strategies and tactics. These games may suggest other variations: for example, balance of power—the politics of equilibrium; class conflict—the politics of domination; stake-in-society—the politics of vested interests; bargaining—the politics of accommodation; miracle, mystery, and authority—the politics of benevolent authoritarianism.[7]

We should remember that the games used in this chapter represent specific cases to illustrate a continuum of political activity. Many other examples could be found throughout history and in the contemporary world that take elements of the three cases used in this chapter. For instance, political activity often combines elements of Machiavelli's cold realism while still holding on to some political ideals to guide action. Keep in mind, also, that the political and legal context in which actions happen affect how we judge those actions. Think of a strike—where an organization or group of people withholds vital services. In the United States, where laws protect unions, the strike is a classic instance of a bargaining tactic that illustrates the accommodation aspect of politics. However, in the early 1980s in Poland, trade union leader Lech Walesa and the Solidarity movement used strikes as a form of civil disobedience that eventually led to the fall of the communist regime in that country and the rise of a new democratic nation.

The games call attention to a number of important ethical, empirical, and prudential problems in politics. They highlight the clash between power and justice. They force us to look critically at "reason of state"—that rationale that prompts leaders of states to protect their nation's vital interests. They force us to ask whether a ruler must accept the "beastly" character of politics and function as both a ferocious lion and an astute fox to protect the state's vital interests. We must decide whether Machiavelli is right in holding that idealism will lead to ruin. The study of these games also entails a deeper look into the ethics and politics of political means. We have to decide if and when the strike is an effective and wise weapon and whether civil disobedience is compatible with majority rule, democratic law, and other time-tested constitutional forms.

Today, we desperately need to clarify the purposes of politics, the uses of power, and the wisdom of policies. In recent years, the ends of political life and the exercise of power have not been keenly criticized. The result has been failure to devise a prudent way to harness power for just and humane purposes. In Chapter 2, we investigate additional scenarios to focus on the problems of political choice.

SUGGESTED READINGS

The following novels, plays, and works of philosophy present a wide variety of additional games that politicians play.

Bolt, Robert. *A Man for All Seasons*. New York: Random House, 1966. Highlights the clash between loyalty to conscience (and God) and to king (and country). Also reveals the nobility—and weakness—of reliance on the law in the face of a powerful, determined, and unscrupulous ruler.

Bradbury, Ray. *Fahrenheit 451*. New York: Simon & Schuster, 2012. First published 1953 by Ballantine. Focuses on how people relinquish control of their lives to government. Originally published in 1953, this science-fiction thriller was in the tradition of Orwell's *1984* in that Bradbury places us in a dystopia that outlaws reading as well as free and critical thought. The focus is on how people relinquish control of their lives to government.

Dostoevsky, Fyodor. "The Legend of the Grand Inquisitor." Book 5, chap. 5 in *The Brothers Karamazov*. New York: Random House, Modern Library Edition, 1950. Contains the grand inquisitor's brilliant (if perverse) argument that a benevolent authoritarian ruler should relieve inadequate humans of the burden of freedom.

Drury, Allen. *Advice and Consent*. New York: Word Fire Press, 2017 (Originally published 1959). Explores the U. S. Senate confirmation of a controversial Secretary of State nominee who was a member of the Communist Party.

Geuss, Raymond. *Philosophy and Real Politics*. Princeton, NJ: Princeton University Press, 2008. Urges students of politics to consider the context and history that define politics and not be held hostage to an otherworldly devotion to ideals.

Golding, William. *Lord of the Flies*. New York: Penguin Group, 1959. Uses a group of shipwrecked boys as an allegory for the evil in all of us and the manner in which we can so easily collectively act on that evil.

Kafka, Franz. *The Castle*. Trans. Willa and Edwin Muir. New York: Knopf, 1930. Addresses the individual's plight in the baffling world of bureaucracy.

Klein, Joe. *Primary Colors: A Novel about Politics*. New York: AOL Time Warner, 1996. The story of an ambitious, womanizing southern politician headed for the White House. Though the book is a work of fiction, its main character bears a remarkable similarity to a recent president of the United States.

Koestler, Arthur. *Darkness at Noon*. Trans. Daphne Hardy. New York: Macmillan, 1941. Illuminates the minds and politics of communist revolutionaries out of power and in power.

Margalit, Avisha. *On Compromise and Rotten Compromises*. Princeton, NJ: Princeton University Press, 2010. An engrossing investigation of when political compromises are a good and when such compromises should be rejected.

Orwell, George. *1984*. New York: New American Library, 1951. Another anti-utopian novel that throws light on the loss of freedom in a totalitarian society.

Shakespeare, William. *Richard III*, 1592; *Julius Caesar*, 1599; *Measure for Measure*, 1604; *Macbeth*, 1605; *Antony and Cleopatra*, 1606; *Coriolanus*, 1607. The games politicians play, as represented in the work of the greatest literary voice in the English language. Highlights political machinations involving the struggle for power and who gets what, when, and how.

Shaw, George Bernard. *Arms and the Man*, 1894; *The Devil's Disciple*, 1897; *Caesar and Cleopatra*, 1899; *Man and Superman*, 1905 (especially that section often produced separately as *Don Juan in Hell*); *Major Barbara*, 1905; *Saint Joan*, 1923. No one play can do justice to Shaw's witty socialist criticism of politics and society. And by all means, read those magnificent lengthy prefaces, which are also great lectures on modern social science.

Sophocles. *Antigone*, c. 441 B.C. A powerful play that illustrates the tragic clash between individual conscience (as informed by a higher law) and public order (as dictated by the need for stability and safety in the community).

Vidal, Gore. *Lincoln, a Novel.* New York: Knopf Doubleday Publishing Group, 2000. Offers a comprehensive, historically accurate account of Lincoln's remarkable career in a lively fictional style.

Warren, Robert Penn. *All the King's Men.* New York: Harcourt, Brace, and World, 1946. Describes the rise and fall of a southern-style political boss. A fictional political novel based loosely on the very real Louisiana governor Huey Long.

GLOSSARY TERMS

accommodation (p. 9)
civil disobedience (p. 18)
conversion (p. 9)
destruction (p. 7)
ethnic cleansing (p. 8)
genocide (p. 12)

justice (p. 10)
lion and fox (p. 14)
players (p. 6)
politics (p. 5)
power (p. 6)
rules (p. 6)

stakes (p. 6)
strategies and tactics (p. 6)
terrorism (p. 7)
wipeout (p. 9)

NOTES

1. Aleksandr Solzhenitsyn, *The Gulag Archipelago, 1918–1956* (New York: Harper Collins, 2002). Originally published in the West in 1974.

2. The description here and in the following paragraphs is derived from *The Complete Writings of Thucydides: The Peloponnesian War*, trans. Richard Crowley (New York: Random House, Modern Library Edition, 1951), 330–337.

3. U.S. State Department, *Country Reports on Human Rights Practices for 1989* (Washington, DC: U.S. Government Printing Office, 1990), 792.

4. Mark Burgess, "A Brief History of Terrorism," *Center for Defense Information*, July 2, 2003, www.pogo.org/our-work/straus-military-reform-project/cdi-archive/a=brief-history-of-terrorism.html?referrer=https://www.google.com.

5. The following discussion is based on Niccolò Machiavelli, "The Prince," trans. Luigi Ricci and rev. by E. R. P. Vincent, and "The Discourses," trans.

Christian Detmold, in *The Prince and the Discourses* (New York: Random House, Modern Library Edition, 1940).

6. See Henry David Thoreau, "On Civil Disobedience," in *Walden and Other Writings of Henry David Thoreau* (New York: Random House, Modern Library Edition, 1937).

7. Karl Marx illuminates the game of "class conflict"; Alexander Hamilton, that of "stake-in-society"; Fyodor Dostoevsky, that of "miracle, mystery, and authority." See, for example, Marx and Engels's *The Communist Manifesto* (New York: International Publishers Company, Incorporated, 1948); Hamilton's state papers; and Fyodor Dostoevsky, "Legend of the Grand Inquisitor," book 5, chap. 5 in *The Brothers Karamazov* (New York: Random House, Modern Library Edition, 1950). On Dostoevsky, see also Neal Riemer, "Some Reflections on the Grand Inquisitor and Modern Democratic Theory," *Ethics* 14, no. 4 (1954–1955): 458–470.

Robert and John F. Kennedy in 1962 during the
Cuban missile crisis.

AP photo

2

POLITICS AND CHOICE

The challenging subject of politics and choice underscores the intimate connection among values, facts, and judgment in the political arena. In this chapter, we examine five dramatic cases that illustrate the dimensions of choice in politics. These cases involve five crucial historical choices: (1) Socrates's choice not to flee Athens to avoid an unjust punishment, (2) James Madison's choice of a new political theory to guide in the creation of the American Constitution of 1787 and the federal republic it undergirds, (3) the choice of the citizens (and key leaders) of Germany to support Adolf Hitler in 1932 and 1933, (4) President John F. Kennedy's choice of a blockade to counter the Soviet Union's placement of offensive nuclear weapons in Cuba in the fall of 1962, and (5) President George W. Bush's choice to invade Iraq in 2003.

FIVE IMPORTANT THEMES

The cases presented in this chapter illustrate that choice in politics can be tragic, creative, perilous, and thoughtful. These examples enable us to see that it is not easy to choose what is right, to break through to a new political understanding, to bear the burden of freedom, or to select the least perilous alternative. As you read, ask yourself what you would have done in each situation:

1. What would you do if you had been lawfully sentenced to death on charges you knew were false and were then offered the opportunity to escape?

2. Would you try a new, untested experiment in government in the face of conventional wisdom that suggested your experiment could never work?

Chapter Objectives

After studying this chapter, you will be able to do the following:

1. Identify five key themes in politics.

2. Discuss the theme of political obligation and the moral life.

3. Describe the tension between liberty and authority in political life.

4. Discuss the burden of freedom in political life.

5. Explain the theme of political power.

6. Recognize the value of accurate information and reasonable assumptions in political decision making.

3. As a German citizen, would you have supported Adolf Hitler's Nazi Party in 1932 and 1933?

4. As president of the United States, how would you have responded to the news that the Soviet Union had placed offensive nuclear missiles in Cuba?

5. Would you have decided to commit American forces to invade Iraq in response to al-Qaida's attack on the World Trade Center and the Pentagon?

Of course, these five cases are not exhaustive. The range of critical choices faced by American leaders are too numerous to list. However, a few might include Thomas Jefferson's decision to purchase the Louisiana Territory from France in 1803, Abraham Lincoln's decision to write and deliver the Emancipation Proclamation in 1863, the Allied decision to undertake the D-Day invasion of Europe in 1944, Harry Truman's decision to drop the Atomic bombs on Hiroshima and Nagasaki, Japan, in 1945, and George W. Bush's decision to invade Afghanistan in order to go after al-Qaida and the Taliban in the aftermath of the 9/11 attacks. The case studies presented here invite special attention because they foster critical thinking about five important and perennial themes in politics.

The first case delves into the theme of political obligation. Why should we obey those who demand our allegiance in politics, particularly those who constitute our government? The second case explores the theme of creativity in politics. Is it possible, in theory and practice, to achieve a new ethical, empirical, and prudential understanding of politics? More specifically, can we devise new ways to reconcile liberty and authority?

The third case explores the theme of the responsible exercise of freedom. Can citizens respond sensibly to social, economic, and political crises? Are we strong enough to bear the burden of freedom? Are we mature enough to exercise freedom responsibly, or do we, under adverse conditions, abandon freedom for authoritarian rule?

The fourth case probes the theme of **power politics**. How do we work out sane, sound strategies and tactics in a nuclear age? Can we avert situations that call for agonizing choices that might lead to nuclear war? In times of crisis can we choose courses of action that preserve our vital interests in peace, national security, and freedom?

The fifth case illustrates the way sound political judgment relies upon accurate information and reasonable assumptions in political decision making. All students of politics must critically consider what is actually happening in the world and from those considerations derive sound assumptions with which to drive policy decisions. Furthermore, rarely are political decisions made on the basis of incomplete information. Politics by its nature deals to a certain degree with the unknown. But a healthy political world has leaders capable of using limited knowledge to make thoughtful decisions. Indeed, this is the basis of sound judgment.

Elaborating the Theme

Each case in this chapter develops one of these key themes, themes that recur throughout this book. Socrates, father of political philosophy in the West, initiates the critical examination of **political obligation**, a concept that explores why people obey or disobey those who demand their political allegiance, such as a government, a law, or a state. His views present a counterargument to those advanced by Henry David Thoreau in Chapter 1. It is a debate that persists today whenever a government's legitimacy is called into question—by American students who protested the Vietnam War, resisted the draft, or left their country in the late 1960s and early 1970s; by Polish members of Solidarity who protested or resisted martial law in their country or fled to avoid tyranny in 1982; by South Africans who opposed apartheid from 1948 to 1989; by Chinese students in Tiananmen Square who demonstrated for democratic reform in 1989; and by protesting Iranians who forced partial vote recounts in their country after accusations of fraud and corruption in the 2009 presidential election. More recently, in 2011, the Egyptian government of Hosni Mubarak was toppled by widespread popular demonstrations and in that same year, citizens of Deraa, Syria began demonstrating against the Assad government demanding the release of political prisoners. Soon, the protests spread throughout the country, and Syria was plunged into civil war. And in early 2018, Iranians once again took the streets challenging their government over the issues of food and fuel prices and corruption. To explore the question of political obligation is to ask what makes a government legitimate—that is, what makes government lawful and entitled to obedience and respect?

Similarly, James Madison, father of the U.S. Constitution, merits our study. He is one of America's most important political theorists—one who was willing to undertake an experiment in constitution-making that remains unfinished even today. He is a rare example of someone who thought at a very high level of political theory, put his thoughts into practice by helping to write the Constitution, and then served in the very real world of day-to-day politics as the United States' fourth president. His ideas help us to understand the formation of the American federal republic, which is the oldest constitutional democracy in the world. A study of Madison's guiding theory illustrates **political creativity**—the achievement in both theory and practice of a more fruitful, ethical, empirical, and prudential understanding of politics—at its best. The task of reconciling liberty and authority remains. It is a problem common to all nations, whether rich or poor; developing or developed; liberal democracy, democratic socialist state, or communist state.

We focus on the fateful choices German citizens made in 1932 and 1933 for several important reasons. Historically, we want to know more about the circumstances that permitted Hitler to attain power and to use that power to unleash World War II and its dreadful consequences. Who voted for Hitler and why? More generally, we want to know what produces **responsible citizenship**, which entails the sensible response of citizens to social, economic, and political tasks and problems. Can people really govern themselves successfully, particularly under adverse conditions? This question can be asked about authoritarian regimes on the left or the right, or about nations emerging from authoritarian rule (such as the republics of the former Soviet Union and the Eastern European nations now freed of communist domination as well as Spain, the Philippines, and Chile, which have thrown off right-wing dictatorships). This question can also be asked about the struggling developing nations of the world and even about supposedly mature democratic regimes in times of crisis.

The Cuban missile crisis merits attention because it brilliantly illuminates key aspects of power politics, or the political pattern of acquisition, preservation, and balancing of power characteristic of the competitive-conflictive behavior of the United States and the Soviet Union. In a world of nuclear weapons, it is important to understand how in 1962 the leaders of the two military superpowers—the United States and the Soviet Union—responded to political crisis. When political actions reached the stage of big-power confrontation in the nuclear age, the fate of the entire globe was at stake.

Finally, the 2003 decision by President George W. Bush to invade Iraq illustrates the dangers of making critical decisions on the basis of inaccurate information and faulty assumptions. Political actors can make decisions that from their perspective are wise and morally correct. But regardless of how "right" the decision may be, if the empirical basis upon which it is made is incorrect the decision runs the risk of failure. Put simply, there is no substitute for accurate information and sound assumptions.

Values, Facts, and Judgment

By exploring these cases and the choices they involved, we discover the intimate relationship of values, facts, and judgment. For example, Socrates's choice is incomprehensible if we do not understand the high value he placed on his birth, education, and citizenship in the Greek polis (city-state). Of course, the unacceptable consequences of escape and life in exile also influenced his decision.

The second case shows that Madison's dedication to republican values of popular rule and basic rights, as well as to effective governance, clarified his quest for a breakthrough to our modern federal republic. Madison's was a **creative breakthrough**, which we define as a significantly fruitful resolution of a problem that conventional wisdom deems insoluble. His understanding of the accepted "facts"—that liberty is possible only in a small state or that a large country cannot be governed on republican principles—did not prevent him from challenging them and articulating a new empirical theory that enabled Americans to reconcile liberty and authority.

The third case depicts how adverse circumstances led Germans to seek political change to give meaning to values such as order, strength, prestige, and prosperity. Many Germans supported Hitler because they sympathized with Nazi promises to help Germany overcome economic depression, avoid the alleged communist menace, and recover from defeat in World War I.

President Kennedy's choice also illustrates the close connection among values, facts, and judgment. His choice in the Cuban missile crisis was dictated by the value of national security; at the same time, it was made agonizing by the danger of nuclear catastrophe if the Soviet Union refused to back down. Key facts—especially the military estimate that a "surgical" air strike could not guarantee the destruction of all Soviet missiles—led him to endorse a blockade, which permitted a firm response and gave the Soviet Union time to reconsider its bold gamble yet held open more militant options if the Soviet Union refused to withdraw its offensive weapons.

Finally, the decision made by President Bush to send thousands of men and women to war in Iraq was one of two military reactions to the 9/11 attacks, the first being the invasion of Afghanistan. As in the case of the Cuban missile crisis, the value of national security seemed to be at stake. America had been directly attacked. But was it a sound decision? Were the empirical facts upon which it was based and rationalized accurate? Without accurate information the ability to make sound political judgments is severely limited.

Our Key Question in examining these five cases is:

KEY QUESTION

1. How does political choice illustrate the intimate connection among values, facts, and judgment?

SOCRATES AND THE MORAL LIFE: POLITICAL OBLIGATION IN ANCIENT ATHENS

The story of Socrates's life and teachings comes to us primarily in the writings of Plato, Socrates's devoted student. Here we focus on the very end of the great teacher's life.

Socrates's Choice

Socrates has been accused of corrupting the youth of Athens and of not believing in the gods. He vigorously denies both charges. He maintains that he is being falsely accused because of his relentless probing of ignorance and pretension among people of repute—particularly rhetoricians, poets, and artisans. This mission, ordained by God, has gotten him into trouble because those who pretend to be wise do not like having their folly exposed.

Socrates sees himself as a "gadfly," "arousing," "persuading," "reproaching," "exhorting . . . to . . . virtue." He has tried to teach his students to put "virtue and wisdom" before their "private interests." He cannot hold his tongue because "this would be a disobedience to a divine command." And he cannot abandon his mission out of fear of death "or any other fear." He cannot give up teaching about the care of the soul. He has never yielded to injustice in either public or private life. His "only fear was the fear of doing an unrighteous or unholy thing." He has taught virtue for its own sake, not for the sake of money. He believes in a higher divinity: "Men of Athens, I honor and love you; but I shall obey God rather than you, and while I have life and strength I shall never cease from the practice and teaching of philosophy."[1]

When he is condemned to die by drinking hemlock, a poison, Socrates refuses to bargain for his life by asking for exile, a stiff fine, or imprisonment. He proposes as his proper punishment that which is his due—his maintenance at public expense! Why should he plead for his life when he cannot be sure that life is better than death? Imprisonment, as a punishment, is intolerable because it is a kind of slavery. He cannot pay a stiff fine because he has no money. Exile, too, is unthinkable: "What a life should I lead at my age, wandering from city to city, living in ever-changing exile, and always being driven out!" On the urging of his friends, he proposes a minuscule fine as punishment.

Socrates does not regret his defense—his "apology." He departs "condemned . . . to suffer the penalty of death." However, Socrates firmly believes those who have condemned him to death will suffer more—"condemned by the truth to suffer the penalty of villainy and wrong."

Crito, one of Socrates's disciples, comes to him in jail with a proposal to bribe the guards and permit him to escape. Crito does not want to lose a dear friend, nor does he want people to think that he did not do enough to save his mentor's life. Appreciative of Socrates's sensibilities, he argues that Socrates should not play into the hands of his enemies. Crito points out that people will respect and love Socrates in exile; that he should not betray his own children, who need him for their education; and that escape will not be disgraceful. Crito knows that he has to make a strong argument to convince Socrates, for at his trial Socrates had already given signs that he would accept his punishment. Socrates had argued that he must always do what is right, that he cannot do anything "common or mean" in his hour of danger; that he would find exile unacceptable and unrewarding, particularly if he could not carry on his mission of critical inquiry; that his death was a meaningful choice; and that his oracle had opposed neither his behavior at the trial nor the verdict of his death.

Socrates responds to Crito's entreaty by arguing the key question: "The only question . . . is . . . whether we shall do rightly either in escaping or in suffering others to aid in our escape." He cannot intentionally injure others; he cannot "render evil for evil to any one, whatever evil [he] may have suffered." In escaping, would he desert the just principles by which he has lived?

Socrates answers his cardinal question by imagining how those who speak for the "laws and the government" would answer it. He cannot be justified in escaping because that action would weaken the laws, the government, and the state. Athens cannot endure if its lawful decisions have no power, if individuals can set them aside at will. Socrates is indebted to his polis—his political community—for birth, for nurture and education, and for fulfillment in citizenship. By his life, growth, and fulfillment in the political community, he has undertaken a contractual agreement that he cannot now violate by escaping. He cannot disobey his parents, "the authors of his education," nor can he disavow his own agreement to obey the commands of the polis—especially when he has not been able to convince the political community that its commands are wrong. He must choose death over banishment; he could not be a "miserable slave," "running away and turning [his] back upon the compacts and agreements [he] made as a citizen." Having been born and having lived and enjoyed citizenship in the political community, Socrates cannot now repudiate that community.

Moreover, Socrates's escape would harm his friends and children and bring him no peace in exile. His friends would lose their property and citizenship and be driven into exile as well. Other good cities would view Socrates as an "enemy," a "subverter of the laws." And he would find no happiness in fleeing from "well-ordered cities and virtuous men." If he lived in disordered cities, could he, having turned his back on his own principles, talk of "virtue and justice and institutions and laws being the best things among men"? Would he deprive his children of Athenian citizenship?

And so, Socrates concludes the argument he has made for law-abiding Athenians and against his escape. Law-abiding Athenians will say the following:

Now you depart in innocence, a sufferer and not a doer of evil; a victim, not of the laws, but of men. But if you go forth, returning evil for evil, and injury for injury, breaking the covenants and agreements which you have made with us, and wronging those whom you ought least to wrong, that is to say, yourself, your friends, your country, and us, we shall be angry with you while you live, and our brothers, the laws in the world below, will receive you as an enemy; for they will know that you have done your best to destroy us.

Socrates's choice not to escape illuminates the problem of political obligation and this key question: Why should we obey the political community that makes claims on our allegiance? Socrates's answer is that because of the contribution that the political community makes to our life, growth, and fulfillment, we are required to obey its laws. He argues that if we cannot persuade the political community that its laws are wrong, we are obligated to obey them.

Socrates was executed in 399 B.C. by the Athenian authorities because of his incessant criticisms of Athenian democracy. Despite being condemned to death, he was unwilling to abandon his city or his friends. Socrates was willing to die for his beliefs, and thus, he offers an example of a man of principle and civic loyalty. Jacques-Louis David, *The Death of Socrates*, 1787.

Questioning Socrates's Choice

Socrates's view, of course, is only one view of political obligation. Thoreau's position, discussed in Chapter 1, represents another view. Thoreau argued that we have no obligation to obey a government that violates a higher law and engages in outrageously immoral action such as aggressive war or human slavery.

The American revolutionaries of 1776 articulated yet another position on political obligation. They held that when a government violates the trust that brought it into being; when it persistently violates the right to life, liberty, and the pursuit of happiness; and when it is not responsive to redress of grievances, the people have a right to revolt and overthrow such a government and establish a new one, based on their consent and dedicated to the protection of their rights. This position rests upon the premise that we owe obedience only to governments of our own making that protect our basic rights and, pursuant to our will, advance life, growth, and fulfillment.

Critical minds will raise questions for Socrates (held to be one of the wisest, most just, and best of human beings), for Thoreau (as we saw in Chapter 1), and even for the authors of the American Declaration of Independence. For example, do we uncritically accept Socrates's statement that "whether in battle or in a court of law" we "must do" as our country orders? Do we accept that "punishment is to be endured in silence"? Even in battle, following orders is no legitimate excuse for violating international law or for committing war crimes, genocide, or other crimes against humanity. Moreover, is there no obligation to speak out against unjust punishment? Some would argue (as did Martin Luther King Jr. and many others—including Socrates—in a long tradition of obedience to a higher law) that to endure injustice in silence is to perpetuate injustice.

Even the theory of political obligation enshrined in the Declaration of Independence has its difficulties. We know that Thomas Jefferson intentionally left certain phrases in the Declaration vague so that people could read into what they believed. How do we more precisely define those "unalienable rights" to life, liberty, and the pursuit of happiness that are to be protected by a government? What conditions justify our conclusion that government is destroying those rights? How do

James Madison, one of the authors of the U.S. Constitution and the fourth president of the United States, was famous for his ability to rethink how republican governments work. Before Madison, it was believed that republics could exist only in small political communities—geographically large and culturally diverse republics like the current United States were inconceivable.

we understand the "consent of the governed" from which "just powers" derive?

African Americans were denied liberty, often life, and certainly the pursuit of happiness when they were enslaved in the United States and then treated as second-class citizens after emancipation. Even today, they may not be treated with genuine equality in all respects. Women in the United States have also been fighting a long battle for genuine equality. Given this record of unequal treatment, do African Americans and women have the same obligation to obey the government as others? How has this question changed, if at all, in the wake of the election of Barack Obama? What about other mistreated minorities? In the wake of 9/11, many Muslim Americans have felt the sting of discrimination as the United States confronts terrorism that now springs from a small subset of Islam. If we extend our democratic theory of obligation—that is, obedience in return for fulfillment of basic rights—to include the right to education, a job, or adequate health care and housing, then the uneducated, the unemployed, the sick, and the homeless may have less of an obligation to obey the government than the educated, wealthy, and well housed. This theory of obligation certainly provides food for thought.

These critical inquiries are disquieting, but they make us see that our judgment about obligation cannot be separated from our evaluation of whether a government is legitimate, whether it honors our rights, and whether it is truly based on the consent of the governed. Depending on their values and their assessment of the facts, different observers may reach different conclusions about political obligation. The young Americans who refused to fight in Vietnam had a different sense of obligation than those who did. African Americans who refused to accept racial segregation in buses, restaurants, movie theaters, and schools had a different sense of obligation than did those who went along with "separate but equal" legislation.

Clearly, an individual's respect for his or her political community—and responsibility to the government—can be interpreted in different ways, and these interpretations are closely related to how the interpreter balances values, ascertains circumstances, and weighs alternatives. James Madison and the constitutional reformers of 1787, for example, felt obligated to disobey the instructions from their states to simply amend the flawed Articles of Confederation that had governed the nation since 1781. In the very interest of improving the young republican union, they drafted a constitution with striking new powers. They undertook what some people consider to be a contradiction in terms—a "peaceful revolution."

MADISON, THE NEW REPUBLIC, AND FEDERAL THEORY: THE STRUGGLE FOR A CREATIVE BREAKTHROUGH IN MODERN POLITICS

James Madison's choice in 1787 was not as simple as Socrates's. Madison's choice represents a theoretical and practical response to a more complicated problem. Between 1776 and 1783, the Americans had fought a revolution to achieve independence as a new nation. But could the new nation hold together? Could the Articles of Confederation, adopted in 1781, cope with four major difficulties that plagued the infant republic: disunion, large size, **faction**, and the antirepublican danger?[2] Would it be enough to patch the Articles of Confederation? Or was a more fundamental change required? And how far should radical reform go?[3]

The Problem: Reconciling Liberty and Authority

These questions led Madison to formulate his key problem as follows: How can we reconcile liberty and authority in a large state? This problem would dominate Madison's thinking throughout his life. It certainly dominated his thoughts and actions in 1787 and 1788 as he battled to draft and win support for a new Constitution. It also influenced key decisions he made in the 1790s in his fight against rich, powerful forces that were unsympathetic to popular interests and to a more generous protection of democratic rights. And, finally, it dominated Madison's thinking and writing in the late 1820s and mid-1830s as he fought the growing forces of nullification and secession. These forces held that a state could nullify an act of the national government and could even secede from the Union that was the United States. (As we will see, these battles in the 1790s and later throw considerable light on the meaning of political obligation.)

Madison's values and the facts of American geography significantly shaped his problem. Madison was strongly committed to popular government and human freedom in a new and large American nation that required power and authority for survival. Madison's problem was most troublesome because the conventional wisdom of his day declared that it was impossible to reconcile liberty and authority in a large state. Large states, such as the United States, must be ruled by monarchs who would necessarily limit personal freedom.

According to conventional wisdom, republican government (based on self-government and liberty) was possible only in a small political community—for example, a city-state such as Athens, Florence, Venice, or Geneva. A large state could be governed only by a monarch or a despot—rulers incompatible with self-government and liberty. How, then, were Americans to deal with this dilemma? Could American republicans have the best of two seemingly contradictory worlds? Could they have self-government and liberty in a republic and also enjoy legitimate power, order, and security in a country as large as the United States?

Other politicians had refused to face up to the problem because they believed it to be insoluble. Patrick Henry and the other Anti-Federalists, who were opposed to the new Constitution of 1787, argued that republican government is possible only in a small political community—this is what traditional political theory had taught for centuries. They did not lift their sights beyond the loose political alliance of the Articles of Confederation. They rejected the desirability of a greatly strengthened central government. On the other side of the political spectrum, men like Alexander Hamilton, who supported the movement for a new and stronger Constitution, initially maintained that only an empire or a strong central government based on the British model could hold together a political community as large as the new American nation. Confederations, they insisted, were notoriously weak, unstable, and detrimental to the interests of justice. Thus, while Henry and his friends argued that great strength in a central government jeopardized republican self-government and republican liberty, Hamilton and his friends held that in the small political community, faction, or a self-interested subgroup, prevailed and jeopardized both the public good and a strong national union.

Neither Henry nor Hamilton challenged the accepted political science of his day or perceived that the traditional understanding of how to reconcile liberty and authority (in the large expanse of the new United States) had to be reexamined. Only Madison challenged the conventional wisdom and was bold enough to look at the problem in a new light and to ask if a new political theory—that of a federal republic—suggested a way out.

Madison's Solution

Madison's theory of the **extensive republic**, the term he used to describe a federal republic governing a large territory, constituted a creative breakthrough in political thought because he proposed that Americans could work out a new synthesis. They could have liberty, self-government, and justice at the local level of state government and also have a powerful central government able to protect the common interests of the whole Union—but only by adopting the model of the new Constitution of 1787. This new federal model allowed the states to control their local affairs while giving the new central government authority in matters concerning all members of the Union. For good measure, the new federal republic operated to control the effects of faction. The Constitution created a central authority—the new federal government—that rested more legitimately on popular consent and the Union's component states yet possessed greater strength than any confederation in history.

The features of the American federal republic are well known today, but in 1787, they constituted a creative breakthrough in governmental theory and practice. The federal republic had such unique features as the division and sharing of powers among Congress, the president, and the Supreme Court; constitutional limitations on national and state governments; a national government with significant powers operating directly on the people; and a strong chief executive. The breakthroughs, moreover, occurred on three fronts.

Ethically, Madison's theory (particularly as fully developed in the 1790s) included broadened concepts of liberty, self-government, pluralist democracy, and the good political life. More specifically, Madison advocated modern principles of religious liberty; freedom of speech, press, and assembly, and other constitutional protections of liberty; an explicit acceptance of interests, parties, and public opinion in the process of self-government; and a more enlightened idea of popular rule, governmental power, and national union.

Empirically, Madison's theory of the extensive republic was designed to explain how Americans could enjoy the best (and escape the worst) of two worlds: how they could enjoy liberty without fear of anarchy and the adverse effects of faction, and how they could enjoy authority without fear of tyranny and the adverse effects of an overly powerful central government. The existence of many different interests in the geographically large political community—farmers, merchants, bankers, and workers—would make it difficult for any one interest to achieve power and work against the public interest. Thus, the negative aspects of factions would be limited and the public good could be achieved.

The large republic would necessitate representation, which would filter the possible evil effects of faction. People would not determine policy in one great mass meeting (where they might easily be inflamed by demagogues). Rather, they would select leaders to represent them. Presumably, these leaders would be chosen because of their virtue, character, and intelligence, and they would, in turn, meet with other comparably chosen representatives to make law. This process would make it difficult for factional interests— interests opposed to the public good—to prevail.

Constitutional limitations on power and the separation of powers were "auxiliary precautions" that would help reconcile liberty and authority in the new republic. Congress would have broad, but not unlimited, powers to tax and spend, to regulate interstate commerce, and to attend to other designated objectives. But a wide range of powers would remain with the states. Moreover, the power given to the central government would not be concentrated in one organ or person; rather, it would be divided among Congress, the president, and the Supreme Court.

In addition, as Madison was to emphasize in the 1790s (in his battle against the alleged plutocratic, antirepublican policies of the Hamiltonian-led Federalist Party), a loyal republican and constitutional opposition party would guard against tyranny at the center. Several factors would protect against the evils of monarchy, plutocracy, and tyranny in the central government and against antirepublicanism and anarchy in the component states: (1) the constitutional operation of majority rule; (2) a sound public opinion, based upon a free press; (3) a healthy two-party system; (4) the federal judiciary; and (5) wise statesmanship that could distinguish between usurpation, abuse, and unwise use of constitutional power. Given the assumptions of this theory, the central government could safely exercise generous and necessary republican power.

Prudentially, Madison's theory constituted sound political judgment on a number of crucial matters not only in 1787 but in the 1790s and later in the 1820s and 1830s. In 1787, Madison saw the need to strengthen the powers of the central government. He wisely insisted on a new federal system that would do a better job of reconciling liberty and authority. The new federal government would be necessarily strong but it would be designed in such a way as to make it unlikely that power was tyrannical. He refused to listen to naysayers who denied the possibility of republican government in an extensive country. And he was willing to settle for a central government that was not as strong as he had wanted because he perceived that the Constitution of 1787 was at least a major step in the right direction. Guided by his political theory, Madison articulated key features of the new federal republic in Philadelphia in 1787 and defended the Constitution effectively in the *Federalist* and at the Virginia Ratifying Convention. After the adoption of the

Constitution in 1789, he authored the Bill of Rights and supported other key legislation to shore up the Constitution. In the 1790s, he led a constitutional opposition party when he became unhappy with the Alien and Sedition Acts and other Federalist legislation. Finally, at the end of his long life, he defended the Union against the advocates of nullification and secession.

Madison took issue with the Sedition Act because it labeled as seditious (stirring up discontent, resistance, or rebellion against the government in power) any hard-hitting criticism, in speech or publication, of the government. For Madison, such criticism was essential to republican government—government based on popular consent and the protection of basic rights. Indeed, Madison maintained, criticism was an obligation of good citizenship.

Nullification and secession were different matters. The Union would be destroyed if single states could nullify national legislation or withdraw from the Union at will. Either action would mean the end of republican government. Nullification and secession could only lead to tyranny and anarchy. Such actions would defeat the creative endeavor to reconcile liberty and authority in a large political community. States had an obligation to abide by majority rule in the national government and to use the U.S. Constitution to seek necessary changes.

Continuing Efforts to Reconcile Liberty and Authority

Madison's republican and federal theory of 1787 constituted a generally successful guide to prudent action throughout his lifetime. His theory demonstrated that Americans could wisely reconcile liberty and authority in a large state. When Americans deviated from this theory, they encountered grave difficulties. The most serious was the American Civil War—civil war being perhaps the worst difficulty that can occur within a political community. Madison's theory illustrates great creativity in politics; the American Civil War represents the failure of politics as a civilizing activity.

The search for new approaches to such persistent problems as the reconciliation of liberty and authority continues, and it occurs all over the globe. This search is apparent in the countries that made up the former Soviet Union. Comparable efforts to reconcile liberty and authority are going on in other central and Eastern European countries as they painfully attempt to achieve constitutional democracy.

Many developing countries in Asia, Africa, and Latin America also struggle to reconcile liberty and authority, often under adverse circumstances. Such struggles can be seen in Cambodia (Kampuchea), the Democratic Republic of the Congo, El Salvador, Indonesia, Lebanon, Liberia, Nicaragua, the Philippines, Russia, Sierra Leone, and South Africa. Many of these countries have suffered the agonies of civil war or acute internal discord.

Will troubled countries be successful in their efforts to reconcile liberty and authority? Can they achieve breakthroughs in politics comparable to Madison's? Such breakthroughs are rare, but the Madisonian example does hold out hope for such countries, and it may stimulate political scientists in their search for creative breakthroughs in politics.

We now turn to another case, which illuminates the burden of choice under adverse circumstances. If Socrates's decision illustrates the tragedy of choice and Madison's illustrates the creative opportunity of choice, then the decision of German citizens in 1932 and 1933 highlights the burden and disastrous consequences of choice.

THE GERMAN CITIZEN AND THE NAZI REGIME: CAN MODERN CITIZENS BEAR THE BURDEN OF FREEDOM?

Freedom is defined as power over one's own destiny. Interpreted negatively, it represents the absence of restraints; interpreted positively, it represents the ability to fulfill peaceful and creative potentialities. The use of the words negative and positive in regards to freedom are not meant as implying an ethical judgment. **Negative freedom**, for instance, does not mean freedom is bad; rather, it means that we are most free when there is nothing restraining us from acting. In this case, the restraining force is usually seen as the government. But it could be other large powerful institutions. Negative freedom can simply mean that the government is not doing much to oppose what you want to do. **Positive freedom** means that you are capable of acting on your potential and government might have a role to play in helping you act on that potential. For example, let's say you appear to be fairly intelligent but you just don't want to learn. You want to sit on the ground all day and watch the clouds. Are you truly free? To those who are most concerned with negative freedom, yes, you are free if there is nothing stopping you from doing just that. For those who ascribe to a positive theory of freedom, you have not developed your potential, and you have no way of judging what more you could achieve in life. You don't know enough to know if your choice to watch the clouds is a good one. For those who think about the idea of freedom, this distinction between negative and positive freedom is an important philosophical question that often leads to debates about what role government should have in fostering free society.

Choice presupposes freedom. And freedom, to be most defensible, requires responsible judgment. But during times of stress, responsible judgment is not always easy. Does the average citizen, especially under difficult circumstances, have the common sense, virtue, wisdom, and strength to choose responsibly? Can we trust the people to make the right choices?

Plato, Socrates's greatest pupil, was skeptical. After all, the people had condemned his beloved teacher to death. Aristotle, Plato's greatest pupil, was also suspicious of Greek democracy, which he understood as rule by the people in their own selfish interest. He argued that only in a polity (which we translate as a constitutional democracy) would popular rule be safe. A polity, he maintained, would be most secure when it rested upon a strong, virtuous, well-educated, prosperous middle class. But what happens when such a middle class does not exist?

Suspicion of the people has endured. In the nineteenth century, the French diplomat, political scientist, and historian, Alexis de Tocqueville, saw democracy as providential and inevitable. The United States, he felt, illustrated the future. Yet, he worried about democratic despotism. Given a favorable Old World inheritance, a favorable

New World environment, and creative statesmanship (illustrated, for example, in the work of people such as Madison and other founders), the United States might make democracy work. But what of countries that lacked these favorable conditions?

John Stuart Mill, in nineteenth-century Great Britain, also worried about the tyranny of the majority. However, he maintained that a sound constitutional, representative government—with excellent political and intellectual leadership—could preserve liberty. His fundamental confidence, despite misgivings, was reinforced by a long tradition of British liberty and by Britain's relative stability and prosperity in the nineteenth century. But, again, how would democracy work in the absence of favorable circumstances?

In the case at hand—Germany in 1932 and 1933—we will focus primarily on the voters who chose the Nazi Party and Adolf Hitler. What circumstances led to their choice? How many, in fact, supported the Nazis and why? We will also ask what other choices—by leaders, voters, and even anti-Nazi forces—contributed to Hitler's triumph. Our treatment will again underscore the interrelationship of values, facts, and judgment.

The political and economic chaos of the 1920s and 1930s made some people believe that individual freedom of expression was dangerous. Adolf Hitler's appeal was based in part on the rejection of intellectual freedom and cultural diversity. Here members of the Nazi youth are shown burning books in Salzburg, Austria, on April 30, 1938.

The Situation in Germany

First, we must examine the adverse circumstances that existed in Germany at the time. From 1919 to 1932, Germany struggled to make democracy work under the least favorable conditions. In Germany, unlike in Great Britain or the United States, constitutional democracy had not put down firm roots before World War I. The new German republic—known as the Weimar Republic because its constitution had been proclaimed in the city of Weimar in 1919—was ushered into the world under severe difficulties. Germany had lost World War I (1914–1918), during which 1,744,000 of its soldiers had been killed and 225,000 of its civilians had died. Economic distress was rampant. The Weimar Republic struggled in the early and mid-1920s to cope with postwar reparations, inflation, and depression. Its modest successes after 1925 were seriously jeopardized by the Great Depression, which began in Germany in 1928. Bad times affected almost every segment of German society: industry, small business, labor, agriculture, and civil service. In a nation of 60 million, 6 to 8 million were unemployed. Farmers revolted; small business owners and craftspeople feared destruction.

From the beginning, the Weimar Republic lacked broad support. Nationalists, National Socialists (Nazis), and reactionary liberals attacked from the right. Communists attacked from the left. The attacks intensified in the early 1930s, and the center (the Weimar coalition of the Social Democrats, which was a center-left party, the Catholic

Center Party, and the Democratic Party) did not hold together. The Democratic Party disintegrated. The Catholic Center Party governed ineffectively in the crucial years from 1930 to 1932. And as one historian noted, the Social Democrats and Communists "devoted far more energy to fighting each other than to the struggle against the growing threat of National Socialism."[4] The Nazis played on the fear of communism and falsely accused the Social Democrats of being responsible for the defeat of 1918, the Treaty of Versailles, inflation, and other German ills. The Nazis condemned the ineffectiveness of the center parties.

Hitler shrewdly took advantage of Germany's disarray to encourage the German people to escape from responsible freedom to a regime of miracle, mystery, and authority. He promised miraculous results that would endure for 1,000 years. The German people had only to follow his authority to see the payoff in jobs for unemployed workers, profits for suffering industrialists, self-respect for an alienated middle class, and power and prestige for a defeated army. The people were not, however, to inquire closely into the mystery whereby the Nazis would accomplish the miracle of the thousand-year Reich.

How many Germans actively supported the Nazis? And how did this support contribute to Hitler's ascent to power? In 1928, only 2.6 percent of the total vote went to the Nazi Party. This figure rose to 18.3 percent in 1930 and to a high of 37.3 percent in the first 1932 election. In the second 1932 election, which was the last free election under the Weimar Republic, the Nazi vote actually fell to 33.1 percent. However, because the left was split (the left-of-center Social Democrats receiving 20.4 percent and the Communists 16.9 percent of the vote), the Nazis emerged with the single largest party vote. The Catholic Center Party had maintained its percentage (16.2), but the other middle-class parties had disintegrated. Even after January 30, 1933, when Hitler was appointed chancellor, the Nazi vote in the spring 1933 election came to 43.9 percent, not a clear majority.[5]

Hitler's appeal was reflected in the first presidential election held in March of 1932, when he polled 11,339,446 votes, or 30.1 percent. Paul von Hindenburg, Germany's leading general in World War I, received 18,657,497 votes, or 49.6 percent. The Communist Party candidate, Ernst Thaelmann, received 13.2 percent, and Theodore Duesterberg, a right-wing candidate, 6.8 percent. On the second ballot in April, the candidates received the following percentage of votes: Hindenburg, 53.0; Hitler, 36.8; and Thaelmann, 10.2.[6]

The rise of the Nazis led President Hindenburg, at the urging of right-wing, conservative advisers—especially his former chancellor, Franz von Papen—to offer Hitler the chancellorship. (The chancellor in Weimar Germany was the equivalent of the British prime minister.) Hindenburg and Papen believed that a cabinet of conservatives would be able to control the policies that Hitler would sell to the country through his party and its propaganda machine. This decision proved to be a fateful mistake.

But how had Nazi strength increased to the point that President Hindenburg and his advisers felt it necessary to bring Hitler in as chancellor? Why did people vote for the Nazis? The choice of Hitler was catastrophic; it doomed German democracy, brought on World War II, made the Holocaust possible, and split Germany into two parts from 1945 to 1990.

"The ideal-typical Nazi voter," wrote Seymour Martin Lipset in *Political Man*, "was a middle-class, self-employed Protestant who lived either on a farm or in a small community, and who had previously voted for a centrist or regionalist political party strongly opposed to the power and influence of big business and big labor."[7] Obviously, those who voted for the Nazis had other common characteristics as well. The Nazis drew some support from every large group of voters. They had success with the middle-class unemployed and with conservative and nationalist voters on Germany's eastern borders. The Nazis also received above-average support from male voters and from younger voters. In general, however, according to Lipset, Nazi votes came "disproportionately from the ranks of the center and liberal parties rather than from the conservatives."

The Nazis were weakest among laborers, residents of big cities, Catholics, women, and older voters. Lipset noted, "With the exception of a few isolated individuals, German big business gave Nazism little financial support or other encouragement until it had risen to the status of a major party. . . . On the whole, however, this group remained loyal to the conservative parties, and many gave no money to the Nazis until after the party won power."[8]

So the heart of Nazi strength was the middle class: small businessmen, small farmers, the self-employed, white-collar workers, civil servants, and inhabitants of small towns. These voters were hostile to big industry, big cities, big unions, and big banks, as well as to the Versailles treaty, Communists, and Jews. Nazi supporters felt threatened by a loss of their status, by liberal values, and by economic depression.[9] They were threatened by key developments of modern society. As David Schoenbaum has noted in *Hitler's Social Revolution*, the Nazis drew on a longing for security, a common hostility to the existing order, and a universal desire for change.[10]

It is extremely important to emphasize that the middle class was not alone in its inability to bear the burden of responsible choice. Choices made by other segments of the German population also paved the way for Hitler. For example, there was the conservatives' disastrous decision to persuade Hindenburg to offer Hitler the chancellorship, as well as the poor policy choices of the Catholic Center Party and its leader, Heinrich Bruning, chancellor from 1930 to 1932. Bruning's deflationary policies (designed to decrease the amount of money in circulation, with a resultant increase in the value of money and a fall in prices) were very unpopular. Many scholars believe that his attempts to govern by decree undermined German democracy. In addition, the Social Democrats were unable to devise a strategy to stop Hitler. German Communists made fateful choices to work against the Social Democrats and thus divided working-class support for the Weimar Republic. Moreover, some army generals (Erich Ludendorff was the most notorious) supported the Nazis early on; others, closing their eyes to Nazi domestic politics and dreaming of the rebirth of German military power, gave their allegiance to Hitler after he became chancellor and then president. Industrialists, fearful of bolshevism and disorder and longing for profits and prosperity through armament sales, also decided, early or late, to support the Nazis. Thus, in one way or another, many Germans proved unable to exercise freedom responsibly.

Lessons of the Nazi Experience

The Nazi experience illuminates the problem of political obligation and the failure of creativity in politics as well as the difficulty of bearing the burden of freedom under adverse conditions. Too few people in Germany were dedicated strongly enough to the Weimar Republic and to democratic values. The Nazi right and the Communist left clearly sought the demise of liberal democracy in Germany. The parties committed to the Weimar Republic—especially the Social Democrats and the Catholic Center—were uncreative and ineffective. Unquestionably, unsettled social and economic conditions led to the poor political decisions that jeopardized German democracy. The Communists hoped that they would come to power with the collapse of the Weimar Republic. The Nazis used the fear of communism to rally support for their cause. Democratic forces were unable to unite effectively and rally the majority of Germans to their side.

The Nazi experience raises the following question: Which values, which circumstances, and which leadership judgments make the responsible exercise of freedom possible—and probable? This question is particularly troubling in many developing nations, especially the younger countries of Asia and Africa. People there may despair of finding democratic solutions for internal strife, poverty, unemployment, and loss of international respect, and may look for authoritarian rulers and solutions. They, too, may seek escape to a regime of "miracle, mystery, and authority."

Comparable difficulties also face many Latin American countries. These nations have longer histories of independence but often lack the social, economic, and political conditions that make for successful democratic and constitutional government. The record of the new regimes in Eastern Europe and the former Soviet Union is a mixed one. Some, like Poland and the Czech Republic, appear to be making successful transitions to democracy, while Russia's democratic record is less clear. Is it possible for such countries to create conditions of peace, human rights, prosperity, and self-esteem that will ease the burden of freedom and facilitate democratic, constitutional, and humane governance?

We now turn to critical decision making in another period of crisis.

JOHN F. KENNEDY AND THE CUBAN MISSILE CRISIS: THE PERILS OF CHOICE IN THE NUCLEAR AGE

On Tuesday, October 16, 1962, at 8:45 a.m., McGeorge Bundy, the special assistant for national security affairs, informed President John F. Kennedy, "Mr. President, there is now hard photographic evidence . . . that the Russians have offensive missiles in Cuba."[11] This disturbing news presented Kennedy with the most difficult choice of his presidency.

He convened a small group of top-level advisers to help him decide on an appropriate response. The news was especially troubling because the Soviet Union had previously stated that it would not place offensive nuclear weapons in Cuba and that any weapons supplied to Cuba were defensive. Despite Soviet insistence, there had been rumors and charges that the Soviets were "up to something" unusual in Cuba. And in late August, the Central Intelligence Agency had reported that "something new and different" was under way. What did those late-summer Soviet shipments to Cuba indicate?

Although in early September the president did not have hard evidence of offensive weapons in Cuba, he had warned that the "gravest issues would arise" if such evidence were found. At his September 13 press conference, he had declared that new Soviet shipments to Cuba did not constitute a serious threat, but he warned that if Cuba were to "become an offensive military base of significant capacity for the Soviet Union, then this country will do whatever must be done to protect its own security and that of its allies."

With evidence of the missiles' arrival, Kennedy felt betrayed. He felt as if his efforts to work toward a more peaceful world had been compromised.

Considering the Alternatives

The Executive Committee of the National Security Council—or ExCom, as the president's group of advisers came to be known—met at 11:45 that Tuesday morning to consider a response. They explored six major alternatives. The United States could (1) do nothing, (2) engage in diplomacy, (3) secretly approach Cuban leader Fidel Castro, (4) blockade Cuba, (5) launch a surgical air attack, or (6) invade Cuba. ExCom operated with the knowledge that the Soviet missiles would be on their launch pads and ready for firing within ten days.

"On the first Tuesday morning the choice for a moment seemed to lie between the air strike or acquiescence—and the president had made clear that acquiescence was impossible," historian Arthur M. Schlesinger observed. The argument for doing nothing was based on the view that the Soviets' ability to strike the United States from Cuba made little difference, given America's vulnerability to missiles already stationed in the Soviet Union. Doing nothing would prevent escalation and avert the danger of overreaction and an eventual nuclear catastrophe. Playing it cool would deprive Nikita Khrushchev, the Soviet leader, of any political advantage from his bold stroke.

Opponents of this alternative raised a number of serious objections. Doing nothing would permit the Soviet Union to double its missile capability, to outflank the U.S.'s early warning system, and to reverse the strategic balance by installing yet more missiles on a base ninety miles from the American coast. Politically, the "do nothing" option would undermine U.S.'s credibility and resolve in the eyes of the world by making the United States appear weak.

Diplomatic approaches—through the United Nations, through the Organization of American States, or directly or indirectly to Khrushchev—required time, and the United States did not have much time. The Soviets could stall or veto action in the United Nations. While diplomats talked, the missiles would become operational. Approaches to Khrushchev might lead to an unsatisfactory deal in the midst of a threatening crisis. A secret overture to Castro ignored the vital fact that the missiles belonged to the Soviet Union and that the key decision to withdraw them was the Soviets' alone.

So the president was initially drawn to the possibility of a surgical strike, an air attack confined to the missile bases. But was there no choice between bombing and doing nothing? If successful, an air strike would eliminate the threat to the United States. But could it be successful? Military leaders at the Pentagon concluded that a surgical strike would still leave Cuban airfields and Soviet aircraft operational. Moreover, the Pentagon could not guarantee that the U.S. Air Force could destroy all the missiles. A limited strike might expose the United States to nuclear retaliation. It would be prudent, militarily, to opt for a large strike to eliminate all sources of danger. So the surgical strike might have to be replaced by a massive strike; but this could lead to loss of Soviet lives and, perhaps, to Soviet retaliation in the divided city of Berlin or in Turkey, where American strategic forces were deployed. Moreover, could the president of the United States, with the memory of Pearl Harbor still relatively fresh in the American mind, order a surprise attack? Was the elimination of the missiles and of Castro worth the cost of a massive strike?

Kennedy's Latin American advisers warned that a massive strike would kill thousands of innocent Cubans and do great permanent damage to the United States in the eyes of Latin Americans. His European advisers warned that the world would regard a surprise attack as an excessive response. And if the Soviets moved against Berlin, the United States would be blamed and might have to fight under disadvantageous circumstances.

An invasion was also risky because U.S. troops would be confronting about 20,000 Soviet troops in the first direct conflict between the forces of the world's two great superpowers. Would such an invasion guarantee a Soviet move against Berlin? Would it bring the world closer to World War III?

On the next day, Wednesday, Secretary of Defense Robert McNamara argued strongly on behalf of another alternative: a blockade, which would provide a middle course between doing nothing and engaging in a massive attack. The blockade would require Khrushchev to respond to a firm but not excessive step; he could avoid a military clash by keeping his ships away. The blockade would set up a confrontation in an advantageous location—the Caribbean. This alternative kept open other options, such as diplomacy or other military action, and it averted the confrontation that brought one's "adversary to the choice of either a humiliating defeat or a nuclear war," as President Kennedy noted.

But there were objections to the blockade. A blockade was an act of war and might be deemed a violation of the UN charter or of international law. Even more seriously, would the blockade bring enough pressure on Khrushchev to remove the missiles already in Cuba? Would it stop work on the bases? Opponents of the blockade maintained that it would lead to a Soviet counterblockade of Berlin and to confrontation with the Soviet Union: if Soviet ships did not stop, the United States would have to fire the first shot, and this might invite Soviet retaliation.

On Thursday evening, President Kennedy met with ExCom. According to Schlesinger's account, the president was leaning toward the blockade:

> He was evidently attracted by the idea of the blockade. It avoided war, preserved flexibility and offered Khrushchev time to reconsider his actions. It could be carried out within the framework of the Organization of American States and the Rio Treaty. Since it could be extended to nonmilitary items as occasion required, it could become an instrument of steadily intensifying pressure. It would avoid the shock effect of a surprise attack, which would hurt us politically through the world and might provoke Moscow to an insensate response against Berlin or the United States itself. If it worked, the Russians could retreat with dignity. If it did not work, the Americans retained the option of military action. In short, the blockade, by enabling us to proceed one step at a time, gave us control over the future. Kennedy accordingly directed that preparations be made to put the weapons blockade into effect on Monday morning.[12]

Making the Choice

The debate between advocates of the blockade and those of the air strike persisted until the formal meeting of the National Security Council on Saturday. After hearing both arguments again, Kennedy endorsed the blockade. But before making his decision final, he wanted one last talk with the Air Force Tactical Air Command to satisfy himself that a surgical strike was not feasible. This meeting was held Sunday morning. The Air Force spokesman told the president that the air strike would have to be massive, and even then it would not guarantee the destruction of all Soviet missiles. The president had been worried that the blockade would not remove the missiles; now it was clear that an air attack could not guarantee that result either.

On Monday, October 22, at 7:30 p.m., President Kennedy addressed the nation (which had known nothing of the crisis that had engaged ExCom since October 16) and set forth his choice. He emphasized that the Soviet missile bases provided the Soviet Union with "a nuclear strike capability against the Western Hemisphere." Soviet action constituted "a deliberately provocative and unjustified change . . . which cannot be accepted by this country, if our courage and our commitments are ever to be trusted again by either friend or foe." The nuclear threat to Americans had to be eliminated. The president then indicated that he had imposed a "quarantine" on all offensive military equipment under shipment to Cuba. Cuba would be kept under intensive surveillance. The president also declared that any missile launched from Cuba would be regarded as an attack by the Soviet Union on the United States and would elicit immediate retaliatory response upon the Soviet Union. He called for a meeting of the Organization of American States to consider the threat to the security of the American hemisphere and for an emergency meeting of the UN Security Council to consider the threat to world peace. Kennedy also appealed to Khrushchev "to abandon the course of world domination, and to join in an historic effort to end the perilous arms race and to transform the history of man."

So the basic choice was made. But before the crisis was over, Kennedy would have to make other key choices: to interpret the blockade flexibly (rather than rigidly), to give the Soviets time to respond to a peaceful solution, and to use diplomacy (rather than force) to accomplish his objective of removing the missiles. By Thursday, Adlai Stevenson, the U.S. ambassador to the United Nations, had effectively destroyed the Soviet argument that the missiles were defensive. Within the Security Council chamber, the following extraordinary exchange took place between Stevenson and Valerian Zorin, the Soviet ambassador to the United Nations:

STEVENSON: "Do you, Ambassador Zorin, deny that the U.S.S.R. has placed and is placing medium- and intermediate-range missiles and sites in Cuba? . . . Don't wait for the translation!"

ZORIN: "I am not in an American courtroom, sir, and I do not wish to answer a question put to me in the manner in which a prosecutor does—"

STEVENSON: "You are in the courtroom of world opinion right now, and you can answer yes or no. You have denied that they exist, and I want to know whether I have understood you correctly."

ZORIN: "Please continue your statement. . . . You will receive your answer in due course."

STEVENSON: "I am prepared to wait for my answer until hell freezes over, if that is your decision. I am also prepared to present the evidence in this room."[13]

Stevenson proceeded to present the aerial photographs that revealed Soviet nuclear installations. The Soviets then probed for a deal, and the Americans responded favorably. The Soviets would remove their missiles under UN inspection, and the United States would promise publicly not to invade Cuba. On Friday, October 26, Khrushchev cabled Kennedy, "If the President and Government of the United States were to give assurances that the U.S.A. itself would not participate in an attack on Cuba and would restrain others from this kind of act, if you would recall your fleet, this would immediately change everything."[14] Kennedy responded by indicating that as soon as work stopped on the missile sites and the offensive weapons were rendered inoperable, a settlement along Khrushchev's lines was in order. U.S. Attorney General Robert Kennedy, in delivering his brother's message to the Soviet ambassador to the United States, Anatoly Dobrynin, indicated that unless the United States received assurances within twenty-four hours, it would take military action by Tuesday.

Saturday night was a disturbing night for President Kennedy as he waited for Khrushchev's reply. At 9:00 a.m., Sunday, October 28, Khrushchev's response came in. Work would stop on the missile sites: the arms "which you described as offensive" would be crated and returned to the Soviet Union. Negotiations would start at the United Nations.

And so, the two-week crisis—perhaps the closest we have come to World War III—ended. President Kennedy's choices in the Cuban missile crisis underscore the dangers and difficulties of achieving national security in the nuclear age. Presidential choices have become more potent for good or ill. Presidents are forced to recognize that the stakes are higher and that their actions affect the vital interests of not only the United States but all humankind. These same thoughts must have troubled the Soviet leaders. This recognition may explain the relative prudence both superpowers demonstrated in respecting each other's vital interests, in achieving arms reduction and arms control agreements, and in limiting the spread of nuclear weapons. In later chapters, particularly Chapters 12 and 14, we examine how prudent such policies actually are.

THE DECISION TO INVADE IRAQ: THE PERILS OF INACCURATE INFORMATION AND FAULTY ASSUMPTIONS

John Kennedy's decision to use a quarantine to force Soviet missiles from Cuba is widely regarded as a brilliant exercise in decision making. Throughout those October days of 1962, President Kennedy constantly questioned his advisers—subjecting their ideas and assumptions to a critical inquiry that led him ultimately to pursue the successful blockade of Cuba. But not all decisions are as successful. To illuminate some of the pitfalls of political choice, we turn our attention to a more recent action, the decision by the United States to invade Iraq in 2003.

On March 20, 2003, U.S. Tomahawk missiles and bombs delivered by F-117s began hitting targets in Baghdad, Iraq. Shortly thereafter, a U.S.-dominated military force of roughly 297,000 troops invaded Iraq, and with the seizure of the Tikrit region north of Baghdad on April 15, coalition leaders declared the military invasion complete. Saddam Hussein's regime was at an end. The swiftness of the victory was stunning, but the euphoria it engendered was short lived.

The first three years of U.S. occupation proved a near disaster. By the end of 2006, Iraq was on the brink of collapse into chaos and civil war. A powerful home-grown insurgency movement, whose primary weapons were roadside and suicide bombs, attacked coalition forces, Iraqi military and police forces, and innocent civilians. Insurgents from outside the country, led by al-Qaida, took advantage of the opportunity to add to the havoc. Within the country, deep-seated distrust and hostility fueled violent conflict between the two largest religious sects—the Sunni, whose Baathist Party had run the country for decades, and the Shiite majority, who under Saddam Hussein had suffered discrimination, persecution, and incredible hardship. As 2006 drew to a close, over 3,000 U.S. troops and over 250 soldiers from other countries in the coalition were dead; thousands more were severely wounded. Iraqi civilian deaths as a result of the war numbered at least in the tens of thousands, perhaps into the hundreds of thousands.[15] By 2007, conditions were so bad that only a radical shift in strategy, accompanied by a dramatic increase in troop strength (dubbed "the Surge"), could begin to reduce the violence that had characterized the previous three years. And even then, the first year under this revised approach saw the deaths of over 1,000 U.S. soldiers.

Why were the first three to four years of the war such a disaster? The answers to this question stem from the powerful yet misguided preconceptions, faulty assumptions, and questionable intelligence that characterized the initial decision-making process. Those flaws contributed to a war that engendered considerable public frustration and disillusionment within the United States and anger among U.S. allies and throughout the Islamic world. The operation has also been enormously expensive, not only in human lives but in U.S. dollars. Estimates of the total cost of the war vary considerably but range from $1 trillion to $3 trillion.

It is worth noting that the final outcome of the war remains unclear. American combat forces have been withdrawn. Iraq still struggles to implement a viable democratic political system. Religious tensions remain high and Shite controlled Iran has become increasingly influential in Iraq's political fabric. Out of the war's chaos, the forces of the Islamic State of Iraq and Syria (ISIS) seized significant Iraqi real estate. After several years of brutal fighting, ISIS lost most of the Iraqi territory that it had seized but the cost both in money and lives was high. For these and other reasons, there is little doubt that the decision to invade Iraq is a compelling case study of how faulty judgments and the inability to gather undisputed facts can lead to questionable actions.

Historical Context

Between 1980 and 1988, Iraq engaged in a brutal war with its larger neighbor, Iran, that resulted in a combined death toll in excess of 1 million. During the conflict, the United States lent support to Iraq and its leader, Saddam Hussein, viewing Iran's recently established Islamic regime a strategic threat to the region. The war ended in a stalemate, and Iraq, having borrowed $40 billion from Kuwait to finance its military adventure, could not repay the debt. When Kuwait refused to pardon the debt, Iraq, seething with anger, invaded its tiny neighbor on August 2, 1990. This action was widely viewed as a clear-cut case of aggression. U.S. president George H. W. Bush declared the invasion unacceptable and set out to reverse it and punish the regime in Baghdad.

In January 1991, a broad coalition of forces led by the United States invaded Iraq and seized roughly half the country. Although it eventually withdrew from the ground, coalition forces established no-fly zones over the predominantly southern Shiite and northern Kurdish regions of the country. Coalition aircraft patrolled these zones until the 2003 invasion. In addition, from August 1990 until May 2003, international economic sanctions were imposed on Iraq. Nonetheless, Saddam Hussein was able to retain power.

The initial response to the 9/11 attacks on the World Trade Center and the Pentagon was a U.S.-led military operation against Afghanistan. Al-Qaida training camps were destroyed, the Taliban government was routed, and the remnants of both groups were left to seek refuge in the rough border regions bridging Afghanistan and Pakistan. While that operation proved largely successful, there was disappointment that al-Qaida leader Osama bin Laden had not been captured. It was at this point, winter 2003, that attention quickly turned to Iraq.

Key figures in the decision to invade Iraq in 2003 included (from left to right) Vice President Dick Cheney, CIA Director George Tenet, President George W. Bush, and Chief of Staff Andy Card.

Rationales for the 2003 Invasion

The administration of George W. Bush offered a number of rationales for taking action against Iraq and bringing down the regime of Saddam Hussein. Iraq was a destabilizing force in the Persian Gulf region, as evidenced first by Saddam's invasion of Iran in the 1980s and then of Kuwait in 1990. Iraq had breached the conditions of the 1991 cease-fire and repeatedly flouted UN Security Council resolutions. Additionally, the very brutality of the regime warranted its overthrow. At the same time, the establishment of democracy in Iraq had the potential to transform the Middle East. Some proponents even saw a linkage between regime change in Iraq and prospects for peace between Israel and the Palestinians. As compelling as these factors might have been, did they constitute sufficient reason to mount a full-scale invasion and replace a sovereign government? Maybe, and maybe not. Regardless, if there were doubts about the salience of these rationales, there were two additional reasons for invasion that, if true, were in the eyes of many, both Republican and Democrat, more than persuasive. By far, the two most powerful arguments the Bush administration made were that (1) there was a likely link between the regime in Baghdad and al-Qaida and (2) Iraq possessed lethal chemical and biological weapons and was continuing to develop nuclear weapons (collectively known as weapons of mass destruction, or WMDs).

Two additional factors helped to motivate the decision for invasion, both with origins stretching back in time to the early 1990s. First, a significant number of officials in the Bush administration felt very strongly that the United States had erred during the first Gulf War in 1991 in not pressing the operation all the way through to Baghdad and ousting Saddam's regime then and there. In the wake of 9/11, perhaps the job could be finished. Second, in September 2002, exactly one year after the attacks on the World Trade Center and Pentagon, the administration had released a revised *National Security Strategy of the United States*.[16] The heart of the doctrine was a new policy for checking the threat of nuclear war. Instead of emphasizing deterrence, as had been policy during the Cold War, the United States would now rely on preemption—that is, where appropriate the U.S. government would employ its military to eliminate WMD programs in other countries. The genesis of the new policy could be traced as far back as 1992, when a group working for then Secretary of Defense Dick Cheney authored a document known as the *Defense Planning Guidance*, which argued that the United States should be prepared to use force to prevent the spread of nuclear weapons.[17]

What Went Wrong?

Good decisions must be made on sound assumptions that in turn are based on accurate information. On both counts, the decision to invade Iraq was sorely lacking. The following are four key assumptions that were made in support of the decision to invade Iraq:

Assumption 1. *Iraq has stockpiles of chemical and biological weapons and a fully active program to develop nuclear weapons.* This assumption proved to be absolutely false. There is no doubt that Iraq had a WMD program at one time. Chemical weapons had been used in 1988 against the Kurdish village of Halabja in a brutal attack resulting in the deaths of thousands of civilians. But after the 1990 invasion of Iraq by coalition forces, firm evidence of a continuing WMD program became scarce. Some of the UN inspectors who had visited Iraq a number of times between 1999 and 2003 were skeptical of claims that Saddam had WMDs.[18] Regardless, Bush administration officials remained convinced that there were WMDs, and the director of the Central Intelligence Agency, George Tenet, even told President Bush that the case for the existence of WMDs was a "slam dunk."[19] British intelligence supported the notion of an active program, and Iraqi defectors had repeatedly told the administration of its existence. What happened? Why was this assessment of Iraq's WMD program so off the mark? Was intelligence manipulated? Was it because our intelligence assets inside Iraq were so limited? Did the administration put too much stock in the word of Iraqi exiles who simply told government officials what they wanted to hear? Was this a case of wishful thinking? Every one of these factors has been offered as an explanation. Space does not allow for a thorough assessment of each here. We will leave it to future historians to sort out exactly what happened. Suffice it to say for present purposes, the assumption that Iraq had WMDs—perhaps the most potent of the arguments given for the decision to invade—proved false.

Assumption 2. *The Iraqi government has close ties to al-Qaida.* This, too, was a powerful argument in favor of invasion. After all, the president had asserted in the wake of 9/11 that those governments that aided and abetted terrorism would be held accountable. While the validity of this assumption remains debatable, the preponderance of evidence suggests that in fact there were no extensive links between al-Qaida and Saddam Hussein's regime. The comprehensive *9/11 Commission Report*, published in 2004, offered no evidence of collaborative ties between Iraq and al-Qaida.[20] And in 2008, the Institute for Defense Analyses released a study based on 600,000 documents captured in post-Saddam

Iraq that drew a similar conclusion: no direct coordination or assistance existed between Saddam's regime and al-Qaida.[21] At most, there may have been some fleeting contacts, but those evidently had little bearing on al-Qaida's terrorist operations.

Assumption 3. *The military operation will be over quickly, political power will be turned over to the Iraqis, a democracy will be formed, and the bulk of American forces will be able to return home after a relatively short period of time.* This assumption was based on what the administration thought the Iraqi people's reaction would be to the U.S. invasion and its perceptions of the physical conditions within the country. Once Saddam was ousted from power, went this version, the U.S. presence would be welcome, order would be quickly restored, and the governance of Iraq would be turned over to the Iraqis themselves. Instead, the Americans found a depressed population brutalized by decades of Saddam's iron rule and an infrastructure—particularly energy grids, fresh water systems, and oil industry—in various stages of decay. The three major ethnic/religious groups in Iraq—Sunnis, Kurds, and Shiites—deeply distrusted each other as well as the Americans. The Sunnis that had dominated the ruling Baathist Party under Saddam Hussein had treated both the Shiites and the Kurds badly. Vengeance and counter vengeance became the rule. Unbelievably vicious warfare broke out between the two largest religious communities, making assassinations and massacres almost daily occurrences. In addition, the United States had to deal with the lethal campaign of insurgents backed by powerful interests outside the country, one which targeted both Iraqis and Americans. Put simply, the country was spinning violently out of control leaving the U.S. military desperate to achieve some degree of stability. The cautious words of Secretary of State Colin Powell to the president before the invasion now rang more clearly than ever: "You are going to be the proud owner of twenty-five million people. You will own all their hopes, aspirations, and problems. . . . It's going to suck the oxygen out of everything."[22] The failure of the administration to accurately assess the likely conditions in Iraq after the initial military success contributed to a complete lack of strategic planning for what became a long, violent, and expensive occupation of the country.[23] Furthermore, the challenges of creating a stable democracy where none existed before proved far more daunting than the administration at first believed. The assumption that democracies are easy to create may have been the worst assumption one could possibly make.

Assumption 4. *A modest-sized force much smaller than the one used in Desert Storm can swiftly and efficiently carry out the invasion.* In his brilliant case study of the Iraqi war decision, Joseph J. Collins of the National Defense University captured the thinking of Secretary of Defense Donald Rumsfeld:

> In retrospect, Rumsfeld wanted to conduct a quick, lightning-like operation in Iraq, followed by a swift handover of power to the Iraqis. He did not want a large-scale, ponderous operation like Desert Storm, which he saw as wasteful and outmoded. He also did not want U.S. troops unnecessarily bogged down in an endless postwar peace operation.[24]

The original Pentagon war plan specified a force of some 140,000 troops, roughly two-thirds the size of the force used in the first Gulf War. This was ultimately increased to a total of 297,000 coalition troops—still 243,000 fewer than in the Desert Storm invasion force of 1990. Rumsfeld was right to a point: His force did prove adequate for a successful lightning-like attack that succeeded in reaching Baghdad in a very short period of time. The problem came in the aftermath of that attack. The force size proved completely inadequate for the job of stabilization. While this fact did not cause the ensuing chaos, it certainly facilitated it. And in the weeks, months, and years that followed, the United States committed numerous additional grievous policy errors in Iraq, though these errors are rightly connected with the execution of the war rather than with the initial decision to invade.

Clearly, political decision making based on inaccurate information and faulty assumptions is a recipe for disaster. Unfortunately, the Bush administration's choice to invade Iraq in 2003 provides us with a powerful case study of this political reality.

CONCLUSION

Our brief examination of these five cases makes clear that wise choices in politics rest on sound values, accurate understanding of political phenomena, and astute judgment. These components are very closely connected. The five cases also emphasize the importance of addressing the problem of political obligation, striving for creative political breakthroughs, learning to bear the burden of freedom, responding wisely to the perils of decision making in the nuclear age, and receiving accurate information and making credible assumptions.

In subsequent chapters, we examine a host of other choices. For instance, in the public policy chapters in Part IV, we illustrate at greater length what contributes to sound judgment. In many instances, the choices to be made are both less momentous and less dramatic than those examined here. Some involve modest personal choices, while others take in a wider range of actors and circumstances. All, however, reveal the intimate connection among values, facts, and judgments.

SUGGESTED READINGS

Allison, Graham T., and Philip Zelikow. *Essence of Decision: Explaining the Cuban Missile Crisis.* 2nd ed. New York: Longman, 1999. A brilliant analysis of a crucial choice, and a penetrating exploration of decision making in general.

Berlin, Isaiah. *Liberty: Incorporating Four Essays on Liberty.* Oxford: Oxford University Press, 2002. Berlin was one of the most important political philosophers to deal with the issue of positive and negative liberty (or freedom).

Browning, Christopher. *Ordinary Men.* New York: HarperCollins, 1993. Examines the lives of members of a German police unit involved in the Holocaust.

Gellately, Robert. *Backing Hitler: Consent and Coercion in Nazi Germany.* Oxford, UK: Oxford University Press, 2002. A thorough scholarly analysis of how and why certain groups supported the Nazi Party.

Hamilton, Alexander, John Jay, and James Madison. *The Federalist* [1787–1788]. Cleveland: World, 1961. Persuasive arguments on behalf of the choice of the new federal Constitution of 1787. Unrivaled in its influence on the fateful choice more than 200 years ago.

Kershaw, Ian. *The Nazi Dictatorship: Problems and Perspectives of Interpretation.* 4th ed. London: Bloomsbury Academic, 2015. Chapter 1 is titled "Historians and the Problem of Explaining Nazism."

Ricks, Thomas E. *Fiasco: The American Military Adventure in Iraq.* New York: Penguin, 2007. An account by a respected *Washington Post* reporter of the American invasion of Iraq and the subsequent occupation of that country.

Riemer, Neal. *Creative Breakthroughs in Politics*. Westport, CT: Praeger, 1996. Explores two genuine and two spurious historical breakthroughs, one contemporary breakthrough still in progress (European Union), and a future breakthrough (protection against genocide).

———. *James Madison: Creating the American Constitution*. Washington, DC: Congressional Quarterly, 1986. Highlights Madison's choices as a nationalist, Federalist, empirical political scientist, and Democrat. Underscores Madison's theory as a creative breakthrough in politics.

Stone, Deborah. *The Art of Political Decision Making*. 3rd ed. New York: W. W. Norton, 2011. Valuable text on the art of decision making with numerous examples of both good and bad decisions.

Stone, I. F. *The Trial of Socrates*. Boston: Little, Brown, 1988. A wonderfully refreshing account by a great journalist. Much more sympathetic to those who tried Socrates and more critical of Socrates than most accounts.

Tuchman, Barbara W. *The Guns of August*. New York: Random House, 1994. Selected by the Modern Library as one of the 100 best nonfiction books of all time. While more recent scholarship challenges some of Tuchman's conclusions, her work remains a brilliant and superbly written account of the events leading up to WWI.

Wilson, Emily. *The Death of Socrates*. Cambridge, MA: Harvard University Press, 2007. A thoughtful account of the death of Socrates and how that event has reverberated throughout history.

GLOSSARY TERMS

creative breakthrough (p. 28)
extensive republic (p. 34)
faction (p. 33)
freedom (p. 37)

negative freedom (p. 37)
political creativity (p. 27)
political obligation (p. 26)

positive freedom (p. 37)
power politics (p. 26)
responsible citizenship (p. 27)

NOTES

1. The quotations in this paragraph and the following are from Plato's "Apology," in *The Republic, and Other Works by Plato*, trans. Benjamin Jowett (Garden City, NY: Doubleday, Anchor Books, 1973), 460–484.

2. In *Federalist* No. 10, Madison defined *faction* as "a number of citizens, whether amounting to a majority or minority of the whole, who are united and actuated by some common impulse of passion, or of interest, adversed to the rights of other citizens, or to the permanent and aggregate interests of the community." See Alexander Hamilton, John Jay, and James Madison, *The Federalist* [1787–1788] (Cleveland: World, 1961), 57.

3. This section draws freely from Neal Riemer's *James Madison: Creating the American Constitution* (Washington, DC: Congressional Quarterly, 1986). For a fuller exploration of creative breakthroughs, see Riemer, *Creative Breakthroughs in Politics* (Westport, CT: Praeger, 1996).

4. Franz L. Neumann, *Behemoth* (New York: Oxford University Press, 1942), 30.

5. For the electoral statistics, see Seymour Martin Lipset, *Political Man: The Social Bases of Politics* (1960; reprint, Garden City, NY: Doubleday, Anchor Books, 1962), 139; and Jeremy Noakes and Geoffrey Pridham, eds., *Documents of Nazism, 1919–1945* (London: Jonathan Cape, 1974), 126.

6. Neumann, *Behemoth*, 30.

7. Lipset, *Political Man*, 138–148. See also David Schoenbaum, *Hitler's Social Revolution: Class and Status in Nazi Germany, 1933–1939* (New York: Norton, 1997); and Noakes and Pridham, *Documents of Nazism*.

8. Seymour Martin Lipset, *Revolution and Counterrevolution* (1968; repr., Garden City, NY: Doubleday, Anchor Books, 1970), 234.

9. Ibid., 234.

10. Schoenbaum, *Hitler's Social Revolution*.

11. Graham T. Allison, *Essence of Decision: Explaining the Cuban Missile Crisis* (Boston: Little, Brown, 1971), 193. See also Graham T. Allison and Philip Zelikow, *The Essence of Decision: Explaining the Cuban Missile Crisis*, 2nd ed. (New York: Longman, 1999). The following presentation draws generously on Allison's study and also on the account by Arthur M. Schlesinger Jr., *A Thousand Days: John F. Kennedy in the White House* (1965; repr., Greenwich, CT: Fawcett Crest, 1967).

12. Schlesinger, *Thousand Days*, 805–806.

13. As it appears in Michael R. Beschloss, *The Crisis Years: Kennedy and Khrushchev, 1960–1963* (New York: HarperCollins, 1991), 505–506.

14. Laurence Chang and Peter Kornbluh, eds., *The Cuban Missile Crisis, 1962: A National Security Archive Documents Reader* (New York: New Press, 1998), 198.

15. Estimates run from a low of roughly 90,000 to a high in excess of 600,000, a figure that appeared in a Johns Hopkins University study in 2006 and reported in the prestigious British medical journal *Lancet*. See Gilbert Burnham et al., "Mortality after the 2003 Invasion of Iraq: A Cross-Sectional Cluster Sample Survey," *Lancet* 368, no. 9545 (October 2006): 1421–1428.

16. Office of the President of the United States, "The National Security Strategy of the United States of America," Washington, DC, September 2002, www.globalsecurity.org/military/library/policy/nation/nss_020920.pdf.

17. Dartmouth College Library, U.S. Government Documents, "Primary Sources Related to the War With Iraq," www.dartmouth.edu/~govdocs/iraq.htm.

18. BBC News, "Blix Skeptical on Iraqi WMD Claim," December 16, 2003, http://news.bbc.co.uk/2.hi/middle_east/3323633.stm.

19. Bob Woodward, *Plan of Attack* (New York: Simon & Schuster, 2004), 249.

20. *The 9/11 Commission Report* (New York: Norton, 2004), 66.

21. Iraqi Perspectives Project, "Saddam and Terrorism: Emerging Insights from Captured Iraqi Documents," www.fas.orga/irp/epring/irazi/index.html.

22. Woodward, *Plan of Attack*, 150.

23. The lack of foresight and planning for the post-invasion period is brilliantly spelled out in Thomas Ricks, *Fiasco* (New York: Penguin, 2006).

24. Joseph J. Collins, "Choosing War: The Decision to Invade Iraq and Its Aftermath," National Defense University, Institute for National Strategic Studies, 2008, 7.

Members of the #MeToo movement protesting sexual harassment in the workplace.

Stephanie Keith/Getty Images News/Getty Images

3

POLITICAL SCIENCE
Components, Tasks, and Controversies

How can we usefully define the discipline of political science? To address this basic question, we begin with a brief discussion of the organizational structure of the discipline followed by analysis of three subjects of great interest to political scientists: political philosophy and **ethics**, the empirical and behavioral study of politics, and public policy.[1] In effect, these three subjects are about how we should act, how we actually act, and how we should work to solve the problems we face now and in the future. These subjects concern the following:

- The good political life and the underlying ethical principles of politics

- A science of politics and an understanding of significant empirical phenomena (facts, circumstances, experiences)

- Political wisdom and judgment in the arena of citizenship and public policy

- The integration of ethics, science, and statesmanship (because the first three concerns are interrelated)

THE BASIC STRUCTURE OF POLITICAL SCIENCE

The discipline of **political science** in the United States is traditionally divided into four subfields:

1. *American government and politics* is the study of how the system of governance in the United States works. At all levels of governance—local, state, and national—how

Chapter Objectives

After studying this chapter, you will be able to do the following:

1. Describe the basic structure of the discipline of political science.

2. Summarize the three major components of political science—ethical, empirical, and prudential.

3. Identify the four major tasks of political science.

4. Discuss how the four major tasks might be interrelated.

5. Discuss some of the continuing controversies in political science.

do we select our leaders and representatives? How are major public policies developed and decided upon? Traditionally, there have been a large number of areas of inquiry subsumed under the American subfield. These include, but are not restricted to, public administration, public policy, political economy, elections, judicial behavior, legislative behavior, and the role of the executive, state, and local government.

2. *International relations* is the study of how countries and other major actors in the international system interact with each other. Some of the more important questions that political scientists working in this area address include the following: Why do countries go to war? Why and how do countries make peace? How do we deal with issues such as global poverty, environmental degradation, terrorism, and nuclear proliferation? As in the case in the American field, there are a large number of specialized fields, including foreign policy, international organization, international law, international political economy, national security, diplomacy, and war and peace studies.

3. *Comparative politics* is the study of political and governance processes in countries around the world. It is a huge field that includes not only the study of specific governments but topics such as ethnic politics, democratization, feminist studies, economic and political development, and the movement of people around the globe (sometimes known as **Diaspora** Studies).

4. *Political theory or political philosophy* is the study of fundamental questions about governance: What should the relationship be between government and the governed? What constitutes legitimate government? Are there fundamental political rights and freedoms? Is one form of government preferable to another? Under what circumstances is the overthrow of a government justified? In the broader sense, political theory is concerned with the idea of justice. Here, great attention is paid to the most influential political thinkers in history, such as Plato, Socrates, Machiavelli, Hobbes, Augustine, Aquinas, Rousseau, Burke, Mill, and Marx. This subfield in many ways bridges the other three subfields of the discipline.

It is important to note that these four subfields are not mutually exclusive. How does one understand American foreign policy without some knowledge of American government? Is the study of energy policy exclusively an international or a domestic concern? The federal budget of the United States mandates consideration of a number of questions that clearly fall under the area of international relations—for example, foreign aid allocations, the size and shape of the military, and funding to fight terrorism.

Beyond the basic organization of the discipline, we note that political scientists who favor the more traditional approaches to their field tend to stress the importance of ethics, history, law, constitutions, formal institutions, and citizenship. Other political scientists stress scientific methodology and human behavior. These latter usually draw on psychology, sociology, economics, and mathematics in their investigations. Sometimes they combine political science and a related discipline to form a subfield such as political economy.

The controversies between approaches have centered on arguments about these emphases. Less traditional political scientists have argued that instead of focusing on questions about the good life and wise public policy, political science should be made a rigorous empirical science like physics or biology; in recent years, the discipline has drawn extensively from the field of economics. Other political scientists counter that such moves are false to the nature of politics, which is inevitably concerned with both the good political life and wise action in the political arena.

To highlight another emphasis, radical political scientists have attacked the empirically oriented students of politics for being not only narrowly scientific but also conservative. They argue that empiricists focus too narrowly on dominant power relationships and ignore the poor, the weak, and the maltreated. Empirical political scientists tend to accept what is normal as what should be. They are often uncomfortable with making normative statements and prefer to stick with describing what is happening and why. Radical political scientists, who may be Marxists, critical social theorists, feminists, or postmodernists, are generally critical of the status quo.

In more recent years, the stark differences between those who want to radically transform politics and those who are committed to simply describing it have grown less sharp. A younger generation of political scientists believe a rigorous set of methodologies can be at the service of informed political discussion by a broader public. These political scientists are engaged with the political world, but not necessarily for radical ends, and believe that their empirical methods provide a powerful tool for explaining human political behavior. They often write blogs, frequently linked to major new organizations, designed to explain political science research to an audience far greater than just other political scientists. At the same time, these scholars publish in traditional political science journals that have a much narrower audience.[2]

Controversies such as these suggest the wisdom of a broad approach. They indicate that any definition of political science that rules out political philosophy and ethics, empirical and behavioral studies, or public policy is inadequate. With this warning in mind, we can attempt a tentative definition of the field: Political science is a field of study characterized by a search for critical understanding of (1) the good political life, (2) significant empirical observations, and (3) wise political and policy judgments. Political science is thus concerned with the search for meaningful knowledge of the interrelated ethical, empirical, and prudential components of that community concerned with the public life.

The central activity of the political community is, of course, politics. Politics, as we saw in Chapter 1, is defined as a process within or between political communities whereby (1) public values are articulated, debated, and prescribed; (2) diverse political actors (individuals, interest groups, local or regional governments, nations, international organizations) cooperate and struggle for power in order to satisfy their vital needs, protect their fundamental interests, and advance their perceived desires; and (3) public policy judgments are made and authoritative actions on crucial public problems are taken. Let us now try to clarify these definitions by addressing the components of political science and the tasks they suggest.

THE THREE MAJOR COMPONENTS OF POLITICAL SCIENCE

Three interrelated components of the study of politics shape the political scientist's major tasks (see Table 3.1). Each of these components represents a major concern or aspect of political science: ethical, empirical, and prudential. Throughout history,

Table 3.1 Three Major Components of Political Science

Component	Main Focus	Main Question	Foundation
Ethical	Political values	What ought to be?	Philosophy
Empirical	Political phenomena	What is (what has been, what will be)?	Science
Prudential	Political judgment	What can be?	Public policy

Source: Compiled by authors.

political scientists have been concerned with the study of the good political life, political institutions, behavior, and wise judgment. Until recently, these emphases were linked. In the post–World War II period, some political scientists argued that these components should be separated for study. Others, however, continued to insist on their integration.

The Ethical Component

The student of politics is concerned with worthy political values—with what ought to be in politics. Specifically, he or she is a student of ethics, which is the study of the nature of moral standards and choices of judgment and behavior. Every community adheres to certain values, is inspired by certain purposes, is dedicated to certain goals, and is committed to certain conceptions of the good life. Critical examination of these norms is a central concern of the political scientist as an ethical theorist or political philosopher. For example, the preamble to the U.S. Constitution expresses the cardinal values of the American political community: "We, the people of the United States, in order to form a more perfect Union, establish justice, insure domestic tranquility, provide for the common defense, promote the general welfare, and secure the blessings of liberty to ourselves and our posterity, do ordain and establish this Constitution for the United States of America." Other constitutions contain similar statements of goals, purposes, and values.

But what do these values mean? This is a question the political scientist cannot avoid; it is a starting point for her or his critical investigation. Although there is widespread agreement at a very general level on such values as life, liberty, peace, justice, and economic well-being, the specific meaning of these concepts in particular circumstances—and their harmony with one another—remains a source of great controversy. Indeed, most political battles center on the meaning given to these values.

Thus, critically examined values provide a standard for judgment in politics. This standard permits us to say that a domestic law is good or bad; that a foreign policy is morally right or wrong; or that the action of a governmental official, politician, or interest group is desirable or undesirable.

The Empirical Component

Political scientists are also concerned with understanding political phenomena—political realities—in the community: events and their causes, conditions of well-being, patterns of conflict and accommodation, institutions, and public policies. In short, political scientists are concerned with political **empiricism**—what has been, what is, and what will be. As social scientists, they investigate empirically significant problems related to politics, such as the causes of war and the conditions that make for peace, the factors influencing democratic or undemocratic rule, and the circumstances connected with justice or injustice within a political community. Political scientists are also interested in the behavior of key political actors (in the United States this would include the president, Congress, and the Supreme Court) and in the role of political parties, the media, and interest groups in the political process.

To investigate these questions, we rely primarily on the methods of empirical science: observation, description, measurement, inductive generalization, explanation, deductive reasoning, continued testing, correction, corroboration, and carefully qualified prediction. Empirical investigations are designed to discover who rules and who benefits in politics and why. Indeed, one famous shorthand definition of the empirical approach to political science is found in the title of Harold Lasswell's influential book, *Politics: Who Gets What, When, How.* In all of these efforts, political scientists strive for the highest degree of objectivity possible. Political mythology, anecdotes, and common wisdom are all antithetical to the empirical approach to political science.

Empirical evidence is used to test hypotheses and to arrive at supportable generalizations. Do businesspeople or farmers or factory workers get the biggest "breaks" from income tax legislation in the United States? Is it really true that the "strong do what they can and the weak suffer what they must" in international politics? Is there an "iron law of oligarchy"—which states that an elite minority will always control any large group—at work in politics as well as in large organizations? In their empirical investigations, political scientists explore these and other questions to arrive at meaningful, coherent, and objectively testable generalizations.

The Prudential Component

Political scientists are also concerned with political **prudence**—that is, with workable public policies developed through wise judgment about the practical tasks of politics, respectful both of sound values and the limitations and opportunities of social reality.[3] How can a political candidate gain enough votes to win an election? How can a nation's leaders most wisely deal with their actual or potential enemies? What actions can a citizen take to influence public officials? How can a nation grapple with problems such as nuclear disarmament, violations of human rights, poverty, unemployment, pollution, crime, drugs, and debilitating diseases such as AIDS? Formulating answers to such questions requires practical judgment, or good sense.

Wise practical judgment must be exercised in making or carrying out public policy and in deciding disputes under the law. But legislators, executives, and judges are not the only political actors who make judgments. Prominent party officials, powerful interest group leaders, and influential members of the media also make key judgments. And beyond even these important decision makers, a variety of economic, social, religious, and educational groups and scores of individuals influence public policy in major or minor ways. Citizens voting in the election booth are making practical judgments. Furthermore, millions of ordinary people are involved in the process of making judgments as they read newspaper stories, listen to political news on their televisions or radios, peruse the Internet, hear political candidates, and contribute to or work in political campaigns.

We will postpone consideration of how these components interrelate until we have examined the four major tasks they suggest.

THE FOUR MAJOR TASKS OF POLITICAL SCIENCE

The major tasks of political science follow logically from an acceptance of the components of the discipline we have examined in the previous section: (1) a concern for what is right or wrong in politics, which leads to the task of ethical recommendation; (2) a concern for political phenomena (facts, circumstances, experiences), which leads to the task of empirical understanding; (3) a concern for what can sensibly be done, which leads to the task of prudential judgment or action; and (4) the theoretical integration of these ethical, empirical, and prudential concerns.

Let us now examine each task in turn.

KEY QUESTIONS

1. How do the three major components of political study translate into discrete tasks for political scientists?

2. What connections exist between the main tasks of political scientists? Is one of the tasks more important than the others?

3. Is it the job of political scientists to advise political leaders, or should political scientists confine themselves to the task of developing a better understanding of the political world through research?

Ethical Recommendation

Political scientists have the important (and admittedly controversial) task of recommending what actions leaders of state, citizens, and all others involved in politics ought to take. They prescribe standards and make critical appraisals that assist political actors in pursuing the good political life. This task also helps political scientists address questions of legitimacy and obligation in politics: For example, which governments or actions are legitimate and therefore entitled to public consent, and which political rights and responsibilities are citizens obliged to honor?

Political philosophers have been concerned about the ideal regime and the best practical political community since the birth of systematic philosophy with Socrates, Plato, and Aristotle in ancient Greece. But what is "best" calls for critical examination. The definitions of key political values—whether justice or the common good or liberty or order or equality or fraternity—are not self-evident. People in politics dispute the meaning of these values. Moreover, the relationship of one value to another—for example, of justice to order, of liberty to equality—cries out for analysis.

In carrying out such a study, political scientists as political philosophers are not completely divorced from the world as it is and as it can be. Their ethical analysis must be compatible with real people, as they now are or as they can sanely become in a real world. Thus, political scientists cannot sensibly recommend political values that are biologically and physically impossible or socially and politically perilous.

Yet political scientists as philosophers are, if not completely unlimited, significantly free to let their imaginations soar. They can raise their ethical sites to discover possibilities undreamed of by pedestrian political actors following the unexamined routes or the bureaucratic ruts carved out by tradition. Political scientists are free to articulate political ideas far removed from the current system. They have the luxury to speculate about an ideal world, see how far we fall short, and then suggest ways to improve the political situation. Arguably, the most important American political philosopher of the latter half of the 20th century, John Rawls, wrote a famous work, *A Theory of Justice*, that offered an ethical standard by which all public policy could be judged. Subsequently, political scientists applied Rawls's keen insights into what *should be* to evaluate specific public policy proposals about what is realistically possible. His work is a great example of how imaginative ideals can inform actual politics. Even if the ideal is never reached, it can serve as a guide to help us navigate to a better, if certainly not perfect, world. They can, for example, imagine a world without war and political communities wherein social and economic justice prevails and policies ensure economic well-being for all. They can conceive of a global physical environment in ecological balance, of a world where disastrous diseases, such as AIDS, have been successfully eradicated. In more concrete terms, they can imagine the reduction and eventual elimination of nuclear arms, poverty, and torture. They can envision good jobs for all persons capable of working, financial security for the aged and the ill, pure water, and the end of racism and debilitating disease.

Critical analysis of values goes beyond a keen appraisal of standards that ought to guide political actors. It includes criticism of actual behavior, institutions, and policies in the light of these standards. Is a given country, for example, engaged in a war? Is it oppressing its own people? Is the U.S. presidency, or the Chinese leadership, tyrannically powerful? Is the United States taking appropriate action to curb terrorism, enhance employment, extend health care, reform the welfare system, ensure educational opportunity, protect the environment, and support fledgling movements for freedom and democracy around the world?

Finally, critical analysis involves examination of sensible alternatives for the future. Can the proliferation of nuclear weapons be avoided? How should this be accomplished? In the near future, should the number of nuclear weapons be reduced to zero? Or would that create its own problems?

As political scientists analyze the protection of human rights, we can ask whether "quiet diplomacy" works best or whether violators should face publicity and strong sanctions. Disturbingly, answers depend on whether the violators of human rights are powerful nations or weak nations and whether they are "friends" or "foes." A classic question that has concerned political scientists for decades is whether engagement, even friendliness, will lead to countries such as China becoming more democratic or should the United States take a hard line with authoritarian governments in hopes that toughness will lead to reform.

And how should Americans weigh alternatives as they seek to overcome global poverty—or whether dealing with global poverty should even be a concern of the United States? Should the poor lift themselves up by their bootstraps suspecting that any aid would lead to a dependency? Or should rich nations (mostly located in the Northern Hemisphere) help poor nations (mostly located in the Southern Hemisphere)? Or should Americans favor a more complex set of policies, one that combines self-help, governmental assistance, and salutary international policies of trade and aid?

And how should Americans respond to the ecological challenges and widespread disease facing the world? Should we rely on science and technology to overcome the dwindling supplies of oil and other precious nonrenewable resources? Or should our focus be on prudent management of natural resources aimed at achieving a "steady-state" society? And how can we successfully treat or even prevent disease?

These questions underscore the connections among ethical recommendation, empirical understanding, and prudential judgment.

Empirical Understanding

Political scientists seek to understand how political actors carry out their business. What really goes on in politics—and why? Here political scientists are concerned with political realities, with what can be scientifically observed, described, confirmed, and explained. Their interest is what has been, is, and will be the case in politics. But they seek more than just the bare facts; they seek comprehensive knowledge and understanding. Although they may begin with description, they hope to end with explanation. A number of important empirical questions challenge the political scientist:

1. How does the larger environment of politics—the geographic world we live in, our biological endowment, our economic resources and activity, our historical memory, our religious beliefs, our scientific and technological achievements, our social mores—influence our political values, patterns of conflict and accommodation, and decision making?

2. Are political values rooted in universal human needs, or are they merely the product of a particular culture's development?

3. Do citizens, as creative political actors, make wise decisions?

4. Why do some political communities succeed better than others at satisfying such values as security, liberty, justice, and welfare?

In attending to these and comparable questions, empirical political scientists seek to establish a general theory that will aid their efforts to order and explain the complex data of politics. As they develop their theories, they follow, as much as possible, the elements of scientific investigation. They examine data systematically and critically to develop fruitful generalizations. Such generalizations enhance the ability of political scientists to grasp connections in the world of political phenomena and even at times to predict future political events.

This, of course, is an ideal portrayal of the empirical task—and one that as yet remains out of reach. Indeed, students of politics must be wary; empirical social scientists frequently "sneak" in unstated assumptions about how the world *should* work instead of merely describing how it in fact *does* work. For example, while political scientists claim to be strictly empirical they often subtly assume that democracy, a political value, is good and desirable. Nonetheless, the empirically oriented political scientist strives to explain how and why political actors formulate political values; accommodate diverse interests and umpire the struggle for power; and exercise judgment (wisely or foolishly) in grappling with problems, making decisions, and administering public policy. Thus, the empirically oriented political scientist is concerned with values and judgment as well as with actual behavior.

Prudential Judgment

Political scientists must provide sensible guidance in political life. This means employing practical wisdom and making decisions in concrete situations. Political scientists may use this capability when they exercise power themselves as politicians or administrators; when they advise leaders of state, legislators, and party officials; when they work as teachers or scholars; or when they function as ordinary citizens.

Political scientists need to be clearheaded about the values—for example, peace, prosperity, human rights, or clean air—they seek to preserve. They need to recognize the factors that threaten (or advance) these values and be able to identify and debate alternative policies addressed toward their protection (or extension). Finally, they need to decide on which of these policies are both most desirable and feasible. We explore these considerations in greater depth in Part IV.

The tasks of ethical recommendation and empirical understanding provide a foundation on which to exercise the task of prudential judgment. Judgment must be guided by critically examined values (for example, respect for human life and human rights) and must recognize the limitations and opportunities of political reality. Yet prudential judgment differs from ethical and empirical tasks in important ways.

In contrast to political scientists who make ethical recommendations and might not be too concerned with being realistic, those engaged in making wise judgments are limited by the constraints of politics, or "the art of the possible." They must tailor their judgments to fit a real, rather than an ideal, world. This does not mean that political scientists have to be timid or rigidly conservative. Bold, imaginative judgments that are nonetheless prudent are possible, even when made, as they often are, in extreme circumstances. Nonetheless, in politics a tension will always exist between the ethically ideal and the politically feasible.

Although feasibility requires political scientists, when exercising prudent judgment, to respect reality, they need only be concerned with that reality insofar as it helps them judge present and future behavior, consequences, and alternatives. Such judgments are not fully scientific because they go beyond knowledge of what is, to what can be, to practical wisdom. Practical wisdom calls for judgment in action—judgment that must usually be made in the absence of complete scientific knowledge. Thus, the judgmental process is not fully scientific, and it entails more than science. Science is, however, indispensable in politics.

Ethical and empirical components are integrally connected with prudent judgments. The interrelationship of these three components brings us now to a fourth task, theoretical integration.

Theoretical Integration

Although political scientists may specialize in any one of the three realms we have discussed—ethical, empirical, or prudential—they must still appreciate how these

Table 3.2 Interrelationship of the Three Major Components of Political Science

Component	Political Values	Political Phenomena	Political Judgment
Ethical	Which political values should exist?	How should political actors behave?	Which public policies should prevail?
Empirical	Which values actually exist in the political community?	How do political actors actually behave?	Which public policies actually exist?
Prudential	Which values can wisely exist in the political community?	How can political actors wisely behave?	Which public policies can be formulated and sensibly implemented?

Source: Compiled by authors.

components interrelate in a unified and coherent discipline. Table 3.2 presents one view of their interrelationship.

Within this framework, the issue of ecological health, for example, would prompt political philosophers concerned with ethics to ask this: Should ecological health be a cardinal value in the political community? Empirical political scientists to ask this: Does such a condition of ecological health actually exist? And students of public policy to ask this: Is ecological health a value that nations can practically achieve?

Other ties among the components of political science are apparent. Indeed, the history of political science and the very nature of politics call for a unified discipline. The great political philosophers—the first creative political scientists—were very concerned with the relationship of ethics to politics. They also saw that politics embraced both empirical understanding and prudent judgment.

Moreover, as we have emphasized, the nature of politics forbids the separation of tasks. Values guide empirical investigation and inform prudent judgment in public policy. Political values make little sense unless they are in accord with actual (or potential) political realities and with creative, but feasible, political decisions. Judgments as to what is feasible influence actual behavior. And judgment is not only informed by the values that motivate political actors but also qualified by the realities of political phenomena. Thus, political science is fruitful because political scientists grapple critically at the highest level of political theory with the interrelationship among articulated political values, empirical data and theory on the actual behavior of political actors (individuals, interests, political communities), and the creative judgments required in statesmanship. In the political life of the real community, these three components, although partially separable in logic and distinguishable for purposes of specialized research, cannot be treated in isolation.

Some additional illustrations will help clarify this interrelationship. Concern for the value of human survival has led inexorably to an appreciation of the disastrous consequences of nuclear war and to a search for prudent ways of controlling and eventually eliminating nuclear weapons. Heightened awareness of the meaning of equality in the United States has led to empirical investigation of racial discrimination, poverty, and sexism, as well as to measures to reduce inequalities (a civil rights act, a "war on poverty," affirmative action). Some programs helped, others worked imperfectly, and still others backfired, often resulting in protests—for example, against such policies as forced busing, forced integration, or reverse discrimination. These consequences sometimes led to a reconsideration of the methods used to fight inequality and of the meaning of equality, and thus to new empirical research.[4]

Political Health as an Example of Theoretical Integration. The tasks of ethical recommendation, empirical understanding, and prudential judgment stimulate political scientists to envisage an ambitious fourth task: integration in the discipline. Such theoretical integration is evident in the concept of **political health**, which can be defined as the political, economic, and social well-being of the political community. Political health encourages integration because it enables political scientists to address the three major concerns—ethical, empirical, and prudential.

There are several ways political scientists could explore political health. First, they could do so as a norm or a standard of the good life. Theoretically, it is possible to refine our definition of political health by judging it in terms of peace and peaceful constitutional change, security, liberty, democratic governance, political and social justice, economic prosperity, and ecological balance.

Second, political scientists could investigate political health in a scientific fashion. Are political communities healthy? Why or why not? What evidence supports an empirical conclusion about their well-being? Here we emphasize that political scientists can move beyond symptoms of political well-being or malaise to empirical generalizations and theories about the healthy political community.

Third, political scientists—guided by an ethical norm and aided by social scientific knowledge—could engage in healing by addressing themselves to wise actions, policies, and judgments designed to maximize political health. They are encouraged as teachers, political advisers, citizens, governmental leaders, or administrators to put their knowledge to work as best they can.

To summarize, the task of theoretical integration involves developing a general theory (for example, of political health) that harmoniously relates the discipline's ethical, empirical, and prudential components and ties together its traditional (and nontraditional) fields of study. Ambitious? Yes. Impossible? No, but certainly difficult!

Historical Theories of Integration. The linkage of political values, social scientific knowledge, and wise action has been noted by key political philosophers such as Plato, Aristotle, James Madison, and Karl Marx as well as by twentieth-century political scientists. In ancient Greece, Plato saw no sharp division between fact and value, or between these two and practical wisdom. For Plato, the good was true, and practical wisdom involved approximating the good as closely as circumstances permitted. Aristotle took a somewhat different position but argued on behalf of the intimate linkage between ethics and politics; he believed that prudence—or practical wisdom—depended on a good goal pursued sensibly in light of existing realities.

In the late eighteenth century, James Madison clearly saw the importance of making republican values central to his thinking. He also recognized the need to advance those republican values within the parameters of America's realities—a nation of large size with diverse interests. Prudence dictated the concept of an "extensive republic"—the present U.S. federal republic—as a wise solution to the problem of reconciling republican liberty and size.

Modern Approaches. In the twentieth century, social scientists (including political scientists) began to systematically gather an enormous amount of empirical data. No longer was the study of politics simply a reflection of personal opinion and beliefs. No longer did people base their political judgments on their own, unscientific impressions of what was going on around them. Instead, people began to survey the world around them a systematic and scientific way. However, this created its own problems. For some, there came a desire to make political science a completely neutral science with no connection to values, ethics, or ideals. For others, the problem was there was just too much data and no way to grasp what the data was showing. One of the great advances in political science was heralded by David Easton. Easton was interested in developing a political science that could make generalizable propositions about politics—to create a "general theory" of political science that made sense of all this information. His most influential work was *The Political System*, and he is famous for arguing that politics is the "authoritative allocation of values for a society." In his work, Easton hoped that political science would be able to use data, combined with theory, to make clear predictive and causals explanations of what was happening in the political world. If students have ever wondered about what all the incredible information we have about politics means—if it somehow fits together—then such an approach is quite appealing.

Practical Applications. Political scientists in all the traditional fields undertake the four tasks we have outlined. To the superficial observer, however, this may not appear to be the case. Ethical recommendation may seem more immediately visible in the field of political theory, empirical understanding more apparent in comparative politics and American politics, and prudential judgment more central in international politics and in public administration and public policy. A more thorough examination of the fields, however, reveals that the ethical and prudential approaches are just below the surface in comparative politics or American politics. Moreover, international politics, public administration, and public policy are clearly guided by ethical norms and must rest on a sound foundation of empirical understanding. And, of course, political theory presupposes both a firm appreciation of political reality and appropriate attention to wise judgment.

Later in this book, we explore more fully the traditional fields of political science and their several approaches. Specifically, we examine political theory in Part II and comparative politics, American politics, and international politics in Parts III and IV. Before turning to a fuller exploration of problems in these fields, however, we must point out here that not all political scientists agree on the approach outlined in the previous pages. Controversy persists on the legitimate subject matter of political science, on proper methodology for the discipline, and on approaches to be taken in the several fields of political science.

CONTINUING CONTROVERSIES IN POLITICAL SCIENCE

Controversies in political science center on the priority to be given to (1) the quest for the good political life, (2) the search for a science of politics, (3) guidance for citizens and leaders of state, and (4) the importance of a unified discipline that can do justice to politics. Political scientists remain divided on key questions within each of these areas of emphasis.

The Quest for the Good Political Life

Some political scientists argue that only ethical reasoning can determine standards for what is right or wrong. Others contend that such norms and standards derive from religious faith and divine revelation as expressed, for example, in the Ten Commandments. Many look to human needs as the root of cardinal values. They insist that human beings elevate their needs for food, shelter, sex, expression, companionship, and fulfillment into preferred values and then into human rights—the rights to life, liberty, property, and so on. Finally, some political scientists maintain that society strongly influences, if not dictates, the ways in which the good political life is understood.

KEY QUESTIONS

1. By what concern for the highest truth should the ethical quest for the good political life be guided: philosophical? religious? scientific? Or should it be led by a quest for the most acceptable opinion?

2. What is the key to unlocking the mysteries of the good political life: philosophical reason? religious revelation? historical experience? human need? societal preference?

The Need for Standards. Renowned political philosopher Leo Strauss argued that the quest for the "best political order" must be central to politics. Politics, he maintained, inevitably requires "approval and disapproval," "choice and rejection," and "praise and blame." Neutrality is impossible; political matters inevitably "raise a claim to men's obedience, allegiance, decision, or judgment." Inescapably, citizens judge political affairs "in terms of goodness or badness, of justice or injustice." Since judgment requires a standard, and sound judgment a sound standard, citizens seek the best standard for the good political life. Only with such a standard of excellence, of virtue, of the best political order can political leaders umpire the "controversies between groups struggling for power within the political community." Here the tie between ethics and statesmanship is explicit. A standard of excellence is necessary if a leader is "to manage well the affairs of his political community as a whole."[5]

Political science, Strauss pointed out, originally meant the skill, art, prudence, and practical wisdom of the excellent leader of state. Such a leader could shape sound public policy only if he or she possessed knowledge about sound political standards and wielded prudential skill. Policies recommended by the philosopher-statesman are normally "a compromise between what he would wish and what circumstances permit. To effect that compromise intelligently, he must first know what . . . would be most desirable in itself." After that, the leader tries prudently to bridge the gap between what is most desirable in itself and what is possible in given circumstances. Those "scientists" and "historicists" who deny the possibility or desirability or primacy of the quest for the good political life, Strauss argued, are the enemies of a true political science.

Robert Dahl, an outstanding and sophisticated empirical political scientist, also addressed the relationship of ethics to politics. He asked, "Can the study of politics be ethically neutral? Should it be?" He framed the "value-fact" controversy, as empirically oriented political scientists and their critics perceive it. This controversy revolves around the question of whether "ought," or value, propositions differ fundamentally from "is," or empirical (factual), propositions. Empirical theorists, Dahl wrote, hold that a "substantial and important aspect of politics is purely empirical, and that this empirical aspect of politics can be analyzed (in principle at least) neutrally and objectively." Dahl sought to find common ground between the conflicting schools and to explain and defend the position of a sophisticated empirical political science.[6]

Ethics Versus Positivism. **Positivism** is a philosophy that holds that human beings can know only that which is based on positive, observable, scientific facts or on data derived from sense experience. "Positivism . . . the dominant and most influential perspective within American political science today . . . is reflected in contemporary political science in what has come to be called the behavioral approach to political phenomena." Some fear that positivism is "an attempt to avoid all normative judgment." Many political theorists, for instance, have never quite accepted this approach and have consistently maintained that politics is a moral activity and we must make important value judgments about what is going on in the political world. Their studies of the great political thinkers inform the kind of questions they ask and suggest that ultimately the political theorist is concerned primarily with what ought to be. But beyond political theorists, many other political scientists, while welcoming the scientific approach to the collection of data, believe that all this data gathering must be at the service of solving social and political problems. We don't just want to describe poverty and know how many people are poor. We want to know how to end the scourge of poverty. And this will create ideological and philosophical debates. To use the example of poverty again, we need to know how many people are poor, and we need to develop an explanation about why they are poor. But once we have done that, different people with different values may argue about what this means and what government should do about it.

The Search for a Science of Politics

Behavioralism. This approach to social science emphasizes empirically observable, discoverable, and explicable patterns of behavior. Some behavioral political scientists maintain that we will progress in political science only if we recognize that our primary business is to state and test hypotheses about relationships in the world of sense experience. Others argue that at the highest level political scientists should follow a physics model, guided by the political science equivalent of Albert Einstein's famous formula, $E = mc^2$. Still, other political scientists contend that we should follow a biological model, guided by the political science equivalent of Louis Pasteur's germ theory of disease to explain health or illness in the body politic. Clearly, quarrels persist on appropriate models and methodology, even as empirical political scientists agree in emphasizing the importance of scientific investigation as a way to proceed.

The Behavioralist Approach. The search for an empirical science of politics in modern America has been closely associated with the behavioral emphasis in the discipline. While scholars continue today to debate how best to approach the study of politics, many of the most important debates on the subject occurred in the 1960s and 1970s between behavioralists and their critics. By the turn of the century, there was a strong consensus that the behavioralist approach was an integral component of the discipline. Most behavioralists share—as David Easton, a leading empirical theorist, pointed out in 1965—a common goal: "a science of politics modeled after the methodological assumptions of the natural sciences." Easton identified eight "intellectual foundation stones" of **behaviorialism**:

1. A belief in *regularities*, "discoverable uniformities in political behavior" that "can be expressed in generalizations or theories with explanatory and predictive value"

2. A commitment to *verification* of such generalizations through testing

3. An experimental attitude toward *techniques*, with the goal of obtaining ever more rigorous means for observing, recording, and analyzing behavior

4. An emphasis on *quantification* where possible, relevant, and meaningful

5. A sophisticated attitude toward *values* and especially a recognition that ethical "valuation and empirical explanation involve two different kinds of propositions that, for the sake of clarity, should be kept analytically distinct"

6. A stress on *systemization*, on the importance of theory in research and in the development of a "coherent and orderly body of knowledge"

7. An acknowledgment of the primacy of *pure science*, as against applied science or practical problem solving

8. An acceptance of *integration* of the social sciences and the value of interdisciplinary fertilization[7]

The use of the **scientific method** in political science is not easy. Perhaps the first of the two most difficult obstacles are that we are dealing with incredibly complex human behavior. In fields like physics, it is possible through the use of highly controlled experiments to limit the number of variables. This is a much more difficult process in the social sciences, and in some cases, it is impossible. When considering why war breaks out or why poverty persists in a region of the world, the number of factors to be considered can be overwhelming. The second difficulty is that we are dealing with human beings—and human beings exhibit an enormous range of emotions, temperaments, and foibles. Neither of these difficulties should be a deterrent to the quest for a more scientific discipline. But they lead us to two realities.

The first reality is that while the scientific method strives to uncover **causality**—that is, the concept that a condition or behavior exists or takes place because of the

influence of another fact (A causes B)—it is in fact far more likely that political phenomena will be explained through **multicausality**—that is, the concept that a condition or behavior exists or takes place because of the influence of two or more factors (A and B cause C).

For example, the collapse of the Soviet Union has been explained by a number of causal factors. Some people believe that the system collapsed because of the decisions made by President Ronald Reagan. His tough stance with the Soviets, his dramatic increase in defense spending, and his push for an enormously expensive antiballistic missile program known as Star Wars drove the Soviets to fiscal disaster. A second assertion claims that it was not Reagan alone who brought the Soviets down. Rather, it was the cumulative pressure of all of the Cold War–era presidents and their relentless adherence to the containment policy that weakened the Soviets. A third explanation centers on Soviet president Mikhail Gorbachev. Gorbachev, a dynamic personality, was not only the first college-educated Soviet

Two key figures in the events leading to the collapse of the Soviet Union and the end of the Cold War were President Ronald Reagan (on the left) and his counterpart Soviet leader Mikhail Gorbachev. Here, they greet each other at their first summit in Switzerland in November 1985.

leader but was also the first to have been born after the Russian Revolution. According to this assertion, it was Gorbachev who looked out over the vast Soviet empire and recognized the extent to which it was overextended and suffering stagnation. Through two policies, *perestroika* (reform) and *glasnost* (openness), Gorbachev set in motion a series of liberal reforms and policies that ultimately took on a life of their own, becoming uncontrollable. Rather than reforming the system, these policies in fact resulted in its total collapse. Finally, there is the assertion that the communist Soviet system itself was fatally flawed and, as a result, simply imploded. Lacking the internal competition and profit motive of the capitalist system, the communist system provided little incentive for quality control or innovation. Over time this caused a serious erosion of the system and eventually its collapse.

So, which factor was it that caused the demise of the Soviet Union? In fact, a very good case can be made that the collapse was caused by some combination of all of these factors. In other words, the case for multicausality is very strong. It is the task of political scientists to understand which factor or factors contributed for a clear understanding of the collapse of the Soviet Union.

A second reality faced by the application of the scientific method to the study of politics is that most causal explanations are probabilistic; while we aim for 100 percent assurance that A caused B, the fact is that we will probably not achieve this. Because we are dealing with human beings in very complex situations, it may be impossible to establish any "laws of politics" or "political axioms" similar to the laws and axioms we find in the hard sciences. The best we can do is to uncover the strongest, causal associations possible. If factor A is present, it is likely or even highly likely that B will occur. Or, if conditions A, B, and C exist, it is probable or even highly probable that D will occur. This does not mean that we lack an explanation or the ability to predict political phenomenon. What it does mean is that explanations deemed highly probable through the testing of hypotheses will be the more powerful as a result.

Finally, the use of a scientific method to better understand politics requires the generation of data that are as objective and value-free as possible. In this regard, tremendous advances have been made by improvements in computer technology. The range of data is enormous. Following is a mere sampling:

1. *Economic data.* Municipal, state, country, and global economic data can be invaluable in better understanding phenomena such as patterns of wealth and poverty or levels of societal frustration. Budgetary data can provide an important window into the political priorities of societies.

2. *Demographic data.* Statistics on population growth and reduction as well as migration patterns can help us to better understand shifting patterns of politics. The distribution of ethnic and racial groupings provides a valuable tool in understanding political tensions within local neighborhoods, countries, and regions of the world.

3. *Voting behavior.* Voting behavior is a critical tool in understanding political values and behavior in democratic societies.

4. *Survey research.* Survey research represents one of the most important types of quantitative political science research. Most commonly, survey research involves the development of a questionnaire that is administered to a sample of respondents from a specified population. This research tool is enormously valuable in our efforts to understand political interests, values, and motives.

5. *Conflict data.* Political scientists with a particular interest in better understanding human conflict find quantitative data on revolutions and wars—their frequency, intensity, geographic patterns, casualty rates, and so forth—of considerable value. Data on military spending and force levels can also be an important resource.

At its height, the controversy between behavioralists and traditionalists involved a number of points. The more radical behavioralists criticized traditional political scientists for not pushing the discipline toward "a science capable of prediction and explanation." Traditionalists, they maintained, did not limit political science to a study of "phenomena which can actually be observed" and did not push quantification more rigorously. The behavioralists also faulted the traditionalists for using unsophisticated methods, for not being interdisciplinary, and for not seeking overarching generalizations about politics. Behavioralists dismissed the legitimacy of the task of ethical recommendation, holding instead that the "truth or falsity of values . . . cannot be established scientifically." Values, they maintained, "are beyond the scope of legitimate inquiry." Behavioralists also tended to reject as illegitimate political scientists' engagement in political reform.[8]

Beyond Behavioralism. Behavioralism is not today's only player. An additional perspective shares the stage. While behavioralism emphasizes the scientific method and uses the natural sciences as a model, **rational choice** or game theory, is inspired by economics. Put simply, rational choice models provide conclusions about how politics works that follow deductively from a simple assumption about political actors such as voters, elected officials, and government administrators.[9] The assumption is that political actors are rational and choose the most efficient means to attain their ends. Behavioralism typically requires political scientists to observe the world and then offer theories about politics. Much emphasis is placed on quantifying political actions. In contrast, rational choice, at least in its purist form, requires only a clear theory about what motivates people and an assumption that people are rational in fulfilling those desires; from the theory and this assumption, simple logic can generate interesting hypotheses about how politics works. The most famous specific example is the **Prisoner's Dilemma**, which shows why two apparently rational actors might not cooperate even though such cooperation would lead to better results. Imagine two accused criminals (A and B) being interrogated separately. If they both stay silent, they will be convicted of a lesser charge and face only a year in prison. If A betrays B and B remains silent, A will go free and B will serve five years in jail (and vice versa). If they betray each other, they will both serve two-year sentences. Notice, if each is acting rationally and pursuing their own self-interest, they will betray each other. Yet, this rational and self-interested outcome produces a non-optimal result for each. (For political scientist interested in this form of analysis, one can put more and more conditions and variation on the game making it very complex—the example just provided is the most basic version). This counter-intuitive result from the game has been used to show how and why real world actors do certain things that at first glance may not appear sensible. For instance, political scientists have used the Prisoner's Dilemma to explain the Cold War. The Soviet Union and the United States spent an enormous amount of resources to build nuclear weapons, which they did not want to actually use. On the face of it, this seems strange. Both sides disarming could result in a much better world of no wasted resources on nuclear weapons and avoid a horrible, civilization-ending war with possibly billions dead. However, both sides building such costly weapons makes sense given a certain kind of rationality in the face of a challenge from the other side and limited knowledge.

Hans J. Morgenthau, a refugee from Nazi Germany and an influential student of politics, once asked, "What, then, ought a political science be like, which does justice both to its scientific pretense and to its subject matter?" Morgenthau's answer handily knit together the multiple perspectives political scientists have championed: Such a political science will profit from the "valuable insights" of philosophical traditions other than the dominant positivism of contemporary political science. It will appreciate that although these insights are not rigorously scientific, they do illuminate a scientific understanding of politics. Such a political science will maintain "ties with the Western tradition of political thought, its concerns, its accumulation of wisdom and knowledge." It will recognize the identity of political theory and political science. It will hold that a "scientific theory is a system of empirically verifiable, general truths sought for their own sake." Political science will also communicate an "objective and general truth about matters political," a truth that holds "regardless of time and place." Such a political science will be guided by a theory whose purpose, of course, "is to bring order and meaning to a mass of phenomena." Contemporary political scientists will wisely recognize that their task is "to reformulate the perennial truths of politics" in the "light of contemporary experience."[10]

Even at the almost certain risk of being controversial, political scientists must grapple with the burning problems and great political issues of society. Here the relevance of political science to statesmanship becomes clear. A "theory of politics presents not only a guide to understanding but also an ideal for action." It maps the political scene "in order to show the shortest and safest road to a given objective."[11]

Guidance for Leaders of State and Citizens

Those concerned with wise judgment and action in politics may concede that there are no scientific answers to the problems that baffle us in politics, yet they seek to enhance our capacity to decide how, for example, to avert devastating wars, to protect human rights, to enhance prosperity, and to guard against ecological disasters. They know that a conscious appreciation of key values and realities is crucial in this endeavor.

Take the issue of poverty and welfare reform in the United States. It is relatively easy to affirm the value of a decent income, decent housing, decent health, decent diet, and decent education for all Americans. It is also relatively easy to identify the poor and those on welfare, the working poor, and the homeless who are destitute and not on welfare. But it is considerably more difficult, although not beyond current capability, to determine why people are poor and why, in some respects, the welfare system fails. It is also difficult to know which rational policies will turn things around. Is the key to sensible welfare reform private sector or community service jobs for those men and women now on welfare who are capable of working, plus an income tax credit for the working poor, plus appropriate health insurance and day care for working mothers and their children? Or is it better education and job training? Is it more generous welfare benefits, or perhaps the abolition of the entire welfare system? Will the costs and benefits of the choices turn out to be politically feasible?[12] Clearly, assessing alternatives is central to sound judgment, even though no one can be absolutely sure which alternatives will be the wisest or which specific qualities make for sound judgment.

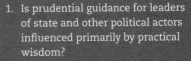

KEY QUESTIONS

1. Is prudential guidance for leaders of state and other political actors influenced primarily by practical wisdom?

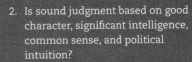

2. Is sound judgment based on good character, significant intelligence, common sense, and political intuition?

Neal Riemer, in *The Revival of Democratic Theory*, attempted to remedy the neglect of prudence by highlighting its special role in politics. He defined prudence as "practical wisdom or that sound judgment which requires conscious and rational adaptation of means to ends." The ends must be proper ends or else the judgment is not prudent but simply clever, narrowly expedient, or basely pragmatic. Prudence requires the ability to judge what is appropriate in a specific situation. It is not to be confused with timidity, priggishness, overcautiousness, weakness, or paralysis. Prudence involves deliberation, awareness of consequences, and appreciation of the relationship of means to ends. Moreover, prudence requires the ability to act in a real world to meet real problems and the strength to make decisions in a morally ambiguous world, where there are only proximate solutions to insoluble problems; prudence can provide a bridge between what ought to be and what is. Most important, prudence may enable the political scientist to focus on fundamental political problems as they are currently illustrated in public policy.[13]

In his important article, "Political Science and Prevision," French political scientist Bertrand de Jouvenal illustrated in more detail the role of the political scientist in providing prudent guidance for leaders of state. He saw the political scientist as "a teacher of public men in activity." Guidance for leaders of state requires, above all, foresight. The political scientist, he argued, "must therefore develop that skill in himself, and in his pupils, and offer it to statesmen he has to advise."[14]

Harold Lasswell also sought to bring political science to bear on problems facing decision makers in politics. The problem-solving approach, he claimed, generates five intellectual tasks: (1) clarifying goals, (2) ascertaining trends, (3) identifying conditioning factors, (4) noting projections, and (5) posing policy alternatives. Political scientists have concentrated on one or more of these tasks throughout the history of their discipline. They will undoubtedly continue to do so as they grapple with unprecedented and far-reaching challenges in the future. Moreover, they will do so in performing their professional roles as teachers, researchers, advisers, managers, and leaders.

Their contribution to what we have loosely referred to as statesmanship and public policy can be more accurately understood in connection with their involvement in every phase of the decision-making process. The phases of this process, as seen by Lasswell, include intelligence (political information); recommendation (promotion of policy); prescription (articulation of official norms); invocation (provisional conformity to policy); application ("final" administration of policy); appraisal (assessment of goal, strategy, and results); and termination (settlement of expectations and claims).[15]

Toward a Unified Discipline of Political Science

Some political scientists emphasize politics as the quest for the good political life. Others stress the search for an empirical science of politics. Still others underscore the importance of prudential guidance for leaders of state. But even if we agree on one focus or another, we must still explore the brand of ethics, the kind of science, and the pattern of leadership involved.

Moreover, we still need to know how the three major components of political science are related to one another in a unified discipline. We need to integrate what ought to be, what is, and what can be. We still need to search for a more systematic theory for the discipline's major emphases and its traditional fields: American politics, political philosophy, comparative politics, international politics, public administration, and public policy. This theory would relate political norms, empirical generalizations, and public judgments. It would reconcile philosophy, science, and public policy without withdrawing from politics, distorting political phenomena, or making faulty efforts to bridge the gap between aspiration and reality.

David Easton, who as we saw earlier urged a systematic study of politics, later advocated for a greater harmony in the discipline. In "The New Revolution in Political Science," Easton outlined a "post-behavioral revolution" to help political scientists integrate their tasks. This revolution would move beyond the important work of behavioral political scientists. Easton called attention to the postbehavioralists's plea for the "constructive development of values" as a key component of "the study of politics." Postbehavioralists, he noted, seek realistic and substantively meaningful empirical research—a political science that will "reach out to the real needs of mankind in a time of crisis." They are, finally, endorsing the need "to protect the humane values of civilization" by taking responsible action "in reshaping society" and by fulfilling their "special obligation" to put their "knowledge to work."[16]

In this account of the postbehavioral revolution, Easton saw a clear relationship between the ethical, empirical, and prudential components of the discipline. The postbehavioralists modestly endorsed the legitimacy of the four major tasks of the discipline. But, clearly, their perspective by no means dominates the field.

Legitimate doubts, difficulties, and dangers will be encountered in this integrative effort, but these problems do not rule out either the desirability or the possibility of using political health as an integrative concept—a concept we explore further throughout the remainder of this book.[17]

CONCLUSION

Despite the continuing debate about the scope, substance, and methodology of political science, we can confidently affirm the reality of three central concerns: (1) an ethical concern for the good political life, for the best political community; (2) a scientific concern for empirical theory, generalization, and explanation relevant to the business of the political community; and (3) a prudential concern for judgment, decision making, public policy, and action. With somewhat less confidence, we can also affirm a fourth concern—a theoretical concern for the integration of the normative, empirical, and prudential components that constitute the leading threads in the design of a complete political science. Each of these concerns underscores significant problems, suggests appropriate methodologies, and leads to fruitful responses, which we explore in succeeding chapters.

SUGGESTED READINGS

Almond, Gabriel A. *A Discipline Divided: Schools and Sects in Political Science*. Newbury Park, CA: Sage, 1989. Argues that some schools of political science ("soft-left," "soft-right," "hard-left," "hard-right") are separate ideological and methodological tables, each with its own conception of political science. Insists that the "overwhelming majority of political scientists" reside in the center—"liberal" and moderate in ideology and eclectic and open to conviction in methodology.

Bryson, Valerie. *Feminist Political Theory*. Basingstoke, UK: Palgrave Macmillan, 2016. A thorough account of the history of feminist political theory and an analysis of contemporary debates concerning feminist politics.

Downs, Anthony. *An Economic Theory of Democracy*. New York: Longman, 1997. Considered the classic statement on rational choice applied to the study of politics.

Easton, David. *A Systems Analysis of Political Life*. New York: Wiley, 1965. Develops the systems approach, which sees the political system embedded in an environment, receiving input (demands and supports), and delivering output (decisions and actions).

Elster, Jon. *Explaining Social Behavior: More Nuts and Bolts for the Social Sciences*. Cambridge, MA: Cambridge University Press, 2015. A revised version of Elster's classic account of how and why people act the way they do. The book deals with the social sciences in general and not just political science.

Gaddis, John Lewis. *The Landscape of History*. New York: Oxford University Press, 2002. Offers a different perspective, from a noted historian, on how to analyze the social and political world.

Goertz, Gary. *A Tale of Two Cultures: Qualitative and Quantitative Research in the Social Sciences*. Princeton, NJ: Princeton University Press, 2012. A recent work that seeks to see how qualitative and quantitative research represent coherent, but different, approaches to the study of the social world. One is not superior to the other.

Goodin, Robert. *The Oxford Handbook of Political Science*. Oxford, UK: Oxford University Press, 2011. A collection of important essays by leading scholars on the major issues and areas of the discipline of political science today.

Katznelson, Ira, ed. *Political Science: The State of the Discipline*. Centennial ed. New York: Norton, 2002. Compilation of essays that avoids the traditional subfields of the discipline but instead focuses on the state, democracy, agency, and inquiry.

King, Gary, ed. *The Future of Political Science: 100 Perspectives*. New York: Routledge, 2009. An interesting collection of 100 brief essays by leading political scientists that offer speculation about where and how political science will develop in the near future.

Lasswell, Harold D. *Politics: Who Gets What, When, How*. New York: Meridian, 1965. One of the most popular definitions of politics by one of America's most creative and versatile political scientists.

Ricci, David M. *The Tragedy of Political Science: Politics, Scholarship, and Democracy*. New Haven, CT: Yale University Press, 1984. Argues that the tragedy of political science lies in the conflict between a commitment to science and a commitment to the good, wise, democratic life.

Riemer, Neal. *Creative Breakthroughs in Politics*. Westport, CT: Praeger, 1996. Examines several historical breakthroughs (Roger Williams and religious liberty and James Madison and the federal republic), two spurious breakthroughs (John C. Calhoun and protection of minority rights and Karl Marx and universal human emancipation), a contemporary breakthrough-in-progress (European Union), and a proposed future breakthrough (protection against genocide).

————. *The Future of the Democratic Revolution: Toward a More Prophetic Politics*. New York: Praeger, 1984. Analyzes the strengths and weaknesses of Machiavellian politics, utopian politics, and liberal democratic politics and argues on behalf of the desirability and feasibility of a model of prophetic politics.

————. *The Revival of Democratic Theory*. New York: Appleton-Century-Crofts, 1962. Analyzes the decline of democratic theory and suggests a case for its revival. Argues that political theory must clarify political values, illuminate empirical political reality, facilitate prudent guidance in politics, and unify the discipline of political science.

Sabl, Andrew. *Ruling Passions*. Princeton, NJ: Princeton University Press, 2002. A thoughtful analysis about how politicians act and lead. In particular, Sabl challenges political theory to think more critically about the actual way democracy works.

Shepsle, Kenneth. *Analyzing Politics: Rationality, Behavior, and Institutions*. 2nd ed. New York: Norton, 2010. An engaging look at rational choice theory by one of its leading proponents.

GLOSSARY TERMS

behavioralism (p. 69)
causality (p. 69)
diaspora (p. 56)
empiricism (p. 59)
ethics (p. 55)

multicausality (p. 70)
political health (p. 65)
political science (p. 55)
positivism (p. 68)

prisoner's dilemma (p. 72)
prudence (p. 59)
rational choice (p. 72)
scientific method (p. 69)

NOTES

1. The word *empirical* may be unfamiliar to some readers. As used here, it means "that which is based on experience and observation." The word *behavioral* refers to those actions, or forms of behavior, that can be observed.

2. Examples include political scientists Seth Masket, Julia Azari, Hans Noel, and their Mischiefs of Faction site (https//www.vox.com/mischiefs-of-faction). See also the *New York Times Upshot* online site. https://www.nytimes.com/section/upshot

3. The concept of prudence was first treated systematically in book 6 of Aristotle's "Nichomachean Ethics." The concept figures prominently in the writings of St. Thomas Aquinas (particularly I–II, Q. 21, A4, 5, 6 of his "Summa Theologica"), Edmund Burke, and James Madison. Charles Merriam, an outstanding American political scientist, devoted a section to political prudence in his *New Aspects of Political Science* (Chicago: University of Chicago Press, 1939), 163–180. Merriam defined *political prudence* as "the conclusions of experience and reflection regarding the problems of politics—wisdom that does not reach the state of science, yet has its own significance" (p. 163). Leo Strauss was well aware of the concept; see Strauss, *What Is Political Philosophy?* (Glencoe, IL: Free Press, 1959), especially pp. 81–82 and 86–87. The concept is also treated prominently in Neal Riemer's *The Revival of Democratic Theory* (New York: Appleton-Century-Crofts, 1962).

4. For an illustrative reassessment of welfare policy in the United States (as it bears on equality, poverty, and unemployment), see the excellent study by David Raphael Riemer, *The Prisoners of Welfare: Liberating America's Poor from Unemployment and Low Wages* (New York: Praeger, 1988).

5. Leo Strauss, "What Is Political Philosophy?" *Journal of Politics* 19, no. 3 (1957): 100–107, especially p. 101.

6. Robert Dahl, *Modern Political Analysis* (Englewood Cliffs, NJ: Prentice Hall, 1964), 100–107.

7. David Easton, *A Framework for Political Analysis* (Englewood Cliffs, NJ: Prentice Hall, 1965), especially pp. 7, 8, 13 ff.

8. Albert Somit and Joseph Tanenhous, *The Development of American Political Sciences* (Boston: Allyn & Bacon, 1967), especially pp. 177–179.

9. Two excellent works in the area of rational choice are Anthony Downs, *An Economic Theory of Democracy* (New York: Longman, 1997); and Kenneth A. Shepsle and Mark S. Bonchek, *Analyzing Politics: Rationality, Behavior, and Institutions* (New York: Norton, 1997).

10. Hans J. Morgenthau, *The Decline of Democratic Politics*, vol. 1 of *Politics in the Twentieth Century* (Chicago: University of Chicago Press, 1962), especially pp. 41, 43, 45, 48, 49.

11. Ibid.

12. See David Riemer, *Prisoners of Welfare*.

13. Neal Riemer, *Revival of Democratic Theory*, especially pp. 60–65. On prudence and political judgment, see also the fine book by Ronald Beiner, *Political Judgment* (Chicago: University of Chicago Press, 1983).

14. Bertrand de Jouvenal, "Political Science and Prevision," *American Political Science Review* 59, no. 1 (1965): 29–38, especially p. 29.

15. Harold Lasswell, *The Future of Political Science* (New York: Atherton Press, 1963), especially pp. 1, 17–26.

16. David Easton, "The New Revolution in Political Science," *American Political Science Review* 63, no. 4 (1969): 1051–1061, especially p. 1052.

17. See Neal Riemer, *The Future of the Democratic Revolution: Toward a More Prophetic Politics* (New York: Praeger, 1984), especially pp. 236–237; and Riemer, "Political Health as an Integration Model in Political Systems Theory," *Systems Research* 3, no. 2 (1986): 85–88.

To come

4

THE PHYSICAL, SOCIAL, AND CULTURAL ENVIRONMENT OF POLITICS

Politics is a creative, but not a completely autonomous, activity. Although political actors are free to make choices in order to fulfill their values, they must make these choices in an environment not entirely of their own choosing. Politics—and political decisions—can be understood only in terms of the physical, social, and cultural environment in which a community is embedded.

PROPOSITIONS AND CHALLENGES

In this chapter, we explore how the larger environment influences politics and political science. Let us first consider some important propositions that may help us to understand the impact of the physical, social, and cultural environment on politics.

1. The *physical coexistence* of all political communities on a single globe rife with nuclear, biochemical, and powerful conventional weapons means that we must learn to live together sensibly or risk dying together in large numbers.

2. Our shared *biological nature* and *biological destiny* should inspire respect for our common humanity—our fundamental equality—and the importance of maximizing cooperation, halting dangerous aggression, and minimizing the conflicts that threaten our existence.

Chapter Objectives

After studying this chapter, you will be able to do the following:

1. Explain how politics is subject to a variety of "nonpolitical" agents.

2. Describe how the physical characteristics and limitations of our world affect politics.

3. Describe some of our basic human characteristics and how they affect the political world.

4. Explore how things like economics, religion, race, ethnicity, science and technology, and history influence the building of our political communities.

5. Discuss how culture can affect politics.

3. *Human needs*, such as security, acceptance, and recognition, suggest the origins of values that provide common purposes, goals, and standards for politics.

4. The *reduction of distance* between people as a result of the communication and transportation revolutions has enhanced global interdependence and cooperative patterns of behavior—political, economic, and scientific.

5. Human *vulnerability to disaster*—military, physical, and ecological—underscores the need for global agreements to avert war, famine, disease, and ecological damage.

6. The rapid *exhaustion of nonrenewable resources* and *the growth of population* beyond what existing resources can support highlight the need for political policies that encourage prudent management of population and resources.

7. The elevation of Earth's temperature, *global warming*, triggering a rise in the level of the oceans and the possibility of catastrophic *climate change*, calls for cooperative action among the world's countries to confront these problems.

8. The *growth of cities* and their suburbs calls attention to a host of problems— inadequate housing, unemployment, poverty, inefficient transportation, crime, and disease—and thus to the need for prudent policy to maintain healthy, vital, and manageable centers of modern civilization.

9. Modern *economic life*—involving industrialization, gaps between rich and poor, periodic recession, and worker alienation—requires policies that ensure full employment, an equitable distribution of income, and mechanisms to protect both workers and consumers.

10. The worldwide **revolution of rising expectation**s, especially in developing nations, is significantly influenced by modern ideology and technology; this phenomenon calls for a wise political balance between hope and possibility.

11. The cyber revolution has posed a whole new set of problems for our world: the protection of personal privacy, the danger of cyber warfare, and the misuse of social media. At the same time, this revolution in communication provides opportunities to foster democracy and undermine secretive authoritarian regimes.

These propositions highlight a number of political challenges:

- Both weapons of mass destruction (WMDs) (nuclear, biological, chemical) and conventional weapons threaten the survival of large numbers of the human species. Scientific and technological developments in combination with political decision making have introduced these threats. Our challenge is to figure out how to control their spread and, ultimately, affect their elimination. This problem is more urgent than ever with the intensification of terrorism.

- Ecological balance is vital; ecological disaster often leads to political disaster. Our challenge is to move away from policies that threaten ecological balance and toward prudent management of resources, population, industry, and everyday activity without sacrificing our standard of living, human integrity, or employment and profits. In recent years, political scientists have become more and more concerned with the concept of *sustainability*. In ecology, sustainability means that biological systems endure and remain diverse and productive overtime. In political terms, we face tough questions about the health of our environment and the enormity of consumption of in contemporary life, particularly in economically advanced countries.

- Current political behavior is based on historical patterns of behavior. Our challenge is to adapt the best of our past while embracing necessary changes to meet evolving conditions—for example, changes that help us to turn away from **racism** and **sexism** and reverse poverty through peaceful, constitutional means.

- Dominant economic systems have often shaped politics, law, and the distribution of wealth. Our challenge is to ensure that the economic system—whether capitalist, socialist, or a combination of the two—serves human needs at the least cost to freedom.

- Politics can be understood in terms of conflict and cooperation among economic, social, ethnic, religious, and political groups. Most often, it is their struggle for power that determines who gets what, when, and how. Our challenge is to umpire this struggle in ways compatible with the public interest.

- Human beings have biological, psychological, and social needs that must be satisfied. Politics can be understood as the effort to work out patterns to meet these needs. Human needs suggest values—goals, purposes, policies—in politics and direct action. Our challenge is to develop appropriate policies.

- Our challenge in connection with a wide range of scientific and technological developments (space exploration, DNA mapping, communication modes) is clear: How can public policy wisely harness the powers of science and technology to benefit humanity?

- In the cultural domain, concerned with the development and refinement of thought, spirit, literature, art, and taste, our challenge is to foster creative imagination in all realms to develop a guiding vision of human excellence.

In exploring the physical, social, and cultural environment of politics, we will outline the factual background undergirding these propositions and challenges. While our treatment is necessarily selective, we nevertheless emphasize here the interdisciplinary setting of politics. After all, political science is only one of many social sciences, and the social sciences themselves constitute only one division of human knowledge and experience. In our treatment of the larger environment of politics, we cannot completely separate the physical and social aspects from the cultural.

For example, anthropology embraces all three worlds—physical, social, and cultural—in that it embodies the concepts, habits, skills, arts, instruments, and institutions of a given people in a given period. Ecology is both a branch of biology that deals with the relations between living organisms and their environments and a branch of sociology (human ecology) that deals with the relations between human beings and their environment. Human biology cannot be discussed in isolation from important societal considerations. The religious setting of politics is both cultural and social. History can be viewed as both a social science and a branch of the humanities. Science and technology are usually located in the physical domain, yet they are products of human society and illustrate culture at work. Clearly, we as students of politics have no choice but to acknowledge our interdisciplinary milieu.

THE PHYSICAL WORLD WE LIVE IN

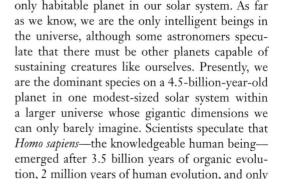

KEY QUESTIONS

1. How do the physical limitations of our world affect politics and policy?

2. How large is Earth's carrying capacity?

3. How does a country's endowment of natural resources influence its domestic politics and relations with other countries?

To the best of current knowledge, Earth is the only habitable planet in our solar system. As far as we know, we are the only intelligent beings in the universe, although some astronomers speculate that there must be other planets capable of sustaining creatures like ourselves. Presently, we are the dominant species on a 4.5-billion-year-old planet in one modest-sized solar system within a larger universe whose gigantic dimensions we can only barely imagine. Scientists speculate that *Homo sapiens*—the knowledgeable human being— emerged after 3.5 billion years of organic evolution, 2 million years of human evolution, and only 5,000 years of historical experience.

Patterns of Population Growth

The success of our species is clear if viewed in terms of reproduction. The planet today is home to slightly over 7.6 billion people distributed unevenly across the globe. But this very success begs these questions: How many more? What is Earth's **carrying capacity**— that is, what size population can it support without suffering deterioration? The answer to this question clearly holds serious implications for politics. Population estimates for 2050 run to approximately 9.8 billion. This population tidal wave is of relatively recent origin. Rapid escalation of the population began with the Industrial Revolution at the end of the eighteenth century. By the turn of the twentieth century, the population had doubled; by the turn of the twenty-first century, it was well over three times what it had been a century before. This phenomenal increase poses momentous challenges for politics. First, it necessitates study of the correlation between a rapidly growing population and other significant human developments—for example, the opening up of new lands in the Americas or revolutions in industry, transportation, medicine, and agriculture. Figure 4.1 illustrates population growth and its correlation with a number of key events, including those that decreased population or slowed growth (war, famine, disease). Information about national populations, when combined with other data (population density, arable land, material resources, economic resourcefulness, political skill), tells us a great deal about nations' political strengths and weaknesses—and potential power.

Figure 4.1   Ten Centuries of World Population Growth (in billions)

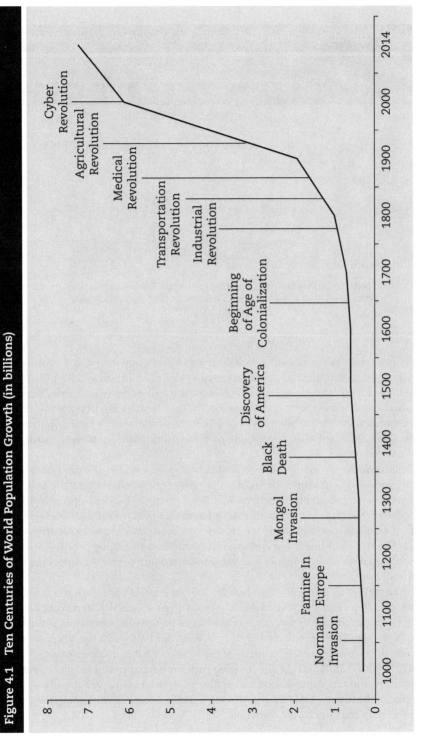

Source: Updated from a report from the Agency for International Development, *War on Hunger* 8, no. 1 (1974): 5.

Table 4.1 World Population Distribution and Projections (in millions)

Region	Year	
	2017	2100
Africa	1,256	4,468
Asia	4,504	4,780
Latin America and Caribbean	646	671
Oceania	39	72
North America	361	499
Europe	742	653

Source: United Nations Department of Economic and Social Affairs, Population Division, *World Population Prospects, 2017 Revisions,* https://esa.un.org/unpd/wpp/Publications/Files/WPP2017_Key Findings.pdf.

As Table 4.1 demonstrates, over half of the world's population is found in Asia, with China being the most populous country at slightly more than 1.37 billion people. In contrast, North America, which includes the United States, Canada, Bermuda, Greenland, and Saint-Pierre et Miquelon, with a combined population slightly in excess of 356 million, is home to only 5 percent of the world's total population. It is especially significant that 80 percent of the world's population lives in the less-developed countries.[1]

Population in terms of absolute numbers and geographic distribution are not the only concerns. The world's population is aging rapidly with potentially enormous consequences for just about every region. This is particularly true in parts of Europe and countries like Japan. People are living longer, and the world is also reaping the results of dramatic increases in birth rates during the late 1940s and 1950s after World War II. The two most important concerns resulting from this aging population are the increased strain on senior support systems in many countries and the shrinkage in the global workforce.

Is the picture all grim? Perhaps not. In 2007, the world's population was growing at a rate of 1.24 percent per year. Today, the growth rate stands at 1.10 percent per year. In fact, there are indications that the average annual increase in population, as measured by crude birthrate, has been declining sharply since the 1960s with the steepest decline occurring in the less developed countries of the world, with the exception of sub-Saharan Africa (see Table 4.1). If current childbearing patterns hold, they will lead to an eventual depopulation. But that depopulation will not begin any time soon, probably not until the latter part of the twenty-first century. Although, it may occur earlier in some parts of the world—in Italy and Greece, for instance.[2]

Finite Resources

The problem of Earth's **finite resources**—that is, resources such as minerals, petroleum, and safe drinking water whose quantities are considered limited—is compounded by the fact that not all of the planet's land areas can produce food. For example, while approximately 29 percent of the planet's surface is land, fully 40 percent of this land is desert or frigid wasteland. Moreover, 33 percent is pasture, forest, marsh, and mountain. Additional amounts must be subtracted for urban areas, leaving a mere 10 percent of Earth's land surface for crop production. And of this, only about 43 percent is in agricultural use.

As Table 4.2 reveals, some countries (for example, Canada, Argentina, Kyrgyzstan, and the United States) have a more favorable population to land ratio than others. Yet this information must be examined with care. Some countries with favorable population to land ratios are not well developed (such as Kyrgyzstan), while some countries with unfavorable ratios are (such as Japan). This fact suggests that factors other than population and land are important and that we can learn a great deal about a nation's politics and policies by examining them.

The United Kingdom and Japan used their human and natural resources to industrialize and to establish global trading networks. Britain's historical devotion to the policy of free trade and freedom of the seas and its long-standing position as a great sea

Table 4.2 Population per Square Kilometer, 2017	
Country	**Population per K² (in millions)**
Canada	4
Argentina	16
Kyrgyzstan	32
United States	35
Egypt	98
Germany	236
United Kingdom	274
Japan	350
India	450
Bangladesh	2,265
Singapore	8,155

Source: www.worldmeters.info/world-population-by-country.

power are intimately connected to its need to import food and raw materials and export finished industrial products. Japan's historical development as a great power, from its opening to the West in the nineteenth century through its defeat in World War II to its emergence as an industrial powerhouse in the late twentieth century, is closely connected to its unfavorable population to land ratio, its need for raw materials for industry, and its need to import food, as well as to the skill and energy of its people. However, both the United Kingdom and Japan remain vulnerable to a cutoff of food, raw materials, and international trade.

The United States is more favorably endowed, and this is unquestionably a source of its political strength. For a period of time, significant increases in the importation of oil were of great concern both in economic and national security circles, particularly as China and India dramatically increased their consumption rates. In 1981, the United States imported approximately 4.2 million barrels of crude oil per day. In 2006, it reached 10.1 million barrels per day. Then things began to reverse through a combination of more drilling, developments in shale oil extraction, and conservation. In 2011, the amount imported was 8.9 million barrels per day, and in 2016, oil imported by the United States dropped to 7.3 million barrels per day.[3] Of course, to many environmentalists this seeming blessing is actual a curse as it delays efforts in the United States efforts to use renewable resources. Asian nations are among the most disadvantaged in terms of balance between population and food. Although large populations can be a source of political strength, they can contribute to political weakness when nations cannot feed their people because food supplies are inadequate, food cannot be imported, distribution is faulty, or the people have no money. These conditions can lead to economic and political crises.

A good distribution system and prudent management of natural resources clearly enhance a nation's strength. Saudi Arabia, for example, was a poor desert country before oil was discovered there. Now oil figures prominently in its economic and political power. Although over dependence on one resource creates its own challenges and concerns, particularly if the resource begins to run out. The location of key resources (for example, water for irrigation, oil, natural gas, coal, and iron ore) tells a great deal about the raw materials of economic, and thus political, power. The locations of some key mineral resources are shown in Table 4.3.

Favorable natural endowments may create difficulties as well as advantages in politics. For example, more powerful nations may covet the natural wealth of weak nations. In the past, this situation led to imperialism and colonialism as European countries sought to conquer and colonize Africa, Asia, and North and South America. Today, richly endowed countries such as Nigeria, Saudi Arabia, and Venezuela may have trouble absorbing and sensibly using their oil wealth. The wisest use of such wealth requires considerable economic and political skill.

Critical finite resources are not confined to valuable minerals or petroleum. Access to safe drinking water is increasingly viewed as a critical resource. The World Health Organization estimates that nearly 21 billion people have no access to improved sources of drinking water; as a result, 842,000 people die every year from intestinal diseases. As countries run out of water, the prospects for interstate conflict over this valuable resource are increasing.[4]

Finally, as we will see in Chapter 15, there is serious concern about humanity's relationship to its global home. In a number of ways, we may be irreparably damaging the

Table 4.3 Leading Producers of Major Resources, 2016 (in order left to right)

Aluminum	China, Russia, Canada	**Nickel**	Russia, Philippines, Canada
Bauxite	Australia, China, Brazil	**Salt**	China, United States, India
Chromium	South Africa, Kazakhstan, India	**Sulfur**	United States, China, Russia
Copper	Chile, Peru, China	**Petroleum (Reserves)**	Venezuela, Saudi Arabia, Canada
Gold	China, Australia, Russia	**Tin**	China, Indonesia, Peru
Iron Ore	Australia, Brazil, China	**Titanium**	China, Japan, Russia
Lead	China, Australia, United States	**Tungsten**	China, Vietnam, Russia

Source: Mineral Commodity Summaries 2017. U.S. Department of the Interior, U.S. Geological Survey. https://minerals.usgs.gov/minerals/pubs/mcs/2017/.

planet. The ozone layer, which protects Earth from ultraviolet rays, is threatened by the release of harmful synthetic gases. Massive industrialization is causing the planet to warm at an alarming rate, endangering coastal regions over the next century. Nearly 16,306 species of animals and plants around the world are considered high risks for extinction.[5] While the world's forests are being managed more efficiently, deforestation remains a critical problem. Between 1990 and 2015, some 129 million hectares have been lost, roughly the size of Texas, California, and Florida combined.[6] The degradation of the environment is critically important.

THE BIOLOGICAL, PHYSIOLOGICAL, PSYCHOLOGICAL, AND SOCIAL CREATURES WE ARE

Human nature significantly influences political values, behavior, and judgments. Many political values are rooted in human needs. We do not have to believe that biology is destiny to recognize that cooperation and conflict may have some relation to our human endowment. And certainly many political actors have decided (foolishly, in our view) that inequality, whether racial or sexual, is somehow rooted in our genes.

Human beings are highly developed primates with four unique species characteristics—large brain size, upright posture, longevity, and thought. These characteristics have permitted human beings to develop a complex language, to reason, and to make ingenious

Human Needs

Although human beings can restructure the natural world, human needs (biological, physiological, psychological, social, and cultural) significantly influence their economic and social life and thus their politics.[7] People need to survive, grow, and develop mentally and socially. To survive, they must satisfy certain material needs, such as physiological needs for air, sleep, water, food, and shelter. Heterosexual intercourse is normally necessary to produce children and perpetuate the species. People also need safety and security.

Human beings have certain social needs as well: belonging, love, affection, and acceptance. They also must have self-esteem and esteem from others. Deficiencies here can impair both life and development. In addition, people have ethical and cultural needs—a need for love, truth, and service; for justice and perfection; and for aesthetics and meaningfulness. The legitimate satisfaction of these varying needs makes life, growth, and development possible. Satisfying these needs calls for considerable social and political cooperation, a fact that has been richly documented in sociobiology, anthropology, and history.

Cooperation Versus Conflict

Some students of human biology, ethology (the study of animal behavior), and anthropology argue that human beings are aggressive by nature and that war is one outcome of such aggression. They maintain that war could not have existed for hundreds of thousands of years if it was not prescribed in our very genetic code. For example, ethologists Konrad Lorenz and Robert Ardrey have posited instinctual human aggression.[8] However, most biologists, anthropologists, and social psychologists think otherwise. Social psychologists such as Leonard Berkowitz contend that human aggression is learned behavior.[9]

Perhaps Julian S. Huxley best summed up the argument against instinctual aggressiveness when he maintained that "human nature . . . contains no specific war instinct, as does the nature of harvester ants." Huxley wrote the following:

> There is in man's make-up a general aggressive tendency, but this, like all other human urges, is not a specific and unvarying instinct; it can be molded into the most varied forms. It can be canalized into competitive sports, as in our own society, or as when certain Filipino tribes were induced to substitute football for headhunting. It can be sublimated into non-competitive sport, like mountain climbing, or into higher types of activity altogether, like exploration or research or social crusades.[10]

Even if war is not the expression of a biological imperative, it remains, wrote Huxley, an ugly and devastating reality for humankind, especially for political leaders. Huxley emphasized that war is "a biological problem of the broadest scope, for on its abolition may depend life's ability to continue the progress, which it has slowly but steadily achieved through more than a thousand million years. . . . War is not inevitable for man." But what is imperative is a politics "to make war less likely."[11]

Political battles over racism, a belief in the superiority or inferiority of a given race, and sexism, a belief in the superiority of one sex over the other, also require an understanding of human beings as biological creatures. In human history, slavery has been justified on the ground that some people are slaves by nature. This view has been thoroughly discredited, but slavery still exists in a few regions of the developing world, as it did in some American states through the middle of the nineteenth century.

Moreover, racial differences, particularly skin color, remain the actual basis for discrimination over most of the world. Racism explains the brutal treatment of Native Americans by the Spanish, the English, and, later, Anglo-Americans; and of Africans and Asians by Anglo-Saxons, Portuguese, Belgians, and French. And, of course, racial doctrines based on false science dominated the Nazi regime and guided its extermination of European Jews.

Although racial discrimination, segregation, and persecution have been repudiated by enlightened public opinion, racism remains a fact of social and political life throughout the world and a continuing problem for public policy. In the United States, for example, immigration policy has historically been prejudiced against Asians and Africans (and even against Caucasians from eastern and southeastern Europe). Battles continue to be fought in American politics over measures to overcome racial discrimination against African Americans, Hispanics, and Native Americans. Arguments continue to rage over such public policies as affirmative action, meant to ensure equality in employment and educational opportunity. In more recent years, there have been a great many debates concerning more subtle forms of racism and the idea of unstated, often unseen, white privilege. Even when formal laws and policies that promote racism are repealed, the problem can persist in other guises. This can be illustrated by the simple act of hailing a cab in a major city, which can be more difficult for minorities than their white counterparts.[12]

Discrimination and persecution based on religion has been a fact of life for centuries and continues to this day. Anti-Catholicism was particularly strong in the United States during the nineteenth century as was anti-Semitism in both the nineteenth and twentieth centuries. Today, feelings of hostility toward Muslims is manifest in both Europe and the United States, particularly after 9/11 and as thousands of refugees from the Syrian civil war and the violence and poverty of North Africa, flooded into Europe.

Sexism, also known as gender discrimination, understood most often as the doctrine of male superiority and the practice of male dominance, is a worldwide phenomenon. Women have been overwhelmingly subjected to unequal treatment before the law, in economic life, and in politics and society. Only in the twentieth century and in liberal democratic and socialist countries have women achieved legal and political equality in theory. However, many of these gains came only after protracted political battles (for example, the fight for women's right to vote in the United States and Great Britain). But even in advanced liberal nations, de facto (actual) discrimination against women persists in the job market, in political life, and in social affairs. In the United States,

KEY QUESTIONS

1. How are the social communities we have built a response to our biological needs and the physical world?

2. How are social communities influenced by psychological needs? By methods of earning a living and carrying out economic relations? By developments in science and technology? By historical memory?

the political impact of women's fight for equality is dramatized by the controversial, ill-fated struggle to ratify an equal rights amendment to the Constitution during the late 1970s and early 1980s. In politics and in society, women have been fighting to overcome the still-widespread social conviction, rooted in a narrow view of biology (and religion), that "a woman's place is in the home." More ominously, the oppression of women and girls endures in many parts of the world where their enslavement, often for sexual purposes, is commonplace. In the United States, for instance, there are debates concerning gender and the recent presidential election. While there were certainly many legitimate reasons to oppose Hillary Clinton, the first female nominee for president of a major party, how much of the opposition was based on misogyny, the fact she was a woman?

Clearly, human biological, psychological, and social characteristics strongly influence the development of social communities. In the course of our discussion, we will pay particular attention to how communities respond to human needs within a political context, to how politics affects human tendencies to cooperate and clash, and to political efforts to deal with both inequality and equality.

THE SOCIAL COMMUNITIES WE HAVE BUILT

Throughout the following analysis of social communities, we will emphasize the ways in which the social environment influences politics.

The Sociopsychological Setting of Politics

Material, social, and cultural needs shape values, behavior, and judgment in society and in politics. Social psychologists contend that these needs include "a frame of orientation and devotion," a sense of roots and of unity, a feeling of "effectiveness," a capacity for "excitation and stimulation," and a guiding "character structure."[13] According to Erich Fromm, these needs can be satisfied in many ways; different political systems represent different modes of satisfaction.

For example, Fromm has noted that the "need for an object of devotion can be answered by devotion to God, love, and truth—or by idolatry of destructive idols." The adulation of Adolf Hitler was the worship of a destructive idol. Other needs can also be answered in different ways. Thus, the "need for relatedness can be answered by love and kindness—or by dependence, sadism, masochism, destructiveness, and narcissism." Nazism again illustrates a flawed political response. "The need for unity and rootedness can be answered by the passions for solidarity, brotherliness, love, and mystical experience—or by alcoholism, drug addiction, and depersonalization." Alcoholism and drug addiction are clearly social matters that call for a public policy response.

"The need for effectiveness can be answered by love, productive work—or by sadism and destructiveness." The former response enhances political trust and economic prosperity; the latter wreaks havoc in the political community. "The need for stimulation and excitation can be answered by productive interest in man, nature, art, ideas—or by a greedy pursuit of ever-changing pleasures." A thoughtless, pleasure-loving society heedless of future dangers bodes ill for ecological and political well-being.

Moreover, the guiding character structure can be principled or unscrupulous, cooperative or combative, altruistic or selfish, democratic or authoritarian. Unscrupulous, combative, selfish, authoritarian people may create political communities that lack agreement on fundamental human rights and are thus prone to exploitation, domination, and war.

Human character can be positively influenced by historical tradition and by coherent inner principles. Vibrant and functional political communities are held together by healthy, political traditions and principles that merit widespread community agreement and by thoughtful discussion about what those principles mean. However, if people are thoughtlessly directed by tradition, they may not be able to adapt politically. For example, ruling aristocrats who are unwilling to alter their ways may invite disaster for themselves by refusing to admit the middle class into political rule. In turn, the middle class may invite a comparable disaster by refusing to admit the working class. The same risk is taken by whites unwilling to admit African Americans or by men unwilling to admit women.

The Economic Environment of Politics

The methods by which we earn a living have always crucially influenced political life. Moreover, the larger economic relationships of society have an enormous impact on politics and public policy. We seek to protect our economic interests, and this leads almost inevitably to politics. The economic influence on politics has been demonstrated by a number of perceptive observers. Aristotle, for example, saw politics in ancient Greece in terms of the struggle between the few rich and the many poor, with the poor often battling to secure a more equitable distribution of wealth and the rich struggling to secure their larger slice of wealth and power.

In seventeenth-century England, James Harrington, a political philosopher, argued that political power rests upon economic power; specifically, he maintained that political power is influenced by the distribution of land. Harrington held that if one man is the sole landlord or if he dominates the people, the result is "absolute monarchy." If a few—the nobility or the nobility and the clergy—own the land or dominate the people, the result is a mixed monarchy, or what we call an aristocracy. But where the people are the landlords or there is a wide distribution of land, the outcome is a commonwealth, a republic, a government of laws and not of men. Although Harrington's understanding of economic power was somewhat limited, he nonetheless perceived that military and political power were clearly related to ownership of land, an important component of economic power in his day.

The importance of economics to politics was a virtual political truism at the birth of the American republic. America's founders understood that British economic policy had triggered the American Revolution. James Madison, the primary author of the

U.S. Constitution, held that "the principal task of modern legislation" was to regulate key interests—those with and those without property, creditors, debtors, manufacturers, merchants, and bankers.

Karl Marx, in nineteenth-century Europe, articulated an even more sweeping view. His philosophy, known as **Marxism,** held that a society's economic structure, especially its system of economic production, was the real foundation upon which the political superstructure and other aspects of the superstructure—such as religion, art, and ethics—rested. For Marx, the power of the ruling class came from its control of economic life. In the nineteenth century, this ruling class was the bourgeoisie (the property owners and capitalists in general). As Marx described it, "The executive of the modern state is but a committee for managing the common affairs of the whole bourgeoisie."

A political scientist need not be a Marxist to recognize the influence of economics. This influence manifests itself in the varying ways that powerful economic interests (for example, farmers, workers, industrialists, large banks, and investment houses) seek to shape public policy at home and abroad through favorable legislative, administrative, or judicial decisions. Such interests, of course, may favor inaction as well as action in the political sphere.

Economics, like biology, throws light on equality and inequality, values always at the heart of the struggle for power that is politics. Some nations are rich and developed while others are poor and developing, or less developed—a gap dramatically illustrated by Table 4.4. Of course, great disparities exist not only between countries but within countries as well. The rich-poor gap within and between nations is an actual and potential source of troublesome conflict and a major challenge to political leaders. Poverty has political consequences. Problems arise from nations' attempts to feed and house their populations; accumulate capital for development; balance needs for defense against those for development and consumers; and, in general, respond to their people's aspirations for a better life. Under certain circumstances, poverty can lead to riots. By intensifying a sense of injustice, poverty can make the poor and their sympathizers more attuned to radical political ideologies and solutions.

Table 4.4 The Development Gap: Developing and Developed Nations, 2015		
	Low-Developing Countries (37 Countries)	**Highly Developed Countries (51 Countries)**
Life Expectancy at Birth	59.3 Years	79.4 Years
Gross National Income/ Capita	$2,649/year	$39,605/year
Avg. Years of Schooling	9.3 Years	16.4 Years

Source: United Nations Development Programme, *Human Development Report 2016*, Table 1. Hdr.und p.org/en/composite/HDI.

Table 4.5 Urbanization in the Developing World (in millions)

City	2000	2016	2030
Mumbai (Bombay), India	16.4	21.4	27.8
Delhi, India	15.7	26.5	36.0
Lagos, Nigeria	7.2	13.6	24.2
Dhaka, Bangladesh	10.3	18.2	27.4
Sao Paolo, Brazil	17.0	21.3	23.4
Karachi, Pakistan	10.0	17.1	24.8
Manila, Philippines	9.9	13.1	16.8

Source: United Nations, *The World's Cities in 2016*. www.un.org/en/development/desa/population/publications/pdf/urbanization_worlds_cities_in_2016_data_booklet/pdf.

Economic and related social problems are particularly acute in less-developed countries. The lack of nutritious food, pure water, good health care, and adequate income seriously threatens human life and decency in many of these countries. In addition, rapid urban growth has created economic, social, and political chaos by straining economic resources and exerting extreme pressure on available jobs and accessibility of adequate food, water, health care, and housing for millions of urban dwellers. Table 4.5 illustrates the recent and projected rapid urbanization of some cities in developing countries.

Our consideration of the economic environment of politics has already overlapped its sociological setting, which is the subject of the next section.

The Sociological Setting of Politics

Economic interests are not the only powerful influences in society—and therefore in politics. Social, ethnic, racial, and religious groups are also players whose efforts to protect vital interests impinge on politics. Indeed, all of these groups are central to politics because public policy often results from their activities. But how else do noneconomic groups influence society? Let us first look at the role of religion in politics.

Religion and Politics. Religion is an enduring source of conflict the world over. Western civilization has been shaped no less by religious conflict than by religious adherence. Since the Protestant Reformation in the sixteenth century, battles between Roman Catholics and Protestants in Western Europe have divided nations and ignited civil wars. Religious persecution was a major factor in the settlement of North America. The United States, at its founding, became a beacon of political ingenuity in its establishment of religious freedom.

The multiplicity and diversity of religious groups in the United States today is a testament to the country's constitutional embrace of religious freedom. And yet, despite the separation of church and state, religious groups have exerted, and continue to exert, a great deal of political influence. For example, religious groups were instrumental in the movement to abolish slavery in the nineteenth century (albeit, split along regional lines). Protestants, especially Methodists, were active in the Anti-Saloon League, which worked successfully for passage of the Eighteenth Amendment that ushered in Prohibition in 1919. The Catholic Church today maintains its strong stand against abortion and continues in its traditional work of advocating for the needy. Religious affiliation extends to matters of foreign policy. For example, American Jews and Evangelical Christians (for quite different reasons) are often strongly pro-Israel.

Beyond the borders of the United States, religious rivalries—and the conflicts arising from them—persist. For example, the violent conflict between Protestants and Catholics in Northern Ireland, known as the "Troubles" lasted for thirty years, 1968 through 1998. A somewhat tenuous peace emerged in the late 1990s that involved power sharing between religious factions. Israeli and Islamic claims on the city of Jerusalem add a religious dimension to complicated nationalistic and political rivalries in the Middle East. From the day of partition, India and Pakistan have endured ongoing flare-ups between Hindus and Muslims—violence directed both at one another and amongst rival sects inside their own borders. Religion, clearly, is a major force in global politics.

One of the more important recent developments in the area of religion and politics has been the growing influence of **religious fundamentalism**. Islamic fundamentalists have received a great deal of attention. So, too, has the Christian right in the United States. We will examine these groups shortly. But first, it is important to note that religious fundamentalism is not confined to these two high-profile cases. Religious fundamentalism has been and remains a factor around the globe. For example, fundamentalist Hindus, Sikhs, and Theravada Buddhists have had a profound influence on the political fabric of India and Sri Lanka, while Latin America has seen the growth of a significant number of Pentecostal communities.

Defining religious fundamentalism is a difficult task. Each religion has its own unique ideological, cultural, organizational, and historical characteristics. Nevertheless, with some caution, we will proceed: Religious fundamentalism is a movement to uphold, defend, and preserve age-old religious traditions and values. In the modern context, fundamentalists adopt new methods, organizational structures, and policies to accomplish their goals. It is here that we see the interface between religious fundamentalism and the world of politics. For a fundamentalist activist, it is not enough "to be merely a conservative or traditionalist in these threatening times."[14] Fundamentalists view modernity as a serious threat to traditional values and the acquisition of political power as an important means to preserve traditional religious practices and values.

Space does not permit a comprehensive discussion of all religious fundamentalist movements and their activities, so we focus our discussion on two such movements, one domestic and one international: the rise of the Christian right in the United States and the emergence of Islamic fundamentalism in many countries throughout the world. While each possesses certain characteristics common to fundamentalist movements, we must emphasize that they also exhibit striking differences—differences to be noted as we consider their respective influences on politics.

The 1973 U.S. Supreme Court decision *Roe v. Wade* legalizing abortion was instrumental in galvanizing a coalition of evangelical leaders to move beyond their pulpits and into action at virtually every level of American politics. Organizations such as the Moral Majority (renamed the Liberty Federation), the Religious Roundtable, and the Christian Voice began to seriously challenge what their members and leaders viewed as an erosion of traditional values. They actively supported conservative candidates for political office and lobbied for action to reverse a variety of societal trends they found objectionable, such as growth in the pornography business, the banning of prayer in schools, moves to allow euthanasia, and wider acceptance of homosexuality. More recently, these objectionable societal trends have included the issue of gay marriage; genetic research that could lead to human cloning; sex education in public schools; the taxing of private Christian schools; and, of course, the legalization of abortion.

Evangelical leaders and their followers do not constitute the entire Christian right, but they can be seen as a vanguard of the movement. There are a significant number of non-evangelical Christians who, at the very least, are sympathetic to the political goals of evangelicals but who may not themselves be politically active. Determining the size of this movement has been difficult. Polling data and conservative Christian book sales indicate that the hardcore Christian right may number no more than 200,000. But, as Grant Wacker of Duke University's Divinity School has noted, "fellow travelers, people who explicitly identify themselves as partisans of the religious right, [range] from ten to fifteen million. Sympathizers who might be mobilized over a specific issue such as abortion or gun control may [number] thirty-five million."[15]

The Christian right now constitutes a major force within the Republican Party. In both the 2000 and 2004 presidential elections, evangelical Protestants accounted for about 23 percent of the electorate; in 2004, 78 percent of them voted for George W. Bush. In the 2008 presidential election, Democrat Barack Obama made small but important inroads into the evangelical vote, receiving approximately 3 percent more of that vote than did Sen. John Kerry in 2004. Perhaps most significant, the greatest gains were achieved among younger evangelicals between the ages of eighteen and forty-four. It appears that this younger group is less tightly bound to the bedrock issues of abortion and homosexuality. The agenda for young Christian evangelicals appears to be broadening to include greater emphasis on the environment, poverty, human rights, and torture.[16] This diversity within the ranks of the Christian right serves as a pointed reminder that political groups evolve and adapt. As is the case with any political group, political scientists can only make generalizations—a fact that should never be overlooked by the student of politics. Still, the Christian Right remains a powerful force within the Republican Party. In the 2012 presidential election, nearly eight in ten white, evangelical Protestants voted for Republican Mitt Romney and delivered roughly the same percentage of votes for Donald Trump in 2016. One interesting aspect of this phenomenon is that the candidacy of Trump caused a huge divide among evangelical leaders, but voters of evangelical persuasion overwhelmingly supported the Republican candidate. The Christian right is active in not only supporting conservative political candidates at all levels but also in lobbying for specific legislation and in pushing for the appointment of conservatives to federal judgeships and other high-ranking positions in government.

While Islamic fundamentalists have been active for decades in various political arenas around the world, the event that brought them into sharp focus was the Iranian revolution of 1979 that toppled the shah of Iran. The revolution was inspired by the strong-minded Shiite Islamic leader, the Ayatollah Khomeini, who, as the seizure of power became imminent, returned triumphant from years in exile in Paris. Khomeini established an Islamic republic in which powerful clerics dominated the government and the conservative values and practices of Islam became the basis of governance. The Iranian revolution energized Islamic fundamentalist movements around the world. Fundamentalists made aborted attempts to seize power in Egypt and Algeria and did succeed in gaining power in Afghanistan where, from 1996 until 2002, the Taliban enforced a strict Islamic code of behavior. Although officially out of power, today the Taliban remains a significant force inside Afghanistan. Where full seizure of power proved unfeasible, Islamic fundamentalist movements sought at least to expand their influence. For example, political leaders in Malaysia, Indonesia, and the Philippines have all had to grapple with the consequences of fundamentalist agitation. In some cases, considerable violence has been the result. Violence may originate from factions within the movements themselves or from brutally repressive campaigns initiated by government officials.

One of the more recent movements is known as ISIS, standing for Islamic State of Iraq and Syria. ISIS is a splinter group of al-Qaida emerging in 2006 out of the chaos of the war in Iraq and the Syrian civil war. As of the end of 2014, the group had seized large amounts of land in northern Syria and northwestern Iraq. Its expressed purpose was to establish a caliphate or Islamic State that erases state borders and eventually declares authority over the world's 1.5 billion Muslims. ISIS rule has proven to be extremely harsh and brutally violent against nonbelievers. By the end of 2017, a coalition of forces that included troops from the Kurdish community, Iraq, and Syria along with Russian, United States, and other NATO air forces regained most of the ISIS-held territory in both Syria and Iraq. This did not result in the elimination of ISIS, however. Significant ISIS cells operate in any number of countries, including Afghanistan, the Philippines, Libya, Bangladesh, Pakistan, and Egypt.

In the wake of violent acts carried out by groups such as Hezbollah in Lebanon, Hamas in the Gaza Strip, and al-Qaida around the world, there has been a tendency in the West to equate Islamic fundamentalism with terrorism. But it is important to note that Islamic fundamentalists are not universally violent. In fact, a genuine sense of social conscience and community characterize many of the movements, as evidenced by the construction of thousands of schools, hospitals, orphanages, and health clinics throughout the Muslim world. Hostile rhetoric and mutual distrust notwithstanding, it is important to note that terrorists who use violent methods to further their political agendas constitute a distinct minority of the Islamic fundamentalist movements.

Race, Ethnicity, and Politics. Race and ethnicity figure prominently in politics. Battles over slavery, emancipation, reconstruction, integration, and affirmative action have characterized U.S. politics. Discrimination against various ethnic groups—Irish, Chinese, Japanese, Jews, Italians, Poles, Hispanics—reverberates throughout American history.

Ethnic minorities in political communities create both dangers and opportunities. The dangers are usually most prominent. The dominant ethnic majority often finds the ethnic minority a thorn in its side; the ethnic minority, which often subscribes to a different religion and may also speak a different language, seeks to preserve its ways and enhance its power. For example, today in Canada a significant proportion of French-speaking Canadians, particularly in the province of Quebec, do not want to be absorbed into an Anglo-Saxon Canada. Their desire for power in Quebec—and perhaps for independence from the rest of Canada—is an ongoing problem for Canadians. Muslims in India, Kurds in Iran and Iraq, Arabs in Israel, Chinese in Malaysia, Basques and Catalans in Spain, and Ibos in Nigeria are comparably situated. Lithuanians, Latvians, Estonians, Georgians, and Ukrainians—all once citizens of the Soviet Union—finally gained their independence; now, ironically, Russians are ethnic minorities in these newly independent states. In the former state of Yugoslavia, violent conflict erupted late in the twentieth century among Serbs, Croats, Bosnian Muslims, and Kosovars of Albanian heritage, creating the worst warfare in Europe since World War II. And, more recently, the ethnic and religious differences in Iraq continue to plague that country.

Governments often overlook the positive opportunities ethnic minorities offer. The key to a thriving pluralistic state is to fashion a multiethnic society where groups can preserve their customs, characteristics, languages, and religions; where political power can be shared; and where social trust ensures peace and constitutionality. Despite its erratic, at times deplorable even, historical record, the United States has gone far in seizing this opportunity. The United States today is a thriving nation distinguished by its diverse cultural fabric, one that includes, among numerous others, Irish, Italians, Jews, Hispanics, Asians, and American Africans. But a truly multiethnic society is sadly more often myth than reality.

Class and Politics. Although anti-Marxists claim otherwise, the influence of **class** on politics is a reality that students of politics and students of sociology must critically explore. Class refers to a division of people by their economic, social, and political standing (usually articulated as upper, middle, or lower). Those who take up Marxism make class struggle, which for them is rooted in economics, the key to their analysis of society and politics. They see a working class and a capitalist class (owners of the means of production and exchange) competing for power. This struggle, Marxists believe, has universal application: It is at work in both developed and developing countries. A study of class struggle identifies the forces competing for power; their basic interests; their values; their economic, social, and political behavior; and their contending public policies.

Some Marxists have even used class analysis to critically analyze communist countries such as the former Soviet Union or North Korea. For example, they have criticized the emergence in such countries of a "new class" of elite rulers in defiance of the orthodox Marxist view of a classless society. Indeed, the 1989 dismantling of Communist power in Eastern Europe revealed that Communist officials in country after country had lived isolated lives of privilege even as the economies they were charged with running collapsed around them.

Some social scientists maintain that class analysis is limited—that it focuses too sharply on one factor. Other social scientists argue that class analysis has been largely neglected. Nevertheless, it should be clear that the Marxist approach to class is only one of several, albeit one of the most powerful.

The Scientific and Technological Environment of Politics

Modern science and technology have significantly affected the world we live in. They have facilitated industrialization and urbanization. They have brought people and goods closer together through rapid transportation and communication. They have increased our economic interdependence. They have led to the development of modern machinery and fertilizers that enable a tiny farm population in a developed country to produce enough food for a huge nation. Through modern medicine, science and technology have assured the growth of population. Most dramatically, they have intensified the destructive powers of war, in particular through development of nuclear weapons. As science and technology have altered our world, they have created problems for politics—just as they have helped policymakers solve problems. In fact, a number of fundamental problems we currently face cannot even be understood without the help of scientists. For example, scientists warn that the planet can sustain only a certain level of population with current resources, or that the effects of carbon gas emissions are especially problematic for global health. At the same time, scientists offer potential solutions, such as holding open the possibility that key ecological problems can be dealt with through the development of solar power or by prudent management of population growth or by increasing the food supply.

Technology has had a particularly profound impact on political communication. While it may not have improved the depth of understanding of political events, twenty-four-hour television cable news has significantly expanded the timeliness and breadth of coverage of both domestic and international news. The Internet permits billions of individuals to communicate directly with each other. It has also become an increasingly important tool in political campaigning, as evidenced by its innovative use in Barack Obama's 2008 presidential campaign. And new forms of cyber communications such as Facebook and Twitter have, among other things, facilitated the transmission of events from inside closed societies. In June 2009, as the Iranian government dramatically suppressed news of widespread antigovernment demonstrations, both descriptive text and dramatic images were transmitted to the outside world via the latest vehicles of communication. In 2017, political unrest once again erupted in Iran with the same combination of actions—individuals employing social media to highlight events and the government attempting to discourage it.

Further, the social media has proven a remarkable tool for political mobilization and change. In 2001, text messaging was critical to the organization of demonstrations in the Philippines that forced Joseph Estrada from office. In the lead-up to the 2004 presidential election in Ukraine, supporters of Viktor Yushchenko, leader of the opposition, used intensive text messaging to organize massive protests that became the Orange Revolution. In Lebanon in 2005, e-mail and text messaging was critical to bringing 1 million demonstrators into the streets to demand that the Syrian government end its military presence in Lebanon. In 2008, an unemployed engineer named Oscar Morales used Facebook and the free Internet-based, telephone service Skype to orchestrate a massive demonstration against the Revolutionary Armed Forces of Columbia, or FARC. A year later in 2009, young people in Moldova, frustrated and angry over the collapse of the economy, used messages on Twitter to turn a small protest of 15,000 people into a global event. As a result, a rigged election was overturned and a new election brought to power the first noncommunist government in more than fifty years. And finally, we note that the protest movements known as the Arab Spring that spanned some seventeen countries in North Africa and the Middle East in 2010 and 2011 saw widespread use of modern cyber-based communications.

But there are a number of major downsides to the cyber revolution. First, the world is witnessing the emergence of cyber technology as a weapon with hackers around the world routinely penetrating the computer data banks of major corporations and financial houses either to steal data or disable cyber networks. In the 2016 presidential election in the United States, American intelligence agencies reported that Russian hackers had among other things, hacked into one of the major Democratic Party computer servers and stolen thousands of emails dealing with the campaign of Hillary Clinton. Further, they launched a significant disinformation campaign on American social media in an attempt to influence the election in favor of Donald Trump. These kinds of operations raise a number of disturbing questions. Is a major international hacking operation an act of war if it is found that a government was behind it? What is the appropriate response to a major attack? How secure from cyberattack are major institutions of infrastructure such as phone networks, subways, power grids, dams, and nuclear power plants? Second, of particular concern to democracies and other open political systems is the loss of privacy that the cyber revolution is bringing. Perhaps the most disturbing example of this has been the extent to which U.S. government institutions like the NSA (National Security Agency) have tapped in and gathered immense amounts of personal data on American citizens as part of the effort to combat terrorism.

The advance of scientific knowledge and technology has had paradoxical results for society and politics. On the one hand, science and technology have encouraged democratic achievements and a revolution of rising expectations—a phrase that exemplifies the hope for a better way of life, especially among peoples in the developing world. The burst of scientific accomplishments in the nineteenth and twentieth centuries coincided with the advent of liberal democracy in the Western world and with significant efforts to overcome backbreaking labor, illiteracy, disease, and famine. On the other hand, science and technology have made possible the totalitarian state and the potential suicide of the human race through nuclear holocaust. Those scientific advances also coincided with an often virulent nationalism and with dreadful patterns of exploitation, mind control, degradation, and death.

Political leaders have to guard against the hubris that scientific mastery can create—specifically, the conceit that technology can fix all of our problems. As noted previously,

AP Photo/Stanley Troutman

Although technology has provided many benefits, it also has a dark side. This is nowhere more dramatically reflected than in the quest by countries to build and deploy WMDs. The awesome destructive power of these weapons was demonstrated by the dropping of the atomic bomb on Hiroshima, Japan, on August 6, 1945. Tens of thousands of people perished, and virtually all the houses and buildings in the city were leveled, with the exception of this movie theater.

technological advances can just as often be used destructively as positively. The atomic bomb can kill as well as protect. Missiles can destroy cities as well as help unravel the mysteries of the solar system. Nuclear plants create dangerous radioactivity even while providing an alternative to expensive oil. Gene splicing (recombinant DNA) can unleash new, virulent microbes or lead to a cure for cancer. Modern drugs can be used to brainwash dissidents in a totalitarian state and to relieve heart attacks. Modern methods of communication may increase the ability of a dictator or an authoritarian state to control thought yet may also permit oppressed people to acquire outside information. Electronic toys may dull our critical senses or open up avenues of excellence in the arts, education, sports, and politics. Clearly, science and technology create problems that impinge directly on politics and call for difficult decisions that require the balancing of benefits and risks. These problems have become an inevitable part of the social and political landscape.

The Historical Setting of Politics

An old adage holds that "political science without history has no root; history without political science has no fruit." Historical roots nourish the societal tree and its political fruits. Historical memory, for example, plays a vital role in social and political communities. A nation's **prescriptive constitution**—that is, its traditional way of conducting social, economic, and political business—originates in a community's history. That history shapes key principles: respect for private property or a belief in public ownership, a belief in separation of church and state or their connection, a primary emphasis on liberty or on equality. These principles often become associated with national patriotism and generate powerful emotions that influence political values and behavior.

Our current social and political environment is an inheritance. To understand that historical inheritance is to understand key forces still influencing the present. Alexis de Tocqueville, the French author of *Democracy in America*, a perceptive nineteenth-century study of the United States, understood this point well. In seeking to explain American society and politics, he called attention to several important factors. He noted the significance of a unique American history, relatively free of aristocracy and feudalism. He stressed the value of an Anglo-Saxon inheritance of constitutional liberty and a sound religious tradition. And he thoroughly appreciated the strategic worth of a bountiful land removed from Europe by 3,000 miles of ocean. These factors, Tocqueville argued, made it easier for creative statesmen to advance democracy and equality in the United States. In contrast to the French in 1789, Americans in 1776 did not have to concentrate great power in a central government to overthrow a monarchy, a nobility, and an established clergy in order to ensure equality and freedom. Americans, Tocqueville contended, had been "born equal." They had already established vital institutions of freedom. This history, he argued, moved Americans toward a more egalitarian democracy. They faced challenges to freedom, but their history promoted the success of their democratic experiment.

The study of history helps students of political science appreciate both change and continuity in politics. Traditions persist, but change and revolution may also occur. Both peaceful change and more violent transformation may be part of a nation's heritage and may influence its politics. Today, for example, the United States, France, and the United

Kingdom are devoted to peaceful constitutional change, but each experienced important revolutions that significantly affected its current politics. The ideological forebears of today's political conservatives were often political radicals. (You might consider had the American Revolution failed, George Washington might be called an eighteenth-century terrorist in books like this one in an alternative universe.)

History shows that nations wax and wane. Empires rise and fall, as do civilizations. These are the truisms of history that stimulate us, as students of politics, to inquire into the dynamics of social and political change. For example, does the study of history help us understand the nature of revolution in general and of specific revolutions in particular? In his classic book, *Anatomy of Revolution*, Crane Brinton examined four major cases: the English civil war in the seventeenth century, the American and French Revolutions in the late eighteenth century, and the Russian Revolution in the twentieth century. He posited that all successful revolutions, including the four he examined, pass through certain stages. They each experience (1) economic difficulties and the desertion of the intellectuals from existing values; (2) a failure on the part of the existing government to maintain its legitimacy, affirm its power, and crush the rebels; (3) the achievement of power by the revolutionaries, with the moderates initially in power; (4) the displacement of the moderates by more radical revolutionaries who undertake a reign of terror; and then (5) a return to more normal, and perhaps even reactionary, behavior after the fires of revolution die down. Not all scholars agree with Brinton, but his investigation stimulates questions about how such historical studies can illuminate past and present revolutions.[17]

History also shows that views of peoples and nations change over time. So, too, does the **civic culture**—the set of attitudes toward citizenship and politics that helps sustain a democratic, stable, and effective nation. Germany is a good case in point. There was no state called Germany before the nineteenth century. As late as the eighteenth century, or even the early nineteenth, German-speaking people were often viewed as easygoing, pacific, and sometimes ignorant and uncultured. They lived in a number of separate states in central Europe. However, by the late nineteenth century, under Prussian domination, a German state had emerged, and Germans were frequently looked on as energetic, militant, intelligent, and cultured. Then, with Hitler's dictatorship (1933–1945), still another transformation took place. German leaders and many German people were characterized as savage, brutal, and sadistic.

After World War II, the Federal Republic of Germany (West Germany) emerged, strongly committed to constitutional democracy. But German citizens did not yet illustrate civic culture at its best. German voters seemed "relatively passive," politically detached, and cynical; hostility between the supporters of West Germany's two largest parties was high and not "tempered by any general social norms of trust and confidence." In 1963, Gabriel A. Almond and Sidney Verba, two students of civic culture, attempted to explain the attitudes of German citizens by noting Germany's "bitter and traumatic political history," its terrible disillusionment with Nazi politics, and "the intense commitment to political movements that characterized Germany under Weimar [the Weimar Republic, after the end of World War I and before the advent of Hitler] and the Nazi era."[18]

Yet in a follow-up study on West Germans and civic culture published in 1980, David P. Conradt demonstrated how more recent history had changed West German attitudes, indicating that the portrait of the West German political culture painted only a decade and a half earlier had "changed in every important respect." By the mid-1970s, Conradt observed, "Germans had greater feelings of trust in government and were more supportive of their political system than mass publics in Britain." (In 1963, Almond and Verba had found the United States and Britain to be exemplars of the civic culture.) Conradt held that the Almond-Verba study was a "dated . . . snapshot of a political culture being remade." Conradt saw signs of a healthy, vital, democratic order and concluded that four historical events accounted for these key changes among West German voters: (1) postwar socialization, (2) the absence of any credible alternative to liberal democracy, (3) postwar socioeconomic modernization, and (4) system performance.[19]

The historical setting of politics thus enables us to see how tradition influences political values, behavior, and judgment and to understand political problems. Our study of history helps us, as students of politics, to appreciate both continuity and change.

THE CULTURAL UNIVERSE WE HAVE CREATED

KEY QUESTIONS

1. Have freedom, reason, and progress held up as keystones of modern culture and politics?

2. Can religion play an integral role in striking a cultural balance? In what way does religion, as a vital part of our culture, influence politics?

In politics, as in other arenas of human endeavor, a people without a vision will perish. This vision of a life to lead—of the good, the true, and the beautiful—comes to all people, including political actors, from a part of our culture understood here as high culture. We distinguish high culture to emphasize the development and refinement of thought, spirit, literature, art, and taste. Thus, our concern is with how philosophy, religion, literature, and art provide insights into human life and creativity. These disciplines call attention to the larger meaning of our world. They underscore the complexity and ambiguity of politics and the wide range and subtlety of human behavior. High culture depicts both the joy and the despair of judgment in human and political life and adds a rich texture to the fabric of societal life and to politics.

The Culture of the Enlightenment

Culturally and politically, Westerners are still children of the **Enlightenment**—the Western-dominated movement committed to reason, freedom, and progress that emerged most clearly in the late eighteenth century, the century of the American and French Revolutions. Despite the cataclysmic events of the twentieth century, most Westerners still share the outlook of the Enlightenment. We still condemn the follies and barbarities of an oppressive and ignorant past characterized by religious intolerance, violations of due process of law, and a rigid class structure. Westerners also look forward to the earthly emancipation of all human beings. The outlook of the Enlightenment has shaped the political philosophy of liberal democracy, democratic socialism, and communism. And despite the hold of traditional cultures in developing countries, this outlook has influenced the viewpoint of intellectuals and leaders in most Asian and African nations as well.

But the culture of the Enlightenment is not without its critics, who assail it as naive and unrealistic and who point out the shortcomings of faith in reason, freedom, and progress. The culture of the Enlightenment, they argue, has refused to face up to human irrationality, the denial of freedom, and political retrogression. The critics call attention, for example, to the decline of belief in eternal truths such as liberty, equality, and fraternity. Looking especially to modern totalitarian regimes, they note that the tradition of civility has been badly wounded in the modern world. They emphasize that the prerequisites for a genuinely democratic society are weak even in developed nations and often nonexistent in others. These critics underscore the failures of both liberalism and communism, pointing out that success in overcoming strife, hatred, poverty, and ignorance is elusive no matter the ideology in play. The dreadful years of instability, war, authoritarianism, and totalitarianism of the twentieth century should refute those who continue to believe in progress, ever upward and onward. And now, in the early years of the twenty-first century, we are faced with the specter of global terrorism. Indeed, the beliefs of terrorists are frequently opposed to the Enlightenment ideals of freedom and progress. Other critics of the Enlightenment emphasize the need for community respect for tradition, and an embrace of spiritual values, which many earlier Enlightenment thinkers appear to slight.

AP Photo/Alessandra Tarintino

Pope Francis—pictured here leaving St. Peter's Square at the Vatican after his weekly general audience in May 2015—has demonstrated an influence on politics since his 2013 election, by drawing attention to issues of world poverty and income disparity.

Striking a Cultural Balance

Naysayers notwithstanding, political thinkers do seem to be striking a balance between the adulation of Enlightenment culture and its harsh criticism. That balance has produced a much more sober and prudent—yet still affirmative—assessment of reason, freedom, and progress than previously existed. In striking that balance, these political thinkers have become conscious of the need to limit the power of political actors, including those with good intentions. They have come to see the dangers that people may face even from those who would usher in a just and peaceful world. The new balance is leading to a keener assessment of citizens' political capabilities—what we can and cannot do—and it is challenging us to seize real opportunities for greater control of our destiny. For example, we may not be able to end all conflicts in human affairs, perhaps not even all warfare, but we may be able to abolish nuclear warfare. Similarly, we cannot eliminate all violations of civil liberties, but we may significantly reduce flagrant and persistent violations, especially genocide. It may be utopian to believe that we can rid the world of poverty and disease, but we can overcome chronic hunger and starvation, and we can prevent a good many afflictions. Overcoming all pollution may be out of the question, but cleaner air and purer water are attainable.

Students of religion and politics argue that too often the religious influences on politics are overlooked. They emphasize that religion has vitally affected our basic philosophy, our deepest aspirations, and our daily commitments. Often religious tradition—whether we are orthodox believers, deists, agnostics, or atheists—has shaped our ideas and practices with regard to birth, education, marriage, and death. Students of religion insist that religion influences our understanding of love, compassion, faith, righteousness, charity, and friendship as well as our notions of peace, liberty, equality, fraternity, and justice. Certainly, they maintain, Judeo-Christian religious conceptions—whether of the covenant or of the biblical commandments—have influenced ideas of constitution and law in the Western world. A comparable account of Islam and other great religions would reveal the political importance of those religious outlooks. For good or ill, the world's great religions have provided a vision for society and politics.

Culture shapes and is shaped by politics. On one hand, religion, literature, and art can influence our political values and behavior. On the other hand, what happens in politics and in society is expressed in religion, literature, and art. These forms thus reveal the creative imagination at work and show integration and disintegration, harmony and alienation, peace and war—among nations, within society, and in the human mind. We can profitably turn to great literary figures—Sophocles, Aristophanes, Dante, Cervantes, Shakespeare, Goethe, Dostoevsky, and Tolstoy—for deeper understanding of people, politics, and society. Novelists such as Charles Dickens, Emile Zola, Charlotte and Emily Brontë, George Eliot, John Steinbeck, Sinclair Lewis, and Virginia Woolf have successfully popularized a host of social issues. Great religious leaders and some students of religion have also profoundly influenced politics. A few examples include Moses, Jesus, Saint Paul, Confucius, and Mohammed; reforming popes such as John XXIII and John Paul II; inspiring women such as Mother Teresa; great religious leaders from the developing world such as Mohandas Gandhi; influential black religious leaders such as Martin Luther King Jr.; and modern students of religion, society, and politics such as Reinhold Niebuhr. Of course, the creators of great world religions stand in a class by themselves, as do the great Protestant reformers Martin Luther and John Calvin. Yet the interpretation of religion—and its impact on politics—goes on.

CONCLUSION

Politics and political science cannot be understood in a vacuum. The activity that is politics and the discipline that is political science exist in a larger world and are affected by a larger environment. In important ways, that larger environment—physical, social, cultural—influences political values, behavior, and judgment and sets the stage on which the political play proceeds. The larger environment calls attention to limits, capabilities, dangers, and opportunities that are the central concerns of those who study politics.

We gain a fuller appreciation of the larger environment of politics from other academic disciplines, ranging from history and physics to literature and art. These disciplines shed considerable light on the political scientist's four major tasks: ethical recommendation, empirical understanding, prudent judgment, and theoretical integration.

These disciplines suggest theories, generalizations, models, methods, and insights that help students of politics address their own significant problems.

For purposes of specialization, we have separated political science from the other social sciences, yet this division is arbitrary and often severs connections that cannot be cut off in the real world. Academic disciplines overlap, just as politics overlaps economics and other human activities. As we come to understand the interdisciplinary setting of politics, we can also understand the importance of focusing on our public life and values, on the struggle for power and patterns of accommodation in the political community, and on public policy judgments.

SUGGESTED READINGS

Armstrong, Karen. *Fields of Blood: Religion and the History of Violence*. New York: Alfred A. Knopf, 2015. A survey of the history of religion and violence. The author asserts that forces like nationalism are far more influential in initiating violence than religion.

Diamond, Jared. *Guns, Germs, and Steel: The Fate of Human Societies*. New York: Norton, 1998. Offers reasons why the Europeans have been in such an advantageous position in the world for so long. A major factor in his thesis is geography.

Freund, Caroline. *Rich People, Poor Countries*. Washington, DC: Peterson Institute for International Economics, 2015. Tells the story of how a new class of billionaires is driving rapid development and industrialization in poor countries but widening the gap between rich and poor citizens in those societies.

Kaplan, Robert. *The Revenge of Geography*. New York: Random House, 2013. A thoughtful and provocative book tracing the powerful impact of climate, topography, and geography on world politics.

Landes, David. *The Wealth and Poverty of Nations*. New York: Norton, 1998. Argues that the key to understanding why there is a gap between rich and poor countries is to be found in the Industrial Revolution. For Landes, cultural values are an important factor.

Levine, Steve. *The Oil and the Glory: The Pursuit of Empire and Future on the Caspian Sea*. New York: Random House, 2007. The story of the rush for oil in Central Asia after the collapse of the Soviet Union.

Maslow, Abraham. *Motivation and Personality*. 3rd ed. New York: Addison-Wesley, 1987. A highly influential hierarchy-of-needs argument that throws a great deal of light on political values and behavior. See also *The Farther Reaches of Human Nature*. 3rd ed. New York: Arkana, 1993; and *The Farthest Reaches of Human Nature*. New York: Peter Smith, 1977.

Naya, Pramodk, ed. *The New Media and Cyberculture Anthology*. New York: John Wiley & Sons, 2010. Incorporates essays by both new and established scholars of digital cultures, including Andy Miah, Eugene Thacker, Lisa Nakamura, Chris Hables Gray, Sonia Livingstone, and Espen Aarseth.

Rothenberg, Paula S. *Race, Class and Gender in the United States: An Integrated Study*. 9th ed. New York: MacMillan Publishers, 2013. One hundred thoughtful and informative essays on the interrelationships between race, class and gender in American society.

Seib, Philip. *The Future of Diplomacy*. 1st ed. New York: Wiley, 2016. Study of the impact of social media and other forms of rapid communications on relations between countries. Draws examples from the Iran nuclear negotiations and the Syrian humanitarian crisis.

Sowell, Thomas. *Wealth, Poverty and Politics*. New York: Basic Books, 2016. A conservative take on issues of wealth distribution in a variety of societies.

Stiglitz, Joseph. *Globalization and Its Discontents*. New York: W.W. Norton & Company, 2017. (First published in 2001 with new edition in 2017.) Stilitz, Nobel Prize economist, makes a powerful case against the way modern globalization works.

Wallis, Jim. *God's Politics: Why the Right Gets It Wrong and the Left Doesn't Get It*. San Francisco: Harper San

Francisco, 2005. An interesting take on religion and politics in America that criticizes both political parties. More recently, Wallis addresses racism in his, *America's Original Sin: Racism, White Privilege, and the Bridge to a New America*. Ada, MI: Brazos Press, 2017.

Yergin, Daniel. *The Prize: The Epic Quest for Oil, Money, and Power*. New edition. New York: Free Press, 2008.

Pulitzer Prize–winning history of oil and its role in international politics. First published in 1991, this is a new edition sweeping in scope and very readable. See also Yergin's *The Quest: Energy, Security and the Remaking of the Modern World*. New York: The Penguin Group, 2011.

GLOSSARY TERMS

carrying capacity (p. 82)
civic culture (p. 101)
class (p. 97)
Enlightenment (p. 102)

finite resources (p. 85)
Marxism (p. 92)
prescriptive constitution (p. 100)
racism (p. 81)

religious fundamentalism (p. 94)
revolution of rising expectations
    (p. 80)
sexism (p. 81)

NOTES

1. Population data from the United Nations, Department of Economic and Social Affairs, Population Division, *World Population Prospects 2017 Revisions*.

2. United Nations, Department of Economic and Social Affairs, Population Division, *World Population Prospects* 2017 Revisions, p. 2. https://esa.un.org/unpd/wpp/Publications/Files/WPP2017_KeyFindings.pdf

3. U.S. Energy Information Administration, 2015, http://www.eia.gov/dnav/pet/pet_move_impcus_a2_nus_ep00_im0_mbbl_m.htm

4. World Health Organization, Water Sanitation Hygiene, 2017. www.who.int/water_sanitation_health/diseases-risks/en/

5. Endangered Species, "The Plight of Endangered Species, 2017. www.endangeredearth.com

6. Food and Agricultural Organization of the United Nations, *Global Forest Resources Assessment 2015*, Executive Summary, p. 1.

7. This discussion follows Abraham Maslow's analysis in *Motivation and Personality*, 3rd ed. (New York: Addison-Wesley, 1987).

8. Konrad Lorenz, *On Aggression* (New York: Harcourt, Brace, and World, 1966); Robert Ardrey, *The Territorial Imperative* (New York: Dell, 1966).

9. Leonard Berkowitz, *Aggression: Social Psychological Analysis* (New York: McGraw-Hill, 1962).

10. Julian S. Huxley, *On Living in a Revolution* (New York: Harper, 1944), 114.

11. Ibid.

12. Cornell West, *Race Matters* (New York: Vintage, 1994), p.

13. This paragraph and the following two cite Erich Fromm, *The Anatomy of Human Destructiveness* (New York: Holt, Rinehart, and Winston, 1973), 230–232.

14. R. Scott Appleby, *Religious Fundamentalism and Global Conflict*, Headline Series (New York: Foreign Policy Association, 1994), ii.

15. Grant Wacker, "The Christian Right," Teacher Serve, National Humanities Center, October 2000, http://nationalhumanitiescenter.org/tserve/twenty/tkeyinfo/chr_rght.htm

16. Lauri Goodstein, "Obama Made Gains Among Younger Evangelical Voters, Data Shows," *New York Times*, November 6, 2008.

17. Crane Brinton, *Anatomy of Revolution* (New York: Vintage Books, 1965).

18. Gabriel A. Almond and Sidney Verba, *The Civic Culture: Political Attitudes and Democracy in Five Nations* (Boston: Little, Brown, 1965), 312–313.

19. David P. Conradt, "Changing German Political Culture," in *The Civic Culture Revisited*, ed. Gabriel A. Almond and Sidney Verba (Boston: Little, Brown, 1980), 246, 256, 264–265.

PART II

POLITICAL PHILOSOPHY AND IDEOLOGY

The three chapters that constitute Part II begin a fuller exploration of the ethical task in political science. Our guiding question is this: How do political philosophy and ideology illuminate our understanding of politics? By political philosophy we mean a critically examined understanding of the values, realities, and judgments of politics—an understanding that is essential to the search for excellence and fulfillment in a just community. By political ideology we mean those beliefs, or ideals, that in a very practical way guide political actors in a given community and the justification of those guiding beliefs.

Chapter 5 presents the contributions of some of the outstanding Western political philosophers to the difficult quest for the good political life and a fuller understanding of politics. Although there is more to political philosophy than the quest for the good political life, there is justification for focusing, at least initially, on this pursuit. It leads to a conscious appreciation of the importance of ethical standards for politics, dictates an empirical search for the necessary and sufficient conditions of the good political life, and encourages students of politics to search for wise public policies.

This question—What constitutes the good life?—is central to politics because answering it leads to the establishment of critical standards. These standards then make it possible to say that a value, a political actor, an institution, an action, or a policy is good or bad—that a judgment is wise or foolish.

Moreover, these questions lead to a critical examination of the great political issues. Here we must confront the nature of human beings, the character of community, and the meaning of human destiny. We must probe frequent conflicts between justice and power, liberty and authority, and individual interest and the public interest. We must ask about the relationship between means and ends, higher law and human law, and personal aspirations and the common good. Intrigued by the elusive character of the good life, we seek to understand the constitutional order, a nation's vital interests, and political obligation, and we try to assess the reality of human fulfillment and the pros and cons of evolutionary versus revolutionary change. In brief, we seek to uncover the meaning—and the necessary and sufficient conditions—of political health.

The brief review in Chapter 5 of how outstanding Western political philosophers have responded to fundamental issues will help you assess the strengths and weaknesses of liberal democracy, democratic socialism, communism, and other alternative outlooks. Chapters 6 and 7 focus on a number of these contemporary ideologies and also on past, present, and future challenges to those dominant belief systems.

Plato and Aristotle as depicted in an early
sixteenth-century fresco by Raphael, the
School of Athens, in the Vatican Museums.

The Granger Collection, New York

5

THE QUEST FOR THE GOOD POLITICAL LIFE

How have the great political philosophers contributed to the difficult quest for the good political life and a fuller understanding of politics? This is the inquiry that will guide us throughout this chapter. Our selective examination will address (1) the problem that prompted their explorations of the good life, (2) their "solutions" and their arguments on behalf of their positions, and (3) the heritage they bequeathed to us. Although this brief treatment cannot do full justice to the richness, complexity, and subtlety of these philosophers' thoughts, it may open the door to deeper study. We encourage you to read further the works of the authors you find interesting.

CLASSICAL GREEK THOUGHT: THE SEARCH FOR POLITICAL EXCELLENCE

Socrates, one of the world's most creative and stimulating teachers, founded Greek political philosophy. His legendary questioning of anyone around him inspired and infuriated others to such a degree Socrates is famous and well known centuries later despite never actually writing anything down. In particular, he wanted to know why people professed certain beliefs and what assumptions they made about the good, the true, and the beautiful. Socrates placed the Greek ideal of *arete*, or excellence, which the Greeks sought to fulfill in all fields of human activity, at the center of thinking and action in the political community. He gathered around him a number of pupils, the most brilliant of whom was Plato, and through relentless examination probed the character of moral life, which was for him the heart of both

Chapter Objectives

After studying this chapter, you will be able to do the following:

1. Explain the differences between the ideas of Plato and his student Aristotle.

2. Compare and contrast the ideas of other significant political thinkers such as Augustine, Aquinas, Machiavelli, Hobbes, Locke, Rousseau, Burke, Wollstonecraft, Mill, and Marx.

3. Explain the significant differences between ancient and modern political thinkers.

4. Analyze the conflict between authority and liberty.

5. Describe differing conceptions of justice.

6. Identify four elements in contemporary political philosophy.

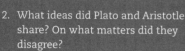

KEY QUESTIONS

1. What are the single most important contributions Plato and Aristotle made to political thought? How relevant is their thinking today?

2. What ideas did Plato and Aristotle share? On what matters did they disagree?

human and communal life. Socrates's passion for excellence in the political community—a concern that required him to articulate an ethical standard, probe political behavior, and seek the wise course of action—remained a central motif in the political philosophy of Plato and Aristotle.

Plato: Justice as the Harmony of Classes and Rule by Philosopher-Kings

Plato's problem in his classic work *The Republic* can be stated simply: What is justice? Plato seeks to rationalize, spiritualize, and universalize the ideal life for the **polis**, the Greek city-state.[1] He seeks to establish the polis on sound principles, suffuse it with excellence, and help it endure. Justice, Plato argues, is the harmonious ordering of the functional classes in the polis: philosophers ruling, soldiers defending, and farmers and artisans providing the necessary food, clothing, and utensils for everyday life. In this fashion, the wise would rule, the brave would defend, and those with basic appetites and talents would sustain the polis with their labor. Plato believes that the philosopher-kings should order the life of the polis in accordance with a vision of the good that their superior intellect allows them to perceive. This intellect permits them to grasp the truth of reality and this ability of knowing is the key to insuring justice. Because of this intelligence—ensured by education and strengthened by the critical examination of ideas—they would govern wisely and ensure excellence. And because each class would do that which it is best endowed by nature to do, each class would receive its due. Conflict would be overcome; justice, or harmony, would prevail.

Plato's preference for the good, for the enduring truth that lies beyond mere appearances, for excellence, for the rational, for the order that is justice, is very clear. In one bold stroke he solves the problem of the clash between justice and power by making the just powerful. Philosophers are entitled to their power because of their knowledge of the good and the supreme truth. Justice cannot be the interest of the stronger, because might does not make right. Justice cannot be expediency, because it must rest on something more enduring than immediate satisfaction or personal advantage. That deeper truth—the idea of the good—provides the proper standard in politics. Plato's theory of ideas illuminates that reality, as the theory holds that ideas—the true "forms"—are the true realities. To grasp these forms we must get past our earthly perceptions of reality, which are actually a debased version of a higher truth. It takes great discipline and learning to see past everyday life to this higher truth—the reality of beauty and justice. And, naturally, those in touch with the higher truth—those who have ascended the ladder of truth to grasp the idea of the good—may wisely guide others in political life.

To the extent that other forms of government move away from the harmony of classes and the rule by philosopher-kings, they are deficient. Plato identifies these deficient forms of government as **timocracy**, **oligarchy**, **democracy**, and **tyranny**. They reveal what the good political life is not. They represent a falling away from **aristocracy**, which is government by the best. Timocracy is government by people of honor and ambition. As aristocracy degenerates into timocracy, so timocracy degenerates into oligarchy—government by the rich and lovers of money (what we would call plutocracy). Oligarchy, in turn, degenerates into what Plato calls democracy, government by the many poor. Democracy emerges "after the poor have conquered their [oligarchic] opponents." Democracy is based on everyone's having "an equal share of freedom and power." Democracy, however, is also unstable. It degenerates into tyranny, which emerges when democratic people, preoccupied with "liberty and equality," lose a sense of **law** and order, a sense of discrimination, and turn to a "champion" to protect them against the rich. Tyranny, the lawless rule of one individual, is the worst form of government and receives Plato's harshest criticism.

Plato's critics attack him as an enemy of the open society, hostile to democracy, a proponent of censorship, and an advocate of a rigid-class society. His supporters defend his commitment to rule by wise people (including women), his affirmation of a standard of a good life as a guide in politics, his dedication to reasoned examination of arguments, and his insistence on moving from popular opinion (doxa in Greek, which Plato thought unreasoning) to knowledge (what is true regardless what the majority might think). Among his critics is his most illustrious student, Aristotle, who, despite differences with Plato, remained indebted to his teacher for many of his own ideas.

Aristotle: Constitutional Government and Rule by the Middle Class

Aristotle criticizes key features of Plato's *Republic* as unrealistic, especially his advocacy of communism for his class of philosopher-kings. Plato favored this system because public ownership would remove a real source of contention—conflicts over private property—among the members of this class. Aristotle thinks such a system of communism is unrealistic and incompatible with human nature.

Aristotle seeks to adjust Plato's severely aristocratic principles to the actualities of life in Greek political communities. But even as he does so, he endorses the need to understand the ideal regime, to relate ethics to politics, and to come as close to the best regime as human nature and political experience permit. Aristotle never loses sight of the anthropological principles holding that the family, the economy, and the local village come into existence to satisfy the bare necessities of life and that the polis then goes on to make the good life possible. The fulfillment of human beings in the political community remains a basic principle. To help guide you in understanding his preferences, Table 5.1 presents Aristotle's famous classification of governments. Note that Aristotle classified regimes according to the number who ruled—the one, the few, the many—and the goals of those rulers, which is ruling for the sake of all or ruling for the sake of oneself or one's class.

Which form of government provides the best practicable good life? Aristotle's answer is the **polity**, or constitutional government—a mixture of democracy and oligarchy. Such a government would rest most securely on a well-educated, reasonably virtuous, sufficiently wealthy, moderate middle class. The middle class is more likely to represent a "golden mean" between poverty and riches. It would not be envied by the poor or feared by the rich. Members of this class would be interested in politics and good

Table 5.1 Aristotle's Classification of Governments

Number Ruling	Rule in Accord With the Common Good	Rule Motivated by Individual or Class Self-Interest
One	Monarchy (government by a virtuous ruler)	Tyranny (government by one lawless person)
The few	Aristocracy (government by the virtuous few)	Oligarchy (government by the rich and noble)
The many	Polity (constitutional government—a mixture of democracy and oligarchy)	Democracy (government by the poor and free)

Source: Developed by authors.

government but would not be overly ambitious. Moreover, the middle class would be able to maintain the rule of law and justice.

Just because Aristotle prefers polity does not mean that he believes it is the ideal choice. In fact, he personally favors monarchy and then aristocracy but acknowledges polity's practicality. All three of these forms of government—polity, monarchy, and aristocracy—are preferable to what he considers the three perverted forms of government: democracy (the most tolerable), oligarchy (a little better than tyranny), and tyranny (the worst of all).

Aristotle recognizes that "the best is often unattainable, and there the true legislator and statesman ought to be acquainted, not only with (1) that which is best in the abstract, but also with (2) that which is best relative to circumstances."[2] Given what is relative to circumstances in Greece, Aristotle favors the polity, in which the middle class is dominant, because such a government would be well administered, would prevent extremism in politics, would be freer of "factions and dissensions," and would be reasonably stable. Aristotle still hopes, however, that his polity would approach his ideal state as closely as circumstances permit. The polis should be small but not too small. Its territory and resources should permit its citizens to live liberally and with abundant leisure. Citizens should be educated, dedicated to wisdom and virtue, and active in the life of the polis.

The Aristotelian heritage is the mixed **constitution**, respectful of the common good and the rule of law, aristocratic in the best sense but willing to come to terms with the legitimate claims of the many poor and the few rich. Yet Aristotle's clear bias against "mechanics" and "tradesmen" and farmers, his justification of slavery, and his exclusion of women from the political process lead modern democrats to challenge those aspects of this heritage.

CHRISTIANITY AND THE GOOD POLITICAL LIFE

As we pointed out in Chapter 4, religion has significantly influenced our understanding of human values, behavior, and judgment. When Christianity became tolerated in the Roman Empire early in the fourth century, its impact was widely felt in the Western world. Christianity's influence grew as it became the empire's favored religion.

Augustine: Incomplete Worldly Peace, Order, and Justice

Augustine (354–430) wrote *The City of God* to defend Christianity against the charge, leveled by pagan Romans, that Christianity caused the fall of Rome in AD 410. He denies the charge, arguing that Roman vice, not Christian virtue, was responsible. In the course of his argument, Augustine writes of two cities—the City of God (the heavenly city) and the City of Man (the earthly city)—that provide two influential standards for judgment, one positive and one negative.

KEY QUESTIONS

1. How does the concept of the City of God help us to understand the good political life on Earth?

2. How do the works of Augustine and Aquinas square with the American doctrine of separation of church and state?

The heavenly city is formed "by the love of God" whereas the earthly city is formed "by the love of self, even to the contempt of God."[3] The City of God is the kingdom of Christ. In this kingdom, composed of the elect, people live according to God in the hope of everlasting happiness. Perfect love, peace, justice, freedom, and fulfillment are possible only in the immortal life of the heavenly city.

The earthly city is the kingdom of Satan. In this city, made up of the damned, people live according to human appetites and seek earthly happiness. Perfect love, peace, justice, freedom, and fulfillment are not possible in this world; indeed, the earthly city is characterized by conflict, injustice, and war. It is a hell on earth.

Augustine maintains that the City of God is not coextensive with the earthly church, even though the church may represent the heavenly city. Church leaders and church members are not necessarily among the elect. Similarly, the earthly city cannot be absolutely equated with Rome or any actual state. Some members of actual states are also citizens of the heavenly city; they are pilgrims sojourning on Earth while awaiting heavenly salvation. On the whole, although the two cities are commingled in any historical state, any actual political community is closer to the City of Man than to the City of God.

Human history will reveal the clash between the two cities and the ultimate triumph of the City of God. That triumph will not take place in this world but in the heavenly one hereafter. The best regime, as the City of God, will emerge only after the end of history. From God's creation of the world and of people, through the Fall (people's turning away from God) and the advent of Christ (offering hope for salvation in God's grace), to the ultimate triumph of the City of God, we can discern God's providence.

But how does this outlook clarify our understanding of the good political life? Augustine's philosophy of history, his idea of human nature, and his view of the two mystical cities lead to a very modest view of the good political life on Earth. Perfection is out of the question. True love—of God and of neighbor—must be professed but cannot be perfectly fulfilled. Justice—which means giving God his due—cannot be realized completely in this world. The Christian commonwealth, in which the one true God is recognized, is Augustine's ideal regime, but it is possible only in the immortal, heavenly city, not in any earthly community. Similarly, perfect peace is not possible on Earth. The good political life in any community is inevitably incomplete. Human nature after the Fall reveals self-love, cupidity, domination, and concupiscence (fleshly lust). Egotism, pride, and lust for money and power lead to dissatisfaction, strife, misery, and war. Even the elect who are intermingled with the damned in this world cannot fully escape the evil consequences of the world of flesh.

According to Augustine's perspective, the best that people in any earthly political community can hope for is an incomplete, although still beneficial, peace and order. The state and its rulers are God's instruments to maintain peace and justice. The political and legal order must restrain human appetites and passions—especially the lust for riches and power—and guide behavior through law and punishment. Political authority is a gift from God to fallen human beings. Even evil rulers must be seen as divinely appointed instruments to govern people after the Fall. Subjects must obey the powers that be. The state's coercive powers are necessary to restrain prideful appetites and conflicts among sinful human beings. Rulers should be resisted only if they command what God's ordinances forbid, and even then resisters must accept punishment.

Citizens in the political community—including the elect on pilgrimage to the heavenly city—see the value of even this incomplete peace, order, and justice. They see the value of law and of ensuring the necessities of human life. Augustine does not ignore the worth of such temporal blessings as health, material possessions, honor, friends, home, and family, but he insists that they are always subordinate to those of the heavenly city.

Augustine leaves a heritage of political realism. Given the nature of human beings—their pride, egotism, cupidity, and lust for power—our efforts to achieve perfect peace or justice in this world cannot succeed. Nevertheless, in our need for peace, order, security, and justice—however incomplete—we can look to government to help maintain a minimum level of civilization. But is Augustine's realism too pessimistic? And can his optimistic faith in God's providence be interpreted differently? Another Christian perspective on politics may provide answers.

Thomas Aquinas: Constitution, Law, Common Good, and Reason

Thomas Aquinas (1225–1274) is more optimistic about the good political life on Earth than is Augustine. He views the political community (and its possibilities for human fulfillment) more positively. Aquinas, like Augustine, endorses the surpassing importance of eternal salvation and other key Christian concepts, but he is more inclined to see the political community as an arena for human development. Following Aristotle,

Aquinas holds that society and government are natural and arise out of human needs. The political community is necessary to fulfill humanity's nature:

> Life in a community . . . enables man . . . to achieve a plenitude of life; not merely to exist, but to live fully, with all that is necessary to well-being. In this sense the political community, of which man forms a part, assists him not merely to obtain material comforts, such as are produced by the many diverse industries of a state, but also spiritual well-being.[4]

Of course, complete spiritual fulfillment is possible only through eternal salvation beyond this mortal life. But the church must do preparatory work in this world, in partnership with the state. Church and state play complementary roles in advancing human fulfillment. The church is primarily concerned with ordering religious life; the state deals with secular life. Both operate within a framework of law: **eternal law**, **natural law**, **human law**, and **divine law**. For Thomas Aquinas, law is "an ordinance of reason for the common good, promulgated by him who has the care of the community."[5]

Eternal law refers to the reason of God ("God's grand design") by which the universe and all things in it are governed. As rational creatures, human beings are able to participate in eternal law through the light of natural reason and to discern what is good and what is evil. Thus, natural law is that part of the eternal law known through reason. Human law is the application, in specific circumstances, of natural law in our earthly affairs. Divine law, revealed by God and found in the Scriptures, helps human beings understand natural law while guiding them toward their supernatural end.

The good political life calls for peace, right action, and life-sustaining necessities. Aquinas said the following:

> Therefore to establish the good life for a multitude, three things are required: first, that the multitude should be brought into the unity of peace; secondly, that the multitude, having been united by the bond of peace, should be directed to good action . . . ; thirdly, that through the care of the ruler there should be provided a sufficient supply of the necessaries for good living.[6]

Adherence to virtue, the common good, a constitutional regime, and the reign of law would lead to peace, right action, and life-sustaining goods. Thomas Aquinas's ideal political regime is monarchy, which requires virtue in rulers and ruled. His best practicable regime is a mixture of monarchy, aristocracy, and democracy. This regime combines a preeminently virtuous ruler, a virtuous governing elite under the ruler, and shared rule. Aquinas holds that "a government of this kind is shared by all, both because all are eligible to govern and because the rulers are chosen by all." This form of mixed government is "the best form of polity." As Aquinas points out in *Summa Theologica*, it is "partly kingdom, since there is one at the head of all; partly aristocracy, in so far as a number of persons are set in authority; partly democracy, i.e., government by the people, in so far as the rulers can be chosen from the people and the people have the right to choose their rulers."

Constitution, law, common good, and reason are inseparable in Aquinas's conception of the good political life. Those who exercise power must do so constitutionally—within limits ordained by law. Such law—whether natural, divine, or human—protects against the arbitrary use of power. Rulers are thus bound up in a system of law. Power is justified only insofar as it serves the common good. Authority is legitimate because it is reasonable and right. As we noted previously, Aquinas defines law as "an ordinance of reason for the common good, promulgated by him who has the care of the community." Thus, unlawful rulers are rebels against God's divine system. In extreme cases, when constitutional redress has been tried and has failed, tyrants can be resisted.

For Aquinas, then, the true end for a human being in the political community is a happy and virtuous life. Such a life contributes to the heavenly life. In a partnership guided by the spiritual leadership of the church, church and state can work together toward human fulfillment in this world and in the next.

Aquinas's synthesis of faith and reason, of Christianity and Aristotle, becomes a mighty medieval resource for modern constitutionalism. His belief in a higher law, a common good, the power of reason, and the importance of earthly (as well as heavenly) fulfillment reinforces efforts to overcome arbitrary power and to make government limited and responsible. His appreciation of the need, in politics, to apply sound principles to specific circumstances ensures his continued appeal to the modern mind. Critics of the "Angelic Doctor" (as Aquinas is known) question what remains of his political philosophy if one lacks his faith in God and his belief in reason. Such skepticism, they argue, undermines the constitutional system Aquinas has created. Niccolò Machiavelli lacked Thomas Aquinas's faith and subscribed to another line of reasoning in quest of a virtuous republic.

THE RENAISSANCE: NICCOLÒ MACHIAVELLI AND THE QUEST FOR A VIRTUOUS REPUBLIC

Machiavelli marks a sharp break from the earlier thinking epitomized by Aquinas; however, it is difficult to understand Machiavelli without a few words about Renaissance politics in his country. During the late fifteenth and early sixteenth centuries, Italy was divided among a number of often-warring states. The papacy was both a religious and a political power. France dominated parts of Italy. Moreover, the Renaissance gave birth to a new secular spirit, which manifested itself in creative activity in literature, art, and architecture and bubbled over into politics, calling traditional religious views into question and inviting bold leaders to demonstrate their talents. Machiavelli, an experienced and resourceful Florentine civil servant, was unquestionably influenced by the energetic mood of the Renaissance as he endeavored to articulate a creative approach to politics.

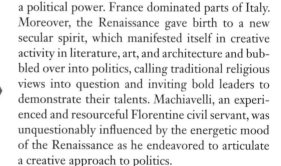

KEY QUESTIONS

1. In what fundamental way does Machiavelli's thinking differ from that of Aristotle? Plato? Augustine? Aquinas? Or does it?

2. How does Machiavellian thinking apply to modern-day politics?

Machiavelli's thought is complex and at times apparently contradictory. He called for a unified Italy, appealing to ethnic pride, praised civic virtue, and believed in virtu. Virtu is an important concept in Machiavelli's thought and means energy or will; however, there is also clearly a masculine connotation to the word and men display virtu. Yet his most famous work, *The Prince*, appears to teach leaders (Princes) how to gain and hold power and excuses the most ruthless actions in pursuing that power. In fact, some political philosophers have called him a teacher of evil and his name has for centuries been a byword to describe people who are cunning and without a sense of morality.

So, what were Machiavelli's actual teachings? As we noted, it is tricky and open to multiple seemingly plausible interpretations. However, his two most famous works, *The Prince* and *The Discourses*, provide a powerful new take on politics. *The Prince* is a brief book that provides lessons for political leaders. At this time in history, there was a tradition of political writing called *mirror of princes*, designed to show young princes how they should rule. This literature often recommended that princes be good Christian leaders and earlier pre-Christian writers recommended being truthful, just, generous, and kind. Machiavelli takes an entirely different approach to his advice. Princes must be tough, at times brutal. They must be wary of flattery. They need to be both a lion (strong) and fox (cunning, deceptive) to seize and maintain power. One of his most famous observations concerns being loved or feared. He writes:

> "A controversy has arisen about this: whether it is better to be loved or feared, or vice versa. My view is that it is desirable to be both loved and feared; but it is difficult to achieve both and, if one of them has be lacking, it is much safer to be feared than loved."[7]

The new ruler "is often forced to act treacherously, ruthlessly, or inhumanely, and disregard the precepts of religion." This last point, to ignore the teachings of Christianity was particularly shocking to his contemporary readers (and to many people today). We must remember that Europe at that time was a place virtually saturated in religion and it was no joking matter to discuss one's immortal soul.

In his somewhat less famous work, *The Discourses*, he writes about how a republic (as opposed to a principality) can be maintained and prosper:

1. A republican government, one that gives the people a significant role in governing themselves, requires a *virtuous people*. They must possess civic virtue: probity, integrity, love of liberty, patriotism, concern for the political community, trustworthiness, and good sense. A virtuous people must be intelligent, confident about public affairs, disciplined, and concerned about the welfare of the republic.

2. A *mixed and balanced constitution* is Machiavelli's preferred constitution. The people will exercise control in policymaking and share governance with nobles under a wise ruler. The balance of people and nobles will contribute to the public good, prevent domination by a single interest, limit power, and keep political actors responsive.

3. *Good laws* are crucial to good republican government. A government under good laws will be stable and prudent. A prince might be superior in making laws, but "the people are superior in maintaining" the laws.

4. *Public opinion and popular participation* are crucial in maintaining the virtuous republic. Freedom to debate and to propose measures for the public good is

most important. It "cannot be wrong to defend one's opinions with arguments founded upon reason, without employing force or authority." Elections give people the chance to choose good, capable rulers and to keep those who hold office responsible. Debate and elections allow grievances to be aired and conflicts to be settled peacefully.

5. Again and again, Machiavelli endorses the value of a *citizen army* for maintaining a republic. People who fight for their own country, government, security, family, and property will be a reliable bulwark for the republic. When they share power in the republic, they will stoutly defend it.

6. Machiavelli articulates the need for *strong and wise leadership*, provided by a public-spirited elite and a virtuous ruler. This leadership will enlighten and guide public opinion. The ruler will be a person of energy, resolve, foresight, and courage, who—along with the elite—will enhance governmental competence and executive vigor.[8]

So, why is Machiavelli central in the history of political philosophy? There are a number of reasons. First, he emphasized a kind of realism in politics. In a sly reference to Plato, he mocks those who "imagined" republics and principalities that have never been or known to exist."[9] Machiavelli would probably scoff at the idea of philosopher kings or the idea that knowledge will lead one to justice. Politics is the pursuit action so man can display their virtu. And this virtu required people to act with power and to dominate and control the political world. Unlike the Ancient Greeks, Machiavelli tells us that politics starts with what is and not with what might or should be. Second, Machiavelli teaches that politics is its own autonomous realm with its own rules. For others—philosophers businessmen, or priests—to tell politicians what to do would be a little like a baseball coach rushing onto a football field and telling the players how to run the bases. Machiavelli is not saying that moralists, religious people, or others are wrong or inferior; however, they have no right to tell princes or citizens how to be political. Machiavelli is elevating politics as worthy in its own right and having its own rules. For instance, one of Machiavelli's most famous lines is, "the ends justify the means." For Machiavelli, this is the way politics works—that is the way politicians think and should think when playing the game of politics. Furthermore, taking these two points together many see Machiavelli as the first political scientist. He observes how people actually do politics and tries to draw valid conclusions. In this way, some believe that Machiavelli is the founder of the science in political science, in the importance of dispassionate observation of the empirical world above all else. His republican vision has influenced modern liberal democratic societies, especially through his argument for a virtuous people, a balanced and mixed constitution, liberty under law, the competition of parties, and creative leadership. Machiavelli's skepticism about absolute truth (whether classical or Christian), his realistic observation of politics, and his Renaissance commitment to will (energetic activity and hard work) can contribute to toleration, pluralism, and wise and bold efforts to protect our vital interests as best we can in this non-heavenly city. But are the people virtuous enough to govern themselves? Thomas Hobbes, the next political philosopher to be discussed—and the first one in modern political thought—did not think so.

MODERN POLITICAL THOUGHT

We may consider the seventeenth century as the beginning of modernity in political thought. It was then that key, modern themes, especially constitutionalism, individualism, and sovereignty, were sounded by philosophers and affirmed in practice. These themes gained even more prominence in succeeding centuries. Constitutional ideas, of course, precede modern times, yet their effective practice had to wait until the late seventeenth century (when Britain's Glorious Revolution of 1688–1689 occurred) and the eighteenth century (when the American and French Revolutions took place).

Thomas Hobbes: The Need for a Supreme Sovereign Leader

The English philosopher Thomas Hobbes, born in the momentous year (1588) that the Spanish Armada invaded the British Isles, experienced the troubled birth pangs of modern constitutionalism. He lived through a civil war (1642–1648); the execution of Charles I (1649); Britain's experiment with a republican government (the commonwealth of 1649–1653); the protectorate of Oliver Cromwell (1653–1658), a military dictatorship; and the restoration of the monarchy with Charles II in 1660. Hobbes died in 1679, a decade before Britain's Glorious Revolution. It is little wonder that he was driven to ask this question: How can one obtain peace and maintain civilization in a troubled time? This question recurs throughout human history and politics. Certainly, it was Hobbes's central problem in mid-seventeenth-century England, wracked as it was by civil war. Hobbes's response to the political crisis of his time can be found in his master work, *Leviathan*, one of the most influential and important works in the history of political philosophy.

To appreciate Hobbes's response, we have to understand what disturbs him. Civil war and the disorder it creates deeply upset him. His image for the unhappy condition of humankind is that of a state of nature, a state prior to society and government, wherein people lived "without a common power to keep them all in awe." Such a state of nature was a state of war, "of every man . . . against every man." Human beings are selfish, self-seeking, materialistic animals. It is no wonder, then, that Hobbes believes this in the state of nature:

> There is no place for Industry; because the fruit thereof is uncertain; and consequently no Culture of the Earth, no Navigation, nor use of the commodities that may be imported by Sea; no commodious Building; no Instruments of moving, and removing such things as require much force; no Knowledge of the face of the earth; no account of Time; no Arts; no Letters; no Society; and which is worst of all, continual feare, and danger of violent death; And the life of man, solitary, poore, nasty, brutish, and short.[10]

KEY QUESTIONS

1. How did the dynamics of the societies where political philosophers like Hobbes, Locke, Rousseau, Burke, Mill, and Marx lived impact their thought?

2. In what way do these philosophers contribute to the concepts and practice of modern-day democracy? How did they view the conflict between liberty and authority?

Thomas Hobbes's concern about the need for peace and order made him a defender of a great and powerful centralized authority, which he called the Leviathan. The front page of his famous book, *Leviathan* (1651), included a fanciful image of **a gia**nt walking the land. A close look shows that the Leviathan is made up of numerous little people. In pictorial fashion, Hobbes says that the individual must give up political power to the sovereign. In return, all can prosper.

In such a world, which lacks sovereign authority, the "notions of Right and Wrong, Justice and Injustice have there no place."

By contrast, the good political life calls for peace and a sovereign power, a "mortal god." Only such a sovereign can maintain peace and order, law and justice. Only such a sovereign can ensure a civilization of industry, agriculture, science, arts, letters, and commodious living. But how can one move from the state of nature into civilized society under the protection of a sovereign power? Hobbes's answer is a particular kind of **social contract** that people can make because they possess reason, which urges them to seek peace and their own self-preservation. Consequently, they contract with each other to give the sovereign the power to make law, ensure justice, and advance civilization.

However, this sovereign is not limited by the people, who have contracted with each other (but not with the sovereign) to grant supreme power. Moreover, Hobbes's sovereign is not limited by divine law—because the sovereign determines the meaning of divine law. (Whatever his personal views were, he was thought of as an atheist at the time.) The sovereign is also not limited by natural law—because the reason of natural law led to the social contract in the first place. Nor is the sovereign limited by civil law, which is the sovereign's own command. Finally, the sovereign is not limited by common law, or custom, because the sovereign assents to common law by his or her silence and also determines the civil law that overrides the common law. Hobbes's logic here is based on the principle that to limit the sovereign is to limit the ability to maintain the very peace and order that the people contracted to obtain.

Of course, the sovereign's common sense will ensure that property and liberty are respected—but only within a framework of peace and order. Beyond the maintenance of peace and order, justice, and national defense, the sovereign need not choose to exercise power. People, therefore, are at liberty "to buy and sell, and otherwise contract with one another; to choose their own aboad [abode], their own diet, their own trade of life, and [to] institute [rear] their children as they themselves see fit."

Hobbes's sovereign may be one person, a monarch (Hobbes's personal preference), or a parliament. What is crucial is not the form of government, but that there be a sovereign power to overcome the "perpetuall war" of "masterlesse men," which jeopardizes security, property, justice, and civilization.

The Hobbesian heritage is mixed. Supporters interested in peace, law, and order understand the logic of a supreme authority that can overcome the war "of every man . . . against every man," which can also be the war of every nation against every nation. They further understand the logic of giving power to an agreed-on authority to protect people from their own self-destructive appetites and egoistic liberties. Many political philosophers believe that Hobbes bequeathed to us the language in which we talk about politics. Many subsequent political thinkers have used his development of the concepts of sovereignty, representation, state of nature, and consent. Others, however, raise serious objections to the way he formulated and developed those influential concepts. They object to Hobbes's unlimited sovereign power and—like John Locke, our next political philosopher—call for another kind of contract to reach most of Hobbes's objectives. Locke sees more virtue and a different kind of reason in people.

John Locke: Popular, Limited, Responsible, Representative Government

If Hobbes saw the need for a sovereign—a Leviathan, a mortal god—to maintain peace and order, John Locke (1632–1704) worried about the absence of limitations on sovereign authority. Hobbes wrote during the turmoil of the British civil war in the mid-seventeenth century, whereas Locke's world was characterized by the monarch's constitutional violations of liberty toward the end of the seventeenth century. Is it possible to reconcile liberty and authority? Can one devise a political system to give sovereign authority legitimate power without sacrificing constitutional liberty? Locke's answer was yes, but only if one opts for a governmental system that is popular, limited, responsible, and representative.[11]

Locke holds that people in the state of nature (a pre-societal state) enjoy certain natural, inalienable rights, especially those to life, liberty, and property. However, these rights are not fully secure. Unfortunately, there is in the state of nature no common superior person, no common judge, no common executive. There is no established, settled, known rule based on common consent; no known and impartial judge to decide disputes; and no fair, impartial organ to execute the laws. Consequently, people—possessing reason and goodwill—recognize the desirability of moving out of the insecure and inconvenient state of nature into a state of civil society where they can enjoy their inalienable rights more fully. They do this by means of a social contract whereby any number of people (capable of abiding by majority rule) unanimously unite to affect their common purposes. They thus establish a society and a body politic. They create governmental organs to make law, resolve disputes, and execute the law. The common legislative and executive power is thus directed toward peace, safety, and the public good.

The government is therefore based on popular consent. The legislature is the supreme power in the commonwealth because the people consent, via the contract, to put trust in the legislature. The government is limited by the very nature of the contract, or constitution—a founding document or documents that spell out the structure and rules of a political system. Neither the legislature nor the king can act arbitrarily. Both are required to act within constitutional limits. The legislature, for example, cannot take a person's property without that person's consent or the consent of his or her representatives. The king cannot hinder the legislature from assembling or acting freely pursuant to its constitutional powers. The government is to be responsible to the people. It must honor the terms of the social contract that empowers it, terms that obligate it to protect

Like Hobbes, John Locke was concerned about the need for peace and order in society. However, he also feared tyranny and believed in the necessity of protecting individual rights, and in particular, the right to property. Locke, who was born in the shadow of a church, also was a proponent of religious tolerance.

life, liberty, and property. Moreover, the government is representative; the people are to judge whether their representatives in the legislature (parliament) and their executive (king) act in accord with their trust.

Revolution is the people's ultimate weapon if government becomes tyrannical and violates the social contract—if it arbitrarily deprives people of life, liberty, and property. The people will, of course, invoke this right of revolution only when the government's violation of its trust is clear to a majority and persists, and when all other constitutional attempts to redress grievances have been tried and have failed.

Locke has been both hailed and condemned as the father of liberal democracy. His supporters argue that liberal democracy rests on the constitutional protection of life, liberty, and property by a government that is limited, representative, popular, and responsible. They maintain that Locke has successfully reconciled liberty and authority. Locke's critics attack the conservative implications of his defense of property, because it leads to inequality of wealth and power and Locke's low estimation of politics as merely protecting our self-interest. There is seemingly nothing grand or glorious in the world Locke envisions. He is the philosopher of the simple, acquisitive property owner. Among Locke's critics is Jean-Jacques Rousseau.

Jean-Jacques Rousseau: Popular Sovereignty Through the General Will

Jean-Jacques Rousseau (1712–1778) criticizes Locke's political philosophy. Rousseau continues to probe the problem of political obligation and to seek a more democratic solution. He asks: What principles of political right make government legitimate, "men being taken as they are and laws as they might be"?[12] "The problem," as he sees it, "is to find a form of association which will defend and protect with the whole common force the person and goods of each associate, and in which each, while uniting himself with all, may still obey himself alone, and remain as free, as before." Rousseau's solution is yet another version of the social contract: a unanimous agreement to associate under the **general will**. "Each of us puts his person and all his power under the supreme direction of the general will, and, in our corporate capacity, we receive each member as an indivisible part of the whole." This social contract also removes people from an inconvenient and inadequate state of nature (where they enjoy only natural liberty) and creates a moral civil society—with a unity, identity, life, and will of its own. In this society people have civil and moral liberty and better opportunity to fulfill themselves. The general will that guides their development is the constant will—the best, long-range will—of the sovereign people; it is the public good or public interest; and it is always right. In this way, sovereign authority becomes (1) legitimate, because it is based on unanimous agreement, not on force; (2) equitable, because it is common to all; (3) useful, because sovereign authority can have no other object than the common good; and (4) stable, because it is guaranteed by the public force and supreme power in the political community.

According to Rousseau, the general will works to the public advantage and is the public's best long-range interest. The general will does not include selfish, private interests. It resides in the majority, yet it is not necessarily identical with majority rule. It may be found by counting votes, yet it is not found simply in counting votes. It is the true will of all the people. The people are sovereign under the direction of the general will. Sovereignty is inalienable and indivisible, and it cannot be represented. Thus, the people cannot be separated from their sovereign power and they cannot allow representatives to make policy on their behalf. The sovereign people control their government's policy and personnel, its form, and its membership. The government merely executes the people's will. In this way the people remain free because obedience to self-prescribed law is liberty. Thus, Rousseau "rediscovers" the democratic political community and its role in advancing the fuller civil and moral liberty of those in the community. Only such a community is capable of the good political life.

Rousseau's political philosophy, too, has its proponents and opponents. Democrats applaud his endorsement of popular sovereignty and a fuller democracy. Advocates of the common good praise his conception of the general will as an idea that can transcend selfish, shortsighted interest and can bind us together in recognition of a public interest that makes fulfillment possible. Libertarians, on the other hand, worry about Rousseau's argument that we can be "forced to be free," that we can be required, under law, to do what is right. They see Rousseau as opening the door to dictatorship or to "totalitarian democracy." Political realists doubt whether Rousseau's concept of direct democracy is either desirable or feasible. Still others wonder if the good political life can be based on so nebulous a standard as the "general will." Edmund Burke, although he had a strong sense of community, did not share Rousseau's radical outlook.

Edmund Burke: Prescriptive Constitutional Government

Edmund Burke (1729–1797) asks whether a prescriptive or historical constitution, prudently interpreted, is the best means to a sane balance that will preserve the right values, principles, and institutions for the political community.[13] This is Burke's central question in the last quarter of the eighteenth century, a period that witnessed the outbreak of two great democratic revolutions—the American Revolution in 1775 and the French Revolution in 1789. Burke's "Old Whig" answer is a resounding yes. But to understand his answer (and his support of the American colonists, his hostility to the French Revolution, and his mixed attitude toward reform in Britain), it is necessary to understand what he means by "prescriptive constitution," "balance," "political community," and "prudence."

A prescriptive constitution, according to Burke, is a constitution—or way of political life—that is the historical choice of successive generations, the successful inheritance of those who have gone before, and the embodiment of the wisdom of the species over time. Such a prescriptive constitution has passed the "solid test of long experience." The British Constitution is one such constitution, which Burke sees as a fortress of genuine natural rights. Justice, private property, instruction in life, and consolation in death are the rights of human beings in and under a prescriptive constitution. Burke contrasts such real rights with the theoretical, abstract rights, such as liberty, equality, and fraternity, delineated in the French Declaration of the Rights of Man. These abstract rights of man did not take sound tradition into account. They ignored other values in society—peace and order, morality and religion, civil and social manners, and the need for a police power and for an effective and well-distributed revenue.

Burke heralds the British Constitution as a **balance of principles**—monarchic, aristocratic, and democratic. It is "a monarchy directed by laws," balanced by an aristocracy (which encompassed the nation's great hereditary wealth, dignity, and leadership), and controlled by the democracy, the "people at large" (in the House of Commons). Burke sees the British Constitution as a successful attempt "to unite private and public liberty with public force, order, peace, justice, and above all, the institutions formed for bestowing permanence and stability" on the nation through the ages. Balance, of course, does not rule out necessary change. Indeed, the British Constitution is based on the principle of progressive inclusion of all politically minded people in the life of the state and on the enlargement of liberty. Only radical innovation is to be avoided.

Burke views the state—the political community—as a high and noble association. It is not to be seen as temporary, perishable, or crassly utilitarian. Such a state deserves to be approached with reverence—even its defects should be viewed with awe and caution. "It is a partnership in all science; a partnership in all art; a partnership in every virtue, and in all perfection." The state is "a partnership not only between those who are living, but between those who are living, those who are dead, and those who are to be born."[14] The people must nevertheless interpret the prescriptive constitution prudently if they wish to achieve the good political life. Prudence, according to Burke, means giving attention to sound principles as well as to circumstances. The people must understand political actualities thoroughly and avoid dogmatic, abstract theorizing. Prudence also dictates that political actors must be aware that society is a very complex creation and that we have only limited understanding of how the various pieces fit together. The law of unintended consequences dictates that we exercise foresight and proceed cautiously when engaged in political reforms. Although they reject radical innovations, prudent people see the need for sensible change. In the case of the American colonies, for example, Burke is convinced that the abstract principle of parliamentary supremacy should not prevent Britain from conceding autonomous home rule to the colonies, thereby creating practical independence within the British Empire. This wise course of action is suggested by both his interpretation of the British Constitution and specific circumstances: the Atlantic Ocean that separates Britain from its American colonies; a flourishing Anglo-American trade; and America's "fierce spirit of liberty" (rooted in British notions of liberty, in popular colonial governments, and in the colonialists' "republican religion"). On the other hand, Burke opposes the French Revolution because he thinks the French revolutionaries are extremists in rejecting the old French Constitution and in ignoring the mandate of prudent statesmanship—to combine "an ability to improve" with a "disposition to preserve."

Burke can be viewed as the father of enlightened constitutional conservatism or an opponent of radical democracy. He makes a powerful case for the prescriptive constitution and for prudent statesmanship. His criticism of radical democratic theory is hard hitting, and he had a keen appreciation for the complexity of political life that often demands a cautious approach to reform. However, his political philosophy may seem too respectful of the status quo, not sufficiently aware of the need for more fundamental change.

Mary Wollstonecraft: Feminism, Education, and the Rights of Women

As the French embarked on their dramatic revolution that caused Burke such concern, many began to question all sorts of things that had previously been accepted largely without question. If society should begin to question why kings and aristocrats ruled, why not question why politics was a solely male activity. Mary Wollstonecraft (1759–1797) was one of those questioners, and in her writings, the foundation of modern feminism was born. Wollstonecraft was born in England and, though originally from a well-off family, her father's squandering of the family fortune led to her taking up various jobs as a governess and eventually a writer. She first came to fame when she published a striking attack on Burke's ideas in her essay *A Vindication of the Rights of Man*. She defended the French Revolution against Burke's condemnation and saw it as being a "glorious *chance* to obtain more virtue and happiness than hitherto blessed our globe." She also spoke for the wisdom of the common people, respected their humble origins, and derided custom and tradition, so dear to Burke, as oppressive. Politics should be about what is rational.

In this regard, Wollstonecraft is a preeminent example of Enlightenment thinking. The Enlightenment, which predated the French Revolution, was an intellectual movement across the Western world, which valued reason, science, believed in progress, toleration, and most of all human freedom. Enlightenment thinkers criticized absolute monarchy, tradition, superstition, and the dogmatic nature of religion. Major figures included Voltaire, David Hume, Adam Smith, Immanuel Kant, and Rousseau. Mary Wollstonecraft is every bit a part of the revolution in thinking these men started.

Her most important work is probably *A Vindication of the Rights of Women*. This work is full of powerful criticisms of other philosophers, most notably Rousseau, and for her belief in education. She first observes, in a very republican way, the problem of being dependent on others and thus lacking independence. Such dependence warps all—those who are dependent and those depended upon. From there, she proceeds to analyze the difficult position of women in European society. She writes,

> Women ought to endeavor to purify their heart; but can they do so when their uncultivated understanding makes them entirely dependent on their senses for employment and amusement, when no noble pursuits sets them above the little vanities of the day . . .[15]

Mary Wollstonecraft English, born Mary Wollstonecraft, was the forerunner of the modern feminist movement and a preeminent example of enlightenment thinking emerging in the nineteenth century.

Women are not by nature drawn to frivolous things but are made that way by the type of upbringing they are given. They have been taught to focus on beauty, fashion, and pleasure (Wollstonecraft's main focus was on middle- and upper-class women—as always many women, like men, spent their time focused on work just to get by.) The key is to give women access to proper and rational education.

"But I still insist, that not only the virtue, but knowledge of the two sexes should be the same in nature, if not in degree, and that women, considered not only as moral, but rational creatures, ought to endeavor to acquire human virtues (or perfections) by the same means as men, instead of being educated like a fanciful kind of half being. . . ."[16]

Wollstonecraft is offended not just as a woman constrained by the customs of society but because she believes it deforms all society. Like many republicans, she believed in virtue and in bettering people—men and women. However, the deformed education women receive hurts not only them but men, too. She writes, "The two sexes mutually corrupt and improve each other." In her day, such ideas appeared quite radical. Wollstonecraft took the political challenges of the day out of the public square and pushed them into the private sphere. At the same time, she urged her readers to see how the private world, where women were prominent in the home, influenced the public one. "Public spirit must be nurtured by private virtue," she observes. And virtue of men or women cannot be sustained by a vapid education. With a good education, women could have true knowledge that would enable them to be truly moral and worthy participants in public life.

Yet, Wollstonecraft is even more radical than this might seem. Today, the assumption is that women have access to education. She insists that women cannot be truly virtuous until they are, in some sense, independent of men. The results of such an education and the resulting independence of women would necessarily lead to a transformed world, and it is hard to predict exactly what that would look like. Truly independent women would be working, living, and loving with truly independent men, and since each sex influences each other, a changed women would result in a changed man. For Wollstonecraft, the Enlightenment meant not only adding new peoples to the mix of politics; it meant thinking on entirely new lines about what politics is. If she did not fully define what that exactly looked like, it was because it would be impossible to say. But she knew it would more likely result in healthier and happier people.

John Stuart Mill: Utilitarianism and Liberty

What principles of liberty and authority best guide the individual's and society's quests for happiness through fulfillment? The answer of John Stuart Mill (1806–1873) provides one influential response. Mill bases his liberal political philosophy on several assertions.

Although recognizing its weaknesses, Mill adheres to **utilitarianism**, the "creed which accepts as the foundation of morals 'utility' or the 'greatest happiness principle.'" This creed "holds that actions are right in proportion as they tend to promote happiness; wrong as they tend to produce the reverse of happiness. By happiness is intended pleasure and the absence of pain; by unhappiness, pain and the privation of pleasure."[17]

Mill insists on a noble interpretation of the utilitarian standard. He outlines a hierarchy of pleasures and absorbs traditional concepts of justice and virtue. According to Mill, "pleasures of the intellect, of the feeling and imagination, and of the moral sentiments" rate more highly than mere sensation or "the animal appetites": "It is better to be a human being dissatisfied than a pig satisfied; better to be Socrates dissatisfied than a fool satisfied." Superior pleasures should be determined on the basis of the "decided preference" of knowledgeable people of taste and discernment. Mill clearly prefers the pleasures of the cultivated mind interested in science, art, poetry, history, and social science. He sees humankind as slowly progressing in its battle against evils of life such as indigence, disease, unkindness, and worthlessness. He sees a harmony between the individual's interest and the public interest. He is convinced that the utilitarian standard will, in time,

MILL'S LOGIC; OR, FRANCHISE FOR FEMALES.
" PRAY CLEAR THE WAY, THERE, FOR THESE—A—PERSONS."

discredit the false "aristocracies of color, race, and sex," as it has already discredited the "injustice and tyranny" of slavery and serfdom.

John Stuart Mill was one of the great defenders of individual freedom, and his most famous work, *On Liberty*, was published in 1859. Mill, who was also an early feminist, wrote a defense of women's rights in "The Subjection of Women" (1869). He always maintained that many of his ideas came from his wife, Harriet Taylor.

Mill endorses representative, constitutional government because of the way it melds liberty and authority. Such a government would permit popular control of the legislature, legislative (or parliamentary) control of the executive, and strong and skilled executive leadership. Mill favors as much popular participation as possible. "But since all cannot, in a community exceeding a single small town, participate personally in any but some very minor portions of the public business, it follows that the ideal type of a perfect government must be representative."[18] The educated and publicly spirited minority should be given a prominent voice in parliament through a system of proportional representation and plural voting.

Liberty, for Mill, is the means to happiness through fulfillment. In *On Liberty*, Mill explores the nature and limits of power—particularly the power that society can legitimately exercise over the individual. His key principle is "that the sole end for which mankind are warranted, individually or collectively, in interfering with the liberty of action of any of their number is self-protection." Mill maintains that "the only purpose for which power can be rightfully exercised over any member of a civilized community, against his will, is to prevent harm to others." Mill is not convinced that an individual's "own good, either physical or moral," is a sufficient reason for interfering with his or her liberty. In brief, a person is to be free in connection with his or her "self-regarding action." Society can interfere only when the individual's action is harmfully "other-regarding." Consequently, Mill defines the sphere of human liberty as that sphere wherein society, as distinct from the individual, has only an indirect interest. He singles out three fields of human liberty: "the inward domain of consciousness" (liberty of belief, thought, and feeling; and freedom of speech, press, and opinion); "liberty of tastes and pursuits"; and "liberty of combinations" (or associations).

Mill seeks a **modified laissez-faire political economy**—that is, an economy without government intervention, one compatible with liberty, the satisfaction of human needs, and the advancement of individual and social happiness. He opposes monopoly and dislikes governmental interference. But he is not blind to the need for sensible regulation of industry to protect workers' health, safety, and welfare. (Here, Mill partly opens the door to the modern welfare state.) In successive editions of *On Political Economy*, he becomes more willing to modify a strict laissez-faire economic system. He moves toward allowing workers greater voice and control, especially through cooperative ventures. (Here, he opens the door slightly to democratic socialism.)

Mill is by no means a radical democrat. He opposes giving the suffrage to the "poorest and rudest class of labourers." Nonetheless, in "The Subjection of Women" (strongly influenced by his wife, Harriet Taylor Mill), he writes a powerful essay on behalf of greater freedom for women. Indeed, Mill can fairly be called one of the most eloquent nineteenth-century sponsors of women's liberation. He argues that happiness for individual women cannot be achieved unless they are given greater opportunity, recognition, suffrage, and equal education—in a word, true equality. The happiness of society depends on women being more fully admitted into the life of the nation. Mill emphatically insists "that the principle which regulates the existing social relations between the two sexes—the legal subordination of one sex to the other—is wrong in itself, and now one of the chief hindrances to human improvement; and that it ought to be replaced by a principle of perfect equality, admitting no power or privilege on the one side, nor disability on the other."[19]

Modern liberal democracy embodies a great many of Mill's principles: his powerful argument on behalf of liberty of thought and discussion, his utilitarian concern for happiness, his preference for representative government, his growing attention to the welfare of workers, and his bold advocacy of women's liberation. Yet his political philosophy still provokes a number of disturbing questions. Is utilitarianism strong enough to protect constitutional democracy, human liberty, and the least free? Is Mill's position too elitist, too aristocratic for the modern world? Does he really come to grips with worker alienation and capitalist abuses? For more radical ideas about liberty and emancipation, we turn to Karl Marx.

Karl Marx: Universal Human Emancipation via Communism

How can universal human emancipation be achieved? This is the radical question posed by Karl Marx (1813–1883).[20] His answer is no less radical: via the proletarian—or communist—revolution. Marx's philosophy is explored in greater depth in Chapter 7; however, it is appropriate to briefly summarize the key points of his views about politics in this chapter because Marx is an important contributor to debates about what the good life means.

First, Marx has a vision for humanity that values human freedom. Freedom will not be complete until the most alienated and oppressed—the workers—have overthrown "all the conditions" that keep people "abased, enslaved, abandoned, contemptible." Marx, in *The Economic and Philosophic Manuscripts*, sees this problem as arising from people's estrangement from what they produce, from their work; this contributes to most people's alienation from their own humanity and their fellow human beings. Human beings by nature like to work and create the world around them. Marx was actually very impressed by the incredible transformative power of capitalism. Yet, this process of producing the civilized world has become oppressive. His vision of the good life is predicated on liberating people from oppression and letting them work on endeavors for which they want to work.

Second, Marx believes that this challenge is best overcome by understanding the economic conditions of society. Thus, he spends an enormous amount of time analyzing capitalism and explaining how it exploits workers—leading to their alienation and limiting human freedom. Capitalists control the means of production, and furthermore, the state, religion, law, and ethics all reflect the values and beliefs of those capitalists who control the world. If the world is viewed in this light, political equality and economic equality become central goals in creating a world in which human beings are free.

Finally, although Marx is persuaded that capitalism's own weaknesses—its lust for profits at the expense of the worker and its vulnerability to economic crisis—create the conditions for its inevitable downfall, to achieve the good communist society, a revolutionary reconstruction of society is necessary. (Capitalism also contributes to this process by creating the working class that will eventually rise up in revolution.) The old bourgeois capitalist order must be destroyed and replaced by a communist order based on worker control of the means of production and exchange. There will be a revolution that occurs in stages: first, the revolutionary overthrow of capitalism; then, the interim "democratic" dictatorship of the proletariat; next, the stage of socialism; and finally, communism. Peaceful reform is not likely to achieve communism; however, Marx did not preclude the possibility of a peaceful transformation of society. He says relatively little about what communism will look like; however, we can get some glimpse of what it means and appreciate its radical egalitarianism by recalling the communist motto: "From each according to his ability, to each according to his needs." The future of communism will be a place in which people are liberated from subjugation and can achieve their true desires in a just world of free workers.

Marx's contribution to modern political thought was to systematically analyze the transformative power of capitalism; provide a compelling vision of an egalitarian society; sketch a theory of history that emphasized materialism; and develop an alluring theory of revolutionary action. To his critics, Marx fails to understand human nature and is too utopian in his call for a classless society. Many others fault his materialist theory of life—saying such a theory places too much emphasis on the economic and physical forces that shape our lives and fails to appreciate the transcendent—God, spirit—in history. Still others believe that Marx failed to appreciate capitalism's ability to adapt to new conditions, and they reject Marx's emphasis on a violent revolution to achieve a better society.

CONTEMPORARY POLITICAL PHILOSOPHY

Contemporary political philosophy, as it becomes intertwined with political ideology, is examined more fully in the following chapters. Here only a few preliminary observations are in order.

First, contemporary political philosophy can only be understood as an outgrowth of the great tradition that we have attempted to sample in the preceding pages. Contemporary political philosophers are deeply versed in the classic tradition. In addressing modern problems and circumstances, they draw inspiration from that tradition. In doing so they often attempt to present a vision of the good political life that, as we have tried to suggest, must deal with political actualities and prudential judgments as well as with ideals.

Second, the great tradition of political philosophy has clearly influenced not only political philosophers but also those who are called political scientists. William T. Bluhm has persuasively argued that "the classic theories furnish the foundations of nearly all the work which is being done today in the field of politics, work which is as vital and varied as the constellation of the classics."[21]

Third, new and creative voices in political philosophy must always be heard. Political philosophers may try to retain the best in the classical and modern tradition while they address the unique problems of the twenty-first century. Indeed, many argue that political philosophy is exactly this ongoing dialogue between our understanding of past thinkers and our ability to think creatively about new problems and challenges.

Fourth, as important as the history of political philosophy is we cannot lose sight of the way many have felt oppressed by that tradition. Numerous current political philosophers are troubled by the way that tradition makes certain unstated assumptions (man should rule or politics is about manly virtu) or don't ask important questions (what if increasing production ruins the planet). Thus, feminism is now one of the most important voices in political philosophical debates. Concerns about nature and how human being live in a world of scarce resources and sustain civilization have given rise to environmental political philosophy. Sometimes, these writers find inspiration from the great thinkers of the past—what if we take seriously Plato's idea of philosopher queens? Other times they react against past philosophers—why did Machiavelli write the "because fortune is a woman, and if you want to control her, it is necessary to treat her roughly."[22] Does Machiavelli's political philosophy demand that man rule? But even this more critical response to the tradition of political philosophy takes seriously the ideas of people like Plato, Aristotle, Machiavelli, or Marx.

The great political philosophers most often wrote in the heat of crisis. Creative political philosophy was born out of real difficulties faced by real political actors and communities. As we assess the contemporary scene, we should be open to the creative work of today's political philosophers and their efforts to address our difficult problems in the light of a great tradition.

CONCLUSION

And so, we return to our guiding question in this chapter: How have the great political philosophers contributed to the difficult quest for the good life and a fuller understanding of politics? They offer critically examined visions of the good life. They force us, whether we agree or disagree, to confront political ideals, political actualities, and prudent judgments. They require us to think through the standards we would employ: justice, the common good, order, happiness, individual fulfillment, liberty, equality, and fraternity.

These political standards are also significant for empirical inquiry. They lead us to examine the use and abuse of power, the proper functioning of institutions, and the consequences of operative ideals. They encourage us to give normative meaning to empirical measurements so that, by assessing relevant facts, we can determine whether we are politically healthy. In this way we can sensibly appraise data about war and peace, poverty and prosperity, slavery and freedom, and inequality and equality. Finally, determining standards for the good political life leads to prudent judgment, which is what we also call political wisdom.

Means can be truly prudent only if they are humanely and rationally calculated to achieve good ends. Guided by critically understood standards of the good political life, we can assess the character of political behavior, politics, and institutions and determine whether they are wise or foolish, feasible or infeasible. The political philosopher, in exploring the good political life, thus facilitates the political scientist's three major tasks—normative recommendation, empirical inquiry, and prudential judgment.

SUGGESTED READINGS

To explore the contributions of the great political philosophers to the good life and to a fuller understanding of politics, there is absolutely no substitute for reading their original writings. They have endured for good reasons. Also see the following:

Arendt, Hannah. *The Human Condition*. Chicago: University of Chicago Press, 1958. A thoughtful attempt to analyze how people work and act together politically. Suffused with reflections about many of the writers discussed in this chapter.

Blackburn, Simon. *Plato's Republic*. New York: Grove Press, 2006. From one of the most distinguished contemporary philosophers, offers a thoughtful interpretation of the most important book of political philosophy.

Brecht, Arnold. *Political Theory: The Foundations of Twentieth-Century Political Thought*. Princeton, NJ: Princeton University Press, 1959. Holds that scientific political theory can contribute to the defense of the good life, enlarge our knowledge of politics, and deepen our "wisdom-of-action" in political affairs. But it cannot establish the absolute validity of ultimate standards.

Dworkin, Ronald. *Sovereign Virtue: The Theory and Practice of Equality*. Cambridge, MA: Harvard University Press, 2000. Well-known and respected political and legal theorist's interpretation of the importance of equality in a democratic and liberal state.

Flathman, Richard, ed. *Concepts in Social and Political Theory*. New York: Macmillan, 1973. A helpful, intelligent introduction to the analytic, linguistic, and conceptual approach to political and social philosophy.

Oakshott, Michael. *Rationalism in Politics*. Indianapolis, IN: Liberty Press, 1991. A classic collection of essays by the foremost conservative political philosopher of the twentieth century.

Rawls, John. *A Theory of Justice*. Cambridge, MA: Harvard University Press, 1971. A highly influential argument on behalf of justice as fairness.

Riemer, Neal. *Creative Breakthroughs in Politics*. Westport, CT: Praeger, 1996. Explores two genuine historical breakthroughs (Roger Williams and James Madison), two spurious breakthroughs (John C. Calhoun and Karl Marx), a contemporary breakthrough still in progress (European Union), and a proposed future breakthrough.

Ryan, Alan. *On Politics: A History of Political Thought*. New York: Norton, 2012. A two-volume work that covers the entire span of Western political thought from Herodotus to the contemporary world written by one of the leading political theorists of the past few decades.

Sabine, George. *A History of Political Theory*. New York: Holt, 1937. A balanced, critical, and humane history, even though written from the perspective of "social relativism."

Tinder, Glenn. *The Political Meaning of Christianity: An Interpretation*. Baton Rouge: Louisiana State University Press, 1989. Concerned with Christianity's contribution to civility via the exaltation of the individual, agape, prophetic hope, liberty, and social transformation.

Wolin, Sheldon. *Politics and Vision*. Boston: Little, Brown, 2004. An influential look at the great tradition of political theory and its relevance to our contemporary concerns.

Woodruff, Paul. *First Democracy*. Oxford, UK: Oxford University Press, 2005. A fascinating account of the main ideas and practices that defined ancient Greek democracy.

GLOSSARY TERMS

aristocracy (p. 110)
balance of principles (p. 124)
constitution (p. 112)
democracy (p. 110)
divine law (p. 115)
eternal law (p. 115)
general will (p. 122)

human law (p. 115)
law (p. 115)
modified laissez-faire political
  economy (p. 127)
natural law (p. 115)
oligarchy (p. 110)
polis (p. 110)

polity (p. 111)
social contract (p. 120)
timocracy (p. 110)
tyranny (p. 110)
utilitarianism (p. 126)

NOTES

1. Plato, *The Republic*, trans. Benjamin Jowett (Garden City, NY: Doubleday, Anchor, 1973).

2. Aristotle, *Politics*, trans. Benjamin Jowett (New York: Random House, Modern Library, 1943), 168–169.

3. Augustine, *The City of God*, in *Readings in Political Philosophy*, ed. Francis W. Coker (New York: Macmillan, 1946), 159.

4. Thomas Aquinas, *Commentary on the Nicomachean Ethics*, in *Theories of the Political System*, ed. William T. Bluhm (Englewood Cliffs, NJ: Prentice Hall, 1965), 196.

5. *Summa Theologica* (1265–1273), I–II, 90.4, in *The Basic Writings of St. Thomas Aquinas*, ed. Anton C. Pegis (New York: Macmillan, 1946), 200.

6. Thomas Aquinas, *Of the Rule of Princes* (1266), quoted in Coker, *Readings*, 200.

7. Niccolo Machiavelli, *The Prince*, trans. Russell Price, edited by Quentin Skinner (Cambridge, MA: Cambridge University Press, 2001), Chapter 17, p. 59.

8. See Niccolò Machiavelli, *The Discourses*, trans. Luigi Ricci and rev. E. R. P. Vincent, in *The Prince and the Discourses* (New York: Random House, Modern Library, 1940).

9. Machiavelli, *The Prince*, Chapter 15, p. 54.

10. Thomas Hobbes, *Leviathan* (New York: Dutton, 1943), 64–65.

11. John Locke, *Second Treatise on Civil Government* (1690). A good critical edition is Peter Laslett's *John Locke: Two Treatises of Government* (Cambridge, MA: Cambridge University Press, 1960).

12. Jean-Jacques Rousseau, *The Social Contract* (1762; repr., New York: Dutton, 1946), 1.

13. See, for example, Edmund Burke, "Reform of Representation in the House of Commons," 1782, in Burke's *Politics: Selected Writings and Speeches on Reform, Revolution, and War*, ed. Ross J. S. Hoffman and Paul Levack (New York: Knopf, 1949). See also Burke, *Reflections on the Revolution in France* (1790) in *The Works of the Right Honorable Edmund Burke*, vol. 3 (Boston: Little, Brown, 1869), 3; and *An Appeal from the New to the Old Whigs* (1791) and "On Conciliation with the American Colonies" (1787) in *Orations and Essays* (New York: Appleton, 1900).

14. Burke, *Reflections*, 359.

15. Mary Wollstonecraft, *A vindication of the Rights of Women*. (New York: Norton,1988), p. 29

16. Ibid., p. 39.

17. John Stuart Mill, *Utilitarianism* (New York: Liberal Arts Press, 1957), 10.

18. John Stuart Mill, "Considerations on Representative Government" (1861), in *On Liberty, Representative Government, the Subjection of Women* (London: Oxford University Press, 1946), 198.

19. Mill, "The Subjection of Women," in *On Liberty*, 427.

20. Of particular value here is Robert C. Tucker, ed., *The Marx-Engels Reader* (New York: Norton, 1971).

21. William T. Bluhm, *Theories of the Political System* (Englewood Cliffs, NJ: Prentice Hall, 1965), preface, vi.

22. Machiavelli, *The Prince*, Chapter 25, p. 87.

A woman votes in Tunisia's 2017 municipal
election, the first since the 2011 revolution.

Middleeastmonitor.com

6

LIBERAL DEMOCRACY

Beginning with this chapter and continuing into the next, we identify and try to clarify the major ideologies that have traditionally dominated contemporary politics—liberal democracy, democratic socialism, and communism. We thus shift from the classical political philosophers and their conceptions of the good political life to modern politics and its guiding views of the good life in the contemporary world.

Political ideologies are the beliefs and practices that guide political actors in political communities. These ideologies reflect the underlying vision of political actors, and studying the ideals that inspire political leaders often illuminates political practice. These ideals—of course—are not always fully achieved, but they help explain the purposes, principles, and rules of politics. Studying ideologies allows us to examine not only what political actors say they *ought to do* but what they actually *do* as well. In addition to identifying and clarifying ideologies, we will address the strengths and weaknesses of political ideologies such as liberal democracy, democratic socialism, and communism by considering them in light of the ideals of the good life advanced by the great political philosophers discussed in earlier chapters.

Our goals in Chapters 6 and 7 are to help readers (1) critically explore the good political life in contemporary politics; (2) locate themselves on the modern political spectrum (left, center, or right; radical, liberal, conservative, or reactionary); (3) understand the reasons for their political positions; and (4) set the stage, through a critical exploration of the meaning of the good political life, for the fuller analysis of comparative politics in Part III and for the more thorough considerations of public policy in Part IV.

What are the strengths and weaknesses of liberal democracy? This is the central question of Chapter 6. In attempting to

Chapter Objectives

After studying this chapter, you will be able to do the following:

1. Summarize the major ideals that define liberal democracy.

2. Explain the historical sources for liberal democracy.

3. Analyze the relationship between liberalism, capitalism, and democracy.

4. Examine the way liberalism as evolved over the years.

5. Critique the versions of liberal democracy that exist today.

answer it, our focus rests primarily on the United States. First, we examine the main ideas that define liberal democracy; next, we analyze its historical roots; we then weigh its strengths and weaknesses; finally, we assess its current liberal and conservative variations.

TOWARD A DEFINITION OF LIBERAL DEMOCRACY

To many readers, this idea that the United States is a liberal democracy might sound confusing. Are there not many conservatives in the United States? Couldn't you call it a conservative democracy? In these chapters on political philosophy, it is important to think and read like a political philosopher. And, in the history of political philosophy, liberal has a somewhat different meaning than in the everyday way citizens talk about liberals and conservatives. Many, if not most, ideas that are associated with what political philosophers call liberal democracy are championed by people who call themselves liberal or conservative in arguing about day-to-day politics concerning Democrats and Republicans. Philosophical liberalism is, thus, greater than the particular way people talk about liberal in everyday politics. (At the end of the chapter, we have a section that discusses conservatism as a distinct philosophy of politics.) The ideal of **liberal democracy**—a constitutional government characterized by popular rule, protection of basic rights, and political and economic competition—is open to continual reinterpretation, there are a number of constants that animate this ideology. As evidenced in its name, liberal democracy embodies two great ideals.[1] The *liberal* ingredients include constitutionalism, protection of basic rights—including the right of private property—political and economic competition, and free choice both at the ballot box and in the marketplace. The *democratic* ingredients include popular rule, freedom, and **equality**.

As an ideology, usually associated with the Democratic Party in the United States, **liberalism** today is a political ideology that favors government intervention in the interest of public welfare, social justice, and fair play. In some ways, what is called conservatism in the United States is really a continuation of an earlier understanding of liberalism, whereby a **laissez-faire** economic approach demanded minimal government interference in the economy. What is called liberalism today represents an evolution of that earlier ideal that actually demands government action to foster freedom and equality. The U.S. Constitution has been interpreted to permit this change. Under either guise, liberalism has always recognized a common good. What has often been at issue is the meaning of that common good and the means to achieve it. Yet, as hard as it is to believe for many Americans, there is a sense in which contemporary American **liberals** and **conservatives** share a common set of concerns that unites them under the broader heading of liberal democracy as defined in this chapter.

The democratic ideals of "freedom" and "equality" are complex and their meanings open to debate and change as well. For example, the call for greater popular participation in politics remains persistent among radical liberal democrats; it is highly unlikely, though, that Americans today will abandon **representative government**—the system by which representative leadership the electorate selected acts on behalf of the citizenry—and move toward any form of **direct democracy**—the system by which citizens vote directly on matters of public policy instead of electing representatives, as once embodied in the seventeenth-century New England town meeting so decisively rooted in the American past.

Combining the ideals of liberalism and democracy helps us comprehend the guiding liberal democratic vision. Such a vision calls for the freest and fullest possible realization of individual freedom within the framework of the common good. Individuals must have the opportunity, within justifiable limitations, to develop the best in themselves. The preamble to the Constitution captures many of the objectives of a liberal democracy when it states that the United States will "establish justice, insure domestic tranquility, provide for the common defense, promote the general welfare, and secure the blessings of liberty." **Liberty**, although a contested concept, can be understood as the right of an individual to act un-coerced by government and to be free from government-imposed unlawful or arbitrary control. The liberal democratic vision is not a single vision; it is a pluralistic vision providing for justice as well as order and for the general welfare as well as liberty. Because many persons, groups, and interests seek fulfillment, a balance must be struck in a highly diverse political community.

The most influential school of liberal democratic thought in contemporary America—the **pluralist school** or **pluralism**—maintains that this balance can best be achieved through a constitutional system of representative democracy, with the help of skillful leaders and resourceful political parties, with the recognition that a rough approximation of the public interest emerges from the clash of contending interests, and in accord with policies that advance the general welfare.

THE IDEALS OF LIBERAL DEMOCRACY

Liberal democrats want their political ideals to be reflected in actual political practice. They endorse pluralism because society includes many interests seeking to protect and advance themselves. The struggles of these contending interests constitute the raw material of politics. Struggles are inevitable because they are rooted in liberty and diversity. Government regulates these struggles on behalf of freedom and the common good.

Operative Ideals

But, liberal democrats insist, government itself must be controlled and politics kept honest, and the struggle for power must be kept within bounds. This struggle must be consistent with justice, domestic tranquility, the common defense, the general welfare, and liberty—it must be civilized. Politics contributes to this civilizing process, which, at its best, allows fuller individual realization. The civilizing process requires fair rules and decent results in politics. Contending interests must accommodate each other. Basic human needs must be satisfied, and there must be opportunities for social, economic, aesthetic, and spiritual enrichment. To advance their vision, liberal democrats support the following operative ideals.

Popular Government. Popular rule requires that the people make political judgments. They must be free to debate and to select among competing leaders, parties, and broad policies. To make choices, the people must enjoy **civil liberties**, rights that permit them to evaluate how the government operates and assess the character and performance of parties and political leaders. Thus, the liberal democratic system is committed to civil liberties and universal suffrage. The system is also committed to an informed and vigilant public opinion, to a diligent and responsible press, to a plurality of contending interests able to articulate their claims, and to competitive parties. Such elements protect the people's vital interests and help fulfill their needs and aspirations.

Rights-Respecting Government. Basic democratic rights are both political and nonpolitical. As we have seen, freedom of speech, press, and assembly, as well as the right to vote, are clearly political and are intimately related to popular rule. People cannot shape public policy unless they can speak, read, and write about public issues; assemble and organize in political parties or other interest groups; and exert political pressure through the vote. They need these rights to rule indirectly and to control the government.

Other freedoms and basic rights are nonpolitical, but they are equally vital to liberal democracy. These religious, cultural, economic, and social rights include, for example, the right to worship according to the dictates of conscience; the right to think one's own thoughts; the right to express one's intellectual, artistic, and scientific ideas; the right to own property; the right to find a job of one's choice; and the right to marry and have children. Of course, this idea of rights is subject to constant debate. Take the right to marry, for instance. Should it be extended to gay couples as is now the case in the United States? There is, then, a realm of activity that must be beyond governmental reach and should be safeguarded by a constitutional government that grants, prohibits, and restricts power.

Constitutional Government. In the liberal democrat's preferred system of constitutional politics, power is granted to government, but it is also limited. Thus, the constitutional rules of the game establish what government can and cannot do and how those with power are to act.

Some powers, such as the powers to tax, to spend on behalf of the general welfare, and to regulate commerce, may be expressly granted. Other powers may be granted if necessary and proper to carry out expressly granted power. Limits on governmental power—explicit prohibitions—exclude government from entering areas such as religion and thought. But even when exercising its legitimate powers, government cannot act arbitrarily; it must follow **due process**—a right that forbids illegal and arbitrary governmental action—to ensure the protection of life, liberty, and property.

Moreover, because of the fear of unrestrained and arbitrary power in the United States, power is divided and shared. The American ideal of constitutional government puts the concept of balance to work in several ways: (1) a balance of governmental organs (in the national government)—two branches of Congress, a president, a Supreme Court; (2) a balance of geographical units (ensured by federalism)—the national government, the fifty states, and the District of Columbia; and (3) a balance of social, economic, and political forces.

Representative Government. Liberal democrats favor representative government because they believe it is the realistic way for the people to govern. Extensive direct democracy—citizens voting directly about policy—is not feasible. In a democratic and constitutional system, the electorate usually chooses representatives with the organizing help of political parties. Governmental leadership is determined, directly or indirectly, by majority or plurality decision.

But what does representative government really mean in liberal democratic theory?[2] Since modern politics occurs in large nation-states, it is difficult to imagine how democracy could function without some form of representation (although there are institutions, such as the referendum and the initiative, in which the people do engage in some form of direct democratic rule). However, the idea of representation is a complicated one. What does it mean when a representative acts? What is he or she representing? Some believe that the representative is simply a *delegate* who should strive to reflect the will of the people in the district. Yet, this does not fully answer the question of what a representative does because it is not necessarily easy to know what the people want. Furthermore, should a representative represent all the people in her district, or just the majority who voted for her? Moreover, there are some liberal democrats who champion a second idea of representation that views the representative not as a delegate but as a *trustee* who uses his best judgment, regardless of the views of the district, to promote the good of the nation as a whole. Finally, most politicians act within some established party system. This means, according to some liberal democrats, that representatives must balance the needs of their districts, their own conscience and judgment about politics, and the demands made on them by party leaders.

Responsible Government. Responsibility in a liberal democracy has several interrelated meanings. Following is a brief overview of these meanings:

1. *Liberal democratic government should be accountable to the people from whom it derives its power.* The way accountability functions varies from country to country. In the United States, the government is complex with nationally elected officials representing districts (the U.S. House of Representatives), states (the Senate), and the nation as a whole (the president). By way of contrast, in Great Britain the government is directly answerable to a majority party or a coalition of parties in the House of Commons and is indirectly answerable to an electoral majority or plurality in the country.

2. *Liberal democratic government should be responsible to political parties.* Parties are responsible for putting candidates and choices before the people, helping to elect a president, ensuring a majority in Congress, and in general facilitating decision-making and public policy. As such, political parties are an integral component of liberal democracy.

3. *Liberal democratic government should be responsible to the Constitution and to the laws and regulations made under the Constitution.* Government may be held accountable if it violates its own operating rules.

4. *Liberal democratic government should be answerable to an authority higher than the people or the Constitution.* Government may be answerable to God, to natural law, or to conscience (as it reflects a higher authority).

5. *Liberal democratic government should adhere to professional standards of conduct and administration.* Those in government—whether they be president, members of Congress, members of the Supreme Court, or millions of bureaucrats—must act in accordance with principles and standards established by their peers, past and present, in and out of government.

In liberal democratic politics, the effort is made to ensure governmental responsibility to "rules of the game" through various means of accountability: elections, public opinion, a free press, party discipline, interest group pressures, an independent judiciary, legislative and administrative investigation, impeachment, and administrative supervision.

General Welfare Government. Modern government in the United States is clearly committed to the idea of advancing the general welfare. As a liberal democratic operative ideal, this means that minimal needs—safety, civil liberties, income, food, housing, health, education—should be satisfied through the democratic process and in a caring and compassionate community. Although the notion of what constitutes "minimal" needs can be debated, liberal democracy has a fervent belief that politics should foster the conditions in which human beings can flourish. The liberal democratic nation stands ready to protect these needs, indirectly and directly, when private organs (the family, the church, and charitable organizations) and **state** and local governments cannot do so. Debate rages, however, on the desirable extent and character of such help.

We should be able to use the foregoing operative ideals to determine whether a nation is a liberal democracy. Affirmative answers to the following key questions characterize a liberal democracy:

KEY QUESTIONS

1. Do most people really have the opportunity, by means of genuinely free elections, to select the people and policies that will govern the nation? Is the government truly based on the consent of the governed?

2. Do the people enjoy the right to speak, write, publish, worship, and assemble freely in order to criticize the government, parties, and leaders in power?

3. Is there at least one independent opposition political party or coalition that is realistically able to supplant the governing leadership if, in a free election, the people turn the incumbents out?

4. Are people protected against the kind of arbitrary and unreasonable action by government that would deprive them of life, liberty, and property without due process of law?

5. Is the state's role limited to certain legitimate and necessary public functions, or does the state dominate the cultural and social life of the community? Is the state, for example, forbidden to dictate which books to read, which plays to see, which radio and television programs to tune in, and which clubs and organizations to join?

6. Is the state willing and able to enhance the physical and environmental safety of its citizens, guard their civil liberties, ensure their minimal income, assist the unemployed, feed and house the needy, enhance health care, and facilitate education? (In other words, is the state willing to advance its people's minimal welfare needs?)

Where did this list of liberal democratic ideals come from? In the following section, we examine the sources; in doing so, we will be in a better position to understand the complexity of these liberal democratic ideals and see how variations are possible.

THE SOURCES OF LIBERAL DEMOCRACY

Political ideologies have a historical life and development, and political ideals and their implementation are significantly influenced by events. Contemporary conceptions of the good life did not emerge full-blown. Many strands have entered into the political ideology known as liberal democracy. Although its roots—in theory and practice—are old, its flowering (despite great growth in the late eighteenth and nineteenth centuries) is a mid-twentieth-century phenomenon.

The Greek Heritage of Democracy. The word *democracy* comes from the Greek words *demos*, meaning "the people," and *krateia*, meaning "rule" or "government." Hence, democracy means "the people's rule." Aristotle understood democracy as government by the many poor, who governed in their own class interest and favored freedom and equality. Democracy meant the rule of the less wealthy and less educated citizen-masses in contrast to that of the plutocratic and aristocratic classes. But democracy in the Greek sense was not constitutional in the modern sense: It lacked effective and regularized restraints on those who wielded power. Moreover, Greek democracy excluded women and slaves from the suffrage. Nonetheless, the Greek democratic ideal did eventually stimulate the imagination of Western Europe. Pericles, a popular Athenian leader, in his great "Funeral Oration," gave a famous accounting of what democracy means when he said it included equal justice, excellence, opportunity, public reverence for the laws, citizen involvement in public affairs, and sound democratic judgment. Although Athenian democracy was incomplete, and to its critics unstable, Pericles's conception perpetuated a noble ideal.

Christian Theology and Roman Republicanism. By insisting on absolute freedom to worship God, Christians began a development that was to culminate, first theoretically and later practically, in constitutional protections against governmental interference with religious worship and in constitutional limitations on arbitrary political power. At first, Christians worried about their right to worship God. However, over centuries this led to a general belief that all people had a right to worship God as they saw fit. People must be free to worship God. Moreover, all men and women are equal under God; they are brothers and sisters under a common deity. Both Christian theology and Stoic philosophy emphasized equality—a concept crucial to liberal democracy in that it emphasizes equal political and social rights or the condition of being neither superior nor inferior. Of course, Christianity's attitude toward women has varied in its accepted practices. Yet, at its heart, Christianity emphasized the equality of all people before God. However, it took a long time for moral equality to become translated into political, social, and economic equality. Slavery characterized the Roman period and was, we must remember, not abolished in the United States until 1865.

The Romans made a twofold contribution. They helped keep alive, at least in theory, the concept of **popular sovereignty**—republican, or popular, rule—and they broadened the concept of citizenship. For the Greeks, all foreigners were barbarians and were excluded from citizenship. The Romans, however, eventually extended citizenship, which brought with it the protection of Roman law, to all who came within the jurisdiction of their empire, whether Roman, Greek, Christian, or Jewish.

Medieval Europe. Constitutional ideas, crucial to the evolution of liberal democracy, were current in medieval political theory. Almost all theorists contended that political rule must be just and in the interest of the people. No earthly ruler was absolute. The theorists insisted that princes (rulers) follow the precepts of a higher law: God's law or natural (moral) law, which could be known by humans possessed of "right reason." Even if political practice in the medieval world fell considerably short of modern canons of democratic and constitutional governance, the notion of limitations of rule by the higher law and God was an invaluable contribution to the development of liberal democratic ideals.

The Protestant Reformation. Martin Luther and John Calvin, the great Protestant reformers, were not modern liberal democrats. In most respects, they shared a medieval Christian outlook about politics. Although they believed in a higher law, they still took a dim view of popular resistance to political tyrants. Nonetheless, their revolt against the Roman Catholic Church, and some of their ideas, set the political and intellectual scene for the emergence of constitutional ideas crucial to liberal democracy. Of special importance were Luther's idea of the freedom of individuals to find God on their own and Calvin's concept of the legitimacy, in very limited cases, of resistance to political rulers by certain magistrates.

The American Republic: The First Great Democratic Experiment. The American Revolution ushered in the world's first large modern republic. Building on Lockean constitutional principles (see Chapter 5), on colonial experience in self-government, and on a physical environment that favored widespread possession of property, the Americans made important contributions to the eventual development of liberal democracy. Americans also drew on the republican tradition. As noted previously, this tradition has roots that stretch back to Rome and was an important aspect of the work of such writers as Niccolò Machiavelli (see Chapter 5) and James Harrington (see Chapter 4). **Republicanism** is a highly contested term, but it has always included some notion of constitutional rule by the many. Despite the property qualifications (actually relatively modest) that prevailed in most states in 1787 and the fact that African Americans, Native Americans, and women were excluded from the ballot and denied other freedoms, the Americans affirmed their general belief in popular rule and the protection of basic rights.

Both the logic of republican, or democratic, theory and the pressure of disenfranchised groups contributed to a growing movement to enlarge the suffrage and expand basic freedoms. In time, the commitment to liberty and equality made slavery unacceptable, revealed the racist treatment of Native Americans, and highlighted sexist discrimination against women. In addition, it underscored the exploitation of workers, the often-perilous economic situation of farmers, and the miserable lot of the poor. Of course, even if the adoption of these ideas was slow to develop and progress was uneven, the idea of popular rule and freedom for all people became the ideal.

The French Revolution of 1789 and Liberal Democracy in Europe. Although the British had pioneered constitutional and representative government, it was the French Revolution of 1789 that most dramatically challenged political absolutism and popularized democratic ideas throughout the European continent. The inspiring motto of the French Revolution, "Liberty, Equality, Fraternity," became the political watchword of European liberal democracy in the nineteenth century.

Nationalism—above all a powerful sense of group identity and loyalty—and liberalism joined in a forceful movement against absolutist governments. For a number of countries, this led to national independence, greater political freedom, and broadened popular rule. Increasingly, more liberal laws and constitutions (guaranteeing basic rights, enfranchising additional groups, and providing for greater popular control of government) were secured. However, setbacks for liberal democracy (Napoleon's dictatorship in France, the defeat of liberal forces in the several revolutions of 1848, and battles against such "iron" chancellors as Germany's Otto von Bismarck) emphasized that liberal democratic forces on the European continent were incomplete and shaky.

In addition to its contribution to democracy, the emergence of nationalism in the late eighteenth century added a psychological dimension to the concept of "country." Specifically, the new term nation-state brought to the political lexicon a way of combining the sense of identity and belonging expressed by nationalism with the legal term for the entity we know as a country—the *state*, which encompasses a people, a territory, a government, and acceptance by the international community.

LIBERALISM, CAPITALISM, AND DEMOCRACY

The rise of the nation-state, at least in Europe, led to the spread of ideas about democracy, constitutional government, and the liberal ideal of individual rights. Of course, liberal democracy had its critics, but the nineteenth century witnessed the continuing intermingling and dissemination of these ideas. This occurred first in Europe and then throughout the rest of the world.

Liberalism began as a movement for political, economic, social, and cultural freedom. It was strongly endorsed by the growing middle class and its allies because such freedom protected and advanced their vital interests. These interests included a stronger role in government; safeguards for religion, speech, press, assembly, and due process; freedom from adverse governmental actions in the economic domain (that is, governmental monopolies, economic regulations, and restrictions); and the opportunity for freer choices in politics, economics, and society.

The French Revolution symbolized the triumph of the middle class—the bourgeoisie—over a royal monarchy, a feudal aristocracy, and an established church. The French Revolution was not only a political triumph of republicanism over monarchy and of more genuinely constitutional government over autocracy; it was also an economic triumph of the middle class over the feudal aristocracy. Further, the revolution was a social triumph of the middle class and its allies among peasants and workers over feudal and church privilege. It was also a cultural and intellectual triumph of largely middle-class writers, artists, and thinkers over monarchical and religious censorship and oppression.

The concurrence of the American and French Revolutions with the Industrial Revolution and the emergence of **capitalism**—an economic system marked by private ownership of the means of production and exchange, a market economy, economic competition, free trade, and consumer sovereignty—is not accidental. The year 1776 saw both the American Declaration of Independence and the publication of *The Wealth of Nations*. Written by Scottish economist Adam Smith, *The Wealth of Nations* became the inspiration for the nineteenth-century liberal policy of restricting governmental interference in economic matters. The new capitalists favored a hands-off policy in the economy, except where it would benefit their enterprise. They wanted governmental policy to favor private enterprise.

The links between liberalism and capitalism, and between liberalism and democracy, are a little clearer than the connection between democracy and capitalism. For example, liberalism and capitalism share a common interest in economic freedom. Similarly, liberalism and democracy share a common interest in freedom, including economic freedom. Of course, capitalists and other members of the middle class share a democratic interest in popular rule and the protection of basic rights, especially when suffrage is limited to people of property and when governmental policy does not interfere with capitalistic enterprise. However, an expanded franchise may lead to policies that protect workers and their needs, and such policies could cut into the power and profits of capitalists. Moreover, capitalists and democrats may disagree on which basic rights to protect and how to protect them. Especially in the United States, middle-class liberals dedicated to freedom, including economic freedom, may join with working-class men and women to fight capitalistic abuses that threaten freedom and jeopardize the fulfillment of human needs.

However, we cannot deny that modern democracy emerged and grew up alongside the economic system of capitalism. Moreover, private ownership of the means of production and exchange, a market economy, economic competition, and consumer sovereignty in the marketplace still command widespread popular support in the United States. Historically, there can be little doubt that liberal democracy—committed to each person's political, economic, social, and cultural freedom—forged ahead with the growth of an essentially capitalistic middle class. Certainly, in Europe, the new middle class used liberal democratic principles to gain greater economic, political, and social powers at the expense of absolutist governments and feudal aristocracies. In the United States, where there was no significant feudal aristocracy to overthrow and where the abundant riches of the frontier beckoned, free and enterprising Americans welcomed the opportunities to advance their economic status in a political economy free of government's interfering hand.

As liberalism, democracy, and capitalism began to interact, the ideal of liberal democracy began to evolve. Many of the debates over the past 200 years have revolved around key questions about the balance between capitalism, democracy, and liberalism (see Key Questions on this page).

KEY QUESTIONS

1. What is the connection between the desire for individual freedom (liberalism) and the rule of the people (democracy)? How do political regimes incorporate both of these values?

2. In what ways do market pressures (capitalism) conflict with democracy? In what ways does capitalism strengthen democracy? How do political regimes strike a balance between these values?

The Changing Character of Liberalism

Liberalism changed significantly between the nineteenth and twentieth centuries. Many nineteenth-century liberals, originally committed to a very limited government, began to believe in the wisdom of more government intervention in economic and social life. Such liberals made this shift in pragmatic response to capitalistic abuses that hurt farmers, small businesspeople, workers, and consumers. Those people who were hurt protested private monopolies, unfair trade practices, tight money, low farm prices, low wages, bad working conditions, and adulterated food. These protests were heard particularly in bad economic times. Legislation to regulate trusts and railroads came at the federal level as early as 1887. Other important legislation—involving, for example, banks and impure food and drugs—came after the turn of the twentieth century. The new twentieth-century liberalism did not fully emerge, however, until the advent of the New Deal, a program initiated by President Franklin D. Roosevelt to fight the Great Depression of the 1930s.

The New Deal ushered in a government strongly dedicated to the general welfare. Government attempted to stabilize prices, provide jobs, stimulate the economy, regulate banking, strengthen labor's right to organize and bargain collectively, provide for unemployment compensation, ensure a fair minimum wage, guarantee a decent retirement income via Social Security, and provide cheaper electric power. In succeeding decades these reforms opened doors to more reforms in education, health, and housing; provided more generously for those in need; ensured the right to vote for African Americans; enhanced cultural opportunities; and protected the environment.

Courtesy of the Library of Congress, Prints and Photographs Division

The Works Progress Administration (WPA) was part of President Franklin D. Roosevelt's New Deal program to put to work those unemployed during the Great Depression of the 1930s. It also marked an unprecedented degree of government activism that changed the way liberalism was understood in the United States. Here, WPA workers construct a playground on Chicago's South Side.

The Changing Character of Democracy

Democracy in the United States has changed significantly in the past 200 years. Although the American founders saw themselves as republicans, they did not extend the right to vote to poor white men, to women, or to most blacks, slave or free. And slavery persisted until the Civil War. Americans adhered in theory to what we today call democratic principles: rule by the people, through majority decision, in a representative and constitutional system that protects individual and group rights and the freedoms of both majority and minority. But in practice their conception of popular rule and basic rights—although remarkably advanced for its day—was not democratic by modern standards.

Although the old fear of democracy as rule by the many poor and ignorant (the classic Greek conception, as Aristotle believed) remained, the republican-democratic demand that suffrage be extended could not be denied. Moreover, the word *democracy* began to replace republicanism as the key concept characterizing the American republic. In 1835, when Alexis de Tocqueville searched for a title for his perceptive study of the young United States, he chose *Democracy in America*. Abraham Lincoln also recognized democracy as popular government in his memorable phrase in the Gettysburg Address: "government of the people, by the people, and for the people."

Yet the wider use of the term *democracy* and a truly universal suffrage had to await the twentieth century. Democracy gained great popularity and prestige in the United States and throughout the world early in the century thanks to President Woodrow Wilson (1913–1921). This began with Wilson's reforms of the U.S. government but was extended by his efforts to characterize World War I as a war to defend democracy. (Although, in a reminder of how complex people are, Wilson's commitment to democracy was accompanied by very racist views that mar his legacy.) Practical and legal obstacles to universal suffrage, however, were not fully overcome until fairly late in the century. American women did gain the right to vote with the passage of the Nineteenth Amendment in 1920: "The right of citizens of the United States to vote shall not be denied or abridged by the United States or by any state on account of sex." But limitations on the right of African Americans to vote persisted into the 1960s. And the poll tax was not outlawed in federal elections until the passage of the Twenty-Fourth Amendment in 1964. (A poll tax is a fixed amount for all adults, and its payment is usually a requirement for voting.)

As people—regardless of sex, race, or property holdings—acquired the right to vote, they also theoretically gained the power to protect their needs and their welfare within a constitutional system used this power to destroy constitutional government, the rule of law, minority rights, or private property, as conservative critics of democracy feared. Instead, they have used their political power to address the content of legislation. They have become increasingly concerned with social and economic laws to advance the fuller life of the many.

With these roots and this evolution in mind, we are in a better position to outline and understand the operative ideals of liberal democracy in the United States today.

VARIATIONS ON THE LIBERAL DEMOCRATIC THEME

Despite the great variety of groups that populate the American political landscape, most Americans are liberal democrats. This may sound odd to many readers; however, despite the important differences in the United States between what we call liberals and conservatives, or between Democrats and Republicans, the average American politician and citizen adheres to the major ideals we have outlined—popular, constitutional, rights-respecting, and responsible government, and even the concept of government dedicated to the general welfare. Of course, they may interpret these ideals differently.

One way of looking at American politics is to divide its practitioners into four groups: liberals, conservatives, **populists**, and **libertarians**.[3] Each of these groups emphasizes a different aspect of the liberal democratic tradition. American liberals see themselves as tolerant, generous, politically progressive, and generally willing to experiment with government action on issues of merit (for example, worker protections). American conservatives see themselves as respectful of traditional values and institutions (private property and enterprise, family, church, and established governmental authority); supportive of liberty over equality when these two ideals clash (for example, in the case of affirmative action); and the preservers of responsible initiative, a richly textured community life, and standards of excellence in a world driven toward uniformity, novelty, and crass materialism. American populists generally tend to favor government intervention in economic affairs and may oppose expansion of some "liberal" personal freedoms. American libertarians consistently oppose government intervention in economic affairs and favor expansion of personal freedoms.

This fourfold classification may bring liberals and populists together on some issues of pro-government action in the economic realm, and conservatives and libertarians together on some issues of antigovernment action in the economic realm. It may also bring liberals and libertarians together on some issues of personal liberty and conservatives and populists together on some issues of personal and social morality.

American liberals, conservatives, populists, and libertarians differ, then, on how to safeguard democratic ideals and the guiding vision of human realization in the American republic. They differ, especially, on three interrelated points: (1) their concern for the least free, (2) their view of the role of government, and (3) their attitude toward change. We concentrate here on the perspectives of American liberals and American conservatives, indicating where they agree or disagree with populists and libertarians.

We should note, though, that American politics is driven by the two-party system. Obviously, there will be difficulties in fitting four major versions of liberal democracy into only two parties. The Democratic Party is now the home of most liberals, and the Republican Party can count on the loyalty of most conservatives. However, when we consider populists and libertarians, the alliances and party loyalties become more complicated.

American Liberals

First, American liberals in general favor a greater concern for the least free and the least powerful in society—poor people, ethnic minorities, women, working people, small farmers, small business owners, and consumers. Like populists, they seek to expand popular power and overcome abuses of economic, social, and political power. American liberals seek to end oppression, injustice, poverty, and inequality. Libertarians, by contrast, are concerned with protecting the individual freedom of both the rich and poor.

Second, American liberals are willing to employ the power of government, especially the national government, to seek changes on behalf of fair play for the least free and the least powerful. Populists, too, favor government action to protect groups such as farmers, workers, or small investors from what they deem the unjust or oppressive action of such powerful economic forces as industrial corporations and banks. American liberals and populists favor broader measures to advance the general welfare. Libertarians are generally opposed to government intervention in economic and social affairs.

Third, American liberals are more favorably disposed to political, economic, and social change to accomplish the objectives mentioned in the preceding paragraphs. They are not afraid to alter the status quo to permit a liberal democratic society to live up to its own ideals. On some economic issues, populists may share with liberals this more favorable attitude to change. Libertarians, as we have noted, take a dim view of governmental changes affecting the lives of people.

American Conservatives

First, while many American conservatives are genuinely concerned about the neediest in society, they are deeply skeptical of the ability of government—particularly the federal government—to solve the problems associated with poverty. They often believe that such programs are wasteful and inefficient. They also may make more distinctions than liberals between who is deserving of help and who may, through their own actions, not be worthy of government aid.

Second, American conservatives generally endorse a laissez-faire position; they are opposed to adverse government interference in their economic, political, and social affairs. Libertarians, more consistently than conservatives, hold to a laissez-faire position. Conservatives do not object when government acts to support private enterprise and profit, which they see as crucial to freedom and prosperity. But conservatives are suspicious of intervention on behalf of the least free (whether in the form of school busing to overcome segregation or of affirmative action programs, which conservatives see as reverse discrimination). Conservatives normally favor a strong defense establishment and a balanced budget.

Third, American conservatives seek to maintain the existing economic, political, and social scheme of things. They are reluctant to abandon that which is known—tried and true and of proven value. They may, however, endorse changes that favor traditional values and institutions. Libertarians take a more consistent position in opposing government economic and social regulations affecting individual or corporate freedom.

Fourth, conservatives tend to support traditional values often reflecting a religious orientation. They believe that conservative values and a conservative temperament provide a basis for social order and foster national unity. Radical change, thus, might be wrong because it is inconsistent with timeless moral beliefs; conservatives might oppose reform because it would undermine national stability.

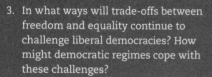

KEY QUESTIONS

1. In what ways has liberal democracy "solved" the political games covered in Chapter 1?

2. How can the liberal democratic state provide security while simultaneously maintaining a healthy respect for personal liberty? How far can and should the state go in providing the security necessary to live one's life?

3. In what ways will trade-offs between freedom and equality continue to challenge liberal democracies? How might democratic regimes cope with these challenges?

AN ASSESSMENT OF LIBERAL DEMOCRACY

Liberal democracy, as we have seen, has different variations. Furthermore, it has critics on both the left and the right. In this section, we evaluate the strengths and weaknesses of liberal democracy. In particular, we examine the following critical Key Questions.

The Defense of Liberal Democracy

Liberal democracy's defenders argue that its guiding vision and ideals enable Americans to achieve a greater measure of civilized life, healthy growth, and creative fulfillment than is possible under any other political ideology. They maintain that more people enjoy more freedom, equality, and prosperity under liberal democratic regimes. A liberal democracy has three key advantages or strengths that make it appealing.[4]

First, it is remarkably adaptive to changing circumstances and it shows a willingness to change and evolve. Democracy's defenders acknowledge its historic and contemporary shortcomings but point out that over time the United States moved successfully toward universal suffrage, freed the slaves, and checked plutocratic abuses of economic and political power. Despite severe trials, democratic institutions demonstrated a remarkable ability to cope with great difficulties. For example, Americans were able to respond to the worst effects of the Great Depression by shaping a state judiciously balanced between liberty and equality, freedom and security.

Second, a liberal democracy is able to effectively respond to the worst examples of tyranny and the abuse of power, so prevalent in the twentieth century. Responding to friendly critics such as Reinhold Niebuhr, who urged liberals to face the harsh realities of evil and power, Americans learned to mobilize countervailing power against abusive forces at home and abroad. For example, laborers formed unions to protect their interests. Demonstrating the organizational ability of a free people in an open society, the United States mobilized to defeat German fascism and Japanese militarism in World War II, a mighty feat of skill and courage. Then with great imagination, the United States helped Western Europe and Japan recover from the ravages of war with remarkable speed. America's foreign policy achievements included leadership in establishing the United Nations, the Marshall Plan to reconstruct war-torn Europe, and the North Atlantic Treaty Organization to protect Western Europe against Soviet aggression.

Finally, a liberal democracy is realistic about politics, and this creates a stable regime. To many students of politics, there is a danger that politics can become messianic—that in the search for the good life unrealistic expectations about what human beings can be and achieve are created. Liberal democracy is not prone to such thinking. The recognition of the rich diversity of life and the acceptance that individuals must be as free as possible to develop themselves as they see fit encourages a tolerance of many perspectives about life and politics. Politically this results in a pluralistic system that values the representation of many interests, balancing those interests and fostering compromise between competing political forces.

To its defenders, liberal democracy is a great historical achievement, a landmark in the evolution of human civilization. It has largely worked out the rules of the political game to strike a proper balance between individual freedom and the common good. It legitimizes government power but provides effective restraints on the exercise of that power to protect individual rights. Government is responsible to the people's representatives, and these representatives are responsive to the people. Liberal democratic politics avoids the worst features of both "lion and fox" and utopian politics, while realistically safeguarding vital community interests.

A Contemporary Challenge to Liberal Democracy: Security Versus Liberty

The war on terrorism has highlighted a certain tension between security and liberty that has always existed at the heart of liberal democracy. On one level, the state

The continued use of the Bagram Internment Facility in Afghanistan for interrogation purposes and the U.S. military base at Guantánamo Bay in Cuba for the detainment of suspected terrorists became a focus of protests during the George W. Bush administration. In January 2009, President Obama signed executive orders closing the facility at Guantánamo, but as of August 2015, the prison facility had not yet been fully closed.

has always made the promise of security and stability. The threat of chaos and the perpetual fear of attacks from without destroy the very fruits promised by liberal democracy: the ability to shape one's life, to prosper economically, to engage in a rich spiritually fulfilling existence, to hold one's elected officials accountable for their actions. It is impossible to imagine achieving any of these goals if one is afraid to leave home. Yet how can the state protect freedom without sacrificing personal freedom to an extent as well? After all, the very idea of liberal democracy is predicated on a notion of limited government. Too much concern for security might encourage the state to limit our very freedoms and significantly expand government powers in general. As Benjamin Franklin said, "Those who would give up essential liberty to purchase a little temporary safety deserve neither liberty nor safety."

This abstract issue became quite real as the George W. Bush administration began its fight to counter terrorism. In recent years, a seemingly endless parade of security versus liberty issues has emerged. What rights should the United States extend toward captured terrorists? Do they have rights of habeas corpus as envisioned under the Constitution? Does it matter where they are captured? Does it matter whether they are a citizen of the United States or another country? Should they be tried by a military tribunal, or should they be tried in traditional civilian courts?

These concerns do not exhaust the issues raised by the question of security and liberty. In an effort to prevent future terrorist acts, how much power should be granted to the U.S. government? How far can the government go in warrantless wiretapping? Indeed, how much monitoring of free citizens should there be? Would it be a good idea to have the type of national identification cards that exist in many other countries?

In dealing with these issues, the Bush administration took an expansive view of what was necessary to contain the threat of terrorism. The demands of security required not just decisive government action; it required strong executive action. Many in the administration believed in a legal theory called the **unitary executive**—the idea that with regard to foreign affairs and national security the president has decisive powers.

At first, Congress went along with many of President Bush's proposals concerning national security—for example, it passed the USA PATRIOT Act (Uniting and Strengthening America by Providing Appropriate Tools Required to Intercept and Obstruct Terrorism) in 2001 in the wake of the 9/11 terrorist attacks. The act put into place a vast array of security and, more controversially, surveillance measures to protect against terrorism. Critics were quick to point out what they claimed were the unconstitutional effects of the act. Many were concerned with both the general increase in government power and the particular increase in presidential authority. Legal controversy ensued. Cases arising from the act took years to work through the federal judicial system. By the time of the Bush administration's second term, they were beginning to reach the Supreme Court. The justices pushed back, forcing careful, though still controversial, legal procedures for captured terrorists. Congress too saw a great deal more debate on the issues, although it did renew the act in 2006.

When elected to the presidency in 2008, Barack Obama pledged to close the Guantanamo Bay prison, a focal point of the heated controversy between those who supported the policies of the Bush administration and those who opposed them, and provide for a more transparent executive branch. Although President Obama did end the use of torture, he did not close Guantanamo Bay prison and his administration continued many of the Bush-era counterterrorism policies such as the widespread use of electronic surveillance. For this reason, in the view of many critics, Obama's record on civil liberties is highly suspect. However, the difficulties raised by the central need for security remain. We are reminded again of Franklin's quote. What, then, is "essential liberty"? And are the measures undertaken to prevent terrorism "temporary," or are they in fact permanent?

The Attack on Liberal Democracy: Left and Right

Radical, democratic, communitarian, and socialist critics on the left contend that American liberal democracy has failed to fulfill its own promise. These critics are concerned that not enough people participate in the modern democratic state. They protest that individuals are not really free but rather are confined in an exploitive economic and social system characterized by inequality that is nourished by racism and sexism and magnified by a lack of genuine concern for the least free. While seeking to protect and expand civil liberties, these critics advocate using the state's powers to advance greater social and economic justice. They are worried about the harmful consequences of a still largely laissez-faire economy and the persistence of the "vandal ideology of liberalism" (an ideology of reckless waste) and the "theory of possessive individualism" (a theory of selfish individualism).[5] They argue that Americans worship private property, profits, and free enterprise at the expense of a healthy society, a meaningful community, and the common good. They emphasize that the United States is an affluent, largely white, democratic nation-state on a globe that is mostly poor, largely nonwhite, and either unprepared for or hostile to liberal democracy.

Aristocratic, individualistic, and capitalist critics on the right worry that liberal democracy has degenerated into mobocracy, serfdom, and socialism. They worry about the threat to such liberal democratic principles as representative democracy and equality of opportunity. They see dangers in participatory democracy: the decline of prudent judgment, submission to the ignorant, and loss of quality. They worry about replacing equality of opportunity with a doctrine of equality of results and about reverse discrimination and other programs of preferential treatment. They worry, too, about the triumph of vulgarity, meanness, and mediocrity in our social and cultural lives. They bemoan the loss of individual moral character and responsibility. They fear that the state's growing bureaucratic power to regulate economic affairs will undermine private property and enterprise as bastions of freedom. These critics deplore governmental controls and the encroachment of centralized state power. They favor limited government and are happiest when governmental power is in their hands and is used only to advance their purposes. They are traditionally opposed to big spending for welfare—unless it is their own welfare.

Certain weaknesses in liberal democracy, according to other critics, need attention and correction: (1) a faulty ethical vision, (2) a deficient empirical understanding, and (3) a timid prudential assessment. These critics do not share the more accepting "realistic" perspective set forth earlier.

Faulty Ethical Vision. Ethically, according to these critics, the vision of liberal democratic politics is faulty. The liberal democratic understanding of American politics has historically excluded Native Americans, African Americans, women, and the poor. Recent efforts to correct this faulty vision are incomplete. Although working people have fared reasonably well, Americans have never forthrightly faced the problem of worker alienation and democratic direction of the economy. Unemployment continues to plague too high of a percentage of the working force, with the unemployment rate among African Americans double or triple the figure for adult whites. As a people, Americans have been wasteful with their natural resources of land, water, timber, and minerals and have demonstrated a shocking disregard for ecological health. Americans may have limited the tyrannical power of government, but they have not seriously questioned abuse of human and natural resources. Americans have not adequately protected against the "vandal" aspects of liberal ideology.

For the critics, the American sense of responsibility for the least free, for the environment, and for the future is weak. Politicians have too frequently been the rich and the powerful. They have lacked concern for the quality of the American union, for a just and caring community. Proponents of liberal democracy have been complacent in appraising it. Americans have been too tolerant of existing evils and have lacked a firm conviction of a common good that would ensure a more desirable political order.

So liberal democratic politics today suffers from a too easy acceptance of the status quo and the prescriptive constitution. Americans too often act as if they have reached the pinnacle of wise political evolution. They tend to accept the rhetoric of liberal democratic ideals as reality and to close their eyes to ugly truths. Those who support liberal democratic politics may forget to dream. Unless prodded, liberal democratic politicians may lose a passionate and imaginative commitment to a better future.

Deficient Empirical Understanding. Empirically, the ideology of liberal democracy is deficient. It has refused to examine how ethics, economics, and ecology influence politics. It has not properly studied how group pressures affect public policy. It has been blind to the reckless and wasteful aspects of liberalism. By focusing too sharply on the status quo, it has neglected the weak, the poor, and the oppressed. It has ignored underlying forces that will become dominant. It has overlooked new possibilities. It has never fully explored the relationship between a capitalistic economic system and a democratic order. Its commitment to incremental change has prevented more radical criticism. It has often failed to acknowledge the gulf between the principles and the practice of liberal democracy.

A powerful existing system often conceals important political forces, seemingly invisible forces that do not come to our attention except in periods of crisis, riot, and revolution. To miss the underlying forces of today that will dominate tomorrow is to miss future possibilities and actualities. This deficient empirical understanding manifests in a wrongheaded view of change. Politics is too often seen in terms of balance and hence in terms of maintaining the status quo. Politics based on progressive change does not allow for radical and rapid change—the kind that may sometimes be needed to handle some crucial contemporary problems.

These generalizations come to life most dramatically in the neglect of African Americans, women, and the poor in an often racist, sexist, and blindly affluent society. Liberal democratic politics also seems congenitally unable to promote satisfaction and creativity in work—human beings' most basic life activity.

Timid Prudential Assessment. Prudentially, liberal democratic ideology is too timid. It is often wrongly conservative instead of rightly conservative; for example, it preserves racism and sexism and prefers property rights to human rights. It is often too hesitant. Liberal democrats are often unwilling to try bold new economic, social, and political experiments. Too frequently, they prefer stability to change, the known to the unknown. They may, for example, have waited too long to clean up the environment and to revive mass transportation. Guided by a timid ideology, liberal democrats have been too slow to attack admitted evils such as the drug problem, homelessness, and AIDS.

Liberal democratic politicians may lack the passion and the vision to act wisely. They may be wrongly convinced that most of the ways ordained by the prescriptive Constitution are sound for the present and future. Consequently, they will be unreceptive to creative political breakthroughs that could, for example, significantly reduce crime, drug abuse, pollution, and cancer as well as assure adequate employment, health care, and housing for all Americans.

Unfortunately, the motto of the liberal democratic politician—"to get along one must go along"—often transforms genuine prudence into weak-kneed timidity and makes bold political action impossible. And so, a desirable tension between what ought to be and what is—one that nourishes courageous judgment in politics—disappears. Modern "realistic" revisions of liberal democratic ideology have hastened the disappearance of this tension. These revisions call for democratic elitism. Such an **elite** system assumes that the people will have a voice in choosing political leaders; however, elites, those few who are better educated, knowledgeable and farsighted, should direct policy. These revisions reflect a lack of faith in the intelligence and capability of the common people, in the possibility of identifying a common good, and in more radical alternatives to the status quo.

There are good reasons to critically analyze these revisions. For example, the judgment of what David Halberstam called the "best and the brightest" turned out to be defective in the Vietnam War.[6] The governing elite's temptation to guard state security by fair means or foul reveals a failure of leadership. Vietnam, the Watergate and Iran-contra scandal, and the foolish coddling of Iraq before the Persian Gulf War in 1991 illustrate the persistence of questionable lion and fox politics in the liberal democratic state.

Seeing public policy as a result of group pressures frequently leads politicians to endorse the order imposed by the powerful. Such an order may benefit the powerful—whether corporations or labor organizations—but does it benefit weaker forces in society? We must ask how it helps the larger public made up of unorganized consumers.

These critical inquiries suggest a need for the bolder judgments that are the very stuff of creative breakthroughs in politics. We are challenged to explore those judgments that might enhance the vitality of liberal democratic politics.

The Case of Conservatism Reconsidered

As discussed throughout this chapter, what many people call conservatism, particularly in the United States, is simply a variation on the political philosophical idea of liberalism. In fact, some in trying to distinguish themselves from contemporary liberals take to identifying them as "classical liberals." But can one make a case for a philosophy and ideology that is distinctly conservative? What would a truly conservative political philosophy look like?

In drawing on the work of Edmund Burke, frequently called the first modern conservative, the twentieth-century, British philosopher Michael Oakeshott and the American philosopher John Kekes, the following ideas emerge as key to a recognizably different view of politics:

1. Tradition and custom are vital to any healthy society. Human life is given form and meaning as we participate in traditions and observe the customs of a place. Many liberals like to imagine what human beings are like if you remove all the trappings of society. There is even an entire school of thought identified as state of nature theorists who use such imaginings as a jumping off point for explaining how politics work and should work. To conservatives, it is a fool's errand to try to imagine a human being denuded of society. People are always situated in a place with ways of doing things significantly influenced by past ways of doing things. As such, traditions and customs should be honored with a great deal of respect, possibly even reverence. Of course, these traditions evolve overtime but the best way for that to happen is slowly, even imperceptibly. Thus, liberals ask why shouldn't gays be allowed to marry— give me a reason to restrict someone's freedom to marry. The perfectly valid conservative response is: Because we have not allowed that before and as far back as anyone can remember. Obviously, the longer something has been done in similar ways, forming a tradition, the more powerful the conservative sees this a good answer. The idea of something being an "instant" tradition is laughable to a conservative, but with continued practice, traditions grow strong and important.

2. Conservatism is, at a very basic level, deeply skeptical. What is skeptical about conservatism? The most important thing is that conservatives are skeptical about is the perfectibility of society. Human knowledge is too limited to know enough to perfect human institutions. Michael Oakeshott vehemently argued against reducing politics to some perfect, rational formula. The best that we can do is combine our intelligence with experience and come to a kind of wisdom about what to do in each unique case. Liberals, according to conservatives, are too apt to think if they just get enough data they will know the answer—be that how to deal with health care, poverty, or the environment. To conservatives, there will never be enough data. This does not mean that they don't believe in taking action but it should be done carefully, in a limited way. If we, as a society, shake things up too much we are bound to disturb this complex society in ways we could not even have imagined. The law of unintended consequences finds its greatest champions among conservatives.

3. Closely related to this second point, there is no such thing as progress. Societies are not progressing anywhere. Societies exist and keep on existing, if they can. There is no such utopian place that we are striving to reach. Conservatives are always quick to identify what they believe is the progressive ideal in liberal thought. Liberals, they are convinced, should also be called progressives, and what this means is that there is some ideal future that we must constantly be working on reaching. Politics, to liberals, is finding the right blueprint that will get us out of "here" and reach "there." Liberals believe that there is something wrong about the way things are right now, and we should be in a hurry about eliminating those wrongs. In contrast, conservatives insist that politics should be about managing matters today, and right here, so that things keep going as well as possible. As Oakeshott wrote, "To be conservative, then, is to prefer the familiar to the unknown, to prefer the tried to the untried, fact to mystery, the actual to the possible, the limited to the unbounded, the near to the distant, the sufficient to the superabundant, the convenient to the perfect, present laugher to utopian bliss."[7]

4. Finally, and this observation follows logically from the previous points, human beings are fallible people. We are prone to making mistakes; we may also do evil things that require moral condemnation and possibly state sanctions. Given this fundamental aspect of human nature, maybe the best we should strive for is avoiding evil. And this avoiding evil is something to endeavor for at the individual and the state level.

These are just the major views that are consensual to many, if not most, people who identify as conservative, political philosophers. One might add other attributes, the importance of religion, for instance, that are frequently mentioned alongside the views considered above. When these ideas are put into practice, different conservatives will often come to different policy suggestions. At times, a conservative might very well agree with others—even liberals—about some proposed government action. To give just one example, there is nothing inconsistent about a conservative being opposed to Social Security when it was first adopted in the 1930s—it was a new idea, that was largely untried, and it would make huge changes to society—and a conservative being in favor of Social Security now. Today, one could easily say that Social Security is now part of society, people expect it and organize their life around it continuing in the future. A sufficiently long-lived conservative could be against it at one time and for at another, later time and this would be based on the same principles and not some change of values.

CONCLUSION

In our presentation of liberal democracy, we deliberately stressed the importance of democratic and constitutional principles. Constitutional principles preceded the liberal democratic state and were incorporated into its politics. These principles will, and must, endure in any future democratic political order.

One of the hallmarks of democratic liberalism is its ability to adapt. Groups that were once excluded from politics, such as African Americans, women, and workers, have used constitutional and democratic principles on their own behalf. Moreover, they may use such principles on behalf of a common good that transcends all classes—capitalist or working class, white or African American, male or female. Historically, excluded groups have broadened both constitutionalism and democracy by demanding inclusion. In spite of being self-interested, these claims enhanced society's understanding of the common good, of legitimate human interests and needs, and of the linkage between democratic power and constitutional protection.

Of course, as we have seen, liberal democracies can be criticized for being overly cautious in expanding democracy at times and a bit too complacent about the inequities created by capitalism. However, at their best, liberal democracies have avoided the horrible excesses of so many other ideologies that captured the imaginations of people in the twentieth century. Thus, the liberal democracies avoided the disastrous policies that were pursued by fascists such as Adolf Hitler or communists such as Joseph Stalin.

Probably one of the greatest challenges facing liberal democracies in the twenty-first century is how to continue balancing freedom and equality. Certainly liberal democracies are wedded to the idea of personal freedom, and this is most powerfully expressed in the freedom allowed by the free market. Yet this very freedom can lead to remarkable levels of economic inequality. At the same time, any effort to alleviate this disparity (through the redistribution of wealth, for instance) can be attacked, particularly by the conservative and libertarian variations of the ideology, as restricting liberty and creating an overly powerful government. This challenge, somewhat successfully met in the past, will remain a persistent problem in the coming years. And, if liberal democrats fail in this task, the call for a more egalitarian politics will emerge with renewed vigor.

SUGGESTED READINGS

Dahl, Robert. *On Democracy*. New Haven, CT: Yale University Press, 1998. An excellent introduction to the key concepts and challenges of the ideal of democracy. Deftly explores the economic questions that pervade recent discussions about the development of democracy.

Fawcett, Edmund. *Liberalism: The Life of an Idea*. Princeton, NJ: Princeton University Press, 2014. A comprehensive look at the idea of liberalism from both a philosophical and empirical perspective.

Fried, Charles. *Modern Liberty*. New York: Norton, 2007. A thoughtful defense of a traditional understanding of liberty and the belief that liberty should not be compromised by the desire for equality.

Grayling, A. C. *Toward the Light of Liberty*. New York: Walker and Company, 2007. A thoughtful discussion of the struggle for freedom and the championing of rights in the West.

Hartz, Louis. *The Liberal Tradition in America*. New York: Harcourt, Brace, 1955. Building on Alexis de Tocqueville's brilliant *Democracy in America* (1835, 1840), emphasizes why and how the United States has avoided the extremes of left and right and adhered most often to the vital center.

Kekes, John. *Against Liberalism*. Ithaca, NY: Cornell University Press, 1997. Argues that liberalism is bound to fail because the very conditions liberalism wants to foster actually lead to many of the evils that liberalism also wants to fight. See also, his *A Case for Conservatism*, Ithaca, NY: Cornell University Press, 1998.

Lowi, Theodore J. *The End of the Republican Era*. Norman: University of Oklahoma Press, 1995. A provocative exploration of the "End of Liberalism," the "Republican Era," the "Conservative Era," the "End of Conservatism," and "Restoring the Liberal Republic." See also Lowi's earlier *The End of Liberalism* (New York: Knopf, 1969)—a critique of interest group liberalism and a plea for the rule of law—and Theodore J. Lowi and Benjamin Ginsberg, *Embattled Democracy: Politics and Policy in the Clinton Era* (New York: Norton, 1995).

Lukacs, John. *Democracy and Populism*. New Haven, CT: Yale University Press, 2005. An important book by a respected historian that examines the troubling relationship between democracy and demagoguery.

Maddox, William S., and Stuart A. Lilie. *Beyond Liberal and Conservative: Reassessing the Political Spectrum*. Washington, DC: Cato Institute, 1984. Convincingly argues on behalf of broadening the ideological categories of liberal democracy to provide room for populists and libertarians as well as liberals and conservatives, with each group defined by its views on government intervention in economic affairs and expansion of personal freedoms.

Niebuhr, Reinhold. *The Children of Light and the Children of Darkness*. New York: Scribner's, 1944. An unflattering and provocative critique of soft-headed idealists, moralists, and pacifists, and a resounding defense of democratic realism.

Parenti, Michael. *Democracy for the Few*. New York: St. Martin's Press, 1988. A sharp, hard-hitting criticism of American politics and society as benefiting primarily the rich and the powerful, the greedy rather than the needy.

Riemer, Neal. *The Future of the Democratic Revolution: Toward a More Prophetic Politics*. New York: Praeger, 1984. In Chapter 4, he assesses the strengths and weaknesses of liberal democracy from the perspective of a model of prophetic politics.

———. *The Revival of Democratic Theory*. New York: Appleton-Century-Crofts, 1962. Bases his case for a reinvigorated democratic theory on eight orienting concepts: (1) political theory as a prudent guide to action, (2) individual realization within the framework of the common good, (3) sensible dimensions of maneuver, (4) the prudential logic of realization, (5) democratic and constitutional accommodation, (6) majority rule, (7) pluralistic and conditional obligation, and (8) constant scrutinization of democracy's well-calculated risks.

Scruton, Roger. *The Meaning of Conservatism*. South Bend, IN: St. Augustine Press, 2014. A compelling analysis, by one of England's leading political philosophers, of conservatism that shows how it is not at all like liberalism. This book's discussion of what true conservatism means may surprise many American readers. The author argues that conservatism is not closely related to the free market or capitalism, nor is it hostile to the state.

Zakaria, Fareed. *The Future of Freedom*. New York: Norton, 2007. Argues that democracy is not always a good thing—that it depends on the right circumstances to flourish and not decline into authoritarianism.

GLOSSARY TERMS

capitalism (p. 144)
civil liberties (p. 137)
conservatives (p. 136)
direct democracy (p. 136)
due process (p. 138)
elite (p. 153)
equality (p. 136)
laissez-faire (p. 136)

liberal democracy (p. 136)
liberalism (p. 136)
liberals (p. 136)
libertarians (p. 146)
liberty (p. 137)
nationalism (p. 143)
nation-state (p. 000)
pluralist school/pluralism (p. 137)

political ideologies (p. 135)
popular sovereignty (p. 142)
populists (p. 146)
representative
    government (p.136)
republicanism (p. 142)
state (p. 140)
unitary executive (p. 150)

NOTES

1. In this and succeeding sections, the senior author drew from his work in the field of democratic theory: Neal Riemer, "Democracy: Merits and Prospects," in *World Affairs: Problems and Prospects*, ed. Elton Atwater et al. (New York: Appleton-Century-Crofts, 1958); *The Revival of Democratic Theory* (New York: Appleton-Century-Crofts, 1962); *The Democratic Experiment* (Princeton, NJ: Van Nostrand, 1967); *The Future of the Democratic Revolution: Toward a More Prophetic Politics* (New York: Praeger, 1984);

James Madison: Creating the American Constitution (Washington, DC: Congressional Quarterly, 1986); *Let Justice Roll: Prophetic Challenges in Religion, Politics, and Society* (Lanham, MD: Rowman & Littlefield, 1996); and *Creative Breakthroughs in Politics* (Westport, CT: Praeger, 1996).

2. See Neal Riemer, ed., *The Representative: Trustee? Delegate? Partisan? Politico?* (Boston: Heath, 1967).

3. See William S. Maddox and Stuart A. Lilie, *Beyond Liberal and Conservative: Reassessing the Political Spectrum* (Washington, DC: Cato Institute, 1984). For Theodore Lowi's classification of the traditions of American political thought, see his *End of the Republican Era* (Norman: University of Oklahoma Press, 1995), Table 1.3.

4. For a recent assessment of liberalism, see Riemer, *Future of the Democratic Revolution,* chap. 4, "Liberal Democratic Politics: The Conservative Politics of Pluralistic Balance."

5. The idea of "possessive individualism" was developed by C. B. Macpherson in his seminal work, *The Political Theory of Possessive Liberalism: Hobbes to Locke* (New York: Oxford University Press, 1962).

6. David Halberstam, *The Best and the Brightest,* 20th anniversary ed. (New York: Random House, 1992).

7. Michael Oakeshott, "On Being Conservative." Rationalism in Politics and other essays (Indianapolis, IN: Liberty Press, 1991), p. 408.

Crowds holding posters of Mao Zedong
in celebration of China's 1949 Communist
revolution.

AP Photo

7

DEMOCRATIC SOCIALISM AND COMMUNISM

Ideologies of the Left

As the twenty-first century dawned, it appeared that liberal democracies had won the day. The ideology that underpins those democracies, which we explored in Chapter 6, had many converts and champions, particularly in the United States and Western Europe. The fall of the Soviet Union indicated that the appeal of communism was waning.[1] Many countries in Eastern Europe adopted some form of democracy and initiated market reforms that might lead to a capitalist system so familiar to Americans.

However, the story of recent politics is much more complicated. A number of countries, such as China, Cuba, North Korea, and Vietnam, still maintain an official allegiance to some form of communism. Even more numerous are the nations that hesitate to embrace all the ideals of liberal democracy, particularly that of a free market. Despite the current popularity of liberalism and democracy, there continues to be a vibrant leftist tradition in nations such as France, Greece, Finland, Belgium, and the United Kingdom that offers a powerful critique of liberalism and, more importantly, capitalism. Furthermore, the left offers its own version of the good life and how to achieve that life with a different set of government institutions and an alternative arrangement of the economic sphere.

Students of politics need to be aware that the triumph of liberal democracy is neither all encompassing nor necessarily permanent. Change is a constant in the political world, where great transformation can occur with little warning, a truth clearly illustrated by the dramatic—and generally unpredicted—collapse of the Soviet Union in 1991. As stated earlier, a powerful critique of the liberal democratic tradition continues to exist. What unites these critics, from moderate socialists to traditional communists,

Chapter Objectives

After studying this chapter, you will be able to do the following:

1. Explain the central ideas that define democratic socialism.

2. Summarize the roots that help shape the evolution of democratic socialism.

3. Describe the main ideas of communism.

4. Summarize the sources of communism.

5. Critique the strengths and weaknesses of democratic socialism and communism.

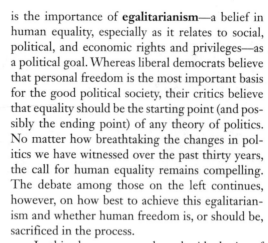

KEY QUESTIONS

1. In what ways do the ideologies of the left offer a powerful criticism of liberal democracy? In what ways are these ideologies compatible with liberal democracy?

2. How are democratic socialism and communism different from each other and from liberal democracy?

3. In what ways do these three ideologies share similar goals and beliefs?

is the importance of **egalitarianism**—a belief in human equality, especially as it relates to social, political, and economic rights and privileges—as a political goal. Whereas liberal democrats believe that personal freedom is the most important basis for the good political society, their critics believe that equality should be the starting point (and possibly the ending point) of any theory of politics. No matter how breathtaking the changes in politics we have witnessed over the past thirty years, the call for human equality remains compelling. The debate among those on the left continues, however, on how best to achieve this egalitarianism and whether human freedom is, or should be, sacrificed in the process.

In this chapter, we explore the ideologies of the left: democratic socialism and communism. Although the two are related and share some common history and, at times, a common set of ideals, they are distinct ideologies with important differences that need to be examined individually. First, we define democratic socialism, describe its intellectual sources, and offer an assessment of its strengths and weaknesses. Next, we provide the same analysis of communism. Finally, we consider the recent changes in democratic socialism and communism and offer some thoughts about the future of each ideology. As you read, keep in mind the Key Questions listed on this page.

DEMOCRATIC SOCIALISM

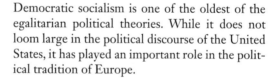

KEY QUESTIONS

1. What are the fundamental tenets of democratic socialism?

2. How is it possible for the basic ideas of democracy and socialism to be compatible with each other?

3. What are the historical sources that contributed to the development of democratic socialism?

Democratic socialism is one of the oldest of the egalitarian political theories. While it does not loom large in the political discourse of the United States, it has played an important role in the political tradition of Europe.

Toward a Definition of Democratic Socialism

Democratic socialism, as the term clearly indicates, combines democracy and socialism. However, because there are many varieties of both democracy and socialism, it is not easily defined. In fact, democratic socialism combines several ideas. *Politically*, it involves a commitment to popular, constitutional rule and the protection of basic rights. *Economically*, it involves a more egalitarian distribution of the community's wealth. To ensure this equitable distribution, key aspects of economic life must be publicly owned or socially controlled. Democratic socialists are especially concerned that workers have a voice in their economic (and political and social) destiny and that human needs (particularly those of the least free) are adequately satisfied. *Socially*, democratic socialism involves the belief that all human beings, in a cooperative community, should have the opportunity to fulfill their good and creative potential.

The Ideals of Democratic Socialism

In their pursuit of social justice, democratic socialists believe that a society must be organized in such a way that all people can develop their basic human potential. In achieving such a society, there are five key ideals that underlie democratic socialist thinking:

1. *Adherence to the main tenets of liberal democracy.* These tenets include such concepts as popular rule and protection of basic rights. Thus, democratic socialists fully accept the principles of parliamentary government, majority decision making, traditional electoral processes and peaceful constitutional change. However, they go beyond these democratic and liberal ideals; traditionally, democratic socialists have sought to advance the cause of economic democracy, and this goal requires strengthening trade unions, passing laws to protect labor, advancing worker voice and control in industry, and encouraging cooperative societies. There is, however, no unanimous, single policy to expand economic democracy. In a fundamental sense, the extension of social democracy involves a continuing battle against social privilege, whether related to an elitist and exclusionary educational system or to social inequalities produced by unearned wealth.

2. *Commitment to public ownership of key aspects of the economy.* Democratic socialists believe that public ownership of key aspects of the economy is essential to public well-being. Their goal is to achieve a **mixed economy**—that is, one in which both public and private control of industries adheres. Although there is no one formula for which industries should be nationalized and countries employ different such arrangements, democratic socialists believe in the viability of some public ownership of major industry. Along with public ownership, governments regulate the economy to foster high employment, economic productivity and prosperity, decent conditions for workers, and a more equitable sharing of the common wealth.

3. *Promotion of an extensive welfare state.* Democratic socialism insists upon an extensive **welfare state**, one that provides social services to ensure a better family life, health care, and housing; protection against unemployment; security in old age; and more recently, a guaranteed minimum income. The latter idea is an old one but has new adherents in recent years. There is a strong belief that the state should protect citizens from cradle to grave, and that any legitimate government must address the realities of poverty.

4. *Assumption of a global perspective.* Democratic socialism champions its ideals for all human beings. Thus, democratic socialists speak of a unity of all workers around the globe, of freedom from imperialism and colonialism, and of world peace.

Attempting to establish unity across political borders can, however, generate many problems because the demands of socialism can easily come into conflict with the appeal of nationalism.

5. *Belief in the centrality of equality.* Democracy, public ownership of the means of production, government regulation, the welfare state, and international unity and peace are designed to enhance the quality of life in a more cooperative community. Democratic socialists are thus concerned with greater equality of individuals on the one hand and an improved quality of life on the other. These socialist ideas have roots in the egalitarian, libertarian, and aesthetic traditions of socialism. Socialists attack privilege, favor greater intellectual and moral freedom, and seek to overcome social barriers and bring people closer together.

THE SOURCES OF DEMOCRATIC SOCIALISM

In this section, we review the roots and evolution of democratic socialism, emphasizing the Key Questions listed below.

KEY QUESTIONS

1. Where did the five ideals outlined in the previous section come from? How did they evolve?

2. How did modern democratic socialism draw on the early liberal democratic and socialist traditions for its own synthesis?

3. How did these ideas contribute to social justice, democracy, public ownership, and the cooperative commonwealth?

In highlighting democratic socialism's fundamental aspects, we draw particularly on its religious, utopian, Marxist, revisionist, Fabian, trade unionist, and reformist roots. We also show how these influences contributed to a growing criticism of the capitalist industrial order and a demand for a new order that would be both democratic and socialist.

We must keep in mind that democratic socialism is the product of ideas and economic, social, and political developments that created an environment receptive to these new ideas. Capitalism and modern industrialism, in particular, created the setting for democratic socialism. Capitalism was sympathetic to liberal democracy and to greater economic, political, and social freedom for the middle class and helped to create the modern working class and trade unions. The condition of workers in modern industrial societies produced many critics, often inspired by the French Revolution and its ideal of extending freedom and equality to all, whose attacks on capitalism significantly shaped intellectual and political opinion and opened people to socialist ideas. The advance of suffrage, made inevitable by liberal democracy, gave workers and their allies' political leverage. The institutions of liberal democracy made it possible for democratic socialists—in time and after many hard-fought battles—to take over the reins of political power. Thus, a number of forces converged to develop a philosophy of democratic socialism. Events (such as the French Revolution and the Industrial Revolution), the development of institutions (such as trade unions and democratic reforms to government), and new ideas (from the thinkers noted below) all contributed to the rise of a new ideology.

What follows are some of the key intellectual and historical sources for democratic socialist thinking.

Religious Roots

The Judaic-Christian prophetic tradition is one source of democratic socialism's ethical ideal. Its emphasis on justice and peace sustained the vision of human beings of integrity joined in a cooperative community where care for the least free—the poor, widows, and orphans—fulfilled God's commandments. This emphasis, reinforced by the primitive communalism of early Christianity, has echoed throughout the history of Christianity. It was reflected in the conviction that covetousness and greed led to evil, which in turn led to conflict, exploitation, and inequality. Religious influences manifested themselves, for example, in the work of Christian socialists such as Charles Kingsley and British Labour Party leaders such as George Lansbury and Clement Attlee. Lansbury wrote in his 1934 book, *My England*, "Socialism, which means love, cooperation, and brotherhood in every department of human affairs, is the only outward expression of a Christian's faith."

In Great Britain, the move to religious freedom was aligned with the desire for greater political freedom. In the seventeenth century, the Levellers—best characterized as radical middle-class democrats—articulated the fundamental argument for universal suffrage (for males, that is) that the Chartists (nineteenth-century political reformers) and others battling for the vote were to repeat in later centuries. As John Lilburne, a leader of the Levellers, put it, people were "by nature all equal and alike in power, dignity, and majesty," and consequently civil authority was to be exercised by "mutual agreement and consent." Although this may sound like common sense to many contemporary Americans, in the seventeenth century it represented a radical demand for social equality.

The modern welfare state has deep roots in the Judaic-Christian tradition's concern for the poor and the needy, its preference for a more cooperative commonwealth, its insistence on fair and just economic rules, and its belief in dignified human life. It should, therefore, not be too surprising that nonconformists, such as the Diggers (or "true-Levellers"), would surface in Britain's seventeenth-century civil war to advocate a primitive communism. Their most prominent spokesperson, Gerrard Winstanley, understood the law of nature as a communal right to the means of subsistence: individuals had an equal right to use and enjoy the earth and its fruits. People should be free to draw upon the common land and the common produce according to their needs. These compassionate and egalitarian ideas continued to find expression in those individuals in the Judaic-Christian religious tradition with a socialist orientation.

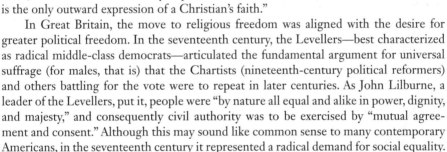

AP Photo/Jon Eeg

Among prominent European democratic socialists is Gro Harlem Brundtland, former premier of Norway (1981, 1986–89, 1990–96), director-general of the World Health Organization (WHO) (1998–2003), UN Special Envoy on Climate Change (2007–2010), and now deputy chair of The Elders, a prestigious group of senior world leaders.

Utopian Roots

The term utopia has come to stand for the perfect political and social order and the ideal of social justice. The **utopian socialists**, who first appeared in the middle of the nineteenth century, stressed cooperation and underscored the possibilities of using education to change the social and economic environment. Frequently, the utopian socialists concentrated on building self-sufficient communities, divorced from the political mainstream. Although the utopians often called for elite leadership to create such communities, democratic principles frequently prevailed in the communities themselves. The comte de Saint-Simon (Claude Henri de Rouvroy), Robert Owen, and Charles Fourier were influential utopian socialists. In some ways, Owen presents the most interesting case of the three.

In *A New View of Society* (1813), Owen looked to a cooperative and integrated agricultural-industrial community to overcome the evils of modern industrial society. Owen favored "villages of cooperation" as models for the new social order. Such planned villages would relieve unemployment by enabling the unemployed to grow their own food. Industrial production, as well as farming, would be communal. Owen's communities would eliminate the squalor of modern industrialism; good working conditions would prevail. Owen's ideas stimulated his followers to raise a number of important questions—for example, whether human nature was compatible with the egalitarian system Owen was trying to establish in his model factory community. They also asked, "Why are working people poor and wretched?" And, "Is the laborer entitled to the whole produce of his labor?"

Owen was a remarkable socialist pioneer with a tremendous faith in the power of education and reform. As early as 1834, he tried, without success, to form a national trade union organization, an "attempt to assemble the entire working class under socialist leadership." He saw his Grand National Union as the means to socialize the economy. Owen also fathered the cooperative movement in Britain—the idea of mutually owned stores selling industrial goods for the benefit of their members. In addition, Owen emphasized the importance of education in shaping people and society. The cardinal premise of his social philosophy was the right environment. "Any general character," he wrote, "from the best to the worst, from the most ignorant to the most enlightened, may be given to any community, even to the world at large, by the application of the proper means; which means are to a great extent at the command and under the control, or easily made so, of those who possess the government of nations."[2]

Marxist Roots

We will discuss Karl Marx's views in greater detail later in this chapter. However, we should note that Marx drew on earlier socialist thinkers in developing his political philosophy, and he, in turn, influenced later socialists. In general, Marx's ethical concerns—for universal freedom, peace and harmony, a more genuine community, and rich human development—were widely shared by all socialists. He also provided socialists with a powerful systematic analysis of how capitalism worked.

There are a number of areas, however, where Marx's views diverged from, or caused problems with, democratic socialism. First, Marx differed from many other socialists in his attempt to establish a more rational, comprehensive, and scientific (as opposed to religious) framework for socialism. Second, and more disturbing to many democratic socialists, Marx's commitment to democracy is questionable. Can socialism be achieved peacefully and by democratic, constitutional means? Marx was ambiguous on this point.

At times he did seem to believe that some countries (many of the advanced industrial nations of Western Europe, for instance) could achieve socialism democratically. However, he never ruled out a violent revolution by the majority against a capitalist minority. He was also vague or silent on the question of minority rights for those who opposed socialist rule. For example, he never clearly addressed the question of socialists being voted out of office in a free election. Apparently, these matters did not bother Marx because he held that the state (as a coercive organ) would wither away and a classless society would emerge under communism. Nonetheless, Marx's lack of concern for the liberal side of politics (respect for the rule of law, elections, civil rights and liberties) is troubling to many democratic socialists.

Revisionist Roots

The **revisionists** shared Marx's general outlook but differed in their economic and political diagnosis. They felt that Marx had to be "revised" in order to advance socialist goals. In this section, we focus on one important revisionist, the German Eduard Bernstein (1850–1932). Bernstein was a social democrat who spent many years of exile in England and whose views reflect the pragmatic and constitutional British tradition and a devotion to ethical concerns that modified his appreciation of the economic and political ideas of Marx.[3]

Ideals played an important role in socialism. For Bernstein, socialism was not inevitable, but it was supremely desirable; ethically it was inspired by Immanuel Kant, as eloquently expressed in the second categorical imperative: "Act so as to treat man, in your own person as well as in that of anyone else, always as an end, never merely as a means." Bernstein's ethical position reflects a break with Marx's strict materialistic outlook.

Politically, Bernstein broke sharply with the revolutionary Marxists. He opted clearly for the peaceful, evolutionary path to socialism and rejected the **dictatorship of the proletariat** as a barbaric idea incompatible with democracy. He accepted the constitutional rules of the game of liberal democracy, although he differed with liberal democrats on how far a democratic state could intervene in the economy. Democracy—understood as popular rule and protection of basic rights—was crucial to Bernstein's political philosophy. Universal suffrage for workers was so crucial that Bernstein was willing to endorse using a general strike to obtain the ballot or guard it against attack. However, once real political democracy had been obtained, the political strike would become obsolete. Bernstein's political strategy rested on building a broad coalition of Socialist Party members, trade unions, cooperatives, and radical members of the **bourgeoisie**. Such a broad electoral base had to rest on democratic principles, class cooperation, and mutual trust. These ideas explain why Bernstein differed with Marx over the "withering away of the state." To Bernstein, these beliefs were unrealistic. Economically, Bernstein adopted a philosophy that called for the coexistence of socialism and capitalism in a mixed economy, not for capitalism's complete destruction. The evidence had not persuaded Bernstein, as it had Marx, that capitalism was going to die, that the middle class was disappearing, and that the workers' lot was becoming ever more miserable. He noted the rising standard of living for many people and recognized the continued vitality and viability of capitalism—its economic strengths, changing character, and susceptibility to democratic reform. Bernstein wanted a more genuine socialist society, but he was content to move gradually toward public ownership and control of the commanding heights of the economy; to favor a mixed economy (partly public, partly private); to endorse government regulation where public ownership was not feasible; and to accept what we today call a welfare state, one that provides key social services for its citizens. Bernstein rejected the complete socialist revolution that meant the abolition of private property and the total destruction of the social privileges and the economic, political, and military power of the bourgeoisie. He thus opted for the reformist posture of class cooperation on the peaceful road to socialism. Greater social and economic equality would come with key social policies such as nationalization of basic industries, social insurance, better housing, and food programs.

Fabian Roots

The Fabian Society, formally constituted on January 4, 1884, grew out of an ethical society called the Fellowship of the True Life that had emerged the previous year. The **Fabians** were a group of British intellectuals committed to the gradual achievement of socialism and motivated in their desire to overcome the injustices of modern industrial societies. The society's numbers included luminaries such as George Bernard Shaw and H. G. Wells and also social scientists such as Sidney and Beatrice Webb. This ethical indignation unquestionably inspired their criticism of capitalism. Their critique uncovered a host of problems involving working people and the maldistribution of wealth and social services.

Whereas the revisionists sought to revise Marx in a more liberal direction, the Fabians sought to revise British liberalism in a more radical, socialist direction. Convinced of the importance of constitutional and parliamentary government, the Fabians advocated a moderate, pragmatic, non-doctrinaire variety of socialism to be achieved gradually. There was no need for violent revolution. The Fabians sought to educate and persuade the leaders of the British middle and upper classes and to provide intellectual leadership for the emerging British Labour Party, which was founded in 1901. They sought practical solutions for practical problems—public control of municipal transport, decent labor conditions in laundries, health regulations in the milk industry, and liquor licensing. They constituted an influential lobby on behalf of social reform and planning. Municipal socialism would lead to government ownership of basic industries. Specific social and economic reforms would create a climate of opinion for broader reforms. Fabians called for reform of the educational system to eliminate social privilege and overcome social inequality. They would build new towns with better housing and amenities for workers.

Trade Union Roots

Democratic socialism is, of course, impossible without popular support. Working people provide the bulk of that mass support. In Britain, the political role of workers and trade unions received a setback with the defeat of the Chartist movement (1838–1848) for universal suffrage and other reforms. Leaders of the working class turned away from political action and began building a strong trade union movement. They did not return to politics until the founding of the Independent Labour Party in 1893. One student of British socialism, Anthony Crosland, has emphasized the importance of the generous ideals of brotherhood, fellowship, service, and altruism in the Independent Labour Party, which anticipated the modern British Labour Party.[4] Members were concerned with working people at the economic bottom of society. This concern for social justice appealed strongly to members of the labor movement. A similar concern, in addition to economic self-interest, motivated the millions of workers who joined trade unions and labor parties in other European countries.

As noted, the present British Labour Party was formed in 1901. With strong trade union support, it began building an electoral following, though it did not adopt a clearly socialist ideology until 1918. In succeeding decades, it came to challenge, and then replace, the Liberal Party as the country's second major party. Trade unions remain a major source of strength of democratic socialism in Great Britain.

Reformist Roots

No account of the roots and evolution of democratic socialism would be adequate if it ignored a miscellaneous group of reformers—from Jeremy Bentham and John Stuart Mill to R. H. Tawney, John Maynard Keynes, and William H. Beveridge—whose ideas and actions helped set the stage for democratic and socialist victories. Some reformers protested the adverse consequences of the Industrial Revolution, particularly the dreadful working conditions. A number of reformers maintained that laborers produced value and were not getting their fair share of what they created. Some protested inequities in the way wealth was obtained and distributed. Many reformers pressed for universal suffrage. Others advocated governmental intervention in the economy to counter depression. Reformers called for social services on behalf of the needy and emphasized the importance of a better quality of life for all. They helped to radicalize elements of the middle class and to unite them with working-class people. They may not have been socialists but their concerns about poverty, the problems of inequality, and the harshness of capitalism meant their ideas contributed to the socialist tradition.

DEMOCRATIC SOCIALISM AS POLITICAL IDEOLOGY: PRO AND CON

To its proponents, democratic socialism constitutes a brave attempt to advance social justice for those traditionally left behind in a free society. To its detractors, it is a failed utopian theory that would lead to economic crisis.

Criticism of Democratic Socialism

Critics insist that democratic socialism is a contradiction in terms. Socialism, they maintain, gives the government too much power, and such great power is the enemy of liberty. In particular, governmental limitations on private enterprise destroy freedom.

Critics on the right argue that socialism is inefficient. In socialized enterprises, production is bound to lag, and services are likely to deteriorate as the generally over-regulated economy crushes incentive, daring, and flexibility, stifling the innovative spirit of capitalism. Socialism is bound to fail because it kills the goose (capitalism) that lays the golden egg (a prosperous economy). In addition, by interfering in the market economy, socialism does not allow full consumer choice in the marketplace. The policies social democrats advocate, critics charge, would often lead to massive government deficits and create a government bloated with bureaucracy. Finally, democratic socialists have not been able to overcome many of the problems of modern industrial society: economic recession, unemployment, troublesome inflation, and declining productivity.

On the left, orthodox communists, and some very left-wing democratic socialists, attack mainstream democratic socialism because they contend that by coexisting with capitalists, democratic socialists failed to carry out the revolution. Democratic socialists are bound to acquiesce in the inequities of capitalism too readily and no great transformation to a more just society will truly occur. Socialist values can only be achieved if capitalist power—economic, political, and social—is destroyed. Under democratic socialism workers cannot be emancipated, the fruits of collective labor cannot be fairly shared, and bourgeois power, values, and policies will still prevail. Although there is much debate on this last point between socialists and communists, many of them believe that some market reforms are compatible with the socialist ideal—a position China appears to be taking with its recent reforms.

The Defense of Democratic Socialism

To its defenders, democratic socialism remains compelling in the twenty-first century because the new global economy, whatever its appeal, still appears to create political and economic inequalities between people (and nations). Indeed, recent concerns about economic inequality led to social protest in the United States called "The Occupy Wall Street Movement." While this movement was not necessarily socialist, it does show a deep concern for the staggering level of inequality in the United States. Furthermore, the unexpected success of Bernie Sanders, an avowed democratic socialist, in fighting for and falling just short of the Democratic Party nomination, shows that there is a significant constituency that is not afraid of some socialist ideas.[5] Social democracy places equality at the center of political discussion and insists that a just society address the problems created by great inequalities of wealth—both in the name of democratic equality and in the fervent belief that the dignity of citizens requires a more equal distribution of wealth.

Pragmatically, defenders of democratic socialism argue that it offers a sane middle ground between capitalism and communism. Under democratic socialism, they insist, freedom and economic well-being can come together. They note that democratic socialist programs have overcome the worst abuses of unregulated capitalism, have transferred wealth to workers and the needy, and have made life more attractive for the mass of people.

COMMUNISM

While democratic socialism represents a powerful criticism of liberalism and the capitalist tradition, there are still stronger critiques of the capitalist system. These are most powerfully embodied in the theory of communism. As we examine communism, consider the Key Questions listed on this page.

Toward a Definition of Communism

Although **communism** shares with democratic socialism a forceful attack on capitalism and a stirring call for equality, it is a distinct political ideology, with its own diagnosis of what ails society and its own solution for achieving a better, healthier society. Communism is, in many ways, an ancient ideal that received its modern definition from Karl Marx. Communism in the modern context means that all people share equally in controlling the production and exchange of things of economic and social value. This ideology demands the end of private wealth and calls for the public ownership of property and the means of production. Communism insists that the exploitation of human beings must end and that freedom must be universally achieved.

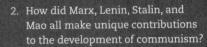

KEY QUESTIONS

1. What does communism have to say about societal institutions, history, and revolution? How might communists explain recent events in politics and the economy?

2. How did Marx, Lenin, Stalin, and Mao all make unique contributions to the development of communism?

3. With the collapse of communism in the Soviet Union and the institution of market reforms in China, is the ideology of communism dead?

The Ideals of Communism

Communist doctrine envisions an earthly paradise in which peace, abundance, community, and fulfillment prevail for all people, regardless of race, color, or sex. Communists claim to stand for freedom as opposed to "slavery"—that is, wage servitude, political oppression, and social subjugation—and promise justice on Earth to the exploited and the abused. Communism, with its vision of a cooperative and altruistic community struggling against an individualistic doctrine of profit making, appeals most pointedly to the oppressed workers, the class of modern wage laborers identified as the **proletariat**.

Communism predicts the eventual rise and triumph of the proletariat, which will not only usher in a classless and conflictless society within a nation but also overcome hostility between nations. Such a society will ensure economic abundance and individual development and realize the ultimate egalitarian principle in the communist motto: "From each according to his ability; to each according to his needs." In this sense, communism is a humanistic philosophy.[6]

Communism is also a philosophy of history. Communism purports to explain rationally the evolution and structure of human society. It describes historical development in terms of clashing material forces related to how people earn a living and conduct their economic activities. Communist philosophy emphasizes that the material environment significantly influences human ideas and behavior. Communism sees history as moving toward a classless society in which the community will own the means of production, distribution, and exchange. Between the revolution, which abolishes the capitalist order, and this final communist society lies a transitional period known as the dictatorship of the proletariat—rule, which may sometimes be coercive, by the overwhelming majority

Karl Marx was one of the most dominant thinkers of the nineteenth century. His varied writings have influenced both democratic socialism and modern communism. Even after the fall of the Soviet Union, Marx's theories about the inequalities generated by capitalism continue to sway political thought.

of workers in their own self-interest. In the final communist community, the state (understood as an instrument of coercion and oppression) will disappear. Communism offers a new order based on worker control of the means of production, the satisfaction of real human needs, and an altruistic pattern of cooperation and development. It has been particularly appealing to radical leaders in poor, formerly colonial nations that seek a rapid path to modernization.

Marx's conception of history is based on three factors: (1) **materialism**, (2) **class struggle**, and (3) **dialectical change**.

1. *Materialism.* For Marx, "life involves before everything else eating and drinking, a habitation, clothing and many other things." History, therefore, requires the production of the means to satisfy these material needs.[7] Materialism is the belief that a society's economic structure, which is shaped by the prevailing mode of production (industrial society, for instance), constitutes the foundation upon which that society's superstructure of law, politics, ethics, religion, philosophy, ideology, and art is built. All these institutions are simply a reflection of the underlying economic forces at work in history.

2. *Class struggle.* History is dynamic, and this dynamism is the result of economic conflict, according to Marx and Friedrich Engels, a German industrialist who frequently collaborated with Marx. Both men saw all history as the result of struggle between the classes. Earlier, the struggle was between "freeman and slave, patrician and plebian, lord and serf, guild master and journeyman, in a word, oppressor and oppressed." In the modern period, the class struggle is between the bourgeoisie (the oppressor) and the proletariat (the oppressed). Here, bourgeoisie refers to the social class composed of modern capitalists, owners of the means of social production and employers of wage-labor. The proletariat, who lack a means of production of their own, are reduced to selling their labor power in order to live.[8] Communists believe that just as feudalism collapsed and was replaced by capitalism, so capitalism will break down and be replaced by communism.

3. *Dialectical change.* Dialectical change is a major societal change arising from the clash of two opposing ideas, forces, or social contradictions. While Marx never employed the rigid dialectical formula of "thesis," "antithesis," and "synthesis" to explain the movement of history, he did underscore the importance of contradictions in a given economic system (whether feudalism or capitalism) that

generate change in that system. For example, the contradictions or challenges that led to the breakdown of feudalism involved new inventions and discoveries that stimulated commercial and industrial production (capitalism) and made individual workshops and the guild economy obsolete. Capitalism produces its own contradictions. Marx emphasized two of them: First, capitalism creates a large class of exploited workers whose labor makes profits for capitalists; these workers become conscious of their exploitation, band together, and eventually overthrow their exploiters. Second, capitalism operates in a faulty, uneven way because it produces periodic catastrophic depressions.

Finally, communism is a strategy of revolutionary action for overthrowing capitalist society and enabling the world's workers to establish the inevitable communist society. This is one of the most controversial aspects of communist thought. How does change occur? As we will see, Marx certainly thought that the point of his political ideas was to effect change in society. But how could such change be advanced? Would it require violent means? In classical Marxist theory, the communist revolution would occur in three stages: first, the overthrow of capitalism; second, the revolutionary dictatorship of the proletariat; and, finally, communism. Capitalism would give birth to the proletarian revolution only after capitalistic society had developed the material conditions necessary to sustain the revolution. A feudal society could not jump to a communist economy without passing through the capitalist stage.

Workers prepare for the revolution by understanding the march of history (from feudalism to capitalism to communism), their own exploitation under capitalism, the weakness of capitalism, and the nature of the class struggle. Workers begin by organizing and unionizing, working with progressive democratic forces, arming themselves, and adopting an independent and militant stance on revolution. They must never lose sight of the ultimate goal of overthrowing capitalism, and they must be wary of being deceived by utopian socialists and liberal reformers, who offer false hopes and no real societal change. Hence, this explains many Communist criticisms of democratic socialists. The communist revolution must be permanent—it cannot merely patch up the bourgeois order; it must give workers control of production and put state power in the hands of the proletariat. In 1872, Marx said that in advanced bourgeois democratic countries, such as the United States and England, workers might be able to "attain their goal by peaceful means." But, he added, "in most countries on the Continent the lever of our revolution must be force."[9] Communists, Marx and Engels claimed, will be the leaders in this class struggle, since they have "the advantage of clearly understanding the line of march, the conditions, and the ultimate general results of the proletariat movement."

THE SOURCES OF COMMUNISM

Communism is clearly identified with several powerful thinkers and political actors. In the following section, we look at the ideas of Karl Marx, V. I. Lenin, Joseph Stalin, and Mao Zedong.

Karl Marx: Master Theoretician

V. I. Lenin, in his essay "The Three Sources and Three Component Parts of Marxism," noted that Germany made Karl Marx a philosopher, France made him a socialist revolutionary, and England made him a political economist.[10] What Lenin neglected to add was that the Enlightenment—which informed German philosophy, French revolutionary theory, and British political economy—made Marx a prophet of the new communist world.

The Enlightenment was a complex and influential movement that dominated Western thought in the eighteenth century, the century of the American and French Revolutions. Many of the *philosophes*—the enlightened ones—condemned the follies and barbarities of an oppressive and ignorant past and looked forward to the emancipation of humanity. Believing in reason, freedom, and progress, they appealed to reasonable people, extolled liberty, and hailed the march of humankind toward a better world. Marx attempted to carry the Enlightenment to what he thought was its logical conclusion: real freedom for all, which for him meant freedom in a classless, communist society.

Marx derived important philosophical ideas from two German philosophers, Georg Hegel and Ludwig Feuerbach. According to Hegel, the principal clue to historical development lay in the clash of opposing ideas—the basis of the Hegelian idea of the dialectic. Marx was impressed with Hegel's concept of the dialectic but disagreed about the opposing forces. Hegel had argued that ideas were the opposing forces, but Marx concluded that material forces—economic classes—rather than ideas explained evolution in history.

From Feuerbach, Marx derived a philosophic materialism (a belief that matter is the ultimate reality) and a radical critique of religion. Both ideas helped him formulate communism. Marx agreed with Feuerbach that religion was an illusion that prevented human beings from focusing on their needs in this world. He also agreed that the critique of religion led to a critique of society. But, Marx held, Feuerbach's materialism was inadequate. One had to move beyond an understanding of the material world to an effort to change that world. As Marx said in his critique of Feuerbach, "The philosophers have only interpreted the world, in various ways; the point, however, is to change it."[11] It was true, as materialist doctrine held, "that men are products of [material] circumstances," but materialists forget "that it is men who change circumstances." The interrelation of objective, material forces and of human thought and action troubled Marx and those who followed him.

Marx drew heavily on French socialist literature, revolutionary theory, and English economists. He was influenced by French social philosophers such as Saint-Simon and by such theorists of the French Revolution as Augustin Thierry, whom Marx regarded as the father of the class struggle in French historical writing. These French thinkers were disturbed about what the capitalist economy was doing, particularly to workers.[12]

Marx also was influenced by the French revolutions of 1789, 1848, and 1871. He saw the revolution of 1789 as the triumph of the French bourgeoisie; the revolution of 1848 as the failure of the bourgeoisie when they had to choose between liberty and property, family, and order; and the revolution of 1871—the short-lived workers' commune in Paris—as a model of the workers' revolution and the dictatorship of the proletariat. Never satisfied with mere intellectualizing, Marx sought to grasp the relationship between theory and practice in order to transform the world to communism.

Marx's stay in England and his wide reading of such British political economists as Adam Smith and David Ricardo made him a well-informed political economist. Engels's firsthand study of British labor conditions, published in 1845 as *Conditions of the Working Class in England*, stimulated Marx's interest in the actual working of industrialism in the most advanced capitalistic country in the world. Marx spent long hours in the library of the British Museum in order to explore and document ideas about capitalism that he had begun to develop (1857–1858) in a vast outline called the "Grundrisse, or Foundations of the Critique of Political Economy." A part of this research was published as *Das Kapital* (Capital) in three volumes.

V. I. Lenin: Master Revolutionary Strategist and Tactician

Lenin's modifications of Marxist doctrine became fundamental components of communist strategy and tactics in his home country of Russia.[13] Lenin's contributions must be viewed in the context of that politically autocratic, economically backward state. Marx had generally assumed that bourgeois capitalism would prepare the way for the communist revolution, and thus he expected the triumph of communism to begin in Western Europe. In tsarist Russia, the bourgeoisie were weak and the industrial proletariat few, especially compared to the peasantry. But World War I offered Lenin a unique opportunity. Losses on the battlefield and widespread discontent on farms and in factories made Russia ripe for revolution. Lenin took advantage of this discontent, winning allies among the peasants and adopting a revolutionary interpretation of Marx. The autocratic and repressive environment of tsarist Russia unquestionably made Lenin's communist strategy sharply revolutionary, conspiratorial, and dictatorial instead of evolutionary, open, and democratic.

In February (or March) 1917, rebels successfully overthrew the tsar, Nicholas II.[14] He abdicated and was replaced by a provisional government interested in establishing liberal, democratic institutions. Eight months later, when the time seemed ripe, the Lenin-led communists overthrew the provisional government and seized power (the October Revolution). A shrewd politician, Lenin promised peace to soldiers, jobs to city workers, and land to peasant farmers.

Lenin was not afraid to adapt Marx to the revolutionary circumstances of Russia. He used the Communist Party to lead the revolution, and he used a minority (party and industrial workers) to lead the majority (peasants, who were not communists).[15] Once in power, Lenin did not hesitate to slow up nationalization and encourage small capitalistic undertakings in agriculture and retail trade when the speed of the communist experiment threatened the regime's existence.

Lenin had argued in his 1902 publication *What Is to Be Done?* that the Communist Party had to lead the revolution. Only such a revolutionary party—equipped with "an advanced revolutionary theory"—could educate and lead the masses to victory. Arguing that such a party had to be united, ideologically homogeneous, limited in membership, and disciplined, Lenin advocated the principle of "democratic centralism," which called for intraparty democracy at the top level of leadership and subordination of the lower levels of the party to that elite. Lenin, thus, accepted a one-party state in which that party monopolized all political power.

Lenin also believed that violent revolution was justified. While such ideas can be seen in Marx's writings, Lenin was much more explicit about the need for such violence. He argued that there can be no liberation of the oppressed proletarian class unless the workers destroy the apparatus of state power built and operated by the ruling class. He insisted that bourgeois state power must be smashed, not merely taken over. He attacked the supporters of gradual reform, who maintained that it was possible to evolve peacefully to socialism. The state, as a repressive agency, however, still had to be used temporarily (now by the proletariat) to wipe out all vestiges of capitalism. During this dictatorship of the proletariat, the liquidation of the bourgeois state and society would continue until completed. Private ownership of the means of production would be abolished, and thus the old exploitation of the worker would end with the public ownership of the means of production. There were other changes that had to occur along with these economic ones: armed citizens had to replace the standing army and police, and the old administrative machinery had to be replaced by a new one, drawn from the people. Thus, Lenin disagreed with the anarchists, who maintained that, with the overthrow of the bourgeois state, coercive power would cease to exist.

Furthermore, during this period—economically the period of socialism—all vestiges of bourgeois society would not immediately disappear. Because socialism could not instantly create an economy of abundance, goods would continue to be distributed according to the amount of work each person did. The socialist motto is, "From each according to his ability; to each according to his work." This is significantly different from the equality embodied in the communist motto, "From each according to his ability; to each according to his needs." However, it was this theorizing about the revolutionary and transitionary period of socialism that marked a key difference between Marx and Lenin.

Joseph Stalin ruled the Soviet Union from 1928 until his death in 1953. Although he oversaw the nation's rise to a modern industrial and military power, he governed principally by terror.

Joseph Stalin: Master Builder of Soviet Power

If "Leninism is Marxism in the epoch of imperialism and of the proletarian revolution" (as Stalin once remarked), Stalinism is Leninism in the epoch of the building of Soviet power. Lenin had appreciated the importance of consolidating the Bolshevik revolution in Russia. Thus, Stalin could cite Lenin's actions to justify his own emphasis on "socialism in one country" Union could survive in a world without immediate communist revolutions in the advanced industrial nations.

As Lenin built upon and altered Marx, so Stalin built upon and altered Lenin. He took from Marx and Lenin those ideas that harmonized with his program and his sense of Russian and world realities, and he abandoned ideas that did not fit.[16] In so doing, Stalin made two important, and controversial, modifications to communism:

1. *Socialism in one country.* Despite his attention to the success of the Russian Revolution, Lenin assumed that the communist revolution in the Soviet Union would be secured by communist revolutions in the advanced industrial countries of Europe. By the time of Lenin's death in 1924, it was evident that communism was not emerging in other countries. Against Leon Trotsky, Stalin argued that socialism had to be built in one country, the Soviet Union, by that country's own efforts, despite its lack of industrial maturity. In theory, Stalin supported world revolution, but practically he emphasized socialism's development in the Soviet Union.

2. *The power of the Soviet state to build socialism.* In several five-year plans, Stalin accelerated industrialization and placed the demands of heavy industry ahead of the production of consumer goods. He defended his use of state power by arguing that the mightiest and strongest form of state power must be developed "in order to prepare the conditions for the withering away of state power" and that the state cannot wither away as long as the Soviet Union remained "surrounded by the capitalist world [and] is subject to the menace of foreign military attack." Stalin's tyrannical dictatorship led to a brutal reign of terror through party purges, phony show trials, mass executions and internments, and the general suppression of all dissent. To his critics, he is the prime example of a totalitarian leader.

Mao Zedong: Founder of Chinese Communism

Mao's main contribution to communism stems from his view of how to achieve power in China and from his concept of the continuing revolution. His primary goal was a united, strong, prosperous, and egalitarian China.[17] He was guided by his belief that China not only had to repel foreign invaders (such as Japan in World War II) but also had to defeat reactionary forces (such as the Nationalist forces of Chiang Kai-shek and China's warlords) that oppressed and divided the country. China had to be strong to prevent future humiliation by foreign powers, had to move out of poverty and into a modern prosperous economy, and had to achieve a more egalitarian society. These objectives, Mao held, could only be achieved by a communism adapted to China's singular history and conditions.

Although Lenin recognized the need to forge an alliance between urban workers and rural peasants, he was sufficiently within the orthodox Marxist tradition to rely on the urban proletariat to make the Soviet revolution. Such a strategy did not make sense to Mao Zedong. China's economy, Mao recognized, was even more agricultural than that of the Soviet Union. The urban workers' movement in China was small. Moreover, Chinese Nationalist leader Chiang Kai-shek had crushed the power of the Chinese communists in the cities at an early stage. Consequently, Mao held that Chinese communists had to build their strength among the peasants and in the countryside of northwest China rather than in the cities and among industrial workers. Aided by the Japanese attack on China before and during World War II, which weakened Chiang Kai-shek's Nationalist regime, Mao and the Chinese communists proceeded—after World War II was over—from their rural base to conquer the cities by military might. Mao successfully used guerilla warfare to maintain his strength until he could muster superior force against the Nationalist regime.

Although the Chinese communists took over the economy when they seized power in 1949, they did not immediately expropriate all private property. Subsequently, however, following Mao's philosophy of the continuing communist revolution, the government moved to exert greater control over the economy, to collectivize agriculture, and to industrialize.

One important ideological difference from classical Marxian theory emerged as Mao began the transition to communism. Mao sought to abbreviate the period of socialism and move more rapidly toward communism (in the Great Leap Forward, launched in 1958) by introducing communes—economic and governmental units for both agricultural and nonagricultural work—which was a policy ultimately doomed to failure.

Later, from 1966 to 1969, Mao attempted a cultural revolution to renew revolutionary vigor, speed up the revolutionary process, avoid bureaucracy, and enhance egalitarianism. The Cultural Revolution illustrates his theory of continuing the revolution under the dictatorship of the people. The Cultural Revolution—which had catastrophic political, economic, and social results—was Mao's effort to continue the communist revolution by resolving the contradictions that he saw in Chinese society: for example, the contradiction between tradition and modernity, between town and country. The revolution was seen as an effort, by societal upheaval and renewal, to move toward an egalitarian, classless society. It was characterized by direct popular action, attempted radical communist changes, and attacks on allegedly corrupt power holders. The Cultural Revolution sought periodic shake-ups to ensure that communism would stay true to its developmental goals.[18]

COMMUNISM AS A POLITICAL IDEOLOGY AND PHILOSOPHY: PRO AND CON

Communism is one of the most controversial theories of politics. In this section, we review arguments in its favor as well as those in opposition.

Criticism of Communism

Communism, as a set of ideas, has been attacked as utopian in theory and totalitarian and Machiavellian in its pursuit of political power (that is, committed to a strategy of "lion and fox") in practice. Moreover, communism's critics argue that it has failed not only as a political and social system but also as an economic system because it cannot produce goods efficiently and abundantly. Finally, it is attacked for its failure to appreciate capitalism's adaptive power: critics contend that communism is not a scientific theory of society. These critics find confirmation in the theory and practice of Marxism-Leninism-Stalinism and in the failure of communism in the Soviet Union.

Communism is utopian because it rests, theoretically, on the unrealistic premise of a classless, conflictless society. No such harmonious society is possible, given human fallibility, liberty, and diversity. The quest for a society that will achieve universal freedom, abundance, and virtue and will banish alienation is a utopian dream. This dream led communists, in the now-defunct Soviet Union, to try the impossible and to be willing (especially, but not exclusively, under Stalin) to pay a terrible price in human freedom and sacrifice to achieve their goals. People in China and other communist countries continue to pay a heavy price for communism's unrealistic aspirations.

Communist theory, in a desperate attempt to attain the impossible, contains elements that can lead to **totalitarianism**—an ideology that espouses the complete political, economic, and social control of people and institutions by a dictatorial, single-party regime—or severely repressive **authoritarianism**—a political stance that favors placing political power in the hands of an elite group or a dictator. Marx's division of the world into an oppressed proletariat and an oppressive capitalist class is the first step toward totalitarian or authoritarian rule. The historical communist commitment to a (generally) violent revolution to overthrow capitalism and establish a dictatorship of the proletariat is an important second step. Lenin's emphasis on the crucial role of the Communist Party is a third step. The momentum of the communist revolution then moves from the dictatorship of the proletariat to the dictatorship of the party (with Lenin) to the dictatorship of the party leadership (the Politburo) to the dictatorship of the key party leader (Stalin). Moreover, given the fear of internal and external enemies, and the herculean job of building socialism, the growth and use of state power seem inevitable.

The communist theory on the dictatorship of the proletariat has been significantly influenced by the Soviet and especially the Stalinist example. Millions of lives were lost during the Soviet Union's dictatorship of the proletariat, which was really Stalin's personal dictatorship. The list of Stalin's victims is endless and includes not only capitalists but liberals, democratic socialists, peasants, and even loyal communists as well. It is easy to blame these excesses on a cruel, despotic, and paranoid Stalin. However, the theory of the dictatorship of the proletariat itself cannot be exempt from criticism, especially as it leads to highly centralized control of the state by the Politburo and, ultimately, control by one person. Any threat to the power of the communist party leadership was ruthlessly put down. The Soviet Union, for instance, did not hesitate to forcefully put down the "liberal" communist revolution against rigid rule in Hungary in 1956; or to send tanks into Prague in 1968 to overthrow the Dubček government when it sought to develop a more democratic, open variety of communism; or to invade Afghanistan in 1979 to prop up a troubled and faltering communist regime.

According to communism's critics, its failure as a political, economic, and social system is clear. This failure is illustrated by the collapse of communism in the Soviet Union and by the disintegration of the Soviet Union itself. The repudiation in free elections of authoritarian communist rulers and regimes in Eastern Europe is additional evidence of communism's failure. The attempt by Chinese rulers to liberalize their economy is further evidence that communist economic ideas do not work. Moreover, political discontent with China's authoritarian political system—as illustrated by the 1989 protest in Beijing's Tiananmen Square—indicates that many Chinese long for greater freedom.

Communism, critics contend, has underestimated the ability of capitalism to adapt to changing circumstances. In the past, communists have been critical of capitalism because values such as peace, freedom, justice, and prosperity were not being fulfilled for the great majority of people. This claim seems less valid today for advanced industrial liberal democracies. In fact, workers in liberal democratic nations have significantly improved their lives. Even if the communist criticism of capitalistic and imperialist abuses is morally justified, it is by no means clear that this ideology offers a realistic way to alleviate the problems of capitalism. Capitalism has not withered away and died. It has, in fact, demonstrated a tenacious staying power.

The Defense of Communism

Communism's beleaguered defenders still maintain that it is a liberating revolutionary philosophy, truly democratic and peaceful, guided by consistent principles, and able to reform itself. They also believe that the history of communism is a great deal more complex than its critics allow.

As Marx pointed out, communism stands for universal human emancipation. In advanced countries where capitalism is overthrown, workers will finally gain control of their economic, social, and political lives and be able to satisfy their needs in the realms of work, education, health, housing, and culture.[19] In new nations, as Lenin anticipated, former colonial subjects will manage their own destinies and, by following the socialist path of development, will lift themselves into the modern world.

Communism, supporters contend, is committed to democratic, peaceful policies. Communism is democratic in that it seeks rule by the overwhelming majority of workers in their own interest. The dictatorship of the proletariat is democratic (the majority exercises power) as opposed to the undemocratic dictatorship of the bourgeoisie (the minority acts in the interest of capitalist exploiters). The use of force and violence in the communist revolution depends on the resistance of those who oppose it.

Wise, consistent Marxist-Leninist principles can still guide communist theory and practice. According to communists, these principles make it clear that the communist victory is inevitable but that circumstances must be considered in moving toward that victory. These circumstances include, for example, a country's stage of economic, social, and political development. Communists maintain that in light of the dangers of nuclear war, peaceful coexistence is the only sane policy. Peaceful coexistence does not, however, bar ideological, economic, and political competition.

Tremendous economic strides were made in many sectors of Soviet society. For all his faults, Stalin presided over a country that saw incredible advances in industrialization; accrued an impressive record in scientific accomplishments; and made significant progress in areas such as education (the elimination of illiteracy is common in many communist regimes), medical care, and housing. All of this was achieved in a largely hostile international environment. Even if, in many areas, standards of living fell short of those enjoyed by Americans, we should consider what was accomplished in light of the backward economic conditions that the Soviet Union inherited from tsarist Russia.

The reform possibilities of communism, its true believers maintain, were tragically cut short in Mikhail Gorbachev's Soviet Union. China, however, as it liberalizes its economy, demonstrates the viability of communist reform.

Finally, because no nation has yet moved to a mature stage of communism, it is difficult to compare theory to actual practice. Marx thought it foolish to describe the details of a full-fledged future communist society. So he did not address problems of freedom, integration, abundance, and community. Marx apparently believed these matters would take care of themselves because society would be based on worker control of the means of exchange, because workers would achieve communist abundance, and because workers would make the leap from the realm of necessity to the realm of freedom. At worst, Marx's deficiency in not spelling out a democratic theory of mature communism is merely an example of naïveté. He was wrong to trust the people to work out the details of a fair and free communist society.

THE RECENT PAST AND FUTURE OF DEMOCRATIC SOCIALISM AND COMMUNISM

The ideologies of democratic socialism and communism have had a tremendous effect on the day-to-day politics of many nations. In this section, we discuss the history and future of these two bodies of thought.

Democratic Socialism

Although it is the case that democratic socialism and communism as political systems have never been adopted in America, their ideas exert an influence in the United States as well as in Europe and elsewhere. Furthermore, if Americans are uncomfortable with the labels of socialism and communism, the values of social justice, greater democracy, a mixed economy, a welfare state, a cooperative community, international freedom, unity, and peace nevertheless have a deep hold on many citizens in the United States. The democratic socialist commitment to democracy links it to liberal democracy. Its commitment to public ownership links it, in part, to communism. From the perspective of a liberal democrat attuned to capitalism, democratic socialists go too far in the economic sphere; from the perspective of orthodox communists, democratic socialists do not go far enough. But have democratic socialists struck the right middle ground in their understanding of the good political life?

We must emphasize that it took a long time to bring together democratic socialist ideas and mass electoral support. Even though, by 1914, socialism had become an important political force on the European continent, no democratic socialist party came to power until after World War I. Even after World War I, the prospects for democratic socialism were grim in the major European powers. Sweden, while not considered a major power, nevertheless provides a striking example of social democratic success. The Swedish Socialist Party came to power in the 1930s and initiated major reforms in social security, equal opportunity, full employment, and national health insurance. In Europe's larger countries, democratic socialism is predominantly a post–World War II phenomenon. Given the democratic socialists' relatively short tenure in power, it is often difficult to compare their professed values with their actual behavior. In general, however, democratic socialists have remained true to political democracy. They have modestly moved in the direction of greater social justice and a more equitable distribution of wealth. They seem to have accepted a socialist version of the welfare state and the mixed economy and to have backed away from more complete nationalization or public ownership. Through educational reform, they have attempted to enlarge opportunities for the less privileged. They have alleviated, if not overcome, a number of key economic problems of modern industrial society: periodic recession or depression, persistent unemployment (particularly among people at the low end of the economic and social ladder), and worker alienation. The golden dream of industrial democracy in a cooperative society has not been fulfilled. Nor have dreams of international freedom, unity, and peace. Yet democratic socialists have unquestionably made life better for working people and the needy. They have helped to tame and harness modern capitalism. And they have kept the costs reasonable.

Nonetheless, democratic socialists still face a dilemma in fulfilling their historic mission. If they are too radical, they will frighten off the middle-class support they need for gaining and wielding power. If they are too conservative, their philosophy and programs will be indistinguishable from those of their political rivals. The rise to political prominence of Senator Bernie Sanders in the United States and the ascent of Jeremy Corbyn as the leader of Great Britain's Labour Party all point to the greater influence of democratic socialist ideas in mainstream politics in those two countries. Although, we should note, Great Britain has always had a significant history of socialism and Senator Sanders socialism is of a more muted variety than is found elsewhere in the world. Democratic socialists strive to develop effective, humane ways to advance social justice, democracy, the satisfaction of human needs, a cooperative community, and human excellence.

Communism: A History

The history of communism encompasses many countries, but we focus on the two most significant cases—the Soviet Union and China.

The Soviet Union. The story of communism, and its future, is even more interesting. Even before Mikhail Gorbachev came to power as general secretary of the Communist Party in 1985, Nikita Khrushchev, who led the Soviet Union from 1958 to 1963, made efforts to reform the communist system. As early as 1956 Khrushchev confronted Stalin's terrorist rule and Stalin's "cult of personality," a phenomenon that makes a "particular leader a hero and miracle worker." He also worried about the advent of nuclear weapons. Khrushchev was cheered by the existence of communist states outside the Soviet Union and the emergence of new nations from among the former colonies of the great powers. In facing up to these developments, Khrushchev attempted to "liberalize" the Soviet Union in various ways, to reject the idea of the "fatal inevitability of war," to highlight "the emergence of socialism from the confines of one country and its transformation into a world system," and to emphasize the possibility of peaceful, parliamentary socialism and communism in the new states of the formerly colonial world as well as in the capitalist world. Gorbachev attempted to follow through on many of these points.

Gorbachev's "new thinking" rested on policies of *glasnost* (openness) and *perestroika* (restructuring) designed to achieve—at home and abroad—something akin to communism with a human face. Gorbachev also stressed the importance of *uskorenie*— the acceleration of reforms in the communist system. There is little doubt that Soviet domestic and foreign policies underwent a significant change between 1985 and 1990. Domestically, Gorbachev sought to move the Soviet Union toward greater respect for the rule of law and other basic freedoms, to reform the distressed economy by opting for "market socialism" (away from a centralized, command economy and toward a decentralized market economy), and to reinvigorate the Communist Party as well as political, economic, and social life in general. In foreign policy, Gorbachev sought to end the Cold War, to reduce arms, to allow the formerly communist regimes of Eastern Europe to go their own ways, and to bring the Soviet Union into a common European home.[20]

Ironically, Gorbachev's efforts at reform placed him in the position of the sorcerer's apprentice who could not stop the actions he had started. The loss of Soviet preeminence in the international communist movement, the end of Soviet dominance in Eastern Europe, a failing and seriously flawed agricultural and industrial economy, and greater freedom for Soviet citizens all contributed to the unraveling of both communism and the Soviet state itself. By the 1990s, the Soviet Union had collapsed, and Russia was under the leadership of Boris Yeltsin, the former mayor of Moscow. For roughly a decade, Yeltsin served as president of the new Russian Republic as it made its transition to democracy and a free market economy. Yeltsin was followed in the year 2000 by Vladimir Putin (Edinstvo Party), a relatively young, energetic, and highly organized graduate of the State University in St. Petersburg. On his path to power, Putin had served as an officer in the KGB, the Soviet Union's foreign intelligence service. Although Putin was temporarily replaced as president by Dmitry Medvedev, he still maintained a great deal of power in the office of prime minister. In 2012, he was reelected as president.

China. After Mao's death in 1976, and under the leadership of Deng Xiaoping, China sought to accept the realities of a market economy and assume a more modern, free, and open worldview. Deng continued to adhere to the famous four principles of Chinese communism: the socialist way, dictatorship of the proletariat, leadership of the Communist Party, and what was called Marxism-Leninism-Mao Zedong thought. But Deng interpreted these principles pragmatically so that they would not interfere with his ideas for the Four Modernizations: in agriculture, industry, science, and defense. Revolutionary class struggle could not be allowed to interfere with sensible economic reform. The Communist Party, of course, would retain control of policy; however, China would move toward a less centralized, less collectivistic, and less bureaucratic communism.

Deng's position would keep China focused on a central point: economic development. The country would persevere in economic reform and open up to the outside world. Economic reform meant "maintaining the system of private agriculture that replaced collective farms, dismantling central planning generally in favor of private entrepreneurship and the market, and fully integrating China into the global economy."[21]

The limits to modernization, and to certain democratic trends in China, were highlighted in 1989 by the Chinese regime's response to the remarkable pro-democracy student demonstrations in Tiananmen Square in Beijing. After tolerating the demonstrations for nearly a month, the Chinese government brutally crushed them and then conducted a campaign of arrests and repression designed to punish the pro-democracy movement and its supporters. Economic reform did not mean political reform in the liberal democratic tradition, and China's future remains problematic. What is particularly uncertain is whether China can modernize economically while resisting political reform (and freedom) and while keeping the Communist Party as the only center of political power. Still, it is clear that as the twenty-first century progresses, China remains a fascinating case of an economically vibrant country that has only sparingly embraced democratic practices.

CONCLUSION

Many former communists have resurrected political careers in Germany, Poland, and elsewhere in Europe. We should not be surprised by this phenomenon. Democratic socialism and communism remain important political forces. They will remain so as long as economic and social conditions create significant inequalities. The demand for some kind of egalitarian politics will not disappear, although it might emerge under different names and in different guises. Indeed, the seeming triumph of global capitalism was seriously called into question by the economic depression, which gripped Europe and the United States starting in 2008. The sluggish recovery from that economic crisis and the continuing high levels of unemployment in the United States and Europe gave added impetus to those who would look again to socialism and Marxism for political and economic guidance. No matter what name it appears under, we can be sure that traditions of criticism developed by socialists and communists will contribute to any new ideology devoted to making people politically equal. Furthermore, as the current leader of China, Xi Jinping has consolidated his power that sparing embrace grows even more uncertain.

SUGGESTED READINGS

Bronner, Stephen. *Socialism Unbound.* 3rd ed. New York: Routledge, 1990. A thoughtful defense of the Marxist tradition.

Cole, G. D. H. *A History of Socialist Thought.* 5 vols. New York: St. Martin's Press, 1953–1960. The richest, most comprehensive account of the roots and evolution of socialism.

D'Amato, Paul. *The Meaning of Marxism.* Chicago: Haymarket Books, 2014. An accessible account of the main ideas of Marx.

Eagleton, Terry. *Why Marx Was Right.* New Haven, CT: Yale University, 2012. From a leading social thinker, challenges many of what he calls myths surrounding Marxism.

Gay, Peter. *The Dilemma of Democratic Socialism: Eduard Bernstein's Challenge to Marx.* New York: Collier-Macmillan, 1962. An illuminating study of one of the most important revisionists and democratic socialists.

Harvey, David. *Seventeen Contradictions and the End of Capitalism.* Oxford, UK: Oxford University Press, 2014. This book examines capitalism and shows how the very nature of capitalism, while incredible dynamic, can also lead to severe economic problems, even collapse.

Gorbachev, Mikhail. *Perestroika: New Thinking for Our Country and the World.* New York: Harper & Row, 1988. Recommended for the remarkable thought of this extraordinary, if tragically flawed, Soviet leader.

Kolakowski, Leszek. *Main Currents of Marxism.* 3 vols. New York: Oxford University Press, 1978. A very rich history and analysis by a Polish scholar sympathetic to Marxist humanism. Vol. 1 (*The Founders*) explores Marxism's origins and other socialist ideas, along with the writings of Karl Marx and Friedrich Engels. Vol. 2 (*The Golden Age*) deals with Marxists such as Karl Kautsky, Rosa Luxemburg, Eduard Bernstein, Jean Jaures, Georges Sorel, George V. Plekhanov, and V. I. Lenin. Vol. 3 (*The Breakdown*) treats the evolution of Marxism from the mid-1920s to the mid-1970s and Joseph Stalin, Leon Trotsky, György Lukács, and key figures in the Frankfurt School—Herbert Marcuse and Ernest Bloch.

McLellan, David. *Karl Marx: His Life and Thought*. New York: Harper & Row, 1973. The authoritative biography. Contains good summaries of Marx's writings.

Pipes, Richard. *Communism: A History*. New York: Modern Library, 2001. A highly critical history of the rise and fall of modern communism from the time of Marx and Engels through the Russian Revolution to the ultimate collapse of the Soviet Union.

Remnick, David. *Lenin's Tomb*. New York: Random House, 1994. A thoughtful and literate account of the collapse of the Soviet Union.

Riemer, Neal. *Karl Marx and Prophetic Politics*. New York: Praeger, 1987. Assesses Marx according to the standard of prophetic politics.

Schram, Stuart R. *The Thought of Mao Tse-tung*. Cambridge, MA: Cambridge University Press, 1989. A balanced, scholarly presentation and assessment of Mao's developing ideas.

Sebestyn, Victor. *Lenin: The Man, the Dictator, and the Master of Terror*. New York: Pantheon, 2017. A recent and very critical view of the founder of the Soviet Union.

Terrill, Ross. *China in Our Time*. New York: Simon & Schuster, 1992. A revealing account of China under Mao Zedong and Deng Xiaoping. Notes that although communism as an idea may be dying, the Communist Party is growing stronger.

Tucker, Robert C., ed. *The Marx-Engels Reader*. 2nd ed. New York: Norton, 1978. An excellent, handy collection. See also Tucker's helpful *The Lenin Anthology* (New York: Norton, 1975) and his brilliant analyses of Soviet leader Joseph Stalin in *Stalin as Revolutionary, 1870–1929* (New York: Norton, 1972), and *Stalin in Power: The Revolution from Above, 1928–1941* (New York: Norton, 1992).

GLOSSARY TERMS

authoritarianism (p. 179)
bourgeoisie (p. 167)
class struggle (p. 172)
communism (p. 171)
democratic socialism (p. 162)
dialectical change (p. 172)

dictatorship of the proletariat (p. 167)
egalitarianism (p. 167)
Fabians (p. 168)
materialism (p. 172)
mixed economy (p. 163)
proletariat (p. 171)

revisionists (p. 167)
totalitarianism (p. 179)
utopia (p. 165)
utopian socialists (p. 165)
welfare state (p. 163)

NOTES

1. For help in understanding the remarkable changes that have occurred in the communist world, see Zbigniew Brzezinski, *The Grand Failure: The Birth and Death of Communism in the Twentieth Century* (New York: Scribner's, 1989); and Adam B. Ulam, *The Communist: The Story of Power and Lost Illusion, 1948–1991* (New York: Scribner's, 1992).

2. See Robert Owen's *New View of Society* (1813), quoted in George Lichtheim, *The Origins of Socialism* (New York: Praeger, 1969), 114.

3. This account draws on Peter Gay, *The Dilemma of Democratic Socialism: Eduard Bernstein's Challenge to Marx* (New York: Collier-Macmillan, 1962). See Eduard Bernstein, *Evolutionary Socialism* (New York: Schocken, 1961); and Leszek Kolakowski's

account of "Bernstein and Revisionism," in *The Breakdown*, vol. 3 of Kolakowski's *Main Currents of Marxism* (New York: Oxford University Press, 1978).

4. Anthony Crosland, *Socialism Now and Other Essays by Anthony Crosland*, ed. Dick Leonard (London: Cape, 1974).

5. Julia Mead, https://www.thenation.com/article/why-millennials-arent-afraid-of-the-s-word/

6. Karl Marx, "Critique of the Gotha Program," in *The Marx-Engels Reader*, 2nd ed., ed. Robert C. Tucker (New York: Norton, 1978), 531.

7. Karl Marx, "The German Ideology: Part 1," in *Marx-Engels Reader*, 155–156.

8. Karl Marx and Friedrich Engels, "Manifesto of the Communist Party," in *Marx-Engels Reader*, 473–474. For definitions of *bourgeoisie* and *proletariat*, see the footnote added by Engels in 1888 in *Marx-Engels Reader*, 473.

9. Karl Marx, "The Possibility of Non-Violent Revolution," in *Marx-Engels Reader*, 523.

10. V. I. Lenin, "The Three Sources and Three Component Parts of Marxism," in *The Lenin Anthology*, ed. Robert C. Tucker (New York: Norton), 640–644.

11. Karl Marx, "Theses on Feuerbach," in *Marx-Engels Reader*, 145.

12. John Plamenatz, *German Marxism and Russian Communism* (London: Longman, 1954), 308. On Marx and the utopian tradition, see Frank E. Manuel and Fritzie P. Manuel, *Utopian Thought in the Western World* (Cambridge, MA: Belknap Press, 1979).

13. See Tucker, *Lenin Anthology*; and Alfred G. Meyer, *Leninism* (New York: Praeger, 1962).

14. The February date is the date according to the Russian calendar, which, until changed by Lenin not long after the Russian Revolution, was about a half month behind the Western calendar.

15. See V. I. Lenin, "The State and Revolution," in *Lenin Anthology*.

16. Joseph Stalin, *Problems of Leninism* (Moscow: Foreign Language, 1940). See also Kolakowski, *Breakdown*.

17. On Mao, see Stuart R. Schram, *The Thought of Mao Tse-tung* (Cambridge: Cambridge University Press, 1989); John Bryan Starr, *Continuing the Revolution: The Political Thought of Mao* (Princeton, NJ: Princeton University Press, 1979); and Ross Terrill, *China in Our Time* (New York: Simon & Schuster, 1992).

18. James R. Townsend and Brantly Womack, *Politics in China* (Boston: Little, Brown, 1986).

19. Some defenders of communism hold that it is a liberating philosophy and that the Soviet Union never truly practiced communism. This raises the question of the relation of Marx's Marxism to the Soviet Union. Kolakowski, in *Breakdown*, writes, "It would be absurd to maintain that Marxism was, so to speak, the efficient cause of present-day Communism; on the other hand, Communism is not a mere 'degeneration' of Marxism but a possible interpretation of it, and even a well-founded one, though primitive and partial in some respects" (p. 26).

20. Mikhail Gorbachev, *Perestroika: New Thinking for Our Country and the World* (New York: Harper & Row, 1988).

21. See Terrill, *China in Our Time*; and (for the quotation) Roderick MacFarquhar, "Deng's Last Campaign," *New York Review of Books*, December 17, 1992, 22.

AMERICAN, COMPARATIVE, AND WORLD POLITICS

In Part III, we begin our examination of the actual political process in the United States and around the world. These chapters explore how politics functions in a diverse set of countries: democracies, communist regimes, and failed states. This is an incredibly varied subject, and in many ways we can touch only on the complex diversity that is politics around the globe.

To fully appreciate how politics works, we need to understand some basic concepts, and Chapter 8 provides an overview of what we identify as the major dilemmas in politics— How do political systems accommodate various interests and resolve conflicts? What is the role political culture and constitutions play in shaping politics? How do political values affect the actions of political actors? Although each country is unique, all political systems must deal with these dilemmas. Chapter 9 specifically deals with the United States, its political culture, and the enduring influence of the Constitution, with its emphasis on separation of powers and the central importance of the Bill of Rights. Furthermore, this chapter explores the way the legislature, the executive branch, and the courts actually function day by day. In Chapter 10, the focus is on comparative politics. To do that, we examine four countries—Great Britain, Nazi Germany, China, and Zimbabwe—that reflect different political systems: parliamentary democracy, authoritarian regimes, mixed political systems, and fragile or failed states. Finally, Chapter 11 explores international politics and the global community. This chapter offers a detailed and specific analysis of the notion of power and how nation-states interact.

Congressmen faced contentious town hall meetings in 2017, particularly over the issue of healthcare.

REUTERS/Lucy Nicholson

8

KEY DILEMMAS
Political Form, Culture, and Values

In the preceding three chapters, we examined philosophical questions about what the good political life looks like. We also investigated the main ideologies that animate contemporary politics—liberal democracy, democratic socialism, and communism. However, in considering the meaning of the good life or acquainting ourselves with political ideologies, students of politics might reasonably wonder if this is all in fact merely talk. Just because theorists of liberal democracy say they value justice and believe in individual freedom, does it necessarily follow that countries professing to be liberal democracies practice what they preach? Because Karl Marx wrote about freedom, equality, and the idea of human development, does this mean communist states actually further those ideals? And even if democratic socialists claim to combine the advantages of democracy with the ideals of socialism, is it the case that social democratic politicians bring this philosophy to bear on their day-to-day actions? In this section, we consider how politics is actually practiced. What are the procedures, structures, and values that shape day-to-day politics? This leads us to consider the Key Questions on the next page.

These questions might seem rather simple to answer. In fact, they are not. Each question focuses on the issue of values and its intersection with the practical world of politics. How, we need to know, do the workings of day-to-day, pragmatic politics interact with the abstract world of ideals? Question 3, in particular, forces us to evaluate the practice of democracy itself.

Chapter Objectives

After studying this chapter, you will be able to do the following:

1. Define the key terms of political values, goals, and political actors.

2. Explain the role of political culture in politics.

3. Examine the main features of constitutional government.

4. Identify the main values found in democracies.

5. Examine the values of political elites and average citizens and the role each plays in politics.

SOME KEY TERMS DEFINED

To get a better grip on how to approach the question of politics and values, we must start by defining key terms. **Political values** are important beliefs about which goals, principles, and policies are worthwhile in public affairs. A **goal** is an objective. It may be peace, security, and order—or war, domination, and power. It may be liberty, equality, justice, and fraternity—or slavery, subordination, tyranny, and enmity. The goal may be a fair return on national investment and international respect—or rampant profit and national self-righteousness. The goal may be democratic and constitutional government—or oligarchic or dictatorial/authoritarian rule. The goal may be economic prosperity for all—or affluence for the few. It may be a healthy environment—or a highly productive society that ignores ecological health. A **principle** is a basic truth or belief that is used as a basis of reasoning or a guide to behavior. It may be belief in peaceful change (ballots)—or violent change (bullets). It may be a commitment to freedom of speech for all—or freedom only for the elite. Principles actually at work in political communities often illustrate compromises among competing ideas. Finally, a **policy** is a course, or general plan, of action designed to solve problems or achieve specified goals. A policy may be aimed at achieving a balance of power, balance of terror, or unilateral disarmament. A policy may be one of universal suffrage—or suffrage limited to rich, well-educated males. It may be in support of a progressive income tax—or a sales tax, a public standard for clean air and pure water—or a hands-off environmental policy. Goals, principles, and policies (which sometimes overlap) often function as norms. They help determine whether certain standards are being met. Consequently, they serve as important guideposts in politics and, as such, merit careful study. When goals, principles, and politics are functioning well the political system is considered **politically legitimate**. Of course, a well functioning society includes a lot of debate. However, if the fundamental goals or principles of a society are called into question or there are such stark differences between groups about them, then political legitimacy can be threatened and society can become unstable.

Where do political values come from? Whose goals, principles, and policies are actually being observed? A **political actor** is the individual or group that expresses and shapes public values, struggles for power, and decides issues of public policy. Governmental, economic, social, and military elites are all examples of political actors. Political parties, **interest groups**, and the mass media—newspapers, television networks, and newsmagazines—are political actors as well. So, too, are individual citizens. In fact, who functions as a political actor at any given time varies widely and comes from all strata of the political world: from political, social, and economic elites to institutions such as political parties, interest groups, and agencies of the mass media to the individual citizen who writes letters, demonstrates, or simply votes.

In a broader sense, political communities themselves are actors. Nation-states constitute one important form of actor in the international system. The United Nations is another type of political community. The subdivisions of nation-states are also political actors: for example, each of America's fifty states, 3,033 counties, 19,492 municipal polities, and 16,519 townships is a political actor. A number of regional and functional organizations—for example, the European Union—are political actors. And so, increasingly, are multinational corporations (MNCs).

This incredibly diverse array of political actors has led students of politics to wrestle with what is sometimes referred to as the "level-of-analysis problem."[1] In attempting to understand international relations, for example, is it more appropriate to concentrate on national governments as the primary actors or on the decision makers who lead the governments? Or should one concentrate on the international system itself and its patterns of military, economic, and political interaction among governments, international organizations, and nongovernmental organizations (NGOs)? In other words, must one operate on a global level to really understand what is going on?

KEY QUESTIONS

1. How do the actual political values of political actors compare with civilized values such as peace, liberty, justice, and welfare?

2. What do the professed values of political actors really mean? Can political actors harmonize different, sometimes competing, values?

3. Finally, how do the values of political leaders differ from those held by common citizens?

In our exploration of the values of political actors in this chapter, we limit our analysis to what we consider to be some of the most important values—national values, popular (citizen) values, and interest group and **class values**. The political values of political actors are rooted in their vital needs, fundamental interests, and perceived desires. The struggle over political values is also conditioned by the differing interpretations of needs, interests, and desires by diverse political actors and by the historical distribution of power. These factors make for both conflict and consensus in politics.

Additionally, the world of politics frequently contains serious gaps between professed values and actual behavior. The gaps exist because political actors—nation-states, governing elites, powerful interests, and citizens themselves—are unable to break out of parochial, rigidly ideological patterns of thought and behavior. Because human resources and capabilities are limited, it is often difficult to narrow these gaps. And, as we have seen in the former Yugoslavia, ancient, historical forces (long-held ethnic grievances) can impose one set of demands on political actors that can come into conflict with other professed values.

Finally, although prediction is hazardous, the future will probably include a major constitutional and democratic struggle between what we might call broad values and narrow values. This struggle will manifest itself in several ways. There will be a contest between broader global or regional human needs and narrower, parochial national interests. There also will be a contest between broad, truly fundamental community interests and narrower, selfish group and individual desires. Finally, there will be a contest between vital individual and local interests and oppressive, centralized interests and desires. This struggle will most certainly require a realistic understanding of vital needs, of compatible fundamental interests, and of modest and prudent desires.

PATTERNS FOR COOPERATION, ACCOMMODATION, AND CONFLICT RESOLUTION

Although we cannot definitively resolve the complex problem of "who gets what, when, where, and how," we may use the question itself to explore patterns of politics. Our hypothesis here and in Chapters 9 and 10 is that successful patterns for furthering cooperation, advancing accommodation, and handling conflicts in politics require the following:

1. *Agreement on the constitutional fundamentals that facilitate consensus and trust.* Without a certain amount of consensus, no political community can carry out its business. Without a certain amount of trust, orderly procedures for discussion and decision would be impossible. Agreement on fundamentals involves accepted rules of the constitutional game (on voting; freedom of speech, press, and assembly; majority decision; due process of law) that enable political actors to civilize the struggle for power. Some political cultures are more effective at reaching agreement on fundamentals because they encourage the education and socialization of the citizenry in sound rules of the political game.

2. *Opportunity to establish needs, interests, and desires.* **Interest articulation** is the expression of political actors' needs, interests, and desires. Articulation is accomplished in any number of ways: for example, by voting, speaking out in public forums, working for a political party, joining interest groups, using the mass media, and contacting elected representatives. Such opportunities facilitate cooperation and accommodation in responsive political systems. Citizens who take advantage of these opportunities are often more knowledgeable about politics and better educated than nonparticipants.

   Massive demonstrations such as the one in support of free press and against terrorism in Paris early in 2014 can be viewed as a form of interest articulation. The demonstration emerged after the January attack on the satirical magazine *Charlie Hebdo* that resulted in the deaths of twelve staff members and two police officers.

3. *Mechanisms for prioritizing.* Some needs and interests are more important than others. Effective prioritizing involves **interest aggregation**—the process by which political actors build support for certain proposals and not for others. Political actors usually find it necessary to work with like-minded individuals or groups to advance the ideas that they believe merit support. Political leaders and parties play key roles in building support for political priorities, but they do not have a monopoly on this enterprise.

4. *Legitimizing policy choice using agreed-upon principles and mechanisms of public obligation.* Why do people obey those who make law and execute public policy? Why, for example, in the United States do citizens accept the result of an election, a law passed by Congress, a decision of the Supreme Court, or a presidential initiative in foreign affairs? Why do people go along with a majority decision? The answer is simple: Without agreement on ideas and ways to obtain approval of the exercise of political power, the struggle for power could easily get out of hand; politics would quickly disappear; and lawlessness, disorder, and civil war would ensue.

5. *Fulfillment of government objectives.* A government that can maintain freedom, law, and order; raise and spend revenue on behalf of agreed-on public purposes; and

ensure the provision of necessary services and benefits is essential. If government cannot modestly fulfill its own objectives—say, of security, liberty, justice, and welfare—its very existence is in serious jeopardy. Political patterns cannot succeed unless they advance effective governance.

6. *Regular and effective controls on government.* Constitutional mechanisms to ensure that government is a wise and limited servant, not a tyrannical master, must be in place.

We will explore our hypothesis by focusing on political culture, constitutional arrangements, and the role of nongovernmental actors in industrialized democratic countries. Throughout our analysis, we will be concerned with whether the political patterns we have examined are voluntary or imposed, humane or barbaric, peaceful or violent. We begin our exploration with a discussion of democratic constitutionalism, with an emphasis on the United States. For comparative purposes, analysis of other countries, including Great Britain, India, and Russia, is also offered. Later in the chapter, we share some thoughts on alternative political systems and political systems that have failed.

DEMOCRATIC CONSTITUTIONALISM

In this section, we look at democratic constitutionalism. Consider the Key Questions on this page.

Political Culture and the Framing of Politics

One way of exploring how political regimes function is to investigate the culture within which they operate. **Political culture** refers to the distinguishing attitudes, habits, and behavior patterns that characterize a political community—the ethos of a particular place. Students of politics can observe important distinctions between the values and beliefs central to one society versus those of another. The ethos of a country may be peaceful or warlike, tolerant or intolerant; it may be altruistic or selfish, trusting or suspicious, cooperative or competitive. The dominant ethos may be genuinely egalitarian or racist and sexist. The people may be cultured, literate, and active in politics, or they may be uncultured, uneducated, and uninvolved. We do not mean to suggest that all people within a given society agree about politics—or even agree with all the traditions and customs of their culture. Furthermore, no society or culture is static—they always evolve and adapt to changing conditions. However, societies do display a dominant set of

KEY QUESTIONS

1. What is political culture, and what are some of the ways it can affect constitutional democratic systems?

2. What functions do constitutions perform, and why are they important to democracies?

3. Why do most proponents of democracy believe that citizen participation, interest groups, political parties, and media are critical nongovernmental actors?

characteristics that enjoys widespread support. In the United States, for example, great emphasis is placed on individual freedom. Other cultures may be less enamored with the idea of personal freedom and more concerned with collective equality or may see too much freedom as threatening social stability.

A political community's culture is significantly influenced by a number of factors. These include the wider environment, as we saw in Chapter 4. The climate, availability of natural resources, and population of a place all affect its political culture. A nation's historical experience and memory clearly shape its culture, as do its language, religion, literature, art, and social mores. Economics (how people earn a living) and geography (especially the prevalence and distribution of resources) influence cultural ethos. Science and technology influence how political business is conducted. These influences in the broader culture dictate certain patterns of cooperation and accommodation, and they set in motion the conflicts that politics must moderate or resolve.

Why Is Political Culture Important?

Some examples may help illustrate the importance of the political culture. In the United States, the acceptance of slavery in the Southern states and the development of an industrial and agricultural economy based on free labor in the Northern and Western states created tension and conflict between the South and the North and West. The outcome was a catastrophic civil war—the worst fate that can afflict domestic politics. But although slavery in the United States made for conflict, the fact that Americans have been a people of plenty—and have lived in a spacious land of abundant resources—has undoubtedly taken the edge off class conflict and made it easier to achieve accommodation in politics. The Civil War and its aftermath also illustrate the way in which political cultures can change and evolve over time.

Russia and the Soviet Union offer the example of a political culture that has proven very difficult to alter. Tsarist Russia lacked a tradition of natural law (or higher law), meaningful representative government, and effective local democracy. (See Chapter 5 for a discussion of natural law.) The despotism of the tsars unquestionably stimulated cruel and conspiratorial responses by the Russian Bolsheviks as they sought the tsar's overthrow in their effort to build a heroic communist society. But authoritarian cultural patterns persisted, most tragically during the period of Joseph Stalin's rule. Finally, in the late 1980s and early 1990s, forces emerged that successfully challenged the centralized power of the Soviet Communist Party. But even today, in the post-communist era, the Russian government under Vladimir Putin continues to struggle with, or even accept, the idea of democratic rule. Today, as economic challenges and ethnic conflict continue, the forces of authoritarianism threaten Russia's fragile democracy.

Great Britain represents a case of successful transition from one political culture to another. For centuries, England was characterized by a highly centralized government controlled by the monarchy and the aristocracy. Today, it enjoys a strong Western democratic political culture in which the monarchy is relegated to largely ceremonial duties. (Though, we should note, ceremony is a vital part of any culture.)

In India, religious, social, geographic, and economic differences have made cooperation and accommodation in politics difficult. After World War II, British India was divided into a primarily Muslim Pakistan and a primarily Hindu India. Despite this political division, differences between Muslims and Hindus have caused great tension in modern India, both between Pakistan and India and within India itself. Kashmir, which is populated largely by Muslims, remains an Indian state and a source of chronic conflict. Throughout the 1990s and continuing to the present, religious differences have led to violence in the region. Caste differences in India—with Brahmins at the top and "untouchables" at the bottom of the social and economic scale—also militate against cooperation in the spirit of equality. India's religious and social system makes reform urgent and yet extraordinarily difficult. On the other hand, Mohandas Gandhi's philosophy of nonviolence and democracy has encouraged peaceful resolution of disputes and the maintenance of traditions such as village industry—much to the dismay of those Indian revolutionaries who believe that the country will not become free and prosperous without a radical, even violent, revolution to usher in a new social and economic system.

Courtesy of the Library of Congress, Prints and Photographs Division.

Black Americans participated in the Northern forces during the American Civil War, inspired by the promise of an end to slavery. Their efforts helped win the war for the Union; however, they were treated far from equally. The black soldiers in this photograph, taken at City Point, Virginia, are clothed in cast-off federal uniforms. Black soldiers such as these were also forbidden to carry arms for the first two years of the war.

A nation's broader culture makes an important contribution to successful (or unsuccessful) patterns of political accommodation. Indeed, the other factors that we will examine—expression of needs and interests, selection of priorities, legitimization of public choices, effective governance, and controls on government—flow from the broader cultural framework.

Agreement on the Fundamentals of Political Culture

The cultural framework of a society is important because it provides the fundamental agreement—and therefore the trust—without which politics cannot advance as a civilizing process. It provides sound rules for the political game. This agreement on fundamentals does not require agreement on all aspects of life. All citizens need not practice the same religion or speak the same language. They do not have to have the same economic, political, or social views. Homogeneous (similar) values may contribute to political trust, but heterogeneous (diverse) values do not necessarily lead to civil war. What is crucial is that there is enough agreement on enough fundamentals to hold the political community together. And there must also be agreement on how to disagree.

Americans may be Protestants, Catholics, Jews, Muslims, Hindu, atheists, or agnostics. They may be capitalists, socialists, or believers in some variety of a mixed economy. They may be Democrats, Republicans, or Independents. They may believe that virtue resides only in the soul of the farmer or that culture is to be found only in big cities such as New York. They may speak English, Spanish, or other languages. They may strongly differ on policies involving abortion, taxation, or disarmament. While at times, the partisan divisions in the United States between Democrats and Republicans make it seem as though there are two Americas with two different cultures and sets of values, there is still a strong sense of fundamental agreement underpinning U.S. politics to make the system work. Some political commentators have worried that recent strains in the United States have reached such levels that American politics is in crisis.[2] (This issue will be discussed in more detail in Chapter 9.) Yet, despite these differences, major parties are still able to work out successful patterns of accommodation because they agree on the basic principles of the American Constitution: government based on the consent of the governed; free elections; freedom of speech, press, assembly, and religion; equal justice under the law; and **majority rule**. Diversity, then, need not lead to failure in coping with the struggle for power. However, learning to cope with diversity is key to successful accommodation.

Different nations have different conceptions of what is fundamental. We will spell out one model, the Western democratic model, which has been called **polyarchy,** or rule by the many. Numerous countries in what is left of the communist world and in the developing world exhibit a political culture quite different from the polyarchy that exists in the countries of North America and Western Europe. The democratic, or polyarchal, framework has the following characteristics:

1. *Commitment to the common good.* Citizens and governments agree to strive for the common good. Although preached more than practiced, this fundamental principle (as understood in terms of security, liberty, justice, and welfare) clarifies the purposes of politics. It requires citizens and the government to cooperate to achieve these purposes. Conflicts must be mitigated through mechanisms that demonstrate respect for these values, safeguard vital human needs, and protect fundamental interests.

2. *Observance of political boundaries.* Citizens and governments agree on certain boundaries for political maneuvers, ruling out patterns of politics such as slavery, genocide, eradication of economic classes, and religious persecution—practices considered evil by most civilized people. Accommodation must be based on an open, not closed, society.

3. *Accommodation to the private sphere.* Citizens and governments agree that an important area for accommodation lies outside the public sphere. They must agree, therefore, on a private sphere in which individuals and groups may work out their problems by themselves, so long as life, liberty, and law are respected and so long as private accommodation does not violate the common good.

4. *Recognition of human diversity and human fallibility.* Citizens and governments agree on the reality of human diversity and human fallibility as well as on the imperative of searching for patterns of accommodation that are helpful, if not entirely perfect. To avoid the imposition of tyrannical or totalitarian truths, people must insist on free expression of ideas and beliefs.

5. *Attainment of judicious balance.* Citizens and governments agree about the need for judicious balance. Often, sensible accommodation calls for striking a balance between contending claims, interests, and units of government—the claims, for example, of producers and consumers; the interests of workers, farmers, and industrialists; and the actions of central and local government.

6. *Adherence to pluralism.* Citizens and governments agree that balancing, harmonizing, and adjusting the purposes and powers of political actors calls for various skills and functions at many levels. This process requires diverse contributions to successful accommodation—hence, pluralism and polyarchy.

7. *Need for political legitimacy.* Citizens and governments agree on how to secure willing obedience to the process of accommodation. This ensures legitimacy— acceptance of key decisions and public policies. In polyarchies, legitimacy is enhanced by widely accepted ideas such as free and competitive elections, the protection of basic rights, opposition political parties, due process of law, and limited government.

Although countries following the polyarchal model may agree on fundamentals, they do not have to have identical political systems. For example, both the British and U.S. systems are democratic. Yet the British have chosen parliamentary supremacy, cabinet government, strong party government, and quasi-unitary government (terms that will be clarified shortly) whereas Americans have opted for **separation of powers**, presidential government, weak party government, and **federalism**.

CONSTITUTIONAL FEATURES

In this section, we present some of the constitutional features that are especially relevant to conflict and accommodation in politics. While political culture provides the backdrop against which the game of politics is played, every society has certain rules for how the game is played. These rules are spelled out in a country's constitution, which, as we saw in Chapter 5, is a founding document or documents that spell out the structure and rules of a political system and reflect the political culture. In some cases, the constitution is a single, clearly written document, such as the U.S. Constitution. In other cases, it is a collection of documents written over the course of many years, such as the British constitution. Despite the amorphous quality of the British constitution, it is real enough and shapes British politics to a significant degree.

Limited or Unlimited Government

One of the first questions we must ask about any political system is the extent to which government is limited. At one extreme, Joseph Stalin's Soviet and Adolf Hitler's German governments exercised almost unlimited domestic power in every sector of society—education, the economy, the arts, and the private lives of citizens. Today, repressive governments are found in several parts of the world with perhaps the most egregious example being North Korea. As noted earlier, liberal democratic and democratic socialist governments (which follow the polyarchal pattern) insist that governmental power be limited. One of the great examples of how government can be limited is found in the U.S. Constitution's Bill of Rights. In that document, various personal freedoms and rights (such as freedom of speech and religion and the right to a fair trial) are clearly protected from government interference. While there can be spirited disagreements between liberal democrats and democratic socialists about the role of government, both groups agree that there must be some clear limits to what a government can do. Without those limits, the specter of tyranny haunts a society.

Representative Government or Direct Democracy

Although governments in the highly developed industrial countries usually depend on the consent of the governed, the people exercise their power through elected representatives—for example, through a president and members of Congress in the United States. Direct democracy—in which the people make laws firsthand—is rare in the United States. It exists primarily at the state or local level, as in the New England town meeting or when the people vote to amend a state constitution or vote on other cardinal issues of public policy through initiatives and referendums. Other developed systems occasionally permit the whole nation to vote on a major issue—for example, in 1973 the British people voted on whether to join the European Common Market. (And more recently, the United Kingdom voted on Brexit, in a national referendum, to leave the European Union.) Though exceptions such as these exist, most democracies primarily rely on some form of representative government.

One of the most important political questions of the twenty-first century asks this: To what extent will former communist countries be able to create representative governments? A related question is this: To what extent will countries that remain formally communist, such as China, be able to adapt certain features of representative government to their own? It is true that in places such as Russia the form of government is ostensibly democratic. Yet policies put into place by Putin during his presidency in the early 2000s, such as censorship of the media and the increased centralization of power, leave the movement toward democratic reform less definite. After serving as the nation's prime minister, Putin was reelected as president of Russia. Although he received 63 percent of the vote, many international observers were concerned about election irregularities. Putin's inauguration was met with a great many protests displaying a deep concern about the fragile hold democracy has in Russia. Either way, it remains an open question as to how democratic Russia really is. Under the circumstances, it is not unreasonable to wonder whether the Russian government simply offers the appearance of representative democracy while masking a fundamentally authoritarian regime dominated by authoritarian-minded rulers. This is a classic example of how culture can influence politics. Although the official laws of a country may be democratic and representative, the actual practice of politics, affected by centuries of tradition and custom, can remain stubbornly undemocratic.

Many developing countries have effective representative institutions, but there is a predominance of authoritarianism in the developing world. This authoritarianism may stem from several factors, depending on the region, history, and culture. Power in a number of developing nations is held by military or political elite that seized control by force and rules without benefit of electoral legitimacy. It is difficult to generalize about so many different countries and regions; however, a few examples will suffice to illustrate the hopes and fears of those who champion democracy. There is ample evidence that the peoples of Central America aspire to democratic forms of government. One democracy of long standing is Costa Rica. However, neighboring countries have for long periods of time been controlled by powerful families, such as the Somozas in Nicaragua from 1937 to 1979, and military strong men, such as Manuel Noriega in Panama from 1983 to 1989. Patterns of imposed authority left over from Spanish colonial rule and a lengthy history of military involvement in politics sustain these trends.

Democracy has had difficulty taking hold in many Asian countries as well. Even highly developed countries such as South Korea have, until very recently, been authoritarian. Singapore, one of the most dynamic economic actors in Asia, remains essentially authoritarian with enormous power vested in the executive. Parliamentary democracy has had a very rocky, unstable, and limited existence in Indonesia. According to Nathan Keyfitz of Harvard, an understanding of the various aspects of Asian culture—the value placed on order, on unity, and on concentration of power, as well as the fear of chaos—is necessary to comprehend these difficulties.[3]

Separation or Connection of Powers

To ensure greater safety amid the struggle for power, a nation's constitutional framework may, in addition to limiting power, also require that different hands hold power. Thus, in the United States power is divided among three branches of government—legislative, executive, and judicial—according to the principle of separation of powers. Constitutionally, Congress enacts all legislation. The president may sign or veto the legislation, but Congress may, by a two-thirds vote, override the president's veto. For good measure, the U.S. Congress consists of a Senate and a House of Representatives, and both chambers must agree on legislation before it can be enacted. Moreover, the U.S. Supreme Court is independent of both the legislative and executive branches and may declare an act of Congress unconstitutional or hold that a presidential action violates a valid law.

Of course, the founders did not intend for the separation of powers to paralyze government. They expected separation of powers to ensure wise governance. The American system thus rests on the premise of cooperation and accommodation. Deadlocks may occur, however, when the president and Congress favor different political philosophies. Such deadlocks make either for sensible compromise or for ineffectual government. The possibilities of conflict in a system of separation of powers have increased the importance of strong and responsible parties that can unite Congress and the president in a common program endorsed by the people. Yet even when government is unified under one-party rule, change can come slowly, if at all. Even with unified government and the passage of a new law, the constitutionality of the 2010 Patient Protection and Affordable Care Act (commonly referred to as Obamacare) still faced a final review by the Supreme Court. In the case of *National Federation of Independent Business v. Sebelius*, June 2012, a deeply divided court upheld the constitutionality of the act. The court could have just as easily struck down this law and the entire process of creating a new health care policy for the nation. In 2017, in the aftermath of the 2016 election, Republicans controlled the presidency and both Houses of the U.S. Congress. However, despite much effort and many public promises to repeal Obamacare (the Affordable Care Act), Republicans could not agree on how to repeal President Obama's signature public policy. Regardless,

England's Conservative Party Leader Theresa May speaking in the English Parliament. May became the second female Prime Minister in 2017 following Margaret Thatcher and was instrumental in pushing for BREXIT, England's separation from the European Union.

the entire process revealed the way separation of powers work. By way of contrast, political power in the British government rests in a prime minister and a cabinet responsible to a majority in the House of Commons. Here we have a **connection of powers**—not a separation. Unlike the American president, who is elected for a four-year term independently of members of Congress, the British prime minister is usually the person who commands a majority of votes in the House of Commons. With that majority, the prime minister and key leaders of his or her party organize a cabinet that runs the British government. The House of Commons and the cabinet are thus connected. British prime ministers lead the government because they have been empowered by a majority in Commons. Losing that majority seriously jeopardizes their ability to remain in power—in fact, it usually means the government falls and new elections are called. The British Parliament must formally enact legislation, but such legislation usually originates in the cabinet.

Theoretically, the British Parliament consists of two branches: the House of Commons and the House of Lords. Constitutionally, however, all effective power resides in Commons. The British also have an independent system of courts; but British courts, in contrast to their American counterparts, have no power to declare an act of Parliament unconstitutional. Consequently, deadlock between the executive and the legislature is impossible in the British system. If the prime minister and the cabinet do not command a majority in the Commons, the prime minister must either resign in favor of someone who will command such a majority or call for new elections that will produce a new majority in Commons and a prime minister who has the confidence of that majority.

The late twentieth century brought a wave of democratic experiments in the developing world. But many of those governments do not incorporate the American principle of separation of powers. Some (for example, India) are close to the British principle of connection of powers, with a prime minister responsible to a majority in the legislature. Others (for example, Mexico) have an independently elected president who rules without effective interference from an elected legislature or an independent judiciary. Nigeria has a long tradition of an independent judiciary that has maintained its role even through periods of military rule. But these examples are more the exception than the rule. Regarding the Asian cultural emphasis on unity and order, Keyfitz observes, "A division of constitutional responsibility between government, parliament, and the courts would be a dispersal of power, a sign that the community was breaking up."[4]

Federalism or Unitary Government

Every large and complicated political community must include cooperation between the national political community and its component parts. There also must be accommodation between the central government and local governments. And conflicts that arise between various levels of government must be handled sagaciously. How does a federal system contribute to successful accommodation? How is the problem of decentralization handled in a unitary political system as compared with a federal system? How is it possible to keep government close to the people?

Federalism is one attempt to reconcile local liberty and national authority. Federalism allows people living in certain localities (in America, the fifty states for example) to manage local problems while leaving to the central government (in which they also have a voice) the power to handle national concerns. A federal system achieves this accommodation by demarcating national and state jurisdictions and powers, by indicating which powers the national government and the state governments may exercise concurrently, and by denying them certain other powers. Federalism is generally a response to the size and diversity of countries such as Canada, India, and the United States. It is designed to balance necessary central authority on behalf of the nation with local liberty and self-government.

A classic federal system exists in the United States. The central, or national, government holds broad but carefully enumerated powers: powers to handle matters of national concern such as defense, foreign relations, taxation, spending for the general welfare, and regulation of interstate and foreign commerce. Some powers (foreign relations and interstate and foreign commerce) are exclusive powers that only the central government can exercise. Other powers (for example, taxation and spending) may also be exercised by the states. All powers neither delegated to the central government nor logically implied as belonging to it come under the jurisdiction of the states (for example, provisions for local schools and police and fire protection). Certain powers are denied to both the central government and state governments (for example, the power to deprive a person of life, liberty, or property without due process of law).

Theoretically, federalism makes it possible for political actors in state and local government to express their needs and interests. They can determine their local priorities—for example, where they want to locate their schools, or what speed limit to impose on traffic. In this way, citizens can keep a close eye on local government and make sure that it is acceptable to them and effective in addressing their concerns. In addition, a federal system keeps the central government from absorbing all power.

The successes of state (and local) government must not be overlooked. State and local governments enhance democracy by keeping government close to the people. People can more easily participate in such governments; they can take initiatives and exercise greater local responsibility. They can respond more quickly to problems. And certain general problems might have specific local causes and unique local solutions, such as welfare. For instance, the causes of poverty may vary by region. Thus, the solutions will vary by region—one state may want to address their poverty problem with increased education funding while another state may upgrade its public transportation to make it easier for people to get to their jobs. In each case, the general problem is poverty but each state has a credible policy to confront that problem. In general, the federal division of powers encourages experimentation, with the opportunity to cancel bad experiments without great losses and to duplicate good experiments nationwide after success at the state level. Thus, a great deal of reform legislation—involving, for example, wages and hours, collective bargaining, unemployment compensation, and welfare reform—has been pioneered in progressive states.

In contrast with federalism in the United States, France and Japan employ a unified approach. In a **unitary government** all major power and policy emanates from the central government. National power includes not only the power to make war or regulate the economy but also the power to shape the educational curriculum of all public schools. So, in France, for example, on any given day in the public school system all children are reading the same books. In France, the prefect, situated in Paris, is the national government's chief administrator in each of the country's ninety-five departments (geographic and administrative units). Elected assemblies in the departments and communes (local governmental units) lack significant power. The national government thus carries out policy at the local level; locally elected officials are pretty much restricted to municipal questions and to bargaining with the Paris-based government and the prefect.

The United Kingdom, which includes England, Scotland, Wales, and Northern Ireland, uses its own unique pattern, one that is situated between a purely federal and purely unitary form of government, although it tends more toward the unitary. Traditionally, all power emanated from the British Parliament located in London. But Northern Ireland had its own parliament before the bloody conflict between Irish Catholics seeking union with Ireland and Protestants insisting on retaining their tie with the British Crown prompted its suspension in 1972 and abolishment the following year. More recently, the Scots and the Welsh have been given opportunities to vote on erecting their own governments within the framework of the British constitution, and the Scots may hold a referendum on independence in 2014. Thus, because of the unique historical composition of the United Kingdom, the centuries-old tradition of local government, and the complexities of the modern welfare state, Britain has seen a great deal of **devolution**—the surrendering of powers to local authorities by a central government. For example, local units of government carry out many national policies. British municipalities govern themselves in local matters, much like American municipalities. And efforts have been made to maximize the voice that the Scots, Welsh, and Irish have in their own geographic domains.

Not all large countries are federal. China, for example, is not. And a number of small countries such as Switzerland and Austria are federal. Nevertheless, the three characteristics of states that make them good candidates for federalism are large size, diverse ethnic and linguistic groups, and a historical tradition of local self-government. In responding to these factors, federal systems can offer effective mechanisms by which to reconcile central authority with local liberty. Successful reconciliation may, however, depend on combining a sense of nationalism with a respect for diversity—a combination difficult to work out at any time.

Majority Rule

Space does not permit a more definitive treatment of all constitutional techniques of accommodation in politics. Yet it is important to treat at least one additional method, one that has figured prominently in the developed countries, is partially employed in communist countries, and plays absolutely no role in purely authoritarian systems: majority rule. We define *majority rule* as the power of one-half of the members, plus one, of any decision-making group to bind the remainder of that group to a decision. This ideal demands that political actors rely on discourse and votes, rather than on edicts and force, in dealing with the struggle for purpose and power. But how many heads are to be counted? In reaching decisions, what percentage of ballots is relied on to identify the winning candidate or policy?

Historically, majority rule has facilitated orderly decision making. Winners have been able to act; losers have abided by the results of the ballot box. Decisions made by majority rule—whether in elections or in the legislative body—have been accepted as legitimate. Majority rule ensures popular and effective government. It avoids the difficulty of having to achieve unanimity on all issues, a difficulty that could lead to a dangerous breakdown in government—and thus to either impotence or anarchy. Majority rule also avoids the un-republican consequences of relying on a minority whose power is based on force, birth, or wealth. Such minority power lacks legitimacy. Minority decisions do not command the will, respect, and peaceful obedience of a population. Instead, they engender popular disrespect for the law and undermine the resolution of conflicts by peaceful and orderly processes, thus threatening political stability and governmental effectiveness. Minorities might resort to force to execute their decisions or to make them stick, but they often lack the means to do so. Furthermore, the difficulty of ascertaining which minority is to rule would produce troublesome conflicts among rich and poor, educated and ignorant, white and black.

The functioning of majority rule in the United States and Britain has not, however, produced "majority tyranny." One discerning historian, Henry Steele Commager, has written, apropos of the United States, that there is no "persuasive evidence from our own long and complex historical experience that majorities are given to contempt for constitutional limitations or minority rights . . . They have not taxed wealth out of existence; they have not been hostile to education or to science. The pulpit, the press, the school, the forum, are as free here as anywhere in the world—with the possible exception of that other great majority rule country—Britain."[5] This is true largely because the constitutional rules of the game in the highly developed nations also require protection of basic rights for all. In the process of resolving disputes by majority rule, a great deal of accommodation goes on. To achieve a majority, conflicting demands must be adjusted to work out sane compromises. This process makes for helpful moderation and desirable reconciliation. The widespread use of majority rule can be illustrated in runoff elections. In France, a runoff election is held when a candidate for president does not receive a majority of votes in the first election. The same is true for the gubernatorial races in some U.S. states. This practice guards against the election of an official by a plurality of votes—that is, by a percentage that is the highest cast though still short of 50 percent. The second election ensures that the winner has the electoral support of a majority of those voting.

Another qualification to majority rule is that a simple majority is not always enough to win. In the United States, the Constitution dictates a two-thirds vote or a three-fourths vote on certain matters. For example, to overturn a presidential veto Congress requires two-thirds of its members to vote in favor of such action. The option of proposing a constitutional amendment requires a two-thirds vote in both houses of the U.S. Congress or the call for a constitutional convention by two-thirds of the state legislatures. Proposed amendments are ratified by a three-fourths vote of state legislatures.

Majority rule, like all political ideals, has its critics. Looking beyond the facade of formal decision making (for example, in a specific election or a specific vote by a legislative body), some students of politics question whether it is the majority that really rules in a democracy. They see instead different varieties of rule by minorities. The strongest criticism leveled against majority rule is from those who posit the existence of what is called the power elite—a cohesive and dominant minority that effectively controls policy. A more subtle attack on the ideal of majority rule is that, although majorities formally control politics, different, shifting minorities control the outcome of specific policy issues.[6] For example, though it may not be true that the oil companies run the United States, they may have undue influence over energy policy and even, some would argue, some aspects of foreign policy.

Majority rule faces difficulties in the developing countries because it presupposes trust among citizens, respect for elections, and a leadership responsive to the popular will. When these are lacking, as they are in many developing countries, majority rule cannot function. Citizens will fight each other and elections will be set aside; in some cases, military leaders will rule by force. Yet some developing countries have successfully employed majority rule in their elections. The late twentieth century saw remarkable advances in the propensity of places as diverse as Eastern Europe and Latin America to use majority rule.

THE VALUES OF NATIONS AS POLITICAL ACTORS

Nations (more accurately, national leaders, ruling elites, or governing parties) generally profess and often seek to protect the **national interest** in foreign affairs and the **public interest** in domestic affairs. They generally interpret the national interest as the vital needs and fundamental interests of the nation as a whole. This would include such concerns as security, liberty, justice, and welfare, all of which are essential to the independence, prosperity, and power of the nation-state.[7] Related to the idea of the national interest is the idea of the public interest, which is the interest of the entire community that transcends the selfish interests of individuals or groups. Public interest expresses the best long-range interests of the nation.[8]

There is considerable historical evidence that many leaders of national governments value survival, security, safety, peace, territorial integrity, defense, prosperity, independence, and power. They value their freedom, their capacity to govern themselves, their control of their own destiny, and their enjoyment of the rights—at home and abroad—that make freedom meaningful. They seek a measure of justice at home and, sometimes, abroad. They profess, at least in most nations, to favor equality before the law, due process of law, and an equitable distribution of wealth. They favor the principle of equal treatment of sovereign nations in the world community and respect for international law and procedure. They claim concern for the welfare of their citizens at home and the afflicted abroad. They often favor policies to enhance national **economic well-being** through growth, production, full employment, decent farm prices, and satisfactory business profits. They support policies that enhance social well-being through literacy, adequate food and housing, and good health and nutrition. They endorse stable institutions and organizations as a way to ensure political well-being.

But—in the critical and truth-seeking tradition of political science—we must probe more deeply. Consider the Key Questions on this page.

Let us now investigate key national values as many leaders throughout the world articulate them. We can, of course, present only a modest portion of the evidence that bears on our questions and might sustain our hypothesis. But such bit of evidence may at least suggest the larger empirical task required for a more rewarding understanding of nations' political values.

KEY QUESTIONS

1. What more specific meaning—in deed as well as in word—do those who exercise power on behalf of nations give to their values?

2. Are such concepts as the national interest and the public interest idealistic myths? Are they cover-ups for naked national power or for dominant elites?

3. Are vital national needs really vital? For whom?

4. Are there serious gaps between civilized (and often professed) values and the actual values revealed in national behavior?

Security and Peace

The leaders of most nations say they believe in security and peace. Yet the history of the twentieth century and early years of the twenty-first are littered with violent conflict—interstate wars, revolutions, assassinations, rebellions, wars of national liberation, ethnic conflict, terrorism, and genocide. While definitions of war vary slightly from study to study, data indicate that over the past fifteen to twenty years, somewhere between thirty and forty wars were raging at any given point in time.[9] The ongoing cost of this behavior is enormous. Though estimates on deaths directly attributable to warfare vary, Zbigniew Brzezinski, in his book *Out of Control: Global Turmoil on the Eve of the Twenty-first Century*, puts the total for the twentieth century at roughly 87.5 million dead—33.5 million combatants and 54 million civilians.[10] M. Cherif Bassiouni, in an article titled "Searching for Peace and Achieving Justice," puts the total even higher at 203 million, including victims of interstate warfare, internal conflicts and victims of tyrannical regimes.[11]

There is a sarcastic adage in international relations that says, "All wars are fought in self-defense." Has each nation engaged only in just wars, defending itself against aggressive opponents and protecting its security against real attack? Or have at least some, using the pretext of protecting their vital interests, attacked and jeopardized the security of other, peace-loving countries? Do wars, or defense preparations, actually serve to protect a nation's security?

Scholars will quarrel about answers to these questions. Evaluations are difficult because there is no agreement on the key terms used in discussions of these matters. For example, there is no common definition of *just war*, *defensive war*, or *aggressive war*, or of *vital interests* or *security*. Also there is no consensus on the meaning, value, and cost of *adequate defense*. The enormous tension and distrustful atmosphere of the Cold War provided a powerful driving force for the building of conventional and nuclear arsenals in the years following World War II. More recently, the dangers of terrorism and nuclear proliferation have complicated the question of security even further. At this point, it is too early to tell how the need to deal with these phenomena will finally affect demands of national security, but in the coming years we can be certain that ensuring security and peace will become even more complex.

There can, however, be little quarrel about the following points: (1) There is a serious gap between talk of peace and the reality of war. (2) Different nations often hold incompatible conceptions of national security. (3) Sometimes nations counter power with power in order to protect vital national interests. (4) National defense expenditures are huge and distort other priorities. (5) The machinery for peace and peaceful change is inadequate.

Adolf Hitler talked of peace but did not hesitate to launch World War II by attacking Poland, then the Low Countries and France, then Britain, and then the Soviet Union. Was Germany's security threatened by the people it attacked? The Soviet Union professed, at its inception in the early twentieth century and in the decades that followed, to be a peace-loving state that respected the national integrity of its neighbors. Yet, in 1956, the Soviets invaded Hungary to put down a revolt against the rigid communist regime that ruled the country. In 1968, the Soviet Union invaded another communist neighbor, Czechoslovakia, to turn back an attempt to liberalize the regime there. In late 1979, the Soviet Union invaded Afghanistan, presumably to defend a recently installed communist regime against alleged internal and external enemies. In these cases, the Kremlin's interpretation of the Soviet Union's national security and national interest clashed with its alleged peace-loving and freedom-loving pretensions, and perhaps with the national and security interests of most people in Hungary, Czechoslovakia, and Afghanistan.

The United States, too, professes to be a peace-loving nation, yet it became involved in a bloody, destructive, and expensive war in Vietnam between 1965 and 1973. Was our action in Vietnam, like our military resistance to Germany and Japan in World War II, based on protecting the legitimate security interests of the United States? More recently, some Americans seriously question why the United States invaded Iraq in 2003. With few links between Iraq and the terrorist organization al-Qaida, and with the failure to find any weapons of mass destruction (WMDs), was U.S. national security sufficiently directly threatened to warrant the invasion? Supporters of American action reply with an unequivocal "yes." Saddam Hussein was a brutal dictator and a dangerous and destabilizing force in a region critical to U.S. security. This debate is likely to persist for years regardless of the outcome of postwar reconstruction and democratization efforts in Iraq.

Clashing conceptions of national security highlight international relations. In the 1930s and 1940s, Japan's "co-prosperity sphere"—as envisaged by Japan, a bloc of Asian nations led by Japan and free of Western powers—clashed with the national security interests of China, Britain, France, and the United States and led directly to the Japanese attack on Pearl Harbor on December 7, 1941. In 1956, presumably to protect their strategic security interests, Britain and France, with Israel's help, seized control of the Suez Canal after Egyptian president Gamal Abdel Nasser nationalized the waterway. Israel has resisted the establishment of a Palestinian state on the west bank of the Jordan River because it fears that the proximity of Arab military forces would jeopardize the security of Israel's cities. Obviously, neither the Egyptians nor the Palestinians agree with these assessments of national security. Whose interpretation is correct?

Recent debates among political scientists have focused on the nature of ethnic and cultural conflicts that persist, sometimes with greater vigor, even as the Cold War has ended. In *The Clash of Civilizations*, Harvard University's Samuel P. Huntington predicted that with the fall of communism different civilizations—Western, Islamic, Latin American, among others—will come into conflict. These civilizations represent great blocs of countries with similar cultural, religious, and political histories. While there is a great deal of controversy about Huntington's theory, it offers a provocative argument about the way to view peace and conflict since the end of the Cold War.[12] Huntington highlights the intersection of values, culture, and security. He posits that different civilizations have different values, springing out of different cultural histories. While that is an interesting hypothesis in and of itself, it leads directly, according to Huntington, to a clash of civilizations as each tries to protect itself. Diverse values, thus, become the source of clashing security concerns.

The discussion in this section does not necessarily prove that all official government policies on military spending are wrong and that the critics are right. We should, however, be leery of automatically accepting what governments profess. The national value of security and peace is subject to differing interpretations. We should be sensitive to the price that is often paid to achieve national security. And we should be aware of the gap that so often exists between professed, civilized values and the actual values expressed through behavior.

Liberty, Human Rights, and Democracy

Most nations profess a commitment to liberty, human rights, and democracy. In fact, with the collapse of the Soviet Union, the world seemed to witness a spectacular rise in the number of democracies. But how do all of these self-proclaimed democracies perform? This is a rather difficult question to answer because just what constitutes a democracy is open to debate. However, if we accept that democracies must have freedom of expression, free elections, and the ability to gather alternative sources of information, the number of democracies has indeed increased in recent years. We should also note, though, that countries might achieve some level of democracy but not complete democracy.[13] Various scholars have tried to create different scales on which countries can be arrayed. Freedom House has developed a means of ranking countries into three categories—Free, Partly Free, and Not Free—and their recent rankings are shown in Table 8.1.

Table 8.1 tells us a number of things. First, there are more democracies than ever before. Second, many countries profess to be democracies and yet are not quite living up to the high standards that democracy demands. Thus, students of politics must continue to investigate the gap between rhetoric and reality. For example, in 1975 the Soviet Union, the United States, and thirty-three other governments signed the Helsinki Pact, which included provisions for respecting human rights. But did the Soviet Union act in accord with its signature? The record reveals the Soviet Union was a place where dissenters were imprisoned, confined to mental hospitals, exiled within Russia, and forced into foreign exile. Soviet citizens were not allowed the right of free emigration, and the free flow of information was impeded. Between 1975 and 1987, Soviet behavior was not consistent with the principles professed in the Helsinki Pact.

Historically, the U.S. record on human rights, although considerably better than that of many other countries, has by no means been exemplary. FBI actions at home

Table 8.1   Countries Rated by Degree of Freedom, 2017

Country	Freedom Status	PR	CL	Country	Freedom Status	PR	CL
Afghanistan	Not Free	6	6	Botswana	Free	3	2
Albania	Partly Free	3	3	Brazil	Free	2	2
Algeria	Not Free	6	5	Brunei	Not Free	6	5
Andorra	Free	1	1	Bulgaria	Free	2	2
Angola	Not Free	6	6	Burkina Faso	Partly Free	4	3
Antigua and Barbuda	Free	2	2	Burundi	Not Free	7	6
Argentina	Free	2	2	Cambodia	Not Free	6	5
Armenia	Partly Free	5	4	Cameroon	Not Free	6	6
Australia	Free	1	1	Canada	Free	1	1
Austria	Free	1	1	Cape Verde	Free	1	1
Azerbaijan	Not Free	7	6	Central African Republic	Not Free	7	7
Bahamas	Free	1	1	Chad	Not Free	7	7
Bahrain	Not Free	7	6	Chile	Free	1	1
Bangladesh	Partly Free	4	4	China	Not Free	7	6
Barbados	Free	1	1	Colombia	Partly Free	3	3
Belarus	Not Free	7	6	Comoros	Partly Free	3	4
Belgium	Free	1	1	Congo, DRC, Kinshasa	Not Free	7	6
Belize	Free	1	2	Congo, Republic of (Brazzaville)	Not Free	7	5
Benin	Free	2	2	Costa Rica	Free	1	1
Bhutan	Partly Free	3	4	Cote D'Ivoire	Partly Free	4	4
Bolivia	Partly Free	3	3	Croatia	Free	1	2
Bosnia and Herzegovina	Partly Free	4	4	Cuba	Not Free	7	6

Country	Freedom Status	PR	CL	Country	Freedom Status	PR	CL
Cyprus	Free	1	1	Guinea	Partly Free	5	5
Czech Republic	Free	1	1	Guinea-Bissau	Partly Free	5	5
Denmark	Free	1	1	Guyana	Free	2	3
Djibouti	Not Free	6	5	Haiti	Partly Free	5	5
Dominica	Free	1	1	Honduras	Partly Free	4	4
Dominican Republic	Partly Free	3	3	Iceland	Free	1	1
Ecuador	Partly Free	3	4	India	Free	3	3
Egypt	Not Free	6	5	Indonesia	Partly Free	2	4
El Salvador	Free	2	3	Iran	Not Free	6	6
Equatorial Guinea	Not Free	7	7	Iraq	Not Free	5	6
Eritrea	Not Free	7	7	Ireland	Free	1	1
Estonia	Free	1	1	Israel	Free	1	2
Ethiopia	Not Free	7	6	Italy	Free	1	1
Fiji	Partly Free	3	4	Jamaica	Free	2	3
Finland	Free	1	1	Japan	Free	1	1
France	Free	1	2	Jordan	Partly Free	5	5
Gabon	Not Free	6	5	Kazakhstan	Not Free	7	5
The Gambia	Not Free	6	6	Kenya	Partly Free	4	4
Georgia	Partly Free	3	3	Kiribati	Free	1	1
Germany	Free	1	1	Kosovo	Partly Free	3	4
Ghana	Free	1	2	Kuwait	Partly Free	5	5
Greece	Free	2	2	Kyrgyzstan	Partly Free	5	5
Grenada	Free	1	2	Laos	Not Free	7	6
Guatemala	Partly Free	4	4	Latvia	Free	1	2

(Continued)

Table 8.1 (Continued)

Country	Freedom Status	PR	CL	Country	Freedom Status	PR	CL
Lebanon	Partly Free	5	4	Mozambique	Partly Free	4	4
Lesotho	Partly Free	3	3	Myanmar	Partly Free	5	5
Liberia	Partly Free	3	4	Namibia	Free	2	2
Libya	Not Free	7	6	Nauru	Free	2	2
Liechtenstein	Free	2	1	Nepal	Partly Free	3	4
Lithuania	Free	1	1	New Zealand	Free	1	1
Luxembourg	Free	1	1	Nicaragua	Partly Free	5	4
Macedonia	Partly Free	4	3	Niger	Partly Free	4	4
Madagascar	Partly Free	3	4	Nigeria	Partly Free	3	5
Malawi	Partly Free	3	3	North Korea	Not Free	7	7
Malaysia	Partly Free	4	4	Norway	Free	1	1
Maldives	Partly Free	5	5	Oman	Not Free	6	5
Mali	Partly Free	5	4	Pakistan	Partly Free	4	5
Malta	Free	1	1	Palau	Free	1	1
Marshall Islands	Free	1	1	Panama	Free	2	2
Mauritania	Not Free	6	5	Papua New Guinea	Partly Free	3	3
Mauritius	Free	1	2	Paraguay	Partly Free	3	3
Mexico	Partly Free	3	3	Peru	Free	2	3
Micronesia	Free	1	1	Philippines	Partly Free	3	3
Moldova	Partly Free	3	3	Poland	Free	1	2
Monaco	Free	3	1	Portugal	Free	1	1
Mongolia	Free	1	2	Qatar	Not Free	6	5
Montenegro	Partly Free	3	3	Romania	Free	2	2
Morocco	Partly Free	5	4	Russia	Not Free	7	6

Country	Freedom Status	PR	CL	Country	Freedom Status	PR	CL
Rwanda	Not Free	6	6	Suriname	Free	2	3
Samoa	Free	2	2	Swaziland	Not Free	7	5
San Marino	Free	1	1	Sweden	Free	1	1
Saudi Arabia	Not Free	7	7	Switzerland	Free	1	1
Senegal	Free	2	2	Syria	Not Free	7	7
Serbia	Free	3	2	Sao Tome and Principe	Free	1	1
Seychelles	Partly Free	3	3	Tajikistan	Not Free	7	6
Sierra Leone	Partly Free	3	3	Tanzania	Partly Free	3	4
Singapore	Partly Free	4	4	Thailand	Not Free	6	5
Slovakia	Free	1	1	Tibet	Not Free	7	7
Slovenia	Free	1	1	Timor-Leste	Partly Free	3	3
Solomon Islands	Free	3	2	Togo	Partly Free	4	4
Somalia	Not Free	7	7	Tonga	Free	2	2
South Africa	Free	2	2	Trinidad and Tobago	Free	2	2
South Korea	Free	2	2	Tunisia	Free	1	3
South Sudan	Not Free	7	7	Turkey	Partly Free	4	5
Spain	Free	1	1	Turkmenistan	Not Free	7	7
Sri Lanka	Partly Free	3	4	Tuvalu	Free	1	1
St. Kitts and Nevis	Free	1	1	Uganda	Not Free	6	5
St. Lucia	Free	1	1	Ukraine	Partly Free	3	3
St. Vincent and Grenadines	Free	2	1	United Arab Emirates	Not Free	6	6
Sudan	Not Free	7	5	United Kingdom	Free	1	1

Source: Freedom House, *Freedom in the World 2017* (New York: Freedom House, 2017).

Note: PR and CL stand for political rights and civil liberties, respectfully; 1 represents the most free and 7 the least free rating. The freedom rating is based on real-world situations caused by state and nongovernmental factors instead of governmental intentions or legislation. Governments are not rated per se but rather the rights and freedoms enjoyed in each country or territory. Two checklists are used—one for questions regarding political rights and one for civil liberties—and countries and territories are given a numerical rating for each checklist. The two ratings are then averaged and used to assign an overall status of Free, Partly Free, or Not Free. A detailed explanation of the methodology for establishing the ratings can be found at www.freedomhouse.org.

and CIA actions both abroad and, more disturbingly, at home have been criticized by civil rights groups, the press, congressional committees, and governmental commissions. The FBI routinely made illegal wiretaps in the 1950s and 1960s. In the mid-1960s and early 1970s, the CIA worked covertly in Chile to influence a presidential election and to overthrow a democratic government led by Salvador Allende Gossens. In the wake of the terrorist attacks on September 11, 2001, civil libertarians in the United States have become increasingly worried about actions taken by the U.S. Justice Department in detaining legal and illegal immigrants. In June 2005, Amnesty International released a report highly critical of the treatment and prolonged detention of Muslim prisoners at the U.S. military base in Guantanamo Bay, Cuba. Of particular concern was the use of "enhanced interrogation" techniques such as shaking, slapping, prolonged standing in shackles (for up to forty hours), and lengthy imprisonment in cold cells. Most controversial was the use of waterboarding, whereby a prisoner is subjected to simulated drowning. To many people, these "enhanced interrogations" are simply a euphemism for torture. Although the concerns about security are real and justified, critics are rightly worried that demands for safety will override the fundamental belief most Americans have in basic individual rights and freedoms.[14] (For a more extensive discussion of this issue, refer to Chapter 13.)

AP Photo/Jeff Widener

A young Chinese demonstrator stands alone in front of a tank column in Tiananmen Square on June 5, 1989. This man was pulled away from the tanks. Hundreds of others, however, were eventually killed or wounded at the square. Still others were later executed or imprisoned as the pro-democracy demonstration was crushed.

A comparable gap between rhetoric and reality exists in many developing countries. In the U.S. State Department's annual *Country Reports on Human Rights Practices*, testimony before congressional committees and documented records of such groups as Amnesty International illustrate this gap. Over the past few decades, the records of such countries as North Korea, Myanmar, Burundi, China, Yemen, Libya, Central African Republic, Somalia, South Sudan, Syria, Pakistan and Gambia have been shocking. The record of the most populous country in the world, the People's Republic of China, has been troubling, particularly during the Cultural Revolution in the late 1960s. As political and economic reform movements swept through the communist world in the 1980s, there was considerable hope that basic human rights and principles of democracy would be part of the Chinese reform movement. Tragically, a stated respect for human rights by the Chinese government lost all meaning as hundreds of students were either shot or crushed under the treads of tanks at Tiananmen Square in Beijing in June 1989 during a peaceful demonstration for democracy. A wave of trials, executions, and long imprisonments followed the defeat of the democratic movement. And up to the present day, China is criticized for its persecution of various minorities and religious groups, such as the Falun Gong. What most of these examples have in common is a belief, cited by many governments, that national security and the need for domestic order justify violations of liberty, human rights, and the democratic process.

Justice, Equality, and Liberty

Justice, understood roughly as "fairness," involves balancing liberty and equality. But justice is perceived in different ways by different nations and by different groups within nations. Developed nations, and the more affluent citizens in all nations, may understand justice in terms of liberty, including the liberty to pursue wealth and protect property. In contrast, communist and developing countries, and the poor in many nations, may understand justice in terms of equality, particularly as signifying a fair share of the national wealth.

Thus, there are many ways to measure a nation's commitment to justice, or fairness. One way is to examine the division of the national "pie"—that is, the way in which income is actually distributed within a nation. Table 8.2 indicates the extent to which overall national income was distributed within a variety of countries, developed and developing. The data represent the distribution of total disposable household income accruing to the wealthiest 10 percent of each country's population.

What is evident from these data is that, in general, the higher the development level, the more equitable the distribution of income within the society. However, even among developed countries, there are significant variations. The United States tends to have a greater gap between the rich and poor than other Western liberal democracies and by all measures is getting worse. A number of factors may contribute to the more skewed distribution of income in the developing world and in the United States. In some cases, consciously designed policies ensure that a small elite retains a higher percentage of wealth. These policies are frequently the result of values held by elites—in the United States, for example, many elites (as well as common citizens) tend to believe that the state should not engage in an aggressive redistribution of wealth.

But other factors—such as limited resources, capabilities, and power structures—may also be relevant. In addition, the larger pie in more affluent countries permits larger slices to be offered to all parts of the population. Nonetheless, despite these limitations, in 2011 a movement called Occupy Wall Street or simply the Occupy movement dominated much political discussion. While this movement was diverse with at times conflicting or unclear goals, the main idea was to question the unfair distribution of wealth and power in the United States. The movement started in New York City and quickly spread to other cities as people staged protests, occupied public spaces, and demanded that the political system address issue of inequality. The common slogan "We are the 99 percent" was designed to highlight the way the top 1 percent of the population were unfairly benefiting unfairly economically by the U.S. capitalist system. This movement was clearly inspired by the economic problems the United States faced in the market collapse in 2008 and aimed to question why so many bankers and economic elites were able to receive generous government help in 2009 and 2010 while millions languished without jobs or a fair wage. No matter what immediate gains, if any, the movement may have realized, it is clear that issues of equality and economic fairness are imperative to many Americans.

The issue of justice and equality goes to the very heart of what values political elites hold. In particular, justice addresses the question of how to balance competing values. For example, Americans believe in equality as well as individual freedom. It is quite possible that the demands of personal freedom—which might require a limited state that

Table 8.2 Income Share Held by Wealthiest 10 Percent and Lowest 10 Percent of Population, 2015

	Income Held Highest 10%	Income Held Lowest 10%
Norway	22.3%	3.5%
Denmark	23.8	3.7
Finland	22.4	3.9
Canada	25.3	2.4
United States	30.6	1.6
Ecuador	34.3	1.6
Cote d'Ivoire	31.9	2.1
Honduras	36.8	1.0
Colombia	40.0	1.3

Source: databank.worldbank.org/data/reports.aspx?source-poverty-and-equity-database.

allows people to do what they want—will come into conflict with the ideal of equality—which might call for the state to limit concentrations of wealth.

Welfare and Economic Well-Being

Most nations endorse (at least in their rhetoric) the welfare and economic well-being of their people.[15] But what do the national governing elites mean by these terms, and how successful are nations in advancing them? **Welfare** refers to government provisions for, or contributions to, individual needs for employment, income, food, housing, health care, and literacy. Economic well-being is the level of income, food, health care, and education that satisfies minimum quality-of-life standards and permits full growth and development. Richer, industrial, developed nations have a much easier time satisfying these needs. They tend to allocate substantially more for education and health care combined than they do for their military. This is not the case for the developing world, where the relative commitment to spending in education and health care is more closely aligned to defense spending. Consequently, in poorer countries, military spending tends to more seriously detract from money allocated for welfare and economic well-being (for example, schools, hospitals, and social welfare programs). Additionally, there is evidence that in poorer countries increases in military spending are associated with slowdowns in economic growth.

Global military spending increased by 50 percent from 1998 to 2013 after having experienced a decline in the immediate post–Cold War years (1990–1995). In 2016, the world's countries spent an astonishing $1.686 trillion on military weapons and personnel. The most rapid growth was in North Africa and the largest increases in spending were in

China, Russia, India, and Saudi Arabia. In addition, recent years have witnessed significant defense cuts in the United States and other Western developed countries.

POPULAR VALUES

So far, we have investigated values from a national perspective. In considering what values nations claim to support, and in thinking about how they may, from time to time, fail to live up to their ideals, we have focused on the actions of elites. However, we also need to consider what citizens believe. In thinking about this, take into account the four Key Questions on this page.

There is considerable evidence that the values of the people who make up political communities are rooted in, and correlated with, a hierarchy of human needs: for sustenance and safety; for belonging and esteem; and for intellectual, aesthetic, and social fulfillment. This proposition is associated with the work of social psychologist Abraham H. Maslow (see Chapter 4, Suggested Readings). A number of social scientists, most notably Ronald Inglehart and Hadley Cantril, have tested Maslow's ideas. Inglehart found considerable empirical evidence in his public opinion surveys supporting Maslow's hypothesis.[16] Cantril's research found that a decent standard of living, a happy family life, and protected health ranked high among popular hopes.[17] Economic, family, and health concerns ranked high among popular leaders, too. Not surprisingly, war loomed large as a major fear among countries that had experienced it. Similarly, political instability was a concern among people whose countries had experienced significant disorders. Inglehart's study found that, with some exceptions, the "priorities of Western publics correspond to a Maslovian model."[18]

However, that is only part of the story. Another important issue in thinking about popular values is whether, among citizens of a given society, there is broad consensus or significant disagreements about certain basic values. For example, party positions, electoral outcomes, and public opinion surveys in all Western democracies demonstrate that the main features of the modern welfare state—for example, unemployment compensation, old-age pensions, health care, and housing support well entrenched. Similarly,

KEY QUESTIONS

1. What shapes the values of citizens?

2. What are those actual values?

3. How do they vary from country to country and within countries?

4. Is there a conflict between the values espoused by elites and those espoused by average citizens? To what degree should elites follow public opinion and respect the basic values of the typical citizen?

most Western democracies are clearly committed to maintaining economic stability (in employment and prices) and to safeguarding law and order.

Figure 8.1 gives us some idea of spending priorities of the American public and specifically the degree to which people are willing to cut or increase spending in a variety of areas. Overall, the data indicate a reluctance to cut. In no case is there a plurality favoring a decrease in spending. On eleven of the fourteen items, a plurality of citizens support an increase with majorities supporting increases in veterans benefits, education, infrastructure, Medicare, and health care.

We should note that sharp disagreements can exist between voters. In the United States, Republicans and Democrats differ substantially on a variety of issues and historically party identification has proven a powerful predictor of voting behavior as well as positions held on many issues. In recent years, there has been a significant surge in citizens identifying themselves as Independents. Has this in any way softened the liberal-conservative partisan divide? Apparently not. Research conducted by the Pew Research Center indicates that most Independents, in fact, express strong partisan leanings on many issues.[19]

In the first decade of the twenty-first century, the American public appeared to be sharply divided over the values reflected in opposing positions on key public policy issues such as abortion, gay marriage, prayer in public schools, euthanasia, genetic research, and

Figure 8.1 Public Preferences for Increasing and Decreasing Spending

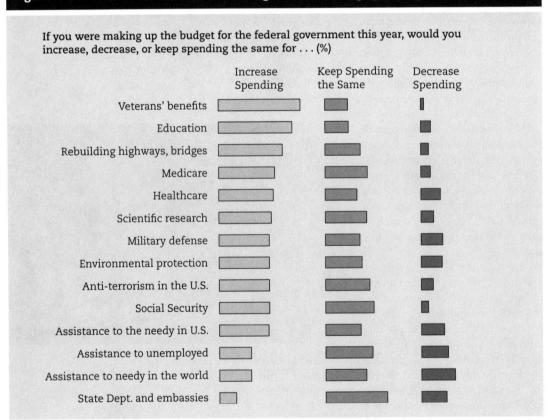

Source: "With Budget Debate Looming, Growing Share of Public Prefers Bigger Government," Pew Research Center, April 24, 2017. http://people-press.org/2017/04/24/with-budget-debate-looming-growing-share-of-public-prefers-bigger-government/.

sex education. The media dubbed the phenomenon the **culture wars** and quickly associated it with the divisions epitomized by the "red" state versus "blue" state analyses of the 2000 and 2004 presidential elections. Throughout the American heartland—supported in part by the increased activism of the Christian right (see Chapter 4)—a swath of red states went to Texan and incumbent president George W. Bush; his opponent, Sen. John Kerry of Massachusetts, took the predominantly blue states of the Northeast and West Coast. But the blue and red labels stood for more than just the Democratic and Republican Parties, or even the simple liberal and conservative designations. These colors, symbols of the deep culture war enveloping the country, signified a battle for the very soul of the United States. Or did they? Not everyone is so sure? In 2004, Morris Fiorina, Samuel J. Abrams, and Jeremy C. Pope asserted that a politically polarized America is a myth, or at the very least grossly exaggerated. Political parties, individual politicians, and elements in the media perpetuate the notion of extreme polarization for their own ends. Despite evidence that, at the elite level, bitter divisions exist, the reality is that most Americans are centrists.[20] In addition, they seem to be shedding their party labels—as more and more American identify as political independents. But as we just noted, the shedding of party label does not necessarily mean the shedding of political leanings associated with the major political parties. Table 8.3 presents a sample of issues reflecting how the divisions have increased since the mid-1990s within the American electorate. The survey includes not only party identifiers but Independents with partisan leanings as well.

The nomination of Donald Trump seemed to reaffirm the notion that the American electorate was becoming increasingly divided on a variety of issues. At the beginning of the nomination process, he faced no less than sixteen Republican opponents, most of whom were "establishment" candidates. Trump took some very hard line positions, some very conservative, and some, like opposition to free trade, seemed to run against traditional Republican thinking. He was against abortion, advocated building a wall along the U.S.-Mexican border to thwart illegal immigration, and rejected globalism, which he believed had been detrimental to American economic interests. He wanted extremely tough changes to immigration policies, including widespread deportation of millions of illegal immigrants and a complete ban on Muslims immigrating to the United States. In the election, he swept the traditional red states through the mid-western farm belt, captured the South as well as Pennsylvania, and took the upper Midwestern states of Michigan and Wisconsin. Candidate Clinton's array of blue states were confined to the far West and the Northeast. Although, getting back to the question of what role majority rule should matter (or in this case plurality rule)—Hillary Clinton won the popular vote by almost 3 million more votes than Donald Trump.

There is little doubt that divisions widened from the mid-1990s to 2017. Positions seemed to harden and the language of political discourse became harsher. But how lasting are these divisions?

One of the common objections to following the values of typical citizens too closely is that their views are fickle and uninformed. Many public surveys confirm that citizens are remarkably ignorant of basic political facts. Surveys of Americans show that people do not know who their congressional representative is, how many senators each state has, and who is chief justice of the United States.[21] When you take this ignorance and combine it with an apparent inconsistency of beliefs—citizens change their views on public policy frequently and seemingly without reason—skeptics of democracy are bound to discount the importance of popular values.[22] However, important studies of American

Table 8.3 Wide Partisan Differences on Many Issues

Issue Percent who agree that:		1994	2017
Government should do more to help the needy even if it means going deeper into debt.	Republican or Leaning Republican	38%	38%
	Democratic or Leaning Democratic	58%	24%
Government regulation of business is necessary to protect the public interest.	Republican or Leaning Republican	33%	31%
	Democratic or Leaning Democratic	49%	66%
Good diplomacy is the best way to ensure peace.	Republican or Leaning Republican	50%	33%
	Democratic or Leaning Democratic	66%	83%
The country needs to continue making changes to give blacks equal rights with whites.	Republican or Leaning Republican	30%	36%
	Democratic or Leaning Democratic	57%	81%
There is solid evidence that the average temperature on Earth has been getting warmer.	Republican or Leaning Republican	59%	52%
	Democratic or Leaning Democratic	79%	92%

Source: Data from Pew Research Center, "Partisan Divide on Political Values Grows Even Wider", October 2017. http://www.people-press.org/2017/10/05/the-partisan-divide-on-political-values-grows-even-wider/.

Note: Pew survey was conducted June 8–18, 2017, with a national sample of 2,504 adults living in all 50 states and the District of Columbia.

politics have found that inconsistency among voters is much less prevalent than originally thought. Benjamin Page and Robert Shapiro, in their book *The Rational Public*, show how basic policy preferences of Americans from the 1940s to the 1990s remained remarkably consistent and not subject to irrational changes. That said, consistent views do not necessarily translate into a culture war.

Of course, just because public opinion on key policies and support for certain basic values are stable does not mean that there are no changes over time. From 1965 to 1973, American public opinion turned against involvement in the war in Vietnam. Similarly, between 2003 and 2005 public support for America's war in Iraq declined significantly.

Over a longer period, comparable or greater change has taken place—change super-charged with meaning for liberty, justice, and welfare. For example, over the past half century or so, U.S. values have altered significantly regarding race relations (attitudes toward African Americans), religious relations (attitudes toward Catholics and Jews), gender relations (attitudes toward women), and labor-management relations. Finally, over the past decade, the speed with which the American public has shifted from a negative view of gay marriage to its acceptance is staggering.

As we noted earlier, Western democratic "publics" and legislators have historically agreed upon the main outlines of the welfare state, although recent conservative governments (for example, Margaret Thatcher's tenure as prime minister in Great Britain and Ronald Reagan's administration in the United States) successfully initiated movements to cut back or reform the welfare state. During the summer of 1996, President Bill Clinton, who had campaigned on a pledge to change welfare "as we know it" and previously vetoed two Republican welfare bills proclaiming them too harsh, finally signed into law sweeping welfare reform legislation largely sponsored by Republican lawmakers. In addition to significant changes in welfare benefits, the law called for a greater emphasis on getting welfare recipients off the welfare rolls and back to work. Finally, the federal government began divesting itself of some of its responsibility for welfare and giving greater responsibility to the fifty state governments. At the same time, the public expects the federal government to take an active role in a host of ongoing problems. Sometimes how a problem is defined significantly affects how popular a proposed solution to it is. In the United States, polls frequently show that there is strong opposition to welfare, yet these very same polls reveal a strong belief on the part of citizens that the government should do more to help the poor. How should we think about the apparent American belief that welfare is bad, but helping the poor is good?

We have little evidence in the matter of public opinion in most communist and developing countries. From 1917 in the Soviet Union, and from the late 1940s in Eastern Europe, to the 1990–1991 collapse of communism, there were no elections involving competing parties to indicate popular responses to the governments in power. Because of the lack of electoral history and general chaos in some of these systems, it may still be too early to make anything more than preliminary assessments. The peoples of the former Soviet Union and Eastern Europe are struggling with campaign and electoral processes they find unfamiliar. Slowly but surely electoral processes did begin to take hold during the 1990s. The 1996 presidential election in Russia was hotly contested by those who constituted the winning majority in support of Boris Yeltsin and the reform movement and those who campaigned vigorously on behalf of Communist leader Gennady Zyuganov. In March 2000, another successful election was held, and Vladimir Putin, of the Edinstvo (Unity) Party, was elected president. By 2005, however, serious questions were being raised about just how democratic the Putin regime really was. Both the Duma elections of 2007 and the 2008 and the Russian presidential election, which brought Putin protégé Dmitry Medvedev the presidency, came under severe criticism by outside monitoring groups. Accusations of irregularity included claims that state employees such as teachers and doctors had been ordered by their superiors to vote for the Edinstvo Party, that voters had been paid to vote for Putin's party, that unequal media coverage had been allotted to the detriment of the opposition, and that unacceptable restrictions had been placed on election monitoring groups. Indeed, in the 2008 election the monitoring group sent by the OSCE (Organization for Security and Cooperation in Europe) refused to observe the election because of the severe restrictions imposed by the Russian government.[23] In 2012, Vladimir Putin was once again elected to the presidency in Russia. It was yet again another controversial election with observers from the OSCE concluding that there were significant irregularities, particularly during the vote counting process.

Recent events in Eastern Europe and the former Soviet Union indicate a profound difference between the long-held values of government officials and values held by the people. For years, communist officials extolled the virtues of the economic systems they led. They publicly justified invasions of Hungary, Czechoslovakia, and Afghanistan. Centrally planned and administered policies were designed to provide adequate food, shelter, and medical care for all citizens. When the Eastern European economies collapsed and the Soviet system faced severe self-criticism under *glasnost*, the differences between the elite and the general population became glaring. To varying degrees, domestic policies in all of these states had failed to provide adequate food, housing, and medical care. The people felt betrayed and bitter. And while Hungarians and Czechoslovakians had obviously resented the Soviet invasions of 1956 and 1968, it now became clear that many Soviet citizens, too, viewed the 1979 invasion of Afghanistan as immoral, destructive, and wasteful, despite years of official pronouncements about its necessity.

CONCLUSION

In studying how politics is actually practiced, we must never lose sight of the ideals and fundamental values of political actors. Politics is, at some level, an attempt to deal with both reality and to aspire to the creation of a humane and just world. This chapter asks you to consider many of the key concepts and dualities that underpin our political world—such as separation of powers and connection of powers, federalism or unitary government, representative or direct democracy. Remember always that these key concepts are open to continual debate and redefinition. Recall also, that there is no one right answer for what works best. Some countries flourish with unitary government while others are almost inconceivable with anything but a federal system. Finally, we ask you to think about the way political values differ between political leaders and those held by the average citizen.

SUGGESTED READINGS

Altman, David. *Direct Democracy Worldwide*. Cambridge, MA: Cambridge University Press, 2014. A recent work that argues that direct democracy and representative democracy are not necessarily at odds in the actual practices of many countries.

Cantril, Hadley. *The Pattern of Human Concerns*. New Brunswick, NJ: Rutgers University Press, 1965. Uses global interviews—and sample survey techniques—to identify popular values. Provides basis for cross-national comparisons. Finds common demands rooted in values of self-preservation, security, order, opportunity for development, and integrity.

Cigler, Allan J., and Burdett A. Loomis, eds. *Interest Group Politics*. 8th ed. Washington, DC: CQ Press, 2015. An informative and varied collection of up-to-date essays on various kinds of interest groups, including both domestic and foreign lobbying efforts.

Dalton, Russell J. *The Good Citizen: How a Younger Generation Is Shaping American Politics*. Washington, DC: CQ Press, 2015. An insightful analysis of the changing American electorate, with particular focus on the 2008 presidential election.

Fiorina, Morris, Samuel J. Abrams, and Jeremy C. Pope. *Culture War? The Myth of a Polarized America*. 3rd ed. New York: Longman, 2010. A serious critique of the notion that the American public is deeply polarized as a manifestation of a great cultural divide. To the contrary, most Americans are centrists or moderates.

Huntington, Samuel P. *The Clash of Civilizations and the Remaking of World Order*. New York: Simon & Schuster, 1996. A provocative look at the post–Cold War era, with an emphasis on the potential for cultural conflict.

Inglehart, Ronald, and Christian Welzel. *Modernization, Cultural Change, and Democracy*. New York: Cambridge University Press, 2005. A magnificent study of social modernization and the way people's beliefs and values change and affect their behavior. In some respects the culmination of work that began with Inglehart's *The Silent Revolution: Changing Values and Political Styles among Western Publics*. Princeton, NJ: Princeton University Press, 1977.

Luce, Edward. *The Retreat of Western Liberalism*. New York: Grove/Atlantic, Inc., 2018. A thoughtful and powerful statement about the decline of Western liberalism that includes a growing ignorance of values that helped to build the West, an arrogance towards those economically less successful and a disturbing complacency since the fall of communism.

Maslow, Abraham H. *Toward a Psychology of Being*. 3rd ed. New York: Wiley, 1998. Also, *Motivation and Personality*. 3rd ed. New York: Addison-Wesley, 1987. Maslow's influential views of the relationship between needs and values and his famous hierarchy of needs. For a keen and penetrating analysis of the concept of human needs, see Patricia Springborg, *The Problem of Human Needs and the Critique of Civilization* (London: Allen and Unwin, 1981).

Page, Benjamin, and Robert Shapiro. *The Rational Public*. Chicago: University of Chicago Press, 1992. A superb account of American public opinion from 1940 to 1990. The authors make a strong case that public opinion is more reasonable and consistent than many critics of democracy allow.

Stimson, James A. *Tides of Consent: How Public Opinion Shapes American Politics*. New York: Cambridge University Press, 2004. Thoughtful and well-written analysis of American public opinion, with some emphasis on opinions that reside below the polling data.

Tilly, Charles. *Democracy*. Cambridge, MA: Cambridge University Press, 2007. A major study of the causes of democracy and the issue of de-democratization by one of our leading political scientists.

GLOSSARY TERMS

class values (p. 191)
connection of powers (p. 200)
culture wars (p. 216)
devolution (p. 202)
economic well-being (p. 204)
federalism (p. 197)
goal (p. 190)
interest aggregation (p. 192)

interest articulation (p. 192)
interest groups (p. 190)
majority rule (p. 196)
national interest (p. 204)
policy (p. 190)
political actor (p. 190)
political culture (p. 193)
political legitimacy (p. 190)

political values (p. 190)
polyarchy (p. 196)
principle (p. 190)
public interest (p. 204)
separation of powers (p. 197)
unitary government (p. 202)
welfare (p. 214)

NOTES

1. J. David Singer, "The Level-of-Analysis Problem in International Relations," in *The International System: Theoretical Essays*, ed. Klaus Knorr and Sidney Verba (Princeton, NJ: Princeton University Press, 1961), 77–92.

2. John Cassidy, "Donald Trump's Crisis of Legitimacy," New Yorker, August 17, 2017. http://www.newyorker.com/news/john-cassidy/donald-trumps-crisis-of-legitimacy

3. Nathan Keyfitz, "The Asian Road to Democracy," in *Comparative Politics: Notes and Readings*, 7th ed., ed. Roy C. Macridis and Bernard B. Brown (Pacific Grove, CA: Brooks-Cole, 1990), 111–117.

4. Ibid., 113.

5. Henry Steele Commager, *Majority Rule and Minority Rights* (New York: Oxford University Press, 1943), 80–81.

6. See Robert Dahl, *A Preface to Democratic Theory* (Chicago: University of Chicago Press, 1956).

7. See Hans J. Morgenthau, *Politics among Nations*, 2nd ed. (New York: Knopf, 1954). See also Charles A. Beard, *The Idea of National Interest* (Chicago: Quadrangle Books, 1966). Beard writes that "it may be said that national interest—its maintenance, advancement, and defense by the various means and instrumentalities of political power—is the prime consideration of diplomacy" (p. 21).

8. For clarification of the concept of public interest, see Richard E. Flathman, *The Public Interest: An Essay Concerning the Normative Discourse of Politics* (New York: Wiley, 1966).

9. Some of the better-known efforts in this area include the work of the Correlates of War Project, directed by J. David Singer, at the University of Michigan; the Stockholm International Peace Research Institute (SIPRI); and the Conflict Data Project at the Department of Peace and Conflict Research, Uppsala University, Sweden.

10. Zbigniew Brzezinski, *Out of Control: Global Turmoil on the Eve of the Twenty-First Century* (New York: Scribner's, 1993), 9–10.

11. M. Cherif Bassouni, "Searching for Peace and Achieving Justice: The Need for Accountability," *Law and Contemporary Problems* 59, no. 4 (1997).

12. Samuel P. Huntington, *The Clash of Civilizations and the Remaking of World Order* (New York: Simon & Schuster, 1996).

13. See Robert Dahl, *On Democracy* (New Haven, CT: Yale University Press, 1998), app. C.

14. On the CIA, for example, see Senate Committee on Foreign Relations, *CIA Foreign and Domestic Activities*, 94th Cong., 1st sess. (Washington, DC: U.S. Government Printing Office, 1974). On Chile, see Robert C. Johansen, *The National Interest and the Human Interest: An Analysis of U.S. Foreign Policy* (Princeton, NJ: Princeton University Press, 1980), chap. 4, "The United States and Human Rights in Chile," 196–281. On the FBI, see Senate Committee to Study Government Operations with Respect to Intelligence, *Intelligence Activities and the Rights of Americans*, Book II, 94th Cong., 2nd sess. (Washington, DC: U.S. Government Printing Office, 1976).

15. Information for these two paragraphs is derived from SIPRI, "Recent Trends in Military Expenditures," 2009, www.sipri.org; Insights, "Military Spending and Development," 2005, www.id21.Org/insights; and UN Development Program, *Human Development Report 2008* (New York: Oxford University Press, 2008).

16. Ronald Inglehart, *The Silent Revolution: Changing Values and Political Styles among Western Publics* (Princeton, NJ: Princeton University Press, 1977). For Maslow's own position, see Abraham H. Maslow, *Toward a Psychology of Being*, 3rd ed. (New York: Wiley, 1998); and Maslow, *Motivation and Personality*, 3rd ed. (New York: Addison-Wesley, 1987).

17. See Hadley Cantril, *The Pattern of Human Concerns* (New Brunswick, NJ: Rutgers University Press, 1965).

18. Ronald Inglehart, "The Nature of Value Change in Post-Industrial Societies," in *Politics and the Future of Industrial Societies*, ed. Leon N. Lindberg (New York: McKay, 1976), 38, 84–85.

19. Samantha Smith, "5 Facts about America's political independents," http://www.pewresearch.org/fact-tank/2016/07/05/5-facts-about-americas-political-independents/

20. Morris P. Fiorina, Samuel J. Abrams, and Jeremy C. Pope, *Culture War? The Myth of a Polarized America* (New York: Longman, 2004).

21. See Benjamin Page and Robert Shapiro, *The Rational Public* (Chicago: University of Chicago Press, 1992), 10–11.

22. Ibid., chap. 2.

23. Radio Free Europe, "Pro Putin Party Wins Landslide in Russian Elections," December 3, 2007, www.rferl.org/content/article/1079222.html; "Election Watchdog Scraps Plans to Monitor Russian Vote," *National Post*, March 19, 2008, www.nationalpost.com/news/world/story.html?id=292473.

President Trump delivers first address to a joint congress.

"REUTERS/XXSTRINGERXX Xxxxx"

9

AMERICAN POLITICS AND GOVERNMENT

This chapter will focus on American politics. As we have noted, the United States is just one of many democracies in the world and in some sense can be seen as just one case study in the broader field of comparative politics. However, it is such an important case study it deserves to be studied on its own. First of all, the United States is arguably the most powerful country on Earth. Its material wealth and military strength make it a political player without parallel. And, even if that changes in the future with the rise of countries like China and India, it is still true today that it is the one indispensable political force that, while it does not control world politics, nonetheless influences politics across the globe. Second, the United States is one of the founding democracies of the modern era. The call for freedom and democracy that started around the time of the American Revolution reverberates to this day. This is not to downplay the significant roles other countries, notably Great Britain and France, played in the ongoing evolution of democracy; yet, we must never lose sight of the fact that modern democracy is fundamentally influenced by the United States, its history and its culture. Finally, the United States deserves study not only for the reasons listed previously—ways in which the United States affects the rest the world—but also because it is in many ways unique and often different from other democracies. The concept of **American exceptionalism**—the idea that America's development is different from other countries, that its democracy is not quite like other countries—is important. Paradoxically, the United States deserves to be studied because it is so much like the rest of the world and intertwined with other countries and because it is also so different from the rest of the world.

Chapter Objectives

After studying this chapter, you will be able to do the following:

1. Identify some of the basic elements of American political culture and their origin.

2. Describe the institutions that make up the basic American government structure at the national level and how they function.

3. Discuss how closely the practice of politics in America squares with some of democracy's agreed upon values.

4. Define the Bill of Rights and how it shapes the way Americans think about politics.

5. Analyze the role that nongovernmental institutions—media, interest groups, political parties—play in American politics.

AMERICAN POLITICAL CULTURE

American Political Culture and the Factors That Shaped It

As we saw in Chapter 8, one of the important concepts to consider when studying any country is what is its political culture? What are the basic habits, customs, traditions, and beliefs of any country? And, we could ask further, what forces shaped those values and customs? How did they develop, and how are they continuing to evolve?

Let us start by considering what Americans believe. There is strong evidence that three key ideas are prevalent in the culture of the United States. First, Americans believe in individual freedom. This is not to say that freedom or liberty is devalued in other countries, but clearly, the evidence is that Americans desire freedom. This idea is evidenced from the very founding of the Republic, with Patrick Henry's famous line, "Give me liberty or give me death" and echoes down the years to New Hampshire's motto, emblazoned on its license plate, "Live Free or Die." Lest one think there is too much emphasis on death, one should note that Americans across the political spectrum champion the political ideal that citizens should be free to control their own destinies, that government power should be treated with a fair amount of skepticism, and that personal autonomy is a vital part of any healthy of politics. Of course, how that freedom manifests itself is often a source of a great deal of political debate. To many, nothing is more emblematic and essential to freedom than the Second Amendment to the U.S. Constitution and its safeguarding of the right to own guns. Others emphasize a woman's right to control her body through the idea of reproductive rights as central to understanding what it means to be free. As you probably know, there is a great deal of debate about gun control and abortion rights—yet, notice how often these debates are framed in terms of personal freedom. In many cultural debates in the United States, the sides that can show they are furthering personal freedom are often the ones who win those debates.

The second ideal that animates U.S. politics is equality. The great French commentator on American politics, Alexis de Tocqueville, once observed, "Americans are so enamored of equality that they would rather be equal in slavery than unequal in freedom." Certainly, economic inequality exists in the United States, and it has actually grown quite extreme in recent years. This has engendered a fair amount of debate and concern among some. Yet, can anyone doubt that Americans believe that at some level everyone is supposed to be equal? No one deserves more privileges or special treatment. We are all equal before the law. While there are many who would point out how the United States falls short of that ideal, it is still true that Americans want to believe it as an aspiration. And it is quite remarkable that no matter what one's wealth or political status, most people claim that they are no better than the "average American." It would be the foolish American politician who claimed otherwise. As with freedom, though, the idea of equality is open to a great deal of debate. This is perhaps best illustrated by the ongoing debate in the United States about Affirmative Action. To its opponents Affirmative Action is clearly wrong because it treats people as unequal. People seeking admissions to college or promotion at work should be treated equally, regardless of skin color. Yet, to its defenders, Affirmative Action is a noble attempt to overcome past discrimination—past actions that denigrated equality and tainted America with a legacy of inequality.

Finally, the third ideal that is part of American culture is democracy. Americans almost instinctively believe that democracy is the way to organize politics. In some ways, this follows logically from the ideals of freedom and equality—particularly equality. All citizens should have a say in how the nation manages its political affairs because we are free and equal to each other. However, we should note that the United States is not democratic in all its practices and procedures and that our history is replete with undemocratic events. Nonetheless, the ideal of democracy has been present from the beginning, and most political scientists would argue that over time America has grown more democratic. Indeed, the title of Tocqueville's famous book is *Democracy in America*, and whatever its flaws, most people see the United States as offering some sort of democracy, certainly in comparison with other countries around world. Furthermore, over time, the United States has implemented more and more democratic pro-

The French political philosopher and historian Alexis de Tocqueville toured the United States in the early 1830s making numerous insightful observations. Among them was that America was "exceptional"— hence the term *American exceptionalism.*

cedures into its politics. When the Republic was founded, senators were elected by state legislatures; however, with the passage of the 17th Amendment to the Constitution they are now elected directly by the citizens of each state. At the state level, many states now have initiatives and referendums that allow the people to create or approve of laws. However, we should not lose sight of the fact that American democracy is, for the most part, representative democracy, and the predominant way the average citizen participates in politics is via the election of officials.

This leads us to think about what factors have shaped American culture. Certainly, three things stand out. First, the United States has been shaped by many discrete historical events. Unlike many other countries whose origins are lost in the mists of time, the United States had a period of a fairly well documented colonization by Europeans in the seventeenth and eighteenth centuries. This was followed by a very clear, and not mythic, revolution with actual Founders (as opposed to legendary figures) who led in the creation of a new nation. There are no lost documents that may never have existed: we know what is in the U.S. Constitution, who wrote it, and when. Later on, many of the failings of the United States—particularly regarding slavery and the ongoing problem of race—led to the Civil War. While the war did not solve all the problems the United States faced, it certainly promoted major changes, and to this day it provides a touchstone for our politics. In the twentieth century, World War II propelled the United States permanently onto the world stage and launched America as a superpower with interests ground the globe. As with any country, certain events reverberate through the years and define generations and shape our politics. The Battle of Gettysburg, the assassination of

Map 9.1   Alexis de Tocqueville's Journeys in America

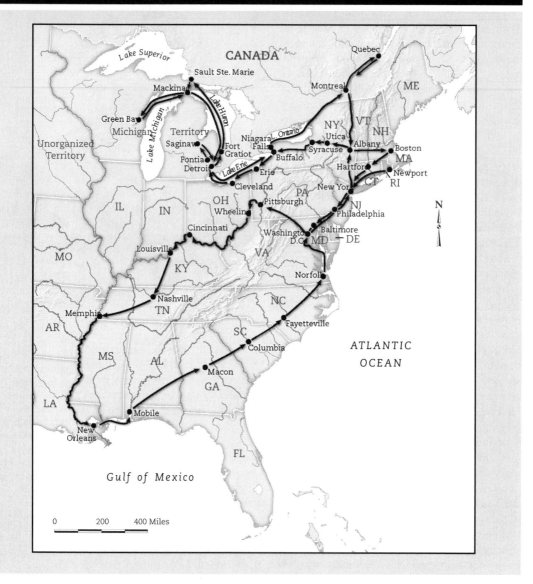

Source: Figure created by production.

John F. Kennedy, 9/11—these are uniquely American events that define us as a people and influenced American politics to this day.

The second factor that has influenced American political culture is that the United States is a nation of immigrants. Each new group carries their own ideas, culture, and aspirations to this continent. Of course, some of these groups, such as most African Americans, were brought here by force. Furthermore, we should not forget that before there were any Europeans here there were more ancient immigrants who we call Native Americans today. (Most such groups actually prefer to be known by their tribal names.) Nonetheless, the key point is that to a degree as great, if not greater, than any other country the United States is a product of a tremendous mixing of diverse peoples.

Finally, the United States culture is shaped its geography. This is, of course, true of all countries. But America is blessed by existing between two large oceans that insulated it from the incessant political infighting of the European powers in the eighteenth and nineteenth centuries. Furthermore, the continent is abundant in natural resources—coal, oil, and timber—that provided the foundation for much of the material wealth that exists to this day.

AMERICAN POLITICAL INSTITUTIONS

Along with its political culture, the United States must be understood through its political institutions. This is most readily understood by thinking about its Constitution. As mentioned in Chapter 8, two of the key concepts that underpin the U.S. Constitution are separation of powers and federalism. The idea of separation of powers means, in the context of the United States, that the national government is divided into three branches—the legislature (the House of Representatives and the Senate), the executive (head by the president), and the judiciary (with the highest court being the U.S. Supreme Court). The American Founders favored separation of powers because they believed that, in the words of James Madison in *Federalist* No. 47, "accumulation of all powers, legislative, executive, and judiciary, in the same hands, whether of one, a few, or many, and whether hereditary, self-appointed, or elective, may justly be pronounced the very definition of tyranny." This institutional structure would safeguard freedom, a fundamental aspect of American political culture from the very beginning (see Figure 9.1).

KEY QUESTIONS

The careful study of American politics raises a number of critical questions to be kept in mind as you work your way through this chapter:

1. How closely does the practice of politics in America square with some of democracy's agreed upon values?

2. How do American institutions, such as the presidency, the Congress, and the courts, function? Does the American system of government produce effective results or does it result in too much conflict and policy gridlock?

3. In what ways does the U.S. Constitution, in particular its Bill of Rights, shape the way Americans think about politics?

4. What role do nongovernmental institutions, such as the media, interest groups, and political parties, play in the way politics operate in the United States?

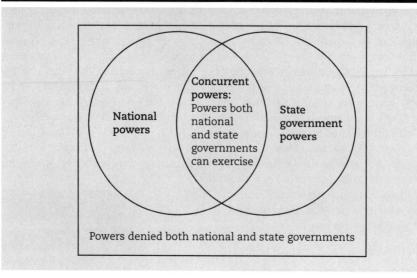

Figure 9.1 U.S. Federal System (Simplified)

National powers

Concurrent powers: Powers both national and state governments can exercise

State government powers

Powers denied both national and state governments

Source: Compiled by authors.

Federalism is the idea that power is shared between the national government and regional government—called states in America. Some matters like foreign policy and defense are under the complete control of the federal government. Others, such as local schools and police, are largely defined by the states. Finally, some policy areas, such as taxation, are exercised by both the national and state governments. Of course, there are continuing debates about what should be a state matter and what should be a national matter. Frequently, this pits local demands to protect certain customary practices against national concerns about justice. A classic example of this type of clash in the United States was the decades-long history of state government discrimination against African Americans. This injustice led in the 1960s to widespread citizen protests and the call by President Lyndon B. Johnson for national action that resulted in congressional passage of legislation to protect civil rights and voting rights for minorities.

To see more clearly how this works, let's take a more detailed look at how the legislatures, executives, bureaucracies, and courts work in the United States. Some of these ideas can be seen in any legislature or executive throughout the world; however, they are certainly true of the U.S. political system.

Legislatures

Legislatures have four main, interrelated functions: representative, deliberative, legislative, and supervisory. In performing these functions, legislatures fulfill most conditions of successful accommodation.

The Representative Function. Legislatures give voice to the political, economic, social, and geographic interests of the political community. The **representative function** of legislators requires that they represent and look out for the interests of the constituents who elected them. However, the typical legislator must balance many different considerations in making political decisions. Legislators feel pressure from their party leadership and the people they represent; at the same time, they must consider their own beliefs and conscience in deciding how to act politically. American legislators typically attempt to balance the interests of constituency, interest group, party, and nation. But because voters are generally interested in only a few subjects, congressional representatives are often freed from their role as "delegates" who do what the dominant interests in the constituency want done. They can function as "trustees" instead, deciding issues by judging what they think is best for the nation. In general, legislators translate key segments of public opinion—and the interests of majority voters, interest groups, and parties—into tangible public policy.

Terms of office vary from country to country in the developed regions of the world. In determining term length for various offices, the architects of a government have to balance the need for politicians to stay close to the people (leading to a brief term) with the need to insulate them from the vagaries of fickle public opinion (leading to a longer term). In the United States, that balancing act can be seen in the different terms of office for members of the House of Representatives and members of the Senate, terms fixed by the Founders in the Constitution. Voters in congressional districts elect members of the House for a term of two years. A statewide constituency elects members of the Senate for a term of six years. As we noted earlier, one-third of the Senate is elected at a time. The types of constituency also matter a great deal in the United States. House members represent relatively homogeneous districts whereas senators typically represent diverse states.

The Senate's influence, in both domestic and foreign affairs, is significant. No law can be enacted without its approval, and it has often provided leadership on legislative programs. Per the language of the U.S. Constitution, the Senate must **advise and consent**—that is, provide advice to the president on treaties and key appointments through the mechanism of hearings and approve these items with a vote requiring a two-thirds majority.

The Deliberative Function. Legislatures manifest their **deliberative function** by providing a forum for debate and formal decision making on issues, thus facilitating the examination of the views of contending parties. Debate may, however, clarify the parties' positions on key issues and thereby educate the public to some extent. In the United States—given the greater independence of Congress—the leaders of the House and Senate organize, separately or jointly, hearings on various issues of concern to members and their constituents as well as to a host of economic, religious, and social interests. Deliberation largely occurs within the committee structure in order to facilitate the articulation of grievances and ideas. This provides Congress with the opportunity to gauge the level of interest of voters and the intensity of voters' feelings. In addition, the committee structure provides the opportunity for members of the executive branch to meet with members of the legislature, usually through the hearing process.

The Legislative Function. Legislatures are expected to exercise the **legislative function**—that is, to carry out their formal responsibility for making law. In passing laws, legislatures not only express interests and shape priorities but also place the stamp of **legitimacy** on public policy. In the United States, the president's signature is required before a bill can become a law. If the president chooses not to sign—that is, she or he vetoes a bill—then a two-thirds vote in both the House and the Senate is necessary for an override. (Figure 9.2 illustrates the cooperation required to enact a bill into law in the United States.) Duly enacted legislation constitutes formal legitimacy—the general acceptance by political actors and citizens that government actions are appropriate and fully accepted. Such legitimacy makes for effective governance. In the United States, the power of Congress to raise and spend money exerts a powerful control over the executive. Money, which must be lawfully raised and spent, crucially affects the exercise of political power.

The Supervisory Function. Legislatures must also carry out a **supervisory function**, which requires them to supervise the work of the executive and the **bureaucracy**. Congressional committees enjoy extensive investigatory powers that they often use to evaluate, and thus control, the functioning of the bureaucracy. Debates in the House and the Senate also provide opportunities for the people's representatives—particularly

Figure 9.2   How a Bill Becomes Law (Simplified)

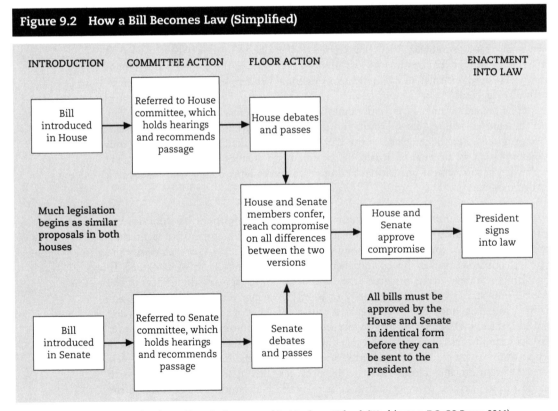

Source: Roger H. Davidson and Walter J. Oleszek, *Congress and Its Members*, 13th ed. (Washington, DC: CQ Press, 2011).

members of the opposition party—to criticize governmental policy. The Senate's agency in giving advice and consent on treaties and other key appointments enables senators to scrutinize policy and personnel. Moreover, the House may impeach (bring charges against) and the Senate try government officials, even the president of the United States, for "treason, bribery, or other high crimes and misdemeanors."

Executives

Secretary of Veterans Affairs Eric Shinseki (left) testifies before the Senate Veterans Affairs Committee in May 2014. The administration was rocked by scandal involving terrible delays in veterans getting appointments and falsification of records. On May 30, 2014, Secretary Shinseki resigned.

The executive, or president, plans, initiates, and implements overall governmental policy. The president is indispensable in the process of articulating vital national needs and fundamental interests. Executives serve to enunciate and gain approval for policies. Their resourcefulness and vigor enable modern governments to do their jobs. Executives also act to control the very bureaucracy they head. In performing their tasks, they must obtain widespread cooperation from legislators, key interests, and citizens in general.

In the United States, the Democratic and Republican Parties choose their presidential candidates. The people of the states then choose the president (indirectly, through the Electoral College—see p. 249), who will serve for a four-year term. Similarly, but independently, the parties choose and the people elect (directly this time) members of Congress, who also serve for fixed terms. Congress must formally enact legislation. The president's signature is required for legislation, unless Congress can override a presidential veto. Constitutionally, presidents cannot force Congress to follow their will; by the same token, if a two-thirds vote to override a presidential veto cannot be mustered in both the Senate and the House, Congress cannot enact vetoed legislation. The president and Congress must cooperate to avoid deadlock. However, politics is frequently dominated by continuing conflict between Congress and the president, as each institution seeks to control the political agenda. This may be true even if the same party controls both branches.

For U.S. presidents, the task of working cooperatively with the legislature can prove challenging. The fact that the president and members of the House and Senate are independently elected makes it possible for the president to be of one party at the same time one or both branches of Congress are dominated by another party. During President Bill Clinton's first term, the Republicans won control of both the House and the Senate in 1994. Two years later, Clinton was reelected, but both houses of Congress remained in Republican hands. In 2000, Republicans initially controlled both Congress and the presidency; however, after Sen. James M. Jeffords of Vermont left the Republican Party and became an Independent, control of the Senate switched to the Democrats. One-party rule was restored in the 2002 elections and reaffirmed in the 2004 elections, when the Republicans won clear, if narrow, majorities. In 2006, the Democrats regained control of both the House and Senate. With the 2008 elections, the Democrats achieved unified control of the Congress and the presidency. Yet two years later, the 2010 midterm elections gave Republicans control of the House of Representatives, while the Democrats maintained a majority in the Senate. Next, in 2014, the Republicans seized control of both houses in the mid-term elections with impressive wins in a number of Senate races. Finally, the 2016 elections brought Donald Trump to the White House and, thus, led to Republican control of all the elected branches of government.

If deadlock occurs between the president and Congress, the American people cannot immediately resolve the conflict by engaging in a new round of elections. The president remains in office for the full four years, House members the full two, and senators the full six. It is also possible for the president's party to lose or to gain control of the House and the Senate during the president's tenure in office, as was the case in both the George W. Bush and Barack H. Obama administrations. Because of separation of powers, there is no constitutional imperative that forces a president and Congress to agree on a common program. And America's relatively weak party system does not build a strong bridge between the legislative and executive branches. Thus, conflict between the U.S. president and Congress is frequent, stormy, and often disruptive. This was evident in 1995 when disagreements over the federal budget between President Clinton and the House of Representatives, led by Speaker Newt Gingrich, resulted in a temporary shutdown of the federal government. This pattern of institutional conflict was repeated in October of 2013, when the Republican-controlled House of Representatives clashed with President Obama over federal spending. For sixteen days, the government was shut down until a compromise could be reached. During his first year in office, Donald Trump's administration marked a new chapter in Presidential–Congressional relations. Despite having the Republican Party in control of both branches, there was a great deal of infighting that hampered the ability of the president and Congress agreeing on policies. Despite the Republican Party promising to repeal Obamacare, they were unable to do so. Some believed that this was because of ideological differences between Republican members of Congress—more extreme conservatives wanted total repeal while moderate Republicans wanted a more limited replacement of the policy. Others noted that President Trump's political inexperience, or even lack of interest, led to a surprisingly disengaged president who failed to consistently push a clear plan. Trump and Congressional Republicans were, however, more successful in passing a major overall and cut in taxes, particularly corporate taxes, later in 2017. Yet, a strong and resourceful president can work out patterns of cooperation. We will shortly examine the resources on which the president may draw to achieve cooperation and exert effective leadership.

The Roles of the President. Box 9.1 calls attention to the multiple roles the U.S. president plays. In many countries, however, the role of ceremonial chief of state (such as the British monarch and the president of the Republic of Italy or Germany) is separate from the real head of government. The sources of the U.S. president's powers are to be found in the Constitution, historical custom and tradition, and court decisions. For example, the president's role as party chief is not laid down in the Constitution; it emerged in the course of American history. Many of the rules that govern how the president acts are based on political norms. These norms are founded on historical precedent and are not required by law. For instance, until the 22nd Amendment to the Constitution was adopted, it was just a custom that presidents only served two terms. This was a tradition initiated by George Washington, reinforced by Thomas Jefferson, and held sway over subsequent presidents until Franklin Roosevelt broke with this custom by seeking a third term amidst concerns about World War II and the U.S. role in a troubled world. Possibly due to his personality and his political inexperience, Donald Trump is a president prone to break with tradition. During the campaign, he criticized judges, something presidents have been loath to do out of deference to the independence of the judiciary and respect for the rule of law. He also failed to release his tax returns—a practice that had been honored by presidents and presidential candidates dating to the 1970s. And, he refused to divest himself of his business interests that was also commonly done by previous presidents. Although none of these actions by Trump are forbidden by law, they have been observed by previous presidents as wise practices. It remains to be seen whether this damages American politics generally or simply reflects a new and different understanding of the office.

U.S. President's Multiple Roles

Chief Executive and Administrator

"The executive Power shall be vested in a President of the United States of America."

"He . . . shall take care that the Laws be faithfully executed." (U.S. Constitution, Article II, Sections 1 and 3)

Commander in Chief

"The President shall be Commander in Chief to the Army and Navy of the United States." (U.S. Constitution, Article II, Section 2)

Party Chief

Based on historical custom and tradition.

Chief Legislative Brain Truster

"He shall from time to time give the Congress Information of the State of the Union, and recommend to their Consideration such Measures as he shall judge necessary and expedient." (U.S. Constitution, Article II, Section 3)

Power to veto legislation. (U.S. Constitution, Article I, Section 7)

Power of patronage. (U.S. Constitution, Article II, Section 2)

Historical custom and tradition.

Chief National Spokesperson

Spokesperson on the "State of the Union."
Historical custom and tradition.

Chief Diplomat

Chief Diplomat. (U.S. Constitution, Article II, Section 1)

"He shall have Power, by and with the Advice and Consent of the Senate, to make treaties, provided two-thirds of the Senators present concur." (U.S. Constitution, Article II, Section 1)

Leader of cabinet—including the Department of State. (U.S. Constitution, Article II, Section 2)

Power to appoint ambassadors. (U.S. Constitution, Article II, Section 2)

Chief Popular Leader

Election, indirectly through the Electoral College, by the people. (U.S. Constitution, Article II, Section 1)

Historical custom and tradition.

Ceremonial Chief of State

U.S. Constitution (implied).
Historical custom and tradition.

Source: Compiled by authors.

BOX 9.1

The U.S. president's powers have evolved largely in response to national problems that called for strong executive leadership—most particularly war and economic crises. To preserve the Union, President Abraham Lincoln had to take extraordinary actions. Without congressional sanction, he called for troops; suspended the **writ of habeas corpus**—literally, "produce the body," a legal document requiring that a prisoner be brought before a court to determine whether he or she is being lawfully held in jail— in parts of Maryland; and imposed martial law on a wide range of civilians. Similarly, during World Wars I and II, Presidents Woodrow Wilson and Franklin D. Roosevelt expanded the powers of the presidency within the broad framework of legislation passed by Congress. During the Great Depression of the 1930s, President Roosevelt boldly assumed a leadership role in initiating legislation and a host of programs to create jobs, lift prices, protect bank depositors, and stimulate the economy.

The challenges of managing the welfare state, which expanded significantly during Franklin Roosevelt's time, remain today. There are, moreover, worldwide problems that underscore the demand for strong leadership to advance security, liberty, justice, and welfare. Indeed, modern executives the world over, whose powers also have expanded to enable them to cope with the demands of the modern world, face what some scholars have called "the statesman's dilemma," which they define as the "dilemma of rising demands and insufficient resources."[1] These problems challenge modern executives and require the critical student of politics to ask if executives can (without abusing their power) plan, initiate, and implement governmental policy successfully.

Planning Public Policy. Modern executives plan on behalf of the nation. Much more so than legislatures, executives possess and use those resources that permit them to plan effectively. These resources include the following:

1. *Comprehensiveness*, or the ability to see a problem in its entirety as a national problem

2. *Foresight*, or the ability to look ahead and anticipate the dangers and opportunities related to proposed policies

3. *Accessibility*, or access to relevant and significant information made available by a command of the bureaucracy

4. *Connectedness*, or the capacity to pull together and coordinate diverse interests on behalf of common programs

5. *Efficiency*, or the ability to act with speed and energy

These ingredients for successful planning do not belong simply to the individual who is the U.S. president, the British prime minister, or the German premier; they belong, rather, to the executive office. While these resources do not inevitably lead to decisions that enhance security, liberty, justice, and welfare, they do in fact increase the likelihood of sensible planning and successful outcome.

Initiating Public Policy. Modern executives also have been called on to use their formidable powers to initiate governmental policy. Indeed, most presidential candidates campaign on an extensive policy agenda and we now expect our presidents or potential presidents to reform policies. The president of the United States, for example, has become the nation's chief initiator of legislation as well as its chief executive. Presidents can base legislative initiative on their constitutional power to recommend "necessary and expedient" measures to Congress. Presidents can also use numerous other powers to mobilize support for legislative priorities. For example, veto power can be used to oppose and defeat legislation that a president does not favor, assuming that the veto will not be overridden by a two-thirds vote in Congress. Even the threat of the veto can influence what actions Congress might take. Presidents can also use their power to make appointments—the power of patronage—to encourage legislators to support presidential policies. Moreover, as head of the party, presidents can draw on party support on behalf of programs. Party regulars know that loyalty can bring them money and support in their reelection campaigns. This point about the president being the leader of his party is strongly underlined by President Trump—a person seen as a party outsider who nonetheless captured the Republican nomination. Despite occasional criticism, Republican leaders in Congress have largely followed the president's lead no matter what their concerns. In addition, both as popular leaders and as public figures, presidents are well positioned to capture the public's attention; using television and radio airtime they can mobilize public opinion on behalf of their preferred policies. More recently, President Trump has been quite adept in using social media to influence the political world. His nearly constant tweeting often captures public attention and becomes the focal point of political discussion. In all of these ways, then, presidents can initiate and push for legislation.

Policy also arises within the governmental bureaucracy. Because legislation cannot possibly spell out every detail of policy implementation, power increasingly is given to the president as head of the administration to interpret legislation that has been passed by Congress. As chief administrator, then, the president can initiate policy in the course of administering the law.

As both initiator and administrator of public policy, the president is strategically positioned to accommodate a wide range of political actors—voters, interest groups, party members, legislators, and bureaucrats. A skillful president who champions sound policy makes U.S. democracy work well. When a president is inept and backs flawed policies, the nation suffers. Sympathetic observers of President Lyndon B. Johnson's domestic programs point to his successes in promoting three civil rights bills, inaugurating the War on Poverty, and improving health legislation. But critics of his foreign policy fault him for involving the nation in a disastrous war in Vietnam and for contributing to inflation by refusing to raise taxes while fighting that war. President Richard Nixon was hailed for his progressive policy in establishing links to the People's Republic of China after twenty-one years of limited, often hostile, contact. Within three years of this policy success, however, the Watergate scandal forced Nixon from office—as the first president to resign the office.

President Ronald Reagan is given much credit for lifting the morale of the American public and reining in spiraling inflation. Later in his presidency, and after he left office, however, he came under severe criticism for allowing the national debt to grow to enormous levels, partly through gigantic military expenditures, failing to monitor and stop a disgraceful scandal at the Department of Housing and Urban Development, failing to recognize and prevent the savings and loan scandal that cost American taxpayers billions of dollars, and allowing the Iran-Contra affair to occur. We might note that many political observers gave Reagan's immediate successor, George H. W. Bush, high marks for the skill with which he built the Desert Storm political and military coalition that retook Kuwait after Iraq's invasion in 1990. Yet in 1992, Bush was denied reelection primarily because Americans believed he had mishandled the nation's economy. In contrast, the public gave President Clinton a vote of confidence when they reelected him in 1996. After a disastrous attempt during his first two years in office to completely redesign the nation's health care system, Clinton rallied and achieved a number of successes—passage of the Brady Bill controlling handguns, family leave legislation, a deficit-reduction bill, a modest increase in the minimum wage, and a peace accord ending the Bosnian conflict. After the attacks on September 11, 2001, President George W. Bush won strong initial support for his war on terrorism that helped propel him to reelection in 2004. But by the end of his administration, the president was under increasing criticism for his initiation of the war in Iraq. President Barack Obama from 2008 well into 2012 had a number of policy accomplishments, including passage of a major health care reform, the initiation of a large stimulus bill to counter the disastrous 2008 recession, a Wall Street reform act, as well as a consumer protection bill. Later still, the Obama administration changed policy concerning gays in the military, and Osama bin Laden was killed in Pakistan by Army Special Forces. However, despite winning reelection, President Obama's popularity declined significantly most likely because the recovery from the Great Recession of 2008 has been slow and less than stellar, particularly when considering personal income for most Americans. However, as the economy continued to improve, Obama's popularity increased. While President Trump's overall approval ratings were low during his first year in office, continued low unemployment, solid job growth, and a soaring stock market eventually led to some improvement in his approval ratings.[2]

Implementing Public Policy. Executives, traditionally, are in charge of implementing policy and managing bureaucracy. The U.S. Constitution requires the president to take care that the laws be faithfully executed. The president also functions as the nation's number one diplomat and as commander in chief of the armed forces. In performing these tasks, the president cannot assume that things will get done automatically. Legislation is not self-executing; orders do not necessarily get carried out. Inevitably, politics impinges on administration. The president, through cabinet members and aides, must follow up on policy, even when forces within the cabinet or wider administration do not see eye to eye on key issues. In Congress, members are especially concerned with policies that affect their home districts or states. In view of these considerations, the president must enlist the support of cabinet members, key aides and bureaucrats, public opinion, affected interests, and members of Congress to carry out administrative duties. In this process—in building and maintaining support and in putting out fires—the president achieves accommodation and facilitates effective government performance.

Bureaucracies

Bureaucracy is an instrument of government; it is composed of the governmental departments, ministries, agencies, and officials that are charged with carrying out public policy. Max Weber, an influential German social scientist and perceptive student of bureaucracy, was one of the first political observers to note the importance of bureaucracy and to delineate the characteristics of the bureaucratic style—rational, efficient, and impartial.[3] Such governance, contrary to our common, pejorative understanding of bureaucracy, was a great advance over government that was often irrational (having no coherent rhyme or reason for policies), inefficient (unable to keep accurate records, collect taxes, and perform services), and based on favoritism and bribes rather than on merit and honesty. Rational, efficient, and impartial treatment of citizens—based on sensible procedures, good record keeping and follow-up and evenhanded behavior—contributes to successful accommodation in the political community.

Of course, government bureaucrats can also be impersonal, inflexible, tangled in red tape, overbearing, inconsiderate, and unhelpful. This type of behavior—all too frequent in every bureaucracy—gives the term its bad name. It is thus easy to associate bureaucracy with government out of control—with abuses of power, rude and offensive behavior, waste, and overregulation. The greater the power of government over our lives, the greater the chance there is for bureaucratic abuse of that power. And there is considerable evidence, in all governments, to support such charges against the bureaucracy.

Despite frequent and often disturbing complaints about how bureaucrats interfere with security, liberty, justice, and welfare, it would be a mistake to ignore their important role in enabling legislatures, and even more so executives, to carry out governmental responsibilities. Indeed, some observers see the top civil servants (often nameless and faceless) as the key policymakers in government. Clearly, government would come to a standstill without a responsible and capable bureaucracy.

Carrying Out Public Policy. The bureaucracy is government in action; it consists of all the departments or ministries, agencies, officials, and commissions required to carry out public policy. It plans, initiates, and implements on behalf of presidents, prime ministers, and premiers. In doing so, the bureaucracy responds to interest groups affected by legislation and regulation, often working out compromises between different interests and the general public. The bureaucracy provides information to executives and legislatures, to the press, and to the public. Lower-level officials may inform senior officials of what is workable. In administering the law honestly and competently, civil servants contribute to approved and effective governance. They may also check on, and work to control, the abuse of power within their domain. There can be little doubt that a well-trained, well-organized, and honest bureaucracy makes an invaluable contribution to modern government. On the other hand, a defective bureaucracy is a prime source of political malaise. Thus, the training and quality of the bureaucracy are vitally important.

In the United States, for example, top civil servants (another name for bureaucrats) usually receive their training at the best universities. Their entrance into government service is typically based on examination, so they constitute a **meritocracy**—that is, members of a bureaucracy who have gained employment and achieved advancement by reason of merit as opposed to patronage or personal favor. Top civil servants are highly intelligent, competent, and honest, and some often spend years considering how to solve problems and implement policy. Clearly, the advantage of this civil service is expertise and knowledge. The disadvantage is that civil servants can become committed to certain established ways of doing things and might be unwilling to think creatively about new solutions to old problems.

Ensuring Governmental Stability and Continuity. In the United States, the number of top administrators who come and go is greater when the party in power changes; even so, a core of permanent civil servants near the top remains to provide vital assistance.

The Courts

In the United States, the courts are extremely powerful and independent. They also serve multiple roles in the political system—from protecting freedom to adjudicating disputes between branches of government and between the national government and the states.

Safeguarding Rights and Liberties. U.S. federal courts protect against federal or state government violation of the basic political and nonpolitical freedoms that ensure the proper functioning of the democratic and constitutional process. The federal courts safeguard a host of crucial rights. Some of them—such as the "privilege of the Writ of Habeas Corpus"—are found in the body of the U.S. Constitution. This famous right protects the people against illegal detention or imprisonment. A prisoner must be brought before a court at a stated time and place so that the court may determine whether the prisoner is being lawfully held in jail. Other rights are found in the Constitution's first ten amendments, popularly known as the **Bill of Rights**—an enduring source of protection of the vital needs and fundamental interests of citizens and groups—and in other crucial amendments. A sampling of rights guaranteed in the U.S. Constitution follows:

> Amendment I: Congress shall make no law respecting an establishment of religion, or prohibiting the free exercise thereof; or abridging the freedom of speech, or of the press; or the right of the people peaceably to assemble, and to petition the Government for a redress of grievances.

> Amendment IV: The right of the people to be secure in their persons, houses, papers, and effects, against unreasonable searches and seizures, shall not be violated, and no Warrants shall issue, but upon probable cause, supported by Oath or affirmation, and particularly describing the place to be searched, and the persons or things to be seized.

> Amendment V: No person shall . . . be deprived of life, liberty, or property, without due process of law; nor shall private property be taken for public use, without just compensation.

> Amendment VI: In all criminal prosecutions, the accused shall enjoy the right to a speedy and public trial, by an impartial jury of the State and district wherein the crime shall have been committed, which district shall have been previously ascertained by law, and to be informed of the nature and cause of the accusation; to be confronted with the witnesses against him; to have compulsory process for obtaining witnesses in his favor, and to have the Assistance of Counsel for his defense.

> Amendment VIII: Excessive bail shall not be required, nor excessive fines imposed, nor cruel and unusual punishments inflicted.

Amendment XIV: All persons born or naturalized in the United States, and subject to the jurisdiction thereof, are citizens of the United States and of the State wherein they reside. No State shall make or enforce any law, which shall abridge the privileges or immunities of citizens of the United States; nor shall any State deprive any person of life, liberty, or property, without due process of law; nor deny to any person within its jurisdiction the equal protection of the laws.

Amendment XV: The right of citizens of the United States to vote shall not be denied or abridged by the United States or by any State on account of race, color, or previous condition of servitude.

The U.S. Supreme Court in 2018. The latest justice selected was Justice Neil Gorsuch. Seated from left in the first row are Associate Justice Ruth Bader Ginsburg, Associate Justice Anthony M. Kennedy (Now retired, replaced with the appointment of Justice Brett Kavanaugh), Chief Justice John G. Roberts, Associate Justice Clarence Thomas, Associate Justice Stephen Breyer, and standing from the left are Associate Justice Elena Kagan, Associate Justice Samuel Alito Jr., Associate Justice Sonia Sotomayor, and Associate Justice Neil Gorsuch.

Other important amendments include the 13th, which eliminated slavery, the 19th, which extended the vote to women, and the 26th, which extended the vote to citizens age eighteen years or older.

Both federal and state courts protect these rights as well as other rights enacted by Congress and state legislatures. It is difficult to overestimate the value of such protections for democratic and peaceful accommodation. Citizens know that they need not resort to force and violence to ensure their rights. They know, too, that the electoral process is available as a way to protect their interests. In safeguarding civil liberties and other basic constitutional rules, the courts ensure agreement on fundamentals essential to the success of democratic and constitutional government.

The U.S. Supreme Court holds a unique position in the developed world because of the American principles of separation of powers, **judicial review**, and federalism. These principles make the Supreme Court one of the most powerful judicial bodies in the world. Under the principle of the separation of powers, the Supreme Court may thus protect its own independent and separate status—its own powers and integrity under the Constitution. Under the principle of judicial review, the Supreme Court may declare an act of government unconstitutional. And finally, under the principle of federalism, the Supreme Court adjudicates issues concerning the division of powers between the national government and the fifty state governments. As a result of these powers, the Supreme Court can significantly influence social policy. One of the most famous examples of this influence is the case of *Brown v. Board of Education* (1954), in which the Court's decision ordering the desegregation of public schools in Topeka, Kansas, fundamentally altered education policy and, more broadly, race relations in the United States. Most recently, in *Obergefell v. Hodges* (2015), a divided Supreme Court ruled that gay couples had the right to marry.

The Supreme Court and the other federal courts umpire the federal system. They do so under rules established in the Constitution and interpreted by Congress, the president, and the courts. Such umpiring is designed to maintain, as Chief Justice Salmon Portland Chase noted in *Texas v. White* in 1869, "a harmonious and indestructible union of cooperative and indestructible states." The federal courts guard against state encroachment on federal power by declaring acts of state legislators and governors unconstitutional or unlawful when they violate the Constitution or federal law. Similarly, if the federal government encroaches on state governments—particularly in ways that threaten their very existence—the Supreme Court has the power, exercised only rarely, to invalidate national legislation that violates the rights and powers given to states. In umpiring the federal system, the federal courts guard against serious conflicts between the nation and the states or among the states. When this umpiring is successful, cooperation and accommodation occur. When rulings are ignored, serious troubles befall American federalism, the most serious and calamitous of which was the Civil War.

Upholding Valid Law and Administration. In the United States, the courts play a vital role in legitimating economic and social public policy under challenge. In a government of limited powers, the Supreme Court serves as a court of last resort in legal actions to test whether Congress has exceeded its powers in passing certain legislation or whether the president has overreached the chief executive's authority in executing duties. In upholding national policy, the Supreme Court gives it a stamp of final constitutional approval. This clearly enhances effective governance by providing definitive rulings on whether the government can, for example, enact Social Security legislation, regulate labor management relations, control the banking system, and subsidize farmers.

In an earlier period, the Supreme Court struck down this kind of legislation at both the state and federal levels—for example, those laws designed to cope with child labor, business monopolies, unfair trade practices, depressed agricultural prices, and lower wages and industrial prices. The Court, at the time in the nineteenth century and up to the 1930s, was very skeptical of government action to that interfered with the economy. Most observers of the Supreme Court now generally agree that these Court actions prevented state legislatures and Congress from attending to problems that needed to be addressed. The Court's rulings hurt the nation's ability to adjust to the realities of an increasingly industrial, urban, and interdependent society, and to achieve social reforms essential to a healthy life in modern society. The Court interfered with the power of voters—acting through their elected representatives—to satisfy basic needs and address fundamental interests. In the 1930s, the Court began to adjust its views on economic and social policy, and its decisions began to reflect this change. Increasingly, it gave state legislatures greater freedom to address their problems. In the field of civil liberties, the Supreme Court maintained its activist role. The late twentieth and early twenty-first centuries have witnessed another change in the Court's attitude toward government regulation of the economy and social life. Although it is too early to say whether this change marks a new era in constitutional law, it is notable that some of the Court's more conservative justices, such as Antonin Scalia and Clarence Thomas, seemed disposed to returning to an older, more skeptical approach to government regulation, particularly when it comes to the actions of the federal government. George W. Bush's appointees to the Court, Chief Justice John Roberts and Associate Justice Samuel Alito, also have a more critical approach. Predicting judicial behavior is a risky business; however, Obama's appointments, Sonia Sotomayor (the court's first Latina) and Elena Kagan have been reliably liberal votes on most decisions. Yet, the difficulty in predicting Supreme Court action was confirmed in late June 2012. President Obama's signature domestic policy achievement—the Affordable Care Act—was upheld by a deeply divided court in a 5–4 vote. Surprising to many, Chief Justice John Roberts wrote the majority opinion that declared much of the act constitutional. However, such a close vote makes it unlikely anyone can safely say how the Court will decide future constitutional controversies. However, in a more recent challenge to this policy, *King v. Burwell* (2015), the court in a 6–3 decision upheld the legality of federal health insurance subsidies, further solidifying the Affordable Care Act's place in our society. The newest member of the court, Neil Gorsuch, appointed by Trump to replace the deceased Antonin Scalia, has so far pleased conservatives with his consistent championing of right-wing positions.

Adjudicating Disputes Under the Law. Just as elections enable citizens to decide contests by counting heads instead of breaking them, so the courts enable individuals, groups, corporations, states, and local units of government to rely on judicial procedures instead of force and violence to resolve conflicts. Here, we concentrate not on disputes between the individual or group and government but on those quarrels involving private citizens, groups, or corporations. Unquestionably, these disputes account for most of the work of U.S. state, county, and municipal courts. These conflicts may involve, for example, the law of contracts or the law of torts. A **contract** is an agreement—usually written and enforceable by law—between two or more people to do something. A **tort** is a wrongful act, injury, or damage (not involving a breach of contract) for which a civil action can be brought. We call attention to the courts' role in handling these disputes to underscore both the existence of a mechanism to deal with conflicts and the cultural habit of resort to the law. Although it is not without its weaknesses, the legal system (when it functions at its best and is respected) provides a valuable means for furthering cooperation, advancing accommodation, and peacefully resolving disputes. Effective judicial systems exist in virtually all developed countries.

BEYOND THE CONSTITUTION: CITIZENS, MEDIA, PARTIES, AND ELECTIONS

Although political culture and constitutional rules have a great influence on politics, nongovernmental actors also are important to the political process. In this section, we consider the following nongovernmental actors—citizens, interest groups, political parties, and the media.

Citizens

In democracies, citizens express vital needs and interests in many ways. They worry about crime, drugs, and the safety of air travel. They complain about high taxes. They attend meetings, write to government officials, and sign petitions. They may also join interest groups that support their positions or participate actively in a **political party**.

There are three key ways in which citizens can influence government. First, they can exercise significant control over government by their right to vote. Political scientists often debate to what extent citizens can influence the day-to-day actions of any government official; however, what is clear is that citizens have the ability to decide who runs government. In this way, they influence what goes on in government. They register disapproval when they vote to "kick the bums out." They also can offer their support of government policy by returning officeholders to power. The second way that citizens can affect government is through the power of public opinion. Public opinion cautions government when it seeks to overturn a popular policy or when it oversteps its bounds. Indeed, if most politicians are concerned about reelection, as many political scientists assume, then a change in public opinion can be just as powerful as an election itself. For example, public opinion polls, by indicating the popularity of key features of the welfare state, may dissuade a conservative government from tampering with the Social Security system. Polls may also indicate support for welfare reform or fiscal responsibility, thus encouraging a government to reduce the federal deficit or crack down on welfare "chiselers." The third way citizens can influence government is through civic activism and even civil disobedience. People can march and protest. Citizens' refusal to pay taxes, to support an unpopular war, or to abide by a hated policy could cripple government. In the United States, for example, the prohibition amendment of 1919 failed because many people—whether a real majority or a very large minority—wanted to drink beer and liquor.

Interest Groups

All political communities include interest groups. (See Table 9.1 for a classification.) In Chapter 8, we learned that an interest group is a public group that organizes in an attempt to shape public policy of special concern to its members. Such groups are more numerous and more powerful in advanced democracies such as the United States. These groups' contribution to political accommodation is a source of controversy.

In the United States, interest groups clearly express their own needs and concerns by providing information, tendering advice, and exerting pressure. They operate through the media, within political parties, before legislative committees, and in the offices of the bureaucracy. They are not bashful in speaking up on behalf of their constituencies or about spending money to advance their concerns. They represent industrialists, farmers, trade unionists, and a wide range of other professional, ethnic, religious, and reform groups. Unquestionably, they constitute a major source of demands on government.

Furniture workers in North and South Carolina want to limit the importation of finished furniture. Ranchers oppose the importation of foreign beef. Environmentalists would like the government to impose tighter controls on air-polluting factories and cars, on strip mining, on clear cutting of timber, and on offshore oil drilling. Industries and unions oppose "overly strict" regulations that threaten profits and jobs.

By the very nature of their self-interested concerns, most interest groups do not hold the broad public good as a high priority. They are not normally in business to unite interests or to reconcile a wide range of claims. In *pluralist theory*, the public good

Table 9.1	Classification of Interest Groups	
Type		**Types of Interests Represented**
I.	Cultural	Friends of architecture, music, opera
II.	Economic	Farmers, manufacturers, retailers, workers
III.	Ethnic	Irish Americans, German Americans, Italian Americans
IV.	Professional	Doctors, educators, journalists, lawyers
V.	Racial	African Americans, Asians, Hispanics, whites
VI.	Reform	Abortion rights advocates and opponents, environmentalists, gun control advocates and opponents, pacifists, prohibitionists
VII.	Religious	Catholics, Jews, Muslims, Protestants

Source: Compiled by authors.

is furthered by the clash of different interest groups, not by the actions of any particular interest group. They do serve a valuable role in providing information to political actors. However, critics charge that powerful interests are able to buy undue power and thwart popular opinion because of their ability to influence political parties and elected officials who need money for campaigns.

Interest groups often are better able to prevent action than to accomplish it. In the United States, the National Rifle Association (NRA) has prevented meaningful national gun control legislation for decades, and AARP (formerly the American Association of Retired Persons) has thwarted efforts by budget-minded legislators to limit or cut Social Security and Medicare benefits. Powerful interest groups cannot always use the political "veto" to block legislation that would adversely affect them, however. It will be interesting to see in the coming years just how powerful the NRA is in blocking gun control legislation in the wake of the Parkland School shooting. Many survivors of that attack have engaged in significant political action. In March of 2018, hundreds of thousands were involved in "March for Our Lives" rallies throughout the country. It remains to be seen whether such activities lead to changes in the laws.

Sometimes when governments take actions that are disliked by key interest groups, those actions are nonetheless effective, particularly if there is widespread support within the country as a whole. For example, in the United States the National Labor Relations Act of 1935 (the Wagner Act), which required employers to recognize as collective bargaining agents unions that had the support of a majority of workers, was unpopular with many industrialists and the groups that represented them (such as the National Association of Manufacturers). Yet the public supported the principle of giving a majority of workers, through their unions, the opportunity to bargain collectively and peacefully with their employers. Despite management's opposition to the Wagner Act and its legal actions to nullify the act's administration, the law was passed.

This analysis suggests how interest groups can influence government by seeking to protect their own interests. They do so by watching for "ill-advised" use of government power—that is, anything that will affect them negatively. They loudly oppose any policy that has an adverse impact on their profits, wages, prices, and benefits. Reform groups, in particular, play a watchdog role. They are on the alert for what they see as violations of civil liberties (the American Civil Liberties Union), good ecological principles (the Sierra Club), and public morality (the Family Research Council). They may challenge government—legally, in the courts; politically, in Congress; or administratively, in the bureaucracy. At their best, interest groups provide valid criticisms of any policy, and the ongoing debate about what a government should do is often helped by the continuing clash of opinion represented by the organized interests.

Political Parties and Elections

Political parties—as they respond to public opinion, help educate the electorate, manage interest groups, and carry on the business of government—are the unsung heroes in the process of furthering cooperation, advancing accommodation, and handling conflicts. Modern democratic politics is impossible without them. But what exactly is a political party? A political party is an organized group that seeks to elect candidates to government office. In so doing, political parties represent "teams" that aim to collectively control government.[4] To some observers party organization is the key to success for developing nations. They maintain that the lack of such organization accounts, to a large extent, for the difficulties facing many developing countries: absence of cohesion; disorder; inadequate integration of people, interests, and government; and ineffective and uncontrolled government.

Here, a comparison of a major political party and an interest group may be illuminating. Like the political party, the interest group wants to obtain, wield, and enjoy the fruits of power. But the interest group desires power not usually for the sake of mastery or prestige but for the sake of advancing its group, economic, and social purpose. The interest group tends, therefore, to be concerned with more specific matters than the political party. For example, the interest group may favor or oppose higher prices for domestic oil, higher wages, or farm price supports. It may oppose or support gun control. The interest group generally does not put up candidates for public office as does the party. In contrast to political parties, most interest groups do not usually have a permanent organization concerned primarily with electing or defeating candidates for public office and with marshaling support in the legislature on a wide range of issues. Unlike the political party, the interest group has little or no responsibility to the electorate for the victory or defeat of its favored candidate.

Political parties serve two key roles in making democracies work. First, they provide a context in which citizens can understand a complex political world. In the United States, for example, which has a two-party system, the two political parties unite numerous social and political groups into either the Democratic or the Republican Party. Furthermore, in the process of selecting their candidates, the parties narrow the field down to just two candidates. (Of course, there are frequently more than two candidates; however, the two major parties dominate politics.) In doing this, the parties encourage accommodation between disparate groups—think of all the different groups that make up the Republican

Party, such as The Club for Growth, whose members are economic libertarians, and the Family Research Council, whose members are social conservatives. Political parties offer clear and distinct policy options to the voters. The second role political parties play is in the translation of election results into government action. When a party wins an election, a team of officeholders can work together to achieve the goals they promised to deliver. Despite a great deal of cynicism about politicians and parties, recent research has shown that most politicians work hard to keep their campaign promises.[5]

American parties, although not as disciplined as parties in other countries because of separation of powers and federalism, can achieve extraordinary things. For example, the election of Franklin D. Roosevelt and large Democratic majorities in the House of Representatives and the Senate resulted in a flood of important legislation in the 1930s: the Agricultural Adjustment Act (1933), the National Labor Relations Act (1933), the Tennessee Valley Authority Act (1933), the Social Security Act (1935), and the Fair Labor Standards Act (1938). These measures were a response to farmers' calls for stable farm prices; to advocates' calls for better electrical power, flood control, and recreation; to labor unions' appeals for collective bargaining; and to workers' demands for unemployment compensation, old-age pensions, a wage floor, and a forty-hour workweek.

During the 1980s, Republican President Ronald Reagan introduced a significant conservative political movement deeply skeptical of an activist federal government. Reagan based his presidential campaign on a promise of deregulation, cuts in spending on social programs, and significant increases in defense spending. The Reagan administration oversaw deregulation of several key industries, most notably the commercial airline system. Funding for social welfare programs such as Head Start, a preschool program for low-income families, was limited. Tough, uncompromising stands were taken against federal employees, such as the federally supervised air traffic controllers, who tried to organize and strike. And consistent with his Republican Party platform, President Reagan proposed and supervised an enormous military buildup, the largest peacetime military strengthening in U.S. history. The first-term George W. Bush administration witnessed a disciplined Republican Party that strongly backed Bush's decision to go to war in Iraq and enacted three major tax cuts championed by the president.

Political parties provide a mechanism for building coalitions. They rally divergent groups on behalf of common programs. In so doing, they can work against narrow and extremist positions. They tie sometimes differing interests together on unifying issues. Thus, they build support for proposals that the party, if successful in elections, may then transform into legislation.

However, the ability to translate election results into coherent government actions is often difficult. In the United States, the principles of separation of powers and of federalism make for a very loosely structured two-party system and, often, deadlock in the national government. Federalism contributes to such a system by creating a number of independent power sources—national, state, and local. Separation of powers reinforces the loose party structure by affirming the independence of the president and members of Congress in their respective spheres. The two major American parties thus emerge as coalitions built around presidential candidates, national party committees, Democratic and Republican members of Congress (or aspirants to congressional seats), state and local parties, officeholders, candidates, rank-and-file partisans, and other key interests seeking a payoff for their support.

Nationally, each party coalition attempts to forge some unity every four years to elect a president, gain majority control in Congress, and enact a party program. It is, however, difficult to achieve unity and carry out a national party program because national interests (most often addressed by the presidential candidates) do not always coincide with regional, state, and local interests. Members of Congress, those seeking election to Congress, and state and local politicians (such as governors and mayors) are often preoccupied with their own elections and with state and local concerns. They are not passionately committed to a national party program. Moreover, our electoral system—rooted in federalism—does not ensure that the president and a majority in Congress will be of the same political party. Additionally, separation of powers ensures the independence of members of Congress in their own sphere of power, which often translates into conflict with the president. Thus, the absence of a cohesive and responsible national party system—with deep and disciplined roots in the country—and the constitutional independence of nationally elected officials frequently create governmental deadlock in Washington.

This deadlock may exist even when the president's party controls both houses of Congress. There is no danger of the government dissolving in the United States if the executive (president) and legislature (Congress) disagree. Representatives and presidents are elected for fixed terms. The president is not responsible to a majority in the Congress, as the British cabinet is responsible to a majority in the House of Commons. In the United States, deadlock does not threaten new elections—and thus encourage agreement between members of Congress and the president.

Nonetheless, the loose coalitions known as the Democratic and Republican Parties in the United States may still make government effective. Under the leadership of inspired presidents such as Franklin D. Roosevelt and Ronald Reagan, American parties have achieved many policy innovations. Furthermore, the party that is out of power, without doubt, can be a strong contributor to responsible and peaceful accommodation. Opposition parties can voice strenuous criticisms of the ruling party and thus contribute to the political debate in a democracy. Today, many political commentators worry that, in the United States, levels of trust and accommodation between the two major parties are dangerously low; however, a mature party system rests on the ideal of accommodation and encourages a humane and civilized politics. This pattern of accommodation ensures a smooth and peaceful transition from one government to the next and, in this way, enormously enhances effective governance and responsible control of government.

When it comes to elections, the United States often uses that most common of practices, majority rules. This how many officials are elected—governors, members of the House or Senate. Majorities do not necessarily decide all elections. Frequently, a plurality of votes proves decisive. This may happen when there are more than two candidates for an office. Even more interesting, in certain circumstances a minority can actually rule. In the 2000 U.S. presidential election, Vice President Al Gore received 500,000 more votes than Texas governor George W. Bush; however, the Electoral College system in use in the United States assured Bush the win with 266 electoral votes for Gore and 271 for Bush. This type of outcome was repeated in an even more striking fashion in 2016. Donald Trump won 306 electoral votes election night and Hillary Clinton won 232. However, Secretary Clinton received almost 2.9 million more popular votes. (See Map 9.2.)

Map 9.2   U.S. Presidential Election, 2000

Gore (D) 266 Electoral votes

Bush (R) 271 Electoral votes

Abstension 1 (Washington, DC)

Source: J. Clark Archer, Stephen Lavin, Kenneth C. Martin, and Fred M. Shelley, Atlas of American Politics 1960–2000 (Washington, D.C.: CQ Press, 2002). Data from National Archives and Records Administration, "2000 Presidential Election: Electoral Vote Results," htttp://www.nara.gov/fedreg/elctcoll/2000res.htm.

Map 9.3   U.S. Presidential Election, 2016

Clinton 232 Electoral votes

Trump 306 Electoral votes

Source: Copyright © 2004-2018 270towin.com.

The Electoral College is a unique system for deciding the U.S. presidency, one that does not take into account majority rule. Instead, each state has a number of Electoral College votes equal to the number of representatives and senators it seats in Washington. Thus, the state of California sends fifty-three members to the House of Representatives based on its large population and, like all states, it has two Senators. Thus, California's Electoral College vote is fifty five. (The District of Columbia, although it has no voting representatives or senators in Congress, has three Electoral College votes.) In most cases when a candidate wins a state, even if by just one vote, that candidate receives all the state's electoral votes. In Nebraska and Maine, the state assigns an electoral vote to the winner of each Congressional district with the overall winning of the state getting the two extra electoral votes of that state. In this system, then, the key is to win individual states—particularly those with large numbers of electoral votes and states in which the two parties are competitive. A candidate who wins enough states and their accompanying electoral votes will gain the presidency even if the candidate has failed to receive a majority, or even a plurality, of the national vote. This does not usually happen. Before the 2000 election, it had occurred on just three occasions, all in the nineteenth century (the elections of 1824, 1876, and 1888). In 2004, Bush won clear, if narrow, majorities in both the Electoral College and the popular vote. And in 2008, Barack Obama won substantial victories in both the popular vote and the Electoral College. In the 2012 election, President Barack Obama was reelected, garnering 332 Electoral College votes over his opponent, Governor Mitt Romney, who won 206 Electoral College votes. The 2012 election was important not just because President Obama won reelection but because of the way it revealed the changing demographics of our society. Not only did Latinos make up a greater percentage of voters overall, 72 percent of Latinos supported Obama.

The 2016 election was interesting because of the ability of Donald Trump to gain just enough white votes (58% according to polls) to offset Clinton's advantage among other ethnic groups. The election was also striking since throughout the fall most experts and polls showed that Hillary Clinton would win, and Trump's victory was quite a surprise election night. The election was also notable because, as we noted earlier, there was a difference in the Electoral College outcome and the popular vote. Given the closeness of the election and the fact the Electoral College result and popular vote were different (although, of course, constitutionally all that matters is the Electoral College vote) many are left to wonder what shaped the outcome. Clinton was dogged by questions about her actions as Secretary of State concerning emails and classified information, and just days before the election, the FBI announced they were re-opening the investigation into these matters. Although no new information was found, many believe it cost her a small but significant amount of support. Even more concerning is the extent of Russian interference in the election. U.S. intelligence agencies all agree that the Russians tried to interfere in the election to help Trump win. What is an open question is to what extent they did this and what, if any, involvement the Trump campaign had in these interferences. In 2017, the Justice Department appointed a Special Counsel, Robert Mueller, a former director of the FBI, to investigate this exact matter. And 2017 and 2018 were taken up, politically, with a great deal of debate about this interference and even the fairness investigation itself. As with so many matters in recent years, the deep divide separating the parties led to recriminations between the parties. Thus, the 2016 election to a greater extent than most elections was controversial.

The Media

The **media** are agencies of communication such as newspapers, magazines, radio, television, and, more recently, the Internet. Depending on the country, the media play an important role in expressing needs and interests, in sharpening priorities, in legitimating government and strengthening its effectiveness, and in guarding against the abuse of power. Where the media are independent, as in developed, democratic countries, their capacity for expression and their ability to influence government is greater than in the communist world or in many developing countries, where the media are often under party or government control.

In the United States, the agencies of mass communication attempt, with varying degrees of success, to give citizens "an account of the day's events in a context which gives them meaning"; to provide "a forum for the exchange of comment and criticism"; to project "the opinions and attitudes of the groups in the society"; and, in general, to reach "every member of the society by the currents of information, thought and feeling" that the media supply.[6] Through editorials, the media can offer judgments about what is happening and urge certain policy outcomes.

Sometimes the media can contribute to the enactment of policy. Such may have been the case in the American humanitarian intervention in Somalia in 1992. Many analysts believe that a major factor in the decision to intervene was the constant barrage of images of war-torn Somalia projected on American television screens—starving children, bodies in the streets of Mogadishu, harried and frightened international relief workers. Dubbed the "CNN effect," these images generated considerable sympathy for the plight of innocent Somalis and contributed to the pressure exerted on President Bill Clinton to do something to relieve the situation.[7]

The media have also played a vital role in guarding against the abuse of governmental power. They have protected freedom of the press against censorship and other violations. They have stood strong on behalf of freedom of speech, assembly, and religion. They have sought to make government, especially in the United States, function in "daylight" by opposing government secrecy (except in very limited cases). They have exposed what happened in important matters—as in the *Pentagon Papers Case*—even at the risk of challenging government contentions that national security mandated such secrecy.[8] But this might have come with a price: some in recent years have questioned whether the 24/7 quality of news coverage and the quickness of the news cycle have contributed to a shallowness and coarseness in American politics.

Constantly on the lookout for government illegalities (as in the Watergate case during the Nixon administration, the Iran-Contra affair and the Housing and Urban Development scandal during the Reagan years, the "filegate" and Whitewater controversies during Clinton's first term, and a CIA agent's outing during George W. Bush's second term), wasteful spending, and shady government transactions, the media play an important role in keeping government honest. But sometimes the price paid for a free and independent press in Western democratic countries is distortion, narrowness, and sensationalism, which the best members of the press deplore.

Finally, we should note some recent trends in the way the media operates. First, there is the rise of overtly partisan news outlets such as FOX and MSNBC. While both networks do engage in traditional news coverage, they do have shows that clearly advance one perspective. FOX is known as a network that advances conservative beliefs while MSNBC champions the liberal viewpoint. Second, many Internet sites are now a key source of political news. The rise of blogs that not only present a strong political view but break news stories is of particular importance. To give just one of many examples, the lawyer and blogger Glenn Greenwald was a key player in reporting that the National Security Agency (NSA) was collecting millions of telephone records. Furthermore, most traditional news organizations—the *Washington Post*, the *New York Times*, the major networks (CBS, NBC, FOX, and ABC) all have Internet sites that often report information before the news is printed or broadcast in its traditional forms. Finally, there are now a number of new organizations that exist solely online—the Huffington Post, Politico, and Real Clear Politics are all examples of this important new media.

Of particular interest is the way President Trump has used social media. The president is a great believer in twitter and tweets frequently. These tweets cover a host of topics but often focus on attacks of his political opponents and the media itself. They also include an obsession about his electoral victory and continual boasting about the nature of his victory. Twitter is a new form of communication and, although President Obama has used it before, Trump was incessant with his tweeting. In fact, in sending out a tweet concerning transgendered people in the military it became a subject of debate about whether his tweets constituted actual policy or not. More generally, as noted earlier in the chapter, Trump has been very critical of the press. While it is true that all presidents have complained about the press from to time, Trump is unique in being both persistent and very public in his attacks on the media. Some critics of the president have even begun to worry that Trump's attacks will undermine the vital role the media plays in helping democracy function. What kind of chilling affects will the president's attacks have on the very necessary investigations of government action that media perform every day? In many ways, despite all of Trump's criticisms, the media has flourished in getting out new and important stories concerning the Trump White House and his administration generally. Yet, as with any new administration, the long-term affects remain to be seen.

CONCLUSION

American politics is both the quintessential example of politics today and, oddly, an outlier that does things quite different. Given its immense power and influence, it deserves to be studied on its own. As we have seen, American democracy has a long history and the country has grown more democratic over the centuries. And this very history has influenced the rest of the world as many other countries adopted democratic systems over the years—particularly in the late twentieth century. There is a strong tradition of representative democracy and protection of individual rights and liberties, and it has a political culture that values freedom and equality. However, it is fitting that in a country with a long history of freedom, particularly freedom of speech, many citizens highlight the way its politics falls short of its ideals. From concerns about the health of civil liberties, rising inequality, the use of torture, and a government that is too powerful and overbearing, many American express their skepticism about the direction of the country. Yet these very criticisms can be seen as an example of the vibrant and robust nature of the political system.

SUGGESTED READINGS

Bessette, Joseph. *The Mild Voice of Reason: Deliberative Democracy and American National Government.* Chicago: University of Chicago Press, 1997. A provocative book arguing that the American system of governance actually does encourage deliberation by lawmakers.

Carp, Robert A., Ronald Stidham, and Kenneth Manning. *Judicial Process in America.* 9th ed. Washington, DC: CQ Press, 2013. A detailed, well-written survey of the court system in the United States—federal, state, civil, and criminal.

Davidson, Roger H., and Walter J. Oleszek. *Congress and Its Members.* 14th ed. Washington, DC: CQ Press, 2013. Thorough accounting of virtually all aspects of congressional politics.

Greenhouse, Linda. *The U.S. Supreme Court: A Very Short Introduction.* Oxford, UK: Oxford University Press, 2012. A thoughtful and brief introduction to the court—both its formal and informal procedures are discussed.

Greenstein, Fred. *The Presidential Difference: Leadership Style from Roosevelt to Barack Obama.* Princeton, NJ: Princeton University Press, 2009. A thorough, accessible treatment of America's highest political office by a premier presidential scholar.

Haskins, Ron. *Work over Welfare.* Washington, DC: Brookings Institution Press, 2006. A thorough accounting of the major 1996 reform of welfare, from one of the participants in the process.

Kingdon, John W. *Agendas, Alternatives, and Public Policies.* 2nd ed. New York: Longman, 2010. Winner of the Aaron Wildavsky Award given by the American Political Science Association, a first-rate analysis of the public policy process in the United States.

Nelson, Michael. *The Elections of 2016.* Washington, DC: CQ Press, 2018. A collection of essays on the 2016 election by leading scholar on American politics.

Neustadt, Richard E. *Presidential Power and the Modern Presidents: The Politics of Leadership from Roosevelt to Reagan.* Rev. ed. New York: Free Press, 1991. An analysis of the presidency that emphasizes the importance of the president's persuasive powers. A classic.

Sabato, Larry, Kyle Kondik, and Geoffrey Skelly. *Trumped: The 2016 Election That Broke all the Rules.* Landover, MD: Rowman and Littlefield, 2017. A look at the 2016 election from perspectives of political scientists and journalists.

Starr, Paul. *Remedy and Reaction: The Peculiar American Struggle over Health Care Reform.* New Haven, CT: Yale University Press, 2013. One of the preeminent scholars on health care traces the various political fights in this policy area.

Wice, Paul. *Judges and Lawyers: The Human Side of Justice.* New York: HarperCollins, 1991. Excellent personal look at those who are in the trenches of the American judicial system. See also Paul Wice, *Chaos in the Courthouse* (New York: Praeger, 1985).

Wilson, James Q. *Bureaucracy: What Governments Do and Why They Do It.* New York: Basic Books, 1991. A classic on the politics of bureaucracy.

GLOSSARY TERMS

advise and consent (p. 231)
American exceptionalism (p. 225)
Bill of Rights (p. 240)
bureaucracy (p. 232)
contract (p. 243)
deliberative function (p. 231)

judicial review (p. 241)
legislative function (p. 232)
legitimacy (p. 232)
media (p. 250)
meritocracy (p. 239)
political party (p. 244)

representative function (p. 231)
supervisory function (p. 232)
tort (p. 243)
writ of habeas corpus (p. 236)

NOTES

1. See Harold and Margaret Sprout, "The Dilemma of Rising Demands and Insufficient Resources," *World Politics* 20, no. 4 (1968): 660–693.

2. CNBC, All-American Economic Survey. "Economic optimism soars, boosting Trump's approval rating: CNBC survey," January 2018. https://www.cnbc.com/2017/12/18/economic-optimism-soaring-helping-trump-cnbc-survey.html

3. H. H. Gerth and C. Wright Mills, eds. and trans., *From Max Weber: Essays in Sociology* (New York: Oxford University Press, 1958), 196–244.

4. See Gerald Pomper, *Passions and Interests: Political Party Concepts of American Democracy* (Lawrence: University Press of Kansas, 1992). See especially chaps. 3, 5, and 6.

5. See Gerald Pomper, *Voters, Elections, and Parties: The Practice of Democratic Theory* (New Brunswick, NJ: Transaction Books, 1988), chap. 9.

6. Commission on Freedom of the Press, *A Free and Responsible Press* (Chicago: University of Chicago Press, 1947).

7. See Stephen Hess, *International News and Foreign Correspondents* (Washington, DC: Brookings, 1996); Johanna Neumann, *Lights, Camera, War: Is Media Technology Driving International Politics?* (New York: St. Martin's Press, 1996); and Robert I. Rotberg and Thomas G. Weiss, eds., *From Massacres to Genocide: The Media, Public Policy, and Humanitarian Crises* (Washington, DC: Brookings, 1996).

8. The *Pentagon Papers Case* involved a secret history of the Vietnam War commissioned by Secretary of Defense Robert McNamara. The document features an extremely candid telling of the story of how the United States became involved in the war and fought it, including distortions and lies told to the American public to justify various Vietnam policies. In 1972, Daniel Ellsberg, a Defense Department employee who helped to write the papers, secretly began feeding them to reporters at the *New York Times*. The papers were also published by the *Washington Post*.

In 2017, the failed state of Somalia was plagued by drought and famine. While the government response was better than the famine of 2011, the effort is severely limited due to insufficient funding and chronic violence.

MOHAMED ABDIWAHAB/AFP/Getty Images

10

COMPARATIVE POLITICS

A variety of forms of government are to be found among the more than 200 countries that inhabit the world. The American system of a three-branch government with a bicameral legislature is only one of innumerable ways that humans govern themselves at the national level. To develop any profound understanding of politics requires one to know at least something about the ways politics is conducted in other countries. As the famous political scientist Seymour Martin Lipset once said, "Those who only know one country, know no country." This chapter is an extended discussion of alternative forms of governance with the understanding that many variations of each can also be found. You need to keep in mind that we are presenting only a few examples of each of these forms of governing. In actuality, every country's system of government is, in some ways, unique. In fact, one of the joys of being a student of comparative politics is to learn, in depth, a different country with its own culture and a political system that may look in some ways like other countries and in other ways is all its own. And comparative politics deals with a host of issues and questions. Comparativists ask such questions as these: How does democracy develop? What is the relationship between economics and politics? What are different regions of the world like? Or, to be very specific, what is politics like in one particular country? As you can see, comparative politics is a huge and varied subfield of political science.

In this chapter, we will focus on four different types of political states and five different countries: Great Britain, Germany under the Nazis, China, and the failed states of Afghanistan and Somalia. Each of these countries represents case studies of different political systems. First, we will discuss parliamentary democracy, which is an important kind of democracy practiced in a great number of countries but does not employ separation of powers as the United States does.

Chapter Objectives

After studying this chapter, you will be able to do the following:

1. Define a parliamentary system of government.

2. Describe an authoritarian system of government.

3. Discuss the unique features of the Nazi form of government.

4. Analyze the mixed form of government by using China as an example.

5. Evaluate the concept of failed or fragile state by using Afghanistan and Somalia as examples.

Second, we will analyze authoritarian regimes that are undemocratic and where power is highly centralized. Third, it is important to look at countries that have a mixed system. In such countries, there may be elements, or possibly just the prerequisites, of democracy and the hope that a fully functioning democratic system could develop; however, the country is certainly not democratic. Also, in many of these cases, the political system appears to be in transition, moving toward something else, yet it is not always clear what that "something else" is. Finally, it is important to consider what are called failed or fragile states. These are countries that are highly dysfunctional. The political system is weak and often the basic services and expectations about government, which we take for granted in the United States, do not exist.

Before proceeding, it is important to again note that there is a great deal of variation within in each general system of governance. Let's take a brief look at one country—Mexico—to illustrate this point. In some ways, Mexico is similar to the United States: Both are considered presidential systems in which the president heads the executive branch and is both head of state and head of government. In addition, there is a separate legislative branch. However, Mexico's presidential system is clearly distinct from the American version. In democratic Mexico, the president has enormous powers.[1]

Mexican presidents are close to being popularly elected dictators, but their power vanishes when their six-year term of office ends. They cannot be reelected. In office, however, they are extraordinarily powerful. It is important to note that Mexico's presidents do face some limitations, the most important being the nations proud revolutionary tradition. They cannot antagonize key interests in the party and in the country: peasant farmers, workers, business, and industry. They cannot too flagrantly offend intellectuals, students, and the church. The recent tradition of civilian leadership inhibits military **dictatorship,** and the limited power and size of the armed forces further discourage military rule by an ambitious president or military junta. Furthermore, Mexico continues to evolve as the once dominant party, the Partido Revolucionario Institucional (PRI), faces off against the Partido de Accion Nacional (PAN) and the Partido de la Revolución Democrática (PRD) in a system of multiparty competition.

PARLIAMENTARY GOVERNMENT

Parliamentary governments are systems ruled by parliaments (another name for legislatures). And they are a very common form of democratic government. Some examples of countries that use parliamentary government include Great Britain, Germany, Italy, Israel, Canada, Australia, and Japan. So what exactly is a parliament? (The word derives from the French *parler*, which means to speak.) Parliaments usually evolved from some ancient council of wise men, or key leaders, such as members of the aristocracy who advised the king about affairs of state. Over time, these bodies became permanent and often began to challenge the unrestricted power of the king. Later still, they changed from being bodies of wealthy and powerful men, often chosen by birth, to being democratically elected bodies selected by the common people.

More specifically, parliaments are legislative bodies that serve to represent people and make laws. In this sense, they are akin to the U.S. Congress. However, whereas the

U.S. Congress is one of the three powerful branches, in countries with parliamentary government the parliament is the most important and powerful branch of government. Indeed, it is in most cases the center of political power. Furthermore, the executive in parliamentary systems is not separate from the legislature, as is the case in the United States. The U.S. Constitution forbids any possibility of members of the executive branch sitting in the legislature. The president of the United States cannot also be a senator at the same time. In parliamentary systems, the executive and his cabinet are also members of the parliament—usually the leaders of whatever party has the most seats in that legislative body.

A key issue to consider when thinking about parliamentary systems is whether they are unicameral or bicameral (there are other possibilities). A unicameral system is one where there is only one chamber or house, and, obviously, a bicameral parliament has two chambers. In some bicameral systems, both chambers have equal or roughly equal powers. In other cases, such as Great Britain, the upper house (the House of Lords) has much less political power. One of the key points in thinking about bicameral systems is what differences exist in selecting members of the two chambers. Sometimes the first chamber is selected directly by the people, and the second chamber is selected by the first. Or the second chamber can be made up of distinguished citizens. Or maybe the second chamber is selected with some geographic considerations in mind and not based solely on the population.

The Case of Great Britain

To better understand parliamentary government, one of the best examples to study is Great Britain, and there are a number of good reasons for this. First, it has one of the oldest, if not the oldest, functioning parliaments in the world. Second, because Great Britain later developed a huge and far-flung empire across the globe, which is now largely disbanded, it often bequeathed to its former colonies its form of politics. For these reasons, Great Britain is frequently called "the mother of parliaments." Today, many countries use what is known as the "Westminster system" because of their conscious efforts to imitate Britain's form of politics. (Westminster is a specific area of London that includes the Houses of the British Parliament.)

Great Britain also represents a case of successful transition from one political culture to another. For centuries, England was characterized by a highly centralized government controlled by the monarchy and the aristocracy. Today, it enjoys a strong Western democratic political culture in which the monarchy is relegated to largely ceremonial duties (though, we should note, ceremony is a vital part of any culture). People in Great Britain enjoy a culture that champions freedom of speech, freedom of religion, and many of the individual liberties that are familiar to citizens of the United States. And that political culture with its evolving respect for what were often called British liberties developed alongside a set of institutions that were increasingly democratic.

The British Legislature and Executive. Political power in the British government rests in a prime minister and a cabinet responsible to a majority in the House of Commons. Here we have a connection of powers—not a separation (see Chapter 8). Unlike the

The British House of Commons, the lower house of Parliament, consists of 650 members of Parliament (MPs), representing constituencies throughout the United Kingdom.

American president, who is elected for a four-year term independently of members of Congress, the British **prime minister** is usually the person who commands a majority of votes in the House of Commons. He or she is the leader of the dominant party in the Commons. With that majority, the prime minister and key leaders of his or her party organize a cabinet that runs the British government; this cabinet becomes the executive branch. The House of Commons and the cabinet are thus connected. British prime ministers lead the government because they have been empowered by a majority in Commons. Losing that majority seriously jeopardizes their ability to remain in power. In fact, in a parliamentary system if the prime minister and the cabinet begin to lose support, for whatever reason, there might be a call for a vote of no confidence. If they lose this vote, a new election is called in a short period of time (a matter of weeks) to see what the citizens want or support. Thus, whereas elections in the United States basically run on a very set schedule—whatever the popularity of the president, he or she is the president until the end of the term—elections in Great Britain, and other parliamentary systems, can occur at almost any time. And if the prime minister of Great Britain achieves some great success, he or she may call for an early election hoping that his popular support will lead to a greater electoral victory and increase the number of seats his party's control—although in Great Britain an election must be called within five years.

The British Parliament must formally enact legislation, but such legislation usually originates in the cabinet. Because important decisions in Britain are made in the cabinet, debate in the House of Commons rarely alters the outcome of legislation. Debate may, however, clarify the parties' positions on key issues and thereby educate the public to some extent. Historically, in both the United States and Britain, legislative control of the purse—the power to provide money for the support of government—has given legislators a major tool for controlling government. Today in Britain, because the cabinet is really the executive arm of a parliamentary majority, legislative control of the purse is no longer an effective safeguard against the executive, the way it was when the British monarch was the executive and government was not responsible to a parliamentary majority.

In Britain the watchdog role falls primarily to the opposition, or minority, party— Her Majesty's **loyal opposition**—whose task it is to criticize, expose weaknesses, and insist on good performance from the party in power. This job is often performed during the question hour in the House of Commons when the prime minister, or other cabinet officers, are queried about the conduct of British policy. Parliament may also investigate key problems or government scandals.

Theoretically, the British Parliament consists of two branches: the House of Commons and the House of Lords. Constitutionally, however, all effective power resides in Commons. The British House of Lords is an unelected body of lords—an aristocracy of intellect, experience, and accomplishment—appointed by the government. (Until recently, the Lords included hereditary members of the British aristocracy; however, reforms begun by Prime Minister Tony Blair and continued by the government of Prime Minister David Cameron significantly changed the makeup of the chamber.) The powers of the House of Lords, however, are minimal. For example, while it may delay for one year the legislation that the British cabinet and the House of Commons wish to enact, it has no power to defeat legislation. Though the hereditary criterion for membership has been largely eliminated, the House of Lords remains a controversial component of British politics, even with recent reforms, because it is not a directly elected body. Although in Britain the cabinet shapes basic policy, Parliament must still officially enact legislation. Parliamentary approval embodies the final act of sovereign legitimacy.

The British Court System. The British also have an independent system of courts; but British courts, in contrast to their American counterparts, have no power to declare an act of Parliament unconstitutional. British courts also protect civil liberties and the rules of the British constitution. They do so under Parliament's legislation, which is the supreme law, and no court can declare otherwise. In 2009, Great Britain created the Supreme Court of the United Kingdom, which is the highest appellate court in the nation. While it does not have powers of judicial review that U.S. courts have, this does not mean that civil liberties are violated at will in Britain. The largely unwritten British constitution, acts of Parliament, and the British legal tradition ensure that basic human rights are protected. It would be unthinkable for the British Parliament to violate the privilege of the writ of habeas corpus (which had its origin in British history) or to deny British citizens the freedoms of religion, speech, press, assembly, or due process of law. British courts thus operate to maintain basic liberties under law. They do not hesitate to rule against British officials who act beyond the law. British courts may also scrutinize governmental actions in appropriate cases to ensure that government obeys the law. They may also raise questions about the meaning of a law passed by Parliament. But once Parliament's position on a law is clear, British courts must respect that law. Thus, they also function to legitimate legislation and to guard against overzealous administration.

British Electoral Politics. As we noted earlier, in the British parliamentary scheme, the cabinet, headed by a prime minister, functions as the executive. The prime minister is a member of Parliament (MP) who has been elected as party leader by the majority party's caucus in the House of Commons. The other members of the cabinet, who are formally selected by the prime minister, are leaders of the majority party (generally members of the House of Commons) who have garnered support within the dominant party. After the 2010 election, though, no one party in Great Britain could form a government. Thus, the United Kingdom was governed by a coalition of the Conservative and Liberal Parties. Although in U.S. cabinet sessions the president's decision prevails (because cabinet members have no authority to override the president as chief executive), in the British cabinet the principle of collective responsibility prevails. The prime minister is powerful and often decisive, yet he or she must have the cabinet's support (or at least that of its majority) to function effectively. A prime minister who acts overly presidential and ignores the collective will of the cabinet may quickly come under attack even from within his own party. They might even lose the support of the party and, thus, lose the office of prime minister itself. In fact, the British prime minister can be replaced without an election. This happened, for instance, when Labour Prime Minister Tony Blair stepped down in 2007 and was replaced by Gordon Brown, another important Labour Party leader. Brown was prime minister for several years before he called for an election.

Cabinet Government in Great Britain. The British cabinet as a group bears responsibility for key decisions. Cabinet members hold major ministerial posts and are responsible for the day-to-day operation of the government. Members may, of course, resign in response to poor decision making; this happened in 2003, when Robin Cook resigned in protest over Tony Blair's decision to support the war in Iraq. Conflict between the cabinet and the majority party in Parliament is impossible insofar as the cabinet is the majority party's instrument to plan, initiate, and implement policy. The cabinet is thus a forceful and cohesive executive, able to govern responsibly and vigorously as long as it maintains majority support in the House of Commons. If the cabinet should lose that majority, however, the prime minister can call for a new round of elections that permits the British electorate to speak and return with their votes a new Parliament with a clear party majority (and a prime minister and a cabinet with authority).

The British cabinet, headed by a strong prime minister, carries the initiative by making policy. Conflicts between divergent interests in the governing party are usually hammered out within or between governmental ministries and then brought to the cabinet for discussion and decision. The cabinet assumes responsibility for enactment of agreed-on policy in the House of Commons.

The British prime minister, like the U.S. president, also uses a number of powers—prestige, ability to influence public opinion, patronage, leadership in the party, and bestowal of benefits—to sustain policy initiatives. In contrast to the U.S. president, the British prime minister can rely on strong party discipline and the threat of new elections to carry policy initiatives. As noted previously, if the majority party does not support the prime minister, the cabinet may fall and a new election would be required; majority MPs risk losing in the new elections. Thus, there is pressure for party members to stick together in support of their party and the prime minister. Pressure works both ways. The cabinet cannot be out of sync with either the majority party or with popular sentiment. The prime minister has at his or her disposal a wide array of tools with which to achieve cooperation, advance accommodation, and mediate conflict. Again, however, a weak prime minister who offers feeble, defective policies is at risk of squandering valuable opportunities. A comparable concern for political support and accommodation is evident in the British cabinet as it carries out public policy. The cabinet is in trouble, for example, if inflation and unemployment rise too high, public or an unpopular tax is proposed. The cabinet must look to the interests whose votes and money sustain it. Thus, a Labour Party cabinet cannot neglect the trade unions and the policies they favor, and a Conservative Party cabinet cannot neglect industrial, business, and farming interests. The party in power must look to its parliamentary majority, paying attention not only to its leading figures but also to its backbenchers, or lesser-known members.

When the party in power has a slim parliamentary majority—and depends for that majority on one or more splinter parties—it must accommodate the members of those parties on vital matters or risk losing power. Indeed, the 2005 elections returned the

Labour Party to power—but with a considerably reduced majority. Speculation immediately ensued about how long Tony Blair would last as prime minister. And, in 2007, Blair stepped down as prime minister and was replaced by another Labour Party leader, Gordon Brown. This occurred, as mentioned earlier, without a general election, and this can happen in parliamentary systems but not in presidential ones. In the recent past, for instance, Conservative leader David Cameron had to share power with the Liberal Democratic Party leader Nick Clegg in a coalition government. As of 2018, the Conservatives maintained power under the leadership of Theresa May. She assumed power when David Cameron resigned after the Brexit vote. The Brexit vote was a national referendum on Great Britain leaving the European Union, and David Cameron strongly campaigned against it. When it passed, meaning Britain would leave the Union, Cameron no longer believed he could lead his party or the nation. In the United States, there is no comparable situation. No one suggested that when President Trump failed to get Obamacare repealed he should resign the presidency. May's power as prime minister was also weakened by a surprisingly poor performance by her party in elections that she called for in June of 2017. She had expected to do fairly well and, instead, the Conservatives lost seats and the Labour Party gained a surprising number of seats. However, it still trailed the Conservatives in MPs. May was able to stay on as prime minister, even though no party had a majority of seats in Parliament, because she was able to work out what is called a "confidence and supply" agreement with another party (in this case the Democratic Unionist Party) to keep her party in power. In such a situation, another, smaller party is not in an active coalition with a larger party with members from both parties sitting in the cabinet working as a team; however, in this case the smaller party agrees to support the dominant party on key votes so that the large party, in this case the Conservatives, can still run the government. In return, the smaller party usually gets some policy concessions. All in all, Prime Minister May found herself in a very precarious situation and her government could fall almost any time.

The British Civil Service. In Great Britain (as in Japan, France, and the United States), top civil servants (another name for bureaucrats) usually receive their training at the best universities. Their entrance into government service is typically based on examination, so they constitute a meritocracy—that is, members of a bureaucracy who have gained employment and achieved advancement by reason of merit as opposed to patronage or personal favor. Top civil servants are highly intelligent, competent, and honest, and some often spend years considering how to solve problems and implement policy. Clearly, the advantage of this civil service is expertise and knowledge. The disadvantage is that civil servants can become committed to certain established ways of doing things and might be unwilling to think creatively about new solutions to old problems.

New administrations in Britain can count on knowledgeable civil servants to carry on while the new cabinet is "tooling up" and on impartial civil servants to assist cabinet members in devising and executing new programs. By thus ensuring continuity of administration, the permanent bureaucracy makes a valuable contribution to the transition from one government to the next and also to public trust in orderly government. In the United States, the number of top administrators who come and go is greater when the party in power changes; even so, a core of permanent civil servants near the top remains to provide vital assistance and stability crucial to effective government.

As you will note, there are many similarities between democracy in Great Britain and democracy in the United States. There is a government accountable to the people with popular elections. There is a competitive party system that makes this accountability work. However, there are numerous differences, particularly when it comes to the structures of government. If we were to go further in this case study (and this is the type of question asked by comparativists), why did politics develop the way it did in Great Britain versus the way it develop in the United States? Does one system function better than the other? What are the comparative advantages and disadvantages of each system?

AUTHORITARIAN GOVERNMENT

Authoritarianism is a form of rule in which the rulers impose their own beliefs or values upon the society regardless of what members of that society think or desire. In this se nse, authoritarianism is a pure form of anti-democracy. The hallmark of liberal thinking—harkening back to John Locke (see Chapter 5)—builds upon the notion of consent. The people must consent to the government, and without that consent the government is illegitimate in the eyes of democrats. However, to authoritarians, government does not require the consent of the governed; indeed, the opinions of the mass of citizens are largely irrelevant to the leaders. Instead, the government's legitimacy rests on other grounds. Sometimes, authoritarians justify their rule on the basis of divine sanction, claiming that God has appointed the rulers. Other leaders may claim a special and personal right to rule that may or may not have anything to do with the divine. Finally, some leaders claim to have a special kind of knowledge that is required to be a ruler. This can take many forms: secret knowledge that cannot be shared, high levels of intelligence that only the few possess, or a kind of wisdom that best discerns what is right. Regardless of how they justify their rule, authoritarians claim that only they can rule, that this is legitimate, and that other forms of politics—such as democracy—are actually illegitimate for the very reason that it rests upon the flawed judgments of the mass of citizens. In the history of political philosophy, Plato is probably the most famous thinker to assert that experts should rule and that democracy is a very poor system of government (but not the worst—see Chapter 5).

Closely related to authoritarianism is the concept of dictatorship. A dictatorship is a form of government in which power is centralized under the control of a single person or possibly a small group of people.[2] There is no separation of power in any meaningful sense—such as the division of power in the United States among the presidency, Congress, and the courts—and there is, in a "perfectly" functioning dictatorship, no way to limit the dictator's rule. It may be very difficult to achieve such tremendous power, and one might argue that there is a continuum on which we could place dictatorships. At one end of the spectrum is the case of a dictator limited by the need to work with the military, respect business leaders, or deal with some powerful national institution. In Spain, for example, from the late 1930s until 1975 the country was ruled by Francisco Franco, who in some ways aligned himself with the Roman Catholic Church in a connection that both bolstered and limited his ability to rule. Dictatorships can also be limited by the very fact that a group is ruling collectively. If there are several leaders sharing power, they will need to develop some procedures for how they come to a decision.[3] Thus, during the French Revolution, France was ruled for a time by the Committee of Twelve. However, even this limit on power does not spring from the people or some other institution; it is merely a procedural issue that must be resolved by a group of dictators. On the far extreme are places like North Korea, where there appear to be few limits on what Kim Jong-un may do in his country, although it is always hard to tell in this secretive land how politics works. In this sense dictatorships should be distinguished from traditional monarchies that in the modern era are limited by a constitution and frequently have to work with some form of legislature; the justification for the dictator's rule centers on the person or persons in question and does not necessarily derive authority from dynastic principle.[4]

Unlike the other political systems, authoritarian systems do not necessarily reflect any fully developed set of political ideas beyond the simple concentration of power, although such ideologies can develop. Authoritarians often arise from some society-wide crisis that may or may not encourage the development of a complex set of ideas to justify their rule. Thus, countries like North Korea are officially communist. In reality, it appears that North Korea is a dictatorship that borders on being a cult of one man. Many also point to Cuba under Fidel Castro, and now his brother Raul Castro, as a dictatorship, although officially Cuba considers itself a communist nation. Little in Cuba apparently changed under the rule of Raul Castro, and Cuba remains a dictatorship. However, in April of 2018 Raul stepped down as president. It will be interesting to see how Cuba changes under new leadership and now that diplomatic relations between the United States and Cuba have been restored after fifty-five years of non-recognition. According to these examples, dictatorships appear to be largely associated with communist and left-leaning countries. Yet in South America for much of the twentieth century, there were a number of dictatorships associated with right-wing political forces that were, to a large extent, friendly to capitalism. This was true, for instance, of Augusto Pinochet's rule of Chile from 1973 through 1989.

Some dictatorships do develop a set of ideas designed to vindicate their ruler and the ruling party, if there is one. Nazi Germany under Adolf Hitler developed a version of **fascism** that, while reprehensible, offered a worldview that competed with liberal democracy, socialism, and communism. This does not mean that the Nazi ideology was rational or even coherent; however, it offered what passed as an explanation for what the Nazis were doing and a racial ideology that was pseudo-scientific. The regimes we discuss in this section do not have such unifying principles as the **rule of law,** an idea based on regularized and consistent laws that are not changed by the whim of leaders or by circumstances such as anarchy, or the belief in freedom and equality that unite Western Europe and the United States. Indeed, one of the hallmarks of authoritarianism, and of dictators, is that leaders can rule arbitrarily. Their "special" skills or knowledge allow them to make decisions that require no obvious justification or explanation to the people. It is this very arbitrariness that strikes liberal democrats as so dangerous. The United States was founded, for instance, by those who saw Great Britain's rule of the American colonies as arbitrary—what the founders of America would have identified as despotic. And it is one of the main justifications for the U.S. system of checks and balances that such a system will make arbitrary government unlikely.

Current or recent examples of dictatorships include North Korea under Kim Jong Il and later his son Kim Jong-un, Iraq under Saddam Hussein, Zimbabwe under Robert Mugabe,

and Uzbekistan under Shavkat Mirziyoyev. We could add to this list a number of places where a tendency toward dictatorship is worrisome. Some commentators, for example, contend that Russia under President Vladimir Putin is increasingly dictatorial. In the mid-summer of 2004, Putin announced plans for sweeping changes in Russia's governance system, namely an extraordinary centralization of power in the Kremlin. The alleged reason for this action centered on the Chechen terrorist problem. Indeed, in September of 2004 Chechen terrorists entered a Beslan school in North Ossetia and held 1,100 hostages for

Vladimir Putin is now serving in his second stint as president of the Russian republic. Many observers of Russia worry about the increasingly authoritarian direction in which the country appears to be going. Putin is an avid outdoorsman and is highly proficient in martial arts, specifically judo.

three days, including 777 children. Russian security forces eventually stormed the building ending the crisis but not before some 385 hostages were killed, including 186 children. But there were earlier signs of a power grab—and for different reasons.

Just a few months earlier, President Putin opened up a war against the so-called oligarchs of the new Russia. These were businessmen who quickly took advantage of the privatization of a good share of the Russia's large business enterprises after the fall of communism in 1990. Some were engaged in questionable business practices. Others were totally legitimate. Regardless, Putin went after them, and over the past few years, the arrest of rich businessmen—as well as the stripping of their assets by the state—has become almost routine.[5]

Putin then began to move on the Russian media that had enjoyed a period of unprecedented freedom in the years immediately following the collapse of the Soviet Union. In 2013, things got so bad that he dissolved the main state news agency, RIA Novosti, and created a new state-run agency to promote Moscow's image abroad.[6]

Finally, we know that Putin himself has ordered all kinds of pressures against some of the former republics of the Soviet Union that are now independent countries. Sometimes the pressure to align closer with Moscow came with the threat of withholding trade or valuable natural gas and sometimes with force as in the case of the 2014 Russian seizure of the Crimean Peninsula, part of Ukraine. The fear of many democratic critics of Russia is that the country is well down the path to a resumption of authoritarian rule and that no matter who is actually in control, the Russian government is not accountable to the people, a primary requirement for any definition of democracy. This leads to a concern that Russia is an example of an authoritarian state in the making. As of 2018, nothing had changed in this assessment, and Putin still appears to have consolidated power with little effective opposition. Opposition leaders are arrested or banned from running. Elections are largely a sham.

We should note that although many authoritarian regimes are reviled, they can also be quite popular for some length of time. Since dictatorships typically emerge during times of crisis, the people often welcome the strong leadership that seems to create stability and stop chaos. There is ample evidence that Hitler enjoyed widespread, although certainly not universal, support for his rule. Many claim that Joseph Stalin was similarly popular in the Soviet Union. We must hasten to add, however, that because dictators have such extensive powers they are frequently able to manipulate the mass media and control their self-image in such a way as to virtually "brainwash" the populace. They are able to eliminate any real or imagined opposition and quash any "negative" history that may have come to light. Thus, the official line taught in school, seen on television, or heard on the radio is that the leader or leaders are right and have always been right. The powers of a modern American president to "spin" a story pale in comparison to the ability of a dictator to control how the general populace perceives his regime. A literary example of this phenomenon can be found in George Orwell's cautionary novel *1984*. The main character, Oceania citizen Winston Smith, has a job rewriting history and destroying documents that might reflect the inconsistencies and failures of Oceania's leaders. Even though this example is found in a piece of fiction, "rewrites" were in fact common under Stalin and Hitler and, more recently, have been documented in the case of Kim Jong Il of North Korea.

There are many different types of authoritarian states—tyrannical, fascist, and totalitarian are just a few. In earlier times, dictatorships were sometimes called despotic. Some political scientists make subtle and nuanced distinctions between all of these terms, while others use them fairly interchangeably. One frequently made and very important distinction is that authoritarianism and totalitarianism are in fact two different forms of government. The authoritarian state maintains political power but might leave other spheres of life relatively untouched. For example, the business community might enjoy freedom to operate as long as it does not challenge the ruler and churches could remain open as long as ministers and priests don't sermonize about political matters. In contrast, in a totalitarian state the regime rigidly controls all aspects of life. In some sense, there might be a virtual eradication of private life and thought all in the name of a strong state, as desired by the ruler or rulers. Even if such total control is as an "ideal" virtually unachievable, totalitarian regimes strive for just such total domination.

The Case of Nazi Germany

Nazi Germany was an example of an authoritarian regime and one that boasted of a certain ideology—namely fascism. *Fascism* is the general term used to describe a totalitarian or authoritarian political ideology characterized by dictatorial leadership; an oppressive one-party system; glorification of the nation-state and its people; aggressive militarism; and political, economic, and social policies designed (allegedly) to overcome the weaknesses of liberal democracy, the threat of anarchy, and the fear of communism.[7] The term *fascism* first came into prominence when used by the Fascist Party, organized by Benito Mussolini, which ruled Italy from 1922 until Mussolini's defeat in World War II. **Nazism** is the particularly virulently racist, militantly aggressive variety of fascism that characterized Germany under Adolf Hitler's dictatorship. **Anti-Semitism**—a prejudice against, or dislike of, Jews that often leads to discrimination or persecution—was a particularly notorious feature of Nazism.

Fascist dictators Benito Mussolini of Italy (right) and Adolf Hitler of Nazi Germany (left) at a military review in Venice, June 14–16, 1934. Both men committed ruthless acts against those they perceived as enemies. However, Hitler's treatment of Jews and other groups was especially heinous.

Why study Nazism—a dead, discredited political ideology that held sway only from 1933 to 1945? There are several reasons. First, Nazism threatened to annihilate the very fabric of modern civilization. For twelve nightmarish years, German power, guided by the insane Nazi ideology, was a mortal enemy of peace, social and political justice, human rights, economic well-being, and human decency. Hitler's Germany aggressively attacked its neighbors and brought on World War II, with its enormous costs in death and destruction. The Nazis barbarically exterminated millions of innocent Jews and others in the **Holocaust**. And they opened the door to repressive Soviet communist power in Eastern Europe.

Second, Nazism posed a mortal challenge to liberal democracy, democratic socialism, and communism. For twelve years, it destroyed those outlooks in Germany, in all areas under its control, and almost throughout the whole of Europe. How could this have come about? By critically examining Nazism, we can learn valuable lessons about its rise and its threats to liberal democracy.

Third, a study of Nazism may shed light on contemporary neo-fascism and right-wing authoritarianism. Although it does not presently appear that Nazism could regain control of a major state, before 1933 (when Hitler became chancellor of Germany) many thoughtful, civilized people believed as well that something like Nazism could not possibly arise. Elements of fascism, and of Nazism, remain evident today, and there are many who still admire Hitler. Neo-Nazis have blatantly attacked and even killed "foreigners" in Germany, where nonwhite immigrant workers have been targeted. Outbursts of anti-Semitism continue to mar a number of European countries. To a large degree in reaction to flow of immigrants and refugees from the Middle East and North Africa and illegal immigrants from Mexico and Central America, the United States and Europe have witnessed the rise of the **alt-right** (alternative right) movement. This is considered by many to be a thinly veiled version of neo-Nazism. The movements believe in white supremacy and anti-Semitism and as such are merely an updating of the Nazi's beliefs about racial hierarchy.

The Operative Ideals of Nazism. Nazism never offered its followers a rational, comprehensive political ideology. The Nazis were opportunistic and shifted ground in the course of their struggle to gain power. As a result, it is not easy to compile a list of consistent Nazi principles. Yet many of the ideas expressed in Hitler's book *Mein Kampf* (My Struggle) were put into practice—with catastrophic effect. Thus, we can identify six major operative ideals around which to organize our presentation of Nazi principles and behavior. With modifications and exceptions, these operative ideals also hold for fascism in general.

1. *The glorification of the authoritarian nation-state.* The Nazis articulated a mystical concept of the nation-state; for them, the German state embodied the good political life. The state expressed the unity, community, power, superiority, virtue, and civilization of the German people. Only through such a state could the German people find fulfillment.

2. *Strong dictatorial leadership.* The Nazis in Germany, like the fascists in Italy, emphatically endorsed the principle of elite leadership, embodied in a single authoritarian party and culminating in *der Führer,* or "the Leader." (In Italy, Mussolini was *Il Duce,* "the Chief" or "the Leader.") This idea illustrates the perverse fulfillment of the "great man" theory. The Nazis emphasized the importance of the leadership principle (*Führerprinzip*), by which the right goals, principles, direction, and discipline could be achieved. All looked to *der Führer,* who embodied the rightful will of the nation. All Germans had to give their obedience to Hitler.

3. *Racial superiority and anti-Semitism.* The Nazis made racial superiority and anti-Semitism—and their monstrous consequence, genocide—into a fanatical dogma. Although the Nazis had scientific trouble in identifying the Aryans, or Nordics, who were to be the superior people (*Volk*), they never doubted that the Jews were inferior. Hitler's talk about the destruction of the Jews and the virulent anti-Semitism of the Nazis were at first translated into a denial of rights. German citizens of Jewish faith and sometimes merely of Jewish ancestry were dismissed from government jobs, teaching, and other professions. Their property was taken away. Then the Nazis went further than a denial of rights. Synagogues were destroyed, and Jews were arrested and imprisoned in concentration camps. In time, the anti-Semitic campaign was extended to all countries that came under Nazi control during World War II and resulted in the dreadful "final solution"—the Holocaust, the extermination of 6 million Jews. Other so-called inferior groups—gypsies, the mentally ill, homosexuals—were also treated barbarically.

4. *Enforcement of conformity at home.* To pursue their objective of a dominant German *Volk*—free of Jewish, communist, liberal, and cosmopolitan "corruptions"—the Nazis required conformity to Nazi political, economic, and social ideology within Germany.

5. *Totalitarianism.* Totalitarianism was a primary objective: total political, economic, and cultural domination. Only one political party, the Nazi Party, was to operate in Germany. Other parties were abolished. Political opponents were killed, jailed, or driven into exile. Opposing political ideas—in the press, schools, trade unions, the military, and business—were suppressed. No independent source of political power—in religion, among labor unions, in the military, or in the business community—was tolerated.

6. *Imperialism, war, and destruction.* The Nazi commitment to struggle against enemies also found expression in Hitler's imperialist policies before and during World War II—policies that brought great destruction to Europe. The Nazis

sought revenge for the lands they had lost in World War I (such as Alsace-Lorraine) and "redemption" of ethnic Germans in Austria, Czechoslovakia, and elsewhere. They also sought *Lebensraum*—"living space"—to the east of Germany. Only military might could achieve these objectives, a military might forged by a cleansed, united, and strong German nation under the resolute leadership of *der Führer*. Fantastic successes included remilitarization of the Rhineland in 1936; *Anschluss* (union) with Austria in 1938; the Munich Pact (1938) and dismemberment of Czechoslovakia in 1939; and the German-Soviet nonaggression pact of 1939. These successes were followed by World War II and incredibly rapid military successes: the defeat of Poland, the overrunning of Holland and Belgium, the capitulation of France, and initial victories in Russia.

Even harder to fathom is the genocidal murder of Jews that went on in towns and cities under German domination and the even more systematic extermination that occurred in the Nazi death camps, a horror revealed to the world when the camps were overrun by Allied troops in 1945.[8]

Of course, this is just one of many authoritarian regimes, and we choose this historical example to illustrate the most horrific example of such regimes. We should note that there are other less brutal and, certainly, less expansionist authoritarian nations. But what is clear is that any authoritarian regime is antithetical to the practices of democracy and the very notion of human rights.

MIXED POLITICAL SYSTEMS

So far, we have investigated two very distinct cases—Great Britain and parliamentary government, and the authoritarianism of Nazi Germany, with a look at Putin and contemporary Russia as a possible authoritarian regime in the making. One could almost call them opposite political systems. However, the world is full of countries that don't neatly fit into one or the other camp. There are countries that exhibit elements of both. These are mixed political systems.

The Case of Communist China

We now take a closer look at one such country—China. With its impressive economic growth and its status as the most populous nation in the world, China occupies an important place in the international order. The Chinese economy is growing at a rate that may soon see the country surpass the United States as the world's largest economy. Judging the size of economies is not easy to do; however, by some measures China already has the largest economy in the world while others show the United States does. (Although, since it has such a large population, the per capita GDP is still significantly lower.) At the same time, China faces numerous challenges as it navigates its way through the twenty-first century. Furthermore, China is still officially a communist system. What exactly does that mean? While communism has faded with the fall of the Soviet Union, it was an important political phenomenon of the twentieth century, and to look at China is not only to see a great power but a great power that is transitioning away from communism (as traditionally understood) into something new. What that new kind of government is, as of yet, unclear.

To appreciate how China works we must first look at its political culture. China was unified long before the advent of the West, and its history spans thousands of years. Consider what this means—a region physically larger and considerably more populous than Europe has been united under a common governance stretching back thousands of years. Its unified governance notwithstanding, there remains a great deal of diversity among the Chinese people. There are fifty-five recognized ethnic groups in China today. What kind of political culture could be common to so many people and for so long? One factor is a widespread commitment to the ideals of Confucianism. The impact and thought of Confucius cannot be summarized adequately in our limited discussion. However, its ideals concerning order, stability, hierarchy, and a deep understanding and overarching belief in the importance of the group over the individual capture the essence of Chinese political culture up to the present day. These values place a heavy emphasis on the need to compromise for the greater good. Chinese culture has always been defined by *luan*—a deep-seated fear of chaos and a desire for stability. In the twentieth century, China was beset with wars that tore the country apart. After the Chinese Revolution (1949), communism became the official doctrine of the state, now known as the People's Republic of China. In spite of this, Confucianism continued to exert a powerful influence. Chinese political culture and its leadership adapted what they found useful in Marxist-Leninism without jettisoning the age-old values of Confucianism. More recently, the Communist Party, while still the only legitimate party to govern, began to import economic reforms based on Western capitalism.

So how does such a complex state, with its long history and recent turbulent past, reach political accommodation and resolve its political conflicts? How does the Chinese government successfully integrate a burgeoning capitalist economy with its traditional Confucian political culture? The answer is that China is a one-party state. Although the Chinese government formally has many of the same departments of government as Western democracies, we must remember that China is first and foremost a nation ruled through the Communist Party. This is strikingly different from Western democracies, where multiple competitive parties seek to control the government. In the case of China, the Communist Party is in sole control of all branches of government. In the West, nations are ruled by multiple parties that compete for power in regular elections. Such overt competition is anathema to Chinese culture, with its ingrained fear of chaos. The idea of a loyal opposition—the hallmark of Western democracies—is alien to the Chinese. The desire for consensus and the need to mediate differences are not processed through competitive elections. Chinese political culture values consensus, and the related fear of chaos precludes forms of government that allow for overt political conflict. This is in clear contrast to liberal democracies, which not only welcome competitive political parties but in fact incorporate institutional conflict, such as that between an executive and the legislature, into their constitutional frameworks. Furthermore, formal separation of powers is unknown to the Chinese. All governance must occur by and within the party. The idea of conflict that is inherent in a system of separation of powers makes no sense to the Chinese. To the Chinese, this is unimaginable. Ideally, party members go among the people to gather ideas. In this way citizens' voices are heard. These ideas are then filtered up through the party where final policy is made. This process reflects an ongoing conversation in which the people are heard and the government responds. China's recent reforms have allowed capitalism to take flight in some parts of the economy; however, thus far reform has been limited to the economic sector. The political process, with rare exceptions, remains largely what it was in the past. Whether the recent economic reforms will lead to a demand for political reform is unclear. Chinese political history and culture being what they are, we might find that China's age-old fear of chaos, desire for stability, and deeply held belief that community takes precedence over the individual preclude wholesale political transformation. Yet, as we shall see, the Chinese have created institutions that, on the surface at least, look like those in the West.

In communist systems, legislatures historically have played a modest role. Representation is formal but ineffective, in the western understanding of legislatures. The primary purpose for the existence of legislative bodies is to rubber-stamp policies as they emanate from the **Politburo** (the Communist Party's principal policymaking and executive committee). Real supervision of government by the legislature is unheard of. Nevertheless, elaborate procedures are followed to elect representatives and hold endless meetings. In the People's Republic of China the key legislative unit is the National People's Congress, consisting of 2,270 deputies. Deputies are indirectly elected for five years by the provincial congresses, autonomous regions, municipalities directly under the central government, and the People's Liberation Army (PLA). The standing committee elected by the Congress is in permanent session. But again, real legislative as well as executive power resides with the Communist Party.

In discussing any communist system, we must distinguish between the formal government executive—specifically, the prime minister and Council of Ministers—and the true executive power—the Communist Party general secretary and the Politburo, which is a small group of high-ranking party officials drawn from the larger central committee. The distinction can be tempered with the knowledge that more often than not there is a high degree of "interlocking membership" between the council and the Politburo. In other words, many of the highest-ranking government executive officials are also members of the party hierarchy.

A further consideration in analyzing executive power in communist systems is the fact that historically they have been vulnerable to what might be called "personalist" tendencies—one person's rise to extraordinary power, often transcending the highest party organs. Certainly, Joseph Stalin epitomized this tendency in the Soviet Union from 1924 until his death in 1953. In North Korea, a highly personalist regime came to power with the rise of Kim Il Sung after World War II and continued with his son, Kim Jong Il, and his grandson today, Kim Jong-un. In the People's Republic of China, Mao Zedong wielded tremendous power for more than two decades after the communists took control in 1949. Though not as charismatic, Mao's de facto successor, Deng Xiaoping, was able to maintain enormous power for many years without holding any official government position.

After Mao's death, the top echelon of Chinese officials sought to alter party power dynamics to prevent the advent of another "personalist" leader. There have since been attempts to share power among top leaders and to develop a consensus model of rule. Chinese political scholar Kenneth Lieberthal characterizes China's ruling model as "fragmented-authoritarianism." Recently, however, some China specialists have noted a reversal of that trend. As of early 2018, the leader of China, Xi Jinping, held a key position of power throughout the system. He was general secretary of the Communist

Party, president of the People's Republic of China, and chairman of the Central Military Commission. In 2016, the party gave him the title of "core leader," something only three of China's previous leaders held (Mao Zedong, Deng Xiaoping, and Jiang Zemin). Xi's immediate predecessor, Hu Jintao, worked in a more collective manner and was seen as a first among equals. Indeed, there is something of a "cult of personality" around Xi with cartoons, books, and songs written about him. More disturbing to believers in democracy, in March of 2018, the National People's Congress adopted a set of constitutional amendments removing the term limits for the president. Xi Jinping could be in power for quite some time to come.

Communist bureaucracies are, in essential respects, similar to the bureaucracies of the developed world. They have, however, greater power than do civil servants in the West simply because the powers of communist governments embrace more areas. Government managers control all major economic enterprises (coal mines and steel mills, automobile plants, collective farms, hospitals, department stores) in addition to collecting taxes, issuing passports, and regulating foreign trade. As systems such as those in the People's Republic of China and Vietnam move toward a free-market economy while trying to maintain Communist Party control, we might expect a weakening of the traditionally strong communist bureaucracy. These efforts to make China more friendly to business have continued under Xi.

Communist bureaucracies tend to be more pragmatic and less ideological than the party that gives rise to them. This trait engenders a more accommodating disposition, a willingness to face facts, and acceptance of scientific guidance over ideological imperative. But Communist Party control of top-level bureaucrats has historically inhibited the ability of professionals in governmental posts—economists, engineers, agronomists, and biologists—to take an independent line, even when they think a policy is wrong.

Courts in communist countries do not generally contribute as significantly to political accommodation as they do in Western democratic countries. Communist courts, in contrast to U.S. courts, have no power to invalidate legislative acts. Their function is to see that the law is obeyed, not to safeguard human rights as they are understood in Western democracies.

Despite the existence in China of seemingly parallel institutions—a legislature, executive, court system, and bureaucracy—we must always remember that China is a one-party state, and that single party, the Communist Party, controls each of these institutions of governance. To the Chinese, working through the party is the way to achieve power; it is through the party that the system maintains legitimacy. In China, in effect, all institutions of government—legislative, executive, judicial, and bureaucratic—exist *inside* the one-party communist system. In contrast, in the West these same institutions of government exist *outside* of parties in the form mandated by national constitutions. Thus, China maintains its official communist party rule with hopes for a more efficient and somewhat market friendly economic system.

FAILED OR FRAGILE STATES

Finally, we turn our attention to what is known as a **failed or fragile state**. As can be readily surmised from our heading, the governments of failed states don't work very well, if at all. Furthermore, the structure of government in these countries is often chaotic and prone to dramatic shifts over time. In a sense, the term *structure* is meaningless, and to summarize official forms of government here is pointless. It would perhaps be more precise to characterize such states by their structural deficits. By definition, a failed state lacks the type of stability that liberal democracies and their communist alternatives take for granted. Failed states are often corrupt; government services are chaotic, if available at all; there is little respect for human rights or the rule of law; the economy is not simply stagnant but declining or even collapsing; and life expectancy is falling with disease rampant. Often, brute force rules the day (see the section in Chapter 1 on wipeout). All in all, a failed state is a land without effective government of any sort or with an extremely repressive government that offers its people little hope and even less justice.

To better understand this phenomenon, we address the two Key Questions on this page.

In failed states, the planning and implementing of public policy is commonly in the hands of a strong leader (Saddam Hussein of Iraq, 1979–2003; Muammar al-Qaddafi of Libya, 1969–2011), a military junta (Argentina, 1976–1983), or a civilian authoritarian figure (François "Papa Doc" Duvalier of Haiti, 1957–1971). This is particularly true in developing regions that do not have strong legislative traditions or where political and economic circumstances require a particularly strong hand. Frequently, legislatures are weak in failed states and likely to be dominated by the president and the leader of the dominant party. In a failed or failing state, the courts offer virtually no support for the political opposition or for common citizens to bring grievances against the government. If courts exist at all, they are usually simply used by the dominant power to maintain its authority.

As we noted previously, it is difficult to generalize in the case of failed states. The causes of the failed or failing state vary widely, and it is these causes that affect the exact ways in which a government has deteriorated or is deteriorating. However, it is safe to say that in most cases a failed state is marked by the collapse of an effective legislature, judiciary, and bureaucracy. The only institution that usually "works" in a failed or failing state is the executive, and this is often because a "strong man" simply maintains his authority—most likely in a brutal and unjust fashion. Eventually, the strong man dies or is overthrown. The failed state then either begins the arduous process of creating stability and a functioning government or it relinquishes control to yet another strong man who has risen to replace the previous leader. Hence, the cycle of violence and injustice continues.

The first ten fragile or failed states ranked in order in 2017 were South Sudan, Somalia, Central African Republic, Yemen, Sudan, Syria, Congo, Chad, Afghanistan, and Iraq.[9] What accounts for the failure of politics in such places? The answer in each case is unique; nonetheless, we can learn much from a brief study of two states: Afghanistan (ranked 9th) and Somalia (ranked 2nd).

The Cases of Afghanistan and Somalia

Afghanistan is a land locked, mountainous country in south central Asia. It lies just north of Pakistan, east of Iran, and south of Turkmenistan, Uzbekistan, and Tajikistan. It is close to Indian and China to the east. Afghanistan is an Islamic country and over 99 percent of its approximately 35 million citizens identify with that religion. Because of its central location along trading routes that tied east to west, it has been the scene of great power conflicts. In the nineteenth century, the imperial rivalries of Russia and Great Britain often centered on Afghanistan, and this conflict was dubbed the "Great Game." However, the people of the country, while often focused on their own internal ethnic and tribal conflicts, are known for their fierce sense of independence. So in one sense, Afghanistan is blessed with an important geographic location and a strong pride in its autonomy. In another sense, though, it has been hobbled by internal conflict and the attention of other powerful countries. So, the struggle to maintain its freedom and sense of cohesion has always been difficult.

These challenges to the stability of the nation took a quite ominous turn in the in the late twentieth century as the country was wracked by a civil war and became the focus on ideological and religious conflicts that threaten its stability to this very day. Although the complete story is very complicated there are number key conflicts that define the country and have created a very fragile state that is beset by problems at all times.

For much of the post–World War II era, Afghanistan tried to develop economically and consolidate national government's power over the country. There were, however, serious internal conflicts that resulted in various chaotic changes in power. At first, its leaders strove to remain neutral in the Cold War conflict. Although, both the United States and especially the USSR made efforts to influence politics. Despite problems, elections were held in the 1960s with a great many parties spanning the ideological spectrum from far right to far left. In 1973, a bloodless coup resulted in the abolition of the monarchy and constitution and the establishment of a republic under Mohammad Daud Khan. Daud Khan failed in his reform efforts, and he was deposed in 1978. The intense conflict between right and left forces ultimately led to a period of chaotic instability and several successive leaders in a short period of time. In December of 1979, the Soviet Union decided to intervene and invaded the country. This led to a civil war with a Soviet-backed central government and various regional groups collectively known as the mujahideen, backed by the United States, China, Pakistan, and Saudi Arabia, fighting for power. Eventually, a group called the Taliban (which is Persian for "students") began to gain power. This group was staunchly Islamic and very opposed to corruption. The Taliban was able to control most of the country and took the capital of Kabul. Ethnic conflicts, however, persisted and the country remained fractured with the Taliban in control over most of the country, but a group called the Northern Alliance was in power in parts. Furthermore, the Taliban's version of Islam was particularly conservative and many human rights advocates worried about is abuses, particularly concerning women. For these reasons, the UN refused to give formal recognition to the Taliban government, although other countries did accept them as the legitimate government.

Matters grew even more dire in the wake of 9/11. Osama bin Laden and his group al-Qaeda were based in Afghanistan and that led the United States and Great Britain to support the Northern Alliance, bombing Taliban strongholds, and eventually U.S. special forces on the ground working alongside militias opposed to the Taliban. The Taliban collapsed, and a new government emerged in 2002 and 2003. Since that time, the government has struggled to maintain control of the country. At times during the past ten years, many believed that the government power was largely confined to the capital, Kabul, and the surrounding areas. Still, a number of elections have been held and gradually the government has been able to expand its ability to control larger regions of the country. That said, there is widespread corruption, the Taliban still exists as a rival force, and the United States continues to have a military presence in the country. Along with the political struggles that have divided the country, Afghanistan is the largest producer of opium-causing, horrible drug problems throughout the world. Opium is one of the few stable sources of income for many people in the country.

The current situation in Afghanistan is virtually a textbook case of a fragile state. Despite some improvements, the central government is weak and local regions have a great deal of autonomy with little interference from the central government. Warlords with their own private militias control significant areas of the country. Modern health care is non-existent in much of the country, access to clean water is problematic for many people, life expectancy is low, and there is only a limited education system. While a central government exists, it is weak, foreign forces remain in the country (including U.S. troops), and at any moment, the precarious political situation could lead to outright collapse. The day-to-day stability and functioning of basic services that Americans take for granted are absent. The story of Afghanistan is one of a fiercely proud set of people who, in the long run, effectively refuse to be ruled by others; yet, at the same time a country that stubbornly fails to unify, given geography and ethnic conflicts, and prone to interference from outside forces.

Somalia is strategically positioned on the Horn of Africa. An arid, predominantly high plains country, it has the longest coastline of any African state and a population of roughly 10 million people. For three years—2011, 2012, and 2013—it topped the list of most fragile or failed states in the world. While it now has at least the institutional semblance of a viable country, the reality is that for fifteen years—1991 to 2006—it had no effective central authority. Instead, it was ruled by various factions, including powerful clans led by warlords. The impact of that central power void was devastating.

Somalia provides another tragic example of a failed state. For centuries, Somalia was a major center of commerce. Then in the middle of the nineteenth century, the Italians and British arrived and established the colonial holding known as British Somaliland and Italian Somaliland. The Italians lasted until 1941, and then the British took over both territories. In 1960, the two regions were merged to form the Somali Republic, an independent country. Strongman Mohamed Siad Barre seized power in 1969 forming the Somali Democratic Republic. Barre adopted policies based on the Chinese communist model—nationalization of banks, industry, and business as well as cooperative farming. Over time, his government became more authoritarian. Among other things he forbid clanism, a social structure deeply lodged in the culture and tradition of the region. Finally, as the economy began to collapse and government policies became increasingly unpopular, Barre's government collapsed in 1991. Resistance to the government had come from a variety of largely clan-based movements often with the encouragement of neighboring Ethiopia. Somalia and Ethiopia had been at odds for years over a territory known as the Ogaden. And as in so many cases similar to this, the country plunged into civil war and chaos ensued for a decade and a half.

With no effective central government, the country was increasingly fragmented. Local authorities, often under the control of warlords, assumed the tasks of governance, not always efficiently. There were a number of attempts to establish a central government, but they did not always succeed. Between 2008 and 2012, the country struggled to put together a stable central government. Finally, in 2012 after years of civil war and arduous negotiations between various factions, what could be termed a reasonably viable central government was in place. But the toll of civil war for so many years was devastating and in some ways continues, though the rebels are not as powerful as they once were. The economy was a shambles, corruption was rampant, and lawlessness was epitomized by well-armed Somali pirates preying upon all sorts of commercial vessels in the shipping lanes off the country's coast. Today, it remains a violent place reflected in a series of horrible truck bombings on October 14 and 28, 2017, in Mogadishu, killing more than 500 people. We should also note that the United States has had extensive military involvement in the country to this day, working with the Somalia government to combat rebels and conduct attacks on terrorist threats. Clearly, here was a case of a failed state largely brought about by first the harsh and destructive policies of an authoritarian leader followed by years of terrible civil conflict.

CONCLUSION

As you can see, the world is filled with a variety of political systems. One of the important tasks done by comparativists is to highlight the unique qualities of any country while at the same time trying to create categories of politics that include many countries. If this latter task is done well, it allows us to see the political world with greater clarity and understanding. Thus, in this chapter we looked at a number of specific cases—Great Britain, Nazi Germany, Russia, Communist China, Zimbabwe, and Somalia. The fascist authoritarianism of Nazi Germany is quite unique in its own way. Yet certain qualities of Nazi Germany make it fruitful to compare with other countries we identify as authoritarian. In this way, comparative politics is the study of the specific in the hopes of highlighting broader political phenomenon.

SUGGESTED READINGS

Almond, Gabriel, G. Bingham Powell Jr., Kaare Strom, and Russell J. Dalton, eds. *Comparative Politics Today: A World View*. 11th ed. New York: Pearson, 2014. Examines Britain, France, Germany, Japan, Russia, China, Mexico, Brazil, Egypt, India, and Nigeria within a framework of system, process, and policy, focusing on political socialization, political recruitment, interest articulation, interest aggregation, and policymaking.

Burleigh, Michael. *The Third Reich*. New York: Hill and Wang, 2000. An extensive study of the development of Nazi Germany.

Coleman, Fred. *The Decline and Fall of the Soviet Empire: Forty Years that Shook the World, from Stalin to Yeltsin.* New York: St. Martin's Press, 1996. Puts fourteen years of journalistic experience in Moscow to good use. The primary assertion seems to be that the Soviet Union was always much weaker and more insecure than U.S. officials ever knew.

Coll, Steve. *Directorate S: The C.I.A. and America's Secret Wars in Afghanistan and Pakistan.* New York: Penguin Press, 2018. A comprehensive work that details the way the United States intervened in Afghanistan and Pakistan to achieve its own objectives to defeat extremists and yet was challenged by Pakistan in that effort. The problems this created in Afghanistan are carefully considered.

Elazar, Daniel J. *Federal Systems of the World.* 2nd ed. New York: Stockton Press, 1994. Fine comparative study by one who is sympathetic to federalism and its contributions.

Evans, Geoffrey. *Brexit and British Politics.* Cambridge, MA: Polity, 2017. A concise work that discusses the way Brexit is changing Great Britain.

Handelman, Howard. *Challenges of the Developing World.* 8th ed. Landover, MD: Rowan and Littlefield, 2016. A thorough analysis of the challenges faced by less developed countries.

Lieberthal, Kenneth. *Governing China.* 2nd ed. New York: Norton, 2003. A great overview of Chinese politics.

MacFarquhar, Roderick. *The Politics of China: Sixty Years of the People's Republic of China.* 3rd ed. Cambridge, MA: Cambridge University Press, 2011. A collection of essays that deal with Chinese politics from many angles—political, economic, and cultural.

Miller, Judith. *God Has Ninety-Nine Names: Reporting from a Militant Middle East.* New York: Simon & Schuster, 1996. An excellent analysis of the Islamization of politics in the Middle East by the former Cairo bureau chief of the *New York Times.*

Moore, Barrington. *Social Origins of Dictatorship and Democracy.* Reprint ed. Boston: Beacon Press, 1993. First published 1966 by Beacon Press. Classic study of governmental forms, including dictatorship.

Norton, Philip. *The British Polity.* 5th ed. New York: Longman, 2010. A lucid, thorough, and highly praised book on the British political system, including discussion of both governmental and nongovernmental actors in the British political fabric.

O'Neil, Patrick, and Ronald Rogowski. *Essential Readings in Comparative Politics.* 4th ed. New York: Norton, 2012. An excellent collection of classical works, recent scholarship, and contemporary journalistic accounts of world politics.

Paxton, Robert. *The Anatomy of Fascism.* New York: Knopf, 2004. A historical study of fascism in both Germany and Italy.

Rothberg, Robert I., and Thomas G. Weiss, eds. *From Massacres to Genocide: The Media, Public Policy, and Humanitarian Crises.* Washington, DC: Brookings, 1996. A series of essays on how media coverage shapes foreign policy and distorts perceptions of the developing world.

Smith, B. C. *Understanding Third World Politics: Theories of Political Change and Development.* 2nd ed. New York: Macmillan, 2013. In addition to a critical discussion of concepts such as dependency, authoritarianism, and modernization, the author provides an excellent review of the literature of development.

Ulam, Adam. *The Communists: The Story of Power and Lost Illusions, 1948–1991.* New York: Macmillan, 1992. A sweeping analysis of the decline of communism by a distinguished Soviet and Russian authority.

GLOSSARY TERMS

alt-right (p. 268)
anti-Semitism (p. 267)
dictatorship (p. 258)
failed or fragile state (p. 273)

fascism (p. 265)
Holocaust (p. 268)
loyal opposition (p. 271)
luan (p. 271)

Nazism (p. 267)
Politburo (p. 272)
prime minister (p. 260)
rule of law (p. 265)

NOTES

1. See Robert G. Wesson, *Modern Governments: Three Worlds of Politics*, 2nd ed. (Englewood Cliffs, NJ: Prentice Hall, 1985), chap. 10.

2. Guy Hermet, "Dictatorship/Dictator," in *The Blackwell Encyclopedia of Political Science*, ed. Vernon Bogdanor (Oxford, UK: Basil Blackwood, 1991), 174–175.

3. See S. E. Finer, *The History of Government*, vol. 1 (Oxford: Oxford University Press, 1999), 76–77.

4. Hermet, "Dictatorship/Dictator," 174–175.

5. Marshall I. Goldman, "Putin and the Oligarchs," *Foreign Affairs*, November–December 2004, http://www.cfr.org/world/putin-oligarchs/p8018.

6. Roland Oliphant, "Vladimir Putin Dissolves Russia's RIA Novosti," *The Telegraph*, Dec. 9, 2013, http://www.telegraph.co.uk/news/worldnews/europe/russia/10505386/Vladimir-Putin-dissolves-Russias-RIA-Novosti.html.

7. Paul M. Hayes, *Fascism* (New York: Free Press, 1973), 23. In our presentation of Nazi roots, we follow, with modifications, Hayes's presentation of eight fascist ideas, 2–119. See also Walter Laquer, *Fascism: Past, Present, and Future* (New York: Oxford University Press, 1996).

8. For a record of Nazi imperialism, war, and destruction, see Karl D. Bracher, *The German Dictatorship* (New York: Praeger, 1970); William L. Shirer, *The Rise and Fall of the Third Reich* (New York: Simon & Schuster, 1960); Lucy S. Dawidowicz, *The War Against the Jews, 1933–1945* (New York: Holt, Rinehart, and Winston, 1975); and Daniel J. Goldhagen, *Hitler's Willing Executioners: Ordinary Germans and the Holocaust* (New York: Knopf, 1996). For a comparative study of totalitarianism, see Bruce F. Pauley, *Hitler, Stalin, and Mussolini: Totalitarianism in the Twentieth Century* (Wheeling, IL: Harlan Davidson, 1997).

9. The Fund for Peace, "The Fragile State Index 2017," http//fundforpeace.ort/fsi/2017/05/14/fragile-states-index-2017-annual-report/

The UN complex in New York City.

11

INTERNATIONAL POLITICS AND THE GLOBAL COMMUNITY

In earlier chapters, we argued that successful patterns of domestic accommodation rest on (1) agreement on certain constitutional fundamentals; (2) meaningful opportunities for the expression of needs, interests, and desires; (3) sound mechanisms for the selection of priorities; (4) acceptable ways for legitimating public policy choices; (5) effective governance; and (6) regular and effective controls on government. In this chapter, we tackle the Key Questions on page 283.

POST–WORLD WAR II AND POST–COLD WAR CHALLENGES

In this chapter, we focus on the patterns of nation-state behavior since the end of World War II in 1945 and the end of the Cold War in 1990. The end of the World War II represents an important divide. To a large extent, the war ushered in a new world, one characterized by (1) the dominance of two superpowers—the United States and the Soviet Union; (2) the advent of the atomic and hydrogen bombs and the globe-girdling missiles, planes, and submarines that deliver these weapons of mass destruction (WMDs); (3) the breakup of the great colonial empires and the subsequent emergence of new nation-states; (4) an economically interdependent global community; (5) a revolution of rising expectations in all parts of the world—developing and developed; and (6) a host of disturbing ecological problems, including rapid population growth; deterioration of the earth's ozone layer; global warming; urban blight; and pollution of the world's rivers, lakes, and oceans.

As profound as these developments were, change continues today, and in the post–Cold War world our focus must

Chapter Objectives

After studying this chapter, you will be able to do the following:

1. Discuss current patterns in international relations.

2. Describe the critical role played by the Cold War in defining the international system.

3. Describe the basic structure and function of the United Nations as an example of multilateralism.

4. Explain the nature and function of regional integration by using the example of the European Union.

5. Define *neutrality*, *nonalignment*, and *isolation* in international relations.

6. Discuss some of the key nonstate actors in the international system—nongovernmental organizations (NGOs), terrorist groups, and multinational corporations (MNCs).

extend beyond the characteristics associated with the post–World War II international environment. In the nearly three decades following the end of the Cold War, the system has been characterized by (1) a large Russian republic struggling with a reduced military capability, a difficult transformation to a market economy, and a resurgence of authoritarian rule after a flirtation with democracy; (2) formerly communist Eastern European countries emerging as new market economies and fledgling democracies; (3) a Western-dominated European Union, rapidly expanding into Eastern Europe right up to the borders of the Russian Republic; (4) the emergence of a militant Islamic fundamentalism, particularly in the Middle East and South Asia; (5) after a dramatic shift from historically authoritarian political systems to democratic systems of government in many parts of the world, a very real struggle for those more open systems to survive; (6) the prospect of a meaningful reduction in nuclear armament by the superpowers coupled with nuclear weapons proliferation in other parts of the world; (7) an alarming increase in civil wars and regional conflicts, many of them emerging out of long-standing ethnic, tribal, and religious resentments; (8) a **globalization** of the international economic system built on the twin pillars of capitalism and computer-based communications; (9) a dramatic increase in the reach and lethality of terrorism, including the specter of biological and chemical weapons; and (10) the rise of new economic powers such as India, Brazil, and particularly China.

Finally, the election of Donald Trump as president of the United States ushered in a challenge to the international order constructed after World War II. His foreign policy seemed built on several assumptions and assertions:

1. The international economic system built on multilateral organizations and free trade was detrimental to the interests of the United States.

2. The system that facilitated the flight of American manufacturing to other countries costs American jobs and must be reversed.

3. Military partners were taking advantage of America by not paying their fair share of military alliance structures and must pay more.

4. The United States cannot play "policeman of the world." It has involved itself in far too many costly regional conflicts.

5. The United States let its nuclear forces deteriorate and are now totally inadequate. Therefore, America's nuclear arsenal must be modernized and increased, reversing years of negotiated agreements reducing the size of the U.S. nuclear forces.

These assumptions and assertions seem to reflect an American retrenchment from American leadership in the world, a hallmark of the post–World War II system.

Earlier we asked whether the present international system could adequately protect the vital needs and interests of nation-states and peoples. But what do we mean by "adequately protect"? We believe that patterns of international politics should accomplish the following four objectives:

1. Prevent a third catastrophic world war, avoid either the accidental or deliberate use of WMDs, curtail the spread of terrorism, and guard against devastating regional and civil wars.

2. Ensure that people live in freedom under governments of their own choice and enjoy basic rights, including the right to govern their own affairs and pursue their preferred lifestyles.

3. Guard against political, economic, and social exploitation of one nation by another.

4. Guarantee that people everywhere have enough food, decent housing, good medical care, basic schooling, and protection against ecological disaster.

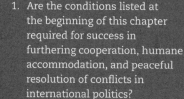

KEY QUESTIONS

1. Are the conditions listed at the beginning of this chapter required for success in furthering cooperation, humane accommodation, and peaceful resolution of conflicts in international politics?

2. Will these conditions maximize security, liberty, justice, and welfare in the global community? Or do vital differences exist between domestic and international politics?

Our guiding hypothesis is as follows: Despite some striking successes in international cooperation, present international patterns do not yet adequately protect the vital needs and fundamental interests of all nations and peoples in the global community.

CURRENT PATTERNS IN INTERNATIONAL POLITICS

In this chapter, we elaborate on our guiding hypothesis by analyzing the strengths and weaknesses of three patterns of foreign policy—**balance of power, domination,** and **multilateralism**. Balance of power and domination find their theoretical roots in realist thought, which emphasizes a pragmatic, national self-interest approach to foreign policy. Multilateralism is more closely, though not exclusively, associated with idealist thought, a body of thought that tends to emphasize accommodation, negotiation, and collective responsibility. Before assessing these patterns, two concepts central to relations between countries should be explored: national interest and power.

The Standard of National Interest

Patterns in international politics are significantly influenced by national interest. A nation will choose a policy based on balance of power, domination, or multilateralism because it offers assurance of protecting the national interest. The national interest is a central concern of leaders in international politics. Leaders must protect the fundamental interests of their nation: its freedom and independence (values), its safety against foreign aggression or subversion (security), its prosperity (welfare), and the rights and welfare of its people (liberty and justice). However, within and between states, debate rages on the more specific meaning of the national interest. That which may be in one nation's interest may not be in another's. U.S. involvement in the Vietnam War between 1960 and 1973 illustrates both aspects of this controversy. Within the United States, some students, legislators, journalists, academics, and other citizens argued that America's national interest was hardly threatened by North Vietnam's effort to take over the whole of Vietnam and unite the country. Other Americans disagreed, believing national interest was indeed threatened: If South Vietnam fell to the North Vietnamese communists, then—like so many dominoes— every country in Southeast Asia would fall, and the United States would be dealt a grievous blow by "international communism." Of course, the governments of the United States and North Vietnam differed on what was in the best interest of Vietnam. The United States sought to contain the spread of communism; the North Vietnamese sought to unify all of Vietnam under the communist banner and rid the country of the foreign interests that had exploited the region for centuries. Needless to say, the rulers of South Vietnam and the rulers of North Vietnam also had conflicting views of national interest.

Similarly, debate remains heated on whether it was in the national interest of the United States to invade Iraq in 2003. As we noted in Chapter 2, some argued that there was more than ample reason for the invasion, not the least of which was that Saddam Hussein—a leader who had used chemical weapons against his own citizens and violated numerous UN resolutions—was a proven destabilizing force in a region of the world critical to the United States. Critics argued that the invasion was not in the national interest, that Saddam did not pose a direct threat to the United States, and that invading a country for the purpose of regime change set a dangerous precedent.

To a large extent, disagreements in international politics involve conflicting concepts of national interest. The standard of the national interest—and not some global standard of the human interest of all peoples—is the primary standard for politicians in international relations.

The Primary Role of Power

Patterns in international politics are also significantly influenced by the distribution and exercise of power. Power, as we noted in Chapter 1, means the ability of one political actor (say, a nation-state) to get another (say, another nation-state) to do (or not do) something. Political realists assert that power must be mobilized and used in a balanced system, either to maintain equilibrium of power between countries or to maintain superiority over an opponent. Similarly, domination cannot be maintained without the threat or employment of power. Finally, true **collective security** requires that peace-loving states employ their collective or multilateral power against aggressive nations that violate the peace or international law. Thus, regardless of the policy they pursue, nations will employ power to maintain national conceptions of security, liberty, justice, and welfare.

Power can be exercised in many ways. It can be military or economic might, sometimes referred to as **hard power**. Or, it can take the form of **soft power**, which involves less-tangible techniques and assets such as persuasion, charisma, and political skill.[1] During the 2008 presidential race, Barack Obama proved a charismatic leader with great personal appeal. Indeed, many of his supporters believed his eloquence and personal history as America's first black president would strengthen the country's soft power throughout the world—a belief evidently shared by members of the Nobel Peace Prize committee who, somewhat controversially, awarded him the Nobel Peace Prize in 2009. But what is also interesting is his use of hard power. During his first term as president, he more than doubled the use of remote armed drone aircraft in the war against terrorism. He also liberally used special operations forces like the Navy SEALs, Army Special Forces, and Delta Force. He increased troop levels in Afghanistan and in 2011, in conjunction with European allies, conducted bombing missions in Libya contributing to the overthrow and death of President Muammar al-Qaddafi. Indeed, President Obama's extensive use of hard power such as armed drones and his bombing of Libya have led his critics to raise questions about overextension of executive power and the possible violation of the sovereignty of countries where the attacks are directed.

Veering away from President Obama's mix of hard and soft power, the first year of President Trump's administration reflected far less reliance on soft power. Trump's budget proposals called for significant cuts in foreign aid and contributions to international organizations like the United Nations. At the same time, we witnessed significant increases in defense spending.

Some political scientists take a more skeptical view of power, maintaining that it is neither good nor evil. Power, they contend, can be equated with many things, for example, the political skill of the experienced diplomat; public opinion, as represented in the views of masses of people putting pressure on decision makers; prestige, as evidenced by the influence of those who are respected on the national and international stage; and authority, as rooted in the law. Thus, power can be military, legal, political, economic, psychological, sociological, or ethical—in essence neutral, with only its particular use or misuse making it good or evil.

Aside from power, a further desire operates in international politics—a desire for mutual benefit. This frequently leads to cooperation, accommodation, and the peaceful resolution of disputes without any military action, economic threat, or political sanction. Thus, nations cooperate on a wide range of practical matters—global communications, ocean and air safety, global health issues, and international postal service are just a few such matters—without the threat of coercive power. Nonetheless, when mutual benefits are not obvious, or when disagreements seriously threaten national interests, the exercise of political, economic, and military muscle will most likely ensue.

BALANCE OF POWER

After the conclusion of World War II in 1945 through the demise of the Soviet Union in 1990, the dominant pattern of international politics involved a balancing of power. While it has many meanings, at its core balance of power is the maintenance of peace through the distribution of power among competing nations so that no single state or combination of states is dominant. Peace is assured when nations' military powers are distributed so that no one state (or combination of states) is strong enough to threaten another state (or combination of states) with its military strength. Stated simply, peace is achieved through equilibrium.

Classic balance-of-power systems are based on the European experience during the seventeenth, eighteenth, and nineteenth centuries. As depicted in Figure 11.1, the system generally had multiple actors of five, six, or seven states. When power is distributed among several nation-states in this manner, it demonstrates **multipolarity**. During most of the post–World War II period, however, the balance-of-power concept was applied to the Cold War rivalry between the United States and the Soviet Union. When power is distributed in this manner, between just two nation-states, it demonstrates **bipolarity**. In the immediate post–Cold War world, some made the case that the distribution of power tended toward **hegemony**, a condition in which one power—in this case the United States—tends to be an overwhelming, dominating, and perhaps stabilizing force. Many analysts now believe, some three decades after the fall of the Soviet Union, that American domination (or at least near domination) is fading and that the international system is once again headed either for a more multipolar distribution of power or perhaps even the emergence of China as a new dominant global power. As we consider the current balance of power in the world, keep in mind the Key Questions on this page.

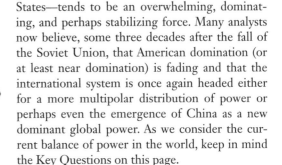

KEY QUESTIONS

1. Which global distribution of power provides the greatest stability for the international system?

2. Is the international system headed toward a new balance-of-power configuration, and, if so, what might it look like?

The Cold War Balance of Power

The forty-five-year ideological-cum-military rivalry between the United States (and its allies) and the Soviet Union (and its allies), and the ramifications of this rivalry across the globe, offers a case study of the bipolar balance-of-power system in its purest form.

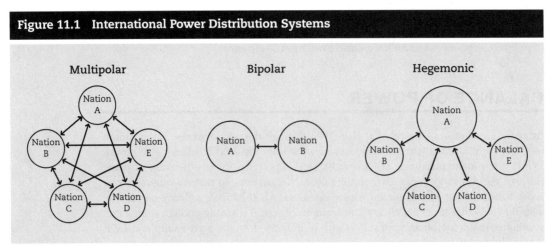

Figure 11.1   International Power Distribution Systems

Multipolar   Bipolar   Hegemonic

Source: Compiled by authors.

The two superpowers sought at the least equality—and preferably superiority—of power relative to the other on the global stage. The United States and the Soviet Union each maintained an arsenal of nuclear weapons designed, so they claimed, to deter an attack by the other. These powerful arsenals still exist, but both parties (the Russian Republic, now, in place of the Soviet Union) have since reduced their overall nuclear capability considerably.

The United States and Its Allies. Crucial to the U.S. balance-of-power policy was its alliance system. The heart of the system was the North Atlantic Treaty Organization (NATO); originating in 1949, NATO signatories affirmed that "an armed attack against one or more of them in Europe or North America shall be considered an attack against them all."[2]

Elsewhere in the world, the United States sought to protect its national interests with other treaties. It extended its protective arm against external aggression over Latin America with the Rio Pact, joined with Australia and New Zealand in the ANZUS Pact, and signed bilateral security treaties with Japan and the Philippines. The Southeast Asia Treaty Organization (SEATO), another Cold War security arrangement, dissolved at the end of the Vietnam War in 1975. In 1986, New Zealand objected to American nuclear warships in its ports, thus crippling ANZUS.

The Soviet Union and Its Allies. In the Warsaw Pact, the Soviet Union allied with Eastern European countries as a counterweight to NATO. The relationship between the Soviet Union and its European allies, however, was clearly coercive. The Soviet Union did not hesitate—as its invasions of Hungary (1956) and Czechoslovakia (1968) made clear—to intervene in its allies' internal affairs to ensure the continuation of reliable communist governments. In protecting its own national interests, the Soviet Union (presumably threatened by a united Germany, rearmed and allied with the West) perpetuated the division of Germany and used a rearmed East Germany as one of its Warsaw Pact allies, just as the United States, beginning in 1955, used a rearmed West Germany as its ally.

By the end of the 1980s, the Soviet Union had begun to reorder its priorities. Enormous resources had been expended in Cold War efforts around the world at the expense of the Soviet economy. Under Mikhail Gorbachev, the Soviets began to dramatically reduce their commitments. They withdrew their military forces from Afghanistan and cut their military and developmental assistance to Angola, Cuba, Ethiopia, Nicaragua, Vietnam, and other client states in the developing world.

Assessing the Cold War

How well did the post–World War II balance-of-power system function? Did it adequately protect the vital needs and fundamental interests of nation-states and of peoples in the global community? Did it further willing cooperation and peaceful resolution of disputes? Did it enhance security, liberty, justice, and welfare? While we have no simple answers to these questions, some replies are possible.

World War III did not erupt. The Soviet Union did not invade Western Europe or attack the United States. And the United States did not attack the Soviet Union or seek to upset any communist government in Eastern Europe. The mutual fear of a nuclear war, or even a conventional war that might escalate into a nuclear war, preserved the post–World War II settlement in Europe.

The Marshall Plan—American economic aid delivered to rebuild a war-ravaged Western Europe—was markedly successful. Assisting in this recovery not only made economic sense for the United States but also contributed to the strengthening of the Western power base as it squared off against the communist bloc in the East. Stimulated by the Marshall Plan, Western European countries banded together in the European Economic Community (EEC) (later renamed the European Union) to overcome former disastrous economic and political rivalries (particularly the Franco-German rivalry). Fear of the Soviet Union and the communization of Eastern Europe served to unite historical enemies (West Germany, France, and Britain) and to keep them in military, political, and economic concert with the United States, primarily through NATO and the EEC. Up to a point, then, these relationships enhanced security, liberty, justice, and welfare for all the contracting parties.

On the other hand, a heavily armed Western Europe, possessing nuclear weapons, created much anxiety. If deterrence failed and NATO used nuclear weapons to stop a conventional Soviet attack on Western Europe, the outcome would have been catastrophic.

As for the Soviet Union, it is now clear that its allies (more accurately, the people of Eastern Europe under communist governments) greatly resented the domination of the Soviet Union in the Warsaw Pact and in Comecon, the communist equivalent of the EEC. Certainly the Hungarian Revolution in 1956, the attempted liberalization of the Czech communist government in 1968, and the Solidarity movement in Poland in the 1980s suggested unhappiness with Soviet domination and no great sympathy with the Brezhnev Doctrine, which asserted the Soviet Union's responsibility to intervene in a communist country to prevent overthrow or liberalization. The dramatic events of 1989, which saw the overturning of Communist Party rule in most of Eastern Europe and the breaking down of the Berlin Wall, confirmed long-held suspicions that most citizens in Eastern Europe were highly dissatisfied with their subjugation.

REUTERS/Wolfgang Rattay

In November 1989, the Berlin Wall crumbled. Dividing the German capital into communist and noncommunist zones, it was perhaps the most striking symbol of the Cold War.

But what about cooperation, accommodation, and peaceful resolution of disputes between the superpowers themselves? During the late 1960s and early 1970s, a policy of **détente**—that is, the relaxation of tensions between nation-states—modestly relieved the worst aspects of the Cold War. The United States and the Soviet Union did agree (1) to stop testing nuclear weapons in the atmosphere; (2) to place no nuclear weapons in space; (3) to sign the Nuclear Non-Proliferation Treaty; (4) to limit the arms race as outlined in the Strategic Arms Limitation Talks (SALT) and reduce the number of strategic weapons through the Strategic Arms Reduction Talks (START); (5) to eliminate all intermediate range nuclear forces (INFs), about 4 percent of the nuclear weapons in their combined arsenals; and (6) to place limits on chemical and biological weapons.

In addition, the nations of East and West also agreed that some Jews could emigrate from the Soviet Union and that some citizens of East Germany could immigrate to West Berlin and West Germany. In the Helsinki Accords on human rights, the West accepted the status quo in Eastern Europe in exchange for human rights concessions from the Soviets. During the 1970s and early 1980s, before Gorbachev's rise to power, the degree of Soviet compliance—or noncompliance—with these agreements aroused considerable controversy in the United States.

Periods of relative calm and progress were, however, interrupted by crisis. In Chapter 2, we discussed the 1962 Cuban missile crisis, when the Soviets installed nuclear-tipped missiles just ninety miles off of Florida. Another crisis occurred in late 1979, when the Soviets invaded Afghanistan; the Soviet Union's prolonged military presence there adversely affected détente.

The Costs and Aftermath of the Cold War

Although it appears that the balance of power at least prevented World War III, the Cold War also had its costs: huge military expenditures, anxiety and fear over the balance of nuclear terror, harsh domination of peoples in Eastern Europe, an abuse of civil liberties in the 1950s as the United States sought out communists within its own borders, costly wars fought in Korea and Vietnam, and the perhaps ill-advised support of right-wing governments by the United States merely because these governments declared themselves anticommunist.

The end of the Cold War raised a critical question about the balance of power. Is the international system realigning itself into a new balance-of-power configuration? No crystal ball can answer this question, but several developments in recent years give some clues. First, the Cold War bipolar balance of power no longer exists. The Warsaw Pact was disbanded in 1991. In the immediate years following the collapse of the Soviet Union, NATO seemed to have lost its primary reason for being—the possible invasion of Western Europe by the forces of the Soviet Union and its Warsaw Pact allies. But as Russia rebuilds its military power and with its annexation of the Crimea Peninsula in Ukraine in 2014, NATO has, in fact, expanded its membership to include some Eastern European countries. In 2018, NATO members included Albania, Belgium, Bulgaria, Canada, Croatia, the Czech Republic, Denmark, Estonia, France, Germany, Greece, Hungary, Iceland, Italy, Latvia, Lithuania, Luxembourg, Montenegro, the Netherlands, Norway, Poland, Portugal, Romania, Slovakia, Slovenia, Spain, Turkey, the United Kingdom, and the United States. There are still some unresolved issues concerning the mission of NATO, beyond providing for European security. How far east should NATO expand its membership? Should NATO concern itself with security issues beyond Europe—for instance, the security of Middle Eastern oil fields?

Second, for roughly a decade the United States emerged as the only world super-power, most notably because of its unique ability to project military power beyond its shores for sustained periods of time. But as we shall soon note, China's rapid emergence as a global economic superstar and Russia's military build-up challenged the whole idea of the United States' status as the *only* superpower. Third, although the major powers still maintain enormous nuclear and conventional military establishments, the world increasingly defines power in economic terms. A new balance between enormous regional economic actors—individual states or regional blocs—may be emerging. We will look more closely at this pattern later in this chapter. Finally, we can make the argument that the diminution of state power has taken place concurrently with an increase in the power of nonstate actors such as multinational corporations (MNCs) and terrorist groups. Certainly, the al-Qaida attacks on New York's World Trade Center and the Pentagon are testament to the growing power of nonstate actors.

DOMINATION

Domination is the policy of exercising direct or indirect control over others. It may be enforced through imperial colonization, conquest, or the exertion of political and economic power. In the nineteenth and twentieth centuries, Great Britain, France, Holland, Belgium, Spain, Portugal, and, to a more limited degree, the United States (particularly in Latin America and the Philippines) practiced imperial colonization. During World War II, Germany and Japan made imperial conquests. Another variety of domination is illustrated by Soviet control in Eastern Europe from 1947 to 1989.

During the Cold War, observers accused the United States and the Soviet Union—and they accused each other—of seeking to dominate the globe. Critics of the Soviet Union built their arguments on communist rhetoric of worldwide triumph. The Soviet Union would achieve this objective, they claimed, in one or more ways: (1) by direct aggression or takeover (as in the absorption of Latvia, Lithuania, and Estonia in 1939); (2) with the help of local communists, fortified by the Red Army, as in Eastern Europe; (3) through peaceful means, as in France and Italy, where communists could poll large numbers of votes; (4) through subversion wherever it was to their advantage; and (5) by encouraging decolonization of the Western imperial regimes, supporting nationalism in the new states and elsewhere, and subsequently taking control in developing countries when communist power and the time were ripe. Similarly, communist and some noncommunist critics of the United States alleged U.S. plans to dominate the world through a capitalist conspiracy, using capitalist puppets to do the bidding of "imperialist" U.S. masters.

Both conspiratorial theories (although grounded here and there in the realities of the Soviet or American struggle for power) are far-fetched. In all probability, neither the United States nor the Soviet Union ever sought, or even had the power, to dominate the world. Given the geographical expanse of the world, its incredible cultural and religious complexity, and its enormous population, global domination by any power is, in fact, a practical impossibility.

Charges of regional domination or significant influence, in varying degrees, are somewhat more persuasive and need to be examined more fully. The Soviet Union dominated Eastern Europe for more than forty years. The United States exercised almost overwhelming influence, particularly economic, over Western Europe, Japan, Latin America, South Korea, and Formosa (Taiwan) for nearly fifteen years after World War II. Today, China moves boldly into the South China Sea establishing airfields and port facilities on the various island complexes in the region. In 2014, Russia annexed the Crimea peninsula, part of Ukraine, and has exercised military force in the Republic of Georgia. It has further put increasing pressure on other independent republics via the withholding of natural gas and the use of cyber attacks, all in an effort to reassert itself into republics that were once part of the Soviet Union.

But even regional domination is increasingly difficult in a world characterized by the rise of new major powers and changing economics. Within the communist world, the Soviet Union reigned supreme until China emerged in the 1950s. In 1989, the Soviets felt that, in view of their collapsing domestic economy, they could no longer afford the high cost of dominating Eastern Europe. Although the United States continues to wield considerable influence in Western Europe, Japan, Latin America, and other countries, it is far from dominating these areas. Indeed, China has recently shown a strong economic interest outside its borders, particularly in Southeast Asia, Latin America, and Africa. Increasingly, the United States must cooperate with its partners as equals, even though it can still limit some of their initiatives. But even this limited power is being eroded by the economic integration of Europe, which creates an immense economic actor that is far less vulnerable to U.S. influence. Even as U.S. military power remains preeminent, the economic strength of the country is equaled by that of a united Europe and will soon be matched and probably surpassed by that of China.

The issue of China's surge toward superpower status raises an interesting question. Should China continue its economic growth and major military build-up, would it conceivably replace the United States as the world's major power and what might be the consequences? One interesting take on this is by Graham Allison who in his book, *Destined for War*, posits that China's rise will probably result in such a shift and that has risks. Allison's focus is on **Thucydides's trap**. Thucydides was the ancient Greek historian and general who wrote about the origins of the war between Athens and Sparta. As Athens rose in power, Sparta became increasingly alarmed to the extent that war was inevitable. Allison examines sixteen cases in which a rising power threatened to displace a ruling power, including England and Holland in the seventeenth century, Germany and Britain in the early twentieth century, and Japan and the United States in the 1940s. In twelve of the sixteen cases, the destabilization of the power shift resulted in war. Though not inevitable, it would appear the Thucydides's trap is something to keep in mind as the world moves through what many believe to be a major power shift.[3]

MULTILATERALISM

Multilateralism involves groups of countries collectively solving problems and conflicts, usually through formal international organizations. These organizations may be global, such as the United Nations, or regional, such as the African Union (formerly, the Organization of African Unity) and the Organization of American States. They may be both regional and economic, such as the European Union, or resource based, such as the Organization of Petroleum Exporting Countries. Multilateralism is most often practiced through the day-to-day operations of international organizations. It can also be conducted through special conferences on any number of issues, ranging from **arms control** to AIDS to pollution of the world's oceans to women's rights to terrorism.

The basic motivation for a strong commitment to multilateralism remains the same, regardless of the problems being dealt with. Decision makers believe that their country's interests will best be protected or advanced through the collective efforts of governments. It is increasingly difficult for individual countries (or even two countries) to deal with the wide range of problems confronting the international system—disease, pollution, global warming, and human rights, to name a few. Most recently, the need for cooperation between states was evidenced in America's efforts to find allies in its global war on terrorism. Although other patterns—balance of power, domination—have not been abandoned in the international system, multilateralism is increasingly seen as a viable technique for advancing the security, liberty, justice, and welfare of states.

In this section, we examine two variations of multilateralism: the work of the United Nations and the economic integration of Europe. In doing so, we investigate the three Key Questions on this page.

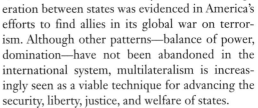

KEY QUESTIONS

1. Can the United Nations be a significant force for world peace?

2. Will regional integration and globalization continue to grow, or will it begin to reverse in the future?

3. Is globalization a force for good?

The United Nations in Theory and Practice

It would be a mistake either to overestimate or to ignore the rhetoric, purposes, and principles of the UN Charter, but they cannot substitute for a critical analysis of UN behavior. As we examine the United Nations (founded in 1945), we must consider its aspirations and ideals, but we must also look candidly at the realities of fulfillment—what the United Nations actually does.

The preamble to the Charter of the United Nations contains an inspiring vision of peoples in nations determined "to save succeeding generations from the scourge of war . . . to reaffirm faith in fundamental human rights . . . to promote social progress and better standards of life in larger freedom . . . to practice tolerance and live together in peace with one another as good neighbors . . . to unite our strength to maintain international peace and security."[4]

Article 1 elaborates on that vision in spelling out the purposes of the United Nations: "To maintain international peace and security . . . to develop friendly relations among nations based on respect for the principle of equal rights and self-determination of peoples . . . to achieve international cooperation in solving international problems of an economic, social, cultural, or humanitarian character, and in promoting and encouraging respect for human rights . . . to be a centre for harmonizing the actions of nations in the attainment of these common ends."

Article 2 lists some of the important principles that guide the United Nations. These guidelines include "the principle of the sovereign equality of all its Members"; a commitment to "settle their international disputes by peaceful means in such a manner that international peace and security, and justice, are not endangered . . . [and to] refrain in their international relations from the threat or use of force against the territorial integrity or political independence of any state"; and a recognition that "nothing contained in the present Charter shall authorize the United Nations to intervene in matters which are essentially within the domestic jurisdiction of any state." Theoretically, according to Article 4, membership in the United Nations is open to all "peace-loving states."

The major UN organs are the General Assembly, the Security Council, the Economic and Social Council, the Trusteeship Council (no longer very important), the International Court of Justice, and the Secretariat. These organs and their functions are outlined in Box 11.1. The only UN body that can pass resolutions with the force of international law is the Security Council. Because of the unique power vested in the council, each of the five permanent members has the right of veto, which means one negative vote from any of these five states defeats the resolution.

How has the United Nations functioned in practice? The United Nations has experimented with a number of approaches to peace—its primary concern—and to related concerns such as human rights, economic and social progress, and self-determination of peoples. Seven such approaches can be discerned: (1) collective security, (2) **peaceful settlement,** (3) **disarmament** and arms control, (4) **preventive diplomacy** (peacekeeping), (5) the **grand debate,** (6) **trusteeship** and **anticolonialism,** and (7) **functionalism.** We use these approaches to explain and illustrate the functioning of the United Nations.[5]

Basic Organization of the United Nations

BOX 11.1

General Assembly

- ☐ Includes all UN members

- ☐ Meets annually

- ☐ May make recommendations on any matter

International Court of Justice

- ☐ Consists of fifteen elected judges representing the world's legal traditions

- ☐ May arbitrate any dispute states are willing to submit to it

- ☐ Located in The Hague, Netherlands

Trusteeship Council

- ☐ Designed to help a number of non-self-governing territories, such as colonies, transition to independence

- ☐ In practice, has almost worked itself out of a job (only one trust territory remains—that of the Trust Territories of the Pacific, held by the United States)

Security Council

- ☐ Consists of fifteen members, five of whom are permanent: United States, United Kingdom, China, Russia, France

- ☐ Does not meet regularly

- ☐ Has primary responsibility for maintaining peace

Economic and Social Council

- ☐ Consists of fifty-four members

- ☐ Produces studies and reports dealing with economic and social issues such as human rights, development, and the environment

- ☐ Meets annually

Secretariat

- ☐ Administrative arm of the United Nations

- ☐ Headed by the secretary-general

- ☐ Staffed by international civil servants from around the world

Source: Compiled by authors.

The idea behind collective security is that all peace-loving nations, including the most powerful, will band together to maintain international peace and law and that they will use their collective strength to deter or punish aggressors who would violate international peace and law. The formation of the United Nations itself represented a move in the direction of collective security but only if the great powers that had banded together to defeat fascism and aggression in World War II could remain united. Given American-Soviet tensions and the veto that the superpowers had in the Security Council, genuine collective security was nearly impossible.

Even the collective action by the United Nations in the early 1950s to prevent a North Korean military takeover of South Korea proved a less-than-perfect example of collective security as envisaged in the UN Charter. The vote in favor of prevention was possible only because the Soviet Union was absent from the Security Council at the time and could not cast its certain veto against UN action on the Korean peninsula. When the Soviets returned, activity related to the "police action" was shifted to the General Assembly where the Soviets had no veto power. Moreover, a powerful police action became possible only because the United States was willing to deploy U.S. personnel and military arms. There is little doubt that the United States would have defended South Korea even if the United Nations had done nothing. In fact, the outcome of the Korean War was only a partial success for the United Nations: the North Koreans were prevented from taking over South Korea by force of arms, but Korea to this day remains divided.

The Iraqi invasion of Kuwait in 1990 constituted the first major post–Cold War international crisis, and for the first time in the history of the United Nations, the collective security machinery operated precisely the way it was designed to. In 1991, twelve Security Council resolutions were passed that together condemned Iraq for its invasion of Kuwait, established a worldwide economic embargo against Iraq, and authorized military action to enforce the embargo and, if necessary, to force Iraq to withdraw from Kuwait. Many observers considered this operation to be a major watershed for the United Nations, since the sanctions and military action were authorized under Chapter 7 of the UN Charter, the document's collective security provision. Under these resolutions, a U.S.-led coalition of military forces successfully forced Iraq to withdraw from Kuwait.

The military invasion of Afghanistan after 9/11 was not specifically mandated by the United Nations. But the UN Security Council did pass a resolution (Res. 1368) that condemned the attacks, labelled international terrorism as a threat to international peace and security, to take all necessary steps to respond to the 2001 attacks, and to combat all forms of terrorism. With this strong language, the United Nations brought international terrorism into the realm of collective security.[6]

Despite its success in the case of Iraq in 1991, however, the appeal of the United Nations to collective security for handling breaches of peace has been disappointing overall. Critics note the many instances in which the Security Council of the United Nations either failed to take meaningful action or did so belatedly and hence proved ineffective. The ethnic cleansing in Bosnia in 1992 and 1993, the Rwandan genocide of 1994, and the widespread rape and killing in Darfur in the Sudan from mid-2003 to 2011 are examples of UN failures.

Peaceful settlement employs inherited techniques such as influence, inquiry, mediation, and conciliation. Here the United Nations—whether through the General Assembly, the Security Council, the secretary-general, or the International Court of

Justice—functions as a third party in the dispute. But success depends on the disputants' willingness to allow the United Nations to work out a peaceful settlement. The techniques may work for unnecessary and essentially avoidable wars but not for the gravest threats to world peace and order.

The United Nations has attempted to facilitate peaceful settlement in a host of cases: for example, in Greece, Palestine, Indonesia, Kashmir, Afghanistan, Iran, and Iraq; in the Balkan conflict involving Serbia, Croatia, and Bosnia and Herzegovina; in the Sudan, where it has sought to resolve not one but two conflicts—the first between the northern Islamist government and the Christian southerners and the second between factions fighting in the Sudan's Darfur region. And most recently, it has attempted to seek a peaceful resolution in the Syrian civil war. The record is mixed. Peace came to Greece in the late 1940s less because of UN actions—aimed at stopping military aid for Greek communists seeking to overthrow the government—than because of U.S. military support for Greece under the Truman Doctrine and because of Yugoslavia's break with Moscow. UN efforts to achieve a peaceful partition of Palestine in 1947 did not succeed. War between Israel and its Arab neighbors broke out, and the region has suffered through a seemingly endless cycle of violence. But the United Nations has successfully facilitated a number of cease-fires and monitored adherence to them. The United Nations played an important role in ending hostilities between Indonesia and the Netherlands and in gaining Indonesian independence. In Kashmir, where Muslims claiming allegiance to Pakistan and Hindus loyal to India have slaughtered each other for decades, the United Nations has helped restrain more open and serious conflict but has not been able to achieve a definitive solution. The most promising developments took place when the United Nations negotiated the withdrawal of Soviet forces from Afghanistan in 1989 and when it mediated a cease-fire in the war between Iran and Iraq (1980–1988); these two efforts are widely considered major successes. In the Darfur region of Sudan, UN efforts resulted in agreements in 2006 and 2011, but the area remains tense, and UN peacekeepers are still present. In 2005, the United Nations had some success in negotiating a cease-fire and peace framework ending years of civil war between the northern Muslim and southern Christian Sudanese communities. In 2011, South Sudan became independent. Despite this success, the border between the two countries, Sudan and South Sudan, remains in the throes of considerable tension and periodic violence. In 2012, UN efforts to stop the terrible violence against protestors in Syria met with little success and the country plunged into terrible civil war. In sum, the United Nations has achieved mixed results in its efforts toward peaceful settlement. Still, the United Nations has acted to minimize violence, making violence less intense and less contagious than it might otherwise have been. To its critics, though, UN actions are often painfully slow.

The processes of arms control, or the negotiation and agreement to limit the production of weapons, and disarmament, or the negotiation and agreement to reduce or eliminate weapons, theoretically lead to peace by significantly reducing and ultimately limiting armaments. The United Nations has attempted to advance the causes of arms control and disarmament without major success. Neither the great powers nor their smaller counterparts have been willing to reduce their propensity for acquiring conventional weapons. As mentioned earlier, both the United States and the Soviet Union (now the Russian Republic) undertook meaningful nuclear disarmament within the framework of START, but this took place outside the auspices of the United Nations.

Dag Hammarskjöld, secretary-general of the United Nations from 1953 until his untimely death in 1961, was a major architect of preventive diplomacy, which, as designed by Hammarskjöld, involved action by the United Nations to help smaller powers settle disputes peacefully before they escalated and involved the United States and the Soviet Union in a dangerous confrontation. The primary mechanism used in preventive diplomacy has been peacekeeping, whereby a multinational UN military force intervenes between conflicting parties, usually at the point of cease-fire. Such UN intervention was designed to keep the superpowers out of conflicts in areas outside their crucial spheres of influence.

Preventive diplomacy can work only if the immediate parties to the dispute will accept the UN peacekeeping role and if the major powers on the Security Council go along with this role. Preventive diplomacy will not work, or will not work well, if one of the major powers with a Security Council veto opposes UN action. Current UN peacekeeping operations are shown in Box 11.2. A more extensive discussion of the UN peacekeeping role can be found in Chapter 12.

BOX 11.2

United Nations Peacekeeping Missions

- UN Truce Supervision Organization (since 1948)
- UN Military Observer Group in India and Pakistan (since 1949)
- UN Peacekeeping Force in Cyprus (since 1964)
- UN Disengagement Observer Force, Golan Heights, Syria (since 1974)
- UN Interim Force in Lebanon (since 1978)
- UN Mission for Referendum in Western Sahara (since 1991)
- UN Organization Mission in the Democratic Republic of the Congo (since 1999)
- UN Interim Administration Mission in Kosovo (since 1999)

- UN Mission in Liberia (since 2003)
- UN Stabilization Mission in Haiti (since 2004)
- African Union–United Nations Hybrid Operation in Darfur (since 2007)
- UN Mission in the Republic of South Sudan (since 2011)
- UN Interim Security Force for Abyei (since 2011)
- UN Multidimensional Integrated Stabilization Mission in Mali (since 2013)
- UN Multidimensional Integrated Stabilization Mission in the Central African Republic (since 2014)

Source: List compiled from the United Nations, 2018, https://peacekeeping.un.org/en.

By serving as an international forum for the grand debate—whereby problems can be raised, discussed, and analyzed; diplomats can meet and test ideas; and the strength of policies can be measured—the United Nations can modestly advance the cause of peace and other UN objectives. Through the constitutional processes of debate and voting, major issues facing the global community can be aired: the danger of nuclear holocaust; the struggle for national independence; ways to overcome poverty, ill health, and illiteracy; and ways to address violations of human rights. Through discussion, standards of international conduct can be articulated, policy propositions advanced, and education furthered. Global consciousness can be raised.

On the other hand, we should not expect too much. Talk is not always salutary; it may exaggerate and intensify mistrust. And UN resolutions are no substitute for peaceful settlement, or the resolution of disputes through such nonviolent means as influence, inquiry, mediation, and conciliation. Some states that find themselves politically isolated may feel beleaguered by the barrage of hostile UN resolutions (Israel is a good case in point) whereas developing nations (a majority in the UN General Assembly) may decline to censure a favored nation for its aggression, domination, or violation of human rights.

Trusteeship, which occurs when a developed nation, most often a colonial power, looks after dependent peoples and prepares them for independence and self-governance, has been an effective UN tool. The United Nations was entrusted with supervising the system of trusteeship and other non-self-governing territories that, a few years after the close of World War II, involved only eleven territories in Africa and some Pacific islands. The United Nations fulfilled its supervisory responsibility reasonably well and suspended operations in 1994 after the last remaining Trust Territory, Palau, achieved independence.

Anticolonialism is a political movement whereby colonies or former colonies become and remain independent nation-states able to govern themselves and achieve economic, social, and political progress. After World War II, the United Nations consistently sought protection of dependent peoples in their struggles with colonial powers. During the 1950s, 1960s, and 1970s, the United Nations functioned as a powerful protector as the process of anticolonialism progressed around the globe. With the adoption of the 1960 Declaration on the Granting of Independence to Colonial Countries and Peoples, the General Assembly emphatically declared that all people have a supreme right to national self-determination. The United Nations was an important, though not primary, cause of the gradual elimination of European empires in what we now call the developing world.

Functionalism is based on the premise that the barriers to cooperation and peaceful resolution of disputes can best be overcome when peoples and nations work together to meet common needs and advance mutual interests. These needs and interests involve practical problems such as trade and shipping, health and literacy, agriculture and fishing, aviation and broadcasting, and nuclear research and development and are primarily nonpolitical.[7] The United Nations has established specialized agencies (actually intergovernmental organizations) to address various functional issues (see Box 11.3).

Specialized Agencies of the United Nations

- Food and Agriculture Organization (FAO)
- International Civil Aviation Organization (ICAO)
- International Fund for Agricultural Development (IFAD)
- International Labour Organization (ILO)
- International Maritime Organization (IMO)
- International Monetary Fund (IMF)
- International Telegraphic Union (ITU)
- UN Educational, Scientific, and Agency Cultural Organization (UNESCO)
- UN Industrial Development Organization (UNIDO)

- Universal Postal Union (UPU)
- World Health Organization (WHO)
- World Intellectual Property Organization (WIPO)
- World Bank Group (WBG): International Bank for Reconstruction and Development (IBRD), International Development Association (IDA), International Finance Corporation (IFC), Multilateral Investment Guarantee Agency (MIGA), International Centre for Settlement of Investment Disputes (ICSID)
- World Meteorological Organization (WMO)
- World Tourism Organization (UNWTO)

Source: List compiled from United Nations, 2015, http://www.un.org/Overview/uninbrief/institutions.shtml

All of these organizations contribute to peace by addressing what some people consider the root causes of war: poverty, illiteracy, disease, and distrust. Some of the work of these agencies along with other special funds and programs is very impressive. The United Nations has eradicated smallpox; immunized millions of children; and funded more than 4,000 projects, including schools, health clinics, communications systems, and food preservation and processing facilities. It has taken the lead in the global fight against AIDS and in efforts to preserve the earth's ozone layer. The successes are heartening, but it is by no means clear that these programs have dealt with the real political problems that create national rivalry, conflict, and war. Still, without the work of the United Nations and its agencies, distress among peoples would probably be greater and tensions more likely to erupt into conflict.

How do we assess the UN contribution to security, liberty, justice, and welfare for the peoples of the globe? Although the system of bipolar balance of power between the United States and the Soviet Union was probably most responsible for preventing a nuclear World War III, the United Nations was able, under extraordinary circumstances, to prevent North Korea from overrunning South Korea. At the same time, it proved unable to bring peace to Vietnam or to prevent any number of conflicts (for example, the Israeli-Arab, India-Pakistan, and Bosnian conflicts, and the civil war in Syria). Its peacekeeping activities, nevertheless, have at times successfully mitigated grave crises. In some instances, as in Indonesia and Kashmir, the UN good offices have either brought peace or reduced violence.

While the United Nations probably spurred movements for national independence in the developing world, it was incapable of preventing Soviet domination of Eastern

Europe or U.S. interference in Chile and elsewhere. The United Nations has raised a standard of human rights throughout the world, although this did not prevent violations in places such as Argentina, Cambodia (Kampuchea), South Africa, the Soviet Union, Rwanda, Bosnia, Myanmar, or Sudan.

Through its functional agencies, the United Nations has contributed greatly to the battle against poverty, disease, and illiteracy—particularly in many developing countries. These activities, while promising, are still inadequate and have not yet acted to dissolve the political rivalries that lead to war.

Regional Integration

Space does not permit us to explore the many and varied regional organizations in the world today. But special attention must be given to at least one such organization—one that has by and large successfully undertaken a functional approach to peace and economic prosperity and, perhaps in the future, to political union. The **European Union** is a regional organization built on a foundation of free trade that seeks total European economic integration. Created after World War II, the European Union emerged from the U.S. Marshall Plan, which sought a reinvigorated Europe organized around economic cooperation and development. The European Union also has roots in the European Coal and Steel Community of 1952, which was designed to tie France and West Germany together economically. In the Treaty of Rome (1957), six nations of Western Europe (Belgium, France, Italy, Luxembourg, the Netherlands, and West Germany) established the EEC and the European Atomic Energy Community (EURATOM). These six nations sought to establish a common market among themselves and a common tariff toward other countries. Their goal was to abolish "obstacles to the free movement of persons, services and capital." They believed that by establishing common agricultural and transport policies they could improve employment and raise the standard of living in member nations.

In 1986, twelve countries of Western Europe (Belgium, Denmark, France, Greece, Ireland, Italy, Luxembourg, the Netherlands, Portugal, Spain, the United Kingdom, and West Germany), building on the success of the EEC, signed the Single European Act (SEA). In doing so, they committed themselves to complete economic integration by the end of 1992. If the unification had been successful by the target date, the collective market would have had a gross national product exceeding that of Japan, South Korea, Taiwan, Hong Kong, and Singapore combined.

Although full integration was not reached by 1992, enormous progress was nevertheless made. In 1994, the three original organs of the movement—the European Coal and Steel Community, EURATOM, and the EEC—collectively adopted the designation of the European Union. The European Union (whose membership as of 2012 is depicted in Map 11.1) has not entirely overcome nationalistic rivalries or mistrust, but it has enhanced economic strength and relative prosperity in Western Europe. Even though the dream of full European economic integration has yet to be fully met, it certainly is in view. The most recent accomplishment, in 2001, was adoption of the European currency (the euro) and, in 2002, its introduction into general circulation.

As successful as the European Union has been, there have been severe strains on the organization. One of the most challenging emerged as a result of what is known as the

Map 11.1 The European Union

GREENLAND
(DENMARK)

ICELAND

SWEDEN

FINLAND

NORWAY

ESTONIA

RUSSIA

LATVIA

LITHUANIA

DENMARK

IRELAND

BELARUS

UNITED KINGDOM

NETHERLANDS

POLAND

BELGIUM

GERMANY

UKRAINE

LUXEMBOURG

CZECH REPUBLIC

SLOVAKIA

MOLDOVA

AUSTRIA

HUNGARY

FRANCE

SWITZERLAND

SLOVENIA

CROATIA

ROMANIA

BOSNIA AND HERZEGOVINA

SERBIA

KOSOVO

BULGARIA

ITALY

MONTENEGRO

MACEDONIA

TURKEY

PORTUGAL

SPAIN

ALBANIA

GREECE

CYPRUS

MALTA

- EU member states
- EU candidate countries
- EU potential candidates

Source: CQ Press/Authors.

European sovereign-debt crisis. European Union and member state economists became particularly alarmed in 2009 when the debt levels of some member countries became so severe that there were serious questions as to whether some national debts could be paid. The most severely affected countries were Greece, Ireland, and Portugal. In May of 2010, the European finance ministers approved a rescue package worth 750 billion euros in an effort to gain greater financial stability in the region, but the crisis continued well into 2012, and despite these and other efforts, the economies of many European countries remained frustratingly sluggish well into 2014. Economic problems were particularly severe in Greece with general unemployment running 28 percent and among young people as high as 60 percent. Since the economic crash of 2008, the country was plagued by constant rounds of strikes and protest demonstrations over strict austerity measures and the European Union and the International Monetary Fund (IMF) prepared three separate bailout programs to try and stabilize the country's economy. The crisis was so severe that it brought into question Greece's continued membership in the European Union.

One of the more important questions raised by the economic crisis in Europe in the early part of this decade is whether economic integration is possible without political integration. In other words, would it have been prudent for the European Union to create a governing council of some sort that had real decision-making power? The existent political body, the European Parliament, is very weak due to member states' desire to maintain their sovereignty.

Another source of strain has been Britain's relationship within the organization reflected in what is known as Brexit, British exit from the European Union. On June 23, 2016, the people of Britain voted 51.9 percent to 48.1 percent to leave the Union. London as well as other major urban centers voted to remain in the EU along with Northern Ireland and Wales. It was in the rural and suburban areas that the vote was clearly in favor of leaving.[8] The actual separation and the conditions surrounding the exit have been subject to long and complicated negotiations with the final break scheduled from March 2019 to December 31, 2020. The reasons for the vote are fairly clear. Many British citizens just do not believe that the EU is a viable economic system, that among other things the differences in economic viability among the member states is just too vast and that Britain was not benefiting from its membership. A second reason for the vote can be broadly characterized as the protection of national sovereignty. For those supporting separation from the Union, membership involved forfeiting just too much national control. Subsumed under this sovereignty argument was the increased nationalism sweeping Europe and the fear of foreign immigration, particularly from North Africa, the Middle East, and South Asia. Indeed, the results of the nationwide British Social Attitudes Survey were published in June of 2017. They revealed that 73 percent of citizens who are worried about immigration voted to leave the EU, while 36 percent of those who did not identify this as a concern voted to leave.[9]

Globalization

Globalization—the rapid and explosive increase in integrative international economic activity—is a term that has risen to great prominence in recent years. For students of globalization, it describes a phenomenon based primarily on the twin pillars of capitalism and high-tech communications. But others have a more expansive definition taking into account the global spread of international travel, cultural endeavors, and politics characterized by the growth of both intergovernmental and nongovernmental organizations. Perhaps its most notable characteristic is the enormous increase in international economic integration and interdependence—in trade, banking, transportation, and investment—that has characterized the past thirty years. The trade figures alone are staggering. The volume of international trade as measured by world merchandise exports has realized a stunning increase in the period since World War II (see Figure 11.2).

As Thomas Friedman notes in *The Lexus and the Olive Tree*, this is not the first era of globalization. "From the mid 1800s to the late 1920s, the world experienced a similar era of globalization. . . . [W]hat is new today is the degree and intensity with which the world is being tied together into a single globalized marketplace. What is also new is the sheer number of people and countries able to partake of this process and be affected by it." Friedman goes on to note that a second element differentiating modern globalization

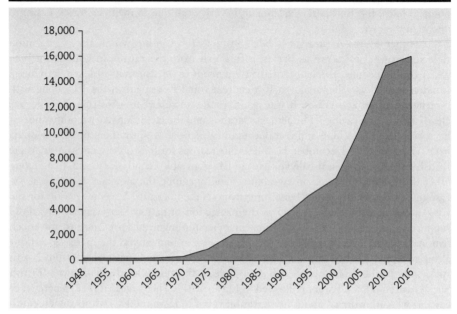

Figure 11.2 Values and Shares of Merchandise Exports and Imports, 1948–2016 (U.S. dollars at current prices and unit exchange rates in millions)

Source: United Nations Conference on Trade and Development, 2018, http://unctadstat.unctad.org/wds/TableViewer/tableView.aspx?ReportId=101.

from its predecessor is computer-based rapid telecommunications.[10] The Internet, cell phones, satellite-based relays—these are the tools that facilitate the enormous increase in global economic integration.

What impact does globalization have on the relations between countries of the world? While space does not permit us an exhaustive examination of this question, we list some pertinent observations made by students of globalization:

1. *A challenge to sovereignty.* Globalization may constitute a threat to sovereignty. A globalized world is one in which countries become increasingly interdependent, and the more we depend on others, the less freedom of movement we have. An example of the global impact of interdependence is the financial collapse of 2008 and 2009 that began in the United States and rapidly spread, becoming a worldwide phenomenon within weeks. Furthermore, a globalized world facilitates the rise of powerful independent nonstate economic actors such as MNCs (discussed in the next section). Finally, the enormously complex, high-speed, computer-based, global communications network is leading to greater transparency. In other words, it is becoming increasingly difficult for countries to hide abuses and isolate themselves from the international system. In June 2009, the world witnessed a poignant example of this in the aftermath of Iran's presidential elections. Protesters were able to use cell phones and the Internet to communicate their anger and

frustrations to a watching world. All of these forces associated with globalization tend to erode sovereignty.

2. *Political instability.* Globalization is a high-speed phenomenon, and some people, countries, perhaps even regions of the world may be left behind. The "have nots" of globalization, those that do not benefit from the enormous profits and increase in standard of living that it can generate, become resentful, angry, perhaps violent, and lash out at forces over which they have little control. This kind of backlash movement has the potential to foment various forms of political instability—riots, rebellions, revolution, terrorism, even war.

3. *Environmental degradation and the plight of labor.* While globalization in one sense can lead to greater order in the world, no central authority governs policies and practices. As a result, excesses are inevitable. One area of great concern is environmental degradation brought on by rapid, unregulated growth in manufacturing facilities, such as those in Mexico along the border with Texas. Another concern has been the treatment of labor. One aspect of this problem is that manufacturing companies enjoy a mobility that labor forces do not have. Entire groups of workers in a country can be left destitute as companies move from country to country in a never-ending search for lower costs and higher profits.

OTHER FORMS OF BEHAVIOR: NEUTRALITY, NONALIGNMENT, AND ISOLATION

Neutrality, nonalignment, and **isolation** are state policies not widely practiced in today's world. While we will not engage in a lengthy assessment of their efficacy, they are nevertheless worth defining. Neutrality is a legally based policy of remaining nonaligned with adversaries for the duration of a war, as Switzerland did during World War II. It can also be practiced in times of peace by the taking of an officially neutral position on a variety of international issues. Isolation is a policy of withdrawal from, and nonparticipation in, world affairs. While recently emerging from its shell, Burma (Myanmar) is one example of a country that attempted to maintain a high degree of isolation for several decades. In general, isolation is an extremely difficult policy to maintain in an age of globalization. Nonalignment, the refusal of states to participate in the struggle between major powers or superpowers, was a policy many nation-states in the developing world adopted during the Cold War. Unlike isolation, it is not necessarily a policy of abstention from world affairs. Nor does it mean, as does the concept of neutrality, that these countries refuse to express preferences in conflict situations. Quite the contrary, nonaligned nations feel a positive responsibility to protect their national freedom and independence, to guard against the dangers of a hot war that will engulf them, and to actively fight for economic and social advancement.

NONSTATE ACTORS

Our treatment of the patterns of international behavior has focused on nation-states and their organizations. But students of politics must be aware of other actors in the international system who are playing increasingly important roles.

Nongovernmental Organizations

A **nongovernmental organization (NGO)** is a private, international actor whose purpose and activity parallel those of domestic interest groups. Many are small, grass-roots organizations working in the rural small towns and villages of poor, developing countries. Others situate themselves in crowded, poverty-ridden urban centers. Still others are spread across continents with hundreds of thousands of members operating within elaborate organizational structures. The foci of NGOs are incredibly varied: cultural preservation, human rights, trade, labor conditions, education, women's rights, health, social services, children's rights, disaster relief, economic development, environment, law, and public advocacy. NGOs attempt to raise public awareness, affect public opinion, and influence the policies of states.

Some of these groups, such as the Anti-Slavery International (fighting slavery), the Union pour le Suffrage des Femmes (the French Alliance of Women's Suffrage, promoting women's suffrage), and the International Red Cross (aiding in disaster relief), have their origins in the progressivism of the middle and late 1800s through the early 1900s. Until recently, the number of NGOs has been small. Roughly a century ago, they numbered perhaps 400. Their growth in recent years has been staggering. In the early 1990s, they numbered perhaps 8,000. Estimates today place the number of NGOs at anywhere between 26,000 and 40,000, with individual membership running well into the millions. It should be noted that this phenomenal increase in the number of NGOs has been facilitated by the revolution in computer-based communications, which has eased not just their formation but their actual efforts as well.

One of the most successful NGOs in the world is Doctors Without Borders (Médecins Sans Frontières), a French-founded organization and recipient of the Nobel Peace Prize. It is noted for sending medical teams into some of the most dangerous, war-torn regions of the world.

The NGO community has been particularly effective in a number of areas. Certainly in the monitoring of human rights, organizations such as Amnesty International and Human Rights Watch have had an enormous impact. NGOs were instrumental in pushing for the establishment of the International Criminal Court (ICC) in 2000. They have also had a large presence at some of the better-known global conferences, such as the 1995 World Conference on Women held in Beijing and the 1992 Earth Summit held in Río de Janeiro, where some 1,500 NGOs were present. Organizations like Oxfam that specialize in development have begun to forge working relationships with the World Bank. Finally, the NGO relief organizations played a critical role in relieving the suffering caused by the tsunami that devastated Southeast Asia in 2005.[11]

Terrorist Organizations

As of early 2018, the U.S. State Department listed sixty-one fully active terrorist organizations around the world. These range in size from very small, regionally based organizations to groups such as al-Qaida, which may have several thousand followers working in cells all over the world.[12]

It is difficult to make a case that these groups in any way advance international security, liberty, justice, and welfare. As the September 11, 2001, attacks on New York's World Trade Center and the Pentagon so aptly illustrate that terrorism is incredibly destructive in many ways. The cost in human and economic terms is enormous, not to mention terrorism's potential as a politically destabilizing force.

Although terrorism was brought home to the people of the United States by the 9/11 attacks, it has been an ongoing problem elsewhere around the globe for decades and one that continues into the present, as evidenced by attacks against the Madrid transit system in 2004; the London transit system in 2005; the Egyptian resort complex at Sharm el-Sheikh, also in 2005; and the multiple suicide and remote bombings in Indonesia and Pakistan over the past few years. There were also horrible school bombings in northwestern Pakistan in 2014 as well as the kidnapping of over 400 young schoolgirls in Nigeria by the group Boko Haram in the same year. One of the most vicious attacks occurred in 2008 in Mumbai, India. Eleven coordinated shootings and bombings were carried out across the city, killing over 160 people. Terrorist attacks in the United States and Europe were particularly devastating in the years 2015, 2016, and 2017. Over those three years, some 13 attacks in the United States resulted in 85 deaths. In Europe, major attacks took place in Brussels, Belgium; Nice, Normandy, and Paris in France; and London and Manchester in Great Britain. And, of course, there were and still are numerous terrorist bombings in Iraq and Afghanistan. Because terrorism is such a destructive and destabilizing force, the student of politics would do well to further study its origins and effects.[13]

The Case of the Islamic State of Iraq and Syria

As noted in Chapter 4, ISIS (the Islamic State of Iraq and Syria; also known as ISIL, the Islamic State of Iraq and the Levant) is a splinter group emerging from al-Qaida and the chaos of the Syrian civil war of 2014. As of late 2015, the group had seized significant territory in northern Syria and northwestern Iraq, and its presence had begun to spread to Libya in North Africa as well as Yemen. An extreme jihadist group, it was particularly barbaric in its treatment of nonbelievers, beheading numerous people who they have held in captivity, including Japanese construction workers, Coptic Christians from Egypt, and American aid workers. It also practiced the buying and selling of young girls as wives for members of its army. By any measure, ISIS had become a threat to regional stability in the Middle East and both Arab countries in the region as well as the broader international community struggle to confront the organization.

In August of 2014, American warplanes began airstrikes against ISIS positions in northern Iraq, and a month later, President Obama put together a coalition of U.S. and Arab allies, including several NATO members, to expand the bombing campaign in support of largely Iraqi and Kurdish ground forces. Eventually, Russia, allied with Bashar al-Assad, the president of Syria, joined the fight but divided its bombing efforts between striking ISIS and Syrian rebel forces opposed to Assad. After months of brutal fighting, the tide began to turn against ISIS, and in October 2017, the Syrian city of Raqaa, the most important power center for ISIS, fell to coalition forces. For all intents and purposes, this marked the defeat of ISIS in Syria and Iraq. It did not, however, mean the end of ISIS. Though seriously depleted by its defeat in Syria and Iraq, in 2017 alone, ISIS carried out or inspired terrorist attacks in Turkey, Afghanistan, Pakistan, Bangladesh, the United Kingdom, Egypt, France, Philippines, Indonesia, Australia, Iran, Spain, and Canada killing over 1,500 and wounding over 7,000 people.

Multinational Corporations

Over the past several decades, perhaps the most powerful nonstate actor has been the large **multinational corporation (MNC)**, a private company such as General Motors, Exxon, SONY, Royal Dutch Shell, or IBM operating in more than one country. If you included nations and corporations on the same list, of the 100 largest economies in the world, thirty-seven are MNCs.[14] The MNC has been both extravagantly praised and witheringly censured. On one hand, it has been commended for its vision of a global market, its recognition of international economic interdependence, its ability to get things done, and its contribution to profits and economic development. On the other hand, it has been accused of exploiting peoples and nations, interfering in nations' internal affairs, and holding back human progress.

How does the MNC affect security, liberty, justice, and welfare around the globe? Does it contribute to voluntary cooperation, humane accommodation, and peaceful resolution of conflicts? Despite its global economic perspective, the MNC lacks the political vision and power to resolve political conflicts or to promote security, liberty, justice, or welfare in the global community. Its primary business is, after all, business: to generate profit for its stockholders. To the extent that profit making is compatible with the security, liberty, justice, and welfare of the peoples in the communities in which it does business, the MNC may enhance these objectives, but they are not its primary objectives. Indeed, profit making may, in fact, lead the MNC to act contrary to those goals. In addition, the MNC is not a political organ; it is a private, elitist organization. And MNCs have often meddled in countries to the detriment of their independence and integrity and to the detriment of the poor in these countries. Chile is a good case in point. There is reliable evidence to support the charge that U.S. corporate actions (those of International Telephone and Telegraph, specifically), in league with the CIA, tried to prevent the democratic election of Salvador Allende Gossens in 1970.

MNCs may play an important role in enhancing global prosperity, but nations must guard against MNC abuses and in fact do so through the passage of regulatory legislation. Ideally, the activities of MNCs should be coordinated with larger developmental purposes and their vision broadened to include the creation of a global mass market based on the fulfillment of human needs. However, because MNCs are not philanthropic organizations and are not responsible political organizations, it is unlikely that these objectives can be fulfilled without government mandate.

CONCLUSION

The global community lacks agreement on fundamentals, except, perhaps, on the horrors of all-out nuclear war. Although the United Nations has emerged as a forum for addressing vital needs and interests, establishing priorities, and legitimizing decisions, it was not intended to be, and does not function as, a global government. Other patterns of politics, such as working through alliances in the balance of power, have achieved only partial success. So how should we assess our guiding hypothesis—that, despite some successes, present international patterns do not yet adequately protect the vital needs and fundamental interests of all nations and peoples?

The bipolar balance of power that existed throughout much of the mid- through late-twentieth century probably prevented an American–Soviet war—a globally devastating World War III fought with nuclear weapons. Yet the peace thus secured for forty-five years was fragile and purchased at a heavy price. This price included the buildup of massively destructive armaments, the domination of Eastern Europe, and conflicts in Berlin and Cuba that were so destabilizing to the bipolar balance that they brought us within a hair's breadth of World War III. There was also the heavy price paid by the developing world, whose struggles for independence almost invariably intertwined with the superpowers' own global interests in a way that led to instability and violence in the so-called third world. Thus, it is fair to say that within the system of bipolar balance of power the vital needs and fundamental interests of Americans or Russians—or of other peoples and nations around the globe—were protected at enormous cost and risk. With the end of the Cold War, the world took a step back from the nuclear abyss. But even so, the continuing proliferation on a multinational scale of these terrible WMDs may once again draw us back to the edge.

Our assessment of balance of power does not appear to offer great hope. Does multilateralism offer more hope—and less risk? Our answer is a qualified yes. The United Nations has set laudable standards for peace, liberty, and economic and social justice and, through its varied approaches to peace, has achieved modest success in a number of cases. It defeated military aggression in two important instances (North Korea in the early 1950s and Iraq's invasion of Kuwait in 1991). The United Nations has promoted peace in Indonesia and Kashmir and was able to keep the superpowers from confronting each other in the Congo, Cyprus, the Middle East, and parts of South Asia. The United Nations has helped dozens of developing countries advance from colonies to independent nations and has aided them in their fights against disease, illiteracy, and famine. It has promoted the economic development of many new states and provided a valuable forum for airing global problems. Today, it plays an increasingly important role in places such as Afghanistan, Angola, Cambodia, Central America, Iran, Iraq, Namibia, and Sudan to bring about and maintain stability and peace. Despite these successes, however, the United Nations did not deal effectively with East–West tensions or prevent dozens of countries from descending into vicious cycles of civil war based on ethnic and religious differences. Nor did the United Nations facilitate political accommodation that might have led to real peace and disarmament in the world.

The European Union has taken significant steps to overcome historic military struggles among its members and to advance economic and political integration. It remains to be seen if these promising results to date can be successfully extended to the rest of Europe.

With the qualification that some forces of multilateralism—an enhanced United Nations, greater economic integration—have had salutary consequences, we must nevertheless conclude that present international patterns do not adequately protect the vital needs and fundamental interests of all peoples and nations. Can we do better? We return to this question in Part IV. In the meantime, we can benefit from a fuller consideration of models and patterns of political decision making.

SUGGESTED READINGS

Allison, Graham. *Destined for War: Can America and China Escape Thucydides's Trap?* New York: Houghton Mifflin Harcourt, 2017. A thoughtful book on the potential destabilizing consequences of one power challenging and replacing another.

Bremmer, Ian. *Every Nation for Itself: Winners and Losers in a G-Zero World.* New York: Portfolio, 2012. Paints a rather bleak portrait of the global landscape, a world without leadership. New powers emerge like Brazil, China, and India, and the world is increasingly plagued by, as Bremmer puts it, "problems without borders."

Collett, Derek, and Samantha Power, eds. *The Unquiet American: Richard Holbrooke in the World.* New York: PublicAffairs, 2011. A series of essays about one of America's most brilliant diplomats, who met an untimely death in 2010.

Dougherty, James E., and Robert I. Pfaltzgraff. *Contending Theories of International Relations: A Comprehensive Survey.* 5th ed. New York: Longman, 2009. One of the most comprehensive, well-organized, and lucid surveys of the major theories of international relations.

Heilmann, Sebastian, and Dirk H. Schmidt. *China's Foreign Political and Economic Relations: An Unconventional Global Power.* New York: Rowman & Littlefield Publishers, Inc., 2014. A balanced and thoughtful analysis of Chinese foreign relations.

Kaplan, Robert D. *The Return of Marco Polo's World.* New York: Random House, LLC, 2018. A series of very interesting essays on the ever-shifting international system by a very thoughtful journalist, historian, and strategic thinker. The first essay on the rise of Eurasia is particularly relevant.

Kissinger, Henry. *Diplomacy.* New York: Simon & Schuster, 1994. A lucid account from the former U.S. secretary of state and national security adviser on the history of diplomacy, with special emphasis on the role of power.

Koops, Joachim, ed. *The European Union as a Diplomatic Actor.* New York: Palgrave Macmillan, 2014. A series of informative and thoughtful essays assessing the diplomatic role of the European Union in the fields of security, human rights, trade and finance, and environment.

Morgenthau, Hans J. *Politics Among Nations: The Struggle for Power and Peace.* 6th ed. Revised by Kenneth Thompson. New York: McGraw, 1985. Classic text that articulates the position of the most influential "realist" in international politics. Morgenthau strongly defended the standard of an enlightened national interest.

National Commission on Terrorist Attacks Upon the United States. *The 9/11 Commission Report.* New York: Norton, 2005. Extremely readable and gripping account of the 9/11 attacks on the World Trade Center and the Pentagon. Penetrating analysis that leads to a series of recommendations for strengthening the nation's security infrastructure and intelligence community.

Shawcross, William. *Deliver Us From Evil: Peacekeepers, Warlords, and a World of Endless Conflict.* New York: Simon & Schuster, 2000. A gripping, firsthand account of the international community, particularly the United Nation's struggle to confront a post–Cold War world characterized by ethnic conflict, massacres, and endless streams of refugees.

Waltz, Kenneth. *Man, the State, and War: A Theoretical Analysis.* New York: Columbia University Press, 1959. A classic statement on the cause of war.

Weiss, Thomas G., David P. Forsythe, Roger A. Coate, and Kelly-Kate Pease. *The United Nations and Changing World Politics.* Boulder, CO: Westview Press, 2007. A well-written and comprehensive textbook on the operations of the United Nations in today's world.

Zakaria, Fareed. *The Post-American World.* New York: Norton, 2009. A thoughtful discussion of the diffusion of power in the world and how the United States will increasingly be only one of several powerful actors in the international system.

GLOSSARY TERMS

anticolonialism (p. 293)
arms control (p. 291)
balance of power (p. 283)
bipolarity (p. 286)
collective security (p. 284)
détente (p. 288)
disarmament (p. 293)
domination (p. 283)
European Union (p. 299)
functionalism (p. 293)

globalization (p. 282)
grand debate (p. 293)
hard power (p. 284)
hegemony (p. 286)
isolation (p. 303)
multilateralism (p. 283)
multinational corporation
  (MNC) (p. 306)
multipolarity (p. 286)
neutrality (p. 303)

nonalignment (p. 303)
nongovernmental organization
  (NGO) (p. 304)
peaceful settlement (p. 293)
preventive diplomacy (p. 293)
soft power (p. 284)
Thucydides's trap (p. 291)
trusteeship (p. 293)

NOTES

1. Joseph Nye offers an extensive discussion of soft and hard power in his thoughtful book *Bound to Lead: The Changing Nature of American Power* (New York: Basic Books, 1990).

2. Article 5, North Atlantic Charter, Washington, DC, April 4, 1949, www.nato.int/doc/basictxt/treaty.htm.

3. Graham Allison. *Destined for War: Can America and China Escape Thucydides's Trap?* (New York: Houghton Mifflin Harcourt, 2017).

4. The Charter of the United Nations, www.un.org/en/documents/charter.

5. Here we follow the excellent analysis of Inis Claude Jr., *Swords into Plowshares: The Problems and Progress of International Organizations*, 4th ed. (New York: Random House, 1984), 236–365. We draw, too, from Claude's equally keen analysis in *Power and International Relations* (New York: Random House, 1962). The analysis has been historically updated with the help of such fine texts as Thomas G. Weiss et al., *The United Nations and Changing World Politics*, 5th ed. (Boulder, CO: Westview Press, 2007).

6. Ben Smith and Arabelle Thorp, "The Legal Basis for the Invasion of Afghanistan," International Affairs and Defence Section, Library House of Commons, UK, 26 Feb., 2010.

7. Two classic works on functionalism are David Mitrany, *A Working Peace System* (Chicago: Quadrangle Books, 1966); and Ernst B. Haas, *Beyond the Nation-State: Functionalism and International Organization* (Stanford, CA: Stanford University Press, 1964).

8. Andrew McGill, "Who Voted for Brexit?," *The Atlantic*, June 25, 2016. https://www.theatlantic.com/international/archive/2016/06/brexit-vote-statistics-united-kingdom-european-union/488780/

9. May Bulman, "Brexit: People voted to leave EU because they feared immigration, major survey finds," *Independent*, 28 June 2017. http://www.independent.co.uk/news/uk/home-news/brexit-latest-news-leave-eu-immigration-main-reason-european-union-survey-a7811651.html

10. Thomas L. Friedman, *The Lexus and the Olive Tree: Understanding Globalization* (New York: Farrar, Straus and Giroux, 1999), xiv.

11. See Brad Knickerbocker, "Nongovernmental Organizations Are Fighting and Winning Social, Political Battles," *Christian Science Monitor*, February 6, 2000; James A. Paul, "NGOs and Global Policy-Making," *Global Policy Forum*, June 2000; Michael Hill, "The NGO Phenomenon," *Baltimore Sun*, January 9, 2005.

12. U.S. Department of State, "Foreign Terrorist Organizations," 2018, www.state.gov/j/ct/ris/other/des/123085.htm.

13. Ibid.

14. Transnational Institute, State of Power 2014, www.tni.org/sites/www.tni.org/files/download/state-of-power-6feb.pdf.

POLITICAL JUDGMENT
AND PUBLIC POLICY

In Part IV, we turn our attention to a third major concern of political science: the development of political wisdom in the public policy arena. How can we sharpen our prudent judgment on key issues of public policy? In the following chapters, we explore the prudential component of political science—the component concerned with wise judgment—by critically examining key issues of public policy. In dealing with such issues as war and peace in the modern world (Chapter 12), the battle on behalf of human rights (Chapter 13), the struggle for economic well-being (Chapter 14), and the imperative of ecological health (Chapter 15), we encourage you to study political judgment and public policy in light of what you have learned about political philosophy in Part II and about the real world of politics in Part III.

As you read, we challenge you to identify and articulate the guiding ethical values that are so crucial to political philosophy and ideology. You will also be asked to assess empirical findings relevant to a science of politics. Prudent judgments—wise judgments—draw on a critical understanding of ethical values and empirical realities. Political actors must act both with purpose and with pragmatism. Prudent judgment also demands a balance between oftentimes competing principles—for example, maintaining freedom while ensuring equality—in deciding issues of public policy.

The chapters in Part IV should thus engage your judgment on a number of controversial problems of the present and the future. These are some of the real challenges of politics: war, violations of human rights, the persistence of poverty, and the environmental degradation of the planet. In addressing momentous issues of public policy, we first explore ethical and empirical factors that help to define each problem. We then identify alternative approaches to the problems and the strengths and weaknesses of those approaches. In setting forth alternative approaches, we must remain alert to the possibility of what we call creative breakthroughs—innovative responses to tough problems that conventional wisdom says cannot be solved. We do not offer these potential creative breakthroughs in order to advance a political agenda. Rather, they are designed to stimulate your thinking concerning possible solutions to difficult problems.

Creative political breakthroughs are rare in history. Roger Williams's concepts of religious tolerance and liberty might be thought of as creative breakthroughs, as might James Madison's formula for the design of a republic with a strong central government that is still able to maintain liberty, self-government, and justice at the state and local levels

Harry Truman's adoption of the Marshall Plan at the end of World War II demonstrated incredible foresight in advancing economic welfare as well as security in Europe and the United States. Under intense pressure, President John F. Kennedy's use of a quarantine as an alternative to a potentially disastrous military strike in the Cuban missile crisis can also be considered a creative breakthrough. In addition, many believe that the European integration movement epitomized by the formation of the European Union will prove a breakthrough as well, particularly in light of the centuries of warfare that have plagued that region of the world.

Students of politics have a major contribution to make in advancing creative breakthroughs. In this section of the book, we invite and encourage you to set forth your own solutions to some of the most difficult problems facing humanity.

The current war in Afghanistan started in 2001
and approaches two decades in duration.

NOORULLAH SHIRZADA/ AFP/Getty Images

12

WAR AND PEACE IN THE MODERN AGE

In developing political wisdom, and then applying it in the public arena, there is no more urgent or important purpose than that of the prevention of war. War, throughout history and up to the modern age, has proven a most tenacious and catastrophic scourge of humanity. The goal of a lasting global peace, while admittedly an extremely complex and difficult challenge, should ever be on the mind of the student of political science. How to think about such a goal, and the creative breakthroughs it demands, is our subject in this chapter.

To begin, we need to define both *war* and *peace* and offer a reminder of what we mean when we speak of *creative breakthrough*. In Chapter 2, we learned that a creative breakthrough is a significantly fruitful resolution of a problem that conventional wisdom deems insoluble. There, we offered the example of James Madison's creation of a republic with a strong central government working in tandem with smaller regional and local governments to effectively manage the affairs of a large and diverse country. In the context of war, the definition of creative breakthrough can be refined to mean an ethical, empirical, and prudential change to promote a more peaceful world order: for example, a higher ethical consciousness of global community, a new or more penetrating scientific understanding of the causes of war, and wiser judgments about how to overcome war and its disastrous consequences. With these examples in mind, we seek in this chapter to answer the following question: What creative breakthroughs can help us achieve a more peaceful world order?

War is defined as military activity, or armed violence, carried out in a systematic and organized way by nation-states (or organized groups that aspire to become nation-states) seeking to impose their will on other nation-states (or organized groups with nationalistic aspirations). While we place considerable

Chapter Objectives

After reading this chapter, you will be able to do the following:

1. Define war and peace.

2. Identify the threat and consequences of nuclear war.

3. Explain the costs and consequences of conventional war.

4. Explain the nature of terrorism in today's world.

5. Define and assess the nature of cyberwar.

6. Discuss some of the alternative approaches for seeking a more peaceful world.

emphasis on this traditional perspective, we also expand our concept of war to include not only wars between states but also domestic wars, such as civil wars; revolutions; intercommunal fighting based on ethnic, tribal, or religious identity; and terrorism.[1]

Peace is the absence of war. Further, it is a condition of harmony between nation-states (or organized groups that aspire to become nation-states) that enables them to cooperatively, lawfully, and voluntarily (through discussion, voting, mediation, conciliation, and arbitration) work out conflicts and deal with disputes.[2] Peace does not mean the end of all conflict, competition, and tension. Rather, we mean the elimination of catastrophic world wars, regional wars, civil wars, and wars of national liberation; the minimization of the level of armed conflict; and the reduction of arms through significant arms control pacts or outright disarmament. In essence, we envision a world in which major disputes (between and within nations) are settled without resort to violence and bloodshed, in which dangerous international tensions are considerably reduced, and in which world energies and monies are used to meet human needs for food, housing, medical care, education, community, and social and cultural development.

ETHICAL AND EMPIRICAL FACTORS

In this section, we elucidate several important factors that affect war and peace in the modern world: the mortal threat of nuclear war, the consequences of conventional war, the burden of arms expenditures, the dangers of the sovereign nation-state system, and the battle against terrorism.

The Mortal Threat of Nuclear War

With the end of the Cold War in 1990, the world seemed to have stepped back from the edge of the nuclear abyss. The immediate threat of a major nuclear exchange between the United States and the former Soviet Union has lessened. The Strategic Arms Reduction Talks (START) and the resulting START I and START II agreements, as well as the 2002 Strategic Offensive Reductions Treaty (SORT), resulted in reductions of nuclear weapons in both the United States and Russia (see Figure 12.1). Additionally, on February 5, 2011, U.S. President Barack Obama and then Russian President Dmitry Medvedev signed the New START Treaty to reduce American and Russian nuclear arsenals even further, limiting each party to 1,550 deployed nuclear warheads. While these actions are to be applauded, the word *deployed* is important. The reality is that both the United States and Russia have significant stockpiles of nuclear warheads over and above those that are ready to use immediately. The United States has an estimated 4,018 such weapons and Russia has approximately 4,500.[3]

But these bilateral steps between the United States and Russia are tempered by other grim realities. The threat of nuclear war is far from over. Nuclear warheads are proliferating the international community, some held by countries in the most volatile regions of the planet. The estimated number of nuclear weapons possessed by countries other than Russia and the United States are as follows: France 300, China 270, United Kingdom 215, Pakistan 140, India 130, Israel 80, and North Korea 10.[4] In addition, for

Figure 12.1 Deployed Strategic Nuclear Warheads

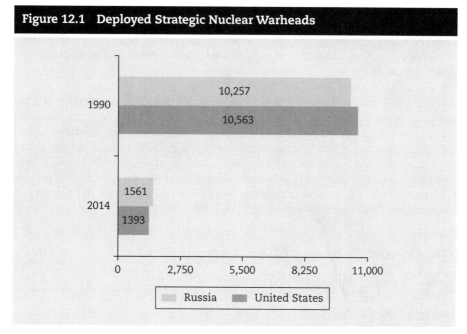

Source: Figure constructed by authors with data from the Arms Control Association, "Nuclear Weapons: Who Has What at a Glance," July 2018, http://www.armscontrol.org/factsheets/Nuclearweaponswhohaswhat.

years Iran actively pursued the means to produce nuclear weapons. In July of 2015, Iran and the group known as P5+1 (United States, Russia, China, France, United Kingdom, and Germany) struck an agreement to curtail Iran's nuclear weapons program. In May of 2018, President Donald Trump announced he was withdrawing the United States from the Iran nuclear deal. The move was not unexpected. Mr. Trump was a long-time critic of the agreement. Regardless, whether or not the agreement holds with the remaining signatories, it is clear that Iran has the technical knowledge and much of the equipment to build such a weapon. It is important to understand the devastating power of nuclear weapons. The single atomic bomb dropped on Hiroshima may have killed as many as 160,000 people. Today's large strategic nuclear warheads are on average 20 to 30 times more powerful. In a worst-case scenario, even with the drastically reduced arsenals of the United States and Russia, all-out nuclear war could destroy a good share of civilization as we know it. Great cities would be flattened, industrial centers destroyed, and water and food supplies contaminated into the distant future. But even if humanity is not literally wiped out in the event of a nuclear war, the devastation wrought by a more limited nuclear exchange of several hundred large warheads in a regional or global war is almost too horrible to contemplate. Assuming urban centers would be prime targets, nuclear warheads would burn everyone—and everything—within a radius of ten to twenty miles. Millions more would suffer grave wounds and would, subsequently and rapidly, perish. Additional millions—burned or mutilated—would suffer a lingering death from their wounds or radiation sickness. The wounded would overrun hospitals, and doctors would be unable to care for them. The networks of modern life—communication, business, factories, agriculture, government, and social life—would unravel. Survivors would face the psychological trauma of loss of loved ones, the dangers to unborn children, and unknown genetic mutations.

Even if the United States and the other major powers are not drawn into a nuclear war, a regional war involving nuclear weapons would kill thousands and most likely cause untold economic damage to the region in which the war would take place. It is also likely that even a limited, regional nuclear war—for instance, between India and Pakistan or Iran and Israel—might very well result in a devastating world depression accompanying the tragic loss of life. Furthermore, there is no guarantee that a regional war, particularly in the Middle East given its oil resources and strategic location, would not spread beyond that region. Thus, a local nuclear exchange could easily evolve into a world war with all the dire consequences that it implies.

The Consequences of Conventional Wars

The record of conventional wars in the twentieth century tells of massive deaths, injuries, and dreadful human suffering. The human, monetary, and political costs of these wars have been devastating.

Human Costs. World Wars I and II alone killed more than 60 million people. The following statistics from World War II offer a unique perspective on war's immense human costs: 1 of every 22 Soviet citizens, 1 of every 25 Germans, 1 of every 46 Japanese, 1 of every 150 Britons, and 1 of every 500 Americans was killed. For a more graphic image of the number of soldiers killed or missing in World War II, picture a parade lasting eighty-nine days (almost thirteen weeks), with a row of ten soldiers passing the reviewing stand every five seconds, day and night.

In addition, more than 40 million soldiers and civilians have been killed in conventional wars since the end of World War II. Civil wars have contributed significantly to these totals. For example, internal wars waged between 1946 and 2000 killed an estimated 212,000 Guatemalans; 300,000 Colombians; 500,000 Indonesians; 1,000,000 Ethiopians; 1,000,000 Sudanese; 1,000,000 Rwandans; 1,770,000 Cambodians; 2,000,000 Nigerians; 6,200,000 Chinese[5]; and roughly 465,000 Syrians died or went missing in their civil war, which began in 2011.[6] One of the tragedies reflected in these terrible statistics is that as war progressed through the twentieth century, armed combatants drew less of a distinction between soldier and civilian.

It is true that worldwide, deaths caused by war-related violence has been declining during the post–World War II era. In the early part of the twenty-first century, war deaths are over half what they were in the 1990s, a third of what they were during the Cold War years, and a hundredth of what they were during World War II. And this decline in war deaths took place as the world population was increasing at a rapid rate.[7] Is this a cause for celebration? Perhaps. There may be some solace in the fact that we have not engaged in a globe spanning war such as WW II. But the reality is that millions of people are still dying in large numbers—in the millions as a result of conventional interstate war, civil war, and terrorism, Further, in addition to directly killing and wounding people, wars also bring death, injury, and suffering from starvation or malnutrition; the ravages of disease; violations of liberty and justice; the plight of refugees; and ecological damage. For example, the Holocaust—the Nazi murder of 6 million Jews and thousands more of other minorities—could not have happened without World War II. The creation of "slave laborers," forced to work for the Nazi war machine, would have been impossible in peacetime. The displacement and dislocation of whole peoples (by the Nazis, the Russians, and also the Americans in the case of Japanese Americans) were another consequence of World War II.

Monetary Costs. War does not come cheap. Reliable estimates put the monetary costs of World War II alone at more than $1.3 trillion, an astronomical figure for the mid-1940s.[8] The estimated combined cost of the Iraq and Afghanistan wars varies widely. As of early 2018, it ranged between $4 and $6 trillion.[9]

Political Costs. War also produces unsettling political effects. For example, it seems quite likely that World War I opened the door to communism in tsarist Russia—to V. I. Lenin and then to Joseph Stalin. World War I also weakened Germany (as it had weakened Russia) and opened the way for Nazism and the triumph of Adolf Hitler. Similarly, World War II enabled Stalin to establish communist regimes in most Eastern European countries and to dominate them thereafter. America's tragic involvement in Vietnam not only led to terrible devastation in that land but also contributed to a sequence of events resulting in the rise of the murderous Pol Pot regime in neighboring Cambodia (Kampuchea), years of wrenching political division in the United States accompanied by a level of civil violence unprecedented since the Civil War, and the decision of a president (Lyndon Johnson) not to run for a second term.

Despite the end of the Cold War, the 1990 Iraqi invasion of Kuwait and the 2014 Russian seizure of the Crimean peninsula, a part of Ukraine, proved that states are still capable of aggression against each other. In addition, many of today's conflicts originated in bitter and long-standing ethnic tensions (see Map 12.1). In recent decades, tribal and clan rivalries in Africa have led to devastating wars in Angola, Burundi, Congo, Ethiopia, Liberia, Mozambique, Nigeria, Uganda, Sudan, and Rwanda. South Asia has been wracked by ethnic, tribal, and religious violence in India, Iran, and Sri Lanka. In the Middle East, terrible violence has plagued Iraq and Syria. And Southeast Asia has not been immune from the plague as evidenced by conflict in places such as Myanmar (Burma) and the Philippines. These kinds of conflicts and tensions are not confined to the developing world. In Europe as well, especially in multicultural societies such as Yugoslavia after the fall of communism and the former Soviet Union today, the potential for widespread violence is ever present. Protests and violent conflict continue to shake the areas comprising the former Soviet Union, most notably in Chechnya inside the Russian Republic itself.

The Burden of Arms Expenditures

Another oppressive reality is the high level of global expenditures on armaments. Economically, politically, and socially, the global quest for weapons is expensive. Global expenditures for arms declined in the years immediately following the end of the Cold War, but during the latter half of the 1990s they began to rise once again, reaching nearly $800 billion by the end of the decade.[10] By 2016, they had reached a staggering $1.69 trillion, or roughly $222 for every man, woman, and child on the planet. U.S. expenditures

Map 12.1 Areas of Ongoing Conflicts, 2018

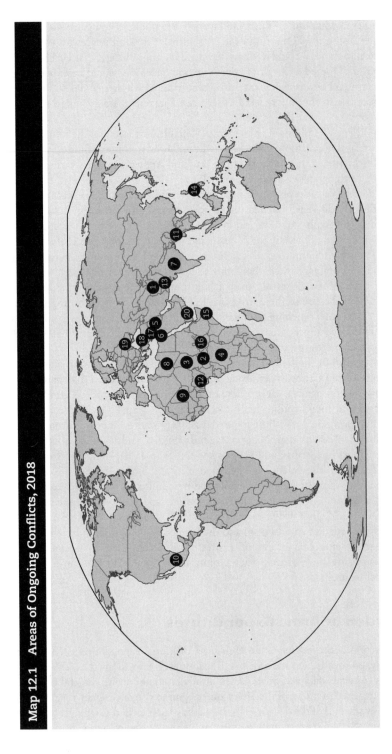

Source: Compiled by authors.

Map	Country	Type of Conflict	Primary Participants
1	Afghanistan	Civil war	Afghanistan government and U.S.-led coalition vs. Taliban.
2	Central African Republic	Civil war	Mulim Seleka vs. anti-balaka Christian militias. Violence rages despite 12 signed peace agreements.
3	Chad	Cross border terrorism	Boko Harem attacks from Nigeria.
4	Democratic Republic of Congo	Civil conflict	On again off again violence for decades with 1.2 million displaced in 2017 along. Over 40 groups fighting.
5	Iraq	Sectarian violence	After U.S. withdrawal, considerable violence continues between Sunni, Shiite, and Kurdish groups.
6	Israeli-Palestinian conflict	Political and territorial conflict	Israel, the Palestinian Authority on the West Bank, and Hamas in the Gaza Strip.
7	India	Ethnic/sectarian violence	Indian government vs. Hindu, Muslim, and Sikh factions. Particularly troublesome are Islamic separatists of Jammu Kashmir Liberation Front (JKLF), Hizbul Mujahideen (HuM), and Lashkar-e-Taiba (LeT).
8	Libya	Civil war	Following the fall of Muammar al-Qaddafi in 2011, Libya plunged into chaos with various ethnic, religious, and political factions violently vying for power.
9	Mali	Civil war	Numerous groups fighting the government for territory and influence. Most important are Ansar Dine Movement, al Qaeda in the Islamic Magrheb, Islamic Movement for Azward, and Signed in Blood Battalion.
10	Mexico	Drug wars	Mexican government vs. numerous drug cartels, including the Sinaloa, Jalisaco New Generation Cartel, and the Beltran-Leyva Cartel.
11	Myanmar	Ethnic cleansing	Government against the Rohingya Muslim minority.
12	Nigeria	Political/religious	Islamic terrorist group Boko Haram terrorizes northern Nigeria and other parts of North Africa and specializes in mass kidnappings.

(Continued)

Map 12.1 (Continued)

Map	Country	Type of Conflict	Primary Participants
13	Pakistan	Terrorism and general civil unrest	Pakistan government vs. Lashkar-e-Taiba (LeT), Tehrik-e-Taliban Pakistan (TTP), the Haqqani Network, and other rebel groups in the Afghan border regions, particularly North Waziristan, Swat Valley, Kyber Agency and Peshawar regions.
14	Philippines	Terrorism and rebellion	Government vs. Islamic separatist group Abu Sayyaf.
15	Somalia	Clan conflict	Regular army and forces of African Union vs. numerous groups, including Al-Shabaab, Hizbul Islam, Hisb al-Islam, Sufi Militia Ahlu Sunna Waljamaca (ASWJ), and Rahanweyn Resistance Army (RRA). Also violence trying to control pirates.
16	South Sudan	Civil war	Since achieving independence in 2011, South Sudan has struggled to maintain political stability. A coup d'etat attempt in 2013 led to widespread fighting. Now over 20 groups vying for territory and influence.
17	Syria	Civil war and secession	Multiple rebel groups began open revolt against President Assad in 2011, and the country was plunged into vicious civil war with hundreds of thousands dead and displaced. Problems compounded when al-Qaida splinter group ISIS (Islamic State of Iraq and Syria) began its violent quest to carve out an Islamic caliphate in northern Syria and northwest Iraq.
18	Turkey	Ethnic Violence	Regular violent clashes between government forces and the Kurdish Workers' Party (PKK) and other less powerful Kurdish groups.
19	Ukraine	Invasion	Russian government invaded and seized Crimean Peninsula in 2014. With support of Moscow, Ukrainians of Russian descent continue to agitate for separation from Ukraine proper. Russians are still fighting in Eastern Ukraine.
20	Yemen	Civil War	Fighting began 2015 with Houthie rebels attempting to seize power backed by Iran. Saudi Arabia and 8 mostly Sunni allies began air campaign. Thousands dead and displaced.

Source: Compiled by authors. The comprehensiveness of this and similar lists varies depending on the definition of conflict. This list is not designed to be inclusive but to provide a reasonable representation of the range of conflicts throughout the world. Sources consulted include Global Conflict Tracker, http://www.cfr.org/global/global-conflict-tracker/p32137#!/?marker=7; Stockholm International Peace Research Institute, http://www.sipri.org; International Crisis Group, http://www.crisisgroup.org; and Wars in the World, http://www.warsintheworld.com/?page=static1258254223.

account for 37 percent of the world total.[11] The costs today of weapons—both nuclear and conventional—are unprecedented. During the 1960s and 1970s, America's frontline fighter planes cost between $2 million and $4 million each. By the 1990s, a mainstay fighter plane in the American inventory such as the F-16 Fighting Falcon cost between $18 million and $31 million, depending on the model and various modification packages. The Lockheed Martin F-117 Nighthawk stealth-attack aircraft runs an astounding $111 to $122 million a copy.[12] Naval vessels are enormously expensive. The DD-1000 USS Zumwalt destroyer runs $7 billion per ship.[13] Nor are strategic weapons systems exactly cheap. The estimated cost of producing a B-2 bomber runs to $1.16 billion per plane.[14] And, according to the Brookings Institution's Nuclear Weapons Cost Project, the price tag for a Trident submarine is a whopping $1.9 billion, with each of its twenty-four Trident II D5 missiles costing $89.7 million.[15]

Perhaps the most distressing aspect of the arms race is that everywhere it drains resources away from basic human needs: for constructive jobs; for food, clothing, housing, education, and medical care; and for social and cultural development. As Ruth Sivard noted when commenting about the Cold War years, "In the 1980s, two governments in three . . . spent more to defend their citizens against military attack than against the everyday hazards of disease, accidents, and ill health; one in three has spent more on military power than on education and health care combined."[16]

Spending in the arms race hurts the battle against inflation and national debt; militates against healthy economic growth; and wastes valuable money, personnel, and resources. In rich and poor countries throughout the world, governments neglect basic human needs in favor of military might and the technology of destruction.

The Dangers of the Sovereign Nation-State System

The threat of nuclear war, the disastrous consequences of conventional wars, and the burden of arms expenditures are all intimately tied up with the sovereign nation-state system. As Robert L. Holmes so eloquently stated in his highly regarded book, *On War and Morality*,

> The threat of nuclear annihilation grows out of the workings of an international system in which, if many realists are correct, the promotion of national interest is the governing norm. And if, as many of them would also have it, national interest ought to be the guiding norm (either of some or of all nations), then we need some accounting of how such a judgment is justified in light of the apparent consequences of its implementation. If one places the highest value upon the survival of the state, and if that survival is jeopardized by the pursuit of national interest, it would seem that pursuit should be abandoned.[17]

The nation-state system requires countries to protect their national interests by relying on their own arms. No peaceful appeal to a supranational authority or global law is required in the event of serious conflict between nations. Nothing prohibits a nation's ultimate resort to war to protect its vital interests. The United States, Russia, Britain, France, China, Israel, India, North Korea, and Pakistan each believes that stockpiles of nuclear weapons and the capability to deliver them are integral to their own vital national interests.

National rivalries have also played a major role in triggering conventional wars. Wars existed before the modern nation-state system took shape with the Peace of Westphalia in 1648. (The treaty, which ended the Thirty Years' War, recognized the independence of the Netherlands and Switzerland and the autonomy of the German principalities.) But wars have become broader and more savage with the development of modern nationalism—and, paradoxically, with the advance of democracy, science, and socialism. Nationalistic rivalries had devastating consequences in the twentieth century. Nationalistic conflicts helped produce World War I. The nationalistic and militaristic ambitions of Germany and Japan were the primary causes of World War II.

Since World War II, wars for national liberation have also been fought. The great nation-states of Western Europe usually did not peacefully relinquish their colonial empires in Asia and Africa. They often fought to protect what they considered their vital national interests in preserving their empires—whether in India, Malaysia, Indonesia, Indochina, Algeria, or the Congo. Sometimes the colonial powers granted independence with reasonable speed and grace, as the British did in India after partitioning the subcontinent between Pakistan and India in 1947. In other instances—the French in Indochina and Algeria, for example—European colonial countries fought bitter and bloody battles against indigenous peoples who felt justified in resorting to arms to gain national independence and freedom.

The great Western nation-states are not the only ones to go to war because of rivalry. Wars between India and Pakistan, between Israel and its Arab neighbors, between Iran and Iraq, between Ethiopia and Somalia, between Vietnam and Cambodia (Kampuchea), and between Peru and Chile indicate that nationalistic rivalries also cause war among less powerful countries. Whether small or large, weak or powerful, the sovereign nation-state defers to no higher law or court to settle disputes affecting its vital national interests.

The imperative of self-defense leads nation-states to arm themselves and thus begins the spiral of the arms race. Nation after nation seeks protection in more arms and more sophisticated (and expensive) weapons—and, if they can manage, even nuclear arms. War, then, remains locked in a deadly embrace with the sovereign nation-state system—a system that is not going to be abandoned any time soon.

The Battle Against Terrorism

After the terrorist attacks on the World Trade Center and the Pentagon on September 11, 2001, President George W. Bush declared that the United States was going to wage a "war on terror." Perpetrators of terror, beginning with Osama bin Laden's network, al-Qaida, would be hunted down, and countries that aided or harbored terrorists would be held accountable. The term *war on terror* proved controversial and has been officially dropped by the government, but nevertheless, it remains in popular use. During the Bush administration, human rights groups increasingly linked the term to such abuses as prolonged incarceration of combatants at Guantanamo Bay in Cuba and the mistreatment of prisoners at Abu Ghraib prison in Iraq. Muslims around the world also increasingly viewed the term as tantamount to a war on Islam. The Obama administration replaced it with the term *Overseas Contingency Operation*. President Donald Trump, under the rationale of "keeping America safe," seemed to exacerbate the tension between the United States and the Muslim World when in January 2017 by executive order he instituted a ban on travelers and immigrants from seven majority-Muslim countries—Iran, Iraq, Syria, Yemen, Somalia, Sudan, and Libya for 90 days, halted refugee resettlement for 120 days, and banned Syrian refugees indefinitely. These actions were initially blocked by lower federal courts and have gone through a series of revisions. In June of 2018, a sharply divided Supreme Court upheld a revised version of the travel ban in the case *Trump v. Hawaii*.

Regardless of the semantics of the endeavor, the United States continues to actively pursue a policy of combating terrorism around the world. Two of the most significant events in this conflict were first the killing of Osama bin Laden inside Pakistan by American SEAL Team 6 special operations forces on May 2, 2011, and the defeat of ISIS in Syria and Iraq in 2018.

A number of characteristics of this "war" make it unprecedented. First, it is not a war between states. It is a war against a number of nonstate actors—terrorist groups—that are part of a series of movements with a variety of purposes. They may seek to drive the United States out of Saudi Arabia, to force the United States to cease its support of Israel, or to bring down governments or establish new ones. This is not to say that states are not involved. They are in a couple of ways. The most obvious is that states are actively trying to stop terrorism. Another way they are involved is in support of various terrorist groups around the world. For example, Iran has consistently supported the terrorist activities of Hezbollah in Lebanon and Hamas in the Gaza strip.

Second, the very transnational nature of the adversary makes the scope of the war less than clear. Even if al-Qaida or ISIS (Islamic State of Iraq and Syria) were to be crushed or severely damaged, how many other terrorist groups do the United States and its allies go after? True, many of the terrorist groups have some affiliation with al-Qaida, but not all of them do.

Third, because the September 11 attacks were on American soil and a domestic catastrophe, waging the war involves a major new domestic security component. The creation of the Department of Homeland Security and appointment of the director of homeland security are indications of that reality. Although domestic security concerns were present during World War II, nothing exceeds the efforts of law enforcement and intelligence arms to root out terrorist cells in the continental United States and to protect the country's infrastructure, including airlines and nuclear power plants. As earlier noted in this book, the greatly enhanced intelligence and security efforts have led to a genuine fear that personal freedom in America is in danger. Massive phone data collection by the National Security Agency (NSA) along with tens of thousands of security cameras deployed throughout our urban centers may make us more secure from terrorist attack. But at what cost? That is a question being debated in the halls of Congress, by think tanks, in academic institutions, and in the living rooms of America.

Cyberwar

Any discussion about the contemporary state of warfare would be incomplete without some attention paid to cyberwar. A fairly widely accepted definition of *cyberwar* is that it is ". . . the use of digital attacks by one country or nation to disrupt the computer systems of another with the aim of creating significant damage, death, or destruction."[18] As clear as this appears, because cyberwar is in its infancy, the reality is that the definition is evolving. For instance, it is important to differentiate between cyberwar and cyberespionage, the latter denoting the penetration of computer systems to steal data such as bank records. Cyberwar involves the destruction or serious damaging of computer systems that control things such as power grids, air traffic and railroad control, medical systems, and the computer systems that control an adversary's weapon systems.

Perhaps the best known case of cyberwar was the unleashing of the American/Israeli designed Stuxnet virus in 2010 against the Iranian nuclear facilities at Natanz. One fifth of the Iranian centrifuges were sent reeling out of control while their status gauges read normal. In 2015, part of Ukraine's power grid was disrupted allegedly by Russian hackers, and in 2015, seven Iranian hackers were accused of trying to shut down the computer system controlling a dam in New York State.[19]

Cyberwar is inherently dangerous because of the damage and chaos that it can cause. But it is particularly dangerous at this point in history because there are few if any accepted "rules" governing the phenomenon. One problem is that of attribution. Do we always know who was responsible for a cyber attack? Was it a government unit? Was it a semi-private group merely associated with a government? Or was it a completely autonomous group of hackers? If the victim country is not sure, where do they direct their retaliation? Another problem is determining the threshold whereby a cyber attack can legitimately be labeled an act of war. Should there be a proportional response or an all out attack on the cyber systems of the attacking country?

Many nations are entering into a cyber arms race not unlike the nuclear arms race of the early Cold War between the United States and Soviet Union. The first ten to thirteen years were particularly dangerous because there were few efforts to limit or control not only the arms race itself, but when and how nuclear weapons might be used. The terror of the Cuban Missile crisis changed that and the two superpowers began talks to try and limit the arms race and establish safeguards to avoid accidental launches. Efforts have been made to establish analogous rules for cyberwar, but they have not been widely accepted by key countries. Under the NATO sponsored Cooperative Cyber Defence Centre of Excellence in the Estonian capital of Tallinn, a group of legal scholars have put together a book of some 154 rules or guidelines for lawyers to apply international law to **cyberwarfare**. But this is a long way from any international acceptance of such guidelines by the world's powerful governments.[20]

ALTERNATIVE APPROACHES TO A MORE PEACEFUL WORLD

In this section, we consider six approaches to a more peaceful world order: (1) a **new balance of power**, (2) the UN **third-party activities**, (3) collective security, (4) global economic **integration**, (5) peace through functionalism, and (6) **nonviolent civilian defense**. These alternatives do not exhaust all the possibilities, and they may sometimes overlap. They do illustrate the strengths and weaknesses of key approaches. While reading this section, consider whether they are truly creative breakthroughs.

A New Balance of Power

The new balance-of-power position is based on the assumption that foreign policy must realistically accept the struggle for power in world affairs generally and between great powers specifically. Great powers will seek to exert and extend their influence on behalf of their vital national interests. Only power can balance power; only strength can deter or defeat aggression. Current trends in the international system indicate that a revision in the balance-of-power system is occurring (see Chapter 11 for our discussion of the various power configurations). While still based on the power-versus-power equation, this new system differs in key ways from the system that characterized the Cold War.

A new balance of power would, first, be multipolar rather than bipolar and, second, place greater emphasis on economic power (though military might would certainly not be abandoned). The United States, Japan, Germany, Russia, China, India, and perhaps some regional units such as Western Europe, Latin America, or Southeast Asia might constitute a new balance-of-power system. Not all of these powers need be equal in strength, and whether all of these actors would have nuclear weapons is uncertain. No doubt all would be capable of arming themselves with such weapons if they chose.

A new, multipolar balance of power might preserve the peace if three conditions were to prevail: (1) All members of the system had sufficient countervailing military power (in nuclear or conventional arms) to deter attack by any other member of the system; (2) all members of the system had adequate economic and political power to defeat nonmilitary threats by any other member of the system; and (3) all members had the political skill, through the use of the diplomacy of accommodation and creative statesmanship, to avoid mistaken judgments about vital interests, to pursue détente (relaxation of tensions), and to build the conditions of international security, human rights, economic prosperity, and social justice that will make free peoples immune to authoritarian rule.

Such a policy is both desirable and feasible, but it will call for strong, astute, and far-sighted statesmanship. It is desirable because it guards the member nations' vital interests, particularly peace and national freedom. The policy provides time to work, step by step, toward arms control, real disarmament, worldwide democracy and constitutionalism, and economic well-being. Peace through a new balance of power is feasible because this policy did work at the bipolar level to prevent World War III. It safeguarded the freedom of Western Europe and West Berlin. It made the United States and the Soviet Union careful about taking actions that would threaten each other's vital interests. It restrained aspects of Soviet-American rivalry that might have gotten out of hand and escalated into a nuclear war that neither party wanted.

The weaknesses of this policy must, however, be recognized. First, a policy of strength calls for armaments, which figured in the arms race during the Cold War years.

At 2 million ground troops, the People's Republic of China maintains the largest infantry in the world. In recent years, it has invested substantially in high-tech weaponry in its pursuit of world-power status.

Creative Breakthrough

Second, even overwhelming strength does not always enable major actors in the system to deter aggression. For example, the old Cold War bipolar balance did not dissuade less powerful actors from acting aggressively, as, for example, when North Korea attempted to seize South Korea or when the North Vietnamese sought to unify Vietnam (first through peaceful means in the form of nationwide elections and then through internal subversion, guerrilla warfare, and military intervention). In Vietnam (in contrast to Korea, where the United States intervened with the blessing of the United Nations), American arms did not prevent the communists from taking over the whole country. Third, it is not always easy to identify vital national interests. Was U.S. involvement in Vietnam dictated by vital U.S. interests? Would a communist Vietnam really have upset the American–Soviet balance of power? Fourth, following the old adage, "Those who possess a gun will eventually use it," a balance-of-power policy based to any degree on military strength increases the probability that at some point power will be used for purposes other than deterrence. Fifth, the balance-of-power mentality may make it extremely difficult to avoid the paranoia that sometimes characterized the Cold War in the 1950s. Sixth, a multipolar balance system is more complex than a bipolar balance system; because there are more major actors, assessing the power of each relative to the others is far more difficult. Seventh, a new emphasis on economic power does not guarantee a lower probability of military confrontation. An economic balance of power can get out of hand. Rather than an arms race, member states might engage in trade wars, using protectionist methods (such as high tariffs and quotas) to counteract the economic power of actors they view as threatening. Of course, economic warfare can lead to military warfare if decision makers believe that vital national interests are threatened. Finally, balance-of-power systems are designed to deal with relations between nation-states. Unfortunately, they do little to confront other forms of violent conflict such as terrorism, revolution, or intercommunal fighting based on ethnic and religious factors.

The United Nations' Third-Party Activities

The end of the Cold War profoundly affected the United Nations. This is most evident in the UN Security Council's ability to agree on a variety of issues that previously sustained frequent vetoes by either the United States or the Soviet Union. The effect is also reflected in the propensity of the major powers to give the organization more genuine power. This raises the possibility of a more vigorous and effective role for the United Nations as a third-party actor or a counterforce to aggression in international conflicts.[21] Third-party activities are conflict-resolution techniques used by the United Nations and other international actors not involved in a given dispute that cover a wide range of essentially ad hoc techniques, including good offices, conciliation, investigation, mediation, arbitration, observation, truce supervision, and interposition (in the case of the United Nations, placing UN forces between the fighting parties). The third party does not participate directly in the conflict but seeks to help both sides resolve a situation. The third party does not coerce; it persuades.

The third-party approach thus relies on the essentially persuasive means of Chapter VI of the UN Charter, "Pacific Settlement of Disputes," rather than on the essentially coercive means of Chapter VII, "Action with Respect to Threats to the Peace, Breaches of the Peace, and Acts of Aggression." That is, third-party intervention looks to such means as "negotiation, enquiry, mediation, conciliation, arbitration, judicial settlement, resort to regional agencies or arrangements, or other peaceful means."[22] It does not rely on economic, diplomatic, and military sanctions. The third party helps opponents work out their disputes peacefully or extricate themselves from military conflicts. For example, the third party may simply help opponents talk to each other. It may dramatize the dangers in failing to reach an accord. The third party may dissolve fears by inspecting danger spots and verifying the absence of aggressive forces. It may provide a neutral buffer between military forces.

Indian peacekeepers highlight the UN third-party role as they patrol in a village in the Democratic Republic of Congo.

Reuters/Finbarr O'Reilly – RTXAUEE

This approach to peace recognizes the realities of current international politics. It acknowledges that the United Nations is not, and was not intended to be, a true collective security organization, in which the overwhelmingly powerful peaceful nations use their collective strength (through diplomatic boycott, economic pressure, or military force) to deter and punish an aggressive state that violates the peace. The third-party approach recognizes that during the Cold War years, veto power made it impossible for the UN Security Council to act coercively against a great power either accused of or guilty of aggression and made it extremely difficult—if not impossible—to act against an aggressive ally of a great power. This approach recognizes that even with the end of the Cold War, it may be difficult for UN members to agree that collective action against aggression should be taken. The UN failure to halt ethnic cleansing in the former Yugoslavia is a case in point. The best the Security Council could muster was a rather ineffective peacekeeping force, UNPROFOR (UN Protection Force), which operated from 1992 to 1995. The "ethnic cleansing" and warfare were not really brought under control until the fall of 1995, when a powerful non-UN force, IFOR (the NATO implementation force), led by the United States and NATO, was deployed in Bosnia to oversee implementation of the Dayton accords, which had been brokered by the United States, not the United Nations.

The UN third-party efforts at the end of the Cold War and beginning of the post–Cold War era were impressive, at least in terms of numbers. Between 1988 and 1994, the United Nations established missions in Afghanistan, Angola, Cambodia (Kampuchea), Croatia-Bosnia-Macedonia, El Salvador, Georgia, Iran-Iraq, Iraq-Kuwait, Haiti, Liberia, Mozambique, Namibia, Nicaragua, Pakistan, Somalia, Uganda-Rwanda, and Western Sahara. In all, there were twenty new missions, involving 70,000 personnel from sixty-six countries.

But the third-party process has not been without problems. For example, in Angola, after successful UN-supervised elections in 1992, the country plunged into renewed civil war. Moreover, as indicated earlier, the United Nations was incapable of stopping Serbian aggression and ethnic cleansing in Bosnia-Herzegovina. While a joint UN-African

Unity force was eventually authorized for Sudan in 2007 to try to deal with the terrible violence in the Darfur region, that effort came under criticism for being far too late and of questionable effectiveness. But perhaps the most serious shortcoming of the United Nations was the total lack of meaningful response to the slaughter of nearly 1 million people in Rwanda in 1994, when members of the Hutu tribe killed Tutsi tribe members by the tens of thousands.

So, despite some success, this third-party approach is not a panacea. In appraising the UN third-party role as a creative breakthrough, we can identify at least eight weaknesses. First, third-party intervention will not work if the parties to the dispute do not consent to such intervention, and in some cases they will not. Second, the veto of a Security Council resolution on third-party activity may weaken the secretary-general's role. Third, the secretary-general and the Security Council may disagree. Fourth, because of the time it takes for the Security Council (or the General Assembly) to act, the secretary-general may have to risk speedy action in a controversial case, which may itself create difficulties. Fifth, a creative, resourceful, and sagacious person may not always hold the office of secretary-general. Sixth, even with the best intentions and the fullest support in the Security Council or General Assembly, third-party activities may not work. Seventh, adequate financial and other resources (including a crisis center, a crisis staff, and a UN police force) may not be available. Eighth, third-party peacekeeping usually attacks the symptoms, not the causes, of conflicts; it does not address the fundamental causes of war.

In addition, it should be noted that the United Nations is having difficulty wrestling with conflicts that some observers have referred to as being in a "gray" area—that is, where neither traditional peacekeeping nor collective security measures seem appropriate. These conflicts—such as those in Bosnia, Haiti, and Rwanda—saw initial UN intervention while violence still raged. Furthermore, these conflicts were basically internal in nature, not classic cases of aggression by one nation against another. In these cases, the secretary-general's neutrality was highly susceptible to compromise since he was forced, almost by the nature of the conflict, to take sides. Whether the United Nations becomes more adept at dealing with these kinds of conflagrations remains to be seen. At the very least, a great deal will depend on the support of the major powers on the Security Council.[23]

Collective Security

Collective security, as we saw in Chapter 11, is the joining of countries into an organization to maintain international peace and law. Their collective strength deters or punishes aggression by member nations. The United Nations is one such organization. In essence, collective security offers protection from "inside" threats. (This differs from a mutual defense agreement, in which the member states agree to protect each other from threats by nonmember states—that is, "outside" threats. A prime example of a mutual defense organization is NATO, which was set up during the Cold War primarily as a defense against the Soviet Union and the Warsaw Pact nations.) Chapter VII of the UN Charter is the collective security provision and the heart of the organization's stated peace and security mechanism. The use of this device requires a two-thirds vote of the

UN Security Council and no negative votes (vetoes) from any of the five permanent members—China, France, Russia, the United Kingdom, and the United States.

Creative Breakthrough

The inability of the United Nations to make full use of collective security during the Cold War was treated extensively in Chapter 11. But the end of the Cold War may have made the collective punishment of aggressors under Chapter VII of the UN Charter more feasible. After all, two superpowers are no longer squared off against each other in the Security Council. But two recent conflicts indicate that it is far too early for a definitive prediction about the future of collective security.

Iraq's invasion of Kuwait in 1991 led to more than a dozen Security Council resolutions condemning the aggressor and levying sanctions. A worldwide economic embargo against Iraq was established, with military force authorized to enforce it. Ultimately, direct military force was used to expel Iraq from Kuwait. Desert Storm was carried out under these resolutions. Later, authorization was granted for UN teams to enter Iraq to find and destroy its stockpiles of and production facilities for weapons of mass destruction (WMDs)—nuclear, chemical, and biological. But it should also be noted that few conflicts in the international arena so clearly threaten the national security interests of so many countries as the Iraqi actions did. For the United States, the European community, and Japan, Iraq's seizure of the Kuwaiti oil fields and the threat to the Saudi oil fields were unacceptable. For many of the Arab states, Saddam Hussein's actions were a clear sign that he was a potential threat to their security.

Still, the collective actions against Iraq might be a cause for optimism, although serious regional problems remain after the U.S. 2003 invasion to displace Saddam Hussein—not the least of which is the Syrian civil war that has spilled over into Iraq with the rise of ISIS. And, as noted earlier, the UN response to the tragedy in the former state of Yugoslavia was anything but heartening. Serbian aggression against the people of Croatia and Bosnia-Herzegovina remained unchecked until U.S.-NATO action in 1995. In this case, the threat to national security interests was not so clear.

At best, it is doubtful whether UN collective security will be an effective instrument for peace on any consistent basis, even with the end of the Cold War. The major obstacle to collective security is no longer an ideologically based veto in the Security Council. The main obstacle now appears to be the international community's lack of will and resources to use the instrument with any degree of consistency, particularly when no clear self-interest of the major powers is evident.

Global Economic Integration

Integration occurs when groups of states, at the regional or global level, expand their economic interaction—trade, finance, transportation, communication—to the point where the separate national economies become increasingly interdependent. Both regional and global integration (globalization) were covered in Chapter 11. We cited there the European Union as perhaps the most advanced example of economic integration in the contemporary world. Some scholars contend that global economic integration, which is well under way, works powerfully against the divisive norms of the nation-state system. The more integrated and interdependent economies become, the higher the cost to be paid for engaging in violent conflict.

Creative Breakthrough

The question, however, is not whether powerful economic integrative forces are operating in the international system and leading to greater interdependence. Obviously, they are. The question is, rather, do economic integrative forces constitute a basis for a new world order that is better equipped to mitigate violent conflict, ensure adequate standards of living for the world's population, and guarantee fundamental human rights?

A certain logic argues that economic integration helps reduce international conflict. In its simplest (indeed, probably oversimplified) form, widespread economic integration means that many countries have economic investments in other countries. Therefore, it is in the interest of all countries to ensure that each other's economies thrive. To injure or destroy another economy is to risk injuring or perhaps destroying one's own economy. If economic integration becomes elaborate enough, warfare will be perceived as benefiting no one. Charles W. Kegley, Jr., and Eugene R. Wittkopf put it this way:

> [G]lobal interdependence may draw the world's diverse components together in pursuit of mutual survival and welfare. Awareness of the common destiny of all, alongside the inability of sovereign states to address many shared problems through unilateral national action, may energize efforts to put aside national competition. Conflict will recede, according to this reasoning, as few states can afford to disentangle themselves from the interdependent ties that bind them together in the common fate on which their welfare depends. From this perspective, then, we should welcome the continued tightening of interstate linkages, for they strengthen the seams that bind together the fragile tapestry of international relations.[24]

Finally, as the integrative process becomes more complex, the need for multilateral diplomacy increases. Group deliberation and decision making about how to manage this complex system become imperative. Most international relations scholars and practitioners would probably agree that economic integration is a positive force in international affairs. But it is not without its problems.

First, it is not at all clear that economic integration can either confront or overcome some of the most intractable problems in international affairs—ethnic, religious, cultural, and territorial tensions and disputes. Second, multinational corporations (MNCs) and financial institutions provide much of the impetus behind economic integration, and despite international efforts to establish behavioral guidelines, there are still serious questions about their accountability. Third, despite the promise of such dramatic patterns as the European Union (which holds out the hope of genuine global integration), critics worry about the limited perspective of such regional organizations. Critics contend that in periods of scarce resources or generally bad economic times, these trade zones could adopt some of the less desirable traits of nation-states, such as protectionism and self-righteousness. Regional associations could be characterized by the same blind loyalties that we have seen in nation-states. Moreover, globally oriented integrationists, such as the functionalists (discussed in the next section), contend that regional associations still do not address humanity's fundamental problems—disease, food production and distribution, shelter, poverty, and environmental quality—from the necessary global perspective.

Peace Through Functionalism

As we saw in Chapter 11, functionalism is a theory positing that the world would be better off if it were organized around the fulfillment of basic human needs such as procurement of food, water, and shelter; delivery of adequate health care; concern for environmental health; and improved communications. These are the "functional" areas of human endeavor. Functionalism stands as an alternative to the nation-state system.

Those who endorse this approach maintain that human beings will move toward world peace if functional organizations can better meet common needs and advance mutual interests. With increased powers, funds, and activities, and by grappling with common problems, these organizations can build a trusting global community. The common problems involve providing decent jobs and increased productivity for workers, farmers, and fishers; furnishing better health care for children, mothers, and workers; building decent housing; developing effective transportation; establishing good schools; developing freer trade; maintaining access to raw materials, credit, and markets; performing scientific research; curtailing crime; limiting pollution; and encouraging cultural development and creative uses of leisure. As such basic problems are resolved, some of the underlying causes of war—distrust, fear, poverty, illiteracy, and disease—will be dealt with. In dealing pragmatically with these problems, humanity can transcend the limitations of national sovereignty and build a workable global system.

In his influential book, *A Working Peace System: An Argument for the Functional Development of International Organization*, David Mitrany made one of the most cogent arguments on behalf of the functional approach.[25] Here we present and, where necessary, modify and update his analysis. The fundamental problem of the present age, according to Mitrany's initial formulation, is to determine how to achieve a new international system. This system must be able to prevent aggression and to organize peace and peaceful change. Without destroying the valuable diversity and freedom of nations, the system must be able to unify a badly divided world. The new world order must also successfully address the world's mounting insistence on social and economic betterment. National loyalties have tended to divide people politically in the modern world, even if they have frequently increased human freedom within the nation-state. On the other hand, the demand for social and economic betterment and the fact of economic interdependence have increasingly bound people together, even if they have also created tensions between the rich and the poor within countries and between countries.

Logically, unity could be obtained by conquest or consent. It could be achieved immediately or over a long period, by revolution or reform. The new world order could result in a centralized world state or a federal state or a global order. The new world order could be pursued according to a formal, constitutional blueprint or by informal, practical pursuit of urgent needs.

On the basis of these considerations, Mitrany reformulates the problem as follows: How is it possible to stimulate a voluntary and progressive evolution of world society that will preserve the valuable aspects of nationality and yet satisfy the legitimate needs of humankind? Mitrany is impressed by the difficulties of the formal, constitutional approach to peace through a new kind of international system. He does not believe that current nations, divided as they are and functioning within the framework of a balance-of-power system, will put aside their differences and agree at some constitutional convention to establish a global world order.

Similarly, he does not believe that the United Nations can do the job required because it leaves untouched the identity and policy of the sovereign nation-states that compose it; the United Nations is too loose an organization to achieve unity in diversity. Theoretically, a federal system of international organization provides the cohesion lacking in a league of sovereign nations. In Mitrany's opinion, the basic community of interest needed for such a federal state does not yet exist worldwide (a condition that appears as true today as when Mitrany first advanced his theory). A federal system would have to operate within the limits of a region or within the framework of an ideological union. However, such a regional or ideological union would be defective because it could divide the world into several potentially competing units.

The primary advantage of the functional approach, according to Mitrany, is that it would "overlay political divisions with a spreading web of international activities and agencies, in which and through which the interests and life of all nations would be gradually integrated."[26] International government, he argues, can be effective only when it coexists with practical international activities. The starting point for a system of peace must be common needs, with momentary disregard for the presence of jealously sovereign nation-states and the absence of a larger political or ideological unity. The proper approach must be experimental and practical, free of insistence on formal blueprints and constitutional requirements.

Mitrany uses the functional approach to deal with the problem of national sovereignty and the insistence of nations on protecting their vital interests through military power. As peoples and nations work together to meet practical and pressing problems—involving trade and shipping, health and literacy, agriculture and fishing, aviation and broadcasting, scientific research and development—sovereignty would be gradually transferred, in the work involved, from the participating nations to the agencies performing the agreed-on job. "By entrusting an authority with a certain task," Mitrany writes, "carrying with it command over the requisite powers and means, a slice of sovereignty is transferred from the old authority to the new; and the accumulation of such partial transfers in time brings about a translation of the true seat of authority."[27] In this way, too, Mitrany maintains, the tough questions of peaceful change, sovereign borders, and vital national interests would be given a new perspective. Peaceful change must come about internationally as it does nationally. We can make changes of frontiers unnecessary by making frontiers meaningless through the continuous development of common activities and interests across them.[28]

Mitrany believes that, in addition to developing the conditions that must underpin the eventual world community, functional agencies could play an important role in advancing the crucial function of security. For example, they could watch over and check activities that lead to aggressive warfare, whether nuclear or conventional, including mobilization of soldiers, deployment of armaments, uses of transport, and accumulation of strategic materials. In conventional wars these agencies might even check those elements threatening aggression by withholding vital services from the potential aggressors.

What are the weaknesses in the purely functional approach to a more peaceful world order? First, functionalism does not deal with the immediately pressing problems of nation-state rivalry that threaten to break out into armed conflict. Second, it does not move the world immediately away from the mortal threat of nuclear war. Third, it has

Creative
Breakthrough

not yet been demonstrated that the functional approach will lead nations to slowly give up dangerous aspects of their sovereign power. Fourth, it is not clear how the functional approach, further down the road, will help transfer national means of defense to a common global authority. Fifth, it is not clear that economic, social, and scientific successes in dealing with poverty, disease, ignorance, and other problems are strong enough to overcome nations' sovereign pride, parochialism, and prejudice or elites' desire to maintain their privileges.

On this final note of criticism, we should mention a vision in the intellectual tradition of functionalism yet different in one important respect. This is **neofunctionalism,** which argues that integration must take place at the political level as well as at the economic, technical, and humanitarian levels.[29] Mitrany's vision of functionalism is essentially nonpolitical; the world must work around the political flashpoints that divide the human race. The neofunctionalists believe that human beings cannot avoid the political problems that divide them. Nor can they ignore the power of nationalism and of national elites. Political union, the neofunctionalists insist, is as important as nonpolitical union.

Nonviolent Civilian Defense

Advocates of peace through nonviolent civilian defense maintain that a breakthrough to a more peaceful world order can be achieved only if nonviolence is seriously considered. From their perspective, traditional means of dealing with conflict have proven inadequate and in some instances disastrous. "Now, more than ever, we need to question some of our basic assumptions about defense, security and peace, and to examine possible new policies that might help achieve those goals." So wrote Gene Sharp in his book, *Exploring Nonviolent Alternatives.*[30] Sharp is critical of the modern military and traditional solutions to political conflict. Military power does not adequately defend a people. Indeed, taken to its extreme—nuclear weapons—military power threatens mutual annihilation.

Another proponent of nonviolent defense, Robert Holmes, questions the basic function and efficiency of violence. He writes the following:

> Destructive force does not automatically add up to social power. . . . Moreover, beyond a certain point increments in the capacity for violence cease to yield increases in power. Beyond that point, in fact, power may decrease, however much destructive force one commands. The United States discovered this in Vietnam. . . . The Soviets did the same in Afghanistan.[31]

Sharp notes that conflict is unavoidable and traditional means of dealing with conflict are inadequate and may be disastrous. These traditional means, according to Sharp, include (1) removal of causes; (2) increased understanding of the opponent; (3) compromise; (4) negotiation, conciliation, and arbitration; (5) democratic institutions; (6) world government; (7) violent revolution; (8) war; (9) avoidance of provocation; and (10) apathy and impotence. Although some of these means may have merit, they are still insufficient. For example, there is not always time to remove the causes of conflict; present conflicts must be dealt with immediately. Understanding does not automatically reduce conflicts; indeed, it may sometimes heighten them. Some compromises are morally and politically dangerous; they may not achieve acceptable results. Democratic institutions are frequently nonexistent, incomplete, or inadequate. World government is, at best, a long way off; it may not be achieved peacefully, and even if it is, it may turn out to be dangerous.

Creative Breakthrough

So, Sharp maintains, nonviolence must be examined seriously. He defines nonviolent action as various forms of protest and noncooperation without physical violence. But can nonviolent action, as a substitute for military armaments, ensure defense, security, and peace? Sharp believes that nonviolent civilian defense is not only desirable but feasible. He maintains that nonviolent action can both deter and defeat aggressors.

Sharp argues that nonviolent civilian defense would actually discourage nuclear attack by eliminating the national lightning rod of nuclear weapons. The very fear that one's opponent might launch a nuclear attack, or perhaps even the fear of a conventional military defeat, might provide the reason for launching a nuclear attack. Civilian defense, which can be used only for defensive purposes, would remove that motive and, hence, if not cancel out the danger, at least greatly reduce it. Moreover, nonviolent civilian defense would deter conventional aggression because the aggressor would know that resistance would take the form of effective nonviolent protest, noncooperation, and intervention.

If aggression did occur, nonviolent civilian defense would defeat it. The invader would have to deal with a population prepared to resist nonviolently. For example, the population could resist the entry of enemy troops by obstructing the docks, refusing to operate railroads, and blocking highways and airports with thousands of abandoned automobiles. Strikes, boycotts, empty streets, shuttered windows, and noncooperation in general would give the aggressor an empty victory.

According to Sharp's philosophy of nonviolent civilian defense, police would refuse to arrest patriotic opponents of the invader. Teachers would refuse to use invader propaganda in the schools. Workers and managers would strike to prevent the enemy from exploiting the country. Clergy would encourage refusal to help the invader. Politicians, civil servants, and judges would defy the enemy's orders, thus denying the use of the community's legal machinery. Underground newspapers and radio stations would support the cause of nonviolent resistance and report only the truth. In these ways, Sharp maintains, nonviolent action would deny the aggressor the obedience needed to make aggression successful.

Nonviolent civilian defense, Sharp concedes, involves risks, dangers, costs, and discipline. It is not easy and takes considerable training and commitment. Robert Holmes elaborates on this point by noting that "nonviolence is no guarantee against bloodshed. No system has such a guarantee. But the use of violence not only allows situations to develop in which bloodshed is inevitable; it entails the shedding of blood."[32]

At its best, then, nonviolent civilian defense would deter and defeat aggression—reducing the level of violence, inhibiting invaders, resisting tyrants, and enhancing peace and freedom. Although not inexpensive, it would permit significant savings. Developed and, especially, developing countries would have more money to deal with unmet human needs. Civilian defense "would very likely become a potent force around the world for liberalizing or overthrowing tyrannical regimes." It would give people greater control over their own destinies. Indeed, "increased confidence in civilian defense and liberation by nonviolent action could produce a chain reaction in the progressive abolition of both war and tyranny."[33]

Critics point to a number of weaknesses in the nonviolent approach. First, given the nature of people and nations, critics say, it is utopian to assume that the nonviolent option can be relied on. Unless there is a miraculous transformation of human nature and of nations, the adoption of nonviolence invites surrender and domination by one's rivals. Second, although nonviolent civilian defense might make a nuclear attack unnecessary, it is not at all clear that nonviolent civilian defense can prevent hostile domination. Third, the notion that it is better to live under an authoritarian regime than not to live at all is cowardly and unacceptable. Fourth, although nonviolent civilian defense might work with humane, civilized, and reasonable opponents, there is no certainty that it would work, at acceptable costs, with brutal barbarians or ideological fanatics.

CONCLUSION

We can now see more clearly the importance—and difficulty—of judging wisely on issues of war and peace. A mere dedication to peace does not produce wise judgments on how to achieve it. Similarly, recognition of the dangers of war does not automatically offer a wise choice about how to secure peace. Costs and benefits are often perceived differently by political scientists, citizens, and policymakers. Yet people must make judgments. They must choose. The failure to judge and choose is itself a judgment and a choice.

Judgment and choice are creative acts. They call for critical acumen; for powers of analysis and synthesis; and for balancing and weighing values, facts, and alternatives. Judgment and choice call for courage because they are not free of doubts, difficulties, ambiguities, and uncertainties.

The widely varying policy options considered in this chapter were chosen to stimulate the imagination and to make choices more ethical, more realistic, and more prudential. The radical alternatives were introduced to provoke thought and to make readers reconsider ethical priorities, reexamine "realities," and reassess wise choices. Only this kind of intellectual endeavor can lead to genuinely creative breakthroughs.

We turn next, in Chapter 13, to the possibility of creative breakthroughs in the battle for the "least free."

SUGGESTED READINGS

Allhoff, Fritz, Adam Henschke, and Jay Strawser. *Binary Bullets: The Ethics of Cyberwarfare*. New York: Oxford University Press, 2016. A thoughtful exploration into the legal and moral issues raised by cyberwarfare.

Biddle, Stephen. *Military Power: Explaining Victory and Defeat in Modern Battle*. Princeton, NJ: Princeton University Press, 2004. Intriguing book on how to win battles in warfare with less emphasis on numbers and technology and more on the manner in which forces are deployed and employed.

Dallaire, Roméo. *Shake Hands with the Devil*. New York: Carroll & Graf Publishers, 2004. Gripping and heart-wrenching story of Lieutenant General Roméo

Dallaire, the UN force commander in Rwanda during the 1994 genocide.

Goldstein, Joshua S. *Winning the War on War: The Decline of Armed Conflict Worldwide*. New York: Dutton Adult, 2011. Insightful analysis of how UN diplomats, aid agencies, and international organizations have increasingly intervened into troubled countries with positive results in reducing warfare of different kinds.

Gurr, Ted Robert, and Barbara Harff. *Ethnic Conflict in World Politics*. 2nd ed. Boulder, CO: Westview, 2000. First-rate study on the wave of ethnic conflict emerging after the end of the Cold War. Central thesis is that ethnic hostilities are often triggered as much by international factors as by domestic influences.

Holbrooke, Richard. *To End a War*. New York: Random House, 1999. Tells the remarkable story, from a career diplomat's perspective, of how he and others brokered a deal to try to end the 1990s war in the Balkans. Superb description of how hard-nosed diplomatic negotiations are carried out.

Holmes, Robert L. *On War and Morality*. Princeton, NJ: Princeton University Press, 1989. One of the finest books in years on the ethics of war. Contains a powerful argument against the realist school and against the "just war" theory, as well as an equally compelling argument for nonviolence.

Mitrany, David. *A Working Peace System: An Argument for the Functional Development of International Organization*. 4th ed. London: National Peace Council, 1946. Still one of the most persuasive arguments for developing an international organization and a functional approach to peace.

Nye, Joseph. *Understanding International Conflict*. 7th ed. New York: Longman, 2008. Excellent survey and analysis of twentieth-century international conflicts.

Pinker, Steven. *The Better Angels of Our Nature: Why Violence Has Declined*. New York: Viking, 2011. A well-known psychologist and neuroscientist, Pinker argues that over centuries humans have become progressively less violent, not more violent. Pinker is always thought provoking.

Seaman, Kate. *Un-Tied Nations: The United Nations Peacekeeping and Global Governance*. Surrey, UK: Ashgate Publishing Co., 2014. Using a number of relevant cases, including the UN interventions into Bosnia, Somalia, Burundi, the Democratic Republic of Congo, and East Timor, Seaman explores how the environment in which these operations took place is changing and how this, in turn, influences the issue of global security governance.

Sharp, Gene. *Exploring Nonviolent Alternatives*. Boston: Porter Sargent, 1971. Sets forth the nonviolent approach that makes the hair on the realist's head stand up straight. Is the world ready for this approach? Can the world endure without it? Also see Sharp's *Civilian-Based Defense: A Post–Military Weapon Defense* (Princeton, NJ: Princeton University Press, 1990).

Shawcross, William. *Deliver Us from Evil: Peacekeepers, Warlords, and a World of Endless Conflict*. New York: Simon & Schuster, 2000. Superb analysis of many of the regional ethnic-based conflicts of the post–Cold War decade and the difficulties of the international community, particularly the United Nations, in dealing with them.

Stiglitz, Joseph. *Globalization and Its Discontents*. New York: Norton, 2003. Discussion on globalization, its principle functions and powers, and its primary institutions. Stiglitz addresses what works and what doesn't in current global policy.

Stoessinger, John. *Why Nations Go to War*. 10th ed. New York: Wadsworth, 2007. Extraordinarily readable treatise on the causes of war, with excellent case studies.

Strachan, Hew, and Sibylle Scheipers. *The Changing Character of War*. New York: Oxford University Press, 2014. This book is the result of a five-year interdisciplinary study at Oxford University highlighting not only the remarkable changes in the way war is conducted but also war's many common characteristics.

Waltz, Kenneth. *Man, the State, and War: A Theoretical Analysis*. New York: Columbia University Press, 1959. A classic statement on the causes of war.

Wright, Lawrence. *The Looming Tower: Al-Qaeda and the Road to 9/11*. New York: Knopf, 2006. A lucid and detailed account of the origins of the modern jihadist movement culminating in the 9/11 attacks.

GLOSSARY TERMS

Cyberwarfare (p. 326)
integration (p. 326)
neofunctionalism
    (p. 335)

new balance of power (p. 326)
nonviolent civilian defense
    (p. 326)
peace (p. 316)

third-party activities
    (p. 326)
war (p. 315)

NOTES

1. Our definition, in contrast to narrower definitions, includes civil wars and revolutionary wars of national liberation. Compare with Francis A. Beer's more traditional definition, in which a clear distinction is made between interstate warfare and domestic violence, in *Peace against War: The Ecology of International Violence* (San Francisco: Freeman, 1981), 6.

2. Again, our conception of peace speaks to the issue of civil wars and revolutionary wars of national liberation. In linking war and peace and the nation-state, we do not ignore criminal violence involving individuals or groups within a nation-state, or troublesome race or class relations. Such violence is not, however, carried on in a systematic and organized way by the political community that has a lawful monopoly on the use of force and violence or by those who aspire to achieve such a monopoly.

3. Arms Control Association. "Nuclear Weapons: Who Has What at a Glance." July 2018. http://www.arms-control.org/factsheets/Nuclearweaponswhohaswhat

4. Ibid.

5. Milton Leitenberg, "Deaths in Wars and Conflicts in the 20th Century," August 2006, Cornell University Peace Studies Program, Occasional Paper No. 29, 3rd ed.

6. Reuters, "Syrian war monitor says 465,000 killed in six years of fighting," World News, March 13, 2017. https://www.reuters.com/article/us-mideast-crisis-syria-casualties/syrian-war-monitor-says-465000-killed-in-six-years-of-fighting-idUSKBN16K1Q1

http://www.nytimes.com/2014/08/23/world/middleeast/un-raises-estimate-of-dead-in-syrian-conflict-to-191000.html?_r=0.

7. Joshua S. Goldstein, "Think Again: War," Foreign Policy, August 15, 2011. Foreignpolicy.com/2011/08/15/think-again-war/#

8. U.S. war costs for World War II came to $664 billion; for the Korean conflict, $164 billion; for the Vietnam conflict, $352 billion. See Beer, *Peace against War*, 122.

9. Jean Sahadi, "The financial cost of 16 years in Afghanistan," CNN Money, August 22, 2017. http://money.cnn.com/2017/08/21/news/economy/war-costs-afghanistan/index.html. Also see Costs of War at http://costsofwar.org.

10. Stockholm International Peace Research Institute, Background Paper on SIPRI Military Expenditure Data, 2012, p. 1.

11. Stockholm International Peace Research Institute, Military Expenditure, World Military. https://sipri.org/research/armament-and-disarmament/arms-transfers-and-military-spending/military-expenditure www.sipri.org/research/armaments/milex.

12. Federation of American Scientists, "United States Munitions and Weapon Systems," 2009, www.fas.org/programs/ssp/man/uswpns/index.html.

13. Deagel Guide to Military Equipment and Civil Aviation, http://www.deagel.com/Fighting-Ships/DDG-1000-Zumwalt_a000550001.aspx.

14. United States Air Force, B-2 Spirit. Fact Sheets. http://www.af.mil/About-Us/Fact-Sheets/Display/Article/104482/b-2-spirit/

15. The Brookings Institution, "The U.S. Nuclear Weapons Cost Study Project."

16. Ruth Leger Sivard, *World Military and Social Expenditures, 1989* (Leesburg, VA: WMSE Publications, 1989), 7.

17. Robert L. Holmes, *On War and Morality* (Princeton, NJ: Princeton University Press, 1989), 89–90.

18. Steve Ranger, "Cyberwar: A guide to the frightening future of online conflict," ZDNET, August 20, 2017. http://www.zdnet.com/article/cyberwar-a-guide-to-the-frightening-future-of-online-conflict/

19. Ibid.

20. CCDOE (NATO Cooperative Cyber Defence Centre of Excellence), Tallinn Manual, 2018. https://ccdcoe.org/tallinn-manual.html

21. For our theoretical observations in this section, we have relied heavily on Oran R. Young's classic book, *The Intermediaries: Third Parties in International Crises* (Princeton, NJ: Princeton University Press, 1967). Updating and additional analysis have come from Douglas W. Simon and Richard Rhone, "United Nations and Conflict Management in the Post–Cold War World," *Harvard Journal of World Affairs* (Fall 1995): 1–12; Michael Klare, "Flawed but Vital: United Nations Peacekeeping Efforts," *Bulletin of Atomic Scientists*, March 1, 1995, 62; and John Terrance O'Neill and Nick Rees, *United Nations Peacekeeping in the Post–Cold War Era* (New York: Routledge, 2005).

22. United Nations, "United Nations Peacekeeping Update," May 1994, Peace and Security Programmes Sector, Department of Public Information, PS/DPI/6/Rev5-May 1994. See also Simon and Rhone, "United Nations and Conflict Management," 3.

23. For a full analysis of this problem, see Simon and Rhone, "United Nations and Conflict Management."

24. Charles W. Kegley Jr. and Eugene R. Wittkopf, *World Politics: Trends and Transformation*, 5th ed. (New York: St. Martin's Press, 1995), 553.

25. David Mitrany, *A Working Peace System: An Argument for the Functional Development of International Organization* (Chicago: Quadrangle Books, 1966).

26. Ibid., 14.

27. Ibid., 9.

28. Ibid., 34–35.

29. Perhaps the leading figure in neofunctionalist thinking is Ernst Haas. See his books *Beyond the Nation-State: Functionalism and International Organization* (Stanford, CA: Stanford University Press, 1964); *The Uniting of Europe: Political, Social, and Economic Forces, 1950–1957* (Stanford, CA: Stanford University Press, 1958); and *Why We Still Need the United Nations: The Collective Management of International Conflict, 1945–1984* (Berkeley: Institute of International Studies, University of California at Berkeley, 1986).

30. Gene Sharp, *Exploring Nonviolent Alternatives* (Boston: Porter Sargent, 1971). Also see Sharp, *Social Power and Political Freedom* (Boston: Porter Sargent, 1980). Another fine example of writing in this area is Robert J. Burrows, *The Strategy of Nonviolent Defense* (Albany, NY: SUNY Press, 1995).

31. Holmes, *On War and Morality*, 272.

32. Ibid., 274.

33. Sharp, *Exploring Nonviolent Alternatives*, 70–72.

Ratko Mladic, the "Butcher of Bosnia," was sentenced in 2017 to life in prison on 10 charges of genocide by the International Tribunal for the former Yugoslavia.

Michel Porro/ Getty Images News/Getty Images

13

THE BATTLE ON BEHALF OF HUMAN RIGHTS

The battle on behalf of human rights has seen significant progress in recent years. Major political actors (the United Nations, the governments of many nations, dedicated nongovernmental organizations [NGOs]) are on record in support of a wide array of human rights. Constitutional democracy, which is built on a crucial respect for human rights, has become an ethical norm for nations around the globe. (Though, the commitment to some constitutional democratic norms has been called into questions in some democracies.) Increasingly, evidence of violations of human rights is brought to the world's attention. And slowly, if not always effectively, political, economic, and military penalties are being employed to combat the worst violations of human rights. Both ad hoc and permanent international courts have been established to hold the perpetrators of **crimes against humanity** accountable for their actions.

Yet, as the reports of the United Nations, the United States, and NGOs such as Amnesty International and Human Rights Watch make clear, much work remains with regard to the protection of human rights. The daunting problems associated with human rights issues necessarily challenge any student of politics. In this chapter, we seek to answer the following question: What wise and effective policies can best offer help in the ongoing and difficult battle to protect human rights around the globe?

In searching for answers to this question, we follow the format adopted in the preceding chapter. After clarifying the problem, we set forth factors that prompt a fuller exploration of our subject. We then present and evaluate alternative approaches to its solution.

Chapter Objectives

After studying this chapter, you will be able to do the following:

1. Discuss various definitions of human rights.

2. Discuss the horrific costs of genocide.

3. Identify other forms of human rights violations such as racism and offenses against women.

4. Identify human rights concerns and violations not only in authoritarian countries but in more open democratic systems as well.

5. Discuss some of the alternative approaches for the advancement of human rights.

CLARIFYING THE PROBLEM

In Chapter 2, we saw that freedom is power over one's own destiny. Freedom can be viewed negatively or positively. Negative freedom means the absence of arbitrary restraints that limit the power to pursue one's destiny. Positive freedom is the presence of opportunities that enable individuals and groups to fulfill their own peaceful and creative potentialities. **Human rights** is, essentially, freedom. That is, it is freedom—legal, political, or moral—from government violations of people's integrity and their civil and political liberties (negative freedom) as well as assurance of the satisfaction of vital human needs such as food, shelter, clothing, health care, and education necessary for life to flourish (positive freedom). The concept of human rights is so closely allied to that of freedom that the terms are frequently used synonymously. What do human rights include? Let us examine this important term further. Cyrus R. Vance, secretary of state during President Jimmy Carter's administration, characterized it as follows:

> *First, there is the right to be free of violations of the integrity of the person.* Such violations include torture; cruel, inhuman, or degrading treatment or punishment; and arbitrary arrest or imprisonment. And they include denial of fair public trial, and invasion of the home.
>
> *Second, there is the right to the fulfillment of such vital needs as food, shelter, health care, and education.*
>
> *Third, there is the right to enjoy civil and political liberties—freedom of thought, of religion, of assembly; freedom of speech; freedom of the press; freedom of movement both within and outside one's country; freedom to take part in government.*[1]

Other definitions of human rights also explicitly include the right to be free of racial or sexual discrimination.

These are working definitions only; there is no universal agreement on the exact meaning of the term. Some scholars interpret human rights narrowly, limiting them to civil and political rights understood as legal claims, which, if violated, legal remedies can uphold. Thus, for example, if the government deprives an American citizen of freedom of speech, through the courts he or she can stop such a violation. Other scholars prefer to interpret human rights more broadly to include economic (and even social and cultural) rights understood as moral, political, and legal obligations that governments are pledged to advance. Thus, in many countries government has a moral obligation to help the destitute, a political obligation to find jobs for the unemployed, and a legal obligation to educate children. A government's capacity to fulfill its legal, political, and moral obligations, however, may depend on the nation's economic development. And, of course, a government's capacity to fulfill legal claims will depend on its constitutional commitments and its political state of health.[2]

Historically, liberal democracies in the West have been primarily concerned with civil and political rights. But with the advent of the welfare state and the advance of democratic socialism, economic, social, and cultural rights have also become prominent. Governments in communist countries and in some developing countries have also emphasized economic, social, and cultural rights. However, whether such rights are actually protected remains a troubling question. In the case of China, for example, it remains to be seen whether the advent of new economic freedoms will lead to greater social and political liberty. Arguments over priorities—and the relationship of one right to another—are central to the battle for human rights. Other questions are also important (see the Key Questions for this chapter).

Before we can sensibly explore alternative approaches to protecting human rights, we need to set forth the key ethical and empirical factors that color our awareness of human rights and influence our choices in considering prudent policies.

ETHICAL AND EMPIRICAL FACTORS

The **least free**—that is, the powerless, the deprived, and the maltreated as well as often the poor, racial, ethnic, and religious minorities, women, and the politically oppressed—have always needed protection. And discourse on the appropriate means of dealing with such oppression has been proffered for millennia. However, in the twentieth century, faced with widespread and flagrant violations of human rights, the world's population experienced an unprecedented rise in ethical consciousness. The existence of human rights violations on a massive scale seized public attention.

When Allied troops overran Adolf Hitler's concentration camps and discovered the horrifying crimes that had been committed there, people around the globe were stunned into considering how such an outrage could have occurred. Other extreme violations of human rights became public knowledge after Soviet Premier Nikita Khrushchev delivered to the Communist Party Congress the now-famous (but in 1956 secret) speech in which he exposed the decades-long crimes perpetrated by Joseph Stalin. After World War II, the struggles of peoples of the developing world for freedom from colonial masters called attention to imperial exploitation and racism. Soviet domination of the countries of Eastern Europe illustrated yet another pattern of imperial control. Racial discrimination in the United States, long a troubling problem, became even more so in a post–World War II America that had just defeated a racist Nazi regime and sought to assume political and moral leadership in a world more nonwhite than white. The contemporary feminist movement, which began in earnest in the 1960s, exposed the reality of sexism—in the United States and around the world. And authoritarian governments of the right and left continued to persecute, imprison, and degrade peaceful dissidents. Even in those countries where the protection of human rights appeared well established, critics worried constantly about their fragility. For example, in the United States after the 9/11 terrorist attacks activists criticized the George W. Bush administration for its policies of detention and interrogation of suspected terrorists implemented as part of the war on terror.

We now investigate in greater detail some of the realities, both historical and contemporary, that have made the problem of human rights so pressing in world politics. Our discussion will examine (1) genocide, (2) the persistence of racism, (3) left- and right-wing violations, and (4) offenses against women.

Genocide

The dreadful reality of the Holocaust—the systematic persecution and murder of 6 million Jews and other minorities during World War II by the Nazis and their supporters—strongly influenced the writing of the UN Universal Declaration of Human Rights in 1948. The Nazis' shocking actions were dramatically revealed when Allied armies entered Germany and the countries it had dominated and liberated the survivors of the concentration camps, the death factories that were the ultimate step in what the Nazis called "The Final Solution of the Jewish Question." At Auschwitz, 2,000,000 had been murdered; at Majdanek, 1,380,000; at Treblinka, 800,000; at Belzec, 600,000; at Chelmno, 340,000; and at Sobibor, 250,000.[3] (See Table 13.1 for estimates of the number of Jews killed in each country.) The full extent of the slaughter—and of the systematic campaign of mass murder—was not immediately apparent but emerged at the post–World War II Nuremberg trials of war criminals and in subsequent investigations. The evidence—in confessions, eyewitness accounts, Nazi records, and pictures of tyranny and terror—of crimes against innocent civilians is incontrovertible and led world opinion to resolve "never again!"

The crimes against Jews perpetrated by Hitler and his supporters started with prejudice fanned by propaganda; advanced to outright political, social, and economic persecution; and, finally, erupted in mass murder. World opinion later came to realize that the crimes against Jews carried out by the Nazis and their supporters were inextricably connected with Nazi violations of the human rights of all civilians—Germans, Poles, Czechs, French, Russians, as well as other Europeans.

It is difficult for us to grasp the terror of this campaign of extermination carried out by "ordinary" Germans in Nazi-occupied lands. In fact, many would argue it is impossible for those who did not experience it to comprehend the living hell of the Nazi concentration camp—the horror, brutality, starvation, degradation, and murder. Again and again survivors have emphasized the point: unless you lived through it yourself, you can never understand. Certainly, those in the outside world who heard reports of the atrocities couldn't understand; nor could the liberators themselves understand— soldiers whose eyewitness reports of piles of corpses of men, women, and children placed squarely before the wider world the catastrophe of the Holocaust; and certainly not today's onlookers, whose window onto the horror of that place and time is limited to the extant photographic and documentary record.

In 1948, in response to Nazi crimes, the UN General Assembly adopted the Convention on the Prevention and Punishment of the Crime of Genocide, which went into force in 1951. Genocide, as we saw in Chapter 1, is defined as the systematic mass destruction of a national, ethnic, racial, or religious group. Genocide includes any of the following acts:

1. Killing members of the group

2. Causing either bodily or mental harm to members of the group

3. Deliberately inflicting on the group conditions of life calculated to bring about its physical destruction in whole or in part

4. Imposing measures intended to prevent births within the group

5. Forcibly transferring children of the group to another group[4]

The Genocide Convention makes a number of actions punishable: genocide itself, the conspiracy to commit it, incitement to commit it, the attempt to commit it, and complicity in it. Genocide is held to be a matter of international concern, a crime under international law. Moreover, by interpretation or amendment, the antigenocide convention should also clearly protect political groups or economic classes from genocidal killing.[5]

Has genocide occurred since World War II? Although nothing quite comparable, at least in sheer numbers, to the Holocaust has occurred, the actions of Pol Pot's Khmer Rouge regime in Cambodia (Kampuchea) can be described as genocidal. "While in power from 1975–1979, the Khmer Rouge (Cambodian communists) compiled one of the worst records of human rights violations in history as a result of a thorough and brutal attempt at restructuring Cambodian society. More than 1 million people, out of a total population of 7 million, were killed or died under the Khmer Rouge's genocidal regime."[6]

Table 13.1 Jews Killed in the Holocaust

Country	Estimated Number Killed
Austria	50,000
Belgium	25,000
Belorussia	245,000
Bohemia/Moravia	80,000
Bulgaria	11,400
Denmark	60
Estonia	1,500
Finland	7
France	90,000
Germany	130,000
Greece	65,000
Hungary	450,000
Italy	7,500
Latvia	70,000
Lithuania	220,000
Luxembourg	1,950
Netherlands	106,000
Norway	870
Poland	2,900,000
Romania	270,000
Russia	107,000
Slovakia	71,000
Ukraine	900,000
Yugoslavia	60,000

Source: *The Holocaust Chronicle: A History in Words and Pictures* (Lincolnwood, IL: Publications International, 2000), 702. Reprinted by permission of Publications International, Ltd.

Courtesy of the National Archives/Newsmakers

Buchenwald concentration camp in Germany was the scene of more than 56,000 deaths at the hands of Nazi officials. The primary objective was to kill prisoners by work, but thousands also perished through torture, beatings, starvation, and lack of hygiene. This picture was taken as the camp was liberated by the U.S. 80th Army Division in April 1945.

Other massive and egregious violations of human rights of a genocidal nature have also occurred. The 1990s saw dreadful attacks in the central African country of Rwanda and in the Balkan countries of Bosnia and Kosovo. "The immediate consequences of the genocide [in Rwanda in 1993 and 1994] were that about 500,000 Tutsi were killed, 10,000 to 30,000 Hutus (also targeted by the *genocidaires*) were killed, and a substantial number of Tutsi women were raped, tortured, and sexually mutilated."[7] Genocide in Bosnia, from 1992 to 1995, took the form of ethnic cleansing, whereby "Muslims were forced from their homes; thousands were placed in compounds reminiscent of concentration camps; hundreds, perhaps thousands, of women were raped; and tens of thousands of citizens were murdered. . . . Before the violence was ended in 1995, as many as 200,000 Bosnian Muslims had perished, and the number of refugees had reached nearly three million."[8] In 1999, a comparable pattern of ethnic cleansing of Kosovar Albanians produced deplorable human rights violations. "Up to 10,000 or so died at Serb hands, mostly innocent civilians; thousands more were raped or otherwise brutalized. Some 800,000 people were forcefully expelled from Kosovo, and hundreds of thousands more were displaced within the territory."[9] Other egregious violations of human rights include, for example, the Indonesian army's brutal assault on the inhabitants of East Timor, on Timor Island, and the savage suppression and murder of Kurds in Saddam Hussein's Iraq. The Darfur region of Sudan has been, and still is to a degree, plagued by what President George W. Bush in 2005 labeled a genocide as thousands of black Sudanese fled the region and nearly 400,000 perished at the hands of government forces or the *Janjaweed*, nomadic Arab militias. Beginning in August of 2017, hundreds of thousands of Rohingya Muslims in Myanmar fled into neighboring Bangladesh. Tens of thousands were internally displaced inside the country and the Myanmar military carried out extensive killings, shelling and arson as part of the ethnic cleansing.[10]

In 2000, UN Secretary-General Kofi Annan challenged the international community to come up with a consensus on the issue of confronting genocide and mass killing. In response to that challenge and the litany of genocidal horrors of recent years, the International Commission on Intervention and State Sovereignty formed by the Canadian government issued a report, known as the **Responsibility to Protect (R2P)**, that outlines a state's responsibilities toward its population and the international community's responsibility if the state fails to protect its citizens.[11] One aim of the R2P is to provide the legal and ethical basis for international **humanitarian intervention**—that is, an internationally sanctioned, multilateral military intervention in a country to prevent or to stop genocide if the country proves unable or unwilling to do so itself. The R2P doctrine was embraced by the UN General Assembly in 2005 at the World Summit in New York City. Whether the doctrine can be translated into meaningful action is open to debate. One concern is the view of a number of developing countries that the doctrine is merely an excuse to allow the United Nations and the countries of the developed world military intervention in the internal affairs of states.

The Persistence of Racism

Racism is an ugly reality. It is rooted in the idea that some races are superior or inferior to others. This judgment becomes a basis for discrimination against the race alleged to be inferior. Such discrimination may be legal, political, economic, or social, or all of these. Racism has promoted slavery, separate treatment, and prejudice in the United States and around the globe. From the late 1940s to the early 1990s, the separation of and discrimination against black South Africans was embedded not only in daily life but also in the legal system. **Apartheid** in South Africa involved the legally sanctioned separation of political, economic, and social life for blacks and whites and was designed to perpetuate white supremacy.

In the United States, slavery ended only in 1865. However, despite the Thirteenth, Fourteenth, and Fifteenth Amendments to the Constitution (amendments passed after the Civil War to protect the civil rights of African Americans), African Americans continued to suffer notorious discrimination. Subsequently, the **separate but equal doctrine**—a doctrine legally sanctioned in the United States from 1896, when the U.S. Supreme Court upheld its constitutionality in *Plessy v. Ferguson*, until 1954, when it was struck down by the Warren Court in *Brown v. Board of Education of Topeka*—held that equality was not violated where blacks were required to use separate facilities in transportation, education, and other public areas as long as the services rendered were equal. After 1938, the Court began to take a more realistic look at so-called separate but equal facilities for African Americans, beginning to strike down separate treatment as unequal treatment in a number of cases. But it wasn't until its sweeping decision in *Brown* that the Court declared unequivocally that "in the field of public education the doctrine of 'separate but equal' has no place because separate educational facilities are inherently unequal."

The *Brown* case set up a series of subsequent legal challenges and Court decisions that fundamentally changed American political, social, and cultural life. All of these legal changes, such as wider access to public spaces and the strengthening of criminal rights, occurred against the backdrop of a heated but ultimately successful civil rights movement. Effective constitutional and legislative reform went hand in hand with the political actions of average Americans of all colors. Among the most important of those reforms was the Voting Rights Act of 1965; a century after the end of the Civil War, African Americans finally received real legal protection for their voting rights. Unfortunately, despite these advances, racial prejudice continues to mar American society. Its extent, and what to do about it, are hotly debated today.

Though the United States did not eliminate slavery until 1865, other countries were even slower to outlaw it. Ethiopia did so only in 1942, Kuwait in 1949, and Qatar in 1952. More disturbing, however, is the fact that slavery, involuntary servitude, and forced labor continue to exist in the twenty-first century. The 2016 Global Slavery Index estimates that there are approximately 45.8 million men, women, and children trapped in various types of modern day slavery—forced labor, domestic servitude, and the sex trade at the hands of human traffickers. Some are young children in debt bondage and some are wives, bought by their husbands and classified as property. Countries with the highest prevalence of slavery measured as a percentage of the population are North Korea 4.37 percent, Uzbekistan 2.97 percent, Cambodia 1.65 percent, India 1.40 percent, and Qatar 1.35 percent. Countries with the highest number of modern slaves are India 19.35 million, China 3.39 million, Pakistan 2.13 million, Bangladesh 1.53 million, and Uzbekistan 1.23 million.[12]

The Charter of the United Nations, the Universal Declaration of Human Rights, and the two international covenants on human rights (discussed later in this chapter) prohibit discrimination on the grounds of race or color. In other conventions, the United Nations has ruled against discrimination in employment (1958) and in education (1960). And in 1965, the General Assembly adopted the International Convention on the Elimination of All Forms of Racial Discrimination. Parties to the convention not only condemn racial discrimination but also agree to eliminate it in all its forms. Parties to the convention also declare that disseminating ideas based on racial superiority or hatred or inciting racial discrimination is punishable by law. They also agree to "declare illegal and prohibit organizations" that "promote and incite racial discrimination" and to "recognize participation in such organizations . . . as an offense punishable by law."[13]

Left-Wing and Right-Wing Violations

Some people might argue that horrors such as the Nazis' genocide and Stalin's destruction of the kulaks (well-to-do peasants) and other real or imagined opponents are things of the past. Stalin in the Soviet Union, Hitler in Germany, Benito Mussolini in Italy, and Francisco Franco in Spain—the dictators of the left or right, communist or fascist, in the 1920s, 1930s, and 1940s—are dead. The worst of Western imperialism and colonialism is behind us. Even racism, which lingers around the globe, has few public defenders.

Unfortunately, although the world has come a long way in articulating standards of human rights, persistent and flagrant violations are still widespread. One of the most recent cases occurred in Syria where President Bashar al-Assad in 2011 and 2012 brutally cracked down on citizens of his country who were protesting against the government in pursuit of greater freedom. As of mid-2012, roughly 8,000 people had been killed by the Syrian government's action. In the subsequent two years, Syria plunged into full-scale civil war with a variety of rebel factions confronting the Assad regime. Against these groups, the government utilized not only the usual array of conventional weaponry but also chemical weapons as well as a particularly devastating device known as the barrel bomb. These are large oil drums filled with explosives, nails, and other sorts of shrapnel and usually dropped from a helicopter. Because they are notoriously inaccurate in their delivery, the chances of innocent bystanders being hit is much greater than with guided munitions. The total number of Syrians killed in the conflict varies widely, but as of 2017, it is thought to be approximately 465,000 of which over 96,000 are civilians.[14] Human rights violations occur in communist countries such as China, Cuba, North Korea, and Vietnam as well as in a number of right-wing authoritarian regimes in Africa, Asia,

Latin America, and the Middle East. Even nations that are considered more democratic—Israel, the United States, and nations of Western Europe, for example—are not entirely immune. These violations (documented in the annual reports of Amnesty International, Freedom House, and Human Rights Watch, and in the U.S. State Department's annual *Country Reports on Human Rights Practices*) include systematic torture, imprisonment, and killing of political opponents, as well as denial of freedom of speech, press, and association. (For a list of countries rated by degree of freedom, see Chapter 8, Table 8.1.)

Efforts to confront terrorism have led to two controversies of note in the United States. The first concerns the **USA PATRIOT Act** (Uniting and Strengthening America by Providing Appropriate Tools Required to Intercept and Obstruct Terrorism), signed by President George W. Bush shortly after the September 11 attacks on the World Trade Center and the Pentagon. The act was designed to enhance the tools available to law enforcement for detecting, tracking down, and prosecuting terrorists and those who aid them. The act actually strengthens protection of certain civil liberties and immigrant groups and constrains some of the new government powers—facts critics often fail to point out.[15] But there is a great deal of controversy over a series of provisions that confer new, and broaden old, surveillance powers of the government. For example, the act permits the government to access information indicating what material people check out of libraries. In addition, critics complain that some of the new powers granted to the government lack transparency and accountability. For champions of civil liberties in the United States, these are serious defects and run counter to the most fundamental rights upon which the nation was founded. Critics maintain that reform is needed; efforts to this end have been periodically undertaken by Congress.[16] In March 2007, the Patriot Act was renewed. The renewed legislation included some curbs on power. But most Democrats and a few Republicans in the House and Senate felt these modifications did not go far enough. Other provisions of the renewed act strengthened the government's powers, particularly in the area of wiretapping. In February 2010, President Barack Obama signed legislation that temporarily extended three very controversial provisions of the Patriot Act for one year: (1) authorization for court-approved roving wiretaps that permit surveillance on multiple phones; (2) court-approved seizure of records and property in antiterrorism operations; and (3) permission for surveillance against a so-called lone wolf, a non-U.S. citizen engaged in terrorism who may not be part of a recognized terrorist group. A year later in February 2011, the Patriot Act was once again extended. Then in June 2013 came the revelations by Edward Snowden, an analyst working for a private firm under contract to the National Security Agency (NSA). The stolen classified documents that he released to the press revealed a vast electronic surveillance program both foreign and domestic involving not only foreign nationals but U.S. citizens. Phone records, e-mails, computer searches, and online purchase patterns were all part of the NSA surveillance efforts with code names like Prism, Muscular, Thin Thread, and Stellar Wind. Communication giants like Verizon, AT&T, Microsoft, Google, Yahoo, and Facebook were pressed to turn over records of their consumers to NSA or allow NSA access to the companies' operational programs. It was a massive invasion of privacy in the name of national security, and the country is still struggling with the problem.

While not related to anti-terrorism efforts, another controversy regarding egregious violation of privacy broke out in 2018. Two years earlier, in 2016, the British political consulting firm Cambridge Analytica obtained copies of private data for roughly 50 million

Facebook users. The company did millions of dollars in political consulting work for Donald Trump's presidential campaign. As of mid-2018, if and how the Facebook data was used is not clear. But the fact that these private files were leaked at all is troubling.

The second controversy concerns the treatment of prisoners seized in the war on terror and held by the U.S. government. During America's intervention in Afghanistan in 2002, which was intended to destroy al-Qaida training camps and bring down the Taliban regime in Kabul, hundreds of enemy fighters were captured and transported to the Guantanamo Bay naval base in Cuba. The United States contended that detention and interrogation of these prisoners were critical for success in the war on terror. Further, the government argued, the prisoners at Guantanamo were outside the United States and therefore not subject to constitutional rights—an argument rejected by the U.S. Supreme Court in 2004. The government also contended that the prisoners were "illegal enemy combatants." But in November 2004, a U.S. district court judge ruled that the Bush administration had exceeded its authority in its stated intention to try the enemy combatants in military tribunals, denying them access to evidence used against them. In July 2005, a three-judge panel of the U.S. Court of Appeals for the District of Columbia Circuit reversed the district court decision, ruling that the military could conduct **war crimes** trials of terrorism suspects. The controversy over the Guantanamo prisoners reached a new level in June 2005, when Amnesty International's secretary general, Irene Khan, labeled the U.S. detention center "the gulag of our times," evoking images of the deplorable prison/labor camps of the former Soviet Union. Many Americans were offended by the charge, including the president of the United States, who countered that it was "absurd." Not unexpectedly, on January 22, 2009, newly elected President Barack Obama took a first step in fulfilling a campaign promise by signing an executive order to shut down the facility at Guantanamo within one year. While the number of prisoners has been significantly reduced, the holding facility was not shut down during the Obama presidency, and President Trump never embraced the idea of closing it. As of early 2018, Guantanamo was still open and all indications were that it would remain open.

In addition to the issue of prolonged incarceration at Guantanamo, a firestorm of controversy swirled around the interrogation of Iraqi prisoners. The issue first emerged with the revelations of the mistreatment of prisoners at Abu Ghraib prison in Iraq in 2004. Both military and CIA personnel had physically and psychologically tormented prisoners, and at least one prisoner, Manadel al-Jamadi, died in Abu Ghraib as a result of his interrogation. The Abu Ghraib actions were denounced by the Bush administration, and various forms of disciplinary action were taken against at least some of the perpetrators. But critics asserted that only lower-level personnel were held accountable and that the responsibility for such treatment rested with staff considerably higher up in terms of authority.[17]

The issue of "enhanced interrogation" reached into the highest levels of government when it was revealed that prisoners at Guantanamo were subjected to "stressful" interrogation, the most controversial technique being the simulated drowning procedure known as waterboarding. The Bush administration prepared various legal positions asserting that "enhanced interrogation," including waterboarding, was not torture and further contended that these techniques had yielded valuable information vital to the war on terror and national security in general. Many critics in the military, legislative, intelligence, and human rights communities disagreed and believed that not only was this a violation of the Geneva Convention on the Treatment of Prisoners of War but that it robbed the United States of moral legitimacy when it complained about human rights abuses in other countries. On January 22, 2009, on the same day he issued the order to close Guantanamo, President Obama issued an order requiring that the CIA use only the interrogation methods outlined in the U.S. Army Field Manual. This, in effect, banned the use of what many considered torture. But some observers believe that the steadfastness of even this seemingly definitive action has been cast in doubt. In April 2009, President Obama appeared not to rule out torture when he said he "will do whatever is required to keep the American people safe." President Trump in both his campaign and as president consistently expressed the belief that torture works and that he supported "enhanced interrogation," including waterboarding. And so, the argument goes on. Is any behavior—including the violation of human rights—justified if a country's security is perceived to be threatened?

It is also important to emphasize the reciprocal connection between freedom and human development (understood in terms of life expectancy, educational attainment, and income). Economically better-off countries generally have a large measure of freedom as well. In fact, it appears that there is "a link between a country's per capita income and the extent of its democratic freedom," even though some rich nations may not rank high on a freedom index and some poor nations may enjoy a high level of political freedom.[18] "People now see freedom as an essential element in human development, not as an optional extra. Political freedom and human development do seem to move in tandem."[19] What is frequently debated, though, is whether freedom leads to economic development or economic development leads to the desire for greater freedom. Among political scientists and policymakers, this has been a hotly debated issue. It has been particularly acute over the last three decades in discussions related to China's dynamic economic reforms. The ramifications for U.S. foreign policy are immense. For example, what policies should we set toward China, an authoritarian communist country undergoing a rapid economic conversion to a market economy, that would best steer it toward greater democratic reform?

Although violations are widespread and flagrant, there is a positive side to the human rights record in the past few years. Mikhail Gorbachev's decision in 1989 to allow the countries of Eastern Europe to pursue their own destinies, free of Soviet domination, signaled the end of the human rights violations that had kept these countries among the least free. The decline of a number of authoritarian regimes in South America in the 1980s signaled another triumph of human rights. Similarly, the end of apartheid in South Africa constituted a significant advance for human rights.

Offenses Against Women

The rights of half the human race continue to be violated on a massive scale around the globe. This is true despite the pronouncements of national constitutions in developed and developing nations and despite the eloquent prohibitions against sexual discrimination in key UN documents. The preamble of the UN Charter endorses the principle of "equal rights of men and women." Article 1, Paragraph 3 declares that one purpose of the United Nations is to promote "respect for human rights and for fundamental freedoms for all without distinction as to race, sex, language, or religion." The same language—"without distinction as to . . . sex"—appears again in Articles 13, 55, and 62. Similar, and even more explicit, guarantees are found in the International Covenant on Civil and Political Rights. These rights relate to such matters as marriage, voting, and public affairs and to protection against sexual discrimination. Both documents affirm that marriage must be entered into with the free "consent of the intending spouses." The International Covenant on Economic, Social and Cultural Rights affirms the principle of "equal remuneration for work of equal value" and equal opportunity in promotion (Article 7), the "right of everyone to education" (Article 13), and the "right of everyone to take part in cultural life" (Article 15). These provisions built on earlier agreements on the rights of women and anticipated the 1967 Declaration on the Elimination of Discrimination against Women.

The 1967 declaration holds that discrimination against women—sexism—is fundamentally unjust and an offense to human dignity. It calls for appropriate measures to abolish discriminatory laws and customs. The document contains several provisions to protect women's status in the family; women's right to acquire, use, and inherit property; and women's right to legal equality. It calls for measures to end prostitution and to give women equal rights with men in education and in economic and social life. It also proposes measures to prevent women from losing their jobs in the event of marriage and supports paid maternity leave and necessary child-care facilities.

The language of the 1967 declaration—and of subsequent conferences—is impressive. But what about the reality? The reality of equal rights for women around the globe shows some progress but remains disappointing. Some women are still enslaved or bought by their husbands and classified as property. Certain marriages—including child marriages—are still arranged in Southeast Asia. The traffic in women for purposes of prostitution still exists.

People who see the persistence of sexism often link the problem to **patriarchy**—the belief in male superiority (and female inferiority). Patriarchy is a powerful cultural norm around the world. Because it is a societal norm, embedded in the heritage of many cultures, it leads to a disturbing set of practices. Such practices often seem normal and are unquestioned by many people. Not only does discriminatory behavior persist in many parts of the world but it is often supported by archaic laws that dictate women's subordinate position in family and society.[20] The double standard of morality (one moral code for men, another for women) that the patriarchal heritage often perpetuates is revealed by the following, lengthy list of sexist practices:

1. adultery (for men only)

2. prostitution (most often for women only)

3. infanticide (girl children only)

4. child marriage (brides even younger than grooms)

5. arranged marriages (veto power to men)

6. illegitimacy (children as property of men)

7. wife selling and wife beating

8. slavery in marriage (divorce available only to men)

9. prohibitions against birth control and abortion[21]

A substantial number of other practices—emphasizing the double standard actually at work in the world—can be identified as well:

1. double duty (women work outside the home and care for the children and home as well)

2. unequal pay for equal work

3. greater number of illiterate women than illiterate men in the world

4. male dominance in policymaking in politics, the corporate world, labor unions, the mass media, and universities

5. no pay for wives for housework

6. female workers in lower-level jobs

Women in every country, Western and non-Western, industrialized and rural, modern and premodern, are underutilized in terms of their numbers, denied access to positions of prestige and power, and expected to find their primary fulfillment as mothers and wives. Women generally are poorer than men. Minority women often bear the twin burdens of race and sex discrimination. The 1977 Declaration of American Women, drawn up at the National Women's Conference, states that women have had "only minor and insignificant roles in making, interpreting and enforcing our laws, in running our political parties, unions, schools and institutions, in directing the media, in governing our country, in deciding issues of war or peace."[22]

Recent UN data reveals alarmingly high levels of violence against women. Worldwide, more than one in three women say that they experienced physical violence in their lifetime and one in ten girls under the age of 18 was forced to have sex.[23]

The severe violation of women's rights has become a particularly disturbing problem with the behavior of two terrorist groups—Boko Haram in North Africa and the Islamic State of Iraq and Syria (ISIS) in Syria and Iraq. Boko Haram has conducted vicious raids in northeast Nigeria, kidnapping and imprisoning well over 2,000 people. In one raid, they took 200 young girls and told them they would be sold in the human trafficking market. While they were in control of northwestern Iraq, ISIS seized young Yazidi women to be sold as wives for ISIS fighters. The Yazidi are one of Iraq's many distinct religious groups.

Also disturbing is the fact that women are far too often the victims of human trafficking or the purpose of promoting pornography and prostitution. Hardly a region of the world has been immune from this plague.

ALTERNATIVE APPROACHES TO SECURING HUMAN RIGHTS

In this section, we examine who does what and how in the realm of human rights. We focus primarily on the United States, the United Nations, important NGOs, and the least free themselves. Some of the questions that the alternative approaches explore are listed on the next page.

Efforts of Powerful States

Jack Donnelly, an astute student of human rights, argues convincingly that "the fate of human rights—their implementation, abridgement, protection, violation, enforcement, denial, or enjoyment—is largely a matter of national, not international, action." Although Donnelly is persuaded of the "moral universality of human rights" and of the importance of authoritative international norms, he maintains that human rights can best be realized through national action.[24] With this perspective in mind, let us consider how one nation, the United States, might act to protect and promote human rights.

The United States can play its role domestically (by respecting human rights at home) and internationally (by promoting the cause of human rights abroad). But what policies should the United States employ to protect international human rights?

Sound international policy begins with a sound commitment. Before World War II, the United States and the other major Allied powers did not do what needed to be done to prevent Hitler's aggressions, particularly his genocidal actions against European Jewry. In 1948, in what one might view as a belated reaction to these horrors, the Allied countries and other members of the United Nations signed the Universal Declaration of Human Rights. It was a significant response to the war's horrible human rights violations. Yet the advent of the Cold War—the U.S.-Soviet rivalry—cast a cloud over American efforts to protect human rights. A forthright policy to protect these rights consistently took a backseat to national security.

In the early 1970s, fed by evidence of substantial violations all over the world, especially in South America, the U.S. Congress did pass important human rights legislation. For instance, laws were passed to prohibit economic and military aid to governments brutalizing their populations. Country reports on human rights practices were required from the State Department. Countries that denied or restricted their citizens' right to emigrate were denied most-favored-nation (MFN) treatment, meaning that a country's right to be granted the lowest possible tariffs in trade relations would be withheld. American representatives on international lending agencies were also required to vote against loans for countries that grossly violated internationally recognized human rights.

In his 1977 inaugural address, President Jimmy Carter declared that the U.S. commitment to human rights must be "absolute" and a "central concern" of American foreign policy. He supported the establishment of human rights machinery in the executive branch as well as congressional initiatives to interpret that commitment and concern. But what fuller philosophy and policies should guide that U.S. commitment to human rights? How does an American president balance the central need to protect vital national interests with the need to enhance the protection of human rights around the globe? If the U.S. commitment to human rights should be a "central concern" of American foreign policy, how "absolute" can that commitment wisely be? Here we can identify two general philosophies.

Prudent realists such as former Secretary of State Henry Kissinger, who served under Richard Nixon and was perhaps the most powerful person to ever hold that office, argue that the United States does, indeed, have an interest in protecting human rights, but this interest must be balanced by the primary need in foreign policy to protect vital U.S. national interests.[25] In February 2009, Secretary of State Hillary Clinton, in an unusually blunt statement, reinforced this realist position when speaking on the issue of human rights in China. While on a visit to Beijing, she asserted that "successive administrations and Chinese governments have been poised back and forth on these issues, and we have to continue to press them. But our pressing on those issues can't interfere with the global economic crisis, the global climate change crisis, and the security crisis." In contrast, *prudent idealists* such as William F. Schulz, executive director of Amnesty International USA (who advocates a "new realism" for our "interconnected age"), argue that defending human rights "benefits us all" and is "in our best own interest."[26]

KEY QUESTIONS

1. Should policy emphasize persuasion; political, economic, and legal redress; or military coercion? What mixture of persuasion and more forceful sanctions makes the most sense?

2. How quickly can actors react when concerns over human rights are raised?

3. Will significant protection require moderate reform or drastic revolution?

4. What political, economic, and social considerations influence what key actors should or can do?

5. What are the strengths and weaknesses of alternative policies, strategies, and tactics?

Ironically, both prudent realists and prudent idealists could find support in the perspective outlined by Carter's secretary of state, Cyrus Vance. Vance suggested that the United States could act on its own or with and through the United Nations. The United States could also work through regional organizations such as the Inter-American Commission on Human Rights. Vance contended that there is a range of policy initiatives available to the United States, including quiet diplomacy, public pronouncements, and the withholding of foreign assistance. He further stated, "Whenever possible, we will use positive steps of encouragement and inducement. Our strong support will go to countries that are working to improve the human condition. We will always try to act in concert with other countries through international bodies."[27]

Creative Breakthrough

According to Vance, "We seek these goals because they are right, and because we, too, will benefit. Our own well-being, and even our security, are enhanced in a world that shares common freedoms and in which prosperity and economic justice create the conditions for peace. And let us remember that we always risk paying a serious price when we become identified with repression."[28] Vance insisted that it was possible to act forthrightly, yet realistically, on human rights. A realistic position would explore violations carefully, consider the prospects of effective action, and avoid self-righteousness.

Vance's well-judged guidelines can be endorsed by prudent realists or prudent idealists. Although the Carter administration's position was closer to an idealistic policy characterized by use of publicity and of **sanctions** (penalties, often economic, imposed on states that violate human rights or international law) than to a realistic diplomacy, liberal critics have, nevertheless, argued that there was more rhetoric than reality in the Carter years. They point out that U.S. policy singled out the Soviet Union and left-wing regimes for criticism. They note that although during the Carter years the United States did cut aid to repressive regimes in Argentina, Ethiopia, and Uruguay, it did not recommend cuts for Iran under the shah, the Philippines, or South Korea—all human rights violators at the time.

Tough-minded realistic diplomacy was the preferred option of the Reagan and first Bush administrations, as it was of the second Bush administration. Critics note that the Reagan and George H. W. Bush administrations did not cut off aid to El Salvador or Iraq—countries with dreadful records on human rights. In those authoritarian regimes, America's alleged security interests conflicted with its human rights concerns. Prudent idealists would avoid the hypocrisy of going easy on national security friends while leaning heavily on national security foes and on little countries that can be scolded with impunity.

Bill Clinton's administration, too, was not without critics on this issue. Although characterized by good intentions and by positive actions in such countries as Haiti, the American government proved inadequate in Rwanda and distressfully slow in responding to dreadful violations of human rights in Bosnia and Kosovo. Belatedly, the United States did move to bring a halt to the fighting in Bosnia with the diplomatic settlement of the Dayton Accords in 1995. And after diplomatic efforts failed with regard to Serbia's actions in Kosovo, the United States joined in the NATO air campaign to end Serbia's ethnic cleansing in Kosovo.[29] However, the Clinton administration eventually backed off on any meaningful action on human rights in China, apparently deferring to the importance of good trade relations and asserting that this policy would help, over time, in "liberalizing" China's human rights record. Moreover, although Clinton in his last days in office did sign the treaty for a new Permanent International Criminal Court (ICC), he did not push energetically for Senate ratification. Of course, it is by no means clear that the U.S. Senate would have approved the treaty even if Clinton had campaigned for its acceptance. In any case, President George W. Bush withdrew the U.S. signature from the Treaty of Rome (which founded the court) in May 2002.

Not unlike many of his predecessors, President George W. Bush actively supported democracy and human rights around the world but was also subject to criticism for his relations with countries with questionable human rights records such as Pakistan, Russia, Saudi Arabia, Tajikistan, Turkmenistan, and Uzbekistan, all of varying importance in the war on terror.

President Obama's human rights record has been characterized by some as "mixed." He did reverse some of his predecessors' practices that advocates of human rights have been critical of, particularly those related to the battle against terrorism. And yet Guantanamo remained open throughout his presidency. He also indicated that his administration would revisit the issue of joining the ICC and encouraged some of the Court's recent actions—including the arrest of the leader of the Lord's Resistance Army (LRA) in the Congo, the referral of Libya to the ICC, and pressure on Sudan to surrender

President Bashir for human rights violations in Darfur. And yet, the White House made no forceful move to ratify the ICC Treaty and join the court. Obama was also inconsistent toward the pro-democracy movements of the Arab Spring. He expressed the view that, "On the issue of genocide, I think 'never again' means that the international community has an obligation, even when it's inconvenient, to act when genocide is occurring."[30] Not unlike many of his predecessors, while Obama spoke for and acted on behalf of the least free, he also demonstrated a streak of prudent realism when it comes to human rights.

During his first eighteen months in office, President Trump came under heavier criticism for his stance on human rights than any recent president. Critics, including some of the leading human rights groups in the world, accused the president of at best ignoring massive human rights violations around the world and at worst, cozying up to various authoritarian leaders with abominable human rights records. Domestically, critics were particularly disturbed by the president's immigration policies and statements. Policies like his ban on immigrants coming from seven Muslim countries, the unwillingness to accept any refugees from violent trouble spots like Syria and Honduras, the separation of children from parents as people from Central America and Mexico attempted to cross the border, and the slashing of emergency funds for refugees, all came under fire. Critics also found many of his statements during the campaign and as president very disturbing, perhaps the most well known is his reaction to the neo-Nazi rally and demonstration in Charlottesville, Virginia, in 2017 when he stated that, *"Well, I do think there's blame—yes, I think there's blame on both sides. You look at—you look at both sides. I think there's blame on both sides. And I have no doubt about it, and you don't have any doubt about it either. . . . But you also had people that were very fine people, on both sides. . . ."* That kind of equivalent assessment of neo-Nazis and those protesting them troubled many people. Finally, his repealing of protections for transgender students, his proposed ban on transgenders in the military, and the appointment of anti-LGBT administrators and representatives to key positions at UN conferences and in the Health and Human Services Department met with considerable criticism. In 2018, President Trump announced the U.S. withdrawal from the United Nations Human Rights Council accusing the body of bias against Israel and the Council's hypocrisy of seating member states with horrible human rights records.

Both prudent realists and prudent idealists may agree that wise judgment is called for in articulating and implementing policy. It is relatively easy to say that decisions call for informed and careful judgment. It is much more difficult to articulate in concrete cases what constitutes wise policy that both protects human rights and is in the national interest.

Prudent idealists argue that the protection and advancement of human rights are a moral imperative. Powerful countries such as the United States should pursue policies that are consistent with their professed values. To do otherwise not only is hypocritical but also serves to undermine the state's moral legitimacy in the eyes of the international community.

Prudent realists, on the other hand, argue for a more proactive policy on behalf of human rights based on the premise that the United States has a vital security interest in their protection. Genocide, especially, is a threat to the security of the international system, and the United States, as a major power, has a responsibility to protect the security of the international system. Moreover, respect for human rights advances the cause of constitutional democracy; it is clear that constitutional democracies do not make war on each other. Put simply, U.S. national security interests, and not abstract morality, must guide foreign policy, including human rights policy. The United States, of course, has an interest in advancing human rights. But the United States must always ask how its actions on behalf of protecting human rights relate to its basic vital interests. Moreover, the U.S. government must always monitor domestic support for its actions on behalf of human rights abroad and assess the human and monetary costs and consequences of those actions. When costs are too high and consequences dangerous, and domestic support is absent, actions on behalf of protecting human rights may not be prudent. One can argue that the failure of the Clinton administration with regard to Rwanda was tied to a belief that there was little domestic support for such action. The early days of the Obama administration revealed a president struggling to move forward in protecting human rights while facing complicated domestic political considerations. For example, when the president proposed the closing of the Guantánamo Bay prison camp and the transfer of captured enemy fighters to prisons in the United States as a first step in a significant change in policy, Democrats and Republicans alike opposed the plan. They feared a political backlash from constituents back home.

In both cases, prudent idealism and prudent realism, there is always the risk that human rights policies will be perceived as, or in reality will become, heavy-handed attempts to impose American values on others.

The United Nations

Another approach to protecting human rights, not necessarily in conflict with national policy, would emphasize working through the United Nations. This argument builds on the UN forthright commitment to human rights. The United Nations exemplifies what is called an *international human rights regime*.[31] The commitment began with the adoption of the Universal Declaration of Human Rights in 1948. Though not a legally binding treaty, it paved the way in subsequent years for adopting a variety of treaties, including the International Covenant on Civil and Political Rights; the International Covenant on Economic, Social and Cultural Rights; the Convention on the Rights of the Child; the Convention relating to the Status of Refugees; the Convention against Torture; the Convention on the Prevention and Punishment of the Crime of Genocide; and two conventions dealing with racial discrimination and discrimination against women.

In many respects, the United Nations has done a remarkable job of articulating common principles—and thus a common standard—for human rights worldwide. Wise and effective implementation is now the major challenge of the United Nations. A host of UN organizations and offices are actively concerned with human rights. These include the General Assembly, which, according to the UN Charter, is to assist "in the realization of human rights and fundamental freedom for all without distinction as to race, sex, language, or religion"; the Security Council, which may be involved if human rights violations endanger international peace and security; the secretary-general; and the Economic and Social Council, which can "make recommendations for the purpose of promoting respect for, and observance of, human rights and fundamental freedoms for all." In 1993, the United Nations established a high commissioner for human rights to work with the UN Commission on Human Rights (replaced in 2006 by the United

Nations Human Rights Council) and other UN groups. But what can these organizations and offices do now to advance human rights principles? What powers do they hold that enable them to fulfill the UN standard? What policy options might become available in the future?

In general, the United Nations has articulated standards and tried to convince nations to endorse them. The United Nations invites compliance reports from parties to its human rights conventions. It receives complaints about violations of human rights from governments, NGOs, and at times individuals. The United Nations may investigate complaints and report on violations—specifically those revealing a gross and consistent pattern of violations of human rights. It may exercise quiet diplomacy or invoke sanctions of one kind or another.

In the first two decades of its existence, "the only systematic activities of the United Nations with regard to the monitoring and protection of individual human rights" related to the trust territories and non–self-governing territories.[32] Beginning in 1967, however, UN organs became more active. They investigated violations in Argentina, Cambodia (Kampuchea), Chile (after the coup that overthrew Salvador Allende Gossens in 1973), Cyprus, El Salvador, Rhodesia (Zimbabwe), South Africa, and Southwest Africa (Namibia). Today, the United Nations is involved in monitoring human rights all over the world, in places like Afghanistan, Eritrea, Haiti, Kazakhstan, Kyrgyzstan, Nepal, Sudan, Uzbekistan, and most recently with an observation mission in Syria. Yet its power to safeguard human rights is constrained—by its limited authority, its reluctance to interfere in the internal affairs of its members (particularly powerful members), the absence of a police force to protect human rights, the veto in the Security Council, and the stubborn defiance of nations that violate human rights.

In view of these considerations, which policy options are available to the United Nations? One course of action would be to strengthen the processes of articulation of standards and the use of quiet diplomacy to gain adherence to those standards. A second course of action would be to focus more sharply on verifying consistent patterns of gross violations through independent UN investigation and on exposing those violations to the glare of public scrutiny. A third course of action would be to place primary emphasis on developing effective political, economic, judicial, and military sanctions to protect human rights.

Each of these courses of action has strengths and weaknesses. Clearly, it is important to move toward a global consensus on human rights standards. But what does consensus mean? Agreement on words? Or fulfillment of principles? Furthermore, rhetorical consensus on standards is one thing; operative respect is another. Nations may pay lip service to rights but ignore them in practice. Quiet diplomacy is certainly a legitimate means and may work, but often it is a code for procrastination. Tact and tactful publicity are often sensible, but sometimes they enable nations to give precedence to alleged national security interests over ethical human rights obligations. Thus, in the past nations have soft-pedaled human-rights violations by their friends. And the United Nations has been reluctant, or unable, to take action against powerful nations.

Verification through UN investigation and subsequent publicity also run into problems. Nations object to interference in their internal affairs and cite the UN Charter in their defense. Investigative visits depend on the consent of the alleged violator of human rights. Public embarrassment may be counterproductive; it may anger the nation whose practices the United Nations is seeking to alter. Compliance reports depend on the good faith of the nation submitting them; no nation guilty of gross human rights violations would willingly incriminate itself.

Given the persistence of the sovereign nation-state system, UN member states will often resist the use of more powerful sanctions to protect human rights. The United Nations has generally been loath, or unable, to invoke sanctions, a matter that falls within the powers of the Security Council, where each permanent member can veto action. In one important exception—Rhodesia (now Zimbabwe)—the great powers agreed to invoke economic sanctions. The 1966 agreement rested not on the issue of human rights but on the fact that the situation there threatened peace. Majorities in the General Assembly can be more easily mustered for resolutions against unpopular members— South Africa, with its former practice of apartheid, has been the best example—but these resolutions lack the teeth of the Security Council's diplomatic, political, economic, and military sanctions. Now that the end of the Cold War has made great power agreement easier, the Security Council may be more likely to invoke sanctions in clear-cut cases, especially when aggressors seek to wipe out the very existence of a previously independent nation (as in the Iraqi invasion and attempted annexation of Kuwait).

In more difficult cases—the protection of human rights in Bosnia-Herzegovina or Kosovo or Rwanda—action is more complicated. UN policy in Rwanda did not stop genocide there. UN military action in Kosovo would probably have been blocked by a Russian or Chinese veto in the Security Council. Nonetheless, the organization has been modestly successful in establishing ad hoc international criminal tribunals for Rwanda and Bosnia; in prosecuting some of those individuals guilty of crimes against humanity, war crimes, and genocide; and even in indicting and bringing to justice a former head of state, Slobodan Milosevic of Yugoslavia.[33] The case of Cambodia was particularly frustrating. Not only did the international community not intervene to stop the slaughter in the mid-1970s but it was not until March 2003 that the United Nations reached a draft agreement with the Cambodian government for an international criminal tribunal to try former Khmer Rouge leaders who had engineered the slaughter of millions of their fellow citizens. The agreement came after only five years of negotiations and twenty-four years after the Khmer Rouge were driven from power.

Crimes against humanity refers to acts of murderous persecution against a group of people and are considered criminal offenses above all others. Genocide is a crime against humanity. War crimes consist of violations of the laws of war as spelled out by various international covenants and include such things as atrocities committed against civilians and the mistreatment of prisoners of war.

Given these difficulties, how should the United Nations best proceed in protecting human rights, particularly from the scourge of genocide? One bold thought experiment envisages the establishment of a global human rights regime, under the auspices of the United Nations, that would (1) significantly strengthen global human rights institutions, (2) be guided by a cogent theory of prudent prevention, (3) utilize an operative theory of effective staged implementation, and (4) employ a wise theory of just humanitarian intervention.[34]

The strengthened institutions would include, for example, an invigorated UN Security Council, the recently established UN high commissioner for human rights, a more proactive UN Commission on Human Rights, and the Permanent International

Criminal Court (ICC), that unlike the International Court of Justice (ICJ), tries individual leaders responsible for crimes against humanity, genocide, or war crimes. As of the end of 2017, the ICC opened investigations into eleven situations in ten countries where serious human rights violations had occurred: Democratic Republic of Congo, the Central African Republic (2 cases), Uganda, Darfur in Sudan, Republic of Kenya, Libya, Mali, Burundi, Georgia, and the Republic of Cote d'Ivoire.[35] Perhaps the case with the highest notoriety is being brought in absentia against Joseph Kony, the alleged commander in chief of the LRA (Lord's Resistance Army) in Uganda. Additional institutions that might be created would include, for example, a UN human rights monitoring agency and a UN human rights protection force, to provide, respectively, watchful eyes and effective muscle in cases of potential or actual genocide. A cogent theory of prudent prevention (designed to prevent genocide rather than cope with it retroactively) would rest on three cardinal principles: the need to develop mature constitutional democracies worldwide, the need to develop the philosophy and practice of deterrence of genocide, and the need to develop the philosophy and practice of preemptive action in the event that deterrence does not work.

AP Photo/Ben Curtis, File

In 2012, the Special Court for Sierra Leone found Charles G. Taylor (left), the former president of Liberia, guilty of crimes against humanity and war crimes. Taylor was sentenced to fifty years in prison, for crimes committed from 1996 to 2002, including murder, rape, slavery, and the use of child soldiers. Here he is shown in 2003 just after handing over the power of the presidency to Vice President Moses Blah.

A workable theory of wisely staged implementation is also imperative. First, such a policy would call for effective machinery for monitoring, investigating, and reporting on potential or actual genocide. Second, such a policy would require that the power of publicity be employed to deter genocidal violations—where there is a clear and present danger of the eruption of genocide—and to solidify global support for just humanitarian intercession to stop genocide in progress. Third, effective remedies—political, judicial, economic, and military sanctions—must be on hand to be prudently chosen and employed to stop genocide. To have any chance of success, such remedies must have the support of UN members willing and able to implement decisions of the UN Security Council. Finally, there is a crucial need to work out the problem of what might be called "human rights consolidation," namely, what it takes to ensure that human rights will continue to be respected after initial efforts at prevention or intervention have been successful.

There is, additionally, a need to articulate and employ a cogent theory of just humanitarian intervention. Such a guiding theory might include the following principles: intervention only by an appropriate authority (such as the UN Security Council); just cause; timely military intervention when other pacific means—political, economic, judicial sanctions—have been tried and found wanting; prudent appraisal of benefits and costs of intervention; expectation of reasonable chance of success in the short term; employment of humane and proportionate means; careful calculation of the reasonable chance of success for the long run. A tall order? Yes. Impossible? No. But how probable?

One school of thought argues that the United Nations has an important job to do in articulating standards for the global community. These standards shape the consensus that will make international freedom a reality. At this time, the United Nations cannot go beyond this important task without meddling in the internal affairs of nations. Perhaps in the future the United Nations will acquire real power to investigate violations of human rights and to fashion effective remedies.

Another school of thought favors developing wise and effective remedies now. Proponents of this school would not only strengthen UN power to investigate complaints but also establish effective machinery to protect human rights after persistent and gross violations have been verified. Interpretation of the UN Charter should clearly allow humanitarian intervention in such cases as genocide.

Political realists are particularly skeptical of the grand thought experiment outlined previously—a global human rights regime. They argue that little can be done; that the world lacks adequate policy, machinery, and particularly will—and that these deficiencies will not be overcome in the foreseeable future; that the costs of intervention and protection are too high; that the United Nations is ill-equipped to handle the tasks outlined; that even well-intentioned nations (looking to their own vital interests) will not cooperate with the United Nations; and that it is unwise, dangerous, and unlawful to meddle in the internal, domestic affairs of sovereign nation-states. The reasons for this skepticism must be understood, but it would be tragic, indeed, if the United Nations were to prove unable to bring a halt to genocide and other serious human rights violations.

Nongovernmental Organizations

Numerous NGOs work tirelessly and effectively to protect human rights. They include Amnesty International, Human Rights Watch, Freedom House, the International League for Human Rights, and the International Commission of Jurists. Amnesty International works to secure the release of prisoners of conscience and, in recent years, to abolish torture and capital punishment. Human Rights Watch is also dedicated to the protection of a wide range of human rights. Freedom House monitors human rights worldwide and reports annually on its findings. The International League for Human Rights drafts human rights standards for the United Nations, forms civil liberties unions around the globe, protects political dissidents and religious minorities, and guards against the extermination of South American Indians. The International Commission of Jurists seeks to preserve the worldwide rule of law, particularly the right to a fair trial.

Image from Amnesty International's *Don't Turn a Blind Eye to Torture* Campaign.

Other NGOs also crusade for human rights. Church, scientific, and professional groups have been involved. The Roman Catholic Church has been in the forefront of the battle for human rights in Latin America, stimulated by the Vatican II meetings of the Catholic leadership to discuss key religious and social issues and the establishment of the Pontifical Commission on Justice and Peace.[36] Protestant organizations such as the World Council of Churches and the American National Council of Churches have also made human rights a priority. In 1976, the American Association for the Advancement of Science formed a human rights clearinghouse to monitor scientific freedom and responsibility. PEN International, a global association of writers, works on behalf of freedom of expression and champions writers, artists, and other intellectuals whose work arouses hostility. Jewish organizations have also worked hard for human rights.

In strategy and tactics, the work of NGOs is threefold. First, many seek to influence the United Nations to draft international human rights standards. Second, some NGOs target for investigating those governments that have allegedly practiced human rights violations, and the organizations publicize the violations. Third, other NGOs, such as Amnesty International, attempt to put direct pressure on governments to obtain legal representation for political prisoners, improve the conditions of prisoners, or stop specific practices such as capital punishment. Some NGOs, of course, adopt all three approaches.

The NGOs are quite strong, particularly in their current roles. They can often obtain reliable information about human rights violations and bring it before the United Nations or a national government. They have made publicity a powerful weapon in the battle for human rights. Because NGOs have no vested national, political, or economic interests to protect, their reports have a degree of credibility that those generated by governments may not. Given their single-minded devotion to human rights, they are not compromised by questions of politics or by the balancing of security and rights in their efforts to report on, and obtain relief for those who suffer human rights violations. The NGO activities often involve hundreds of thousands of people directly. Their consultative status with the United Nations allows NGOs to engage in private diplomacy, and they can directly approach offending governments to seek information about and redress for violations of human rights. Their activities have raised global consciousness, made governments more hesitant to violate rights, secured the release of persons unjustly imprisoned, and mitigated the punishment of others.

Political scientists who are impressed by the NGOs argue that the organizations' careful work in documenting and publicizing violations has helped protect human rights by making violating governments take notice. The NGOs cannot perform miracles, but they can make actual or potential offenders think carefully about their practices. In fact, these organizations may have prevented violations that would otherwise have occurred, and they have secured the release of at least some victims.

Other scholars, who applaud the limited good that NGOs do, nevertheless are quick to emphasize their weaknesses. These critics note, for example, that although the NGOs can organize influential and even mass memberships in the United States and Western Europe, they cannot do so in China, Iran, Iraq, or North Korea. Unlike states, they cannot invoke political, economic, or military sanctions.

Creative
Breakthrough

Efforts of the Least Free

What role will the least free play in their own emancipation? Some scholars are persuaded that human rights for the least free cannot be achieved without significant transformation in the global community or without major reform or radical revolution within the countries that now violate their own people's human rights. The victims of genocide, colonialism, racism, political repression, and sexism themselves have to be involved in the changes essential to securing their rights. For example, to guard against another Holocaust, Jews already in Palestine joined forces with refugees from Europe to found the modern state of Israel as a homeland for persecuted Jews everywhere, a strong haven against genocide. They established a nation with the power to make "Never again!" a reality. Jews who prefer to remain citizens of other countries must actively defend their constitutional rights and vigorously support the freedom of their coreligionists in Israel and elsewhere in the world.

Efforts on the part of citizens in authoritarian regimes to advance freedom are never easy. It takes courage, personal sacrifice, and oftentimes the suffering of physical abuse to effect change. In places where freedom was curtailed for certain periods of time, such as El Salvador, Argentina, and South Korea, indigenous challenges were not entirely futile. Through the use of civil disobedience, public demonstrations, or outright revolt, significant changes in these countries improved protection of human rights. In more authoritarian countries such as Iran, North Korea, Sudan, and Syria, it is far more difficult for citizens to effect significant change in pursuit of human rights protection. One recent development that offers some reason to be optimistic is the advent of new technologies such as Internet and cellphone use inside such countries; their use may allow oppressed peoples to quickly and cheaply inform the wider world about abuses occurring inside their countries. This was in clear evidence in the case of Iran in June 2009, when suspect election results fomented widespread—and ultimately well-documented—protest. It was also evident during the Arab Spring in 2010 as it swept through seventeen North African and Middle Eastern authoritarian regimes, toppling governments in Tunisia, Libya, Egypt, and Yemen. In all, there were seventeen countries that to varying degrees experienced the Arab Spring. Unfortunately, it was only in Tunisia that some real reform seems to have taken hold. In the remaining countries, either authoritarian forces have prevailed against the protests or as in the case of Libya and increasingly in Yemen, power vacuums were formed and the countries were plunged into uncertainty and chaos.

Specifically, what can the people in these countries do to protect their human rights? Will strategies vary for different regimes, depending on whether they are totalitarian or authoritarian? Will tactics that enable U.S. citizens to cope with violations of civil liberties work in China, Iraq, or Vietnam? These questions are not easily answered, but they call attention to the important and difficult work of the least free and their allies around the globe. A process of liberalization initially did overturn an authoritarian Soviet Union (although as time passed, Russia under Putin increasingly reverted to authoritarianism and remains very suspect in its protection of human rights); most countries in South America are now free of military rule; and some repressive regimes (such as that of Ferdinand Marcos in the Philippines) have been overthrown with the help of "people power" and massive nationwide protests.

It is also important to realize that philosophies such as liberation theology—rooted in a particular interpretation of Christianity and drawing on Marxist social analysis—can help people struggling to ensure their human rights. Liberation theology interprets Christianity as a gospel of freedom and justice for the oppressed. It also uses a Marxist analysis to highlight capitalism and imperialism as sources of economic, political, and social oppression. Critics still ask which understanding of liberation theology is to be chosen by the least free with this religious commitment. They also wonder how effective liberation theology will be in both theory and practice.[37]

For all the oppressed peoples of the world, a basic policy choice exists: change through peaceful means versus change through violent means. Another fundamental choice is between incremental, constitutional reform and radical, extralegal revolution. Combinations of these choices are, of course, theoretically possible. In making their choices, the least free have to face the most difficult task of judgment—the balancing of costs and benefits. Violence, for example, may lead to the loss of life, and a militant revolution often calls for a sacrifice of liberty. It is extraordinarily difficult to balance the human rights sacrificed and the lives lost under a repressive regime against the human rights and lives potentially saved by a revolutionary regime of the least free. And there is always the danger that a revolution will simply replace one repressive regime with another. Similarly, it is unusually difficult to balance the sacrifices in human rights of slower, incremental, constitutional, peaceful reform against the gains of speedy, wholesale, extralegal, violent revolution. The choices are agonizing. Perhaps a top priority of any strategy by the least free should be to avoid, or minimize, any sacrifices of human rights or lives.

Other tasks in the battle of the least free are less agonizing. For example, the least free have to realize their plight and position. They must achieve self-identity and self-reliance. They must also organize to enhance their collective strength. They need to reach out to allies and form coalitions to maximize their strength. And they need to realistically assess the strengths and weaknesses of the institutions that oppress them. At the right time, they must focus their power to extend their freedom.

This is easier said than done. Yet there are success stories to juxtapose against the failures and the incomplete successes. Racism is by no means completely absent in the United States; yet, as we noted earlier, in a remarkable civil rights "revolution" in the 1950s and 1960s, the separate but equal doctrine, which was an integral part of the American South, was defeated. While this revolution involved the actions of tens of thousands, it was sparked by courageous African Americans such as Martin Luther King, Jr., head of the Southern Christian Leadership Conference; Thurgood Marshall, the lead attorney arguing the *Brown v. Board of Education* case of 1954; and Rosa Parks, the seamstress who in 1955, in segregated Montgomery, Alabama, refused to give up her seat in the middle section of a bus so that a white man could sit there.

The Holocaust was a dreadful reality; yet the state of Israel was founded in its wake and thrives through the efforts of the Jewish people. Apartheid, the government-sanctioned separation of races in South Africa, no longer exists—in no small measure because of the work of people such as Archbishop Desmond Tutu and Nelson Mandela. Through the protests and other political activities of people such as Lech Walesa in Poland, Andrei Sakharov in Russia, and Vaclav Havel in Czechoslovakia, the groundwork was laid for the eventual elimination of communist rule and establishment of democracies in Eastern Europe and the Soviet Union.

Sexism pervades the modern world, with women enslaved; prostituted; battered; and denied education, the vote, and equal pay for equal work. But in some countries, women have made significant gains in education, politics, and social life. In the United States, for example, Elizabeth Cady Stanton and Susan B. Anthony led the nineteenth- and early-twentieth-century movement to gain legal rights for women, including the right to vote (achieved in 1920). The U.S. women's movement of the 1960s and 1970s went further, demanding economic, political, and personal equality and significant progress has been made over the past few decades. But despite all the progress, in late 2017, the **"Times UP" and "Me Too" movements** emerged consisting thousands of women in the United States and Europe revealing their experiences as victims sexual assault and harassment. Internationally, four global conferences on women's issues were held in the last three decades of the twentieth century: in Mexico City, Mexico (1974); Copenhagen, Denmark (1980); Nairobi, Kenya (1985); and Beijing, China (1995). These conferences were instrumental in facilitating communication between women around the world and in developing strategies to obtain basic rights.

Supporters of peaceful incremental reform believe that it is important to establish and then build on institutions of freedom in all countries. They concede that the battle will be easier in countries with a constitutional tradition than in countries where authoritarian regimes persevere. Still, whatever the form of government, supporters of this approach believe reform will be less costly and more beneficial if it is achieved by peaceful means rather than violent revolution.

Supporters of a more militant policy point out that those who keep the least free powerless will not easily permit peaceful, constitutional change. Repression will continue until power is mobilized to overturn it. Because those who now oppress the least free use explicit violence, violence in turn may be necessary to defeat them. The degree of militancy will depend on the character of the oppressor, and different strategies may be required for different categories of the least free—for example, blacks or women or political dissidents—as they confront different types of repressive regimes.

CONCLUSION

If politics is viewed as a civilizing process, creative breakthroughs to policies that can enhance the freedom and human rights of the least free must be explored. Students of politics must understand the values, behavior, and judgments that make such breakthroughs possible. Ethically, a civilizing politics must give top priority to helping the least free and to opposing the worst evils: nuclear war, genocide, brutalizing racism, savage torture, and inhumane sexism. Systematic, persistent, and gross violations of human rights must be opposed and ended. A civilizing politics should prefer lawful, constitutional, nonviolent means to protect human rights.

Next, we focus on one important ingredient of human rights that merits its own chapter: economic well-being.

SUGGESTED READINGS

Evans, Gareth. *The Responsibility to Protect, Ending Mass Atrocity Crimes One and For All.* Washington, DC: Brookings Institution Press, 2009. Former Australian foreign minister and now president of the International Crisis

Group, was the primary architect of the Responsibility to Protect Doctrine. Cannot get better than reading about this doctrine than from its author.

Donnelly, Jack. *Universal Human Rights in Theory and Practice.* 3rd ed. Ithaca, NY: Cornell University Press, 2013. Argues on behalf of human rights as universal moral rights. Emphasizes the connection between human rights and Western liberalism, and rebuts various relativist challenges, favoring priority of national action in implementing human rights. A very persuasive analysis.

Freedom House. *Freedom in the World: The Annual Survey of Political Rights and Civil Liberties, 2011–2012.* New York: Freedom House, 2012. Ranks countries on a scale of 1 to 7, where 1 means "most free" and 7 "least free."

Howard, Rhoda E. *Human Rights and the Search for Community.* Boulder, CO: Westview Press, 1995. Favors a conception of rights that embraces economic as well as civil and political rights.

Human Rights Watch. *Human Rights Watch World Report 2017.* New York: Human Rights Watch, 2017. Annual publication that describes and analyzes significant human rights developments in sixty-five nations.

Morsink, Johannes. *Inherent Human Rights: Philosophical Roots of the Universal Declaration.* Philadelphia: University of Pennsylvania Press, 2009. Written by a major historian of the Declaration of Human Rights, traces the philosophical roots of the Declaration back to the Enlightenment and to a shared revulsion of the horrors of the Holocaust.

———. *The Universal Declaration of Human Rights: Origins, Drafting, and Intent.* Philadelphia: University of Pennsylvania Press, 1999. Award-winning historical and philosophical account of the development of the declaration.

———. *The Universal Declaration of Human Rights and the Challenge of Religion.* Colombia: University of Missouri Press, 2017. Morsink's third book on the Universal Declaration of Human Rights. Like the first two volumes in this series, it is both well written and challenging.

Neier, Aryeh. *The International Human Rights Movement: A History.* Princeton, NJ: Princeton University Press, 2013. An extremely well-written account of the history of the movement by a historian who helped to make the history he writes.

Power, Samantha. *A Problem from Hell: America and the Age of Genocide.* New York: Basic Books, 2002. Award-winning account of twentieth-century genocide and the American response.

Riemer, Neal. *Protection against Genocide: Mission Impossible?* Westport, CT: Praeger, 2000. Contains articles on the case for a global human rights regime, crucial changes in the international system, Rwanda, economic sanctions, the Permanent International Criminal Court, a proposed UN constabulary, and humanitarian intervention.

Schulz, William F. *The Future of Human Rights.* Philadelphia: University of Pennsylvania Press, 2009. Schulz recounts and laments how the United States has regressed from its progressive position on human rights manifest at the end of the Cold War.

Sikkink, Kathryn. *The Justice Cascade: How Human Rights Prosecutions Are Changing World Politics.* New York: Norton, 2011. Illustrates how recent decades have seen former and sitting heads of state brought before various national and international courts and tribunals and how this is a marked change from earlier eras when these officials were largely immune from prosecution for human rights violations.

Teitel, Ruti G. *Humanity's Law.* New York: Oxford University Press, 2011. Brilliant treatise on the shift in international law from "state security" (e.g., borders, statehood, territory) to "human security," or the protection of people.

U.S. Department of State. *Country Reports on Human Rights Practices.* Washington, DC: U.S. Government Printing Office. The State Department's yearly report to Congress. Informative, measured. Should be supplemented by reports of NGOs such as Amnesty International.

GLOSSARY TERMS

apartheid (p. 349)
crimes against humanity (p. 343)
humanitarian intervention (p. 348)
human rights (p. 000)
least free (p. 345)

patriarchy (p. 354)
Responsibility to Protect (R2P) (p. 348)
sanctions (p. 358)
separate but equal doctrine (p. 349)

"Times UP" and "Me Too" movements (p. 368)
USA PATRIOT Act (p. 351)
war crimes (p. 352)

NOTES

1. Cyrus R. Vance, "Law Day Address on Human Rights," in *Human Rights and American Foreign Policy*, ed. Donald P. Kommers and Gilburt D. Loescher (Notre Dame, IN: University of Notre Dame Press, 1979), 310.

2. For an excellent, balanced, and critical discussion of this issue, see Jack Donnelly, *Universal Human Rights in Theory and Practice*, 2nd ed. (Ithaca, NY: Cornell University Press, 2002).

3. For estimates of those murdered in Nazi concentration camps and elsewhere, see Lucy S. Dawidowicz, *The War against the Jews, 1933–1945* (New York: Holt, Rinehart and Winston, 1975), 149. See also Martin Gilbert, *The Holocaust: A History of the Jews of Europe during the Second World War* (New York: Holt, Rinehart and Winston, 1985); Daniel J. Goldhagen, *Hitler's Willing Executioners: Ordinary Germans and the Holocaust* (New York: Knopf, 1996); and Eric A. Johnson, *Nazi Terror: The Gestapo, Jews, and Ordinary Germans* (New York: Basic Books, 1999).

4. See the text of the United Nations Convention on the Prevention and Punishment of the Crime of Genocide, in Neal Riemer, *Protection against Genocide: Mission Impossible?* (Westport, CT: Praeger, 2000), app. 1, 161–164.

5. On this point, see Leo Kuper, *Genocide: Its Political Use in the Twentieth Century* (New Haven, CT: Yale University Press, 1982), especially 9–10 and chap. 8, "Related Atrocities," 138–160.

6. U.S. Department of State, *Country Reports on Human Rights Practices for 1989* (Washington, DC: U.S. Government Printing Office, 1990), 792.

7. See Helen Fein, "The Three P's of Genocide Prevention: With Application to a Genocide Foretold—Rwanda," in Riemer, *Protection against Genocide*, 57.

8. Douglas W. Simon, "The Evolution of the International System and Its Impact on Protection against Genocide," in Riemer, *Protection against Genocide*, 23.

9. Ivo H. Daalder and Michael E. O'Hanlon, *Winning Ugly: NATO's War to Save Kosovo* (Washington, DC: Brookings, 2000), 3.

10. Human Rights Watch, Rohingya Crisis, 2018. www.hrw.org/tag/rohingya-crisis

11. International Commission on Intervention and State Sovereignty, *Responsibility to Protect: Report of the International Commission on Intervention and State Sovereignty* (Ottawa, Canada: International Development Research Center, 2001).

12. The Global Slavery Index 2016, www.globalslaveryindex.org/findings.

13. Moshe Y. Sachs, *The United Nations: A Handbook of the United Nations, Its Structure, History, Purposes, Activities, and Agencies* (New York: Worldmark Press, 1977), 101.

14. Reuters, World News, "Syrian War Monitor says 465,000 killed in six years of fighting," May 13, 2017. www.reuters.com/article/us-mideast-crisis-syria-casualties-war-monitor-says-465,000-killed-in-six-years-of-fighting-idUSKBN16K1Q1

15. Stephen J. Schulhofer, *Rethinking the Patriot Act: Keeping America Safe and Free* (New York: The Century Fund Press, 2005), 2.

16. Ibid., 6.

17. For an extensive discussion of the Abu Ghraib abuse case, see David Levi Strauss and Charles Stern, *Abu Ghraib: The Politics of Torture*, The Terra Nova Series (Berkeley, CA: North Atlantic Books, 2004).

18. United Nations Development Programme, *Human Development Report 1992* (New York: Oxford University Press, 1992), 27.

19. Ibid., 32.

20. See Lynne B. Iglitzin, "The Patriarchal Heritage," in *Women in the World*, ed. Lynne B. Iglitzin and Ruth Ross (Santa Barbara, CA: Clio Books, 1976), 7–8. For updates that substantially confirm these conclusions, see Kelley D. Askin and Dorean M. Koenig, eds., *Women and International Human Rights Law*, 3 vols. (Ardsley, NY: Transnational, 1999–2001); United Nations Department of International and Economic Affairs et al., *The World's Women, 1970–1990: Trends and Statistics* (New York: United Nations, 1991); and Padmini Murthy and Clyde Lanford Smith, *Women's Global Health and Human Rights* (Sudbury, MA: Jones & Bartlett, 2009).

21. Iglitzin, "Patriarchal Heritage," 14. Here Iglitzin is quoting or citing Carol Andreas, *Sex and Caste in America* (Englewood Cliffs, NJ: Prentice Hall, 1971), 74.

22. National Women's Conference, "1977 Declaration of American Women," in *The Spirit of Houston: The First National Women's Conference (An Official Report to the President)* (Washington, DC: National Commission on the Observance of International Women's Year, 1978).

23. Somini Sengupta, "U.N. Reveals 'Alarmingly High' Levels of Violence Against Women," *New York Times*, March 9, 2015, https://www.kff.org/news-summary/violence-against-women-reaches-alarmingly-high-levels-globally-u-n-report-says/.

24. Donnelly, *Universal Human Rights.*

25. Henry Kissinger, *Does America Need a Foreign Policy? Toward a Diplomacy for the 21st Century* (New York: Simon & Schuster, 2001).

26. William F. Schulz, *In Our Own Best Interest: How Defending Human Rights Benefits Us All* (Boston: Beacon Press, 2001).

27. Vance, "Law Day Address on Human Rights," 314.

28. Ibid.

29. On Rwanda, see Fein, "Three P's of Genocide Prevention"; on the Dayton accords, see Richard Holbrooke, *To End a War* (New York: Random House, 1998); on NATO intervention in Kosovo, see Daalder and O'Hanlon, *Winning Ugly.*

30. Remarks by President Barack Obama (United States) and Chancellor Angela Merkel (Germany), Dresden Castle, Dresden, Germany, June 5, 2009.

31. The Universal Declaration of Human Rights and various covenants associated with the declaration provide the norms of what Jack Donnelly terms a "global human rights regime," a system of rules and implementation procedures centered on the United Nations. The principal organs of this regime are the UN Commission on Human Rights and the various human rights committees. See Donnelly, *Universal Human Rights*, 206.

32. See Nigel S. Rodley, "Monitoring Human Rights by the U.N. System and Nongovernmental Organizations," in Kommers and Loescher, *Human Rights and American Foreign Policy.*

33. See Michael P. Scharf, *Balkan Justice: The Story behind the First International War Crimes Trial since Nuremberg* (Durham, NC: Carolina Academic Press, 1997). Scharf deals with a key early case handled by the international tribunal for the former Yugoslavia. Subsequently, more prominent individuals involved in crimes in the Bosnian conflict have been indicted, including Milosevic.

34. See Neal Riemer, *Creative Breakthroughs in Politics* (Westport, CT: Praeger, 1996); and Riemer, *Protection against Genocide*, chaps. 1 and 8. In addition to the United Nations (a global regime), there are regional human rights regimes: for example, a European regime and an inter-American regime. There are also single-issue regimes, which concern themselves with such issues as workers' rights, racial discrimination, torture, or women's rights. See Donnelly, *Universal Human Rights.*

35. The International Criminal Court, Situations and Cases, 2018. https://www.icc-cpi.int/#

36. See Jo Renee Formicola, *The Catholic Church and Human Rights: Its Role in the Formulation of U.S. Policy, 1945–1980* (New York: Garland, 1988).

37. On interpretations of liberation theology, see José Miguez Bonino, *Doing Theology in a Revolutionary Situation* (Philadelphia: Fortress Press, 1975); Philip Berryman, *Liberation Theology: The Essential Facts about the Revolutionary Movement in Latin America and Beyond* (New York: Beyer, Stone, 1987); Ivan Petrealla, *The Future of Liberation Theology: An Argument and Manifesto* (Norwich, UK: SCM-Canterbury Press, 2006); and Petrealla, *Beyond Liberation Theology: A Polemic* (Norwich, UK: SCM-Canterbury Press, 2008).

Child laborers carry stones on the outskirts of Gauhati, India.

AP Photo/Anupam Nath

14

THE STRUGGLE FOR ECONOMIC WELL-BEING

As noted in Chapter 13, many people consider economic well-being to be a basic human right—the right to fulfill vital needs for food, shelter, health care, and education—one so important it deserves its own chapter. Economic well-being is closely related not only to human rights and freedom but also to peace. War can harm or destroy economic well-being. Nations attack each other's soldiers (and, too often, civilians) and each other's economic systems—factories, transportation, and sources of strategic raw materials. Modern wars destroy food and housing along with guns, tanks, planes, ships, and munitions. Even the mere threat of war is damaging. The arms race consumes valuable resources (such as capital, labor, scientific skill, and organizational ability) that could be better used to fight poverty, disease, illiteracy, and inadequate housing. Many scholars also believe that economic well-being and war are connected in another way: the frustration of economic deprivation facilitates war.

Economic well-being and ecological health are also closely connected. For example, economic well-being calls for a sensible balance between population and resources, and both pollution and the imprudent use of resources affect the quality of economic and social life. We touch on these ecological problems in this chapter but defer a fuller discussion to Chapter 15. In this chapter, we seek to answer the following question: What creative breakthroughs can promote greater economic well-being?

In responding to this problem, we focus primarily on the world's poor, especially those who live in developing nations—the least developed ones in particular. But we cannot forget the pockets of poverty and the problems of unemployment, homelessness, inflation, and industrial stagnation that continue to plague the developed world. Given the interrelatedness of the world economy, unhealthy economies in industrial, developed

Chapter Objectives

After studying this chapter, you will be able to do the following:

1. Define different conceptions of economic well-being.

2. Discuss the extent of poverty in the world today.

3. Identify the causes and devastating consequences of poverty.

4. Explain the concept of economic inequality not only as it applies between countries but within countries as well.

5. Define and discuss some of the alternative approaches to economic well-being.

6. Explain the role of the international community in matters of economic well-being.

nations adversely affect the developing areas as well. For similar reasons, we cannot close our eyes to economic performance and social well-being in the communist world. The post–World War II record of China, Cuba, the Soviet Union, Vietnam, and the communist countries of Eastern Europe was at best mixed and at worst disastrous.

DEFINING ECONOMIC WELL-BEING

In Chapter 8, we defined economic well-being as the level of income, food, health care, education, shelter, and quality of life that satisfies minimum standards of life and decency and permits full growth and development. In contrast, **poverty** is that level of income, food, health care, education, shelter, and quality of life below minimum standards of life and decency. Poverty usually precludes full growth and development. People living in poverty—as we will see more clearly in the second section of the chapter—are undernourished. They may die in periods of famine. They are vulnerable to disease. They are often illiterate. They live in substandard housing, are ill clad, and are poorly equipped to move up the economic and social ladder. They are often unemployed or underemployed and poorly paid. They usually do not participate in politics. Indeed, politics might be seen as a luxury they cannot afford.

Geographically, a large percentage of the poor live in countries in the Southern Hemisphere and the southern part of the Northern Hemisphere. Collectively, they are known as developing countries; in 2018, there were 139 states designated as such.[1] Of these, 47 are classified as **least developed countries (LDCs)**.[2] These are the world's poorest countries, a high percentage of which are found in Africa. Most of the world's affluent nations, the **developed countries**, which are both highly industrialized and technologically advanced, are in the Northern Hemisphere. This neat, albeit not entirely precise, hemispheric geographic division leads to use of the terms *North* and *South* to designate developed and undeveloped nations, respectively. The poorest nations and peoples are in sub-Saharan Africa and South Asia. The richest nations tend to be in North America and Europe and also include Japan, Australia, and now China. In addition, there are several dynamic and relatively prosperous Asian economies, sometimes referred to as the **newly industrialized economies (NIEs)**; they include Singapore; South Korea; Taiwan; and, increasingly, Thailand. Finally, in Eastern Europe there are what are now called **emerging economies**—countries such as the Czech Republic, Hungary, and Poland that were formerly members of the Soviet bloc.

In exploring the struggle for economic well-being, we set forth the ethical and empirical factors that prompt exploration of the problem. These factors are grim and sobering. They underscore the absence of political, economic, and social resources that people need in order to cope with economic malaise. They pose troubling ethical and prudential questions—involving the calculus of costs and benefits—for policymakers seeking wise and humane choices.

After examining these ethical and empirical factors, we consider some major alternatives facing policymakers in the United States and elsewhere in the West, in the developing countries, and in communist China as they deal with economic challenges. These alternatives present a number of broad options that involve varieties of capitalism, communism, and democratic socialism. We will consider options that favor the nation-state and the current economic world order as well as options that look toward a different world order. Finally, we challenge readers to devise their own solutions on the basis of their critical analysis.

ETHICAL AND EMPIRICAL FACTORS

The sense of urgency that guides our analysis here was summed up by UN Secretary-General Kofi Annan in his *Millennium Report of the Secretary-General of the United Nations*, issued in 2000:

> How can we call human beings free and equal in dignity when over a billion of them are struggling to survive on less than one dollar a day, without safe drinking water, and when half of all humanity lacks adequate sanitation? Some of us are worrying about whether the stock market will crash, or struggling to master our latest computer, while more than half our fellow men and women have much more basic worries, such as where their children's next meal is coming from.

> Unless we redouble and concert our efforts, poverty and inequality will get worse still, since the world population will grow by a further two billion in the next quarter-century, with almost all the increases in the poorest countries.[3]

The Persistence of Poverty

There is no question that, over the past several decades, and particularly since Kofi Annan made the preceding statement almost two decades ago, enormous progress has been made in terms of eradicating poverty in many regions of the world. Mortality rates have been drastically reduced in a number of developing countries. Life expectancy has increased worldwide. The number of malnourished children has been drastically reduced. Enormous strides have been made in reducing illiteracy, and per capital income has dramatically increased.[4] As Nicholas Kristof of the *New York Times* recently put it in a 2018 column, "Every day, the number of people around the world living in extreme poverty (less than about $2 a day) goes down." And he goes on to say, "Just since 1990, the lives of more than 100 million children have been saved by vaccinations, diarrhea treatment, breast feeding promotion, and other simple steps."[5]

But it must also be recognized that while great progress was made over the life of the Millennium Development Goals program, 2000 through 2015, not all the goals were fully met and further, the distribution of gains was anything but even. Many of the enormous gains that were made in lowering poverty occurred in East and Southeast Asia, while sub-Saharan Africa, while making some gains, remains a poverty-laden region. Within the developing world, there are serious discrepancies. For instance, the poorest children have made the slowest progress in terms of improved nutrition. Opportunities for full and productive employment remain slim for women. Rural populations lag far behind that of the cities and towns in sanitation improvement and access to safe drinking water.[6]

And despite all the progress, the gap in economic welfare between the richest and poorest regions remains wide as demonstrated in Table 14.1.

Where do the poor live? Using the $1.25 per day income as a measure of extreme poverty, Figure 14.1 indicates that the largest concentrations of poverty are in sub-Saharan Africa, South Asia, and East Asia and the Pacific.

This picture of poverty is made even more disturbing when we realize that there are substantial pockets of poverty in affluent countries as well. In the United States, significant numbers of poor can be found in the inner cities, the Appalachian region, and rural areas of the South. Of course, many of these people seem, in relative terms, better off than many of the destitute in developing countries. Yet poverty in the midst of affluence, like affluence in the midst of the developing world's terrible poverty, should sensitize critical students to probe for reasons and solutions. Thus, the issue of poverty is both an international and domestic political challenge. This issue is striking in China. Overall, China is now a very wealthy nation. China has either the largest or the second

Table 14.1 Comparison of Poor and Affluent Countries, 2016			
Nation (Ranked by HD1)[1]	Per Capita GNI (US$)[2]	Expected Years of Schooling	Life Expectancy
Switzerland	56,364	16.0	85.1
United States	53,245	16.5	79.2
Spain	32,779	17.1	82.8
Greece	24,808	17.2	81.1
Mexico	16,383	13.3	17.0
Indonesia	10,053	12.9	69.1
Philippines	8,395	11.7	68.3
Ghana	3,839	11.5	61.5
Bangladesh	3,341	10.2	72.0
Haiti	1,657	9.1	63.1
Dem. Rep. Congo	680	9.8	59.1

1. HDI (Human Development Index) is calculated by the UNDP based on a variety of indicators.

2. GNI (gross national income) is the aggregate income of an economy generated by its production and its ownership of factors of production, less the incomes paid for the use of factors of production owned by the rest of the world, converted to international dollars using purchasing power parity (PPP) rates, divided by midyear population.

Source: United Nations, Human Development Report, International Development Indicators, 2016. Hdr .undp.org/en/countries.

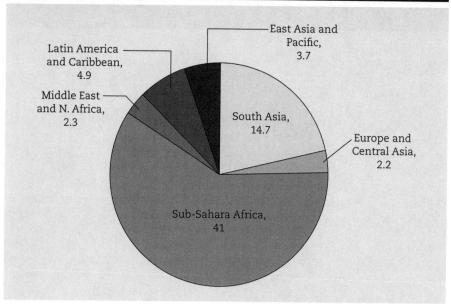

Figure 14.1 Concentration of Poor in Developing Regions, 2016 (Percent of each region's population living on $1.25 per day)

East Asia and Pacific, 3.7

Latin America and Caribbean, 4.9

Middle East and N. Africa, 2.3

South Asia, 14.7

Europe and Central Asia, 2.2

Sub-Sahara Africa, 41

Source: The World Bank, The Data Blog Chart: How Does Extreme Poverty Vary by Region. http://blogs.worldbank.org/developmenttalk/2017-global-poverty-update-world-bank.

largest economy in the world. (Economists use different methods to measure the size of economies and the issue of comparing the wealth of countries is a complicated one.) However, in many regions, particularly in rural areas, tens of millions of Chinese are extremely poor.

The poor frequently lack money because they are unemployed, underemployed, or not receiving fair pay for their labor. Unemployment is particularly acute in many developing countries (see Table 14.2 for stark contrasts between developed and developing countries). Yet in both worlds, unemployment remains a chronic problem, mirroring economic ill health. That ill health is reflected in industrial stagnation, sectional depression, economic recession, low agricultural productivity and rates of growth, and inadequate use of human and material resources. Economic troubles in the developed world hinder economic well-being in the developing world.

The plight of women in the poorest countries is particularly distressing. In poor households, women often shoulder a much greater workload than do men and have considerably fewer chances to earn money. The latter problem has, ironically, become worse in developing areas where modern technology—such as computer-based mass production—has led to even lower female employment. Furthermore, the relative lack of educational opportunities for women hinders their ability to gain managerial positions.

Poor housing—inadequate space, sanitation, and protection—is the lot of millions, particularly in poor developing nations. Reliable statistics are difficult to obtain, but the

Table 14.2 Comparative Unemployment in Developed and Developing Countries, 2017 (Estimates in percentages and countries in rank order of development utilizing the Human Development Index)

Switzerland	4–6%
Australia	4–6%
United States	4–6%
Iran	9–13%
Turkey	9–13%
Brazil	9–13%
Egypt	9–13%
Sudan	13–17%
Yemen	13–17%
Botswana	17%+
Mozambique	17%+

Source: International Labor Organization, World Employment and Social Outlook, Explore employment trends around the world, 2017. http://www.ilo.org/global/about-the-ilo/multimedia/maps-and-charts/enhanced/WCMS_541385/lang--en/index.htm.

plight of the world's poor in rural areas and urban slums is familiar to experienced world travelers. In many crowded cities in the developing world (and even in developed world cities such as Chicago, Paris, and London), some poor people sleep on the streets. The loans that the **World Bank** has made to rehabilitate slums and build low-cost housing testify to the inadequacy of, and need for, housing.

Hunger remains an agonizing problem for the world's poor, despite the fact that world food stocks are more than adequate to feed all people. The food problem is largely one of inadequate purchasing power and inadequate and inequitable distribution. Whatever the reason, the problem is immense: Almost 800 million people in the developing world do not get enough food.[7] Hunger and malnutrition, however, are not absent from rich, developed countries. For example, the estimated number of undernourished people in the developed countries of the world is slightly less than 15 million.[8] People need either money to buy food or the ability to produce their own food. Poorer nations unable to grow food must be able to import it for reasonable prices. To increase their own production, they require fertilizers and appropriate farm equipment. Most experts agree that many developing countries would benefit significantly from agrarian reform, understood as more equitable distribution of land and income. They would also benefit from adequate transportation and educational services to ensure that nutritional food is locally available at reasonable cost. Finally, in periods of famine, many developing nations desperately need shipments of food from richer, food-exporting countries.

Malnutrition and starvation lead to serious health problems and death, as does disease. Perhaps the greatest health scourge facing the developing countries of the world is HIV/AIDS. While the HIV epidemic appears to have stabilized and infection rates have fallen, worldwide there remain roughly 36.7 million adults with HIV/AIDS, with 1.8 million new infections reported in 2016. The preponderance of cases is in the poorer regions, with sub-Saharan Africa particularly hard-hit.[9]

In the developing world, poverty and hunger, the lack of clean water and effective sanitation, the absence of immunization programs, and the shortage of trained health workers all contribute to high infant and child mortality, to a host of debilitating diseases, and to shorter life expectancy.

While the number of illiterate persons has fallen over the past decade, 750 million adults and children worldwide cannot read and an additional 250 million youth are failing to acquire basic literacy skills.[10]

The Causes and Consequences of Poverty

There are numerous explanations offered for the persistence of poverty in the developing world. Some analysts point to the vagaries of geography and demography, a major thesis of Jared Diamond in his widely read book *Guns, Germs, and Steel: The Fates of Human Society*.[11] For Diamond, the geography and general environment of Eurasia made it more conducive (than the more tropical southern regions) to efficient food production via the domestication of plants and animals, the evolution of populations more resistant to disease, and ultimately the development of complex communication and political systems.

Other writers point out that adverse trade and financial conditions also affect most developing regions of the world. Many developing nations suffer economically because they are so dependent on the export of commodities—coffee, tea, rubber, or copper—whose prices fluctuate and thus may not produce steady, reliable income. Compounding the problem, prices for raw materials such as wood, minerals, petroleum, and grains generally increase more slowly than prices for processed or manufactured goods. At the same time, developed nations, seeking to protect domestic sectors of their economies, frequently place extraordinarily high tariffs on manufactured or processed goods from developing countries, which makes these products noncompetitive. Because of these adverse trade conditions and the net outflow of capital, most developing countries carry alarmingly high debt levels, making it difficult to find new capital for investment and expansion of their economies.

Many people, particularly in the developing world, believe that these conditions are merely carryovers from European colonialism during the nineteenth and twentieth centuries. The European colonial powers—Belgium, Britain, France, Germany, Holland, and Italy—did not have the economic well-being of the native people as a prime objective. Colonial powers were interested in profits and their own national security, not in developing balanced economies. Because colonial powers did not care about social justice, they perpetuated patterns of domination and dependence. In the eyes of many scholars, those same patterns exist today in the form of **neoimperialism**, whereby multinational corporations (MNCs), owned and controlled by powerful forces in the developed North, take unfair advantage of the poor, developing countries in the South by exploiting cheap labor, squandering natural resources, and reaping enormous profits. These corporations reinvest little of those profits in the infrastructure of the developing countries.

Regardless of the cause, chronic poverty has consequences that go beyond the kind of human suffering we have already chronicled. Political instability has characterized many of the developing nations, and we cannot discount the probable relationship between deprivation and political turmoil. Burundi, Congo, Liberia, Nigeria, Rwanda, Sierra Leone, Somalia, Sri Lanka, Sudan, Syria, and Yemen, among others, have been plagued by civil wars, coups, revolutions, and wars with neighboring states.

A high percentage of developing countries lack stable, cohesive, and responsible political leadership. A number of them have struggled to establish democratic political systems, but many have been and continue to be ruled by an army strongman, a military junta, or a powerful single political party with low tolerance for dissent.

The Question of Economic Inequality

Linked to the issue of poverty is that of economic inequality. For many years, the concern about inequality focused at the global level on the economic disparities between the wealthier industrialized countries and the poorer developing countries and the extent to which the policies of the developed countries may have perpetuated the gap between rich and poor. As noted earlier in this chapter, there has been some closing of this gap as reflected in the reduction in poverty levels, although globally the progress has been somewhat uneven. What is now of increasing concern is the distribution of wealth and income both globally and particularly within countries. In global terms, according to the Credit Suisse Global Wealth Report 2017, the world's richest 1 percent own half of the world's wealth. In contrast, the 3.5 billion poorest adults, 70 percent of the world's working age population, account for just 2.7 percent of global wealth.[12] At the national level, within the developing world, many individual countries suffer debilitating income and wealth inequality, countries such as the Central African Republic, Botswana, Haiti, and Namibia.[13]

Income inequality varies greatly across world regions. The lowest is to be found in the countries of Europe and the greatest in the Middle East followed closely by Sub-Saharan Africa along with Brazil and India. Over the past few decades, income inequality has increased in almost all countries of the world. Of particular concern has been the increasing income and wealth gap within some of the more affluent countries, most specifically the United States.[14]

In the United States in 2015, the top 10 percent of earners took roughly half of the country's overall income, the highest proportion recorded since 1939. Wealth inequality has also been increasing with 1 percent of the population controlling roughly 37.[15] Numerous studies have clearly confirmed that since the late 1970s, real earnings have fallen for many families, with globalization, the decline of unions and technological innovations eroding workers' wages. At the same time, earnings have soared at the very top among big Wall Street investors, corporate executives, and the founders and executives of the high-tech firms.

For an increasing number of financial institutions, both private and public, as well as academic institutions and think tanks, the issue is important on more than moral or ethical grounds. More and more economists are raising the question of whether income and wealth inequality contribute to growing poverty, exacerbate recessions or financial collapses, and make economic recovery more difficult. For the political scientist, the issue revolves around a shrinking middle class, traditionally a bulwark of an effective democratic system.

The Calculus of Costs and Benefits

The benefits in the struggle for economic well-being are reasonably clear: ending degrading poverty, providing jobs and decent income, ensuring adequate food and good health, advancing literacy, and sharing the common wealth more fairly. But at what costs—as reflected in which policies—might those benefits be obtained?

Debate rages about whether the poor developing nations can lift themselves with enough speed and at acceptable costs. How dependent will the developing countries be on the richer nations to assist them in conquering poverty? Will the richer nations be willing to provide significant enough resources to wage an effective war on poverty?

Controversy has also surrounded the role of various political and economic models in the struggle to achieve greater economic well-being. Developing nations might follow a communist, totalitarian, and egalitarian model. They might also opt for a capitalist, authoritarian, and non-egalitarian model such as the one Brazil used for most of the 1970s and 1980s. Or they might ask whether a liberal capitalist or democratic socialist path is possible. We now turn to some approaches and assess their potential for a creative breakthrough in mitigating poverty.

ALTERNATIVE APPROACHES TO ECONOMIC WELL-BEING

Which policies adopted by which political actors will bring about economic well-being? First, we examine a liberal capitalist and liberal democratic option characteristic of the United States. Next, we present the strengths and weaknesses of the Chinese communist and Brazilian capitalist models of development. Finally, we consider a democratic socialist model. We present these models to stimulate thought about how to achieve economic well-being, particularly for the poor in developing countries. Numerous variations on each model are possible.

Liberal Capitalism and Liberal Democracy

It is impossible in a few pages to present a definitive statement on the liberal capitalistic and democratic approach because there is no universal agreement on all aspects of that model. There are, however, a few common basic elements. In general, supporters of this model maintain that the way to overcome poverty and related ills is to increase the size of the economic "pie" (agricultural and industrial production) and to encourage a more equitable distribution of income and services. Robert S. McNamara, former president of the World Bank, held that "the basic problem of poverty and growth in the developing world can be stated very simply. . . . The growth is not equitably reaching the poor. And the poor are not significantly contributing to growth. Development strategies, therefore, need to be reshaped in order to help the poor become more productive."[16]

A threefold strategy is required. First, poor people and nations must help themselves. Second, richer nations such as the United States must help developing nations in a variety of ways. Third, private enterprise (including multinational or transnational corporations) must assist in crucial ways. Working together, these forces can contribute to balanced growth and equitable distribution within a framework of freedom.

Developing nations need a stable and reasonably efficient political and administrative structure that can encourage greater agricultural and industrial productivity and thus increase profits, jobs, and income. They require a social, educational, and medical infrastructure (transport, communications, schools, and health services) to deliver basic services (decent housing, clean water, and literacy) in the interest of basic human needs. As necessary, these nations also have to undertake agrarian or social reform to give poor people a greater stake in their productivity and a decent share in the common wealth. Such reform must include conscious decisions to bring population and resources into a better balance and to avoid spending valuable money and resources on excessive military armaments.

The United States and other rich Western nations can play an important role by extending credit and aid, stabilizing prices of commodities from developing nations at a reasonably remunerative level, relieving some of the crushing international debt levels of poorer countries, and allowing trade to flow freely. They can also help by ensuring lower food prices and by working toward a global energy policy to make oil (or energy substitutes) available at fair prices. These wealthy nations must encourage the kind of self-help outlined in the preceding paragraph. These acts are not mere kindness. In the long run, it is essential for the United States and the other affluent countries to assist in the developing world's economic improvement because their vital interests cannot really be secure in a world containing so much poverty and discontent.

Private enterprise, by adopting a more enlightened view of economic well-being in developing nations, can see that sensible profits and the battle against poverty are not incompatible. Increased productivity and trade and a vast new army of consumers can be linked to reasonable profits and to the satisfaction of basic human needs. Wise private investment and credit can aid in the struggle for economic well-being. Multinational (or transnational) corporations, operating under sensible rules to ensure that productivity, technology, and profits redound to benefit the poor in the host country, can also help overcome poverty.

The strengths of this option are considerable. It emphasizes peaceful, evolutionary development within a democratic and constitutional framework, and it emphasizes the value of political, economic, and social freedom. This model taps people's interest in their own improvement. It connects the self-interest in reasonable profits to the satisfaction of human needs. Historically, it has also proven to be the most powerful engine of economic growth. And economic success, some scholars believe, attacks one of the most serious problems now plaguing the developing world—enormous population growth. The **demographic transition theory** posits that as societies grow economically and become more industrialized, population growth begins to subside as it did in Europe and North America when the Industrial Revolution took hold.

With the end of the Cold War, the world has witnessed an enormous effort to encourage variations of this model within the developing world as part of the whole globalization movement. Actually, the movement started long before the 1990s, with the rejection of a protectionist trade system and the push to establish a system of free trade after World War II. The problem was that for decades the primary participants in this system were the developed countries of the noncommunist world—only a very limited number of developing states participated. When the Soviet empire collapsed, Eastern European states and a preponderance of the developing countries that were run on some variation of the socialist model almost immediately began the shift toward free market capitalist systems. At the same time, more than 100 developing countries ended military or one-party rule and moved toward more democratic political systems.[17] How have they fared? For the Eastern European countries, the so-called emerging economies, the shift has been by and large successful. However, many fear backsliding toward more authoritarian governments—in Poland and Hungary for instance. For the developing world, the results are mixed. Developing countries in East Asia along the Pacific Rim, such as Indonesia, Malaysia, Vietnam, the Philippines, and Thailand, are good examples of limited to outstanding success. In this part of the world, trade is up, jobs have been created, significant amounts of direct investment by MNCs have taken place, burgeoning indigenous manufacturing has taken root, and standards of living have generally improved.

Other parts of the developing world have not fared so well, despite the adoption of capitalist and democratic models. This is particularly true of Africa, which not only lags far behind the developed countries of the world but also significantly behind other regions of the developing world. To be fair, some regions of Africa are doing better, experiencing remarkable economic growth rates due in part to significant increases in foreign investment. China's large presence has improved the continent's infrastructure and increased the manufacturing sector and countries such as Brazil, Turkey, Malaysia, and India have also made significant investments. But the limited successes must be placed in perspective. Many of the continent's countries remain riddled with poverty, governed by noxious regimes, and plagued with political instability and violence.[18]

Its successes notwithstanding, the weaknesses of a liberal capitalism and liberal democracy model must also be seriously considered. The most fundamental criticism is that capitalists are motivated by profits, not economic and social justice. Because capitalists have a tendency to stress short-run payoff rather than long-run development, they are, and will be, unwilling to adopt those policies necessary to overcome poverty. Critics contend that liberal democratic capitalists are financially, too, tied into the dominant system of exploitation to respond to the claims of the least developed.

Even putting aside or rejecting this criticism, we are left with other points of contention. Liberal capitalism, the critics claim, may not overcome the economic and social inequities of the developing country. Indeed, many observers assert that by its very nature, liberal capitalism increases socioeconomic divisions within countries. Moreover, this option may presume too much wisdom and self-control on the part of the people and leadership of developing nations. It may also presume too much enlightened self-interest and long-range perspective on the part of affluent nations. This option may overestimate the intelligence of capitalist entrepreneurs, both inside and outside the developing country. Finally, its critics say, this option fails to come to grips with old-fashioned capitalistic exploitation or economic imperialism. Despite the lowering of trade barriers, other unfair trade practices have retarded economic development that would benefit the poor people of the developing countries.

How desirable and how feasible is the liberal capitalistic and democratic alternative? How do we assess, more exactly, its costs and benefits? Without actual testing of this model, it is difficult to judge. But we may look to the past performance of the United States, of other liberal capitalistic and democratic nations, and of countries in the developing world for clues. Past behavior does not dictate the future, but it may help the prudent policymaker to judge the chance for significant change.

Egalitarian Communism

One might assume that with the end of the Cold War, communism is "dead" as a viable economic or political model. Perhaps. But it would appear that not all countries are faring well under a new capitalist experiment, and as frustration grows, the temptation to seek out other models could be powerful. It is not beyond the realm of possibility that various communist models might guide the struggle for economic well-being in developing nations. There are a number of real-life case studies to pick from: Chinese, Cuban, Soviet, and Vietnamese. Because conditions in most developing countries are closer to those in China than to those in the former Soviet Union, we will examine the case of China. In doing so, however, we must recognize that China, like several other communist countries, is a nation in profound transition. From about 1949 to 1976, China's political and economic system was what might be termed a Maoist version of communism. After Mao's death in 1976, China began to institute very tightly controlled changes in the economic system, with emphasis on free market reforms. The following analysis takes these changes into account.

In the periods before the major market reforms, again roughly 1949 to 1976, the Chinese egalitarian model had several fundamental elements. The economic system was characterized by virtually no (or very little) private property. The major means of production were owned by the state. The regulation and management of virtually the entire economy—industry, agriculture, transportation, communications, and finance—were by the state. Finally, there was an underlying premise that society was a collective, and maintaining the welfare of the entire community is the fairest, most equitable, and most just means of running the economy. The political system, of course, was under the complete control of a single party, the Communist Party.

In the early years, from about 1949 to 1957, China followed the conventional Soviet model of development, emphasizing heavy industry and rapid industrialization. Beginning in 1958, Mao placed his imprint on China's development policies, which—as we noted in Chapter 7—featured the terribly disruptive and costly Great Leap Forward and the Cultural Revolution. The Maoist period, which ran from 1958 to 1976, emphasized all-around industrial and agricultural development: self-reliance and communes in the countryside; mass mobilization of the people and heroic, if not brutal, labor policies to increase productivity; the primacy of politics and party to guide the revolution; and decentralization to stimulate local initiatives.

The post-Mao model, which began with the Chinese leader's death in 1976 and continues to the present, is attempting to achieve what are known as the "four modernizations": in agriculture, industry, national defense, and science and technology. It is a mixture of communist doctrine and free market reform requiring a number of crucial balances—specifically five.

First, the post-Mao model seeks to balance egalitarianism and excellence. That is, without giving up the effort to satisfy the basic needs of all, the Chinese are attempting to enable those individuals with expertise to address specialized problems in industry, agriculture, science, and education. Second, the post-Mao model attempts to balance central direction and local initiative. Here, without squelching local originality and effort, the Chinese are trying to follow a national plan of development. Third, China today seeks to balance party control and order on one hand with greater freedom and legality on the other. Without party control, the Chinese leadership believes, there can be no coherent development, yet people need to be free of oppressive control if they are to contribute their best to national development.[19] Fourth, the current Chinese model strives to balance the old Maoist emphasis on self-reliance with a modern reliance on foreign trade, credits, and investment. The present leadership recognizes that China needs scientific, technological, and economic help from countries such as the United States and Japan, yet China strives to be as self-reliant as possible as it develops modern capability in a number of fields. Finally, the Chinese are attempting to balance public ownership of land with small private agricultural plots. They recognize that the small plots can significantly enhance agricultural productivity without completely relinquishing the principle of communal ownership and operation.[20]

In 1980, the Chinese leadership decided to slow down the four modernizations but not abandon them. In 1986, priority was given to reform and expansion of the open-door policy—that is, the policy that encourages foreign investment. This involved decentralizing the economic system and relinquishing the state monopoly on foreign trade. In addition, six "special economic zones" were established to promote foreign investment and trade. Finally, major reforms were begun in banking, pricing, labor law, and agriculture.

AP Photo/Ng Han Guan

While tremendous increases in standards of living have been achieved in China, particularly along the coastal regions, interior provinces still suffer from considerable poverty.

As implemented in China, egalitarian communism holds out the hope (if not the promise) of significantly improving the economic well-being of the developing nations that choose it. If China is at all typical, the basic human needs of most of the world's people might be met. Between 1975 and 2005, China's per capita growth rate, as measured by its GDP, ran a superb 8.4 percent; between 1990 and 1999, the growth rate was an astounding 9.5 percent. In 2018, it had fallen to a still formidable 6.9 percent.[21] By comparison, the average for high-income countries in 2017 was 3.2 percent and 2.6 percent for the United States.[22] However, it should be noted that higher growth rates are more easily achieved in smaller economies that start with a great many inefficiencies to be fixed. Nonetheless, Chinese growth was quite impressive. The welfare of a majority of Chinese living today has progressed significantly. China's adult literacy rate is 96.4 percent. Life expectancy went from 67 years in 1980 to 76 years in 2017, and the infant mortality rate (below five years) dropped from 59 per 1,000 births in 1980 to 9.2 per 1,000 births in 2017. Expected years of schooling for adults over 25 years of age went from 3.7 in 1980 to 13.5 in 2017.[23]

On the subject of population growth, it must be noted that China's has been enormous. China had 570 million people in 1952 and 928 million in 1975; today there are 1.41 billion people. However, with the help of family planning, easily accessible abortion, and bonuses for small families, the rate of growth has been slowed. Between 1975 and 2010, the annual population growth rate was a low 1.2 percent, and in 2017, stood at a still relatively low 1.61.[24] Yet that reduction in the rate of population growth was made possible at least in part by the implementation in 1980 of policies restricting the number of children that couples could have. In 1982, when census figures revealed that China's population had topped 1 billion, a ruthless enforcement policy was enacted: a national standard of one child per couple was established. It should be noted that the national goal of limiting population growth came at the expense of personal freedom. Grim stories of forced late-term abortions, infanticide, and child abandonment began to appear. In recent years, there have been some signs that the strict quota system is softening.

The strengths of the communist model are appealing. In China, life has improved for the vast majority. The worst ravages of starvation have been overcome. Abject poverty has subsided. People have better nutrition, health, and housing. Literacy continues to spread. The economy—especially industry—grows rapidly and holds out hope for larger slices of a bigger pie. Income is distributed more fairly. But this rosy picture must be tempered with the understanding that the economy, while certainly not 100 percent capitalist, has been shifting increasingly toward major free-market reforms. Although progress in human welfare was made during China's more purely communist phase of development, our assessment of the strengths of the communist economic model is severely affected by the spread of free market mechanisms. Estimates as to how much of the current Chinese economy is state owned vary wildly. At the low end, some economist believe that the government owns at least 30 percent and an even higher percentage of particular sectors, perhaps 50 percent of the industrial sector and almost 100 percent of banking.[25] Regardless, the reality is that in many ways, the private owned enterprises have far outstripped the government owned enterprises in terms of performance.

One disturbing trend has emerged. Parts of China, in particular the coastal provinces of Fujian, Guangdong, Jiangsu, and Zhejiang, have benefited enormously from a shift away from a strict communist economic system to one featuring free enterprise market economies. The benefits for these regions have been remarkable, but that success has caused economic disparity; the poorer, largely rural interior provinces of China have not fared as well. Recently, China has seen signs of unemployment, something that is not supposed to happen in a communist system.

In sum, advocates of the egalitarian communist model maintain that the benefits outweigh the costs. This model's ability to improve the economic well-being of the overwhelming majority of people in a developing nation, they argue, is greatly preferable to the exploitation and loss of freedom that comes with a capitalist-based model. Proponents suggest further that a more humane communism than that of the former Soviet Union or China is possible.

Yet despite what appear to be some successes, critics contend that the grave weaknesses of the communist regime itself must be faced. One weakness is the continuing high cost of the communist revolution, which includes destruction of the regime's opponents; the terrorization of those who do not follow the leaders' or party's current line; and authoritarian control of speech, press, and culture. These costs include the regime's willingness to sacrifice millions in one generation for gains to be achieved in the next. Communist regimes also have to worry about bureaucratic centralization of power and failures of the master plan. Above all, communist systems do not rely on individual incentives as a prime motivator, and some critics argue there are few if any other incentives to work harder, produce more, or innovate. In the case of China, the government faces a constant struggle as it strives to adapt some of the incentive structures of capitalism while maintaining strict communist party rule. Without individual incentives, people tend to do only what is necessary, to play it safe, to be more concerned with security than production. The most graphic example of the limitations of this kind of system can be seen in the Soviet economy, which by 1990 was near collapse. Similarly, the Cuban communist system has not fared well since the end of the Cold War, when economic aid from the Soviet Union came to a halt.

Illiberal Capitalism and Right-Wing Authoritarianism

There are many varieties of what we call illiberal capitalism. This form of capitalism emphasizes capital growth at the expense of, or in disregard of, economic and social justice. Variations on this model may be found in Chile (under Augusto Pinochet from 1973 to 1989), the Philippines (under Ferdinand Marcos from 1972 to 1986), South Korea (under a variety of military strongmen during the post–World War II period), Indonesia (under military strongman General Suharto from 1966 to 1998), and Singapore (under Lee Kuan Yew, who, after his election as the country's first prime minister in 1965, ruled the island country for decades with an iron hand). This option rests on the assumption that economic growth, an enlarged GNP, and capitalist profitability precede and create the conditions for greater economic and social justice. Wealth must be created before it can be equitably distributed. And there must be a favorable environment for those who can create it—the capitalist entrepreneurs.

Right-wing authoritarianism complements illiberal capitalism in the sense that economic growth requires political, economic, and social stability. Left-wing agitation is not allowed to get out of hand. Strikes are not permitted in essential industries. Adverse criticism of the nation's rulers, if it goes too far, may be subject to punishment. When "national security" is at issue, civil liberties may be jeopardized by the intervention of the military, as was the case in countries such as Brazil, Chile, the Philippines, and South Korea.

In illiberal capitalist and right-wing authoritarian systems, the government encourages a high rate of growth in the GNP. The state plans, regulates, and directs the economy to accomplish this purpose. It may even own and operate basic industries crucial to capitalistic growth. The state must be willing, if necessary, to impose wage controls in the fight against inflation. It must be willing to make the poor wait, to defer the satisfaction of basic economic needs. Leaders of the regime seek to advance the nation's economic growth, military strength, and security. They will cooperate with, but try to avoid over-dependence on, rich capitalistic countries and MNCs. This variety of illiberal capitalism seeks a big enough pie to ensure, in time, larger slices for all. Then, presumably, the people's basic need for greater economic well-being can be satisfied.

Brazil's record from 1964 to 1985 illustrates the illiberal capitalism and right-wing authoritarianism model's pattern, its key results, and its continuing problems. In 1964, in a military coup, the democratically elected government of President João Goulart was ousted. In 1979, General João Baptista de Oliveira Figueiredo was sworn in as president after winning a two-party contest in late 1978 and promising a return to liberalization and democracy. In 1985, General Figueiredo's government was replaced by an elected civilian government, which ruled with a fragile coalition. In 1988, a new, substantially liberalized constitution was approved. The essentially authoritarian military or military-backed regimes that held sway from 1964 to 1985 worked closely with capitalist entrepreneurs, the upper-urban bourgeoisie, and technocratic civil servants. The Brazilian leadership sought to maintain economic and political order and thus make possible the "economic miracle."

From 1967 to 1974, Brazil's economy grew at an impressive rate. For example, Brazil's GDP rose an average of 11.3 percent per year during this period. Between 1975 and 1980, the annual growth rate was 6.5 percent, the slowdown partly due to the OPEC oil crisis. Investment poured into Brazil.[26] The country's GNP (in U.S. dollars) climbed from $125,600,000,000 in 1976 to $250,568,000,000 in 1986. And per capita, GNP rose from $1,088 in 1976 to $1,809 in 1986.[27]

There is little doubt Brazil achieved significant aggregate economic growth. But how this growth affected human welfare is debatable. At the end of this period of illiberal capitalism, were the people of Brazil any better off than the people of Latin America in general? Not really. Using 1986 as the base year for comparison, we note the following: Only 78 percent of Brazil's people were literate, compared with 80 percent for all of Latin America. Life expectancy in Brazil was sixty-five years; for all of Latin America it stood at sixty-six years. Brazil's annual infant mortality rate was sixty-three deaths per 1,000 live births; for Latin America as a whole, it was fifty-six deaths per 1,000 live births. GNP per capita for Brazil was $1,809; for Latin America overall, it was $1,872.[28] In 1986, a substantial percentage of the Brazilian population still lived in poverty in both the country and city. Finally, there was a severe maldistribution of wealth. In 1984, twenty years after the beginning of the illiberal capitalist period, 10 percent of the population controlled nearly 50 percent of Brazil's household income.[29]

The Brazilian experience helps point up the strengths and weaknesses of this model. Rapid economic growth can occur, particularly in capital-intensive industries. As a result of the groundwork laid during the period of illiberal capitalism, Brazil now produces consumer products—automobiles, refrigerators, and television sets—for its affluent minority. The hope is that sooner or later the larger economic pie—the increased GNP—will benefit more people, including the poor.

The Brazilian model, like the Chinese one, requires present sacrifice for future gain. Economic and social justice—especially for the poor—is postponed. Although a new Brazilian Constitution has been adopted to reduce the power of the president, abolish censorship, and generally expand civil liberties, it remains to be seen whether wealth can be more fairly distributed. Brazil's twenty-one-year authoritarian experience was relatively mild in comparison with the illegal arrests, imprisonment, and torture that characterize other right-wing regimes. In Brazil's case, as in other right-wing regimes, the ruling elite maintained that its economic and political policies were necessary but temporary. But one must ask: How necessary? How temporary?

Defenders of this model are firmly convinced that the economic pie must be enlarged considerably before the basic human needs of the poor can be satisfied. They believe that postponing political, social, and economic justice is a necessary, but temporary, sacrifice. They concede that capitalist economic growth may immediately favor the affluent minority, but they emphasize that all citizens benefit a little from a larger GNP and that eventually those who are less well-off will benefit much more than they would have under communism. Proponents also maintain that right-wing regimes offer greater opportunity for eventual political liberalization than do left-wing regimes.

Democratic Socialism

This option rejects communism, liberal democratic capitalism, and right-wing authoritarian capitalism. The possibility of public ownership of key economic and social services is assumed. Agriculture may be communal and genuinely democratic (say, on the model of the Israeli kibbutz), or it may be private. Other aspects of the economy—small businesses and service industries—remain in private hands. This option assumes, moreover, a two-party or multiparty system, political competition, and civil liberties. It assumes central guidance in areas essential for satisfying human needs (such as education, health, or housing) that will not be met by the private sector.

Consequently, the democratic socialist state will not hesitate to nationalize monopolies or regulate fundamental industries (banking, railroads, and key services) to ensure sensible growth, equitable distribution, and key services in the interest of the majority. Top priority is given to employment, sustainable income levels, literacy, health care, and housing. Because of widespread rural poverty in the developing world, there will be substantial agrarian reform, development of cooperatives, attention to labor-intensive production, and balanced industrial growth. Better urban planning is also necessary to ensure decent housing, sanitation, and transportation. Education is crucial to both rural and urban development.

The democratic socialist model for the developing world requires family planning and population control to prevent imbalance between population and resources. Balanced agricultural and industrial growth is also important. Low or modest expenditures for national security are most helpful; resources can thus be used for healthy economic growth and attendance to basic human needs.

Democratic socialist governments seek to maintain both freedom and equality. The difficulties most developing nations face hamper these attempts. Those on the right complain that freedom and egalitarianism breed disorder. Those on the left complain that excessive concern for individual freedom inhibits egalitarian social policy. There are few, if any, genuinely successful democratic socialist governments in the developing world. The post–Cold War emphasis on free market systems and privatization in much of the developing world has resulted in significant movement away from democratic socialist (and communist) models.

The strengths of the democratic socialist option lie in its commitment to meeting basic human needs as quickly as possible and within a framework of freedom. Supporters argue that this model is the only one that makes sense in developing countries. They state that democratic socialism is the only policy that can strike the right balance between liberty and equality and between economic growth and satisfaction of basic needs. A certain amount of central planning is required to direct a nation's resources; increase production; and tackle problems such as hunger, disease, and illiteracy. Moreover, only a government truly respectful of people's liberties and needs can enlist their energies in a successful program of development.

Democratic socialism may be vulnerable to attacks from the left or the right. The extreme left believes that democratic socialist governments fail to achieve a truly egalitarian society. The extreme right is frightened by socialism and democracy, by the commitment to more equitable distribution and to freedom. These two types of opposition were dramatically demonstrated in the early 1970s. In 1971, extreme leftists mounted an unsuccessful armed rebellion against the democratic socialist government of Sirimavo Bandaranaike (the world's first-elected, female prime minister) in Sri Lanka. Two years later a right-wing military coup overthrew the democratic socialist government of Salvador Allende Gossens in Chile. Both left and right believe (for different reasons) that democratic socialist governments lack strength and are too easy on rightists and leftists, respectively. The left holds that democratic socialist governments lack the courage to wipe out capitalistic domination. The right maintains that democratic socialist governments frighten away private investment by threatening profits.

The economic crisis that hit Europe in 2011 and 2012, a follow-on to the global crash of 2008, also gives pause to carefully examine the democratic socialist model. Several countries, including Greece, Spain, and Italy, found themselves in economic trouble, particularly Greece. The cost of achieving and maintaining basic human needs for an entire country is considerable. If that spending gets out of hand and reaches levels far exceeding already high taxation levels, enormous debt can incur and threaten the entire economy. Whether this scenario is entirely the fault of the basic structure of the democratic socialist model, the impact of the global recession that hit in 2008, or merely a case of exceedingly bad management is open to debate. But it is probably fair to say that the model itself is vulnerable to excessive spending that could reach dangerous levels and deserves close scrutiny.

THE CRITICAL ROLE OF THE INTERNATIONAL COMMUNITY

This chapter has concentrated on presenting and evaluating fundamental economic political models for developing states to overcome the problems of poverty. We would be remiss, however, if we did not discuss the role of some actors in the broader international community who are key to the development process, regardless of which model is adopted. Efforts toward development are very complex, and there is no way that any discussion included here can be comprehensive. So a few brief comments about three key actors are useful to help flesh out the picture. These actors include international organizations, nongovernmental organizations (NGOs), and state-based, foreign-aid programs.

International Organizations

Multilateral assistance plays a vital role in today's development process. Although some foreign assistance is channeled through regional organizations, by far the most critical activities in this area are to be found in the efforts of various organs within the UN system. Several of the specialized agencies, such as the Food and Agriculture Organization (FAO) and the World Health Organization (WHO), are instrumental in development efforts. But the following three organs are absolutely central to development efforts and are particularly worth noting.

The World Bank (also known as the International Bank for Reconstruction and Development, or IBRD) is headquartered in Washington, D.C., and is in the business of making loans to countries for development purposes. The World Bank's strategic priority is to meet the **Millennium Development Goals** (outlined later in this section). The World Bank's support to developing countries rose from $52.6 billion in 2013 to $59 billion in 2017.

The **International Monetary Fund (IMF)**, also headquartered in Washington, D.C., is composed of 189 member countries. Its activities are concentrated on stabilizing financial systems, promoting international monetary cooperation and exchange stability, and helping to manage excessive debt load. The IMF efforts to wrestle with the enormous debt loads assumed by many developing countries in the mid- to late 1980s have been controversial. In providing debt relief through loan modification (for example, by lowering interest rates over a longer payback period), the IMF has insisted on certain fiscal conditions. These conditions are designed to impose fiscal discipline and increase the probability that the loans will be paid back. Debtor countries may find that the amount of money they are permitted to spend is strictly limited. In some cases, critics argue, these circumscribed conditions are both repressive and injurious to economic growth. The IMF has reviewed a number of cases and in some instances eased conditions. The controversy continues, however.[30]

The **United Nations Development Programme (UNDP)** provides development advice and grant support. Its advisory role concentrates on assisting countries in drafting development reports and adopting development programs that integrate both public and private programs and projects. One of the principle coordinating mechanisms is the UNDP resident representative, stationed in each recipient country, who acts as an onsite coordinator of development activities.[31]

At the UN Millennium Summit held in 2000, there were 189 governments that adopted the Millennium Declaration, which established a set of eight goals. The Millennium Development Goals, designed to drastically reduce or even eliminate global poverty in the twenty-first century, are as follows:

Goal 1. Eradicate extreme poverty and hunger by halving the proportion of people whose income is less than $1 per day by 2015.

Goal 2. Achieve universal primary education by 2015.

Goal 3. Promote gender equality and empower women by eliminating gender disparity in primary and secondary education, preferably by 2005, and to all levels of education no later than 2015.

Goal 4. Reduce child mortality (the under-five mortality rate) by two-thirds between 1990 and 2015.

Goal 5. Improve maternal health (the maternal mortality ratio) by three-quarters between 1990 and 2015.

Goal 6. Halt and reverse the spread of HIV/AIDS by 2015 as well as the incidence of malaria.

Goal 7. Integrate the principles of sustainable development into country policies and programs and reverse the loss of environmental resources and halve the proportion of people without sustainable access to safe drinking water and sanitation by 2015. Also, significantly improve the lives of at least 100 million slum dwellers. (For a discussion of the concept of sustainable development, see Chapter 15.)

Goal 8. Develop a partnership for development between international organizations, countries, and the private sector.[32]

By the end of 2015, the international community had made significant progress in achieving many of the Millennium Development Goals. But it is also true that the results were mixed a great deal depending on geographical region and specific country. Keeping that in mind, the following can be said:

Poverty: Enormous strides were made in reducing poverty. In 1990, roughly 1.9 billion lived in extreme poverty. By the end of 2015 that had been reduced to 836 million.

Hunger: Significant progress was made in reducing hunger, but the Millennium Development Goal of halving the percentage was not achieved.

Education: Significant increases occurred in the number of young girls in school in developing regions of the world and literacy rates improved dramatically. Net primary school enrollment in developing regions reached 91 percent in 2015, up from 83 percent in 2000. Child mortality: Child mortality has been almost halved, dropping from ninety deaths per 1,000 live births in 1990 to forty-three in 2015.

HIV/AIDS, malaria, and other diseases: Significant progress was made reducing the number of people newly infected with HIV, and people with HIV are living longer due to the expansion of antiretroviral treatment. Antiretroviral therapy for HIV-infected people may have saved as many as 6.6 million lives between 1995 and 2015.

Environmental sustainability: Unfortunately, while global awareness of global environmental degradation has increased and some progress has been made in the development and use of alternative fuels, the major factors that threaten environmental sustainability march on. Global carbon emissions continue to rise. Millions of hectares of forest are lost every year while many species are being driven closer to extinction and renewable water resources are becoming scarcer.[33]

The work to achieve the Millennium Development Goals came to an end in 2015, and on January 1, 2016, a new, more ambitious set of goals were adopted, called the **Sustainable Development Goals**. In all, there are seventeen goals as opposed to the eight in the Millennium effort. While some of the new goals continue the work of the earlier program, such as the elimination of poverty, promotion of gender equality, zero hunger, good health and improved education, the Sustainable Development Goals place added emphasis on improving the environment, encouraging urban viability, striving for industry innovation and improved infrastructure, and greater efforts at partnership in order to achieve the goals. The target date for completion of the Sustainable Development Goals is 2030.[34]

Nongovernmental Organizations

NGOs have become a major part of the efforts to promote development and combat poverty in the developing world, and their number has increased dramatically over the past thirty years. The range of development concerns of these organizations is almost limitless. A few examples include the following:

Arab Council for Childhood and Development

Asian Women in Cooperative Development

Care International

Center for Development Services

Egyptian AIDS Society

Habitat for Humanity International

Human Rights Watch

International Association of Planned Parenthood

International Cartographic Association

International Centre for Human Rights and Democratic Development

International Rural Housing Association

International Save the Children Alliance

Maryknoll Sisters of St. Dominic, Inc.

Mercy Corps International

Oxfam

Population Council

United Methodist Church—General Board of Global Ministries

World Energy Council

© Howard Davies/CORBIS

One of the keys to successful development efforts in poor countries is the use of appropriate technology. In this photograph, Oxfam development workers and villagers sink a well for a Cambodian village.

State-Based Foreign Aid Programs

There are a number of myths, or at least misconceptions, about foreign aid given from the developed countries of the North to the developing countries of the South. To be sure, the aid has been generous, over a trillion dollars since the end of World War II. But several points must be considered.

First, not all foreign assistance is in the form of grants or outright gifts. A significant percentage is in the form of loans, which lenders expect to see paid back. Second, a significant amount of foreign aid is in the form of military aid. Third, some of the major aid programs, such as those of the United States, tend to be highly concentrated. For example, Israel and Egypt receive an enormously disproportionate percentage of American bilateral foreign assistance. Nevertheless, this constitutes a very small percentage of the U.S. budget.

Fourth, while attacking poverty and promoting development are part of major aid programs, there are other significant considerations. Foreign aid is an instrument of influence, and donor countries by and large want something in return—political allegiance, military basing rights, support in international organizations, and friendship. Donors may also demand changes in behavior, such as improvements in human rights or democratic reforms. Not that any of these conditions are necessarily bad, but one should remember that more often than not foreign aid comes with a price.

Finally, it should be noted that the end of the Cold War has had a significant impact on foreign aid programs. Within the developing world, the shift toward free market capitalist models has caused donor states to reconsider their aid programs and to question whether, with the increases in trade and the influx of foreign investment into developing countries, aid programs are still necessary, at least at the levels of the past.

CONCLUSION

The need for creative breakthroughs that will result in greater economic well-being, particularly for the world's poor, is clear and present. The persistence of poverty, unemployment, hunger, ill health, illiteracy, poor housing, and inequality is well documented. What is not clear is how to overcome these agonizing problems and how to deal with the troublesome task of balancing costs and benefits in proposed policies. All of the alternatives that we have examined pose difficulties. The challenge facing the decision maker is to select the alternative that will quickly maximize benefits for the world's poor at acceptable costs to those in developing and developed countries.

Policies for economic well-being must be worked out by most developing nations (where most of the poor live) in the face of severe problems. Most developing nations lack the prerequisites for significant and humane development. They often have no democratic and constitutional consensus. They do not enjoy political stability. They are short on effective party and administrative organization, trained personnel, good transportation, and schools. They face enormous obstacles in the very evils they seek to overcome: low incomes, malnutrition, disease, illiteracy, and inadequate housing.

Scholars concerned with advancing global economic well-being must also question the foresight, will, and judgment of the richer nations of the developed world. Too often, these nations fail to adopt long-range policies to help the world's poor; too often, their policies are foolishly motivated by short-range interests that are frequently identified with national security. The richer nations seem incapable of speeding up the process of economic development for the poorer developing nations. What assistance they do provide is often not in tune with freedom and humane treatment for the poor. Moreover, the domestic policies of rich nations such as the United States do not offer attractive models for economic well-being. Indeed, while the standard of living in the United States remains high for most people, there are indications that the gap between the "haves" and the "have nots" within the country is widening.

Minimal economic well-being in a totalitarian state is not appealing either. Nor is lopsided and unjust economic growth in a right-wing authoritarian regime. Both models call for present sacrifices to achieve future gains. A democratic socialist model and a more genuinely liberal capitalist and democratic option are more attractive, as is the world order option, but how attractive, and how feasible, are they?

Ethically, political scientists recognize the need for sane and humane policies to deal with the empirical realities of economic malaise, but we find it hard to make prudent decisions that can help balance acceptable costs and clear-cut benefits on the road to greater economic well-being. Our consciences compel us to search for creative breakthroughs. Empirically, we appreciate the difficulties of achieving greater economic well-being, particularly for the world's poor, but we have not yet developed empirical explanations to help us, prudentially, overcome economic malaise rapidly and satisfactorily.

In Chapter 15, we concentrate on the imperative of ecological health, an issue vitally related to economic well-being.

SUGGESTED READINGS

Bhagwati, Jaquati. *In Defense of Globalization*. New York: Oxford University Press, 2007. From an eminent economist, lays out a powerful case on behalf of globalization, particularly its positive impact on some developing countries.

Easterly, William. *The Tyranny of Experts: Economists, Dictators, and the Forgotten Rights of the Poor*. New York: Basic Books, 2015. A scathing critique of the "top down" approach to development that facilitates the continued power of autocratic leaders and exploits the world's poor.

Hulme, David. *Global Poverty: Global Governance and Poor People in the Post-2015 Era*. Abingdon, UK: Taylor and Francis, 2015. A multidisciplinary approach to understanding contemporary poverty in a world of terrorism, climate change, and access to natural resources.

Moyo, Dambis. *Dead Aid: Why Aid Is Not Working and How There Is a Better Way for Africa*. New York: Farrar, Straus and Giroux, 2010. Critique as to why billions of dollars sent from wealthy countries to the developing countries of Africa has not worked.

Sachs, Jeffrey. *Common Wealth: Economics for a Crowded Planet.* New York: Penguin Group, 2010. An assessment of how environmental degradation, population growth, and poverty threaten global peace and prosperity.

———. *The End of Poverty: Economic Possibilities for Our Time.* New York: Penguin, 2006. A widely read and important book on the problem of poverty. Makes a strong case for putting critical infrastructure in place to facilitate the growth of market-economy mechanisms.

Smith, Stephen C. *Ending Global Poverty: A Guide to What Works.* New York: St. Martin's Press, 2005. Smith, a development economist at George Washington University, responds to the question: How should people allocate their charitable giving to groups that aim to reduce poverty? Emphasis is on the various traps that keep people mired in poverty such as poor nutrition, illiteracy, and lack of health care.

United Nations Development Programme. *Human Development Report.* New York: Oxford University Press.

A valuable annual analysis of the human condition in the world. Combines economic indicators and assessment of political welfare.

Weatherby, Joseph W., et al. *The Other World: Issues and Politics of the Developing World.* 10th ed. New York: Taylor and Francis Longman, 2017. An interdisciplinary approach to the most fundamental issues and problems of development. Includes regional briefings on Asia, Latin America, the Middle East, North Africa, and sub-Saharan Africa.

White, Gordon. *Riding the Tiger: The Politics of Economic Reform in Post-Mao China.* Stanford, CA: Stanford University Press, 1993. A first-rate analysis of those forces that brought about the remarkable economic changes in China since the late 1970s.

World Bank. *World Development Report.* New York: Oxford University Press. Excellent and authoritative annual world development picture. Statistical tables are invaluable.

GLOSSARY TERMS

demographic transition theory (p. 383)
developed countries (p. 374)
emerging economies (p. 374)
International Monetary Fund (IMF) (p. 391)

least developed countries (LDCs) (p. 374)
Millennium Development Goals (p. 391)
neoimperialism (p. 379)
newly industrialized economies (NIEs) (p. 374)

poverty (p. 374)
Sustainable Development Goals (p. 393)
United Nations Development Programme (UNDP) (p. 391)
World Bank (p. 378)

NOTES

1. International Statistical Institute, Developing countries, Based on World Bank Classifications, 2018. https://isi-web.org/index.php/resources/developing-countries

2. United Nations Committee for Development Policy, Department of Economic and Social Affairs, List of Least Developed Countries, 2018. https://www.un.org/development/desa/dpad/wp-content/uploads/sites/45/publication/ldc_list.pdf

3. Kofi Annan, *Millennium Report of the Secretary-General of the United Nations* (New York: United Nations, March 2000).

4. United Nations, *The Millennium Development Goals Report 2011* (New York: United Nations, 2011).

5. Nicholas Kristof, "Why 2017 Was the Best Year in History," *New York Times,* January 7, 2018, p. 9.

6. United Nations, The Millennium Development Goals Report 2015. http://www.un.org/millenniumgoals/2015_MDG_Report/pdf/MDG%202015%20rev%20(July%201).pdf

7. World Hunger, 2016. World Hunger and Poverty Facts and Statistics. https://www.worldhunger.org/2015-world-hunger-and-poverty-facts-and-statistics/#hunger-number

8. Ibid.

9. UN AIDS, Fact Sheet, 2016, www.unaids.org/en/resources/fact-sheet

10. UNESCO, Literacy, https://en.unesco.org/themes/literacy

11. Jared Diamond, *Guns, Germs, and Steel: The Fates of Human Society* (New York: Norton, 1997).

12. Rupert Neale, "Richest 1% own half the world's wealth, study finds," *The Guardian*, November 14, 2017. https://www.theguardian.com/inequality/2017/nov/14/worlds-richest-wealth-credit-suisse. See also: The Credit Suisse Research Institute, *Global Wealth Report 2017*. http://www.credit-suisse.com/corporate/en/research/research-institute/global-wealth-report.html.

13. Inequality Datablog, *The Guardian*. "Inequality index: where are the world's most unequal countries?" April 26, 2017. https://www.theguardian.com/inequality/datablog/2017/apr/26/inequality-index-where-are-the-worlds-most-unequal-countries

14. Racundo Alvaredo, et.al., World Inequality Report 2018, World Inequality Lab, 2018. http://wir2018.wid.world/files/download/wir2018-summary-english.pdf

15. World Wealth and Income Data Base, http://wid.world/country/usa/

16. Robert S. McNamara, *The Assault on World Poverty* (Baltimore: Johns Hopkins University Press for the World Bank, 1975), v.

17. UNDP, *Human Development Report 2004* (New York: United Nations, 2004), 10.

18. The World Bank, "Economic Growth is on the Upswing Following a Sharp Slowdown," Press Release, April 19, 2017. http://www.worldbank.org/en/news/press-release/2017/04/19/economic-growth-in-africa-is-on-the-upswing-following-a-sharp-slowdown

19. In recent years, the Chinese leadership has leaned toward party control and order, as the massacre at Tiananmen Square demonstrated (see Chapter 7).

20. Our discussion of China has benefited from the keen analysis of James R. Townsend and Brantly Womack, *Politics in China*, 3rd ed. (Boston: Little, Brown, 1986); Gabriel Almond et al., eds., *Comparative Politics Today: A World View*, 7th ed. (New York: Longman, 2000); and Gordon White, *Riding the Tiger: The Politics of Economic Reform in Post-Mao China* (Stanford, CA: Stanford University Press, 1993). Also of great value was the *Europa Yearbook* (London: Europa Publications, annual).

21. Trading Economics, China GDP Annual Growth Rate, 1989–2018 Data. https://tradingeconomics.com/china/gdp-growth-annual

22. Department of Commerce, Bureau of Economic Analysis. U.S. Economy at a Glance, 2018. https://www.bea.gov/newsreleases/glance.htm

23. United Nations Development Program, Human Development Indicators. http:hdr.undp.org/en/countries/profiles/CHN#

24. World Meters. China Population, 2018. http:www.worldmeters.info/world-population/china-population/

25. Gao Xu, "State owned enterprises in China: How big are they?" The World Bank, East Asia & Pacific, January 19, 2010. http://blogs.worldbank.org/eastasiapacific/state-owned-enterprises-in-china-how-big-are-they and Christopher Balding, "China takes on state-owned firms." Bloomberg News, August 10, 2017. https://www.bloomberg.com/view/articles/2017-08-10/china-takes-on-state-owned-firms

26. Peter L. Berger, *Pyramids of Sacrifice: Political Ethics and Social Change* (Garden City, NY: Anchor Books, 1976), 155.

27. Ruth Leger Sivard, *World Military and Social Expenditures, 1981* (Leesburg, VA: World Priorities, 1981), 25; Sivard, *World Military and Social Expenditures, 1989* (Washington, DC: World Priorities, 1989), 50.

28. See Sivard, *World Military and Social Expenditures, 1989*, 47–55.

29. World Bank, *World Development Report 1990: Poverty* (New York: Oxford University Press, 1990), 127.

30. For more information, go to the IMF website at http://imf.org.

31. For more information, go to the UNDP website at www.undp.org.

32. UNDP, *Human Development Report 2004*, 135–136.

33. United Nations, Sustainable Development Goals, 2018, http://www.un.org/sustainabledevelopment/blog/2015/12/sustainable-development-goals-kick-off-with-start-of-new-year/

34. Ibid.

A polar bear floats on an ice floe in the rapidly melting Arctic.

Stock photo © Coldimages

15

THE IMPERATIVE OF ECOLOGICAL HEALTH

Ecological malaise, or environmental illness, has emerged as a major concern in world politics. Scientific data are making it increasingly clear that ecological degradation has consequences as bad as those of poverty or human rights violations; indeed, it may be even more dangerous than modern warfare.

At its worst, ecological ill health threatens humankind's biological existence. It affects both developed and developing nations. The depletion and waste of resources; population growth wildly in excess of needed resources such as food, land, water, and energy; and **global warming** are all real threats to hopes for a better tomorrow. In particular, ecological dangers may prevent developing nations from overcoming poverty and threaten the prosperity of developed nations.

In examining the imperative of ecological health, we see again the linkage between the values of peace, human rights, and economic well-being that we have been considering in Part IV of this book. For example, war not only destroys human beings but it also destroys the countryside, poisons the air, and wastes vital resources. Economic well-being is vitally related to a stable population, adequate resources, and clean air and water. Human rights are violated if people starve to death because population outruns food supply or if they have no clean air to breathe or clean water to drink. In the interests of biological existence, societal growth and development, and the cultural quality of life, political actors must understand and respond to threats to ecological health. Hence, the question we seek to answer in this chapter is this: What creative breakthroughs can help humanity achieve ecological health?

Ecological problems cannot be considered apart from political philosophy and practical politics. The ideologies of liberal democracy, democratic socialism, communism, and

Chapter Objectives

After studying this chapter, you should be able to do the following:

1. Define several of the world's major environmental problems.

2. Discuss the possible link between climate change, scarce resources, and armed conflict.

3. Understand the environmental challenges facing policymakers.

4. Evaluate the international responses to major ecological problems.

5. Discuss some of the alternative approaches to ecological health.

right-wing regimes are based on ideas of growth and abundance intimately related to the world's ecological difficulties. Thus, the ecological challenge is also a challenge to the world's prominent political philosophies and to the ideas and institutions that stem from them. In brief, the ecological crisis suggests (at least to some critics) that both capitalism and communism may have fatal flaws. Liberal democracy and democratic socialism may also be in trouble because some of their key ideas (individualism, freedom, social justice) may be severely threatened by ecological crisis and responses to it. A number of political problems, then, may have to be rethought as the world examines and responds to the ecological crisis.

Ecology is concerned with the relationship between organisms and their environment. Human ecology deals with the relationship between people and their larger physical, biological, social, economic, and political environment. For human beings, ecological health is the relationship between people and their larger environment that allow people to flourish. Ecological health means clean air, pure water, the prudent use of natural resources, and a sensible balance between population and resources. It means respect for the planet, a partnership between people and resources. Ecological health calls for people to manage their "household"—the household of the human race—in a caring way.

Let us now consider some of the key factors that prompt our critical exploration of ecological health. Then we examine some leading approaches to ecological health. Finally, we encourage the reader to make wise judgments that may move us toward creative policy breakthroughs on ecological health.

ETHICAL AND EMPIRICAL FACTORS

Our search for key factors is part of a search for a sound ecological philosophy to guide humankind toward sane public policy judgments. We have to reconsider whether, and to what extent, traditional political and economic philosophies are adequate. We have to ask how we can respond to factors that bear upon ecological health. Although controversy rages between ecological pessimists and optimists about responses to these factors, the challenges are generally recognized by all.

Many people see the depletion of the earth's **ozone layer**, global warming, depletion and misuse of scarce and **nonrenewable resources**, air and water pollution, and the imbalance of population and resources as the five major threats to quality of life and life itself. They endanger those now living as well as future generations. They constitute direct ecological threats, present and future, to the biosphere and indirect political threats to human freedom. Humankind could be overwhelmed by an ecological catastrophe brought on by the slow (in human terms) degradation of the planet caused by poisoned water and air; it could be rendered poverty stricken by the disappearance of vital nonrenewable resources; or it could be dehumanized by populations wildly in excess of the resources necessary to sustain adequate living conditions. Efforts to cope with these ecological difficulties could accentuate selfish nationalism and international tensions between "have" and "have not" nations or could intensify class conflicts between rich and poor within both developed and developing nations.

Depletion of the Ozone Layer

In the mid-1980s, scientists confirmed long-held suspicions that something ominous was happening to the ozone layer, the thin layer of ozone that encircles the earth's stratosphere and protects the planet from the full force of the sun's ultraviolet rays. The planet's ozone shield was dissipating. The most observable phenomenon was a 15 million-square-kilometer hole above Antarctica. Will Steger and Jon Bowermaster articulate the seriousness of this situation in their book, *Saving the Earth:*

> The problem with ozone loss is that it increases the amount of one form of
> ultraviolet light—UV-B—that reaches the Earth. Each 1 percent drop of ozone
> allows 2 percent more UV-B to reach the ground. This, in turn, increases the
> potential for skin cancer by 3 to 6 percent. If ozone depletion continues at
> the current rate, and if CFC [chlorofluorocarbon] usage continues unabated,
> the EPA [Environmental Protection Agency] predicts more than 60 million
> additional cases of skin cancer and about one million additional deaths among
> Americans born by the year 2075.[1]

Loss of ozone increases people's vulnerability to infectious diseases through suppression of the immune response system. Furthermore, unchecked ozone depletion will disrupt the food chain. Field studies of soybeans have demonstrated that ozone depletion of up to 25 percent could decrease crop yields by more than 20 percent.[2] The death of microscopic organisms in the world's oceans—another danger with ozone depletion—will seriously endanger other marine life. Finally, climate will be dramatically affected. Ozone depletion will cause a cooling of the stratosphere, perhaps altering global wind patterns.[3]

The cause for this potential ecological disaster is the continuing release of chlorofluorocarbons (CFCs) and bromine from gases called halons (fire-extinguishing agents). The CFCs are used as sterilizing agents in the production of plastic foam products and as propellants in aerosols. Roughly, forty-two tons of CFCs were released into the world's atmosphere in 1950. By 1988, that figure had increased to an astounding and dangerous 1,260 tons.[4] Over the following eight years, however, the amount of CFCs released into the atmosphere fell to 141 tons.[5] How did this change come about?

Because the threat to life on Earth was so great, the international community moved quickly in its attempt to rectify the problem. In 1987, twenty-four nations and the European Economic Community (EEC) signed the Montreal Protocol on Substances That Deplete the Ozone Layer. Most of the major producers and consumers of CFCs and halons signed the agreement, which froze world CFC production and called for overall consumption to be reduced 50 percent by 1999. The agreement further called for a freeze on halon production beginning in 1992—the freeze to be effective at the 1986 level of production.

Even before the Montreal meeting, however, the ozone layer was found to be disappearing at a rate far faster than expected. In response to this development, parties to the Montreal Protocol met in London in May 1992 and agreed to a 100 percent ban for developed nations by the year 2000, with a ten-year time lag for developing nations. This agreement included new chemicals, such as carbon tetrachloride, that had only recently been recognized as contributors to ozone depletion.[6] The size of the ozone hole continued to grow over the next few years to a maximum of 28.7 million square kilometers in 2000 and then began to shrink. Whether the Montreal actions were responsible for this development is open to debate. Some studies indicate that through 2014, the primary reason for the reduction in the size of the hole was weather, not CFC reductions. Regardless, the same studies assert that the Montreal action were absolutely necessary and will begin to have a meaningful impact during the period between 2015 and 2030.[7]

The greatest responsibility for reversing the ozone crisis clearly rests with the world's developed nations, which produce roughly 70 percent of the world's total harmful gases. Not all international environmental problems generate responsible international political action. The depletion of the ozone layer may be an exception. Yet, like most complex policy issues, our understanding of the problem is subject to continual investigation. Political scientists should always be aware of this. In 2018, scientists discovered evidence that the ozone layer may not be recovering quite as well as we expected at a lower level of the stratosphere. It is too early to tell how worrisome this problem is, but it deserves more study and possibly more political action.[8]

Global Warming

In the view of the preponderance of the world's leading climatologists and environmental advocates, the most serious environmental problem facing the planet is global warming, a theory asserting that because of the emission and trapping of heat-absorbing gases the planet's temperature is rising. Global warming is caused by the **greenhouse effect**, whereby the earth's heat is trapped in the atmosphere by such heat-absorbing gases as carbon dioxide, CFCs, methane, nitrous oxide, and ozone. Coal burning, vehicle emissions, and large-scale clearing of tropical forests each add to increased carbon dioxide levels in the atmosphere. Global carbon dioxide (CO_2) emissions from fossil fuel combustion rose from 1.6 billion tons in 1950 to more than 37 billion tons in 2017.[9]

A number of scientific reports have been issued in recent years, each building on previous findings and adding new data. In 2017, a particularly disturbing report was released by scientists and climatologists from 113 federal agencies of the United States. Titled the *Climate Science Special Report, National Climate Assessment, 2017*, it drew some very troubling conclusions with serious implications for the planet and the United States. The following are just a few taken from the report:[10]

1. Global annually averaged surface air temperature has increased by about 1.8° F over the 115-year period 1901–2016. This period is now the warmest in the history of modern civilization . . . and the last three years have been the warmest years on record for the globe.

2. This assessment concludes, based on extensive evidence, that it is extremely likely that human activities, especially emissions of greenhouse gases, are the dominant cause of the observed warming since the mid-twentieth century. For the warming over the last century, there is no convincing alternative explanation supported by the extent of the observational evidence.

3. Global average sea level has risen by about 7–9 inches since 1900, with almost half (about three inches) of that rise occurring since 1993. Human-caused

climate change has made a substantial contribution to this rise since 1900, contributing to a rate of rise that is greater than during any preceding century in at least 2,800 years.

4. Global average sea levels are expected to continue to rise by at least several inches in the next fifteen years and by 1–4 feet by 2100.

5. Heatwaves have become more frequent in the United States since the 1960s, while extreme cold temperatures and cold waves are less frequent.

6. The incidence of large forest fires in the western United States and Alaska has increased since the early 1980s and is projected to further increase in those regions as the climate changes, with profound changes to regional ecosystems.

7. Annual trends toward earlier spring melt and reduced snowpack are already affecting water resources.

8. The magnitude of climate change beyond the next few decades will depend primarily on the amount of greenhouse gases (especially carbon dioxide) emitted globally. Without major reduction in emissions, the increase in annual average global temperature relative to preindustrial times could reach 90° F or more by the end of this century.

The international community's response to global warming has been mixed and certainly cautious. At the **Earth Summit**, a global environmental conference held in Rio de Janeiro, Brazil, in June 1992, a Convention on Climate Change was drafted that proposed international action to prevent carbon dioxide and other greenhouse gases from building up in the atmosphere to levels that could cause damaging climate changes. It established financial aid for developing countries, as well as institutions to review and update commitments. However, after twenty-three years, the impact of the convention has been negligible. The major problem with the treaty is that it contains no specific emission targets, and carbon dioxide concentrations as measured by parts per million have increased steadily from a low of 356.2 in 1992 to 400 in 2016.[11]

In December 1997, some 160 nations met in Kyoto, Japan, and drew up the Kyoto Protocol to the Framework Convention on Climate Changes. By 2000, emissions had fallen slightly, to 6,299 million tons, thanks to efforts spearheaded primarily by the emerging economies of the former eastern bloc nations. In contrast, during the same time frame the industrial nations of the West, including the United States, failed to reduce carbon emissions. About ten countries share responsibility for roughly two-thirds of the world's carbon emissions—led by the United States and China. As of early 2018, 192 countries had ratified the agreement. Only three countries have not, Afghanistan, Sudan, and the United States. As a follow-up to Kyoto, 196 countries met in Paris in 2015 and negotiated the Paris Climate Agreement. One of the criticisms of the Kyoto Agreement was that it set no targets or goals. The Paris Agreement sought to at least make an effort to correct that by having each country voluntarily establish goals for limiting greenhouse gas emissions. The overall goal was to limit the temperature increase to 1.5° C. A temperature increase of 2.0° or more is widely considered to be very dangerous for the planet. In June of 2017, President Donald Trump announced that he would withdraw the United States from the agreement.

The overwhelming preponderance of the world's scientific community has reached the conclusion that the greenhouse effect is real. But it would be incorrect to say that this belief is unanimous. One reason is that the greenhouse effect, unlike the hole in the ozone layer, is not clearly observable. Many of the greenhouse predictions come from complex computer models. Additionally, there is disagreement on whether a global disaster will result; some scientists believe nature will intervene and compensate for the abuse of the planet. One body of thought argues that even if global warming is linked to the release of greenhouse gases, clouds will shift in a manner to counter much of the temperature increase and preserve the equable climate.[12] Still, we should note that much of the debate in the scientific community revolves around how quickly and severely the problems associated with global warming develop – not the reality that the climate is changing, getting warmer overall, and that human activity contributes to this phenomenon.

Clearly, the issue of global warming and the related greenhouse effect raises serious questions for policymakers throughout the world. How much longer can fossil fuels be relied on as the primary source of energy in the industrialized world? Will developing nations, as they become more industrialized, use more fossil fuels? Are such energy sources as hydropower, wind power, geothermal power, solar power, and biomass power realistic alternatives? How would a drastic reduction in the use of fossil fuels affect the world economy? Can the destruction of the world's great rainforests in places such as Brazil be allowed to continue?

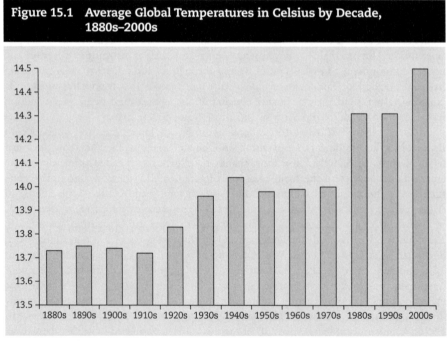

Figure 15.1 Average Global Temperatures in Celsius by Decade, 1880s–2000s

Source: NASA, Goddard Space Flight Center, "GISS Surface Temperature Analysis (GISTEMP)," http://data.giss.nasa.gov/gistemp.

Pollution

Modern warfare, especially when it involves nuclear weapons, has had a devastating effect on ecological health. Radiation poisoning, which killed one of every five people who ultimately died at Hiroshima, has also taken lives in the peacetime testing of nuclear weapons, and it remains a hazard in all nuclear plants and waste dumps. Herbicides used in Vietnam to defoliate jungle cover not only devastated millions of acres of natural foliage and farmland but also caused severe medical problems for soldiers and civilians alike.

AP Photo/EyePress, File

Air pollution has proven to be a major problem for China as its manufacturing-based economy has rapidly grown over the past three decades.

As contaminating to the environment as war is, massive pollution over extended periods of time has mostly been caused by modern industrialization and agriculture. Industrial cities suffer from smog. Acid rain may fall hundreds or thousands of miles from a factory or coal-burning energy plant and injure lakes, streams, buildings, and antiquities. Automobiles are among the worst polluters, filling the air with noxious fumes, including lead. The pollution of rivers and oceans and air by factory smoke, industrial chemicals, and agricultural pesticides threatens people, animals, and fish. Shorelines are desecrated when millions of gallons of oil spill from tankers that run aground. How long can the earth sustain this kind of injury? How long will people tolerate it?

Insults to the environment are found in every industrial society. Europe, which is densely populated and highly industrial, faces pollution problems even worse than those in the United States. The Baltic and Mediterranean Seas and the Rhine River are heavily contaminated. Oil spills have plagued European shores. Acid rain falls on Scandinavia. Ironically, Japan's very economic success in the second half of the twentieth century contributed to its severe pollution problem. An illustration of this problem was the tragedy in Minamata Bay in the early 1950s. Mercury poisoning from industrial sources is believed to have caused the death of more than 600 people and the severe illnesses, including paralysis, of approximately 1,300 more. In 1989, as the cloak of secrecy surrounding much of Eastern Europe was lifted with the fall of the Soviet Union and the development of democracy in that region, it became painfully clear that the industrialized communist countries had not been immune to ecological problems and damage. Areas of Bulgaria, Poland, and Romania turned out to be ecological disaster zones. The Communist Soviet Union had been no better able to deal with insults to the environment than the United States or other capitalistic countries. Indeed, some of the most treasured natural assets of the former Soviet Union, such as Lake Baikal, may be irredeemably polluted. It should also be noted that India and China, in particular, suffer from extreme air pollution as a result of their rapid industrial modernization.

Depletion of Valuable Resources

For much of humanity's time on Earth, scarcity, not abundance, was the rule. The idea of endless abundance is relatively new, associated with the discovery (dated to 1492) by Western peoples of "virgin" and abundant lands and resources in Africa, the Americas, and Asia. Until quite recently, science and technology seemed to hold out the hope of limitless development of resources.

The impression of limitless clean air and water nourished the impression of bountiful lands and resources. Given abundant nature and scientific genius, many Westerners concluded that they could overcome scarcity throughout the world. With hard work and the opportunity to accumulate capital, human beings could produce abundantly and overcome the traditional hardships of nature. Per capita income could grow enormously. Abundant energy sources—whether human labor, hydroelectric power, coal, or oil—could make production and growth zoom. It seemed as though the Malthusian fears of population growing in excess of food supply unless checked by war, disease, famine, or birth control had finally been laid to rest. Liberals and capitalists shared these high hopes with democratic socialists and communists. All of them assumed that the economy—rightly directed—could produce abundantly and (given the right political and social direction) enhance freedom and justice. In this period dominated by the idea of growth and progress, few people saw that the earth was finite and limited, that exponential growth—unless checked or controlled—might seriously threaten the carrying capacity of the globe.[13]

Today, the idea of scarcity as a problem is widely accepted. Humanity may be producing too many people, whose increasing appetites may mean running out of the resources necessary to sustain their lives. Some natural resources, such as oil, are nonrenewable resources—resources that, once used up, are gone forever. Indeed, some oil analysts believe we may soon reach peak production—often called Hubbert's Peak, after Dr. M. King Hubbert, the geophysicist who first noticed the nature of production over time—and less and less oil will be extracted after that point. His observations have been criticized as some experts note better technology may lead to the greater recovery of oil from existing fields. Still, these resources are finite. Certain nonrenewable resources, such as coal, may be plentiful at present, but even they will not last forever. Moreover, these types of resources will be depleted even faster if present practices of consumption continue. And these are the practices on which current economic growth and lifestyle depend. Thus, the supplies of key nonrenewable resources can be exhausted at exponential rates. As nonrenewable resources decline, their prices increase. When key energy sources become excessively expensive and are depleted, a major ingredient of modern growth and life will be denied. Which energy source will then run the modern industrial plant? What fuel will automobiles use? What about the jobs of automakers? What will happen to the world's system of highways?

Wasteful and imprudent use of **renewable resources**, which are resources that can be reused or replaced such as soil and trees, could also produce terrible consequences. The land could become exhausted, wasted, and ruthlessly exploited. Trees could be recklessly cut down and not replanted. Water and air could be poisoned.

One of the most valuable resources on the planet is fresh, safe water, sometimes known as potable water. Technically water is a renewable resource because of rain cycles. But three things contribute to what is considered a growing global crisis. The first is obviously climate change. With the planet warming, the frequency of severe drought is increased significantly. Second, safe water is not evenly distributed on the earth. Some regions, such as in the tropics, have an abundance of water. Other regions like the water-scarce Middle East and North Africa consider water an incredibly valuable resource. The third factor is widespread contamination of water in certain regions. Roughly, 844 million people have no access to safe drinking water and every ninety seconds a child dies of a water-related disease.[14] It is also important to point out that access to freshwater is not exclusively a concern of countries in the developing world. Concerns about water play a significant role in the United States. States like Texas and Oklahoma have suffered from huge water shortages for irrigation for a number of years, and from 2011 through 2017, the agriculturally rich state of California faced a severe water crisis with the possibility of long-term drought. From 2014 through 2018, the city of Flint, Michigan, suffered a devastating problem of lead pollution of its fresh water supply.

The picture of the imprudent use of renewable resources has been dramatically captured by Garrett Hardin's ecological metaphor, the **tragedy of the commons**, which calls attention to the overuse and eventual destruction of commonly held resources.[15] The commons is the communal grazing plot. If all farmers seek to exploit the free grazing of their herds on the communal plot, the grass will soon be gone and will be incapable of renewal, and all the farmers will lose. Tragically, individual farmers are unable to abstain from overgrazing because while they might abstain, selfish competitors will nevertheless continue to graze. In this case, then, immediate self-interest trumps long-range concern. In the end, of course, the grass is destroyed, the commons cease to benefit anyone, and all farmers and animals suffer. (This is a good real-world example of rational choice theory or game theory we explored in Chapter 3. In the tragedy of the commons, individuals acting in their personal self-interest will, in the end, create less than optimal outcomes.)

The global degradation of land is alarmingly illustrated by what has become known as deforestation, brought on by humanity's seemingly unquenchable need for wood and wood products and for new arable land. Global forests are roughly half of what they were 8,000 years ago. Fifty percent of original forest have been destroyed in the last fifty years with 15 billion trees cut down annually. Seven countries of the world account for roughly 60 percent of the total deforestation on the planet. These include Brazil, Canada, the United States, Indonesia, China, Russia, and the Democratic Republic of Congo.[16]

We may already be in the process of losing hundreds of species of wildlife. Nearly 20,000 species of animal and plant life are threatened on the planet, according to Richard Pearson of the American Museum of Natural History.[17] For example, oceanic and freshwater fish are terribly overexploited; in time, this could significantly reduce catches, and nets may come back to the boat empty. Other renewable sources, such as clean air and water, are threatened just as the commons are.

The tragedy of the commons is now a global tragedy. So, unless the global community can discover new resources or employ science to find substitutes for current resources, the earth faces ecological scarcity. As shortages loom, prices are bound to inflate, living standards are bound to suffer, and inequalities are bound to worsen. The waste of scarce resources hurts the present generation but may deal an even more devastating blow to posterity. The present recklessness may doom future generations to a lack of adequate food, clothing, shelter, energy, clean air, and pure water. Poverty may be intensified; the hope of overcoming it in developing areas may be dashed. Tension between the relatively rich and poor may increase and with it, perhaps, conflict and repressive measures to perpetuate the inequalities that can no longer be relieved by a bigger "pie."

Climate Change, Scarce Resources, and Armed Conflict

Finally, there is the specter of armed conflict that finds its origins in climate change. Outright war over access to scarce resources is a possibility as well as the disruption brought on by the mass migration of people because of the lack of resources in areas where they work and reside. In 2015, the Proceedings of the National Academy of Sciences reported just such an occurrence. It concerned the horrible civil war in Syria that began in 2014. Scientists compiled statistics showing severe water shortages in Syria, Iraq, and Turkey killed livestock, drove up food prices, and sickened children. The result was a mass migration of 1.5 million rural residents to Syria's already densely packed cities at precisely the same time as that country was exploding with immigrants from the Iraq War. While the analysts readily admit that there were multiple causes of the Syrian civil war, the sudden and massive increases in urban population exacerbated already bad conditions, including corruption, inequality, high unemployment, and the government's inability to curb human suffering. The link to climate change is pretty convincing. After examining meteorological data, the scientists determined that natural variability alone was unlikely to account for the terrible droughts.[18]

The Danger of Population Imbalance

Our mania for growth is also reflected in the population explosion. As we saw in Chapter 4, world population began a steep climb with the onset of the Industrial Revolution (at the end of the eighteenth century) and continued that climb during the revolutions in transportation, medicine, and agriculture in the nineteenth and twentieth centuries. The world's population doubled between 1850 and 1950, moving up from about 1 billion to 2 billion, and now stands at roughly 7.6 billion.

Even though population growth has slowed in many developed and industrial countries (to an average annual increase of 1.3 percent), the overall picture remains disturbing, largely because of the increasing birth rates in poor, mostly undeveloped countries. The African continent alone is expected to explode from 1.26 billion in 2018 to 2.53 billion by the year 2050.[19] We must keep in mind that the trouble comes from population growth in excess of resources—food, energy, water, nonrenewable resources, space, and heat.[20] Globally, there may not be enough food to sustain the growing population. Countries with high growth rates may also have to double industrial and agricultural production to keep up with population—an almost impossible feat and a further strain on an already damaged environment.

While agricultural output in East Asia and Latin America has substantially increased at rates keeping up with population, the same cannot be said for two other regions of the developing world—the Indian subcontinent and sub-Saharan Africa. Table 15.1 lists some of the most severely affected countries as reflected in underweight children.

The task of feeding so many (particularly in poorer countries) may not be impossible but will be difficult. And if population does not stabilize, there may be as many as 9 or 10 billion people on Earth by the middle of the twenty-first century. Feeding these people will be even more difficult. Earth's population is likely to put enormous strain on the planet's carrying capacity. And clearly, scarce resources accentuate the problem.

Of course, it may be possible to expand necessary resources and to limit population through family planning. The prospects here are bleakest in the most vulnerable segments of the globe: the poorest regions of South Asia and Africa. The greatest successes will probably occur in countries with richer resources and the lowest birthrates. Other "solutions" for the imbalance of population and resources—war, famine, and disease—are possible, of course, although none are appealing.

The Challenges of Ecological Politics

The challenges that face policymakers depend on the fundamental diagnosis of the ecological plight. These ecological challenges are also political challenges. They challenge liberalism and socialism, capitalism and communism, nationalism and internationalism. They challenge democratic and constitutional government. If ozone depletion, global warming, pollution, ecological scarcity, and the imbalance of population and resources are realities—and if they cannot be offset by a natural leveling-off process or by science and technology—then a number of questions must be faced:

1. Can peoples and nations adjust to the idea of (at least relative) scarcity, which undercuts modern belief in growth and requires a new lifestyle of prudent ecological balance? Can we adjust to the idea that population growth must slow or stop because it imperils resources? Can we accept the idea that pollution threatens the quality of life on Earth?

Table 15.1 Hunger in Developing Countries, 2007–2014	
Country	Underweight Children, 2007–2014 (Percentage of those under 5 years
Bangladesh	45.1
Burundi	29.1
Ethiopia	25.2
Niger	37.9
Pakistan	21.6
Papua New Guinea	27.9
Sudan	32.2

Source: World Health Organization, World Health Statistics 2015, pp. 102–110.

2. Is laissez-faire economics—with individuals, businesses, and corporations relatively free to produce, consume, and trade as they please—tolerable any longer? Or must government—in recognition of the dangers of scarcity, of the population explosion, and of pollution and in pursuit of a common ecological good—act to safeguard the globe? Will ecological philosopher-kings have to coerce selfish and thoughtless people to save them and the planet? Can democracy endure under these conditions?

3. Even if the people own the means of production and exchange (as in socialism and communism), can they avoid the consequences of scarcity, population growth, and pollution? Will communist regimes have to be more coercive in order to ration scarce resources, control population, and curtail pollution?

4. Can developing nations fulfill their dreams of overcoming poverty and achieving democratic development if they cannot fulfill plans for economic growth? Will the need to adopt some form of ecological balance—to husband resources, to limit population growth—doom their aspirations for a better life? And what setbacks will occur if richer nations cannot extend needed help to developing nations?

These questions point toward difficult judgments on public policy. If the ecological optimists are correct, these questions will not be so troubling. If a world of abundance can still be counted on, if population growth will stabilize, if pollution can be overcome, the ecological future will be brighter. There may still be some worries, but given the genius of modern science and technology and sound political decisions, perhaps the scenario of the doomsday prophets can be avoided.

ALTERNATIVE APPROACHES TO ECOLOGICAL HEALTH

It is, of course, entirely possible to adopt a do-nothing, hedonistic, or piggish approach to ecological health. One could ignore ecological problems, assuming they will go away. One could also embrace the hedonistic philosophy of "eat, drink, and be merry, for tomorrow we die." Or the leaders of currently rich and powerful nations could try to perpetuate their dominance by continuing to exploit the poor. They could try to isolate themselves from growing scarcities, booming populations, and growing pollution. Although all of these responses are possible—and, indeed, are likely in some nations—we shall presuppose a more rational and ethical response.

Liberal Conservation

Those who adopt the liberal approach to conservation maintain that modest reform can do the job. They emphasize the feasibility of conserving scarce resources, limiting family size, and safeguarding the environment. They point to actual policies and developments in countries such as the United States to highlight the possibilities of reform.

During the 1970s and 1980s, a number of steps were taken to conserve energy in the United States: for example, a fifty-five-miles-an-hour speed limit; smaller, gas-efficient cars; lower temperatures in heated buildings; less joyriding. Unfortunately, the mid-1990s witnessed a reversal of several of these steps. On a more positive note, efforts to recycle paper, aluminum, glass, and other valuable resources enjoy considerable popularity, although recycling could be increased still further. In 2009, President Barack Obama moved toward achieving even tougher fuel efficiency standards for automobiles and trucks that among other things would require all vehicles to average 54.5 miles per gallon average by 2020. He also instituted a variety of additional measures to improve the environment. But it is also important to note that during his first year in office, President Trump, primarily through executive orders, rescinded the Obama administration's miles per gallon requirement and dismantled many of the environmental policies that not only President Obama had instituted but other previous presidents as well. However, given the federal nature of the U.S. system, many states are pursuing their own environmental initiatives. America's largest state, California, is taking bold action regardless of what the federal government does. See Chapter 8 for a discussion of the concept of federalism.

Much more can be done. Water and land can be used more prudently. Educational programs can successfully encourage water conservation. Better farming practices, food control, and reforestation can save soil and trees. The conservation of nonrenewable resources and the prudent care and replacement of renewable resources can go a long way toward achieving ecological balance. Most of these actions can be done voluntarily, but in some instances democratic government may have to intervene on behalf of the common good. Yet such actions always raise concerns of conservative Republicans who prefer limited government intervention in the economy.

Family planning is easier in the developed world, where the higher level of well-being reduces the pressure for large families and where education, literacy, and the relative emancipation of women encourage birth control. But the industrialized nations can encourage family planning in other nations through education about birth control, better programs of health and welfare, and efforts to improve economic well-being. Such measures may reduce the need for more radical and controversial means of limiting population, including vasectomy (the operation that prevents passage of sperm from the testes to the penis), tubal ligation (the cutting and tying off of the fallopian tubes), and free abortions on demand.

Environmental protection can also work. Sensible legislation to protect against flagrant polluters already exists. Resources must be protected against those who would pollute the air, water, and land. It is not too much to ask of chemical companies to safely dispose of contaminating wastes. It is not too much to insist that factories and power plants release fewer pollutants through their smokestacks. It is not too much to require strip miners to restore the earth after they have removed the coal.

The strengths of this reform alternative are many. There can be little argument about the need for conservation, family planning, and environmental protection—especially when they are undertaken voluntarily. When good habits are widespread, they contribute enormously to ecological health. Democratically agreed-on, wise regulation on behalf of these objectives is desirable.

Creative Breakthrough

But are reforms that build on existing policies enough? Here we uncover some of the weaknesses of this alternative. Critics maintain that these reforms do not come to grips with the true scarcity, overpopulation, and pollution. These critics believe that current conservation only postpones the day of reckoning. They hold that present reforms have not seriously addressed the problem of useless, wasteful, destructive production. They say that these reforms do not address the scandalous fact that the developed countries use a disproportionate share of the world's resources to maintain their high standard of living. Moreover, these reforms cannot balance population and resources in the poorer countries or cut pollution in any significant way. The critics gravely doubt that present measures can work fast enough to ensure the planet's continued ecological health. They believe that the reformist approach makes too many compromises, such as accepting pollution to avoid the loss of industrial jobs and succumbing to the mania for growth to maintain prosperity. In particular, many critics of compromise worry about a "tipping point" in the near future—a point after which it will be too late to overcome the ecological degradation of the planet. These considerations suggest to some that bolder and more radical policies are in order.

Guarded Optimism and Economic Growth

Scholars such as Herman Kahn, Julian L. Simon, Dennis T. Avery, and Bjørn Lomborg take a guardedly optimistic approach toward ecological health.[21] Kahn and two of his colleagues at the Hudson Institute, Leon Martel and William Brown, set forth their views in a widely read book, *The Next 200 Years: A Scenario for America and the World*. Although published more than three decades ago, it remains perhaps the most compelling work of the guarded optimists. First, these scholars believe that many of the pessimistic environmental projections are exaggerated, temporary in nature, or patently false. Additionally, they maintain that to the degree some of these problems do exist they can be overcome. Guarded optimists argue that to the extent they exist, the problems of population, hunger, energy, disappearing raw materials, and pollution are solvable in the future and that the principal means to their solution is cutting-edge technology and economic growth. Indeed, many of these problems are the temporary problems of a world in transition from poverty to prosperity. Guarded optimists further maintain that neither the world nor the United States must suffer from long-term shortages of energy or resources.

The guarded optimists and growth enthusiasts do not accept conventional wisdom about patterns of population growth. For Avery, currently a senior fellow at the Hudson Institute, the world's population is "not spiraling out of control. What we are seeing is a one-time surge. In fact, the world is in the final stages of the third—and probably last—human population surge."[22] Avery notes that the first surge began 10,000 years ago with the invention of farming. The second surge occurred with the Industrial Revolution and was associated with increases in human wealth. We are now in the final surge, which is linked to vast improvements in medical science and public health systems. He concludes,

> The current population surge is expected to be over before the year 2050. Total fertility rates in the poorest countries have already come more than 60 percent of the way to stability, essentially in one generation![23]

As the population stabilizes, hunger will be drastically reduced and ultimately eliminated. The optimists do not see a growing gap between demand and supply. Rather, they see abundant food in the future. Poor weather, natural disasters, bad policies, and inadequate distribution have led to malnutrition, hunger, and famine in some areas of the world, but there is enough land, water, and fertilizer to sustain the present and future populations, particularly as we continue to make advances in high-yield crops and sophisticated irrigation techniques.

In the eyes of the guarded optimists, global energy problems are to a large extent attributable to bad luck, poor management, and general waste. Future energy is not dependent on an endless supply of fossil fuel. Given scientific breakthroughs, there is every reason to believe that the world will have an inexhaustible supply of energy, including solar, wind, hydroelectric, geothermal, and nuclear. Many optimists believe that a milestone was reached with University of Houston professor Paul Chu's discovery of a compound that is a near-perfect conductor of electricity at high temperatures—the superconductor. Superconductivity is the process of transmitting energy with limited or no loss of energy. The potential of this technology is revolutionary. As Robert M. Hazen describes it,

> Powerful and efficient lightweight magnets and motors, compact computers faster than any now in existence, magnetically levitated bullet trains able to travel hundreds of miles per hour, money-saving power transmission cables linked to safe, remote nuclear and solar generators, long-term energy storage systems, and a multitude of other devices are all possible in theory through the utilization of superconductivity.[24]

Hazen continues,

> Superconducting motors could be smaller and more powerful than conventional designs. Battery-powered automobiles with light, efficient superconducting electric motors could revolutionize society and its dependence on fossil fuels.[25]

Indeed the age of the superconductor motor may be upon us with an increasing number of practical applications such as naval, cargo, and cruise shipping.[26] There is also optimism about other raw materials, which guarded optimists believe will be abundant for future generations. They reject the idea of exhausted vital resources and emphasize the potential of mining the oceans and even of extraterrestrial mining. Recycling, conservation, and substitution can secure vital materials now in short supply.

As far as pollution is concerned, the guarded optimists hold that short-term problems can be solved. They place their faith in technology, money, time, and intelligent self-restraint. They believe that in the not-too-distant future, human beings will look back proudly on ecological achievements. The enormous progress made over the past twenty years in reducing air pollution in U.S. cities and in the nation's waterways is proof of what can be done to improve the environment.

Finally, the guarded optimists and growth enthusiasts are obviously committed to economic growth, but they believe such growth will taper off somewhat over time.

Creative
Breakthrough

Despite some stubborn pockets of poverty, continuing overall economic growth will benefit all.

The strengths of this philosophy of guarded optimism and economic growth are considerable. If true, this orientation provides hope for a future wherein science and technology, prudently joined with wise public policies, can cope with scarce natural resources, balance population and resources, and provide a clean environment. Growth and prosperity can continue to progress.

The weaknesses of this alternative are found in its assumptions: that population growth will level off fast enough and be in balance with abundant and deliverable food supplies; that resources, especially energy, will be available at reasonable costs to keep industrial and agricultural machinery operating; and that pollution can be overcome. But if population does not level off; if food supplies do not reach hungry people; if no new natural resources can be found; if the sun, the wind, the rivers and oceans, and the earth cannot be tapped for energy; and if pollution continues and is too expensive to curtail, then humankind is clearly at grave risk. Will we have both the scientific genius and political will to do all that Kahn and his associates see as essential?

Critics of technological solutions point to the alarming costs involved in scientific efforts to cope with scarcity, population, and pollution. For example, nuclear power, science's answer to fossil fuel use, is expensive and potentially dangerous. The partial meltdown at the Three Mile Island reactor in Pennsylvania in 1979, the reactor explosion at Chernobyl in the Soviet Union in 1986, and the Fukushima nuclear power plant disaster in 2011 clearly demonstrate that serious accidents at nuclear power plants can happen and can release harmful radiation. The disposal of radioactive waste remains a troubling problem. The widespread use of nuclear power complicates the problem of the proliferation of nuclear weapons.

Alternative sources of "clean" energy, such as solar power, are not easily or inexpensively obtained. (Though, we should note, prices for solar panels have come down remarkably in recent years.) Hydroelectric power is a possibility only for countries fortunate enough to be able to tap the potential of falling water. Geothermal power, which is comparatively benign but not entirely pollution free, is by no means universally available. Only wild optimists predict that geothermal energy will constitute more than 20 percent of the world's future energy supply. The loss of cheap, abundant energy is particularly damaging to the dream of a technological solution to the ecological crisis, because so much industrial and agricultural productivity relies on such energy. Cheap energy, for example, has fueled growth and affluence in many industrial, developed nations. The green revolution that significantly increased the food supply now requires increasingly expensive fertilizer (itself dependent on oil) for success. Even with remarkable discoveries such as superconductivity, skeptics conclude that there are decided limits on how far science and technology can go in overcoming the fundamental problems of scarcity, the imbalance of population and resources, and pollution.

A Sustainable Development Model

In 1987, under the auspices of the United Nations, the World Commission on Environment and Development published *Our Common Future*.[27] The report lays out several clear theses. First, the world is under severe environmental stress. Second, sound ecological management is not incompatible with development. In fact, economic growth can and must continue. The question is, "What kind of growth leads to ecological problems and what kind of growth is compatible with sound environmental management?" Third, there is linkage between environmental protection and world peace. Environmental crises present a threat to national security in two ways. Obviously, the threats to the biosphere, oceans, fresh water, and other resources are a danger to human welfare. Beyond this, arms expenditures siphon off valuable resources that could be used for environmental protection.

Stock photo © iShootPhotos LLC

Wind-powered generators are an example of alternative energy sources favored by the guarded optimists who believe that the earth's supply of fossil fuel is not infinite.

The strategy that *Our Common Future* proposes for both development and environmental management is called **sustainable development**, a rational and equitable approach to development that attempts to balance societal needs against environmental limitations. The concept has been widely accepted in UN circles and the wider environmental community.[28] As the report notes, sustainable growth contains two key concepts: "the concept of 'needs,' in particular the essential needs of the world's poor, to which overriding priority should be given" and "the idea of limitations imposed by the state of technology and social organization on the environment's ability to meet present and future needs."[29]

Sustainable development is really a call for what the commission sees as a more rational and equitable approach to development. Growth in the more industrial regions of the world has been highly material and energy intensive, putting enormous strain on the environment. Similarly, but for different reasons, poverty, as found in the developing regions of the world, "reduces people's capacity to use resources in a sustainable manner; it intensifies pressure on the environment."[30] High birthrates along with seemingly desperate overuse of land are but two manifestations of this.

Sustainable development depends on a two-pronged management approach. First, there must be a high degree of responsible and rational growth at the national level. Educating people on the damage done by short-term, irrational development is crucial. Second, "sustainable development can be secured only through international cooperation and agreed [upon] regimes for surveillance, development, and management in the common interest. . . . Without agreed [upon], equitable, and enforceable rules governing the rights and duties of states in respect to global commons, the pressure of demands on finite resources will destroy their ecological integrity over time."[31]

Numerous international efforts at different stages of development highlight the possibilities of international cooperation. The oceans are governed under the Law of the Sea Treaty, the International Whaling Commission, and the 1985 Convention on Prevention of Marine Pollution by Dumping of Wastes and Other Matter. Space is regulated by the UN Global Environmental Monitoring System and by an outer space treaty that states that outer space is not subject to national appropriation. Antarctica has been the subject of several agreements, beginning with a 1959 treaty that confined the continent to peaceful uses and extending to the 1964 Agreed Measures for Conservation of Antarctic Fauna and Flora, the 1972 Convention of Conservation of Antarctic Seals, the 1980 Convention on the Conservation of Antarctic Marine Living Resources, the 1989 Convention on Transboundary Movements of Hazardous Wastes and Their Disposal, the 1992 Convention on Biodiversity, and the 1994 Convention to Combat Desertification. To these we can add the Montreal Protocol, the Kyoto Treaty, and the Paris Agreement on Climate Change. These kinds of efforts to build effective regimes for managing the earth's ecological welfare are only a start. The future is clearly a multilateral one, and much needs to be done to expand and strengthen these regimes as well as to create new ones.

Creative Breakthrough

The basic principles of environmental protection and sustainability must be fully absorbed into the ethos of our industrial civilization and into every aspect of our economic life and behavior. As represented in Figure 15.2, sustainable development represents the reconciliation of environmental, societal equity and economic demands. The idea of the Venn diagram is to reinforce the notion that these three pillars of sustainability, environment, equity and economic, overlap, are not mutually exclusive and can actually reinforce each other.

The sustainable development argument is appealing. It does not reject the notion of growth. Advocates of sustainable growth claim that development in the poorer parts of the world must proceed and that economic growth in the developed world cannot be halted but must be more environmentally sound. Sound national policy must be

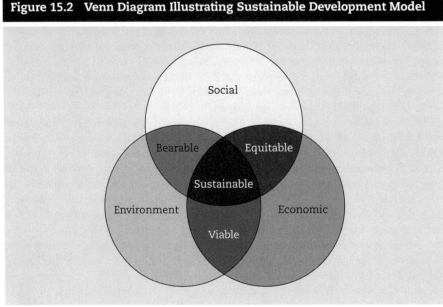

Figure 15.2   Venn Diagram Illustrating Sustainable Development Model

Source: United Nations, 2005 World Environmental Summit, Rio de Janeiro.

combined with more international programs committed to planetary management. To fund national and international efforts, resources now devoted to other priorities, such as the military, must be reallocated.

Critics of sustainable development have serious doubts about the model. Is there not, they query, an element of "having one's cake and eating it too" in this philosophy? Are developed countries willing to drastically change their energy-intensive and materially driven economies if such change means they must lower their standards of living? Will the countries that compose the international community be willing to grant international organizations and programs the power necessary to effectively manage the earth's ecological systems? Can governments realistically reach practical accords on the environment? These critical questions raise the possibility that the problems of planet management may require even more radical solutions.

A Steady-State Philosophy

The concept of a steady state closely relates to that of sustainable growth, but the emphasis is different. Clearly, economic growth and development are more important to sustainable growth than to a steady state. Advocates of a steady state are convinced that the present ecological crisis is a deep-seated, ongoing reality and cannot be dealt with through superficial reform and democratic muddling or by relying on a scientific and technological fix. Adopting the minimum, frugal steady state will require radical ecological, political, and economic changes. William Ophuls forcefully advanced this argument in his 1977 book, *Ecology and the Politics of Scarcity: Prologue to a Political Theory of the Steady State*, and again in his 1992 follow-up volume, *Ecology and the Politics of Scarcity Revisited: The Unraveling of the American Dream*, co-authored with A. Stephen Boyan, Jr.[32]

Ophuls argues that ecological scarcity adversely affects the political system. It seriously challenges policies of liberal reform. Such liberal policies, he argues, can only briefly postpone the day of reckoning. Our planet's finite character, set against humanity's unchecked exponential growth, materialistic appetites, and indifference to pollution, presages a severe and alarming crisis, for which there is no scientific and technological fix. The crisis really focuses on environmental demand versus carrying capacity. Ophuls estimates that the saturation point will be reached by 2036. Ecological scarcity involves shortages of food and of mineral and energy resources. Our ability to use technology to increase resources can only go so far. Earth is a finite planet with limited and increasingly costly resources and technology.

The only sane response to the ecological crisis, according to Ophuls, is a steady-state philosophy. He defines a steady-state society as "one that has achieved a basic long-term balance between the demands of a population and the environment that supplies its wants."[33] Such a society calls for a healthy biosphere, careful use of resources, wise limitations on consumption, long-term goals to guide short-term choices, and a respect for future generations. Human beings must learn to live within their annual incomes and thus avoid eating up the world's capital. They must manage the planet prudently so that it continues to nourish this generation and future generations.

Ophuls believes that swift action in the right way can achieve transition to a high-level steady state. Otherwise, a lower-level steady state may result, or people may even be forced back to a premodern, agrarian way of life. The philosophy of the steady state requires that we physically tune into the cycle of nature that we try to replenish what we withdraw. It is vital that we maintain population within our planet's ecological carrying capacity.

We must also consider the sociopolitical characteristics of the steady-state society. Politically, Ophuls favors the Jeffersonian ideal: small, self-governing communities associated with a federal government pursuing clearly defined national purposes. As people turn away from the rape of the globe, from mindless growth, they will find economic, social, and political satisfaction and personal fulfillment. Humanity will have to move away from rampant individualism to place a higher priority on community and the common good. The community will need authority to enforce its demands on individuals. Although authority need not be remote, arbitrary, and capricious, and although basic rights will have to be retained in a constitutional system, the right to ecological destruction will have to be curbed. Ophuls anticipates a shift from egalitarian democracy toward political competence and stratification. He looks to agreed-on governmental values—"aristocratic principles"—favoring the common interests of the steady state. Ideally, a class of elites, under constitutional restraints, would govern in accord with a steady-state philosophy of virtuous restraint. Liberal, laissez-faire, muddling-through politics will no longer do. Courageous political decisions will have to be made on behalf of ecological health. Such health will not result from the free play of market forces; such free play has produced only the tragedy of the commons.

Ophuls also sees diversity as a characteristic of the steady-state society. He looks forward to a greater role for small-scale enterprise. He anticipates great opportunities for people at the local level.

The steady-state society will more genuinely embrace the principle of holism—the interrelationship of the whole global system. A new, more virtuous and spiritual morality will characterize the steady-state philosophy. Ophuls believes that people will cultivate a more mature economy to protect precious resources and the quality of life. Care for the earth will reward humanity with beauty and amenity as well as ample sustenance. The modern age of thoughtless growth will come to an end.

Ophuls's steady state offers a happy mean between degrading poverty and wasteful abundance. He insists that the steady state is not stagnation—that it does not oppose all forms of growth. Rather, it seeks a dynamic equilibrium affording ample opportunity for ethical, cultural, and scientific growth. Ophuls is sympathetic to small-scale and self-sufficient enterprises that help individuals control their own economic lives.

Creative Breakthrough

What can we say of the strengths and weaknesses of this philosophy of the steady state? The vision of a harmonious balance between people and resources is most attractive. So, too, is a world of ample sufficiency that provides generous scope for artistic, intellectual, moral, scientific, and spiritual fulfillment. A philosophical review of materialistic and aggressive appetites (toward other peoples and nations as well as toward the planet) has long been in order. The philosophy of growth and progress needs critical analysis, as does our often unthinking reliance on science and technology. A fundamental transformation of our worldview may be required to meet the ecological challenge.

But are the steady-state philosophers correct in their empirical analysis of the ecological crisis? And if they are right, is their prescription desirable and feasible? These questions call attention to possible weaknesses. The guarded optimists, in particular, disagree with Ophuls's empirical analysis. They see population stabilizing, hence no exhaustion of resources; and they believe pollution can be controlled. They insist that Ophuls's extrapolations about exponential growth are misleading and, furthermore, believe that economic growth will slow in ample time to avert disaster. Above all, science and technology will ensure abundance and defeat pollution.

Even if Ophuls's analysis is correct, and assuming that the steady-state society is desirable, can such a society be achieved? Critics maintain that people lack the will to cut back to a more frugal economics. People are simply not willing to pay the costs of the steady state: reduced economic growth, more modest lifestyles, and the expenses of pollution control. Furthermore, it is not clear that ecological health on the model of the steady state can be achieved without coercive governmental decisions to limit population, direct economic production, avert the tragedy of the commons, and stop pollution. Other critics find Ophuls's preference for "small is beautiful," "aristocratic principles," decentralization, and less government to be reactionary, authoritarian, and contradictory. These critics insist that the clock cannot be turned back on larger economic and political organizations. A central government is needed to ensure the common good; we may need more governmental powers acting on behalf of ecological health rather than fewer.

Benevolent Authoritarianism

Some contemporary critics are convinced that the dangers of ecological ill health cannot be met in a democratic and constitutional way. They maintain that only benevolent authoritarianism can prevent disaster.[34] They argue that the masses cannot understand the dangers of ecological disorder and that even if they could, neither they nor the governing elites would be willing to adopt steady-state measures to curb population, protect resources, and stop pollution. Consequently, a benevolent elite (which understands the ecological dangers, has the common good and posterity in mind, and has the courage and will to act) must use coercive, authoritarian means to rescue humankind. Such "medicine" will not be pleasant, but it must be taken. If education and propaganda succeed, people will take the medicine voluntarily. If not, the benevolent authoritarian elite must step in.

If people can voluntarily—with the aid of bonuses for small families—limit family size through late marriage, abstinence, contraception, sterilization, and sensible abortion, then stronger compulsory measures may not be necessary. But if population growth threatens the carrying capacity of the planet, then sheer survival may dictate harsher measures. Some worried observers even raise the prospect of triage. According to this concept, the peoples of the world would be divided into thirds: those who can survive with no help, those who can survive with reasonable help, and those considered to be beyond help no matter what is done for them and so will be left to die.

Compulsion will be required to conserve the planet's resources and to overcome pollution. Wasteful production will be prohibited. Government will have to allocate scarce resources equitably. Recycling will be compulsory. Automobile travel will be severely curtailed in favor of mass transportation and bicycles and will be heavily taxed. Polluters will face significant tax burdens or, in the worst cases, be put out of business.

The benevolent authoritarian government will seek to lower birthrates by lifting the level of economic well-being, emphasizing education, and ensuring social security. And it will reach to obtain relatively pollution-free energy (such as solar power) and to use the best scientific and economic knowledge in the interest of ecological health.

Creative Breakthrough

This approach appeals to those who believe that a "strong doctor" willing to dispense "strong medicine" is needed to restore ecological health. Proponents maintain that certain democratic freedoms may have to be abandoned in order to deal with the ecological crisis. A kind of ecological constitutional dictatorship may have to be instituted to handle the coming period of great peril. Strong measures may have to be taken to curb population growth, curtail the reckless use of resources, and develop a new set of ecological habits. The alternative may be mass starvation, an increasing gulf between rich and poor, and other social explosions.

Opponents of benevolent authoritarian government feel that the medicine is worse than the disease, that ecological health can be regained in ways more compatible with democratic and constitutional government. They worry about the competence and trustworthiness of the ecological philosopher-kings who would be in charge. And, of course, those who doubt the reality of such deep ecological trouble are even less inclined to support benevolent authoritarianism.

CONCLUSION

In June 1992, more than 20,000 people representing 172 governments, 1,400 nongovernmental organizations (NGOs), and hundreds of news media gathered in Rio de Janeiro, Brazil, for the UN Conference on Environment and Development, otherwise known as the Earth Summit. Attempts to evaluate this conference illustrate the enormous complexity of global ecological problems and related political difficulties. Some people believe the conference heralded a new beginning and was cause for hope. These people base their optimism on the unprecedented level of participation and the growing scientific consensus on the seriousness of our environmental problems. Other observers do not assess the conference so charitably. True, there was a good deal of consciousness-raising. But the fine print of the documents produced—the Rio Declaration, Agenda 21, the Convention on Climate Change, the Convention on Biological Diversity, and the Forests Charter—contains no specific targets or timetables. The documents are filled with good intentions but little more. Can the world's nations find the political will and funding to go beyond Rio to address the ecological dilemmas outlined in this chapter?

Two additional global conferences have taken place. Earth Summit 2002 took place in Johannesburg, South Africa, and Earth Summit Rio+20 took place in 2012. It remains to be seen whether more meaningful progress toward effective management of the planet's ecological systems emerged from these conferences in comparison with the disappointments of the Rio conference ten years earlier.

Few observers deny the imperative of ecological health. But, as we have seen, many do disagree about the urgency of our short-term problems and the accuracy of long-term predictions. Some of these disagreements may fade as the future confirms or denies trends and forecasts. There can be little doubt, however, that we must work to preserve the home—planet Earth—on which we all live. The form this care must take arouses political dispute. As we have seen, our ecological problems require a momentous political response that taxes the human capacity for wise judgment. In responding to the imperative of ecological health, we must rethink our political values; study the empirical realities of ecology, economics, and politics; consider alternatives and their costs and benefits; and ultimately choose a prudent course of action.

SUGGESTED READINGS

Bsumek, Erika Marie, David Kinkela, and Mark Atwood Lawrence, eds. *Nation-States and the Global Environment: New Approaches to Environmental History*. New York: Oxford University Press, 2013. A thoughtful series of essays highlighting both global and regional environmental crises we are facing.

Chellaney, Brahma. *Water, Peace, and War: Confronting the Global Water Crisis*. New York: Rowman & Littlefield Publishers, Inc., 2015. A pioneering and authoritative study considers the impact of the growing global water crisis on international peace and security.

Goodell, Jeff. *The Water Will Come: Rising Water, Sinking Cities and the Remaking of the Civilized World*. New York: Little Brown, 2017. An extremely well-reviewed exploration not only of rising sea levels but how that will reshape our world.

Gore, Al. *An Inconvenient Truth: The Planetary Emergency of Global Warming and What We Can Do About It*. Emmaus, PA: Rodale Book, 2006. The former vice president and Nobel Prize–winner's book on the threat of global warming. Sound narrative and terrific graphics. Also note his later book, *Our Choice: A Plan to Solve the Climate Crisis* (Emmaus, PA: Rodale Books), 2009.

Hardin, Garrett E. *Exploring New Ethics for Survival*. New York: Viking, 1973. The philosophy of the author of "The Tragedy of the Commons." Will we have to move toward the benevolent authoritarianism that Hardin sees as necessary to cope with harsh ecological realities?

Kahn, Herman. *The Next 200 Years: A Scenario for America and the World*. New York: Morrow, 1976. Articulates the argument of the guarded optimist, who is sympathetic to the technology-and-growth enthusiast and opposed to the guarded pessimist and the convinced neo-Malthusian. Who is right? And what is the price of being wrong? See also Julian L. Simon and Herman Kahn, eds. *The Resourceful Earth: A Response to Global 2000* (New York: Blackwell, 1984).

Kolbert, Elizabeth. *The Sixth Extinction*. New York: Henry Holt, 2014. A fascinating look at the phenomenon of mass extinction and the possibility that we are now living in a sixth such extinction largely driven by human action. The book won the 2015 Pulitzer Prize for general non-fiction.

Lomborg, Bjørn. *Solutions for the World's Biggest Problems*. New York: Cambridge University Press, 2007. An optimistic view of our environmental future. See also Lomborg, *Smart Solutions to Climate Change*. New York: Cambridge University Press, 2010.

Ophuls, William, and A. Stephen Boyan, Jr. *Ecology and the Politics of Scarcity Revisited: The Unraveling of the American Dream*. New York: Freeman, 1992. A follow-up to Ophuls's initial volume, *Ecology and the Politics of Scarcity: Prologue to a Political Theory of the Steady State* (San Francisco: Freeman, 1977), argues that American and democratic values and institutions are "grossly maladapted" to the era of ecological scarcity. Hope for the United States lies in moving toward a politics of the steady state.

Simon, Julian L. *Hoodwinking the Nation*. Edison, NJ: Transaction Publishers, 2006. Reinforces the anti-dooms-day environmental position.

Strong, Maurice. *Where on Earth Are We Going?* New York: Texere, 2001. A superb treatise on the state of the world and a powerful case for sustainable development by a highly respected former under-secretary-general of the United Nations.

Worldwatch Institute. *State of the World*. New York: Norton. An influential annual publication covering a variety of global environmental problems.

———. *Vital Signs: The Trends That Are Shaping Our Future*. New York: Norton. Published annually, an excellent companion to the *State of the World* series. Examines over periods running from forty to forty-five years key indicators—environmental, economic, military, and social—that have a major impact on the condition of the planet. Extremely valuable use of statistical data, graphs, and charts.

GLOSSARY TERMS

Earth Summit (p. 403)

ecology (p. 400)

global warming (p. 399)

greenhouse effect (p. 402)

nonrenewable resources (p. 400)

ozone layer (p. 400)

renewable resources (p. 406)

sustainable development (p. 415)

tragedy of the commons (p. 407)

NOTES

1. Will Steger and Jon Bowermaster, *Saving the Earth: A Citizen's Guide to Environmental Action* (New York: Knopf, 1990), 31.

2. Environmental Protection Agency, Office of Public Affairs, "CFCs and Stratospheric Ozone," briefing paper, Washington, DC, December 1987.

3. Steger and Bowermaster, *Saving the Earth*, 31–32.

4. Worldwatch Institute, "CFC Production Continues to Plummet," contributed by Molly O'Meara in *Vital Signs 1998: The Environmental Trends That Are Shaping Our Future* (New York: Norton, in association with Worldwatch Institute, 1998), 70–71.

5. Ibid.

6. Beatrice Lacoste, "Saving Our Ozone Shield," *Our Planet* 4, no. 4 (1992): 5.

7. Anthony Watts, "AT AGU, NASA Says CFC Reduction Is Not Shrinking Ozone Hole—Yet," Watts Up With That?, December 11, 2013. http://wattsupwiththat.com/2013/12/11/at-agu-nasa-says-cfc-reduction-is-not-shrinking-the-ozone-hole-yet

8. Chris Mooney, "It looked as if Earth's was healing nicely—until now." *Washington Post*, February 6, 2018. https://www.washingtonpost.com/news/energy-environment/wp/2018/02/06/a-key-part-of-earths-ozone-layer-is-failing-to-recover-and-sci entists-dont-know-why/?utm_term=.b334ce01a88c

9. Craig Welch, "Carbon Emissions Had Leveled Off. Now They Are Rising Again," *National Geographic*, November 13, 2017. https://news.nationalgeographic.com/2017/11/climate-change-carbon-emissions-rising-environment/

10. Climate Science Special Report, National Climate Assessment, 2017. The full report can be downloaded at: https://www.nytimes.com/interactive/2017/11/03/climate/document-Climate-Science-Special-Report-2017.html

11. Institute of Oceanography, Mauna Loa Observatory, Cripps CO2 Program, Carbon Dioxide Measurements in 2017. http://scrippsco2.ucsd.edu/. Also see: Brian Kahn, "The World Passes 400 ppm Threshold. Permanently," Climate Central, 2017. http://www.climatecentral.org/news/world-passes-400-ppm-threshold-permanently-20738

12. Justin Gillis, "Clouds' Effect on Climate Change Is Last Bastian for Dissenters," *New York Times*, May 1, 2012.

13. Much of this discussion is based on William Ophuls, *Ecology and the Politics of Scarcity: Prologue to a Political Theory of the Steady State* (San Francisco: Freeman, 1977); and William Ophuls and A. Stephen Boyan, Jr., *Ecology and the Politics of Scarcity Revisited: The Unraveling of the American Dream* (New York: Freeman, 1992).

14. water.org. The Water Crisis, 2018. https://water.org/our-impact/water-crisis/

15. Garrett E. Hardin, "The Tragedy of the Commons," *Science*, December 13, 1968, 1243–1248.

16. World Preservation Foundation, Archive for Deforestation, 2018. http://worldpreservationfoundation.org/environment/deforestation/

17. Richard Pearson, "Are We in the Midst of a Sixth Mass Extinction?" *New York Times*, June 3, 2012.

18. Craig Welch, "Climate Change Helped Spark Syrian War, Study Says," *National Geographic*, March 2, 2015. https://news.nationalgeographic.com/news/2015/03/150302-syria-war-climate-change-drought/

19. United Nations Economic and Social Affairs, Population Division, World Urbanization Prospects: The 2017 Revision Database, https://esa.un.org/unpd/wpp/Download/Probabilistic/Population/

20. These are the six types of resources that Paul Ehrlich and Anne Ehrlich deem essential to the survival of human populations. See their *Population, Resources, Environment* (San Francisco: Freeman, 1972), 59. See also Dennis Pirages, *Global Ecopolitics: The New Context for International Relations* (North Scituate, MA: Duxbury Press, 1978), especially 14–23.

21. Herman Kahn, Leon Martel, and William Brown, *The Next 200 Years: A Scenario for America and the World* (New York: Morrow, 1976); Julian L. Simon, *The Ultimate Resource* (Princeton, NJ: Princeton University Press, 1981); Simon, *Population and Development in Poor Countries* (Princeton, NJ: Princeton University Press, 1992); Simon, *The State of Humanity* (Oxford, UK: Blackwell Publishing, 1996); Dennis T. Avery, *Saving the Planet with Pesticides and Plastic*, 2nd ed. (Indianapolis, IN: Hudson Institute, 2000); S. Fred Singer and Dennis T. Avery, *Unstoppable Global Warming: Every 1,500 Years, Updated and Expanded* (New York: Rowman & Littlefield, 2008); Bjørn Lomborg, *Smart Solutions to Climate Change* (New York: Cambridge University Press, 2010); Lomborg, *Cool It: The Skeptical Environmentalist's Guide to Global Warming* (New York: Knopf Doubleday Publishing, 2010).

22. Avery, *Saving the Planet*, 50.

23. Ibid., 52.

24. Robert M. Hazen, *The Breakthrough: The Race for the Superconductor* (New York: Summit Books, 1988), 8.

25. Ibid., 257.

26. Katrina C. Arabe, "Superconductors May Claim New Applications," Thomas Net: Industrial News Room, March 30, 2004, http://news.thomasnet.com/IMT/archives/2004/03/superconductors.html.

27. World Commission on Environment and Development, *Our Common Future* (New York: Oxford University Press, 1987).

28. Four examples of environmental studies adopting a sustainable development model are Lester R. Brown et al., *State of the World 1993: A Worldwatch Institute Report on Progress toward a Sustainable Society* (New York: Norton, in association with Worldwatch Institute, 1993); Al Gore, *Earth in the Balance: Ecology and the Human Spirit* (New York: Houghton Mifflin, 1992); Maurice Strong, *Where on Earth Are We Going?* (New York: Texere, 2001); and Melissa Leach, Andrew Charles, Charles Sterling, and Ian Scoones, *Dynamic Sustainabilities: Technology, Environment, Social Justice* (Abingdon, UK: Taylor & Francis, 2012).

29. World Commission on Environment and Development, *Our Common Future*, 43.

30. Ibid., 49.

31. Ibid., 261.

32. Ophuls, *Ecology and the Politics of Scarcity*; and Ophuls and Boyan, *Ecology and the Politics of Scarcity Revisited*.

33. Ophuls, *Ecology and the Politics of Scarcity*, 113.

34. Writers who express the need for such an alternative include Hardin, "Tragedy of the Commons," 1243–1248; Hardin, *Exploring New Ethics for Survival* (New York: Viking, 1972); Robert L. Heilbroner, *An Inquiry into the Human Prospect: Updated and Reconsidered for the 1990s* (New York: Norton, 1991); Buckminster R. Fuller, "An Operating Manual for Spaceship Earth," in *Environment and Change: The Next Fifty Years*, ed. William R. Ewald, Jr. (Bloomington: Indiana University Press, 1968); B. F. Skinner, *Walden Two* (New York: Macmillan, 1948); and Skinner, *Beyond Freedom and Dignity* (New York: Knopf, 1971). For an analysis of the ecological problem that favors benevolent authoritarianism, see Chapter 4 of Ophuls, "The Politics of Scarcity," in *Ecology and the Politics of Scarcity*.

CONCLUSION

How will the study of politics as a civilizing enterprise be carried on in the twenty-first century? To answer this final, crucial question, we may find it helpful to recall the four key concerns we posed in our Introduction that highlight the features of our approach to the study of politics and political science. Concern for these features must be central to the challenging study of politics in the twenty-first century.

1. *Can we as citizens and students of politics articulate and defend a view of the good political life and its guiding political values?* At the level of political ethics, we must continue to explore values, institutions, behavior, and policies that maximize life, growth, and fulfillment. We must continue to define such civilizing values as peace, liberty, democracy, human rights, justice, economic well-being, welfare, and ecological balance. Moreover, we must investigate those institutions and behavior patterns that advance voluntary cooperation and accommodation and that resolve conflicts in peaceful and constitutional ways.

2. *Can we develop a science of politics to help us understand significant political phenomena—the empirical realities of politics?* In the twenty-first century, we remain concerned with what advances the good political life and politics as a civilizing process. We seek to understand conflict and cooperation; force and reason; and the interests of key political actors, including nations, interest groups, regional organizations, and the United Nations. We pursue a better empirical understanding of what promotes peace, freedom, justice, and welfare—and what encourages war, tyranny, poverty, and ecological malaise. Students of politics must be cognizant of both the bright and the dark sides of the powerful—and challenging—forces that have shaped modern civilization and that will continue to do so.

3. *Can we bring a high level of political prudence or wisdom to bear on judgments about politics and public issues?* A wide range of political actors can benefit from an increased capacity for such prudence as they strive to make ethical and rational choices about war and peace, economic welfare, human rights, and environmental degradation. Exercising restraint and asking the tough questions underscore the difficult tasks of prudent judgment.

4. *Can citizens and students of politics creatively address the future of politics?* Our concern with political breakthroughs calls attention to a concern for the future of politics as a whole. Political scientists try to learn from the past and attempt to deal with present problems. But they are shortsighted indeed if they do not look into both the immediate and the long-range future. This requires an appreciation of the future effect of values and knowledge of emerging realities that will transform politics. It also requires an awareness of the need for wise judgments about potential problems and choices.

For our final thoughts on the challenge of politics, we now direct our attention to this task of future projection. Students of politics must be ready to venture beyond mere wisdom and prudence and search for creative breakthroughs that address the most intractable of political problems. Such breakthroughs, as we know, are rare; nevertheless, they do occur. James Madison's breakthrough to the federal republic in the United States and Roger Williams's breakthrough to religious liberty are two historic examples. A present-day example is the founding and continuing evolution of the European Union. Are future creative breakthroughs possible? Breakthroughs that would allow us to confront our demons, including war, genocide, poverty, and environmental degradation?

No one can predict the exact character of future politics. But we are certainly deficient as political scientists and as citizens if we do not think about the future. If politics is to remain a civilizing enterprise, we need to be concerned about how future developments will affect key values and people's vision of the good political life. We must be prepared for whatever unfolds—good or bad. By thinking about the future, we are reminded that politics is about what is possible. As Robert Kennedy, the former U.S. attorney general and U.S. senator, repeatedly said during his 1968 presidential campaign, "Some men see things as they are and say why. I dream things that never were and say why not."

Let us consider some scenarios that evolve from current developments. Then, in the interest of stimulating the creative imagination in politics, we will move on to a prophetic planetary scenario. We will view these scenarios as "thought experiments" designed to prepare people for the future.

A BEST-CASE SCENARIO

A best-case scenario, based on current developments, presents the fullest consequences of the end of the Cold War. Significant nuclear disarmament would continue, perhaps to the point of a nuclear-free world. Humane, democratic, and prosperous regimes would emerge in Russia and the other republics of the former Soviet Union. Effective constitutional democracies would triumph in all of Eastern Europe. All the former republics of the Soviet Union would live together peacefully and thrive economically. All of Europe would profit from a common, mutually beneficial market and unitary monetary system. China's market-based economy would continue to expand, and perhaps a transformation from communism to democracy would begin. North and South Korea would achieve a peaceful reunification under a democratic and constitutional government. Israel and the Palestinians would achieve peace and freedom, fostering a renewed sense of security and prosperity that may lead to a general peace throughout the Middle East. New democracies would replace old autocracies in that region. The countries of the African continent would know peace, and poverty that plagues so much of the region would be eradicated. A settlement would be arranged between India and Pakistan over the province of Kashmir.

We, the authors of this book, cannot confidently predict that this best-case scenario will be fulfilled. The end of the Cold War did bring about many positive results, but it is by no means clear that all aspects of this rosy scenario will come to pass as the future unfolds. Russia faces a difficult battle in achieving a democratic and constitutional polity and a prosperous, free-market economy. A measure of arms reduction has taken place in recent years, but major powers appear once again to be significantly increasing their defense budgets and more countries seek to add nuclear weapons to their arsenals. While European economic unification has thus far been impressive, the prospects for continued economic integration are in some doubt and the movement for political unification still lags far behind. China's path toward a greater measure of domestic freedom will be halting. The displacement of other authoritarian regimes will not occur easily. The Israelis and Palestinians may hammer out a peace of sorts, but a fully harmonious and prosperous Middle East will still have to withstand resistant hardliners. Revolution in the developing world may diminish, but violence, poverty, and authoritarian rule will probably still characterize many of these nations. Civil wars—such as those in Afghanistan, Syria, South Sudan, and the Democratic Republic of the Congo—will continue. Although it took some first baby steps toward democratic rule, Iraq seems to be slipping into civil war, and Afghanistan's political future remains uncertain.

For the United States, while overall prosperity will be maintained, the recovery from a disastrous recession in 2008 and 2009 has proven difficult. Entitlement programs, such as Social Security and Medicare, will face limited resources and rising costs. The nation will continue to struggle to improve its educational system and to combat crime and drugs. Internationally, the United Nations will modestly strengthen its war prevention, peacekeeping, and rights protection capabilities. But it may still have trouble moving from rhetorical resolutions and modest actions to more complete fulfillment of the laudable objectives of its charter.

Perhaps most troubling is the hardening of left and right political positions in the United States on a variety of issues such as climate change, abortion/right to life, gun control, immigration, LGBT rights, deficit spending, the size and intrusiveness of the federal government, and separation of church and state. This hardening of positions has led to a legislative gridlock in Washington to the point where large segments of the public believe the federal government, at least the legislative branch, is totally dysfunctional. And skepticism about presidential leadership, by a large segment of society, is worrisome to the long-term health of the nation. A loss of faith in the government, its legitimacy, is a dangerous possibility for democracy.

A WORST-CASE SCENARIO

As they face the future, resourceful students of politics would be wise also to anticipate worst-case scenarios that could develop from present realities. A worst-case scenario would envisage a resumption of great-power rivalry among developed nations and all of its debilitating consequences. Authoritarian rule would resurface in Russia as its democratic experiment collapses. Democratic gains in Eastern Europe would wither away something we are already witnessing in Hungary and Poland. Tensions between the People's Republic of China and the Nationalist government of Taiwan would escalate into a full-blown conflict, drawing the United States into a violent exchange with mainland China in the Taiwan Straits. China's continued militarization of the South China Sea would also result in violent confrontations. North Korea, seeking to take advantage of the chaos, would launch a military attack on South Korea.

The arms race would accelerate. Horizontal proliferation of nuclear weapons would transform limited nuclear powers, such as India, Iran, Israel, North Korea, and

Pakistan, into major players. The probability of weapon deployment would increase significantly.

European tensions would once again resurface as some of the countries in Eastern Europe face economic failure. The Balkan region would once again erupt in a vicious cycle of ethno-nationalistic violence. Economic depression would sweep through Europe, fracturing the carefully constructed European Union. Tensions would lead to a military standoff in Eastern Europe as the Russian Republic seeks to reestablish its sphere of influence on a scale to match that which was held by the Soviet Union. The hope for peace and justice following the end of the Cold War would evaporate. Poverty and authoritarian rule would sweep through large parts of the developing world, reversing much of the progress of the years since the end of the Cold War. Violent revolution, civil war, and aggressive war would return to many areas of the globe. Iran would ultimately dominate the Middle East, control world oil prices, and dominate the Islamic world. Because of a failure by major economic powers to collectively plan for their energy needs, including the development of alternative fuels, tensions over access to fossil fuels would turn into a violent war for natural resources. The moderate governments of Algeria, Egypt, Saudi Arabia, and other Islamic countries would topple to Islamic religious fundamentalism.

The United States would fail to get its economic, political, and social act together. Its budget and trade deficits would grow menacingly larger. The nation would slide into a persistent recession. Unemployment would continue to rise. Racial unrest would explode in the nation's cities. Health care would decline, and housing would deteriorate. Educational reform would fail. Drugs and crime would be rampant. Economic inequality would continue to grow worse and severely weaken the democratic foundation of the nation as the wealthy used their power to manipulate the system.

The change in our planet's climate would continue and even accelerate as the earth warmed. The major economic powers would fail to reach any agreement about how to deal with this problem, and the world would face an unprecedented and likely horrible transformation of the only planet we have.

The United Nations would be incapable of dealing with the difficult issues dividing the great powers. The financial strains on the organization would be so great that it would, in effect, declare bankruptcy and collapse.

Will such a worst-case scenario really materialize? Probably not. But it would be foolish to ignore the underlying realities that might produce such a scenario, or at least its key parts. These realities include the persistence of great-power rivalries and the rivalries of other nations. They also include Russia's difficulties in achieving economic and political reform and, as a result, a stable society; the comparable difficulties facing some Eastern European nations trying to overcome a legacy of political and economic authoritarianism; mainland Chinese aspirations to regain control of Taiwan; and the festering violence between Israel and the Palestinians. Meanwhile, a number of countries continue their efforts to build nuclear or chemical and biological warfare capabilities. And the global society continues to consume natural resources at an alarming rate.

In sum, the world is filled with the realities of frustrated nationalistic and ethnic aspirations and ambitions, weapons acquisition, chronic poverty, and authoritarianism in many developing countries; environmental degradation on a planetary level; and the very limited capabilities of even the best-intentioned nations to address these problems.

A more balanced assessment of the realities of the U.S. political experience suggests that the United States will probably not slide into economic, political, and social disaster.

Historically, the nation has demonstrated a pragmatic ability to deal with problems once it perceives that they must be faced. The odds are highly favorable that the United States will control its finances, shore up its social and health care infrastructures, revitalize its economy, improve its educational system, and in all other respects avert a worst-case scenario. Many of the problems the United States faces do not concern a lack of resources or knowledge; rather, they are the result of a lack of political will. So, too, a worst-case scenario will probably not see the United States disintegrate in economic ruin.

A PROPHETIC PLANETARY SCENARIO

It is also possible to move beyond the best-case scenario presented here. It is possible to envisage a transition to a twenty-first century characterized by planetary prophetic politics. Here, we come to the greatest challenge confronting political scientists as they approach the future: Can ethical, scientific, and prudential resources really be used to usher in a world without catastrophic war, flagrant violations of human rights, egregious poverty, or dangerous ecological malaise? This scenario envisages a world in which conflicts are handled in a genuinely constitutional way; in which prevention would make political, legal, and military remedies for violations of human rights unnecessary; in which people and communities work together for economic well-being; and in which the steps necessary to ensure ecological health have been taken. This scenario imagines a world in which nations and regional, functional, and global communities cooperate fully and generously to advance the creative situations outlined in our discussion of a best-case scenario.

The steps necessary to move toward these goals call for numerous creative breakthroughs in politics. Although political scientists would not be the only ones involved in such breakthroughs (humanists, physical and biological scientists, and social scientists from other disciplines would also participate), they would play a leading role. And as creative breakthroughs to a more prophetic politics occurred, individuals all over the globe would be able to cultivate that excellent quality of life that is the supreme mark of politics as a civilizing enterprise.

Is such a scenario possible? Yes, because we can envision it. Is it probable? Given our current understanding of political realities, it is not highly probable. Nonetheless, we may be able to take significant strides toward fulfilling key features of this scenario. How far we can go will depend on the creative steps we take now and in the future.

It is possible to be both bold and prudent in politics. The possibilities of creative human endeavor encourage people to be bold. The limits to human endeavor—the dangers of pride—encourage us to be prudent. Sometimes, however, the prudent course is the bold course, and the bold course is the prudent course. Genuine and effective worldwide arms reduction is both bold and prudent. Establishing global constitutional machinery to protect human rights is also bold and prudent. Similarly, it is both audacious and wise to adopt policies and develop programs to advance economic well-being, particularly for poor people in developing countries. It is both courageous and sensible to move globally toward some version of a balanced ecological order. Our success in these creative endeavors is a test for a creative political science in the twenty-first century.

SUGGESTED READINGS

Falk, Richard. *On Humane Governance: Toward a New Global Politics*. University Park, PA: Pennsylvania State University Press, 1995. Articulates the views of one of the most perceptive advocates of a global politics that can overcome key weaknesses of the present sovereign nation-state system.

Friedman, Thomas. *Thank You for Being Late: An Optimist's Guide to Thriving in the Age of Acceleration*. London: Picador Press, 2017. The latest work by the famous *New York Times* columnist and commentator on the current political and social world.

Fukuyama, Francis. *The End of History and the Last Man*. New York: Free Press, 2006. Presents fascism and communism as defeated, feudalism and monarchy as relics of the past, and democracy as the last man standing.

Huntington, Samuel. *The Clash of Civilizations and the Remaking of the World*. New York: Simon & Schuster, 2011. Asserts that future world conflict will not be between nation-states but by much larger cultural- or ethnic-based regions.

Kaplan, Robert. *The Coming Anarchy: Shattering the Dreams of the Post Cold War*. New York: Random House, 2000. A grim yet fascinating view of the global political environment now and in the future. See also his recent collection of essays, *The Return of Marco Polo's World: War, Strategy, and American Interests in the Twenty-first Century*, New York: Random House, 2018.

Mershiemer, John. *The Tragedy of Great Power Politics*. New York: W. W. Norton, 2002. Argues that the end of the Cold War changed very little and international life will continue to be the brutal competition for power.

Pinker, Steven, *Enlightenment Now: The Case for Reason, Science, Humanism, and Progress*. New York: Viking Press, 2018. A Harvard professor of psychology argues that the current world is still a product of the enlightenment and that by many important measures the world is getting better.

Sen, Amartya. *The Idea of Justice*. Cambridge, MA: Harvard University Press, 2000. Nobel Prize–winning economist gives his conception of the theory of justice.

Strong, Maurice. *Where on Earth Are We Going?* New York: Texere, 2000. A superb treatise on the state of the world and a powerful case for sustainable development by a highly respected former under-secretary-general of the United Nations.

GLOSSARY

accommodation: Political behavior that seeks a compromise between competing interests and is marked by cooperation, bargaining, and balloting.

advise and consent: Process by which the U.S. Senate provides advice to the president on treaties and key appointments through the mechanism of hearings and approves these items with a vote requiring a two-thirds majority.

alt-right: Short for alternative right. A broad and contested term that is used to describe a loosely connected collection of neo-Nazis, neo-fascists, racists, and other far-right hate organizations and individuals.

American exceptionalism: The idea that America's development is different from other countries, that its democracy is not quite like other countries.

anticolonialism: Political movement seeking to achieve independence for colonies, thus permitting countries to govern themselves.

anti-Semitism: Prejudice against, or dislike of, Jews often leading to discrimination or persecution.

apartheid: Former South African legal system of racial discrimination—separate political, economic, and social life for blacks and whites—designed to perpetuate white supremacy.

aristocracy: A privileged, educated, and powerful upper class that rules society. Interpreted by Plato and Aristotle as government by the best.

arms control: Negotiations and agreements that limit the production of weapons by nations.

authoritarianism: Anti-democratic political stance that favors placing political power in the hands of an elite group or a dictator.

balance of power: The maintenance of peace through the even distribution of power among competing nations so that no single state or combination of states is dominant.

balance of principles: Edmund Burke's view of the British constitution as a monarchy directed by laws, balanced by an aristocracy, and controlled by the democracy.

behavioralism: Approach to social science that emphasizes empirically observable, discoverable, and explicable patterns of behavior.

Bill of Rights: The first ten amendments to the U.S. Constitution, which establish such individual rights as freedom of speech and religion.

bipolarity: The distribution of power between two nation-states.

bourgeoisie: For Marx, the social class composed of modern capitalists, owners of the means of social production, and employers of wage-labor. In general, the middle class in a capitalist society.

bureaucracy: Governmental departments, ministries, agencies, and officials that carry out public policy, ideally in a rational, efficient, impartial, and stable manner.

capitalism: Economic system marked by private ownership of the means of production and exchange, a market economy, economic competition, free trade, and consumer sovereignty.

carrying capacity: Ability of the Earth to support life without suffering deterioration.

causality: The concept that a condition or behavior exists or takes place because of the influence of another factor.

civic culture: Set of attitudes toward citizenship and politics held by those in a particular nation.

civil disobedience: Doctrine advocating that an individual may peacefully, publicly, and selectively disobey a morally outrageous government policy, although the individual must be prepared to face the consequences for such disobedience.

civil liberties: Rights that allow citizens to evaluate how the government operates and to assess the character and performance of parties and political leaders.

class: Division of people by their economic, social, and political standing, such as upper class, middle class, and lower class.

class struggle: In the modern period, conflict between the bourgeoisie (capitalist oppressors) and the proletariat (working oppressed).

class values: Political interests shaped by social classes, such as worker or capitalist.

collective security: Joining of countries into an organization to maintain international peace and law. Their collective strength deters or punishes aggression by member nations. The United Nations is one such organization.

communism: Ideology that upholds equality by demanding an end to private wealth and insisting on public ownership of property and the means of production.

connection of powers: Connection of political power among governmental bodies, as opposed to the separation of powers.

conservatives: In the American context, proponents of traditional values and institutions, including private property, enterprise, and family. Generally favor liberty over equality.

constitution: Founding document or documents that spell out the structure and rules of a political system and reflect the political culture.

contract: An agreement, usually written and enforceable by law, between two or more people to do something.

conversion: The peaceful transformation of a political opponent through voluntary agreement and free choice. The instruments of conversion include love, conscience, and reason.

creative breakthrough: The significantly fruitful resolution of a problem that conventional wisdom deems insoluble.

crimes against humanity: Acts of persecution, including genocide, against a group of people; considered criminal offenses above all others.

culture wars: Term that came into use during the first decade of the twenty-first century to describe sharp divisions within the American public over fundamental values as reflected in disagreements over such issues as abortion, gay marriage, prayer in public schools, euthanasia, genetic research, and sex education.

cyberwarfare: The use of digital attacks by one country or nation to disrupt the computer systems of another with the aim of creating significant damage, death, or destruction.

deliberative function: That part of the legislative process consisting of discussion and debate on issues.

democracy: Rule by the people, usually via elected representatives, under a constitution that provides for the protection of basic rights and majority rule. Interpreted by Plato and Aristotle as government by the poor.

democratic socialism: Ideology committed to popular, constitutional rule and the protection of basic rights while maintaining that key aspects of economic life must be publicly owned, or socially controlled, to ensure an equitable distribution of the community's wealth.

demographic transition theory: Theory that posits that as societies economically grow and become more industrialized, population growth begins to subside. This occurred in Europe and the United States after the advent of the Industrial Revolution.

destruction: Political game in which violence and other instruments of force are used to annihilate one's opponent.

détente: A relaxation of tensions between nation-states.

developed countries: Affluent, highly industrialized, and technologically advanced nations located predominantly in the Northern Hemisphere.

devolution: Surrendering of powers to local authorities by a central government.

dialectical change: Major societal change arising from the clash of two opposing ideas, forces, or social contradictions.

diaspora: The dispersion or scattering of people from their original homeland.

dictatorship: Form of government in which power is centralized under the control of a single person or possibly a small group of people.

dictatorship of the proletariat: Rule, sometimes coercive, by the overwhelming majority of workers in their own self-interest.

direct democracy: Form of democracy in which citizens vote directly on matters of public policy instead of electing representatives.

disarmament: Negotiations and agreements whereby countries agree to reduce or eliminate weapons.

divine law: Law revealed by God and found in scripture that helps humans understand natural law while guiding them toward their supernatural end.

domination: Policy of exercising direct or indirect control, sometimes despotic, over others.

due process: Right that forbids such governmental action as the systematic destruction of a religious group, race, or class or such spurious legal action as a trial based on false evidence or coerced confession.

Earth Summit: Global environmental conference held in June 1972 in Rio de Janeiro, Brazil. A number of other world environmental conferences have since taken place.

ecology: The relationship between organisms and their environments.

economic well-being: Level of income, food, health care, and education that satisfies minimum quality-of-life standards and permits full growth and development.

egalitarianism: Political goal that stresses a belief in human equality, especially as it relates to social, political, and economic rights and privileges; political thought that unites socialists and traditional communists.

elite: Select group, often characterized by superior political, economic, social, or cultural skills or power.

emerging economies: Economies of former communist bloc countries that began shifting to a free market system with the end of the cold war. Hungary, Poland, and the Czech Republic are examples of emerging economies.

empiricism: Approach to social science concerned with political phenomena—what has been, what is, and what will be. Methods of empirical science include observation, description, and reasoning.

Enlightenment: Eighteenth-century, Western-dominated movement that believed in reason, freedom, and progress.

equality: Concept that emphasizes equal political and social rights or the condition of being neither superior nor inferior.

eternal law: The reason of God ("God's grand design") by which all things are governed.

ethics: The study of the nature of moral standards and choices of judgment and behavior.

ethnic cleansing: Forceful displacement of a group from a given territory based on their religion, ethnicity, race, or nationality. May involve a variety of methods, including mass murder, military force, or intimidation through torture or rape.

European Union (EU): Regional organization built on the foundation of free trade. Seeks total European economic integration.

extensive republic: Madison's term for a federal republic governing a large territory.

Fabians: Group of British intellectuals in the nineteenth and twentieth centuries committed to the gradual achievement of socialism.

faction: Self-interested group that acts in ways inconsistent with the common good.

failed or fragile state: A country in which there are serious questions (both on the part of the international community and many of its own citizens) about governmental legitimacy.

fascism: Authoritarian political ideology characterized by dictatorial leadership, an oppressive one-party system, strong nationalism, and aggressive militarism.

federalism: Governmental system that combines central authority for nationwide concerns with state, provincial, or regional authority for local concerns, with certain powers shared by, and certain powers denied to, both levels of government.

finite resources: Resources such as minerals, petroleum, and safe drinking water whose quantities are considered limited.

freedom: Power over one's destiny, interpreted negatively as the absence of restraints and positively as the ability to fulfill peaceful and creative potentialities.

functionalism: Concept in international politics that asserts that the barriers to cooperation and peaceful conflict resolution can best be overcome when peoples and nations work together to meet common needs and advance mutual interests. Emphasis is on such functional areas as trade, health, agriculture, transportation, and environment.

general will: The constant will of the sovereign people; the public good or public interest that is always right.

genocide: Systematic mass destruction of a national, ethnic, racial, or religious group.

globalization: Rapid and explosive increase in integrative international economic activity—trade, investment, and banking. Built on the twin pillars of capitalism and high-tech communications.

global warming: Theory that posits that because of the emission and trapping of heat-absorbing gases, such as carbon dioxide, CFCs, methane, nitrous oxide, and ozone, the planet's temperature is rising.

goal: An objective.

grand debate: Function of the United Nations whereby problems can be presented, discussed, and analyzed; ideas can be tested; and the strength of policies can be measured.

greenhouse effect: The trapping of heat-absorbing gases within the earth's atmosphere, which increases the temperature of the planet. *See also* global warming.

hard power: Military or economic influence. Stands in contrast to soft power, which involves less tangible elements such as persuasion, political skill, and public opinion.

hegemony: Circumstance in which one nation-state has overwhelming, dominating power.

Holocaust: The systematic extermination of 6 million Jews and other minorities during World War II by the Nazis and their supporters.

humanitarian intervention: An internationally sanctioned, multilateral military intervention in a country to prevent or to stop genocide if the country proves unable or unwilling to do so itself.

human law: Application, in specific circumstances, of natural law in our earthly affairs.

human rights: Freedom—legal, political, or moral—from government violations of people's integrity and civil and political liberties (negative freedom) as well as assurance of the satisfaction of vital human needs such as food, shelter, clothing, health care, and education (positive freedom).

integration: Occurs when groups of states, at the regional or global level, expand their economic interaction to the point where the separate national economies become increasingly interdependent.

interest aggregation: Means of selecting priorities in which political actors build support for specific proposals, usually by working with other like-minded individuals or groups.

interest articulation: Expression of political actors' needs, interests, and desires through voting, speaking at public forums, or joining political parties or interest groups.

interest group: Members of the public who organize in an attempt to shape public policy on issues of concern to them.

International Monetary Fund (IMF): Specialized agency of the United Nations concerned with stabilizing national financial systems, promoting international monetary cooperation and exchange stability, and managing debt.

isolation: Policy of withdrawal from, and nonparticipation in, world affairs.

judicial review: The ability of the U.S. Supreme Court to declare an act of Congress or a state legislature unconstitutional.

justice: Variously defined as fairness, rightfulness, giving persons their due, and a balancing of liberty, equality, and fraternity.

laissez-faire: Economic policy in which commerce receives minimum interference from government.

law: Rule established by authority or custom; according to Thomas Aquinas, "an ordinance of reason for the common good, promulgated by him who has the care of the community."

least developed countries (LDCs): World's economically poorest nations.

least free: The powerless, the deprived, and the maltreated; often the poor, racial minorities, women, and the politically oppressed.

legislative function: Formal responsibility of legislatures to make laws.

legitimacy: The general acceptance by political actors and citizens that government actions are appropriate and fully accepted.

liberal democracy: Constitutional government characterized by popular rule, protection of basic rights, and political and economic competition.

liberalism: Modern political ideology that favors government intervention in the interest of public welfare, social justice, and fair play.

liberals: In the American context, proponents of liberal democracy who emphasize tolerance, generosity, and a willingness to experiment; advocate progressivism.

libertarians: In the American context, proponents of liberal democracy who oppose government intervention in economic and personal affairs; believe in the maximization of personal freedom.

liberty: Freedom from slavery, imprisonment, captivity, or any form of unlawful or arbitrary control; the sum of rights of a free individual or group.

lion and fox: Game of politics in which a state's vital interests are at stake and must be protected by the use of both force and craft; political strategy first articulated by Niccolò Machiavelli in *The Prince.*

loyal opposition: Name given to the opposing, or minority, party in the United Kingdom.

luan: An important term in Chinese culture describing a deep-seated fear of chaos and a desire for stability.

majority rule: Power of one-half of the members plus one of any decision-making group to bind the remainder of that group to a decision.

Marxism: Political philosophy developed by Karl Marx that posits a class struggle rooted in economics as the key to understanding societal structures and political oppression.

materialism: Belief that a society's economic structure is the underlying force behind all societal institutions, including law, politics, ethics, religion, philosophy, ideology, and art.

media: Agencies of communication such as newspapers, magazines, radio, television, and, more recently, the Internet.

meritocracy: Members of a bureaucracy who have gained employment and achieved advancement by reason of merit as opposed to patronage or personal favor. Often applies to systems of personnel recruitment in government by civil service examination.

Millennium Development Goals: A set of eight development goals to drastically reduce or even eliminate global poverty in the twenty-first century; adopted by the United Nations in 2000.

mixed economy: An economy that is both privately and publicly controlled.

modified laissez-faire political economy: Economy without government intervention; compatible with liberty, the satisfaction of human needs, and the advancement of individual and social happiness.

multicausality: The concept that a condition or behavior exists or takes place because of the influence of two or more factors.

multilateralism: Groups of countries operating through international organizations and engaged in collective problem solving and problem resolution.

multinational corporation (MNC): Private company operating in more than one country.

multipolarity: When power is distributed among several nation-states.

national interest: Vital needs and fundamental interests of nations, such as security, liberty, justice, and welfare, essential for independence, prosperity, and power.

nationalism: Strong sense of cultural belonging and group loyalty generally used to achieve political, economic, and social freedom.

nation-state: Term used by political scientists to label countries. Combines the legal term "state" with the more psychological term "nation," which implies a strong sense of group identity.

natural law: That part of the eternal law known through reason, such as the ability to discern good from evil.

Nazism: Virulently racist, anti-Semitic, and militantly aggressive variety of fascism that characterized German politics under the dictatorship of Adolf Hitler.

negative freedom: The idea that people are free when they are not constrained, usually by government restrictions.

neofunctionalism: Theory that argues that integration must take place at the political level as well as at the economic, technical, and humanitarian levels. Working within traditional international organizations, neofunctionalists, unlike traditional functionalists, do not avoid political problems or nationalism.

neoimperialism: Body of thought that asserts that multinational corporations, owned and controlled by powerful forces in the developed Northern Hemisphere, take advantage of poor, developing countries in the Southern Hemisphere by exploiting cheap labor, squandering natural resources, and reaping enormous profits.

neutrality: Legally based policy of remaining nonaligned with adversaries for the duration of a war. Can also be practiced in times of peace on a variety of international issues.

new balance of power: New multipolar balance of power that may include a number of major nation-states as well as regional organizations. While military might would be retained, greater emphasis would be placed on economic might. *See also* balance of power.

newly industrialized economies (NIEs): Several of the dynamic and relatively prosperous Asian economies along the Pacific Rim, exclusive of Japan. They include South Korea, Taiwan, Singapore, and Thailand.

nonalignment: Policy whereby states refuse to participate in the struggle between major powers or superpowers.

nongovernmental organization (NGO): A private international actor whose purpose and activity parallel those of interest groups.

nonrenewable resources: Irreplaceable resources, such as fossil fuels.

nonviolent civilian defense: Body of thought that maintains that a breakthrough to a more peaceful world can be achieved if nonviolence is seriously considered. Espouses the notion that traditional means of dealing with conflict are inadequate and in some cases have proved disastrous.

oligarchy: Generally understood as government by the few, especially for corrupt and selfish purposes. According to Plato, it meant government by the rich and money loving.

ozone layer: Thin layer of ozone that encircles the earth's stratosphere and protects the planet from the full force of the sun's ultraviolet rays.

patriarchy: Belief in, or practice of, male superiority or domination.

peace: The absence of war. A condition of harmony between nation-states (or organized groups that aspire to become nation-states) that enables them to cooperatively, lawfully, and voluntarily (through discussion, voting, mediation, conciliation, and arbitration) work out conflicts and deal with disputes.

peaceful settlement: Resolution of disputes through such nonviolent means as influence, inquiry, mediation, and conciliation.

players: Contestants in the game of politics who win or lose, who compete or cooperate in pursuit of certain goals, who exercise power or will, who enjoy or suffer.

pluralist school/pluralism: Political school maintaining that balance in diverse political communities is best achieved through a representative democracy acting in accord with policies that advance the general welfare, while still recognizing that a rough approximation of the public interest emerges from the clash of contending interests.

policy: In the context of political science, a government course or general plan of action designed to solve problems or achieve specified goals.

polis: Greek city-state.

Politburo: a small group of high-ranking Communist Party officials drawn from the larger Central Committee.

political actor: Individual or group that expresses and shapes public values, struggles for power, and decides issues of public policy.

political creativity: Achievement in both theory and practice of a more fruitful, ethical, empirical, and prudential understanding of politics.

political culture: The distinguishing attitudes, habits, and behavior patterns of a political community.

political health: The political, economic, and social well-being of the political community judged in terms of peace and peaceful constitutional change, security, liberty, democratic governance, justice, economic prosperity, and ecological balance.

political ideologies: Beliefs and practices that guide political actors in real political communities.

political legitimacy: The idea that the authority of the government is accepted by people because the society's basic rules are correct and right.

political obligation: Concept that examines why people obey or disobey those who demand their political allegiance, such as a government or a state.

political party: Organized group that seeks to elect candidates to government office; a "team" that seeks to control government.

political science: Field of study characterized by a search for critical understanding of the good political life, significant empirical understanding, and wise political and policy judgments.

political values: Important beliefs about which goals, principles, and policies are worthwhile in public affairs.

politics: Process whereby public values are debated, political actors cooperate and struggle for power, and policy judgments are made and implemented.

polity: Constitutional government—a mixture of democracy and oligarchy. Form of government believed by Aristotle to provide the best practicable good life.

polyarchy: Rule by the many in a democratic and constitutional system.

popular sovereignty: Constitutional rule by the many; also known as republican rule. *See also* republicanism.

populists: In the American context, proponents of liberal democracy who favor government intervention in economic affairs and may oppose expansion of some "liberal" personal freedoms. *See also* liberals, liberalism.

positive freedom: The idea that people are most free when they are acting rationally and acting to further their potential as human beings. This often requires an active government to help people reach such potential.

positivism: Philosophy stating that human beings can know only that which is based on positive, observable, scientific facts or on data derived from sense experience.

poverty: Level of income, food, health care, education, or shelter that is below minimum quality-of-life standards; may preclude full growth and development.

power: Political, legal, economic, military, social, or moral ability of one political actor to get another political actor to do or not to do something.

power politics: Political pattern characterized by the acquisition, preservation, and balancing of power. Most often used to describe the competitive-conflictive behavior of the United States and Soviet Union during the cold war.

prescriptive constitution: Successful and proven ways of conducting social, economic, and political business that originate in a community's history.

preventive diplomacy: Action by such groups as the United Nations to help states, often smaller ones, settle disputes peacefully before the disputes escalate and involve major powers.

prime minister: Executive in the British parliamentary system, elected by the House of Commons.

principle: Basic truth or belief that is used as a basis of reasoning or a guide to behavior.

prisoner's dilemma: An intellectual "game" that shows why individuals, acting rationally, might not cooperate even if it was in their interest to do so.

proletariat: Class of modern wage laborers.

prudence: Wise judgment about the practical tasks of politics, respectful both of sound values and the limitations and opportunities of social reality.

public interest: Community interest that transcends the personal interests of individuals or groups and expresses the best long-range interests of the nation.

racism: Belief in the superiority or inferiority of a given race resulting in discrimination against, or maltreatment of, the supposed inferior.

rational choice: A model that provides conclusions about how politics works that follow deductively from a simple assumption about political actors such as voters, electoral officials, and government administrators.

religious fundamentalism: A movement to uphold, defend, and preserve age-old religious traditions and values.

renewable resources: Resources, such as forests, that can be replaced.

representative function: One of the roles performed by legislative bodies. Legislators represent and look out for the interests of their constituents who elected them to office.

representative government: Constitutional system in which government leadership is determined, directly or indirectly, by decisions of the electorate.

republicanism: Constitutional rule by the many. *See also* popular sovereignty.

Responsibility to Protect (R2P): Report of the International Commission on Intervention and State Sovereignty that outlines a state's responsibilities toward its population and the international community's responsibility if a state fails to protect its citizens.

responsible citizenship: The sensible response of citizens to social, economic, and political tasks and problems.

revisionists: As related to socialism and Marxism, adherents to an intellectual tradition that agrees with Karl Marx's outlook but opts for a peaceful, evolutionary path to socialism; led by Eduard Bernstein. *See also* Marxism.

revolution of rising expectations: Phrase characterizing the hope for a better way of life, especially among peoples in the developing world.

rule of law: Idea of regularized and consistent laws that are not changed by the whim of leaders or by circumstances like anarchy.

rules: Agreed-on procedures that regulate the conduct of the political game.

sanctions: Penalties, often economic, imposed on states that violate human rights or international law.

scientific method: Pattern of reasoning used in the systematic search for knowledge; involves identifying the problem, articulating a guiding hypothesis, obtaining evidence to test the hypothesis, and validating and explaining the significance of the hypothesis and the findings that support it.

separate but equal doctrine: Constitutional doctrine in the United States from 1896 to 1954 that held that equality was not violated if blacks were required to use separate facilities in transportation, education, and other public areas as long as the services rendered were equal.

separation of powers: Division of powers into legislative, executive, and judicial in the U.S. government.

sexism: A belief in the superiority of one sex over the other, resulting in discrimination based on gender.

social contract: Agreement in which a number of people unite for a common purpose.

soft power: Influence exercised by less tangible means than raw power, such as persuasion, public opinion, and political skill. Stands in contrast to hard power, which is the application of military or economic power.

stakes: That which can be gained in victory or lost in defeat.

state: Legal term for the entity commonly known as a country; requires people, territory, government, and acceptance by the international community.

strategies and tactics: Plans of action, schemes of attack or defense, and judgments that bring about victory or defeat.

supervisory function: The legislative responsibility to monitor and oversee the work of the executive and the bureaucracy.

sustainable development: Rational and equitable approach to development that attempts to balance societal needs against environmental limitations.

Sustainable Development Goals: Goals adopted in 2016 as a follow-up to the Millennium Development Goals that came to an end in 2015.

terrorism: The use of violence against civilians to achieve political goals.

third-party activities: Conflict resolution techniques used by the United Nations and other international actors not involved in a given dispute. They include good offices, conciliation, investigation, mediation, arbitration, observation, truce supervision, and interposition.

Thucydide's trap: A particularly dangerous time when a new rising power seeks to surpass an established dominant power and the dominant power resists the new power. Instability ensues and there is a higher possibility of war.

Times Up and Me Too Movements: Broad-based movements emerging in 2017 protesting sexual harassment and sexual assault. Principle action was women publically revealing their experiences as victims.

timocracy: Government by people of honor and ambition.

tort: A wrongful act, injury, or damage (not involving a breach of contract) for which a civil action can be brought.

totalitarianism: Ideology that espouses the complete political, economic, and social control of people and institutions by a dictatorial, single-party regime.

tragedy of the commons: Ecological metaphor calling attention to the overuse and eventual destruction of commonly held and used resources.

trusteeship: Commission from the United Nations to a country to look after a region, territory, or colony until the people of that land are believed ready for independence and self-government.

tyranny: Lawless rule by one leader.

unitary executive: Legal theory that asserts that with regard to foreign affairs and national security the president has decisive power.

unitary government: Form of government in which all major power and policy emanates from the central government.

United Nations Development Programme (UNDP): Specialized agency of the United Nations that provides development advice, planning, and grant support to countries of the developing world.

USA Patriot Act: Legislation passed in the wake of the September 11, 2001, attacks on the World Trade Center and the Pentagon that is designed to enhance the tools available to law enforcement for detecting, tracking, and prosecuting terrorists and those who aid them.

utilitarianism: Creed that accepts utility and the search for happiness as its foundation.

utopia: Perfect political and social order.

utopian socialists: Nineteenth-century writers who stressed cooperation and the possibilities of using education to change the social and economic environments.

war: Military activity or armed violence carried out in a systematic and organized way by nation-states (or organized groups that aspire to become nation-states) seeking to impose their will on other nation-states (or organized groups with nationalistic aspirations).

war crimes: Violations of the laws of war as spelled out by international covenants; include atrocities committed against civilians and the mistreatment of prisoners of war.

welfare: Government provisions for, or contributions to, individual needs for employment, income, food, housing, health care, and literacy.

welfare state: Society that provides social services to ensure better family life, health care, and housing; protection against unemployment; and security in old age.

wipeout: Pattern of politics in which one player, insisting on total domination, encounters resistance and employs brute physical force to destroy an opponent.

World Bank: Specialized agency of the United Nations, also known as the International Bank for Reconstruction and Development (IBRD), that makes loans to countries for development purposes.

writ of habeas corpus: Literally, "produce the body"; legal document requiring that a prisoner be brought before a court to determine whether he or she is being lawfully held in jail.

PHOTO CREDITS

CHAPTER 1

Photo 1.1:	REUTERS/Pool New
Photo 1.2:	Courtesy of the Library of Congress, Prints and Photographs Division
Photo 1.3:	AP Photo/Bob Daugherty
Photo 1.4:	Courtesy of the Library of Congress, Prints and Photographs Division

CHAPTER 2

Photo 2.1:	AP Photo
Photo 2.2:	The Granger Collection, New York
Photo 2.3:	Library of Congress
Photo 2.4:	AP Photo
Photo 2.5:	AP Photo/Eric Draper

CHAPTER 3

Photo 3.1:	Stephanie Keith/Getty Images News/Getty Images
Photo 3.2:	AP Photo/Scott Stewart

CHAPTER 4

Photo 4.1:	©iStockphoto.com/danielvfung
Photo 4.2:	AP Photo/Stanley Troutman
Photo 4.3:	Pacific Press/LightRocket/Getty Images

CHAPTER 5

Photo 5.1:	The Granger Collection, New York
Photo 5.2:	The Granger Collection, New York
Photo 5.3:	www.constitution.org
Photo 5.4:	www.constitution.org
Photo 5.5:	The Granger Collection, New York

CHAPTER 6

Photo 6.1:	European Parliament/Flickr
Photo 6.2:	Library of Congress
Photo 6.3:	AP Photo/Susan Walsh

CHAPTER 7

Photo 7.1:	AP Photo
Photo 7.2:	AP Photo/Jon Eeg
Photo 7.3:	Courtesy of the Library of Congress, Prints and Photographs Division
Photo 7.4:	Courtesy of the Library of Congress, Prints and Photographs Division

CHAPTER 8

Photo 8.1:	REUTERS/Lucy Nicholson
Photo 8.2:	Courtesy of the Library of Congress, Prints and Photographs Division
Photo 8.3:	REUTERS/Handout
Photo 8.4:	AP Photo/Jeff Widener

CHAPTER 9

Photo 9.1:	REUTERS/XXSTRINGERXX Xxxxx
Photo 9.2:	The Granger Collection, New York
Photo 9.3:	REUTERS/Jonathan Ernst
Photo 9.4:	Thr Supreme Court Historical Society

CHAPTER 10

Photo 10.1:	MOHAMED ABDIWAHAB/AFP/Getty Images
Photo 10.2:	© UK Parliament/Jessica Taylor
Photo 10.3:	AP Photo/RIA Novosti, Alexei Druzhininl
Photo 10.4:	Courtesy of the Library of Congress, Prints and Photographs Division

CHAPTER 11

Photo 11.1: Stock photo © Stockbyte
Photo 11.2: REUTERS/Wolfgang Rattay
Photo 11.3: SIA KAMBOU/AFP/Getty Images

CHAPTER 12

Photo 12.1: NOORULLAH SHIRZADA/ AFP/ Getty Images
Photo 12.2: AP Photo/Vincent Yu
Photo 12.3: REUTERS/Finbarr O'Reilly

CHAPTER 13

Photo 13.1: Michel Porro/Getty Images News/ Getty Images

Photo 13.2: National Archives/Hulton Archive/ Getty Images
Photo 13.3: AP Photo/Ben Curtis
Photo 13.4: Michael Stephens - PA Images/PA Images/Getty Images

CHAPTER 14

Photo 14.1: AP Photo/Anupam Nath
Photo 14.2: AP Photo/Ng Han Guan
Photo 14.3: © Howard Davies/CORBIS

CHAPTER 15

Photo 15.1: ©iStockphoto.com/Coldimages
Photo 15.2: AP Photo/Eye Press
Photo 15.3: ©iStockphoto.com/iShootPhotosLLC

INDEX

Elite system, 153
Emerging economies, 374
Empirical component of political science, 58–59, 66, 67–68
See also Theoretical integration
Empirical understanding and liberal democracy, 152–153
Employment, 355
Endangered wildlife, 407
"Ends justify the means," 118
Energy sources, 413, 414, 415 (photo)
Engels, Friedrich, 175
"Enhanced interrogation," 352–353
The Enlightenment, 102–103, 125–126, 174
Environmental influences
  academic disciplines, 104–105
  aggression and, 88–90
  challenges, 80–81
  cultural balance, 103–104
  economic influences and, 91–93
  Enlightenment, 102–103
  finite resources, 85–87, 85 (table), 87 (table)
  global degradation, 86–87, 303
  historical setting of politics, 100–102
  human nature and, 87–90
  physical world, 82–84, 83 (figure), 84 (table)
  propositions, 79–80
  sociological setting of politics, 93–97
  sociopsychological setting of politics, 90–91
  technology and science, 98–100
Environmental protection, 411
  See also Ecological health
Equality
  challenge of balancing with freedom, 156
  as democratic, 136
  economics of, 92–93, 92 (table), 93 (table), 389–390
  justice and liberty and, 213–214
  lack of. *See* Racism; Sexism
  obligation theory and, 32
  social democrats' belief in, 162, 164
  as U.S. ideal, 226–227
Eternal law, 115
Ethics
  as component of political science, 58, 63, 66
  ethical and cultural needs, 88
  liberal democracy and, 152
  positivism *vs.*, 68
  standards and, 67–68
  See also Theoretical integration
Ethiopia, 276–277
Ethnic cleansing, 8, 329
Ethnicity and politics, 96–97

EURATOM (European Atomic Energy Community), 299
Europe
  colonial empires in, 324
  liberal democracy in, 143
  population growth, 84, 84 (table), 85 (table)
  tensions in, 427
  See also European Union; *specific country*
European Atomic Energy Community (EURATOM), 299
European Coal and Steel Community, 299
European Economic Community (EEC), 288, 299, 401
European Union
  as breakthrough, 425
  challenges of, 282
  economics of, 299–301, 300 (map), 390
  global economic integration, 331–332
  pollution problems, 405
  successes of, 307
ExCom (Executive Committee of the National Security Council), 42, 43
Executive branch of government
  about, 233–234
  in Great Britain, 259–261, 262–263
  impeachment of presidents, 233
  legislature's role and, 232–234, 232 (figure), 237–238
  roles of presidents, 234–238, 235 (box)
Executive Committee of the National Security Council (ExCom), 42, 43
Exploring Nonviolent Alternatives (Sharp), 335–336
Extensive republic, 34–35

Fabian Society, 168
Facebook data, 352
Factions, 33
Failed/fragile states, 256 (photo), 258, 273–277
Fallibility of humans, 154–155
Family planning, 411
Fascism, 265, 267–270
Federalism (unitary) government, 200–202, 241–242
  See also American Civil War
Feminism, 125–126, 126–128, 128 (image), 130
Feuerbach, Ludwig, 174
Filipino tribes, 88
Fiorina, Morris, 217
Foreign aid programs, 394
Fragile states. *See* Failed/fragile states
"Fragmented authoritarianism," 272–273
France
  Committee of Twelve, 265
  constitutional features, 202, 203
  Declaration of the Rights of Man, 124–125

oligarchs of, 266
Russian Revolution, 101
Tsarist Russia, 194
See also Cold War; Communism; Lenin, V. I.; Marx,
   Karl; Soviet Union
Rwanda, 12, 294, 329, 348, 360, 362

Saint-Simon, Henri de, 166, 174
Sanctions, 358, 362
Sanders, Bernie, 182
Saudi Arabia, 86, 87 (table)
Saving the Earth (Steger and Bowermaster), 401
Schlesinger, Arthur M., 42, 43
Schoenbaum, David, 40
Schulz, William F., 357
Science of politics
   behavioralism, 68–69
   behavioralist approach, 69–71
   investigations, 62
   multiple perspectives, 72–73
   rational choice (game theory), 72
   scientific method, 69–71
   See also Empirical component of
      political science
Scotland, 202
Security Council, 329–331, 360, 362
Security *vs.* liberty in war on terror, 149–151
Sedition Act, 36
Separate but equal doctrine, 349
Separation of powers, 197, 199–200, 229,
   234, 248, 271–272
   See also Court systems; Executive branch of
      government; Legislatures
September 11 attacks, 13, 47
   al-Qaeda and, 275–276
   interrogation techniques, 212
   security *vs.* liberty issues in war on terror, 149–151
   USA PATRIOT Act, 150–151, 351
Serbia, 12, 329, 358
Sexism, 81, 89–90, 345, 353–355, 367–368
Shapiro, Robert, 218
Sharp, Gene, 335–336
Shiites, 46, 47, 49
Shinseki, Eric, 233 (photo)
Sierra Leone, 363 (photo)
Singapore, 199
Slavery
   justifications for, 89
   moral equality and, 141
   movement to end, 142
   persistence of racism and, 349–350
   political culture and, 194
   Thoreau's civil disobedience and, 18–20

Smith, Adam, 144, 175
Snowden, Edward, 351
Social Democrats, 38–41
Socialism, 169–170
   See also Democratic socialism
Social media, 98–99
Social needs, 88
Social Revolution (Hitler), 40
Social sciences, 81–82
Social Security example, 155
Societal influences, 67
Sociological setting of politics, 93–97
Sociopsychological setting of politics, 90–91
Socrates
   choices of, 28, 31–32
   execution of, 31 (photo)
   moral life and obligation, 29–31, 31 (photo)
   passion for excellence, 109–110
   political obligation and, 26–27
Soft power, 284–285
Somalia, 251, 256 (photo), 276–277
Sophocles, 18
South Africa, 349
South Korea, 199
Sovereignty
   challenges to, 302
   dangers of nation-state system, 323–324
   Hobbes on, 119–121
   problems of, 334
   Roman concept of, 142
   Rousseau on authority, 122–123
Soviet Union
   arms control, 295–296
   balance of power, 327–328
   biopolar balance of power, 307
   collapse of, 70
   Helsinki Pact, 207
   history of communism in, 182–183
   invading Afghanistan, 289
   public opinion in, 219–220
   recent wars of, 206
   United Nations, 298–299
   See also Arms race and arms control;
      Cold war; *specific Soviet leader*
Spain, 264
Sparta, 10, 291
Spending priorities of U.S., 215–216,
   216 (figure)
Sri Lanka, 94
Stakes, 6
Stalin, Joseph, 7–8, 176–177, 176 (photo),
   180, 194, 267, 272, 345
State government, 201, 230, 230 (figure)

Unitary executive/government, 150, 200–202, 241–242
United Kingdom. *See* Great Britain
United Nations
  agencies of, 298 (box)
  approaches to peace, 293–299
  charter of, 350, 353–354
  collective security, 330–331
  Conference on Environment and
    Development, 420
  Economic and Social Council, 360
  functions of, 292–293, 293 (box)
  General Assembly, 330, 350, 360
  Genocide Convention, 347
  Human Rights Council, 359
  human rights record, 360–364
  Millennium Report of the Secretary-General, 375
  Mitrany on, 334
  nongovernmental organizations and, 365
  Security Council, 329–331, 360, 362
  Stevenson and Zorin exchange, 44
  successes of, 307–308
  third-party activities, 328–330, 329 (photo)
  Universal Declaration of Human Rights, 346, 350
  violence against women and, 355
United Nations Development
    Programme (UNDP), 391
United States
  arms control, 295–296
  balance of power, 138, 307, 327–328
  branches of government, 199
  British political systems comparison, 197
  civil service, 263–264
  Congress and parliament comparison, 258–259
  conservatives, 136
  deadlock, 247–248
  Declaration of Independence, 31–32, 144
  discrimination based on religion, 89–90
  domination during Cold War, 290–291
  economic well-being of, 395
  as egalitarian democracy, 100
  ethnicity and politics, 96–97
  fundamental freedoms, 195–196
  future scenarios, 426, 427–428
  geography of, 33
  House of Representatives, 231
  human rights and, 207, 212, 356–360
  inequalities, 64–65
  liberals, 136
  modern democracy influenced by, 225
  multinational corporations and, 306
  nuclear war threats, 316–318, 317 (figure)
  as only superpower post-Cold War, 289
  political culture, 226–229

  popular values, 215–216, 216 (figure)
  poverty, 376
  presidential election of 2016, 99
  recent wars, 206
  religious freedom, 93–95
  resources, 86, 87 (table)
  Senate, 231
  slavery in, 349
  spending priorities, 215–216, 216 (figure)
  study of American government and
    politics, 55–56
  Supreme Court, 241–243, 241 (photo)
  United Nations and, 298–299
  See also Cold War; Executive branch
    of government; *specific war*
United States Constitution
  Anti-Federalists' views on, 34
  Bill of Rights, 197–198, 240–241
  economic influences, 91–92
  majority rules, 203
  obligation theory and, 32
  reconciling liberty and authority, 33–36
  separation of powers, 229
  values expressed in, 58
Universal Declaration of Human
    Rights, 350, 360
Unlimited *vs.* limited government, 197–198
USA PATRIOT Act, 150–151, 351
Uskorenie, 182
Utilitarianism, 126–127
Utopian socialists, 165–166

Value-fact controversy, 67–68
Values
  empirical investigation and, 64
  human needs as, 67
  judgments and, 64
  national interests *vs.* public
    interest, 204–205
  security and peace, 205–207
  as standard for judgment, 58
Vance, Cyrus R., 344, 357–358
Venezuela, 86, 87 (table)
Verba, Sidney, 101
Veto power, 237
Vietnam War, 206, 284, 328
A Vindication of the Rights of Man (Burke), 125
A Vindication of the Rights of Women
    (Burke), 125–126
Violence, 176
  See also War
Virtu, 116–117, 118
Virtuous people, 117